PREFACE TO POETRY

Charles W. Cooper

WHITTIER COLLEGE

IN CONSULTATION WITH

John Holmes

TUFTS COLLEGE

hb

HARCOURT, BRACE AND COMPANY

NEW YORK

PRINTED IN THE UNITED STATES OF AMERICA

To E. B. C.

FOREWORD

There are three men who stand in special relationships to this *Preface to Poetry*. Dr. I. A. Richards, distinguished psychologist and literary critic, now of Harvard University, is the source of many of the linguistic ideas that undergird it, and has generously given both encouragement and counsel. Dr. Albert W. Upton, professor of English at Whittier College, long-time friend and colleague, has served as motivation and guide in this work throughout the years in which it has gradually taken shape. Professor John Holmes of Tufts College, poet and critic, has during this final year of revision and enlargement, not only stimulated the author with general and detailed comments on the manuscript, but also supplied a wealth of suggestions and enriching materials. In humility, falling short of what each of these men has certainly expected, the author feels that ordinary thanks is by no means enough.

But the author is deeply grateful also to many other persons who, having read the preliminary edition or revised version of this *Preface to Poetry,* contributed their numerous comments and critical suggestions: to Dr. O. B. Baldwin and Dr. Alfred L. Baldwin, professional psychologists, father and son, for their helpful reading of BOOK ONE; to John L. Sweeney and Roberta Forsberg, orthologists East and West, for their critical comments; to Leila Glover and Ted Robins, instructors in English, for their helpful consideration of the preliminary edition; to Professor Richard B. Sewall of Yale University and Professor I. J. Kapstein of Brown University for stimulating notes on successive revisions; to the late William H. Wright for advice as regards song-lyrics and their airs; to Benjamin G. Whitten, librarian, for a final reading of the proofs; to Edris B. Cooper and Clara Dallas for help in the preparation of the manuscript and publication of the preliminary edition; to Miriam N. Post and Betty Gardner, senior students, for a systematic reading of the final manuscript; and to the classes of lower and upper division students who, by invitation, have been so engagingly frank in their oral and written comments upon the preliminary edition and the revised chapters. To them all, again, thanks.

But no book making use of modern poetry is without its deep obligation to those various persons and publishers who, for fee or friendship, have granted permission for the reprinting of copyrighted materials. To the requisite acknowledgments, which follow, is added sincere thanks, both to the firms and individuals listed, and also to the many courteous and helpful persons who conduct the permissions correspondence for the various publishers and literary agents. And the hope is expressed that oversight in the recognition of literary property, if such has occurred, will be forgiven.

The instructor may wish to turn at once to the Open Letter addressed to him, to be found in the Appendix. Others may prefer to glance through the acknowledgments and preliminary tables as further prelude to—the inevitable *page one*.

C. W. C.

Acknowledgments

D. APPLETON-CENTURY COMPANY, publishers, for courtesy in regard to "I Love to Love" by Marion Ward, and for versions of "O Bury Me Not on the Lone Prairie" and "Joshua Fit de Battle ob Jerico" from Blair and Chandler's *Approaches to Poetry*.

WILLIAM ROSE BENÉT and NORMAN HOLMES PEARSON, editors, and OXFORD UNIVERSITY PRESS, for a prose comment by Vachel Lindsay on "The Congo" from *The Oxford Anthology of American Literature*.

THE BOBBS-MERRILL COMPANY, publishers, for "Keep a-Goin'!" from *Songs from Dixie Land,* by Frank L. Stanton, copyright, 1900, 1927. Used by special permission of the publishers, The Bobbs-Merrill Company.

BRANDT & BRANDT, literary agents, for a selection from *John Brown's Body* by Stephen Vincent Benét, copyright, 1927-1928, by Stephen Vincent Benét, published by Farrar & Rinehart, Inc.; for "Chansons Innocentes," copyright, 1923, by E. E. Cummings, from *Collected Poems of E. E. Cummings* published by Harcourt, Brace and Company; for "Euclid Alone—," copyright, 1920, by Edna St. Vincent Millay, from *The Harp-Weaver and Other Poems,* published by Harper & Brothers; for "What Lips My Lips—," copyright, 1920, by Edna St. Vincent Millay, from *The Harp-Weaver and Other Poems,* published by Harper & Brothers; for "When It Is Over," copyright, 1941, by Edna St. Vincent Millay; for "Counter-Attack" from *Counter-Attack,* by Siegfried Sassoon, published by E. P. Dutton & Co., Inc., copyright, 1940, by Siegfried Sassoon.

STANTON A. COBLENTZ, editor, and CELESTE T. WRIGHT for "Thumbprint" from *Wings, a Quarterly of Verse* (Winter 1942).

CAMBRIDGE UNIVERSITY PRESS DEPARTMENT of the Macmillan Company for a selection from *The Tragedies of Sophocles* translated by Richard C. Jebb; for courtesy in regard to "Song of the Ungirt Runners" from *Marlborough* by Charles Hamilton Sorley.

COWARD-MC CANN, INC., publishers, and ROBERT PENN WARREN for "The Wrestling Match" by Robert Penn Warren from Alfred Kreymborg's *Lyric America: an Anthology of American Poetry*.

THOMAS Y. CROWELL COMPANY, publishers, and WINFIELD TOWNLEY SCOTT for "The U. S. Sailor with the Japanese Skull" from *To Marry Strangers* by Winfield Townley Scott, published by Thomas Y. Crowell Company.

THE CREATIVE AGE PRESS, publishers, for "The Praying Mantis Visits a Penthouse," from *That's All That Matters* by Oscar Williams, copyright, 1945, by Oscar Williams.

DAILY NEWS of Los Angeles, California, for "Final Touches Put on Pageant," news story of July 20, 1943.

SMITH DAWLESS for "Conversation Piece" from the *C.B.I. Roundup.*

DODD, MEAD & COMPANY, publishers, for "The Soldier" from *Collected Poems* by Rupert Brooke; for "Jesse James: American Myth" from *Man Possessed* by William Rose Benét; for "Accident in Art" by Richard Hovey; for "Non sum qualis eram bonae sub regno Cynarae" by Ernest Dowson, reprinted by permission of Dodd, Mead & Company, Inc.

DOUBLEDAY, DORAN, AND COMPANY, INC., publishers, for "The Amateur Botanist" from *Tobogganing on Parnassus* by Franklin P. Adams, copyright, 1911, by Doubleday, Doran and Company, Inc.; for "I Hear America Singing," "So Long!" "When I Heard the Learn'd Astronomer," and a selection from "Song of Myself" from *Leaves of Grass* by Walt Whitman, copyright, 1924, by Doubleday, Doran and Company, Inc.

DUELL, SLOAN & PEARCE, INC., publishers, and JOHN HOLMES for "Evening Meal in the Twentieth Century" from *Map of My Country* by John Holmes, reprinted by permission of the publishers, Duell, Sloan & Pearce, Inc.

ROBERT DYE and GUY FRANK for the lyric and music of their song "Alma Mater" from *We Want It Our Way.*

FARRAR & RINEHART, INC., publishers, for "The Ballad of William Sycamore" from *Ballads and Poems, 1915-1930,* by Stephen Vincent Benét, copyright, 1930, by Stephen Vincent Benét, and reprinted by permission of Farrar & Rinehart, Inc., publishers; for "Speech to Those Who Say Comrade" from *Public Speech,* copyright, 1936, by Archibald MacLeish, and reprinted by permission of Farrar & Rinehart, Inc., publishers.

FIRST THE BLADE, the Editors, William S. Ament, and Margaret Yale, for "Some Things There Are" by Margaret Yale, from *First the Blade,* volume XVI, copyright, 1943, by Scripps College.

ROBERT FROST for special permission to print the unpublished draft of "Stopping by Woods on a Snowy Evening."

HERMANN HAGEDORN and the REV. and MRS. JOHN G. MAGEE for "High Flight" by John Gillespie Magee, Jr., from *Sunward I've Climbed,* copyright, 1942, by Hermann Hagedorn, The Macmillan Company, publishers.

HARCOURT, BRACE AND COMPANY, publishers, for "La Figlia Che Piange," "The Love Song of J. Alfred Prufrock," "The Hollow Men," and section 2 of "The Waste Land" from *Collected Poems of T. S. Eliot,* copyright, 1936, by Harcourt, Brace and Company, Inc.; for a selection from *The People, Yes,* by Carl Sandburg, copyright, 1936, by Harcourt, Brace and Company, Inc.; for "Edgar A. Guest" from *Selected Poems and Parodies of Louis Untermeyer,* copyright, 1935, by Harcourt, Brace and Company, Inc.; for "Ich weiss nicht, was soll es bedeuten" from *Heinrich Heine: the Poems* translated by Louis Untermeyer, copyright, 1937, by Harcourt, Brace and Company, Inc.; for a selection from "Food and Drink" from *Food and Drink* by Louis Untermeyer, copyright, 1932, by Harcourt, Brace and Company, Inc.; for "And to the Young Men" from *The Noise that Time Makes* by Merrill Moore, copyright, 1929, by Harcourt, Brace and Company, Inc.; for a prose selection from *Modern American Poetry* edited by Louis Untermeyer, by permission of Harcourt, Brace and Company, Inc.; for "Daemon & Lectern & a Life-Size Mirror" from *Poems 1930-1940,* copyright, 1941, by Horace Gregory, by permission of Harcourt, Brace and Company, Inc.; for "Monologue at Midnight" from

Selected Poems 1923-1943 by Robert Penn Warren, copyright, 1944, by Harcourt, Brace and Company, Inc.

HARPER & BROTHERS, publishers, for "An Afternoon in Artillery Walk" from *Guinea Fowl and Other Poultry* by Leonard Bacon, published by Harper & Brothers; and for courtesy in regard to "Robin-a-Thrush" from *Speech Choir* by Marjorie Gullan, published by Harper & Brothers.

HENRY HARRISON, publisher, for a selection from "Twentieth Century Songs" by Elsa Gidlow from *California Poets.*

HENRY HOLT AND COMPANY, INC., publishers, for "The Listeners" and "The Huntsmen" from *The Collected Poems of Walter de la Mare;* for "To an Athlete Dying Young," "The Lads in Their Hundreds," and "Is My Team Ploughing" from *A Shropshire Lad* by A. E. Housman; for "Mending Wall," "Out, Out—," "The Road Not Taken," "Once by the Pacific," "To Earthward," "Stopping by Woods," "Birches," and "Death of the Hired Man" from *The Collected Poems of Robert Frost* and "Our Hold on the Planet" from *A Witness Tree* by Robert Frost; for "The Harbor" and "Chicago" from *Chicago Poems* by Carl Sandburg; for a prose comment by Louis Untermeyer from *Come In and Other Poems* by Robert Frost, published by Henry Holt and Company, Inc.

HOUGHTON MIFFLIN COMPANY, publishers, for "Ars Poetica" and "The Too-Late Born" by Archibald MacLeish, and for selections from *The Hamlet of A. MacLeish;* for "Patterns" and "Night Clouds" by Amy Lowell; and for selections from the works of John Greenleaf Whittier, Henry Wadsworth Longfellow, Ralph Waldo Emerson, and John G. Saxe.

BURGES JOHNSON for his poem "The Service" from *Harper's Magazine* (CXXX, 397).

THE KENYON REVIEW and JOHN L. SWEENEY for a selection from "Basic in Reading," by John L. Sweeney, *Kenyon Review,* Winter, 1943.

ALFRED A. KNOPF, INC., publisher, for "Peter Quince at the Clavier" reprinted from *Harmonium* by Wallace Stevens, copyright, 1923, 1931, by Alfred A. Knopf, Inc.; for "Proem" and "Epilogue" reprinted from *Weary Blues* by Langston Hughes, copyright, 1927, by Alfred A. Knopf, Inc.; for "Fighting South of the Castle" reprinted from *170 Chinese Poems* translated by Arthur Waley, copyright, 1918, by Alfred A. Knopf, Inc. Reprinted by permission of Alfred A. Knopf, Inc.

LITTLE, BROWN & COMPANY, publishers, for "I Died for Beauty" from *The Poems of Emily Dickinson,* edited by Martha Dickinson Bianchi and Alfred Leete Hampson, reprinted by permission of Little, Brown and Company; for "The Purist" from *I'm a Stranger Here Myself* by Ogden Nash, reprinted by permission of Little, Brown & Company.

LIVERIGHT PUBLISHING CORPORATION for "Helen" from *Collected Poems of H. D.,* by permission of Liveright Publishing Corporation; and for "E. P. Ode pour l'élection de son sepulchre" and "Ballad of the Goodly Fere" from *Personae* by Ezra Pound, by permission of Liveright Publishing Corporation.

JOHN A. LOMAX for selections from the music and lyric of "The Dying Cowboy" from *Cowboy Songs,* published by The Macmillan Company, copyright, 1938, by John A. Lomax.

MC LAUGHLIN & STICKLES, counsellors at law, and the administratrix of the Estate of Carolyn Wells Houghton for "There Was a Young Fellow Named Tate" by Carolyn Wells.

THE MACMILLAN COMPANY, publishers, for "The Lake Isle of Innisfree" from *Collected Poems* by William Butler Yeats; for "Mr. Flood's Party" from *Collected Poems* by Edwin Arlington Robinson; for "The Daisies" from *Collected Poems* by James Stephens; for "The Death of Oenone" from *Poetical Works* by Alfred Tennyson; for "Poetry" from *Selected Poems* by Marianne Moore; for "The Fog" from *Salt Water Farm* by Robert P. T. Coffin; for "The Ghosts of the Buffaloes" and two sections of "The Congo" from *Collected Poems* by Vachel Lindsay; for "New Year's Eve" and "Ah, Are You Digging on My Grave" from *Collected Poems* by Thomas Hardy; for "Dover Beach," "The Last Word," and "Philomela" from *Poetical Works* by Matthew Arnold; for "Say Not the Struggle Nought Availeth" by Arthur Hugh Clough from Hill's *The World's Great Religious Poetry;* for "Sea-Fever," "The Racer," and a prose comment on "The Racer" from *Poems* by John Masefield;

for a selection from the Introduction by Matthew Arnold to Ward's *English Poets*. By permission of The Macmillan Company, publishers.

VIRGIL MARKHAM for "The Man with the Hoe" and "Outwitted" from the poems of Edwin Markham, reprinted by permission.

MUSIC PUBLISHERS HOLDING CORPORATION for the lyric of "Begin the Beguine" by Cole Porter, copyright by Harms, Inc., reprinted by special permission.

OXFORD UNIVERSITY PRESS, publishers, and MR. A. T. A. DOBSON for "I Intended an Ode" and "Ars Victrix" from *The Complete Poetical Works of Austin Dobson;* Oxford University Press and the Poet's family for "The Windhover" and "The Leaden Echo and the Golden Echo" from *The Poems of Gerard Manley Hopkins.*

PACKARD AND COMPANY, publishers, and E. MERRILL ROOT for "Chicago Idyll" from *Bow of Burning Gold* by E. Merrill Root.

POETRY: A MAGAZINE OF VERSE and JOHN CIARDI for "P-51" from *Poetry,* May, 1945.

RANDOM HOUSE, INC., publishers, for "Shine, Perishing Republic" and "Coast Road" by Robinson Jeffers; for "Oh Young Men, Oh Young Comrades" by Stephen Spender; for "In Memory of W. B. Yeats" by W. H. Auden; for courtesy in regard to the work of Francis Thompson. Reprinted by permission of Random House, Inc.

I. A. RICHARDS for a prose selection from *Science and Poetry,* Psyche Miniatures, London, 1935.

TED ROBINS for "The Dive" from *Forms and Fragments* by Ted Robins.

MRS. ADA RUSSELL, literary executor, and the HARVARD COLLEGE LIBRARY for the facsimile of the first draft of John Keats' "On First Looking into Chapman's Homer" from *John Keats* by Amy Lowell, copyright, 1925, by Amy Lowell, published by Houghton Mifflin Company.

G. SCHIRMER, INC., music publishers, for the melody line of Samuel Barber's setting of "The Daisies" by James Stephens, copyright, 1936, by G. Schirmer, Inc.

CHARLES SCRIBNER'S SONS, publishers, for "One Star Fell and Another" from *Preludes for Memnon* by Conrad Aiken; for "Polo Grounds" from *Summer Landscape* by Rolfe Humphries; for "Heresy for a Class Room" from *Out of the Jewel* by Rolfe Humphries; for "Again the Native Hour Lets Down the Locks" by Allen Tate from *New Poems, 1943;* for courtesy in regard to the poems of R. L. Stevenson and W. E. Henley. Reprinted by permission of Charles Scribner's Sons.

FRANK M. TOWNE for "Reconciliation" from *Five Poems* by Frank M. Towne.

THE UNIVERSITY OF CHICAGO PRESS, publishers, for a selection from *How People Look at Pictures* by Guy Buswell.

THE VIKING PRESS, INC., publishers, for "Tom Mooney" from *A Son of Earth, Collected Poems,* by William Ellery Leonard, copyright, 1928, by The Viking Press, Inc.; for "The Creation" from *God's Trombones, Seven Negro Sermons in Verse* by James Weldon Johnson, copyright, 1927, by The Viking Press, Inc.; for "Brothers—American Drama" from *Saint Peter Relates an Incident,* copyright, 1935, by James Weldon Johnson, reprinted by permission of The Viking Press, Inc., New York; for "Go Down, Moses" from *The Books of American Negro Spirituals* by James Weldon Johnson and J. Rosamond Johnson, copyright, 1925, 1926, by The Viking Press, Inc., New York.

OSCAR WILLIAMS, editor, for "Sonnet" by William Empson from *The War Poets,* copyright, 1945, by Oscar Williams, published by The John Day Company.

YALE UNIVERSITY PRESS, publishers, for "The Hammer-Throw" and "A Boxer Called Panther" from *Connecticut River and Other Poems* by Reuel Denney.

As some of the above permissions were specifically limited to the reprinting of the poems in books for sale in the United States alone, the following additional permissions have been secured to cover the reprinting of these poems in books for sale also in Canada:

CAMBRIDGE UNIVERSITY PRESS, publishers, Cambridge, England, for a selection from *The Tragedies of Sophocles* translated by Richard C. Jebb; and for "Song of the Ungirt Runners" from *Marlborough* by Charles Hamilton Sorley.

FABER AND FABER, LTD., publishers, London, for "La Figlia Che Piange," "The Love Song of J. Alfred Prufrock," "The Hollow Men," and section 2 of "The Waste Land" from *Collected Poems of T. S. Eliot.*

MC CLELLAND AND STEWART, LTD., publishers, Toronto, for "The Soldier" from *Collected Poems* by Rupert Brooke.

THE SOCIETY OF AUTHORS, literary representative of the Trustees of the Estate of the late A. E. Housman, and JONATHAN CAPE, LTD., publishers, London, for "To an Athlete Dying Young," "The Lads in Their Hundreds," and "Is My Team Ploughing" from *A Shropshire Lad* by A. E. Housman.

STEPHEN SPENDER, the poet, for "Oh Young Men, Oh Young Comrades."

JAMES STEPHENS, the poet, for "The Daisies" from *Collected Poems of James Stephens.*

ARTHUR WALEY, the poet, for "Fighting South of the Castle" from *170 Chinese Poems* translated by Arthur Waley.

A. P. WATT & SON, London, as authorized by Mrs. W. B. Yeats, and THE MACMILLAN COMPANY OF CANADA, LTD., for "The Lake Isle of Innisfree" by William Butler Yeats; A. P. WATT & SON and the Executors of the Estate of Charles L. Dodgson for "Jabberwocky" from *Through the Looking-Glass* by Lewis Carroll.

TABLE OF CHAPTERS

TABLE OF POEMS

An Author Index with Titles

BOOK ONE

The Preface

Good wine needs neither bush nor preface
To make it welcome.   SCOTT

PART ONE

Orientation to Poetry

1

PRECONCEPTIONS AND POINTERS

> For those who like it, no preface to poetry is necessary;
> and for those who don't, no preface will serve to make it
> welcome.

If this seeming paradox were true, the present volume might well
conclude with its beginning. But it is certainly not true, or at best
it is only true in part. For those persons already favorably disposed
toward poetry are often eager to know more about it; and those
who are ill disposed toward it, may be willing to undertake a study
of it that is bound to shed some new and perhaps interesting light
upon their language behavior. Nor is it impossible that, with increased understanding, there will come a greater measure of enjoyment as well as of appreciation.

Each individual reader of this *Preface to Poetry* will, of course,
come to it with a different body of experiences in this one of the
language arts. For one person will say, "Yes, I like poetry; I read
the Poet's Corner in the evening paper." Another may respond, "Of
course I like poetry; I started writing verse when I was in gram-
mar school." A third, "I read and reread *The Golden Treasury* of
poetry, and love it all." It may be seen at a glance that these persons
are not liking the same thing, and that their "poetry" is abstracted
from widely different experiences.

I. PREJUDICES AND PRECONCEPTIONS

Those who honestly do not care for poetry also have had widely
different experiences. Their prejudices often stem from early child-

3

hood and school days. In some cases they may be traceable to the well-meaning efforts of particular teachers who enforced the memorization of unwanted poems, or the mechanical scansion and analysis of verse, or the unilluminating study of word history and figures of speech that may have set up an early antipathy toward poetry. Or these often enthusiastic mentors may have cloyed the taste of their young charges with verbal sweetmeats; they may have read verse that was utterly removed from their pupils' lives, or labored the hidden meanings of esoteric poems.

In early experiences such as these may sometimes be found the sources of deeply entrenched adult prejudices, particularly among men. Three such not uncommon attitudes toward poetry are these: first, that poetry is sentimental and effeminate; second, that poetry is a waste of time; third, that poetry is for the intellectuals and highbrows.

There is no use denying it if you are one of those who does not like poetry. It will be far better to face the fact squarely, and to smoke out the prejudice upon which the dislike may be based, tracing it to its source when that is possible. It may even be of value to air your prejudice in discussion with others, describing it rather than defending it, explaining it rather than arguing about it. And then, with the skeleton out of the closet—put it quietly back in again. For it is possible to put prejudice aside, quite consciously, and to give poetry another chance.

But only some of the readers of this book will have the prejudices suggested above. We must now turn to a quite different group of preconceptions found among some persons who like poetry as well as among those who don't.

One of these is the notion that poetry is a mass of authors and titles and dates and periods and influences and summaries of substance, the whole seasoned with selected quotations, critical opinions, and a few rare anecdotes. " 'To a Mouse' by Robert Burns (1759-1796) was written in November 1785 following an experience indicated in the subtitle, 'on turning her up in her nest with the plough'; and was published the following year. . . ." These are facts *about* poetry; they are a part of literary history, which is an

y to avoid the pitfalls, making use of the pointers given
ve paragraphs?

THE SERVICE
Burges Johnson

as the third man running in a race,
nd memory still must run it o'er and o'er:
  The pounding heart that beat against my frame;
e wind that dried the sweat upon my face
nd turned my throat to paper creased and sore;
  The jabbing pain that sharply went and came.

eyes saw nothing save a strip of road
hat flaunted there behind the second man;
  It swam and blurred, yet still it lay before.
legs seemed none of mine, but rhythmic strode
nconscious of my will that urged, "You can!"
  And cried at them to make one effort more.

en suddenly there broke a wave of sound,—
rowds shouting when the first man struck the tape;
  And then the second roused that friendly din;
hile I—I stumbled forward and the ground
ll wavered 'neath my feet, while men agape,
  But silent, saw me as I staggered in.

sick in heart and flesh I bent my head,
wo seized me and embraced me, and one cried,
  "Your thudding footsteps held me to the grind."
d then the winner, smiling wanly, said,
No dream of records kept me to my stride—
  I dreaded you two thundering behind!"

(1915)

THE HAMMER-THROW
Reuel Denney

y he will close the book, walk toward the window,
ch, shift, and turn, and saunter down

interesting study in its own right; but surely these facts are not the poetry itself.

A second preconception is that poetry is primarily a body of other facts, definitions, formulae, rules, and arbitrary distinctions: "Ninety per cent of all English poetry is iambic. . . . A feminine ending is an unstressed syllable added to a line normally ending with a stressed syllable. . . . The Spenserian stanza is iambic and rimes $ababbcbc^5c^6$. . . . The rules do not permit a poet to use homonyms as rime words. . . . *Wert* and *eve* are poetic words, but *butcher* and *skunk* are not. . . ." The facts, definitions, and formulae are, again, facts *about* poetry; they are a part of that science of poetry known variously as versification, metrics, prosody, or poetics. The arbitrary rules and distinctions are among the camp followers of Poetry; surely they are not the poetry itself.

Yet a third preconception is that poetry is essentially long-faced, the more solemn the better. Poetry, so conceived, should deal only with the conventional sentiments regarding Death, God, Nature, and Love; a good poem should always have a message, a neat moral on the up-lift side. This notion results from the confusion of Poetry with Homiletics, but it does as much injustice to the one art as it does to the other.

And there are yet other preconceptions held by some persons: "It's not poetry unless it rimes." . . . "Free verse, of course, isn't poetry at all." . . . "No real poetry has been written since Tennyson." . . . "If it's popular, that's a good sign it's not poetry." . . . These notions, together with the identification of poetry with literary history, with versification, and with pretty sermonettes, must also be left at the check-stand before going further.

2. PITFALLS AND POINTERS

Having put aside these hampering ideas and attitudes, the reader should be further prepared for the journey he is about to take. Some pitfalls lie ahead. A few positive suggestions may keep the reader from stumbling into them. For convenience these pitfalls and pointers will be grouped as five friendly imperatives:

1. *Read poetry slowly.* One of the pitfalls into which the reader of poetry may easily stumble, is rapid reading. Indeed the trend in the past few years has been to emphasize speed, and only a certain sort of comprehension, in the teaching of silent reading. People have been urged to overcome their tendency toward vocalization, those lip movements and whisperings that betray consciousness of the oral sound and feel of the words and that slow down silent reading. But the full effect of a poem is in great measure dependent upon the sound and feel of the words. If you read a poem as rapidly as you do the morning paper, you will miss one of the richest pleasures of poetry. A couple of centuries and more ago, William Walker wrote this couplet:

> Learn to read slow: all other graces
> Will follow in their proper places.

Well, at least certain other graces may be the reward of slower reading.

2. *Read poetry over and over again.* It is a mistake to think that a single reading of a poem will suffice. A really good poem will call for several readings—a first reading to spy out the land and to get the feel of the thing; a second reading to get the sense of it here and there where the meaning is not at once apparent; another reading or so to get the full flavor of it. And this suggestion should be carried further: Go back to your favorites among the great poems, not merely to be lulled by the memory of your previous thoughts and feelings, but to be challenged and stirred afresh. It is a test of greatness in poetry that it will have something new to say each time you come to it.

3. *Read poetry aloud.* Many people have fallen into the habit of reading only silently. Now, in poetry, language is used in a way calculated to appeal particularly to the ear. Unless you have had unusual experience in reading much poetry aloud or in listening to the reading of others, you will not be able to get full enjoyment from poetry when reading it silently. But here is a pointer: You need not necessarily read it *to* anyone; for, particularly at first, you will probably sound better to yourself than to others. Try to make use of tones of voice, pitch variations, rates of utterance, and

changes in volume that are appro... Do not tra-la-la it monotonously, b... ing. Then let yourself go, and rea...

4. *Read poetry with an alert m...* fall of your easy chair and radio... lazily on the end of your spine. N... are too rigorous for a hammock on... pointer for what it is worth: W... appropriate physical posture in favo... may not always want to stand up, ... edge of your desk; but you will ... movements when you do so. Abov... obvious clues and suggestions wit... "good things" get by you. And d... posture for reading some poetry *is* ... tall grass.

5. *Read poetry with emotional re...* upon the reading of poetry as a sp... selected problems in interpretation a... is aimed more often at the heart t... reader, will do well to relax, and le... upon what used to be called your ... derstand: this is not a suggestion t... sentimentality, or the cheap satisfa... ever, it seems to be true that man... veloped a certain amount of em... obduracy against various stimuli, ... But it seems equally true that, ur... feelings to be stirred by the great ... in reading them at all.

3. A PAIR OF ...

So much, then, for these prelimi... Now for a poem or two. Need I s... prejudices for the time being, and ...

Through the afternoon that brings the leaves down slowly,
To kick those leaves before him through the town.
As he comes out he feels all loosely made,
His jaunty striding wears the very sun;
And he seems golden-jointed, and new-eyed.
Legs, arms, and lungs are all a happy one.
The wide and level field becalms the daylight
Except when airs bring in the sudden sound
Of shoutings dimmed in sleepy distances.
He rubs his hands. He walks upon the ground.
On spike, and nervy, and the nostrils sharpened,
Won by the weight as the weight is whirled by him,
He pivots!—and the nerves cry out their question,
Centrifugal to heart and every limb,
Whether the world complete might be so lifted,
Whether it could be drawn so into the dervish
Of these locked knuckles and senses tight with joy:
Until, let slip, the iron leaps from hand,
And from his throat a noise, a kind of laughter,
Follows from that spent body, robbed and trembling,
The way the ball flies, with the chain drawn after.

(1939)

Did you read "The Service" and "The Hammer-Throw" slowly and thoughtfully? Are there any places, not clear at first reading, that became clear on a second or third reading? Did you read them out loud? And if so, do you feel that you got into the swing of the lines? Were you conscious of responding physically to the strains and tensions suggested in the poems? Did you experience any emotion at all as you read the concluding lines of either of the two poems?

These two poems, both by modern American poets and both related to athletic experiences, are really very different, as a close study of them might indicate. Nor are they, for many readers, of equal validity or worth. Further discussion of them, however, will give way to three questions suggested by an earlier paragraph in this opening chapter:

Would it seem to you that the writers of these poems are effemi-

nate? Or that reading them is just a waste of time? Or that they
are somehow addressed to the highbrows?

I believe not.

SUGGESTIONS FOR STUDY

1. *A Poetry Inventory.* Before undertaking this "psychological orientation to language-art," the reader will do well to inventory his acquaintance with particular poems, to check over his varied experiences
with poetry, and to take note of his "favorites" and "pet aversions."
Such a stock-taking may help the reader to determine just where he
stands, for it is from this point that every journey must begin.

(a) First, turn to the "Title Index" at the end of this book, and
check down the list four times with these questions in mind, and record
the number of your responses:

1. How many of the titles do you *recognize* at all?
2. How many of the poems have you *read but forgotten?*
3. How many have you read or studied, and *remembered?*
4. How many have you at some time *memorized?*

(b) But you certainly have read some other poems that you may
remember by title. List them in your notebook, and then check down
the list with the above second, third, and fourth questions in mind.
Record the number of your responses, and list them opposite the numbers you recorded from the "Title Index" count. Total these numbers
both vertically and horizontally.

(c) Now read down the next list of questions, and record your responses with an enumerated list of simple *yes*'s and *no*'s:

1. Did you hear poetry read aloud during your childhood?
2. Did any of your teachers read poetry aloud effectively?
3. Does your own or family library include books of poetry?
4. Do you ever listen to radio programs of poetry?
5. Do you read such magazine verse as you encounter?
6. Do you ever read books of poetry voluntarily?
7. Have you ever listened to good poetry recordings?
8. Have you taken a course in oral interpretation or verse choir?
9. Have you taken a course in English or American Literature?
10. Have you ever written any verse of any kind?
11. Have you submitted verse in a contest or for publication?
12. Have you "placed" in a contest, or had verse printed?

For how many of these questions did you make an affirmative response?

(d) List your "favorite poems" and your "pet aversions." Be candid,
and feel no obligation to rationalize your feelings. Count and record

the total number of poems you might consider as belonging in each list.

(e) A comparative study of the above responses with those of other readers will give some indication of your individual point of departure as you embark upon a reading of this *Preface to Poetry*.

2. *Preferences and Preconceptions.* The three poems here brought together are different in many ways. After reading them several times, decide which one you like the best; then seek reasons for your preference, and write a one-page "rationalization" of your choice. A comparison of your reasons with those of other readers may bring out into the light your particular preconceptions about poetry.

A RED, RED ROSE
Robert Burns

O, my luve is like a red, red rose,
    That's newly sprung in June.
O, my luve is like the melodie,
    That's sweetly played in tune.

As fair art thou, my bonie lass,
    So deep in luve am I,
And I will luve thee still, my dear,
    Till a' the seas gang dry.

Till a' the seas gang dry, my dear,
    And the rocks melt wi' the sun!
And I will luve thee still, my dear,
    While the sands o' life shall run.

And fare thee weel, my only luve,
    And fare thee weel a while!
And I will come again, my luve,
    Tho' it were ten thousand mile!

(1796)

THE HARBOR
Carl Sandburg

Passing through huddled and ugly walls,
By doorways where women haggard

Looked from their hunger-deep eyes,
Haunted with shadows of hunger-hands,
Out from the huddled and ugly walls,
I came sudden, at the city's edge,
On a blue burst of lake—
Long lake waves breaking under the sun
On a spray-flung curve of shore;
And a fluttering storm of gulls,
Masses of great gray wings
And flying white bellies
Veering and wheeling free in the open.
(1914)

HOLY SONNET X
John Donne

Death, be not proud, though some have callèd thee
Mighty and dreadful, for thou art not so;
For, those whom thou think'st thou dost overthrow,
Die not, poor Death, nor yet canst thou kill me.
From rest and sleep, which but thy pictures be,
Much pleasure; then from thee much more must flow;
And soonest our best men with thee do go,
Rest of their bones, and soul's delivery.

Thou art slave to Fate, Chance, kings, and desperate men,
And dost with poison, war, and sickness dwell,
And poppy or charms can make us sleep as well
And better than thy stroke. Why swell'st thou then?
One short sleep past, we wake eternally,
And death shall be no more. Death, thou shalt die!
(1609, 1633)

3. *Rereading a Favorite Poem.* It has been suggested in the text that the reader go back to his old favorites, not merely to be lulled by the memory of previous pleasant reading experiences, but to be challenged or stirred afresh. Now look up one of your favorite poems, perhaps the first one on your list above. While checking the Index you may have noted that it is reprinted in this volume; or you may prefer to use a well-worn book from your library; or you may need to hunt it up in

the Library.[1] In rereading this favorite poem, make use of the five numbered suggestions in the text of this chapter. Then write a short paper discussing your experiences with this poem: when you first encountered it, what in it appealed to you, why it continued to attract you, how your experience with it has changed.

4. *A Pair of Poems.* Of these two poems based on the same story, one is relatively easy to read, the other relatively hard. Some readers find the first more enjoyable; but the second is likely to provoke more discussion. Review the five pointers and pitfalls before proceeding.

Leigh Hunt, who wrote the first of the two poems, was a liberal journalist and friend of the leading poets of his day. He borrowed his story from Schiller's "Der Handschuh," but refers his readers to two French sources. The King of the poem is the French monarch of the early sixteenth century.

THE GLOVE AND THE LIONS
Leigh Hunt

King Francis was a hearty king, and loved a royal sport,
And one day, as his lions fought, sat looking on the court.
The nobles filled the benches, with the ladies in their pride,
And 'mongst them sat the Count de Lorge, with one for whom he
     sighed:
And truly 'twas a gallant thing to see that crowning show,
Valor and love, and a king above, and the royal beasts below.

Ramped and roared the lions, with horrid laughing jaws;
They bit, they glared, gave blows like beams, a wind went with their
     paws;
With wallowing might and stifled roar they rolled on one another,
Till all the pit with sand and mane was in a thunderous smother;
The bloody foam above the bars came whisking through the air;
Said Francis then, "Faith, gentlemen, we're better here than there."

De Lorge's love o'erheard the King, a beauteous lively dame,
With smiling lips and sharp bright eyes, which always seemed the
     same;

[1] If you remember the name of the poet, you can easily find the poem in the author's Complete Works, if such is available. If you forget the name of the poet, you may discover it by checking the title in *Granger's Index to Poetry and Recitations*. If you can only remember an oft-quoted line or phrase, you may be helped by using the *Home Book of Quotations* or Bartlett's *Familiar Quotations*.

She thought, "The Count, my lover, is brave as brave can be;
He surely would do wondrous things to show his love of me;
King, ladies, lovers, all look on; the occasion is divine;
I'll drop my glove, to prove his love; great glory will be mine."

She dropped her glove, to prove his love, then looked at him and
    smiled;
He bowed, and in a moment leaped among the lions wild;
The leap was quick, return was quick, he has regained his place,
Then threw the glove, but not with love, right in the lady's face.
"By Heaven," said Francis, "rightly done!" and he rose from where he
    sat;
"No love," quoth he, "but vanity, sets love a task like that."

(1836)

The second of this pair of poems was inspired by the first, and was
written a few years later by Robert Browning. From title to final
couplet, it presents a quite different interpretation of the romantic incident. Peter Ronsard, who is assumed to relate the story, was one of
a group of poets in the time of King Francis, as was *Clement Marot*.
The *Naso* referred to is more usually encountered as Ovid, the Roman
love poet.

THE GLOVE
Robert Browning

(PETER RONSARD *loquitur*)

"Heigho," yawned one day King Francis,
"Distance all value enhances!
When a man's busy, why, leisure
Strikes him as wonderful pleasure:
'Faith, and at leisure once is he?
Straightway he wants to be busy.
Here we've got peace; and aghast I'm
Caught thinking war the true pastime.
Is there a reason in meter?
Give us your speech, master Peter!"
I who, if mortal dare say so,
Ne'er am at loss with my Naso,
"Sire," I replied, "joys prove cloudlets:
Men are the merest Ixions"—

Here the King whistled aloud, "Let's
—Heigho—go look at our lions!"
Such are the sorrowful chances
If you talk fine to King Francis.

And so, to the courtyard proceeding,
Our company, Francis was leading,
Increased by new followers tenfold
Before he arrived at the penfold;
Lords, ladies, like clouds which bedizen
At sunset the western horizon.
And Sir De Lorge pressed 'mid the foremost
With the dame he professed to adore most.
Oh, what a face! One by fits eyed
Her, and the horrible pitside;
For the penfold surrounded a hollow
Which led where the eye scarce dared follow,
And shelved to the chamber secluded
Where Bluebeard, the great lion, brooded.
The King hailed his keeper, an Arab
As glossy and black as a scarab,
And bade him make sport and at once stir
Up and out of his den the old monster.
They opened a hole in the wire-work
Across it, and dropped there a firework,
And fled: one's heart's beating redoubled;
A pause, while the pit's mouth was troubled,
The blackness and silence so utter,
By the firework's slow sparkling and sputter;
Then earth in a sudden contortion
Gave out to our gaze her abortion!
Such a brute! Were I friend Clement Marot
(Whose experience of nature's but narrow,
And whose faculties move in no small mist
When he versifies David the Psalmist)
I should study that brute to describe you
Illum Juda Leonem de Tribu.
One's whole blood grew curdling and creepy
To see the black mane, vast and heapy,

The tail in the air stiff and straining,
The wide eyes, nor waxing nor waning,
As over the barrier which bounded
His platform, and us who surrounded
The barrier, they reached and they rested
On space that might stand him in best stead:
For who knew, he thought, what the amazement,
The eruption of clatter and blaze meant,
And if, in this minute of wonder,
No outlet, 'mid lightning and thunder,
Lay broad, and, his shackles all shivered,
The lion at last was delivered?
Ay, that was the open sky o'erhead!
And you saw by the flash on his forehead,
By the hope in those eyes wide and steady,
He was leagues in the desert already,
Driving the flocks up the mountain,
Or catlike couched hard by the fountain
To waylay the date-gathering Negress:
So guarded he entrance or egress.
"How he stands!" quoth the King: "we may well swear,
(No novice, we've won our spurs elsewhere
And so can afford the confession,)
We exercise wholesome discretion
In keeping aloof from his threshold;
Once hold you, those jaws want no fresh hold,
Their first would too pleasantly purloin
The visitor's brisket or surloin:
But who's he would prove so fool-hardy?
Not the best man of Marignan, pardie!"

The sentence no sooner was uttered,
Than over the rails a glove fluttered,
Fell close to the lion, and rested:
The dame 't was, who flung it and jested
With life so, De Lorge had been wooing
For months past; he sat there pursuing
His suit, weighing out with nonchalance
Fine speeches like gold from a balance.

Sound the trumpet, no true knight's a tarrier!
De Lorge made one leap at the barrier,
Walked straight to the glove,—while the lion
Ne'er moved, kept his far-reaching eye on
The palm-tree-edged desert-spring's sapphire,
And the musky oiled skin of the Kaffir,—
Picked it up, and as calmly retreated,
Leaped back where the lady was seated,
And full in the face of its owner
Flung the glove.

        "Your heart's queen, you dethrone her?
So should I!"—cried the King—"'t was mere vanity,
Not love, set that task to humanity!"
Lords and ladies alike turned with loathing
From such a proved wolf in sheep's clothing.

Not so, I; for I caught an expression
In her brow's undisturbed self-possession
Amid the Court's scoffing and merriment,—
As if from no pleasing experiment
She rose, yet of pain not much heedful
So long as the process was needful,—
As if she had tried in a crucible,
To what "speeches like gold" were reducible,
And, finding the finest prove copper,
Felt the smoke in her face was but proper;
To know what she had *not* to trust to,
Was worth all the ashes and dust too.
She went out 'mid hooting and laughter;
Clement Marot stayed; I followed after,
And asked, as a grace, what it all meant?
If she wished not the rash deed's recalment?
"For I"—so I spoke—"am a poet:
Human nature,—behooves that I know it!"

She told me, "Too long had I heard
Of the deed proved alone by the word:
For my love—what De Lorge would not dare!
With my scorn—what De Lorge could compare!

And the endless descriptions of death
He would brave when my lip formed a breath,
I must reckon as braved, or, of course,
Doubt his word—and moreover, perforce,
For such gifts as no lady could spurn,
Must offer my love in return.
When I looked on your lion, it brought
All the dangers at once to my thought,
Encountered by all sorts of men,
Before he was lodged in his den,—
From the poor slave whose club or bare hands
Dug the trap, set the snare on the sands,
With no King and no Court to applaud,
By no shame, should he shrink, overawed,
Yet to capture the creature made shift,
That his rude boys might laugh at the gift,
—To the page who last leaped o'er the fence
Of the pit, on no greater pretence
Than to get back the bonnet he dropped,
Lest his pay for a week should be stopped.
So, wiser I judged it to make
One trial what 'death for my sake'
Really meant, while the power was yet mine,
Than to wait until time should define
Such a phrase not so simply as I,
Who took it to mean just 'to die.'
The blow a glove gives is but weak:
Does the mark yet discolour my cheek?
But when the heart suffers a blow,
Will the pain pass so soon, do you know?"

I looked, as away she was sweeping,
And saw a youth eagerly keeping
As close as he dared to the doorway.
No doubt that a noble should more weigh
His life than befits a plebeian;
And yet, had our brute been Nemean—
(I judge by a certain calm fervour
The youth stepped with, forward to serve her)

—He'd have scarce thought you did him the worst turn
If you whispered "Friend, what you'd get, first earn!"
And when, shortly after, she carried
Her shame from the Court, and they married,
To that marriage some happiness, maugre
The voice of the Court, I dared augur.

For De Lorge, he made women with men vie,
Those in wonder and praise, these in envy;
And in short stood so plain a head taller
That he wooed and won . . . how do you call her?
The beauty, that rose in the sequel
To the King's love, who loved her a week well.
And 't was noticed he never would honour
De Lorge (who looked daggers upon her)
With the easy commission of stretching
His legs in the service, and fetching
His wife, from her chamber, those straying
Sad gloves she was always mislaying,
While the King took the closet to chat in,—
But of course this adventure came pat in.
And never the King told the story,
How bringing a glove brought such glory,
But the wife smiled—"His nerves are grown firmer:
Mine he brings now and utters no murmur."

Venienti occurrite morbo!
With which moral I drop my theorbo.

(1845)

Before rereading "The Glove," glance through this paragraph of
notes. The *theorbo,* of the last line, is a double-necked lute, a stringed
instrument not unlike a mandolin; the next to the last line, of *Latin,*
is translated, "Go to meet approaching ills." The earlier *Latin* line:
"That lion of the tribe of Judah." *Ixion:* a legendary Greek king who
dared to love Hera (Juno), and was bound to a revolving wheel for
punishment. *Bluebeard:* a lion so named actually was kept at a zoo near
Browning's home. *Marignan:* an Italian town. *Kaffir:* one of a South
African tribe of noted hunters. *Nemean:* Hercules slew the Nemean
lion as one of his "twelve labors."

Now go back to the poem and read it carefully. Is it perfectly clear
to you what happens in the second half of the poem? who marries

whom? and then what happens? And what the attitudes and reactions are of the several characters in this romantic drama: De Lorge, the "dame," the King, Ronsard, the "youth," and the "beauty"? [2]

Note on the dating of poems: The date following each poem is usually that of first publication, but sometimes of the first publication in book form; italic numerals indicate date of composition. The *c.* is here an abbreviation of *circa* (about) rather than of *copyright.* Thus, (*c.1600, 1623*) means: written about 1600, first published in 1623. Dating poems is often difficult, at times impossible, with any certainty; and (*? c.1400*) will indicate a very approximate date.

[2] The curious student may wish to go further and study various interpretations of the poem, such as those to be found in W. Clyde DeVane, *A Browning Handbook,* F. S. Crofts, 1935, and in a number of articles from the *Explicator,* May, 1943; November, 1943; December, 1943; February, 1944.

2

IN SEARCH OF POETRY

The question "What is poetry?" tempts one to formulate an elaborate, hard-and-fast definition. But the essential thing, "the real poetry of it," slips through one's fingers, like the pearl of medieval allegory, to be lost in the growth of verbal weeds and grasses.

So we shall start out in our Search for Poetry by reading a poem, and then by asking some questions about it. "Sea-Fever" by John Masefield, English seaman and poet laureate, is probably well known to you. It has been chosen for that reason. As you now read it, slowly and aloud, whole-heartedly and repeatedly, try to have as full and rich an experience of it as you can.

SEA-FEVER
John Masefield

I must go down to the seas again, to the lonely sea and the sky,
And all I ask is a tall ship and a star to steer her by,
And the wheel's kick and the wind's song and the white sail's shaking,
And a grey mist on the sea's face and a grey dawn breaking.

I must go down to the seas again, for the call of the running tide
Is a wild call and a clear call that may not be denied;
And all I ask is a windy day with the white clouds flying,
And the flung spray and the blown spume, and the sea-gulls crying.

I must go down to the seas again to the vagrant gypsy life,
To the gull's way and the whale's way where the wind's like a whetted
 knife;
And all I ask is a merry yarn from a laughing fellow-rover,
And quiet sleep and a sweet dream when the long trick's over.

(1902)

Go back, now, and read it yet again before continuing with the next paragraphs.

"Sea-Fever," I am sure that you will agree, is *a poem*. Certainly, if someone asked you the question, "What is poetry?" you might well reply, "Why, 'Sea-Fever' is poetry—'Sea-Fever' is a poem." But what do you mean when you call it *a poem;* and what are you referring to by the *"it"* when we call *it* "a poem"?

When you speak of the *poem* "Sea-Fever," are you thinking of the printed verses, the words here on the page? Or are you thinking of what the words stand for—what they stood for in Masefield's experience, what he meant by the words? Or are you thinking of what the words do to you—what they mean to you?

I. SENSES OF THE WORD "POEM"

One cannot dismiss these questions with an indifferent shrug, or with the casual comment that the three things implied in these questions are really one and the same. Look at the following statements referring to "Sea-Fever" and using the word *poem*. You will note that the word is being used in three quite different senses:

(a) "Masefield's poem 'Sea-Fever' grew out of his deep hunger for life."
(b) " 'Sea-Fever' is one of the poems found in most anthologies."
(c) "This poem carries me away—down to the sea in ships. It is the richest of my dreams, the essence of my wanderlust."
(d) "It is a poem both sentimental and sing-songy—I don't like it!"
(e) " 'Sea-Fever' used to be my favorite poem, but no longer. It has lost its old magic."

Notice that in the (a) statement the word *poem* clearly refers to Masefield's experience, or to what the writer of it believed Masefield's experience to have been. But in the (b) statement the word *poem* refers quite as clearly to the printed verses. In the statements (c) and (d) the word *poem* refers to two different readers' experiences, both stimulated by the same printed verses. But what very different experiences they were! What very different *poems* are referred to! And notice how, in the (e) statement, the word *poem* refers to previous pleasant experiences and to a present unpleasant experience, at one and the same time.

So it is that, although nearly everyone would agree that "Of course 'Sea-Fever' is *a poem,*" some persons will mean one thing and some will mean quite other things when using the words. Therefore, in this *Preface to Poetry,* when it is important to call attention to the particular sense in which the word *poem* is being used, somewhat cumbersome phrases will be employed to indicate which sense is intended. The following phrases or their equivalents will recur frequently in these pages: "the poet's experience," "the printed verses," and "the poem-reading-experience." [1]

A few additional comments should be made about this poem "Sea-Fever" before proceeding further. (In what sense or combination of senses am I using the word at this moment?)

When we think more closely of the poet's experience, for which the printed verses stand, we are faced with a very real problem. Do we mean his experience when the idea for the written poem first flashed into his mind? Or when he scratched out the verses with his pen (or worked them out in his head) riming "denied" with "tide," echoing "gull's way" with "whale's way," repeating consonant sounds in "wheel," "white," "whale," "whetted," "when"? Or do we mean Masefield's experience when, the labor of composition done, he put down his pen and read over what he had written, with a certain feeling of satisfaction? Or do we mean that later experience, prompted by some uncertainty, which led him to question the opening phrase of each stanza.[2] No one but Masefield himself will ever know exactly what the poet's experience was at any one of these times, and exactly what thoughts and feelings he intended to communicate to his future readers. And the chances are that, when asked, he would merely repeat the words of the printed poem, with perhaps a few random comments.

[1] For some readers the simple symbols $poem^p$, $poem^v$, and $poem^r$ would serve to distinguish the three senses of the word.

[2] The first line of each stanza of "Sea-Fever" is sometimes printed, "I must down to the seas again . . .;" and sometimes, "I must go down to the seas again. . . ." John Masefield now prefers the latter reading and, in response to enquiry, writes, "I always insert the word 'go' when I speak the line; and prefer to print it in the published versions."

When we turn to the printed verses under the title "Sea-Fever," again we are presented with a problem. Do we mean the printed verses in your copy of this book? Or the somewhat different printed page in Masefield's *The Story of the Round House*, with its somewhat different style of type, different line breaks, different punctuation? Or should we mean the poet's original handwritten MS, with whatever crossings-out and writings-in may have been a part of his creative effort? And in the case of "Sea-Fever," is the printed poem the "I must down" version or the "I must *go* down" version of the text? When we speak of the poem "Sea-Fever," we must, then, be alert to the fact that we may be referring to a particular set of printed verses in a particular book, or we may be referring to an abstraction based upon various printings or even various texts.

When we think of the poem-reading-experience, even closer attention must be given to the problem of reference. For each and every reader, the poem "Sea-Fever" will, of course, be different, though they may all be reading the same or identical copies of the printed poem. For the poem-experience is a complex pattern of the reader's thoughts, feelings, and other internal goings-on, his amazingly individual subjective response stimulated by the poem on the page. Indeed the poem-experience "Sea-Fever" will vary each time it is read, even by the same reader.

Let us think, for a further moment, about "Sea-Fever," and the relationship of the poet's experience, the printed poem, and the reading-experience. I cannot know anything about the printed verses except by experiencing them; and almost all that I will ever know about the poet's experience is what I can find out about it by a careful interpretation of his words.

It should be your aim, then, to achieve an experience as nearly like that of the poet as you can, and you must not forget that the poem on the page is the link between the two.

2. ASPECTS OF THE POEM-EXPERIENCE

Before pursuing the matter further, it might be well to read another poem. But first, a few words about this particular poet's experience.

He was a young man who liked, you may think strangely, to read great literature. A friend had borrowed a rare old volume, the *Iliad* and the *Odyssey* translated into the full-throated, salty English of Drake and Shakespeare. The two young men sat up most of the night reading aloud and by turns the exciting passages about the Trojan War and the wanderings of Ulysses—stories that they had previously known only in the dandified translation of Alexander Pope still current in their time. Finally, and toward dawn, John Keats walked home with stirring thoughts of the rich demesnes (or realms) of that ancient world, of the western islands out beyond what we call Gibraltar, of the many other noble works in classical literature, of the patron god of manly youth and of poetry, of the planets and stars, of the discovery of the New World and of the vast ocean beyond it as seen from the Isthmus. And before going to bed, he wrote out a poem, which he sent next morning to his friend, Charles Cowden Clarke.[3]

Read the poem slowly several times, but *do not,* for a reason that will be clear later, read this particular poem out loud.

ON FIRST LOOKING INTO CHAPMAN'S HOMER

John Keats

Much have I travell'd in the realms of gold,
    And many goodly states and kingdoms seen;
    Round many western islands have I been
Which bards in fealty to Apollo hold.
Oft of one wide expanse had I been told
    That deep-brow'd Homer rul'd as his demesne;
    Yet did I never breathe its pure serene
Till I heard Chapman speak out loud and bold:

Then felt I like some watcher of the skies
    When a new planet swims into his ken;
Or like stout Cortez when with eagle eyes
    He star'd at the Pacific—and all his men
Look'd at each other with a wild surmise—
    Silent, upon a peak in Darien.

(1816)

[3] See Amy Lowell, *John Keats,* Houghton Mifflin, 1925, vol. I, pp. 176 ff.

Now, in talking about the poem "On First Looking into Chapman's Homer," I can only describe my own experience. I cannot tell you what you thought, felt, and "saw." Nor shall I presume to tell you what you *ought* to have experienced. It is true that some readers are more skillful than others in the interpretation of poetry, that some readers have richer backgrounds or more active imaginations or more sensitive feelings; but, even among such especially qualified readers, poem-experiences will be of marked variety. Still, a short description of the present writer's poem-reading may be of some value and interest to those engaged upon this chapter.

Although my experience in reading "On First Looking into Chapman's Homer" possesses a notable unity, there are some six interrelated aspects that may be profitably distinguished: The *first* of these was my "seeing" the printed verses. This resulted from the pattern of stimulation upon the retina of my eyes. This "seeing" of the poem on the page was important, because the other five aspects of the reading experience were a response to it.

The *second* aspect of my experience was the "hearing" of the words in my mind's-ear, and my "feeling" them, almost as if they were rolling off my tongue. This consciousness of what the words would sound like, and of the feelings that would accompany their articulation, was definitely pleasing to me. I was also conscious of an underlying surging and variable rhythm, and an additional interest attached to the recurrence of the riming sounds: the "gold," "hold," "told," and "bold"; etc.

A *third* aspect of this experience consisted of the pictures that I "saw" in my mind's-eye. There were several such views that were especially clear, particularly that of an excited astronomer peering into his telescope, and the awe-struck explorer who realized his discovery of a vast uncharted sea. But there were other fleeting images that emerged with the interpretation of individual words: the textbook pictures of Homer, old and blind; a similar picture of Apollo Belvedere; and tropical island scenery. And there were related images, not visual, but the imagined sound of "loud and bold" speech, and the imagined smell of the clear fresh air of the mountain peak.

A *fourth* part of my total experience stimulated by the printed verses, was the stream of my thoughts about the meanings of the words. The way in which our thoughts serve to point to, or to refer to, things—"things" in the broadest sense—is an interesting problem that will be suggested in another chapter. It is enough at this moment to point out this intellectual stream due to the activity of the Central Nervous System, these thoughts of the things for which the words stand, this following of the *sense,* of what it is all about. It was as though I had made a rapid-fire running-comment on the words as they streamed by in my consciousness. "Oh, yes, *bards* is used to mean *poets,* like Milton and Tennyson and John Masefield . . . *fealty,* a strange word, Medieval society, yes, the faithful relationship of vassal to overlord . . . *Apollo,* classic myths, Greek gods, Sun-god? (Doesn't fit in here), good-looks? (No), *god of poetry!* . . . *Homer*—he wrote the *Odyssey;* Penelope and her suitors, Ulysses and the Cyclops. . . . *Chapman*—Shakespeare's rival poet (?), wrote *Eastward Ho!,* translated Homer. . . . *Cortez* (ha! it was Balboa; I remember that)—well, *explorer* anyway. . . . *Darien*—where's that? Oh, yes, Isthmus of Panama. . . ." So much for the side comments, here only very crudely suggested. The sense of my poem-experience seems to piece itself together and, in substance, may be represented by the following summary:

John Keats says, "I have been a wide reader of great books, but I had no knowledge of Homer till I came upon his works as put into clear, strong English by Chapman. Then my feelings were like those of the man who sees some new star for the first time, or like the feelings of Cortez (= Balboa) and his men when, from the mountain top in Panama, they had their first view of the great Pacific Ocean."

This will suffice for the present discussion of the sense of the poem in my reading.

The *fifth* aspect of the poem-experience is the emotional stream of activity that, for many persons, goes deeper than the thoughts of the sense, and seems at times to involve the reader's whole being. For me, at any rate, there is a succession of vague and fleeting feelings caused by past associations with particular words, and I might suggest some of them in this way: "I certainly *do like* to

travel . . . *pretty* scenery, green islands against golden sunset . . .
didn't *care* much for the classic myths, but like Greek sculpture
. . . Homer: Ulysses' *good times* at the Court of Alcinoüs; the
sports and races were *exciting* . . . clean mountain air makes me
feel good all over. . . ." So I might go on with a record of these
feelings that trail along, in my experience, with the senses and images and sounds of the words. But it is the over-all feeling evoked
that is of greatest importance to me in this poem-experience. I have
experienced this emotion before: the tingling excitement I have had
in the sudden discovery of the amazing and the new. The sheer
thrill of my first precipitate in the high school chem lab; the first
view of the Sierra Nevada back-country from Kaiser Ridge; my
first sight of a spouting whale off South Laguna; my discovery of
Walt Whitman. And I believe that my feelings are somewhat like
John Keats' feelings when he discovered in Chapman's translation the bracing and invigorating air of Homer's epic poems.

But there is a *sixth* and final aspect to my experience. It might
be called the residuum, if by that we mean not only the bits of
experience that may remain in the memory for conscious recall, but
also the personality changes or shifts in attitude that may have resulted as a part of the poem-reading-experience. In addition to such
phrases as "deep-brow'd Homer" and "the pure serene," and such
mind-pictures as that of the astronomer and that of the explorer
with his men, which are subject to recall from the vaults of my
remembrance, I venture to say that "On First Looking into Chapman's Homer" has left me somehow changed in my disposition,
more alert to discover and to be moved by the awesome, whether
in literature or in life.

In these six paragraphs, then, I have described a particular poem-
reading-experience—my own. A further consideration of some of
the problems therein suggested will form the substance of Part
Two of this book.

3. VALUE AND VARIETY

So far in our Search for Poetry, we have asked the question,
"What is a poem?" and, after discovering several answers to that

question, we have begun an exploration of the poem-inside-the-skin. Let us now turn our attention to a pair of poems that will serve to carry this introductory orientation a step further.

The first of these two poems narrates an incident from the naval Battle of the Nile (1798) in which the British under Nelson defeated the French in Abukir Bay. When the French admiral, Brueys, was killed, Louis de Casabianca took command, was wounded, remained at his post, his son with him, and was blown up with his ship.

CASABIANCA
Felicia Hemans

The boy stood on the burning deck,
  Whence all but him had fled;
The flame that lit the battle's wreck
  Shone round him o'er the dead.

Yet beautiful and bright he stood,
  As born to rule the storm;
A creature of heroic blood,
  A proud, though child-like form.

The flames rolled on; he would not go
  Without his father's word;
That father, faint in death below,
  His voice no longer heard.

He called aloud, "Say, father, say,
  If yet my task be done!"
He knew not that the chieftain lay
  Unconscious of his son.

"Speak, father!" once again he cried,
  "If I may yet be gone!"
And but the booming shots replied,
  And fast the flames rolled on.

Upon his brow he felt their breath,
  And in his waving hair,
And looked from that lone post of death
  In still, yet brave despair;

And shouted but once more aloud,
  "My father! must I stay?"
While o'er him, fast, through sail and shroud,
  The wreathing fires made way.

They wrapped the ship in splendor wild,
  They caught the flag on high,
And streamed above the gallant child,
  Like banners in the sky.

There came a burst of thunder sound;
  The boy,—oh! where was he?
Ask of the winds, that far around
  With fragments strewed the sea,—

With mast, and helm, and pennon fair,
  That well had borne their part,—
But the noblest thing that perished there,
  Was that young, faithful heart.

                                    (1829)

The second of these two poems, written about a century later,
takes the suggestion for its title from Macbeth's words when he
hears of his Queen's death.[4]

"OUT, OUT—"
Robert Frost

The buzz-saw snarled and rattled in the yard
And made dust and dropped stove-length sticks of wood,
Sweet-scented stuff when the breeze drew across it.
And from there those that lifted eyes could count
Five mountain ranges one behind the other
Under the sunset far into Vermont.

---

[4] See *Macbeth*, V, v, 16-28 for the full passage.
        . . . Out, out, brief candle!
    Life's but a walking shadow, a poor player
    That struts and frets his hour upon the stage,
    And then is heard no more; it is a tale
    Told by an idiot, full of sound and fury,
    Signifying nothing.

And the saw snarled and rattled, snarled and rattled,
As it ran light, or had to bear a load.
And nothing happened: day was all but done.
Call it a day, I wish they might have said
To please the boy by giving him the half hour
That a boy counts so much when saved from work.
His sister stood beside them in her apron
To tell them "Supper." At the word, the saw,
As if to prove saws knew what supper meant,
Leaped out at the boy's hand, or seemed to leap—
He must have given the hand. However it was,
Neither refused the meeting. But the hand!
The boy's first outcry was a rueful laugh,
As he swung toward them holding up the hand
Half in appeal, but half as if to keep
The life from spilling. Then the boy saw all—
Since he was old enough to know, big boy
Doing a man's work, though a child at heart—
He saw all spoiled. "Don't let him cut my hand off—
The doctor, when he comes. Don't let him, sister!"
So. But the hand was gone already.
The doctor put him in the dark of ether.
He lay and puffed his lips out with his breath.
And then—the watcher at his pulse took fright.
No one believed. They listened at his heart.
Little—less—nothing!—and that ended it.
No more to build on there. And they, since they
Were not the one dead, turned to their affairs.

(1916)

The fact that these poems were presented as a pair may have made the reader attentive to the similarities and differences in the two reading experiences. Both of the poems are narrative—they involve characters "doing things." Both depict the death of a boy. And there, for some readers, the similarities cease, and the many differences begin. It is not to our purpose now to enumerate the various sorts of differences that readers might point out—romantic, realistic; heroic, commonplace; past, present; remote, immediate; sentimental, restrained; etc., etc.—but to introduce another problem.

Despite the fact that "Casabianca" was long an elocutionary favorite—"Eating peanuts by the peck," from the parody, still comes readily to tongue—it is what many people today would call a "bad" poem. Despite the fact that "Out, Out—" may never enjoy such popularity, it is what many people today would call a "good" poem.

The first poem is a bad one for many because it is the stimulus for mediocre poem-experiences; the second poem is a good one because it is the stimulus for valuable poem-experiences. "There is nothing either good or bad," says Hamlet in an often carelessly interpreted speech, "but thinking makes it so." In their thinking about a poem, in making their value judgments and in rationalizing them, readers will find themselves at wide variance one with another. Some readers are surprised to find that competent scholars, critics, and editors disagree in their evaluation of particular poems. But that they disagree in many instances is not so surprising as that they often do agree, though their general agreement may result from widely different intuitive and rational processes.

But a further discussion of the Evaluation of Poetry must wait until Part Three. Now a concluding comment will indicate the direction that the reader should go from there, when he undertakes further reading and study of poetry.

The eleven poems so far included in this volume have been widely different. Each of them was written by a different poet, and their dates and places of composition spread over three and a third centuries and across the Atlantic. Some of these poems are called lyrical, some narrative; each of them is in a different form, though there are some close similarities in this regard. But more important, the reading-experiences occasioned by these poems have been of amazing variety: in subject matter and in theme, in mood and in style; in the swing of their "music," in the nature of their imagery, in emotional content. And, as has just been pointed out, these poems have certainly been of varying value.

Keats speaks of "the realms of gold," of "many goodly states and kingdoms," of the "western islands . . . Which bards in fealty to Apollo hold." It is the purpose of this volume to open up to the reader the wide and varied expanses of Poetry where he too may make exploration and discovery.

SUGGESTIONS FOR STUDY

1. *Variations in a Poem.* "A Red, Red Rose" by Robert Burns, reprinted in the first chapter, begins with these lines:

> O, my luve is like a red, red rose,
> That's newly sprung in June.
> O, my luve is like a melodie,
> That's sweetly played in tune.

But sometimes it is printed in a version with the following first line (and third line to match):

> O, my Luve's like a red, red rose. . . .

Occasionally one sees—

> My love is like a red, red rose. . . .

Sometimes the "O" is "Oh," and the "luve" or "Luve" is "love" or "Love."

Consider the question: Just what effect might the apparently slight variations in the printed poem have upon the poem-experience for a particular reader? (a) As you read the entire poem, how do you feel that it "goes"? Which of the readings seems best to fit the swing of the lines? Which seems to you the most "musical"? (b) Are you inclined to pronounce "luve" and "love" identically? Is there, for you, any difference in the overtones of their meaning? Which is more likely to suggest "the girl loved," and which "the emotion of love"—*my luve* or *my Luve?*

2. *The First Draft of Keats' Poem.* We have said that it should be the reader's aim to achieve an experience as nearly like that of the poet as he can. The incident in Keats' life that led up to his writing the sonnet "On First Looking into Chapman's Homer" was narrated above in an effort to bring the reader a step closer to the poet's experience. It may be of somewhat similar help to the reader to study the facsimile reproduction of the first draft of the poem.[5]

Compare this version of the poem with the one given in the text. What are the principal verbal differences? What can you deduce from

[5] First published by Amy Lowell, *John Keats,* Houghton Mifflin, 1925 (vol. I, op. p. 180), it is here reprinted by special permission of Mrs. Ada Russell and of the Harvard College Library.

them about the poet's creative activity? Amy Lowell, herself a poet, has traced many of the "bits and tittles of thought and memory" out of which Keats made his sonnet, and the student especially interested in the poet's experience may well refer to her study of *John Keats*, volume I, pages 176-83. There he will find the likely source of the "pure

Facsimile of the first draft of Keats' "On First Looking into Chapman's Homer"

serene" that Keats added in revising the first draft, and the various bits of reading from which Keats' creative talent fashioned the bold similes in the last lines of the poem.

3. *A First Look into Chapman's Homer.* Keats wrote the sonnet after his first reading from George Chapman's translation of Homer's great epic poems, *The Iliad* and *The Odyssey*.

(a) Refresh your memory of these two works, of which you have doubtless some knowledge already, by consulting a ready reference book, such as the *Oxford Companion to Classical Literature,* or one of the standard encyclopedias. Which of the epics seems to you to have been most influential in shaping Keats' poem?

(b) Among the passages in Chapman's translation that, according to Clarke, gave Keats especial pleasure, is the one here reprinted, depicting the shipwreck of Ulysses.

from THE ODYSSEY Book V
Homer, translated by George Chapman

This spoke, a huge wave took him by the head,
And hurl'd him o'er-board; ship and all it laid
Inverted quite amidst the waves, but he
Far off from her sprawl'd, strow'd about the sea,
His stern still holding, broken off, his mast
Burst in the midst, so horrible a blast
Of mix'd winds strook it. Sails and sailyards fell
Amongst the billows; and himself did dwell
A long time under water; nor could get
In haste his head out, wave with wave so met
In his depression . . . ; but gat at length again,
Wrestling with Neptune, hold of her; and then
Sat in her bulk, insulting over death,
Which, with the salt stream prest to stop his breath,
He scaped, and gave the sea again to give
To other men. His ship so strived to live,
Floating at random, cuff'd from wave to wave. . . .

Ino Leucothea, . . . she with pity saw
Ulysses justled thus from flaw to flaw,
And, like a cormorand in form and flight,
Rose from a whirl-pool, on the ship did light
And thus bespeak him: ". . . Thou shalt not be unwise
To leave thy weeds and ship to the commands
Of these rude winds, and work out with thy hands. . . .
Take here this tablet, with this riband strung,
And see it still about thy bosom hung;
By whose eternal virtue never fear
To suffer thus again, nor perish here.
But when thou touchest with thy hand the shore,
Then take it from thy neck, nor wear it more;

But cast it far off from the continent,
And then thy person far ashore present."
     Thus gave she him the tablet; and again,
Turn'd to a cormorand, dived, past sight, the main.
     Patient Ulysses: ". . . Not with thoughts too clear
Will I obey her; but to me appear
These counsels best; as long as I perceive
My ship not quite dissolved, I will not leave. . . ."

     While this discourse employ'd him, Neptune raised
A huge, a high, and horrid sea, that seized
Him and his ship, and toss'd them through the lake. . . .
     Then did Ulysses mount on rib, perforce,
Like to a rider of a running horse,
To stay himself a time, while he might shift
His drenchèd weeds, that were Calypso's gift.
When putting straight Leucothea's amulet
About his neck, he all his forces set
To swim, and cast him prostrate to the seas. . . .

                    . . . Two nights, yet, and days
He spent in wrestling with the sable seas;
In which space, often did his heart propose
Death to his eyes. But when Aurora rose,
And threw the third light from her orient hair,
The winds grew calm, and clear was all the air,
Not one breath stirring. Then he might descry,
Raised by the high seas, clear, the land was nigh. . . .
Then labour'd feet and all parts to aspire
To that wish'd continent; which when as near
He came, as Clamour might inform an ear,
He heard a sound beat from the sea-bred rocks,
Against which gave a huge sea horrid shocks. . . .
The shores, the rocks, and cliffs, so prominent were.
"O," said Ulysses then, "now Jupiter
Hath given me sight of an unhoped-for shore,
Though I have wrought these seas so long, so sore. . . .
And should I swim to seak a haven elsewhere,
Or land less way-beat, I may justly fear
I shall be taken with a gale again,
And cast a huge way off into the main. . . ."

While this discourse he held,
A cursèd surge 'gainst a cutting rock impell'd
His naked body, which it gash'd and tore,
And had his bones broke, if but one sea more
Had cast him on it. But [Pallas] prompted him,
That never fail'd, and bade him no more swim
Still off and on, but boldly force the shore,
And hug the rock that him so rudely tore;
Which he with both hands sigh'd and clasp'd till past
The billow's rage was; which scaped, back so fast
The rock repulsed it, that it reft his hold,
Sucking him from it, and far back he roll'd. . . .
Quite under water fell he; and, past fate,
Hapless Ulysses there had lost the state
He held in life, if, still the gray-eyed Maid
His wisdom prompting, he had not assay'd
Another course, and ceased t' attempt that shore,
Swimming, and casting round his eye t' explore
Some other shelter. Then the mouth he found
Of fair Callicoe's flood; whose shores were crown'd
With most apt succours; rocks so smooth they seem'd
Polish'd for purpose; land that quite redeem'd
With breathless coverts th' others' blasted shores. . . .

Then forth he came, his both knees faltering, both
His strong hands hanging down, and all with froth
His cheeks and nosthrils flowing, voice and breath
Spent to all use, and down he sunk to death.
The sea had soak'd his heart through; all his veins
His toils had rack'd t' a labouring woman's pains.
Dead weary was he. But when breath did find
A pass reciprocal, and in his mind
His spirit was recollected, up he rose,
And from his neck did th' amulet unloose,
That Ino gave him; which he hurl'd from him
To sea. It sounding fell, and back did swim
With th' ebbing waters, till it straight arrived
Where Ino's fair hand it again received.
Then kiss'd he th' humble earth; and on he goes,
Till bulrushes show'd place for his repose,

Where laid, he sigh'd, and thus said to his soul:
"O me, what strange perplexities control
The whole skill of thy powers in this event! . . . "

(*?c.850 B.C.;* 1614)

From the deep sleep into which he falls, Ulysses is awakened by the beautiful Nausicaä, princess of the land, and her handmaidens, who, having washed clothes and bathed in the river, are enjoying a frolicsome game of ball. Taken by her to her father's court, Ulysses is hospitably entertained with food and song and athletic contests.[6]

To John Keats, the Elizabethan translation of Chapman came like a breath of fresh air in a stuffy room, for he was accustomed to the translation of Alexander Pope, a few lines of which are here given for ready comparison with the final verse paragraph above:

from THE ODYSSEY Book V

Homer, translated by *Alexander Pope*

That moment, fainting as he touch'd the shore,
He dropp'd his sinewy arms: his knees no more
Perform'd their office, or his weight upheld:
His swoln heart heaved; his bloated body swell'd:
From mouth and nose the briny torrent ran;
And lost in lassitude lay all the man,
Deprived of voice, of motion, and of breath;
The soul scarce waking in the arms of death.
Soon as warm life its wonted office found,
The mindful chief Leucothea's scarf unbound;
Observant of her word, he turn'd aside
His head, and cast it on the rolling tide.
Behind him far, upon the purple waves,
The waters waft it, and the nymph receives.
Now parting from the stream, Ulysses found
A mossy bank with pliant rushes crown'd;
The bank he press'd, and gently kiss'd the ground;
Where on the flowery herb as soft he lay,
Thus to his soul the sage began to say:

[6] *The Odyssey* is readily approached through other translations. A recent prose translation is by T. E. Shaw (Lawrence of Arabia); the standard prose translation is that of Butcher and Lang. The verse translation of William Cullen Bryant is still widely read.

"What will ye next ordain, ye powers on high!
  And yet, ah yet, what fates are we to try? . . ."

(1725)

(c) Now reread Keats' sonnet thoughtfully yet again. How has the poem changed for you as a result of your own "first looking into Chapman's Homer"?

4. *First Thoughts.* Read the following short poem a time or two.

SO WE'LL GO NO MORE A-ROVING

George Gordon, Lord Byron

So we'll go no more a-roving
  So late into the night,
Though the heart be still as loving,
  And the moon be still as bright.

For the sword outwears its sheath,
  And the soul wears out the breast,
And the heart must pause to breathe,
  And Love itself have rest.

Though the night was made for loving,
  And the day returns too soon,
Yet we'll go no more a-roving
  By the light of the moon.

(1817)

Now jot down some notes about the poem as you experienced it, your first thoughts: what scenes and persons came to mind? what was the meaning of it to you? what emotional response did you feel?

5. *Second Thoughts.* The above poem was sent by Lord Byron from Venice to his friend Tom Moore in a letter, dated February 28, 1817, that read in part as follows: "At present, I am on the invalid regimen myself. The Carnival—that is, the latter part of it, and sitting up late o' nights, had knocked me up a little. But it is over,—and it is now Lent, with all its abstinence and sacred music. The mumming closed with a masked ball at the Fenice [a theatre in Venice], where I went, as also to most of the ridottos [masquerades with music and dancing], etc., etc.; and, though I did not dissipate much upon the whole, yet I

find 'The sword wearing out the scabbard' [an old French saying], though I have but just turned the corner of twenty-nine."

Reread Byron's poem against the background of this letter, and make some fresh notes. Then look back over your First Thoughts. In what particulars is your experience now a different one?

Compare your notes with those of other readers. Are your Second Thoughts more nearly alike than your First Thoughts?

6. *Experiencing a Poem.* The following is part of section #47 of the long poem Walt Whitman wrote and rewrote over a period of a dozen years. He gave it his own name as a title, but it is frequently called "Song of Myself." (a) Glance back over the pointers in Chapter 1 (pp. 6-7), and try to put them to use in reading this selection. (b) After reading and rereading it, think over the six interrelated aspects of the poem-reading-experience as they have been distinguished in this chapter.

from SONG OF MYSELF
Walt Whitman

I am the teacher of athletes;
He that by me spreads a wider breast than my own, proves the width
    of my own;
He most honors my style who learns under it to destroy the teacher.

The boy I love, the same becomes a man, not through derived power,
    but in his own right,
Wicked, rather than virtuous out of conformity or fear,
Fond of his sweetheart, relishing well his steak,
Unrequited love, or a slight, cutting him worse than sharp steel cuts,
First-rate to ride, to fight, to hit the bull's eye, to sail a skiff, to sing
    a song, or play on the banjo,
Preferring scars, and the beard, and faces pitted with small-pox, over
    all latherers,
And those well tann'd to those that keep out of the sun.

I teach straying from me—yet who can stray from me?
I follow you, whoever you are, from the present hour;
My words itch at your ears till you understand them.

I do not say these things for a dollar, or to fill up the time while I
    wait for a boat;
It is you talking just as much as myself—I act as the tongue of you;
Tied in your mouth, in mine it begins to be loosen'd. . . .

The young mechanic is closest to me—he knows me well;

The woodman, that takes his axe and jug with him, shall take me with him all day;

The farm-boy, ploughing in the field, feels good at the sound of my voice;

In vessels that sail, my words sail—I go with fishermen and seamen, and love them.

The soldier camp'd, or upon the march, is mine;

On the night ere the pending battle, many seek me, and I do not fail them;　·

On the solemn night (it may be their last,) those that know me, seek me. . . .

(1855-67)

3

LANGUAGE AND ART

There are an amazing number of waking hours during which we make use of language—conversing with our friends, listening to lectures or broadcasts, reading books and papers, taking notes and writing letters or reports. We carry on our business with words —conferences, letters, contracts. Our entertainment is largely verbal—cinema, radio, magazines. Our religious practices are in some ways essentially linguistic—Mass, prayer, sermons, meditation. Our scientific knowledge is developed, controlled, and transmitted by language—hypothesis, classification, exposition. And we must not forget that the chief cumulative record of the great Human Comedy is to be found in Literature.

In the past, people were all so busy making use of language in their daily lives that they didn't pay much attention to exactly *how it worked*. During recent years, however, with the widespread application of psychology to various fields of activity, there has developed a better understanding of our language behavior. We can now see how advertising slogans work upon us; we are alert to the uses of propaganda; we may be more cautious in making generalizations and in using abstractions. The word "semantics" has come into general use. The *Tyranny of Words* and *Language in Action* have been best-sellers.[1] Popular articles in the press and journals have followed upon the growing body of critical literature, extending our knowledge of this new science of language. C. K. Ogden and I. A. Richards, pioneers in this work, began publishing their language studies some twenty years ago.[2] It is to this new movement in linguistic thought that this *Preface to Poetry* belongs.

[1] Stuart Chase, *The Tyranny of Words,* Harcourt, Brace, 1938; S. I. Hayakawa, *Language in Action,* Harcourt, Brace, 1941.
[2] *The Meaning of Meaning* (Harcourt, Brace, 1923) is now in its fourth edition.

I. THE ART FUNCTION OF LANGUAGE

Let us begin by pointing out that language has three distinct functions. Look closely at the following examples:

FINAL TOUCHES
PUT ON PAGEANT

Finishing touches were put on the stage of Hollywood bowl today for the pageant "We Will Never Die," which tomorrow night will be given its only performance in the west.

The cast of 1000 will be headed by Edward G. Robinson, Edward Arnold, Akim Tamiroff, Jacob Ben-Ami, John Garfield. . . .

The mass memorial for more than 2,000,000 Jewish civilians killed in Europe was written by Ben Hecht, with musical score by Kurt Weill.

Hollywood bowl has been converted for the performance into a huge place of worship, draped in black, with the Ten Commandments inscribed on two 40 foot tablets on the stage.

All races and creeds have endorsed the pageant. Cochairmen include Archbishop John J. Cantwell, Bishop W. Bertrand Stevens and Rabbi Edgar F. Magnin, and Dr. E. C. Farnham, executive secretary of the Church Federation, has lent his support to the production.

Now for the second example:

. . . "What does a person do when he looks at a picture?" This question is obviously a very general one which may be restated as a series of specific questions relating to the nature of the processes of perception and attention while studying any work of art. Certain of these questions relate to the characteristics of the picture being observed. For example, what is the effect of color or lack of color? What are the main centers of interest in looking at a picture? Does the pattern of perception re-

flect the way the various parts of the picture are balanced? Other questions might be asked relating to the characteristics of the persons
looking at a picture. . . . Still other questions might have to do with
the conditions under which a picture is observed. . . .

Here is a third example:

FLOWER IN THE CRANNIED WALL
Alfred, Lord Tennyson

Flower in the crannied wall,
I pluck you out of the crannies,
I hold you here, root and all, in my hand,
Little flower—but *if* I could understand
What you are, root and all, and all in all,
I should know what God and man is.

(1869)

In the first example above, from the *Daily News,* language is
used solely for the purpose of *communication.* Such is the infor-
mational function of journalism. Here the facts gathered by the
reporter are put into words printed on news stock, delivered at the
door, and read at the breakfast table. If the reporter has been reasonably skilled, if no serious smudges blur the printing, and if
one is a relatively able reader, the main facts about the forthcoming
pageant are communicated by means of language.

Note, however, that in the second example language functions
differently, or at least you may observe an added function. Here,
Guy T. Buswell, in his book *How People Look at Pictures,* is
using language as a device for *problem-solving.* He is, as a heading
points out, stating and clarifying his problem, and he does this by
asking a general question for which he will try to find a scientific
answer. He then proceeds to ask a series of more specific questions,
some of which are here omitted. Asking these questions was a part
of Professor Buswell's problem-solving. "What does a person do
when he looks at a picture?" Well, Buswell hypothesizes, that may
depend upon the kind of picture looked at, upon the person who
looks at it, and upon conditions at the time. Then he proceeds to

gather scientific data bearing upon the questions. After interpreting these data and sorting them out, he comes to certain conclusions, which form the last three pages of the text of his book.

In the third example, "Flower in the Crannied Wall," language serves what we shall call the *art function* of "emotional adjustment." Its chief purpose is not to communicate information, nor to proceed with the solution of a problem. Here we find words carefully chosen and arranged in such a way as to achieve a special sort of effect in the reader. This special sort of effect is that complex combination of rhythmic and sound patterns, image pattern, meaning pattern, and feeling pattern outlined in the last chapter and there called a poem-reading-experience. Whereas in the news item and in the paragraph above about how we look at pictures, language was used primarily to make statements and to ask questions of fact, in Tennyson's poem language is used primarily to stimulate in the reader an experience of a special sort, to suggest searching thoughts, to stir feelings, and to shape attitudes.

When we put the sense of the news item into other words, nothing of great importance seems to be lost:

Last minute details were completed at the Hollywood Bowl for the staging of "We Will Never Die," which will be given tomorrow night, one time only in California. . . .

The facts, by and large, are presented in this rewrite. So, too, when one puts the sense of Mr. Buswell's paragraph into other words:

"What is one's behavior while in the act of seeing a painting?" That question takes in more than may be answered at one time. So let us put a number of special questions about the make-up and operation of our sense system and attention when an art-thing is under observation.

Here again, other words, or the same words differently arranged, serve well enough. The substance of the exposition remains virtually unchanged. But look at a similar rewording of Tennyson's poem:

The writer says, as if to a small flower, "I have taken you up by the roots, from between the stones in this wall, and have you here in my *hand*. That was not hard to do. But if I had in my *mind* all the facts of your plant structure, growth and development, and your place in the design of things, I would be full of the knowledge of God and of man, and of their relation one to the other."

In the first place, the reader may not be satisfied that the above prose paraphrase is an accurate transcript of the sense of the poem. In the second place, he will say at once that, granting the mere *sense* of Tennyson's words has survived, or has even been made clearer, "the real poetry of it" has been lost. The paraphrase, using nearly twice as many words, seems to do only half as much work. The special form of the poem to the eye is, of course, lost; the patterned flow of the simple words, with the recurrent syllable stress and sounds; the sharpness of the central image; the contrast between the unmistakable meaning of the opening lines and the enigmatic suggestion of the close; the deep stir of wonder and humility—these things have evaporated in the translation! And these things *are* the poem-reading-experience—or, at least, the most characteristic parts of it!

2. THE PROBLEM OF MEANING

Before continuing our discussion of how words do their work, let us observe another example of language in action. Remember the pointers given in the first chapter (pp. 6-7), and read this poem slowly and aloud, alert in mind and with an open heart. But read it only once or twice before going on with the paragraphs that follow it.

EUCLID ALONE HAS LOOKED ON BEAUTY BARE
Edna St. Vincent Millay

Euclid alone has looked on Beauty bare.
Let all who prate of Beauty hold their peace,
And lay them prone upon the earth and cease
To ponder on themselves, the while they stare
At nothing, intricately drawn nowhere
In shapes of shifting lineage; let geese
Gabble and hiss, but heroes seek release
From dusty bondage into luminous air.

O blinding hour—O holy terrible day,
When first the shaft into his vision shone
Of light anatomized! Euclid alone
Has looked on Beauty bare. Fortunate they
Who, though once only and then but far away,
Have heard her massive sandal set on stone.

(1920)

This poem, unlike "Flower in the Crannied Wall," may have given you a bit of trouble in the reading. Perhaps some of the words were strange or unusual to you, or you didn't get the sense of them here or there. *Euclid* is, of course, the ancient Greek, the "father of geometry," that branch of mathematics concerned with the relationship of lines, angles, surfaces, solids. The capitalization of a word like *Beauty* may mean, either that the writer is giving emphasis to his notion of an abstract thing, or that the abstraction is personified—imagined as being a person. The word *prate* is often used in the sense of idle or foolish talk or prattle. The phrase *hold your peace* is common in Shakespeare as an order to be quiet, "hold your tongue." *Prone,* as the opposite of "supine," usually bears the sense of face downward. The word *lineage* is sometimes pronounced as having three syllables, (lĭn'ê·àj) or (lĭn'ê·ĭj), and sometimes as two (lĭn'ĭj). It is often used to mean the line of one's descent, one's ancestors; it is also used, with disyllabic pronunciation, to refer to lines of printed matter, or to one thing's being lined up with another; but in the poem, of course, the word may be used in some other and perhaps quite obvious sense. *Anatomize* may be used to mean to analyze or to dissect something so as to show its structure.

When Edna St. Vincent Millay was a student at Vassar College in 1914, a new theorem was discovered by a member of the Mathematics Department, and this may, in the opinion of the poet's biographer Elizabeth Atkins, have "brought home to Millay the consciousness that the mathematician, as well as the word-wielder, may be a poet." [3] She may also have been reading Bertrand Russell, who had just written: "The true spirit of delight, the exaltation,

[3] Elizabeth Atkins, *Edna St. Vincent Millay and Her Times,* University of Chicago Press, 1936, pp. 32-33.

the sense of being more than man . . . is to be found in mathematics as surely as in poetry." Mathematics, Philosophy, Literature were among the subjects of Edna St. Vincent Millay's study at Vassar. Her first volume of poetry was entitled *Renascence,* and it is no mere accident that "Euclid Alone—" is cast in a favorite form of the Italian Renaissance, the sonnet, and that it echoes Shakespeare more than once in its language.

Now your general store of relevant information has been somewhat enriched, but without your being told what the lines of the poem mean, or in which sense certain words are being used. So, return to a careful rereading of the poem, which, for your convenience, is here again reprinted:

> Euclid alone has looked on Beauty bare. .
> Let all who prate of Beauty hold their peace,
> And lay them prone upon the earth and cease
> To ponder on themselves, the while they stare
> At nothing, intricately drawn nowhere
> In shapes of shifting lineage; let geese
> Gabble and hiss, but heroes seek release
> From dusty bondage into luminous air.
>
> O blinding hour—O holy terrible day,
> When first the shaft into his vision shone
> Of light anatomized! Euclid alone
> Has looked on Beauty bare. Fortunate they
> Who, though once only and then but far away,
> Have heard her massive sandal set on stone.

Did this second reading go better? There may still be some particular questions raised by this poem that might well be discussed. But before doing so, let us take a general look at the way in which the language is doing its work.

The meaning of a poem—or of a news story or of a technical book—is a very complex thing. That meaning will consist of the meanings of the individual words and of their special relationships to one another in the utterance. But the over-all meaning of the work will often seem to be greater than the mere total of these separate meanings, and this is especially so in the case of poetry.

Now, a word has *meaning* only when it is at work in a sentence, and its meaning is dependent upon its particular use—upon the words round about it; its relation to them, and to the general drift of what has been said; its relation to the time and the place; and its relation to both the vital and the verbal experience of the person using it. But there is still a common misconception that words have absolute meanings. It is only in the technical vocabularies of the exact sciences that certain words, each coined to name one definite thing, are used under the formula: one word = one meaning. And even these words, like "vitamin," get out into the nontechnical world and quickly acquire new senses. No, for the most part, words do not have absolute meanings; words have particular meanings only in context. Take *lineage,* for instance, as used in the poem above.[4] We are, truly, sense-making mechanisms; and our effort to make sense out of the words before us, led to the rejection of the "ancestor" sense and "printer's line" and "alignment"—senses of the word recorded in the dictionaries. But the preceding words, "shapes of shifting—," and the general drift of what's been said about Euclid, and our experiences with geometry—geometric figures, angles, lines—give us an appropriate sense: *lineage* = simply "lines."

That's what it means to the writer of this book. What did it mean to Edna St. Vincent Millay?

Well, to the poet, the word *lineage,* the phrase "In shapes of shifting lineage," meant what she meant it to mean! (Notice how the word "meant" here shifts its meaning.) And we will never know what she meant for certain, really and absolutely, even if Edna St. Vincent Millay were to write out an explanation of her meaning—for we should then be faced with the problem of interpreting her explanation. So as careful readers, anxious to come as close to the intended meaning as possible, we make use of all the relevant parts of the background of our experience, acquiring new bits of information as needed, and keeping ourselves alert to all the clues to be found within the work itself.

It has been recognized that words may operate with double

---

[4] By the way, how did you decide to pronounce the word? How many syllables do you feel are called for by the "swing" of the line?

meanings. When language is functioning purely for communication, this possible ambiguity is a great hazard, and the writer whose business it is to "give us the facts" will make every effort to avoid those word-relationships that will be open to two equally self-consistent interpretations. He is a downright knave, of course, if he tricks us with an outwardly innocent statement that, once accepted, is turned to sinister account. So, too, when language is used as a tool in problem-solving, the writer will make an effort to pin down his critical terms with working definitions, and strive to avoid those constructions in his writing that may leave his sentences open to several interpretations. For ambiguity is a fault when language is serving these two functions.

But not so when language is serving its art function. The amazing capacity of words to suggest two or more equally suitable senses in a given verse, to operate with two or more senses at the same time, to convey a central meaning but with overtones and undertones of other senses—this is the great "resourcefulness of language," to use I. A. Richards' phrase. And poets have been especially skillful in making use of the full carrying power of language, supercharging their words often with a great pressure of meaning.

It is also important to point out that the sense of an utterance is only one aspect of its full meaning, which may be looked upon as a very rich compound of intention, tone, and feeling, as well as the mere sense of it.[5] The good reporter and the scientific writer will use language in such a way as to communicate the facts in the case, avoiding those "emotive" words that will show their strong feelings about the subject and that will arouse similar feelings in their readers. Not so the editorial writer and the feature writer, or the popularizer of scientific material. They will make use of a language well loaded with feeling, whether it is excitement or prejudice, propaganda or sarcasm, for their intention will be to play, at least in part, upon the readers' feelings and to establish in them certain attitudes. They will be using words for "emotional adjustment," very much as it is used in poetry. It is in language serving this art function that the meaning will be the richest—and

[5] This matter will be considered in some detail in Chapter 7.

about which there may be widest difference of opinion among equally competent readers.

But let us return to Euclid—and to Beauty. *Friday*

3. THE PROBLEM OF BEAUTY

The following paraphrase, in an intentionally controlled vocabulary, is not set forth as *the* meaning of "Euclid Alone—." It is only one reader's understanding of the sense of the poem, presented here as a challenge to other readers who should develop their own interpretations.

Euclid is the only man who has had a clear idea of what "the beautiful" truly is. Let the teachers of art-theory put a stop to their foolish talk about art-values—and, face down upon the earth, with no thought of their feelings, let them keep their eyes shut and give attention to the lines and angles of geometry formed in the mind's-eye. *Small* persons will go on making their foolish noise, like common fowl running about among the dirty farm buildings. But the *great* men, stretching their wings, will get above the dust and up into the free light air.

It was truly a blinding hour, a day of holy fear, when Euclid suddenly "saw" the beautiful relation of line to line, angle to angle, the basic facts of geometry. Euclid is the only man who has had a full view of "the Beautiful," in person and unclothed. To other persons, by chance—once only and from a distance—no more than the sound of her footfall!

And indeed the reader will come forward with his questions and objections: "Where do you get the 'teachers of art-theory'? Any one may 'prate of Beauty'—and most people do! And it's 'Beauty,' not 'art-values,' of which they prattle." . . . "Edna St. Vincent Millay doesn't tell them to shut their eyes. How do you get 'lines and angles of geometry' out of 'shapes of shifting lineage'?"[6] . . . "Is

[6] "Generally the sonnet is read as if concerned with geometric discoveries, but patently the lines 'When first the shaft into his vision shone/ Of light anatomized' have reference to an optical discovery," writes E. R. M. in *The Explicator,* October, 1942, wondering "what bearing Euclid's 'Optics' may have upon the lines in question." Other comments in explication of the lines are to be found in the next issue of the same publication.

it a 'holy terrible day' for Euclid or for mankind?" . . . "Why interpret 'Beauty' as personified at the end of the poem when you
don't so interpret it at the beginning?" . . . So the reader will not
be satisfied with any interpretative paraphrase except his own—and
he will probably not be quite satisfied even with that!

Without commenting upon the "music" aspect of the experience
of this poem, upon the pictures evoked in the mind's-eye, upon
the feeling that it may stir, or the way it may readjust attitudes
either toward geometry or esthetics, let us proceed with another
poem, again by a contemporary American. The first three sections,
of this somewhat longer poem, will serve as a unit.

TWENTIETH CENTURY SONGS
Elsa Gidlow

I

Will ever the perilous dip of a plane's wing
Shake us like the swoop of a gull?
The roar of a plane's engine pass and leave us desolate,
Like a gull's cry, for something wild, lost and beautiful?
Will ever a building flung against the sky
Have power to halt the breath like a tree?
Or the great moan of a city, its ominous moan
Trouble the soul like the moan of the sea?

2

There is no telling what elder man will become,
What will stir him, what fire his marrow
Till he is shaken; nor, for him, from what bow
Will be shot Beauty's impalpable arrow.
He will be nourished at a sterner breast
Than that we sucked; the guiding mother-command
Will come from a steelier throat; he will pluck flowers
That rain down golden from the riveter's hand.
Steel, rhythm of steel, harsh courage of steel
Will be in him, and men bred on these
(Let us suppose) will vibrate to steel's beauty
And have small need for trees.

3

Man must be drunken, he must see his world
Now and again, through chaos. He must reel
Smitten somehow by Beauty. . . . Our wines paling,
He will get drunk on steel;
And on another, a keener wine—speed—
Wine of the stars inebriate in space.
Already, it confuses his blood; already he hears
The winds of high heaven laughing against his face.

(1932)

If for Edna St. Vincent Millay the secret of Beauty is sublime perception of abstract spatial relationships, what is it for Elsa Gidlow, who considers herself a little old-fashioned, and for "elder man," as she calls the men of this age of steel?

The thoughtful consideration of the question, "What does *Beauty* mean in these two poems?" would serve two purposes: First, it would again illustrate for the reader the fact that the meaning of a word is dependent upon its context. Second, it would introduce him to the central and most troublesome problem in the field of the arts. And of this troublesome problem, Beauty, we shall say a few words—even at the risk of prating!

Let us launch this brief discussion with a few working definitions, and say that *poems* taken all together make up *Poetry* (with a capital P), and that Poetry is one of the three great branches of *Literature* (with a capital L), and that Literature is one of the *Arts*. Other ones of the Arts, let us go on, are Music, Theater Art, the Dance, Painting, Sculpture, and Architecture, each of which may be looked upon as comprising all of the art works of its particular sort. So Architecture is the total of all "well-designed" buildings; Painting, all "artful" pictures; Music, all "significant" compositions; and so on. Notice the weasel adjectives gnawing at the *all!*

For many people at least, only the beautiful buildings, only the beautiful pictures, only the beautiful music may be called art. And so too, for these persons, only the beautiful poems should be called poems at all—the others to be dismissed as "mere verse."

There is much to be said in favor of this comfortable point of view. It suggests that there is some mysterious—nay, beautiful—

kinship that makes a great cathedral cousin to the symphony, a noble painting kinsman to the poem. It brings all of the finest fruits of the human spirit into the great family of Art.

But there are some difficulties involved in this assumption. Some people maintain that there is *no thing* in the outer world that *is* Beauty, and that it is a mistake of the same sort to look for Beauty as an indisputable quality of certain objective things. First, they will say, no two equally competent observers will identify this presumed quality as possessed by the same things, or as possessed in the same degree in a certain thing. Second, different generations and peoples of different civilizations will have markedly different tastes for the salt, the bitter, and the sweet. There indeed will be no telling from what bow, for elder man, "Will be shot Beauty's impalpable arrow." And third, some things are considered art-things by persons who would not think of calling them "beautiful." In fact, the gargoyles, those grotesquely sculptured waterspouts of the great cathedrals; theatrical comedy and verse satire; as well as certain works in modern painting, architecture, and music are looked upon by many people as works of art without "beauty," as they use the word and understand its use.

It might therefore be better to use the word *beauty,* not to name the dubious property of certain works of art, but to name one of the unique qualities of some art-experiences—and of certain not-art experiences as well. If my breath is caught short by reading that "Euclid alone has looked on Beauty bare"—if I am set atingle, a surging rush and excitement within me, a special kind of burning intensity—I must remember that life outside of and away from books and Art will also bring these significant and memorable moments.

So, in poetry, language is serving primarily its art function, and it may provide us with complex and rich experiences, one of whose special qualities may well be designated "the beautiful."

SUGGESTIONS FOR STUDY

1. *Close Attention to the Meaning.* Turn back to Elsa Gidlow's "Twentieth Century Songs." (a) Reread the first two sections care-

fully. What is the meaning of "shake us" (line 2)? of "elder man" (line 9)? of "impalpable" (line 12)? of "sterner breast"? "mother-command"? "steelier"? (b) Now study the third section and write out, in the form of a simple and unambiguous prose paraphrase, your understanding of the sense of it.

2. *Poem-Reading and Poem-Singing*. Among the American cowboy ballads, the following is one that has enjoyed a wide popularity.

THE DYING COWBOY

O BURY ME NOT ON THE LONE PRAIRIE

Anonymous

"O bury me not on the lone prairie."
These words came slowly and mournfully
From the pallid lips of a youth who lay
On his cold damp bed at close of day.

"O bury me not on the lone prairie,
Where the wild coyote howls mournfully,
Where the cold wind weeps and the grasses wave;
No sunbeams rest on a prairie grave."

He has wasted and pined till o'er his brow
Death's shades are slowly gathering now;
He thought of his home with his dear ones nigh,
As the cowboys gathered to see him die.

Again he listened to well-known words,
To the wind's soft sigh and the song of birds;
He thought of his home and his native bowers,
Where he loved to roam in his childhood hours.

"I've ever wished that when I died,
My grave might be on the old hillside;
Let there the place of my last rest be—
O bury me not on the lone prairie!

"O'er my slumbers a mother's prayer
And a sister's tears will be mingled there;
For 'tis sad to know that the heart-throb's o'er,
And that its fountain will gush no more.

"In my dreams I say"—but his speech failed there;
And they gave no heed to his dying prayer;
In a narrow grave six feet by three,
They buried him there on the lone prairie.

May the light-winged butterfly pause to rest
O'er him who sleeps on the prairie's crest;
May the Texas rose in the breezes wave
O'er him who sleeps in a prairie's grave.

And the cowboys now, as they roam the plain
(For they marked the spot where his bones were laid),
Fling a handful of roses over his grave,
With a prayer to Him who his soul will save.

(?c. 1875)

(a) For this, as for many other folk ballads, widely different printed versions are to be found. See Carl Sandburg, *The American Songbag,* Harcourt, Brace, 1927; John A. Lomax and Alan Lomax, *Cowboy Songs,* Macmillan, 1938; Frank Luther, *Americans and Their Songs,* Harper, 1942; etc. (The first line is often used as the title of this song.)

(b) Now sing this ballad—or whistle the tune or hum it as you read the stanzas again; or re-create the melody in your imagination so that you hear it in the mind's-ear.[7]

"Oh, bur - y me not on the lone prai - rie." Those... words came low and mourn-ful - ly · From the pal - lid lips of a youth who lay On a dy - ing bed at the close of day.

(c) In what way does your experience change as you combine melody and verse?

3. *The Art Function of Language.* This next poem, quite different in kind, might well be read several times before proceeding with the questions given below.

[7] The tune here given is from Lomax, *Cowboy Songs,* and is reprinted by special permission of John A. Lomax and The Macmillan Company, publishers.

THE SONG OF THE UNGIRT RUNNERS
Charles Hamilton Sorley

We swing ungirded hips,
And lightened are our eyes,
The rain is on our lips,
We do not run for prize.
We know not whom we trust
Nor whitherward we fare,
But we run because we must
    Through the great wide air.

The waters of the seas
Are troubled as by storm.
The tempest strips the trees
And does not leave them warm.
Does the tearing tempest pause?
Do the tree tops ask it why?
So we run without a cause
    'Neath the big bare sky.

The rain is on our lips,
We do not run for prize.
But the storm the water whips
And the wave howls to the skies.
The winds arise and strike it
And scatter it like sand,
And we run because we like it
    Through the broad bright land.
                    (1916)

(a) Consider this poem in terms of the art function of language as you now understand it. How might writing the poem have effected an emotional adjustment in the poet? How might reading the poem effect an emotional adjustment in the reader?

(b) Charles Hamilton Sorley was a young Englishman just completing his education at the outbreak of the first World War. Though he was critical of all false patriotism, he enlisted at once and attained his captaincy at the age of twenty. He was killed in action a few months later. His few poems were gathered together and published posthumously by his father.

As you reread the poem with this data added to your background for interpreting it, how does the meaning change for you?

4. *Puzzling Ambiguities.* Often a simple poem contains ambiguities that go unnoticed, for the reader may assume that "obviously" the poem-experience is the same for all readers.

ROSE AYLMER

Walter Savage Landor

Ah, what avails the sceptered race,
    Ah, what the form divine!
What every virtue, every grace!
    Rose Aylmer, all were thine.
Rose Aylmer, whom these wakeful eyes
    May weep, but never see,
A night of memories and of sighs
    I consecrate to thee.

(1806)

Objectify your interpretation of this poem by answering the following multiple-choice questions. (For some of them, no one of the suggested responses may seem to you to be satisfactory. In such cases jot down what you think would be appropriate.)

1. After one or two readings, is the *meaning* of this poem: (a) perfectly clear to you, (b) clear as to its main idea, (c) obscure at certain points, (d) not clear at all?
2. Does the *first line* mean: (a) Who can win a race with a spirit? (b) Why should one set himself against royalty? (c) What use is it to be of noble family?
3. What word from the first line is implied in the *second:* (a) what, (b) avails, (c) sceptered, (d) race?
4. Does the phrase *form divine* bear the sense of: (a) God's image, (b) holy works, (c) a figure like a Greek goddess, (d) shaped by the gods?
5. Does *virtue* here communicate the sense of: (a) chastity, (b) good qualities, (c) strength of character?
6. Does *all* in line 4 mean: (a) everything, (b) all men, (c) grace, virtue, form divine, and sceptered race?
7. Does *consecrate* here carry the sense of: (a) packing a lot into a small space, (b) setting aside, (c) dedicating and making holy, (d) setting on fire?
8. *What* does the poet consecrate: (a) the night, (b) the memories and sighs, (c) himself, (d) Rose Aylmer?

9. Why are the eyes *wakeful:* (a) because they burn with tears, (b) because they peer out into the night, (c) because the poet can't sleep on account of thoughts of his beloved, (d) because the poet wants to stay awake and think over the good times he's had with Rose?

10. Do you judge that *Rose Aylmer* is: (a) now married to or in love with another, (b) way off, in another land perhaps, (c) removed from the poet because of some disgrace, (d) dead?

11. Is the *time* of the poem: (a) dawn or just before dawn, (b) morning, (c) noon, (d) afternoon, (e) evening, (f) about midnight?

12. Which statement best suggests your understanding of the poet's *tone* and *feeling?* (a) You were a great little kid, Rose; and our love was swell while it lasted! (b) Why does a beautiful girl— talented, noble and good—have to die so young! (c) Although I lament your loss, now that I can't see you, at least I can spend this night in thinking about you.

(Turn to the Supplementary Note at the end of this chapter for some relevant facts about Rose Aylmer, but not until you have completed your independent interpretation.)

5. *A Pair of Poems* for comparative study.

I WANDERED LONELY AS A CLOUD
William Wordsworth

I wandered lonely as a cloud
That floats on high o'er vales and hills,
When all at once I saw a crowd,
A host, of golden daffodils;
Beside the lake, beneath the trees,
Fluttering and dancing in the breeze.

Continuous as the stars that shine
And twinkle on the Milky Way,
They stretched in never-ending line
Along the margin of a bay:
Ten thousand saw I at a glance,
Tossing their heads in sprightly dance.

The waves beside them danced; but they
Outdid the sparkling waves in glee:
A poet could not but be gay,

In such a jocund company:
I gazed—and gazed—but little thought
What wealth the show to me had brought:

For oft, when on my couch I lie
In vacant or in pensive mood,
They flash upon that inward eye
Which is the bliss of solitude;
And then my heart with pleasure fills,
And dances with the daffodils.

(1804)

PETER QUINCE AT THE CLAVIER

Wallace Stevens

1

Just as my fingers on these keys
Make music, so the self-same sounds
On my spirit make a music, too.

Music is feeling, then, not sound;
And thus it is that what I feel,
Here in this room, desiring you,

Thinking of your blue-shadowed silk,
Is music. It is like the strain
Waked in the elders by Susanna:

Of a green evening, clear and warm,
She bathed in her still garden, while
The red-eyed elders, watching, felt

The basses of their being throb
In witching chords, and their thin blood
Pulse pizzicati of Hosanna.

2

In the green water, clear and warm,
Susanna lay.
She searched
The touch of springs,

And found
Concealed imaginings.
She sighed,
For so much melody.

Upon the bank, she stood
In the cool
Of spent emotions.
She felt, among the leaves,
The dew
Of old devotions.

She walked upon the grass,
Still quavering.
The winds were like her maids,
On timid feet,
Fetching her woven scarves,
Yet wavering.

A breath upon her hand
Muted the night.
She turned—
A cymbal clashed,
And roaring horns.

3

Soon, with a noise like tambourines,
Came her attendant Byzantines.

They wondered why Susanna cried
Against the elders by her side;

And as they whispered, the refrain
Was like a willow swept by rain.

Anon, their lamps' uplifted flame
Revealed Susanna and her shame.

And then, the simpering Byzantines
Fled, with a noise of tambourines.

4

Beauty is momentary in the mind—
The fitful tracing of a portal;
But in the flesh it is immortal.

The body dies; the body's beauty lives.
So evenings die, in their green going,
A wave, interminably flowing.

So gardens die, their meek breath scenting
The cowl of Winter, done repenting.
So maidens die, to the auroral
Celebration of a maiden's choral.

Susanna's music touched the bawdy strings
Of those white elders; but, escaping,
Left only Death's ironic scraping.
Now in its immortality, it plays
On the clear viol of her memory,
And makes a constant sacrament of praise.

(1923)

(a) Upon a first reading, these two poems may seem in no way comparable. But each has something to say about Beauty.

Wordsworth's poem is an easy one. But the following notes regarding the poet's experience may be of interest. He was living with his wife and sister in the beautiful Lake Country of northern England. "The daffodils," Wordsworth later wrote, "grew and still grow on the margin of [Lake] Ullswater, and probably may be seen to this day as beautiful in the month of March, nodding their golden heads beside the dancing and foaming waves." And his sister, Dorothy Wordsworth, wrote in her Journal, April 15, 1802: "When we were in the woods beyond Gowbarrow Park we saw a few daffodils close to the water-side. . . . As we went along there were more, and yet more; and, at last, under the boughs of the trees, we saw there was a long belt of them along the shore. . . . I never saw daffodils so beautiful." And she wrote further of the way they "tossed, and reeled, and danced." In his famous Preface, Wordsworth says, "Poetry is the spontaneous overflow of powerful feeling; it takes its origin from emotion recollected in tranquillity; the emotion is contemplated till, by a species of reaction, the tranquillity gradually disappears, and an emotion, kindred to that which was before the subject of contemplation, is gradually produced, and does itself actually exist in the mind."

Wallace Stevens' poem is, for some persons at least, a "difficult" one. The following notes may be of some slight help: *Peter Quince:* the rustic director of "Pyramus and Thisby" in *A Midsummer-Night's Dream. Clavier:* a forerunner of the piano. The *first lines* of the poem suggest such other poems as Browning's "Abt Vogler" and Adelaide Procter's "A Lost Chord." *Susanna and the Elders:* The story is found in *Daniel,* 13, of the Douay (Catholic) Bible, and in the *Apocrypha,* "The History of Susanna." Joakim's beautiful wife, Susanna, attracted the attention of two elders, judges who were staying at Joakim's house. Knowing that she walked daily in her husband's garden, they contrived to hide and watch her while she (dismissing her attendants) bathed. They confronted her, and tried by blackmail to win her to their lusts. But she preferred to face the accusation that they threatened. So the elders cried out, and belied Susanna before her returning attendants, saying that they found her with a young man. In the trial that followed, young Daniel contrived to save her by entangling the elders in their false witness; and they were put to death. (The subject has been treated by various painters and poets.)

(b) Now, after a thoughtful rereading of these poems, turn your attention to what you consider to be these poets' thoughts regarding Beauty. And reconsider in this connection Edna St. Vincent Millay's "Euclid Alone—" and Elsa Gidlow's "Twentieth Century Songs."

6. *A Supplementary Note.* The reader who puzzled the ambiguities of "Rose Aylmer," may be impatient to know which ones of his interpretations—or guesses—are "right." The following facts may bring him a step closer to the answer: Rose Aylmer, daughter of Sir Henry Aylmer, was a friend and companion of Landor's youth in Wales (1795-98). She shortly went to India, and died there in 1800. Landor wrote this elegy in 1806 at the age of 31. (Interesting comment on this poem, by R. H. Super, will be found in the *Explicator,* February 1945.)

PART TWO
Anatomy of the Poem-Experience

4

SEEING THE POEM ON THE PAGE

In Chapter 2, while we were "In Search of Poetry," a preliminary analysis was made of the poem-reading-experience, the poem inside the skin. Each of its six aspects was described briefly in a single paragraph. They will now be given more extended treatment in Part Two of this book, under the general heading "Anatomy of the Poem-Experience," the first chapter of which is concerned with what happens when one *sees* a poem on the page.

The impression of the printed verses upon the retina of the reader's eye is of more importance than most people assume, because it is this pattern of retinal stimulation to which all the parts of the poem-reading-experience—the "seeing" of the page, the music and imagery, meaning and emotion—are a very complex response. The "retinal image" is the sensory link between the page and the experience.

But sight is not the only possible link between the printed verses and a poem-experience. You may hear a poem read or recited by some other person, either directly or over the radio, or from a record; then the auditory sense will be used in the place of the visual. But there will be more difference than that: some other person then comes between you and the printed verses; and this other person will not, indeed cannot, be a merely mechanical speaker; he will be an interpretative artist striving to communicate to you *his* full poem-experience. We all know this, of course, having listened to poetry read aloud, though we may never have given it much thought. Nor have most of us considered the fact that sensitive finger tips link the blind to poetry through the use of Braille.

However, we are now concerned with the visual link, the seeing of the poem on the page.

I. THE SEEING PROCESS IN READING

Let us begin with an example of the thing we shall be discussing. In reading Stevenson's "Requiem" you should pay particular attention to what your eyes are doing. But have an enjoyable experience with the poem at the same time.[1]

REQUIEM

Robert Louis Stevenson

> Under the wide and starry sky,
> Dig my grave and let me lie:
> Glad did I live and gladly die,
>   And I laid me down with a will.
>
> Here may the winds about me blow;
> Here the clouds may come and go;
> Here shall be rest for evermo,
>   And the heart for aye shall be still.
>
> This be the verse you 'grave for me:
> *Here he lies where he long'd to be;*
> *Home is the sailor, home from sea,*
>   *And the hunter home from the hill.*

(1884)

What are some of the things that happen when you *see* the printed verses on this page?

The page, by the way, consists of relatively white paper in the center portion of which there is an arrangement of black marks. Most of the light that strikes the pattern of black printing is ab-

---

[1] The title "Requiem" is a Latin word meaning *rest,* and is the first word of a Mass said for the dead: "Give eternal rest to them, O Lord." The last two lines of Stevenson's poem mark his grave in Samoa.

sorbed, and most of the light that strikes the negative pattern of white space is reflected. With the book held at the proper angle, this pattern of light is reflected from the page into the eye.

It passes through the glassy outer surface (or cornea), through the adjustable shutter (the iris with its pupil), and through the lens, which reverses and inverts the pattern before the light rays strike the retina. The retina is the inner lining of the back of the eyeball, in which are imbedded optic nerve-ends that are sensitive to light. The pattern of light falling on the retina—the retinal image of the printed page, of the white space surrounding the words—stimulates the optic nerve-ends (the rods and cones), and they transmit impulses, by way of the optic nerve, to the visual center of the brain, where the actual *seeing* of the visual image [2] is said to take place.

But this process of seeing the poem on the page is complicated by the fact that the retina is not all equally sensitive. There are no nerve-ends at all at what is called the blind spot, so that light rays fall without effect upon that part of the retina. But at the center, opposite the lens, there is a hypersensitive spot (the fovea), a small depression crowded with nerve-ends. That which is brought into focus upon and near this center point is seen with clear vision, while surrounding things are seen less clearly.

It is necessary, then, to bring groups of printed words into focus near this most sensitive part of the retina in order to see them clearly enough for reading. To do this, the complex sets of outer eye muscles are called upon to make amazingly subtle adjustments of the position of the eyeballs in their sockets. In three or four jerky movements from left to right, with four or five brief pauses, the successive groups of words in the printed line are brought into focus upon and near the sensitive fovea. Then the eyes are moved back to the left and down a bit so as to bring the first part of the next line into focus. And the succession of saccadic movements and fixations, as they are called, is repeated. The process reminds one of the movements of a typewriter carriage when one is typing a

2 *Visual image* in the sense of visual tied-imagery, imagery tied to immediate sensation. Visual free-imagery will be considered in Chapter 6.

list of very short words. It is during the momentary pauses, or as a result of the nerve stimulation during these pauses, that the *seeing* of the words takes place.

T his **and** the   t he following line s   a re spaced ou t
s o as **to** cal l   a ttention to th e   s accad**ic** movemen t s
o f the **read**er's ey e s. I n each **group** of wor d s t hree **letter** s
h a ve **been** set i n   i n bold-faced typ e   s o as **to** provi d e
d e finite **points** fo r   s u ccess**ive** fixatio n s   a t the **same** tim e
e m phasizing th e   c l arity of **one**'s visi o n   a t the **fove** a.
H a ve you **not**iced th e   t he **phrases** as h e r e   h e re **print**e d
a t times **overl**a p?   S o it **will** be a s   a s one **reads** alon g:

the successive fixations may overlap, but you won't actually *see* the word the second time, as your attention will have passed beyond it. You welcome, no doubt, this return to normal printing, but the above may have given you some insight into what your eye-move-ments are when you read.

2. EYE-MOVEMENT IN READING VERSE

Let us proceed, however, and come more directly to the pattern of eye-movements peculiar to the reading of poetry.

THE TWENTY-THIRD PSALM
David

The Lord is my shepherd; I shall not want.

He maketh me to lie down in green pastures:
  he leadeth me beside the still waters.
  He restoreth my soul: he leadeth me
    in the paths of righteousness for his name's sake.

Yea, though I walk through the valley of the shadow of death,
  I will fear no evil: for thou art with me;
  thy rod and thy staff they comfort me.

Thou preparest a table before me in the presence of mine enemies: thou anointest my head with oil; my cup runneth over.

Surely goodness and mercy shall follow me all the days of my life: and I will dwell in the house of the Lord for ever.

‘ (*bef. 150 B.C.; tr. 1611 A.D.*)

These familiar words *look* like poetry and *read* like poetry as printed here [3]—indeed they *are* of the highest poetry in whatever arrangement, though some of the "poetry" is obscured for many readers in the traditional typography.

David's trust in God,   **PSALMS, 25**   *and confidence in prayer.*

PSALM 23

David's confidence in God's grace.
A Psalm of Dă'vid.

THE LORD is *a* my shepherd; *b* I shall not want.

2 *c* He maketh me to lie down in 2 green pastures : *d* he leadeth me beside the 3 still waters.

3 He restoreth my soul : *e* he leadeth me in the paths of righteousness for his name's sake.

4 Yea, though I walk through the valley of *f* the shadow of death, *g* I will fear no evil : *h* for thou *art* with me ; thy rod and thy staff they comfort me.

5 *i* Thou preparest a table before me in the presence of mine enemies : thou 4 *k* anointest my head with oil ; my cup runneth over.

6 Surely goodness and mercy shall follow me all the days of my life : and I will dwell in the house of the LORD 5 for ever.

PSALM 24

1 *God's lordship in the world.* 3 *The citizens of his spiritual kingdom.* 7 *An exhortation to receive him.*
A Psalm of Dă'vid.

THE *a* earth is the LORD'S, and the fulness thereof; the world, and they that dwell therein.

2 *b* For he hath founded it upon

a Is. 40. 11.
Jer 23. 4.
Ezek. 34. 11, 12, 23.
John 10. 11.
1 Pet. 2. 25.
Rev. 7. 17.
b Phil. 4. 19.
c Ezek.34.14.
2 Heb. *pastures of tender grass.*
d Rev. 7. 17.
3 Heb.*waters of quietness.*
e Ps. 5. 8 ; 31. 3.
f Job 3. 5 ; 10, 21, 22 ; 24. 17.
Ps. 44. 19.
g Ps. 3. 6 ; 27. 1; 118. 6.
h Is. 43. 2.
i Ps. 104. 15.
4 Heb. *makest fat.*
k Ps. 92. 10.
5 Heb. *to length of days.*

a Ex. 9. 29;
19. 5.
Deut. 10. 14.
Job 41. 11.
Ps. 50. 12.
1 Cor. 10. 26, 28.
b Gen. 1. 9.
Job 38. 6.
Ps. 104. 5 ;
136. 6.
2 Pet. 3. 5.

1017.]
c Ps. 15. 1.
d Is. 33. 15,16.
6 Heb. *The clean of hands.*

10 Who is this King of glory? The LORD of hosts, he *is* the King of glory. Sĕ'lah.

PSALM 25

1 *David's confidence in prayer.* 7 *He prayeth for remission of sins,* 16 *and for help in affliction.*
A Psalm of Dă'vid.

UNTO *a* thee, O LORD, do I lift up my soul.

2 O my God, I *b* trust in thee : let me not be ashamed, *c* let not mine enemies triumph over me.

3 Yea, let none that wait on thee be ashamed : let them be ashamed which transgress without cause.

4 *d* Shew me thy ways, O LORD ; teach me thy paths.

5 Lead me in thy truth, and teach me : for thou *art* the God of my salvation ; on thee do I wait all the day.

6 Remember, O LORD, *e* 8 thy tender mercies and thy lovingkindnesses ; for they *have been* ever of old.

7 Remember not *f* the sins of my youth, nor my transgressions : *g* according to thy mercy remember thou me for thy goodness' sake, O LORD.

8 Good and upright *is* the LORD : therefore will he teach sinners in the way.

9 The meek will he guide in judg

How very different is the *seeing* of these two arrangements of the same poem!

[3] A number of modern editions of the Bible print the poetic sections in the form of free verse: the Moulton arrangement of English Revised Version, *The Modern Reader's Bible;* the new translation of Moffatt; etc.

As I read the first one, my eyes fix on the title, then jog down to the poet's name for a longer pause. Down they jog again and over left to the beginning of the first line, which is taken in three pauses, with two jumps. And then they sweep back and down for the second line: . . . jump . . . jump . . . back-again-and-down; . . . jump . . . jump . . . back-again-and-down; . . . jump . . . jump . . . back-again-and-down. And so it goes, with the rhythmic pattern of my eye-movements varied as I take in the longer lines with an extra stride.

But follow my eyes as I read these verses in the traditional arrangement, and as I pursue them with a plodding attention. My eyes "fix" on "The Lord *is*," jump and fix on "*ᵃ*my shepherd; *ᵇ*I." Then they jump back as my attention is attracted by the odd type (the italics) of *"is"*; and they jump to the superior *a* and then to the superior *b*; thence over to the central margin, where I fix on the first of the cross references and jog down the others one by one. Then (for I am *not* turning to *Isaiah,* 40:11 at this moment) my eyes jump back to the beginning. This time, they take in the first line in two quick fixations and sweep back for the remainder of the sentence on the second line. Now back to fix on the beginning of the third line. . . . And so on, with a variety of jumps as I fix on the verse number, the superior letters and numerals, indices of cross references and literal translations.[4]

There are many factors, of course, that determine the pattern of eye-movements, the duration of fixations, and the span of apprehension, as the width of word-grouping is called that can be taken in during one fixation. Some of these factors are the reader's aptitude and training; his attention and fatigue; his interest and the difficulty of the material to be read. Other factors include the various details of typography: the size and style of type, the width of the lines and margins, the space between the lines, and so on. Psychologists, educators, and publishers have given much attention to these matters in recent years. It is not generally recognized, how-

---

[4] It is possible, of course, for the reader to withhold his attention from these at times distracting stimuli, and thus simplify the pattern of eye-movements in reading from such a complex page.

ever, that the patterns of eye-movement are especially important in the reading of poetry.

But, in its first reprinting above, "The Twenty-third Psalm" is not the usual sort of poem; nor is it, as given the second time, the usual sort of prose. Let us therefore turn to a poem that in every way does look like a poem. Richard Lovelace, its author, was one of the Cavalier poets. He was imprisoned for presenting the "Kentish Petition" to the Long Parliament of 1642.

TO ALTHEA, FROM PRISON
Richard Lovelace

When Love with unconfinèd wings
  Hovers within my gates,
And my divine Althea brings
  To whisper at the grates;
When I lie tangled in her hair
  And fettered to her eye,
The birds that wanton in the air
  Know no such liberty.

When flowing cups run swiftly round
  With no allaying Thames,
Our careless heads with roses bound,
  Our hearts with loyal flames;
When thirsty grief in wine we steep,
  When healths and draughts go free,
Fishes that tipple in the deep
  Know no such liberty.

When, like committed linnets, I
  With shriller throat shall sing
The sweetness, mercy, majesty,
  And glories of my king;
When I shall voice aloud how good
  He is, how great should be,
Enlargèd winds, that curl the flood,
  Know no such liberty.

> Stone walls do not a prison make,
>   Nor iron bars a cage;
> Minds innocent and quiet take
>   That for an hermitage;
> If I have freedom in my love
>   And in my soul am free,
> Angels alone, that soar above,
>   Enjoy such liberty.

(1649)

This poem calls for eye-movements that are fairly typical for the reading of verse. In the experience of many, there will be established a *rhythmic pattern* of alternating eye-fixations and eye-movements—about three fixations for each of the longer lines and about two for each of the shorter lines. But this will vary with individuals, depending upon their acquired skill in reading, upon the speed and degree of attention in their reading, and upon the extent of their vocalization (a matter to be taken up in the next chapter).

Certainly the particular pattern of eye-movements is part of the unique character of each poem-experience.

UPON HIS DEPARTURE HENCE
Robert Herrick

> Thus I
> Pass by
> And die,
>
> As one
> Unknown
> And gone.
>
> I'm made
> A shade
> And laid
>
> I' the grave;
> There have
> My cave.

Where tell
I dwell.
Farewell.
(1648)

Occasionally there is some special relationship between the pattern of eye-movement and the other aspects of the poem-experience, which will be dealt with in the following chapters. For instance, in "To Althea, from Prison" the eye-rhythm of alternating three-fixation and two-fixation lines is played against the ear-rhythm (metrical pattern) of four-stress and three-stress lines. But in "Upon His Departure Hence" the eye-movements are simply *down* the page, one line, or (for some readers) two lines or even a whole stanza of three lines, at a time. And this eye-rhythm will coincide, rather than be played against, the ear-rhythm of one-stress lines. For some readers of this poem there will also be a notable relation between the pattern of eye-movements and the meaning—for just as the eye moves swiftly down the page and is done, so the poet observes that he moves swiftly down the road of life and then is gone. And this entire poem experience, even the visual imagery and the reader's emotional response, may be colored by the simple process of seeing the poem on the page.

But look now at some of the long sweeping lines, the so-called septenarius couplets, of Leigh Hunt's "The Glove and the Lions," which was presented in the first chapter (p. 13).

King Francis was a hearty king, and loved a royal sport,
And one day, as his lions fought, sat looking on his court.
The nobles filled the benches, with the ladies in their pride,
And 'mongst them sat the Count de Lorge, with one for whom he sighed:
And truly 'twas a gallant thing to see that crowning show,
Valor and love, and a king above, and the royal beasts below.

Here the eye sweeps along the line, in a series of long strides, then away back to start again. How very different the reading-experience is, however, when the verses of the poem are printed (as they are on the next page) as though they were the fours and threes of ballad meter!

King Francis was a hearty king,
   And loved a royal sport,
And one day, as his lions fought,
   Sat looking on the court.

The nobles filled the benches, with
   The ladies in their pride,
And 'mongst them sat the Count de Lorge,
   With one for whom he sighed:

And truly 'twas a gallant thing
   To see that crowning show,
Valor and love, and a king above,
   And the royal beasts below.

It is more than a mere difference in the patterns of eye-movements, for (to some ears) the "music" is subtly affected. For most readers the long lines will have seven stresses; but some will feel that four stresses dominate the line, with the in-between stresses secondary; and the effect will be that of a metrical gallop, keeping pace with the swift succession of eye-movements and suggesting the swift succession of dramatic incidents. But the change in typographical form will affect this in the experience of many readers, for whom the "music" will now be based upon a strongly marked alternation of four-stress and three-stress verses.

But we must proceed to another aspect of seeing the poem on the page.

3. RETINAL IMAGE AND POETIC FORM

While the eye focuses sharply on the successive phrases, there is a vague image of the rest of the page on the periphery of one's vision. This is of some importance in the reading of poetry. From this general image, the reader will be conscious of the printed form of the stanza and of the whole poem. A few poems, like George Herbert's "Easter Wings," are so written that the form of the printed verses will suggest the subject matter.

EASTER WINGS
George Herbert

Lord, who createdst man in wealth and store,
  Though foolishly he lost the same,
    Decaying more and more,
      Till he became
        Most poor;

        With Thee
      O let me rise
    As larks, harmoniously,
  And sing this day Thy victories:
Then shall the fall further the flight in me.

My tender age in sorrow did begin:
  And still with sicknesses and shame
    Thou didst so punish sin,
      That I became
        Most thin.

        With Thee
      Let me combine,
    And feel this day Thy victory,
  For, if I imp my wing on Thine,
Affliction shall advance the flight in me.

(1633)

Give the book a quarter turn to the right, and the two pair of wings will become more apparent. Poems like this, in which typographical form is representational, are rare; and indeed they have been called a form of false wit. The device is known as *carmen figuratum,* and an amusing example is the "long and sad tale" of the Mouse in *Alice in Wonderland.* " 'It *is* a long tail, certainly,' said Alice, looking down with wonder at the Mouse's tail, 'but why do you call it sad?' And she kept on puzzling about it while the Mouse was speaking." The typography of the tale is amusingly tail-like.

But *all of the so-called poetic forms,* to be considered later,[5] *owe something of their special character to typographical form,* the configuration of the printed verses upon the page. And this printed form is grasped from the vague retinal image of the page as the eye-movements bring the successive phrases into focus upon and near the fovea.

When one takes up a new poem, this typographical form may be taken in at a glance—a glance followed by some purely exploratory eye-movements. Look at the following poem, and try to take it in as a whole. Then look it over carefully, giving your attention to details of its typographical form, but without even trying to read it.

> Io mi senti' svegliar dentro a lo core
> un spirito amoroso che dormia:
> e poi vidi venir da lungi Amore
> allegro sì, che appena il conoscia,
> dicendo: "Or pensa pur di farmi onore„;
> e'n ciascuna parola sua ridia.
> E poco stando meco il mio segnore,
> guardando in quella parte onde venia,
>
> io vidi monna Vanna e monna Bice
> venire inver lo loco là 'v'io era,
> l'una appresso de l'altra maraviglia;
> e sì come la mente mi ridice,
> Amor mi disse: "Quell'è Primavera,
> e quell'ha nome Amor, sì mi somiglia„.

What are some of the features that distinguish the typographical form of a poem?

(1) The *width* of the poem on the page; that is, the length of the lines. (This poem, two-thirds the page-width as here set, is made up of lines that are longer than those of "Requiem," but not so long as those of "The Glove and the Lions.")

(2) The *length* of the poem. (The length of this poem is nearly

---

[5] See Suggestion for Study #5 at the end of this chapter (p. 86), and the further discussion in Chapter 17.

the same as its width; whereas "To Althea, from Prison" is about page-length.)

(3) The *relative line-length;* that is, the length of the lines in relation to each other. (For this poem they are of approximately the same length; not alternately longer and shorter as in "To Althea.")

(4) The *indentations,* some lines being set in from the left-hand margin farther than others. (In the first part of this poem, every other line is indented, and there are two degrees of indentation in the second part; but there are no indentations at all in "Upon His Departure Hence.")

(5) The *divisions,* if any, separation of groups of lines by additional white space. (There are two divisions here, but of unequal size; whereas almost all of the other poems in this chapter are made up of stanzas, similar groups of lines.)

But let us turn to another poem—this one in English—and read it without regard to the visual experience of its typographical form. Read it aloud and slowly, alert of mind and open of heart.

THE SOLDIER
Rupert Brooke

If I should die, think only this of me:
    That there's some corner of a foreign field
That is for ever England. There shall be
    In that rich earth a richer dust concealed;
A dust whom England bore, shaped, made aware,
    Gave, once, her flowers to love, her ways to roam,
A body of England's, breathing English air,
    Washed by the rivers, blest by suns of home.

And think, this heart, all evil shed away,
    A pulse in the eternal mind, no less
        Gives somewhere back the thoughts by England given;
Her sights and sounds; dreams happy as her day;
    And laughter, learnt of friends; and gentleness,
        In hearts at peace, under an English heaven.

(1915)

"The Soldier" by Rupert Brooke is one of the poems of the First World War. Brooke was born at Rugby, England, where his father was assistant master. Grown up, he was six feet tall, good-looking, athletic, and fond of life. He traveled and wrote poetry. Then came the war. He fought in Belgium, and embarked with the ill-fated British Mediterranean Expeditionary Force. His sonnet-sequence, *1914,* of which this poem is a part, was published only a few weeks before the poet's untimely death.

Have you now read and also reread the poem? Are there any points at which your thoughts about the sense of it aren't clear? If there are, the following paraphrase may be of some help. But if the meaning of the poem is perfectly clear, skip the paragraph and read on.

If I go to my death, let your thought of me be this: A certain small bit of field in a strange country will be a part of England for ever, because my dead body is there. In the good earth of that land, there will be mixed a still better dust—dust that England gave birth and form to, made conscious of beautiful things, flowers and roadways; a body that became a part of England, breathing its air, swimming in its rivers, bathing in its warm sun.

But at the same time, have this other thought: My spirit, now free from evil, a part of the Eternal Mind, in the same way gives back somewhere the thoughts given it by England, the beautiful views and sounds, the dreams as happy as spring days, the laughing got from friends, and the kind ways of peace-loving men living under the English sky.

But now we must return to our consideration of the typographical form of this poem, and see whether the visual image of the printed page may bear any relation to other aspects of the poem-reading-experience.

A person widely read in poetry will probably have seen at a glance that this poem, like the Italian poem printed above, is a *sonnet.* His quick exploratory eye-movements, which we earlier detailed, revealed the relative page-width, the almost equal length, the comparable line-lengths, the pattern of indentations, and the larger and smaller divisions of the poem. And the reader may have coupled these observations with some tentative judgments: the *width* may be the ten-syllable lines of the sonnet's iambic pentameter; the *length* looks about right for the fourteen lines requisite for a sonnet; the alternative *indentations* in the first part and the two degrees of indentation in the second part may be clues to the rime-scheme, and suggest a variation of the so-called Italian form of the sonnet; and the unequal *divisions* may be the eight- and six-line parts of that form.[6]

Even an experienced reader may not make all of these observations and judgments as he takes up a new poem. But if he does, and recognizes "The Soldier" at once as a sonnet, a variation of the Italian form, he is likely to be conscious of a slightly different music, with a fuller appreciation of the deviations from the metrical expectancy, a melody colored and made rich by his past reading of sonnets by Wordsworth, Milton, and Shakespeare. He will be prepared for some sort of balance in the development of the thought of the poem through the eight-line and six-line sections. He may even be disposed to have a particular sort of emotional response to the poem.

So it is that readers of poetry learn to recognize certain of the poetic forms at a glance—blank verse, short couplets, heroic couplets, the ballad, the Spenserian stanza, the limerick, and the sonnet. Of these forms no more will be said in this place; but it has been necessary to introduce them here, as poetic form is dependent in part upon the general retinal image and exploratory eye-movements.

4. SOME VISUAL PROBLEMS

There are several special problems, however, that call for brief mention before this chapter is brought to a close.

Self-deception is within the experience of all of us. Who cannot recall instances in which he has been tricked by "seeing" something that wasn't there! The witnesses of a traffic accident conscientiously report quite different observations. It must be remembered that we don't "see" with the eye. The *retinal* image, as we have called it,

---

[6] All sonnets are not printed with these indentations and in two divisions, but some are. Look at Donne's "Holy Sonnet X" (p. 12), Keats "On First Looking into Chapman's Homer" (p. 25), and Millay's "Euclid Alone—" (p. 46). The sonnet will be considered in some detail in Chapter 17.

is to be distinguished from the *visual* image that we *see,* as pointed out in an earlier paragraph (p. 67). So occasionally we "see" the words that we expect to see rather than the ones reflected upon the retina of the eye from the printed page. This will cause misreadings, sometimes amusing or embarrassing. Byron's "So We'll Go No More a-Roving" has at times been misread "So we'll go no more a-rowing," with notable alteration in the sense of it and in the visual imagery. And Stevenson's "Requiem" is frequently misread, "Home is the sailor, home from *the* sea," even when there is not a second *the* on the page.

Another special problem may be created for the reader by the vague peripheral image of things other than the poem printed on the same page. There may result an unhappy mixing of "rose buds" with the indefinite "sea gulls" and "Death" of other poems. Reading poetry in a double-column anthology is like looking at pictures in a crowded gallery. It is difficult to keep surrounding poems and pictures sufficiently screened out to allow for an uncontaminated "seeing." So, too, as one is reading a poem, the cat dozing by the fire or the flickering flames may come in through the tail of one's eye and mix into the poem-experience, sometimes with unusual results. Some people find a special pleasure in reading poetry in particular places—out in the woods or overlooking the sea or in their gardens—and it is probably true that the peripheral images of the outdoor sights may have some bearing upon the experience that they thus have in reading poetry.

A third special problem is the effect of the general appearance of the book page. There can be no doubt that the color and quality of the paper, the size and style of the type, the color of the ink, the spacing, and the width of the margin—all contribute to the general retinal image. And pleasant visual sensations will predispose the reader to a generally pleasing experience. At this point the art of the printer joins hands with the art of the poet. And sometimes, as with William Blake and William Morris, the two artists have been one and the same person.

As a final illustration for this chapter on the process of seeing the poem on the page, read "Chansons Innocentes" by E. E. Cummings, a modern American experimental poet who abandoned conven-

tional punctuation and capitalization, and centered his attention
upon arbitrary typographical form. The general visual image of this
poem and the unusual pattern of eye-movements as one reads it,
are indeed very important parts of the reading-experience.

from CHANSONS INNOCENTES
E. E. Cummings

in Just-
spring   when the world is mud-
luscious the little
lame baloonman

whistles   far   and wee
and eddieandbill come
running from marbles and
piracies and it's
spring

when the world is puddle-wonderful

the queer
old baloonman whistles
far   and   wee

and bettyandisbel come dancing
from hop-scotch and jump-rope and

it's
spring
and
    the
              goat-footed

baloonman   whistles
far
and
wee

(1923)

SUGGESTIONS FOR STUDY

1. *Observing Eye-movements.* (a) As the necessity for eye-movement in reading is bound up with the anatomy of the eye, it is desirable to have some understanding of the eye-ball and the retina. Glance back at the opening section of the chapter; then make a cross-sectional sketch of the eye as you imagine it to be. Check this against the diagram to be found in a standard anatomy text, reference work, or dictionary.

(b) Observe the eye-movements of another reader. Sit across the table from him with the book and a small mirror flat on the table between you. (This will be an easier position than having him hold his head and book up to your eye-level.) (1) Ask him to read some prose from the text; count the number of fixations per line. (2) Ask him to read "The Twenty-third Psalm" in both versions. (3) Watch him as he reads "Upon His Departure Hence," the long lines of "The Glove and the Lions," and "Easter Wings."

(c) Work with yet another person reading the same poems. Be alert for differences both as regards exploratory eye-movements and the saccadic movements.

2. *The Valley of the Shadow.* Concerned with the physiology of reading, the reader may not have given much attention to the possible meaning of the poems reprinted in this chapter.

(a) Several of them suggest (at least to me) the poets' attitudes toward approaching death: Stevenson's "Requiem," Herrick's "Upon His Departure Hence," and Brooke's "The Soldier." Reread these poems carefully. Write a one-page paper in which you compare and contrast the attitudes as you interpret them.

(b) Now turn your attention briefly to "The Twenty-third Psalm." It, too, suggests an attitude toward death, as do also several poems in the first three chapters—Donne's sonnet (p. 12), Hunt's and Browning's poems (pp. 13-19), Hemans' and Frost's poems (pp. 29-31).

3. *On Wings of Song.* Return to a closer study of George Herbert's "Easter Wings."

(a) Reread it thoughtfully and paraphrase the sense of it. Here are a few notes that may be helpful. *Store* in line 1: abundance. The *fall* of line 10: the "decay" and decline of the first five lines, with perhaps an allusion to the Fall of Adam. The *first* stanza begins with the decline of Man; the *second,* with the decline of the poet. *Combine* in line 17: join. *Imp,* line 19: in falconry, to graft a feather or wing onto another wing. *Affliction,* line 20: the "sicknesses and shame" of line 12.

(b) Now turn your attention to some other aspects of the meaning.

What about the *wings:* the larks' wings, a hawk's wings, "my" wings, God's or Christ's wing? Then what is the possible meaning of the title, "Easter Wings"?

(c) What is the relation of the general retinal image to the meaning of the poem? Note the pattern of saccadic eye-movements as you read the decreasing line-lengths in the first half of each stanza, and the increasing line-lengths in the second half. What is the relation of this to the progress of the thought? Does "Most poor" suggest to you depth of degradation? And does "Then shall the fall further the flight in me" suggest to you empyreal heights?

4. *Three Poems.* The poems that are here reprinted together will probably give rise to rather different reading experiences. As you read them do not force yourself to compare or contrast them. Consider each one separately.

Homer's *Odyssey* recounts the adventures of Ulysses on his return trip home from the Siege of Troy. In his sea wanderings he was driven about the Mediterranean for some ten years before reaching Ithaca, his kingdom and his home. There Penelope, his patient wife, awaited him. After slaying the importunate suitors for his wife's hand, he settled down by his home fire; but the fever came upon him to be off again, so he gathered his old remaining companions and seamen, and thus addressed them:

ULYSSES

Alfred, Lord Tennyson

It little profits that an idle king,
By this still hearth, among these barren crags,
Match'd with an aged wife, I mete and dole
Unequal laws unto a savage race,
That hoard, and sleep, and feed, and know not me.
I cannot rest from travel: I will drink
Life to the lees: all times I have enjoy'd
Greatly, have suffer'd greatly, both with those
That loved me, and alone; on shore, and when
Thro' scudding drifts the rainy Hyades
Vext the dim sea: I am become a name;
For always roaming with a hungry heart
Much have I seen and known: cities of men,
And manners, climates, councils, governments,
Myself not least, but honour'd of them all;
And drunk delight of battle with my peers,

Far on the ringing plains of windy Troy.
I am a part of all that I have met;
Yet all experience is an arch wherethro'
Gleams that untravell'd world, whose margin fades
For ever and for ever when I move.
How dull it is to pause, to make an end,
To rust unburnish'd, not to shine in use!
As tho' to breathe were life. Life piled on life
Were all too little, and of one to me
Little remains: but every hour is saved
From that eternal silence, something more,
A bringer of new things; and vile it were
For some three suns to store and hoard myself,
And this grey spirit yearning in desire
To follow knowledge like a sinking star,
Beyond the utmost bound of human thought.

This is my son, mine own Telemachus,
To whom I leave the sceptre and the isle—
Well-loved of me, discerning to fulfil
This labour, by slow prudence to make mild

A rugged people, and thro' soft degrees
Subdue them to the useful and the good.
Most blameless is he, centred in the sphere
Of common duties, decent not to fail
In offices of tenderness, and pay
Meet adoration to my household gods,
When I am gone. He works his work, I mine.

There lies the port; the vessel puffs her sail:
There gloom the dark broad seas. My mariners,
Souls that have toil'd, and wrought, and thought with me—
That ever with a frolic welcome took
The thunder and the sunshine, and opposed
Free hearts, free foreheads—you and I are old;
Old age hath yet his honour and his toil;
Death closes all: but something ere the end,
Some work of noble note, may yet be done,
Not unbecoming men that strove with Gods.
The lights begin to twinkle from the rocks:
The long day wanes: the slow moon climbs: the deep
Moans round with many voices.
Come, my friends,

'Tis not too late to seek a newer
    world.
Push off, and sitting well in order
    smite
The sounding furrows; for my
    purpose holds
To sail beyond the sunset, and the
    baths
Of all the western stars, until I
    die.
It may be that the gulfs will wash
    us down:
It may be we shall touch the
    Happy Isles,
And see the great Achilles, whom
    we knew.
Tho' much is taken, much abides;
    and tho'
We are not now that strength
    which in old days
Moved earth and heaven; that
    which we are, we are;
One equal temper of heroic hearts,
Made weak by time and fate, but
    strong in will
To strive, to seek, to find, and not
    to yield.

                (1842)

A PSALM OF LIFE
Henry Wadsworth Longfellow

WHAT THE HEART OF THE YOUNG
MAN SAID TO THE PSALMIST

Tell me not, in mournful num-
    bers,
    "Life is but an empty dream!"
For the soul is dead that slumbers,
    And things are not what they
    seem.

Life is real! Life is earnest!
    And the grave is not its goal;
"Dust thou art, to dust returnest,"
    Was not spoken of the soul.

Not enjoyment, and not sorrow,
    Is our destined end or way;
But to act, that each tomorrow
    Find us farther than today.

Art is long, and Time is fleeting,
    And our hearts, though stout
    and brave,
Still, like muffled drums, are
    beating
    Funeral marches to the grave.

In the world's broad field of battle,
    In the bivouac of Life,
Be not like dumb, driven cattle—
    Be a hero in the strife!

Trust no Future, howe'er pleasant;
    Let the dead Past bury its dead.
Act—act in the living Present—
    Heart within, and God o'erhead.

Lives of great men all remind us
    We can make our lives sublime,
And, departing, leave behind us
    Footprints on the sands of
    time—

Footprints that perhaps another,
    Sailing o'er life's solemn main,
A forlorn and shipwrecked brother,
    Seeing, shall take heart again.

Let us, then, be up and doing,
    With a heart for any fate;
Still achieving, still pursuing,
    Learn to labour and to wait.

                (1839)

NUNS FRET NOT AT THEIR CONVENT'S NARROW ROOM

William Wordsworth

Nuns fret not at their convent's
  narrow room;
And hermits are contented with
  their cells;
And students with their pensive
  citadels;
Maids at the wheel, the weaver at
  his loom,
Sit blithe and happy; bees that
  soar for bloom,
High as the highest Peak of
  Furness-fells,
Will murmur by the hour in fox-
  glove bells:
In truth the prison, unto which
  we doom
Ourselves, no prison is: and hence
  for me,
In sundry moods, 't was pastime
  to be bound
Within the Sonnet's scanty plot of
  ground;
Pleased if some Souls (for such
  their needs must be)
Who have felt the weight of too
  much liberty,
Should find brief solace there, as
  I have found. (1807)

5. *Three Sorts of Form.* These three poems may serve to illustrate three general categories of poetic form. (a) Tennyson's "Ulysses" is in one of the *continuous forms;* that is, the lines follow each other continuously with only occasional paragraphing as in prose. Browning's "The Glove" (p. 14), Robert Frost's "Out, Out—" (p. 30), Whitman's "Song of Myself" (p. 40), and Chapman's translation of Homer (p. 35) are all in different ones of the continuous forms. They call for comparable sorts of eye-movement in the process of reading. (b) Longfellow's "A Psalm of Life" is in one of the *stanzaic forms;* that is, the poem is made up of groups of similar lines identical in number and related by means of a rime-scheme (to be discussed in the next chapter). However different the stanzaic forms (and many different ones have been encountered thus far in this book), they all have something in common for the reading process: the vague retinal image of the stanzaic form and repetitive patterns of eye-movement. (c) Wordsworth's "Nuns Fret Not—" is in one of the *special forms;* that is, the poem as a unit is fashioned in one of the forms which have developed in literary tradition. Only the sonnet, among these special forms, has been thus far encountered; others will be introduced later in this volume. Donne's "Death Be Not Proud—" (p. 12), Keats' "On First Looking into Chapman's Homer" (p. 25), Millay's "Euclid Alone—" (p. 46), and Brooke's "The Soldier" (p. 77)—all of these are sonnets of one sort or another. The eye-movements and general retinal image involved in the process of reading a sonnet have been sufficiently suggested in the text; other special forms may call for somewhat comparable reading.

6. *A Note on Typography.* Double-column typography has been introduced in the reprinting of these three poems. (a) Look back at the "Ulysses," and observe closely the changed pattern of eye-movements as you leave the single-column printing and begin on the double-column. What effect may this have upon your total reading-experience? (b) Now turn your attention to Wordsworth's sonnet as printed above, and compare the general retinal image and eye-movement with that experienced when you read the poem as here again reprinted:

> Nuns fret not at their convent's narrow room;
> And hermits are contented with their cells;
> And students with their pensive citadels;
> Maids at the wheel, the weaver at his loom,
> Sit blithe and happy; bees that soar for bloom,
> High as the highest Peak of Furness-fells,
> Will murmur by the hour in foxglove bells:
> In truth the prison, unto which we doom
> Ourselves, no prison is: and hence for me,
> In sundry moods, 't was pastime to be bound
> Within the Sonnet's scanty plot of ground;
> Pleased if some Souls (for such there needs must be)
> Who have felt the weight of too much liberty,
> Should find brief solace there, as I have found.

7. *The Three Poems as Regards Meaning.* Again we must recall ourselves from a technical consideration to study the meaning of these three poems.

(a) Reread Tennyson's "Ulysses" after glancing back at the selection from Chapman's translation of *The Odyssey* (pp. 35-38), and after reconsidering your review of the entire epic. What do you view as the chief points in Ulysses' attitude toward life as Tennyson interprets him?

(b) After going back to "The Twenty-third Psalm" and rereading Longfellow's "Psalm of Life," contrast the attitudes of "the Psalmist" and of "the Young Man." Note how important the subtitle of the poem is to an interpretation of its meaning. Pay close attention to the first line; it is ambiguous: does *in mournful numbers* mean "ye numerous sorrowful people" or "in somber lines of poetry"?

(c) Look back at Lovelace's poem, "To Althea, from Prison," remembering his actual imprisonment. Then consider Hamlet's remarks to his old schoolfellows when he first meets them on their return to Denmark: [7]

[7] Shakespeare, *Hamlet*, II, ii, 241-254.

HAMLET. . . . what have you, my good friends, deserved at the hands of Fortune, that she sends you to prison hither?

GUILDENSTERN. Prison, my lord!

HAMLET. Denmark's a prison.

ROSENCRANTZ. Then is the world one.

HAMLET. A goodly one; in which there are many confines, wards, and dungeons, Denmark being one o' the worst.

ROSENCRANTZ. We think not so, my lord.

HAMLET. Why, then, 'tis none to you; for there is nothing either good or bad, but thinking makes it so: to me it is a prison.

Next, reread Wordsworth's sonnet "Nuns Fret Not—." As a stimulus to the reader's independent interpretation of the poem, the prose paraphrase of another reader's understanding of the sense of it is here given:

Women who have given themselves to the Church, make no protest because their rooms are narrow. Men who have gone off by themselves, living only with their thoughts, are happy in their small dark rooms. And men of learning have the same feeling about being among their books. Young women seated at their thread-making, and cloth-makers at their machines, are not bitter but happy. Bees that, looking for flowers, go up to the very mountain top, will be happy-sounding for hours within the bell of the "foxglove."

It is a fact that the prison into which we put ourselves freely, is not truly a prison at all. Therefore [says Wordsworth] when I have been of a certain mind, I have got great pleasure from writing verse within the narrow limits of this special form. I have been happy in the thought that to others (who, like me, have become tired of being completely free) there might come the same feeling of peace in reading my "sonnets," that I have had in writing them.

Now give some thought to the attitudes of Lovelace, Hamlet, and Wordsworth toward imprisonment—actual, imagined, and self-imposed.

(d) Even though you were warned not to force comparison of "Ulysses," "A Psalm of Life," and "Nuns Fret Not—," you may have been unable to avoid doing so. Each of them does, for many readers, communicate a philosophy of life. In what ways do you think them similar? dissimilar?

(e) Give some consideration to the question: What relation does the typographical form of each of these three poems, as you interpret them, have to its meaning?

8. *Form and Music.* (a) Turn back to E. E. Cummings' poem "Chansons Innocentes" (p. 81). Read it aloud and silently several times, until you feel that you have had a full and rich experience of it. Then observe the relationship of the typographical form to the "music" of the poem in your mind's-ear and to the meaning aspect of the full poem-experience. Note especially the effect of the wide   spaces within certain of the lines, the effect of the namesruntogether and the hyphenated-words, the effect of the

successive

descending

indentations.

(b) E. E. Cummings has made a recording of this poem on a disc entitled "Poem, or Beauty Hurts Mr. Vinal" (Harcourt, Brace record). If it is available, study the relation of the poet's oral reading to the typographical form of the printed verses.

9. *Form Past and Present.* (a) Browse in the poetry stacks of the library or the shelves of a used-book shop, and observe the typography of the older editions. Bring in such curiosities of printing as come to your attention that may have some bearing on visual image and eye-movement in the reading of poetry. (b) Browse also with the object of finding what you consider excellent examples of modern typography in this connection. (c) Glance through a dozen different magazines that you think may print some verse, and note their typographical treatment of it.

10. *Brief Solace.* To conclude this chapter, read MacLeish's "Ars Poetica." It is here presented without prefatory note for your thoughtful enjoyment.

ARS POETICA

Archibald MacLeish

A poem should be palpable and mute
As a globed fruit

Dumb
As old medallions to the thumb

Silent as the sleeve-worn stone
Of casement ledges where the moss has grown—

A poem should be wordless
As the flight of birds

.   .   .   .

A poem should be motionless in time
As the moon climbs

Leaving, as the moon releases
Twig by twig the night-entangled trees,

Leaving, as the moon behind the winter leaves,
Memory by memory the mind—

A poem should be motionless in time
As the moon climbs

. . . .

A poem should be equal to:
Not true

For all the history of grief
An empty doorway and a maple leaf

For love
The leaning grasses and two lights above the sea—

A poem should not mean
But be.

(1926)

5

THE MUSIC OF POETRY

Long before writing was devised, man had developed the amazing capacity to speak. There are many languages for which there has never been a native written form. The American Indian, for instance, had no alphabet until Sequoia invented one for the Cherokees a hundred and fifty years ago. Now, the written or printed words, which the eye picks up from the page, are symbols, first and foremost, for word-sounds, which in turn are the symbols for thoughts. The living language of a people is indeed its tongue, not its books.

However, much of our training today condemns vocalization, the mouthing or whispering of words as a part of the process of silent reading. In going over the daily paper or skimming through a popular magazine, vocalization does indeed slow the reader down without adding significantly to the value of his reading experience. One can and should learn the shortcut from "word to sense," so as to avoid the longer way around from "word to sound to sense" when glancing through an article or book.

But it is also true that, unless *the reader of poetry* develops the capacity to realize the full oral flavor of written language, he will miss much of the possible richness of the poem-reading-experience.

Vocalization, so much condemned, may be a necessary step toward that silent reading in which, without the actual activity of tongue and lips, one *feels* the words upon "the mind's-tongue" and *hears* them sounded in "the mind's-ear." These articulatory and auditory images may follow quite immediately upon one's "seeing" the retinal image of the words on the page. I. A. Richards, the psychologist and literary critic, calls them "tied imagery," and, in his little book *Science and Poetry,* says, "These together give the *full body,* as it were, to the words, and it is with the full bodies of words that poets work, not with their printed signs."[1]

When you read a poem aloud, or when you hear someone else reading it or listen to a recording, you are well aware of the speech tune. It may be a very monotonous droning, or a rich poetic melody; it may be inarticulate and halting, or intelligible and free-flowing; it may be singsongy and stilted, or variable and sensitive. However, it is not the purpose of this chapter to consider the special problems of oral interpretation, but to deal primarily with the speech sounds not actually uttered by the voice and not actually heard by the ear, the tied articulatory and auditory imagery, the second aspect of the poem-inside-the-skin that comes with silent reading. And this, as we shall use the phrase, is "The Music of Poetry."

I. ARTICULATORY TIED-IMAGERY

To begin with, let us give our attention briefly to vocalization and articulatory imagery.

The following poem comes from the very end of Shakespeare's *Love's Labour's Lost,* where Armado introduces it as "the dialogue that the two learned men [the Schoolmaster and the Curate] have compiled in praise of the owl and the cuckoo." The one side is Spring which, he says, is upheld by the cuckoo-bird; the other is Winter which is upheld by the owl. The cuckoo, be it remembered, is that bird noted for laying its eggs in the nests of other birds; and the word, in the form of "cuckold," came to be applied to the man whose wife has been unfaithful.[2]

Read this double lyric aloud, trying to catch on to how it goes, its particular swing and movement. Listen carefully to the rising and falling of your voice, for the recurrence of particular sounds,

---

[1] I. A. Richards, *Science and Poetry,* second edition, London, 1935, pp. 17-18. See also Richards, *Principles of Literary Criticism,* fourth edition, Harcourt, Brace, 1930, pp. 118-21.

[2] A few other notes may be helpful: *Lady-smock* and *cuckoo-bud:* used to name various flowering plants, a bitter cress, ragged robin, and wood sorrel. *Turtle:* the turtledove, of course. *Tread:* to mate, said of birds. *Rooks and daws:* crow-like birds. *Keel:* to cool, by stirring or skimming. *Saw:* a proverb or maxim.

for the qualities of tone and their sequence that make the rhythmic
patterns of this poem unique.

SPRING and WINTER

from LOVE'S LABOUR'S LOST, V, ii

William Shakespeare

SPRING

1

When daisies pied and violets blue
   And lady-smocks all silver-white
And cuckoo-buds of yellow hue
   Do paint the meadows with delight,
The cuckoo then, on every tree,
Mocks married men; for thus sings he,
          Cuckoo;
Cuckoo, cuckoo: O, word of fear,
Unpleasing to a married ear!

2

When shepherds pipe on oaten straws,
   And merry larks are ploughmen's clocks,
When turtles tread, and rooks, and daws,
   And maidens bleach their summer smocks,
The cuckoo then, on every tree,
Mocks married men; for thus sings he,
          Cuckoo;
Cuckoo, cuckoo: O, word of fear,
Unpleasing to a married ear!

WINTER

3

When icicles hang by the wall,
   And Dick the shepherd blows his nail,
And Tom bears logs into the hall,
   And milk comes frozen home in pail,
When blood is nipp'd, and ways be foul,

Then nightly sings the staring owl,
Tu-who;
Tu-whit, tu-who—a merry note,
While greasy Joan doth keel the pot.

4

When all aloud the wind doth blow,
And coughing drowns the parson's saw,
And birds sit brooding in the snow,
And Marian's nose looks red and raw,
When roasted crabs hiss in the bowl,
Then nightly sings the staring owl,
Tu-who;
Tu-whit, tu-who—a merry note,
While greasy Joan doth keel the pot.

(*c. 1590*, 1598)

It has been suggested that you read this poem aloud and give your attention to how the "music" of it sounds. Now direct your attention to the process of articulation, and to how it feels to "make the music."

The phenomenon of human speech is an amazingly complex activity. It involves the entire breathing mechanism of chest, diaphragm, and abdomen, and the skillful control of exhalation; subtle muscular adjustments of the vocal bands, and the production of voice tones; the amplification of these tones by resonation through nasal and other near-by cavities and structure; the altering and shaping of these tones by the articulators—palate, tongue, teeth, lips.

Read aloud, with vigor and gusto, the first stanza of the cuckoo's defense of Spring, and take note of your *breathing*.

When daisies pied and violets blue
And lady-smocks all silver-white
And cuckoo-buds of yellow hue
Do paint the meadows with delight,
The cuckoo then, on every tree,
Mocks married men; for thus sings he,
Cuckoo;

> Cuckoo, cuckoo: O, word of fear,
> Unpleasing to a married ear!

Were you conscious of strong inhalation of breath just before you started? of abdomenal tonicity as you read, particularly as you uttered the plosive and stressed sounds? of running out of breath? of quick inhalations? At what points in the poem did you take shallow and deep breaths?

As you reread the second stanza, aloud and forcefully, sharpen your consciousness of the process of *phonation* and *resonation*. Slow down and linger on such sounds as "straws" and "daws," and upon the cuckoo's call.

> When shepherds pipe on oaten straws,
>   And merry larks are ploughmen's clocks,
> When turtles tread, and rooks, and daws,
>   And maidens bleach their summer smocks,
> The cuckoo then, on every tree,
> Mocks married men; for thus sings he,
>   . Cuckoo;
> Cuckoo, cuckoo: O, word of fear,
> Unpleasing to a married ear!

Did you feel the vibration of muscles around the larynx? Did you feel the resonation of tones in the nasal structure?

In rereading the third stanza, isolate the *articulatory* activity for special observation by whispering vigorously and distinctly. There will still be strong breathing, but without vibration of the vocal bands.

> When icicles hang by the wall,
>   And Dick the shepherd blows his nail,
> And Tom bears logs into the hall,
>   And milk comes frozen home in pail,
> When blood is nipp'd, and ways be foul,
>   Then nightly sings the staring owl,
>   Tu-who;
> Tu-whit, tu-who—a merry note,
> While greasy Joan doth keel the pot.

Did you feel the proximation of your tongue and teeth on the "the"? tongue and palate on "wall"? the lip activity on "blows" and "bears"? Did you distinguish the articulatory feel of the *n* and *m* sounds in "nail" and "milk"? of the *sh* and *s* sounds in "shepherd" and "sings"? Did your lips round as you articulated "tu-who"? Did you pronounce "greasy" with an *s* or a *z* sound?

Reread the fourth stanza *silently*. Your breathing will now assume a pattern of inhalation and exhalation that may bear quite a different relation to your reading of the lines. Your vocal bands will be relaxed; and the articulators will also be at rest—or almost so, for there may be rudimentary and vestigial movements of tongue and lips for the reader who likes the feel of words. There is, indeed, no sharp line between fully vocalized and silent reading.

> When all aloud the wind doth blow,
>   And coughing drowns the parson's saw,
> And birds sit brooding in the snow,
>   And Marian's nose looks red and raw,
> When roasted crabs hiss in the bowl,
> Then nightly sings the staring owl,
>   Tu-who;
> Tu-whit, tu-who—a merry note,
> While greasy Joan doth keel the pot.

While reading this stanza in silence, you were probably conscious of those goings-on in the mind that we called tied imagery in an earlier paragraph—the *feel* of the words upon the mind's-tongue and the *sound* of the words in the mind's-ear.

So, *as you read a poem silently, this awareness of sounds unuttered yet felt in the mind, together with the sounds unperceived yet heard, is the "music" of poetry, which for many persons is one of its chief pleasures.*

2. AUDITORY TIED-IMAGERY; PROSE AND VERSE

But let us now leave articulatory imagery, and proceed to a more lengthy consideration of *tied auditory imagery*.[3]

---

[3] For the distinction between *tied* imagery and *free* imagery, see the opening paragraphs of the next chapter.

The most conspicuous feature of the music of a poem is likely to be its *rhythm*. The rising and falling of the voice, as heard or imagined, in an undulating though interrupted flow of tone, provides the reader with a pleasurable sensation something like music. This alternate rising and falling, which is a more notable feature of spoken English than of some other languages, results from the stressing of the more important words in a sentence and from accenting certain syllables. For we emphasize key words and syllables by uttering them with greater *force,* with longer *time,* and with higher *pitch* than that used for the adjacent unstressed syllables. These word sounds, because they are higher, louder, and longer, stand out as "points of interest" in the flow of an utterance either heard or imagined. And the *un*-stressed words and *un*-accented syllables—for the most part lower in pitch, softer, and shorter—find their place in the background of our attention.

The word *rhythm* is here used to name the peculiar sort of feeling that may accompany the apperception of repeated points of interest. As one LIStens to the FLOW of SPEECH SOUNDS, or HEARS them in the MIND'S-EAR while READing, one's atTENtion is CAUGHT by the ACcented SYLlables and STRESSED WORDS that THUS beCOME POINTS of INterest; and THIS GIVES RISE to the FEELing that we here call "RHYTHM."

The syllables printed in ALL-CAPS are those that are stressed, as the writer conceives of their being spoken. But stress is entirely a relative matter, and there are innumerable *degrees* of stress. So this use of caps and small letters is, like the traditional systems of scansion,[4] a very crude means of indicating the undulating rise and fall of the voice, let alone the other variables of speech melody. But crude as it is, look again at the second sentence in the last paragraph. You will notice that the stresses (accented syllables and stressed words) appear at very irregular intervals in the flow of speech. Several of the stressed words stand next to each other, but

---

[4] Scansion is the process of marking off the stresses and accents as they occur, or "should" occur, in verse. There are several systems that are in common use, such as the marking of acute accent (´) and breve (˘) above the stressed and unstressed syllables. All of the two- and three-valued systems, like the use of all-caps in this text, are very crude devices at best.

usually there are one to three unstressed syllables or short words intervening, and in one case there are five.

Language of this sort is called *prose*. It is the ordinary language of our conversation, the newspapers, textbooks. But many works of language-art also are in prose. One of the great branches of Literature may be called Prose Literature. It includes the Novel, Biography, the Essay, and so on. And much of another great branch of Literature, Dramatic Literature, also is in prose. There are two features that distinguish prose as a sort of language: One is the quite irregular pattern of stresses, so irregular that for some persons there arises no feeling that they would call rhythm. The second feature is to be seen in the written and printed form of prose; the words fill out each line from margin to margin, even with the division of a word at the end of the line when necessary to complete the printer's measure.

Such is prose, with its relatively irregular rhythm. The other sort of language is called verse.

THE LADS IN THEIR HUNDREDS
A. E. Housman

The lads in their hundreds to Ludlow come in for the fair,
　　There's men from the barn and the forge and the mill and the fold,
The lads for the girls and the lads for the liquor are there,
　　And there with the rest are the lads that will never be old.

There's chaps from the town and the field and the till and the cart,
　　And many to count are the stalwart, and many the brave,
And many the handsome of face and the handsome of heart,
　　And few that will carry their looks or their truth to the grave.

I wish one could know them, I wish there were tokens to tell
　　The fortunate fellows that now you can never discern;
And then one could talk with them friendly and wish them farewell
　　And watch them depart on the way that they will not return.

But now you may stare as you like and there's nothing to scan;
　　And brushing your elbow unguessed-at and not to be told

They carry back bright to the coiner the mintage of man,
The lads that will die in their glory and never be old.

(1896)

Here the stresses (the accented syllables and stressed words) appear quite regularly in the flow of speech.

The LADS in their HUNdreds to LUDlow come IN for the FAIR,
There's MEN from the BARN and the FORGE and the MILL and
the FOLD,
The LADS for the GIRLS and the LADS for the LIQUor are THERE,
And THERE with the REST are the LADS that will NEVer be
OLD.

There are two unstressed syllables between the stresses within the line, though only one at the beginning of each line. This, you have noted, is not ordinary language. It is *verse,* the sort of language used in Poetry, which is the third great branch of Literature. But verse is also found in many works of Dramatic Literature, in many of the greatest. There are two features that distinguish verse as a sort of language: First, the relatively regular pattern of stresses, sufficiently regular that for many persons there arises a strong feeling of rhythm. Second (and observed in the last chapter), this sort of language, when written or printed, is set off in lines of varied and arbitrary length without regard to the printer's measure and the usual margins. And each of these lines of poetry is called *a verse*.

Mr. Jordan, in Molière's *The Would-Be Gentleman,* was astounded when his Philosophy Teacher told him that, in language, "All is prose that is not verse, and all is verse that is not prose." And he was delighted to learn that he had been talking prose all his life.

But it is not so easy to draw a sharp line between prose and verse as it might seem. For some prose is much more regularly rhythmical than other prose, and some verse is very much less regularly rhythmical than other verse. Free verse, for instance, is quite as irregularly rhythmical as much prose; yet it is set off in lines of varied and arbitrary length. But let us put "free verse" aside for the time being; its music will be different from the music of the more usual verse, or "bound verse" as it has been called.

It was said that the most conspicuous feature of the music of a poem is its rhythm—the feeling that may result from the apperception of repeated stresses at fairly regular intervals in the undulating flow of the verses. We shall call this the *poetic rhythm,* for though it is the chief rhythm that may be felt, there are other rhythms too. But these subordinate rhythms will be taken up later in this chapter; now our attention will be given to the principal rhythm, the poetic rhythm.

3. POETIC RHYTHM; EXPECTANCY AND DEVIATIONS

Let us take another poem to carry forward our discussion of the *poetic rhythm,* one aspect of the auditory tied-imagery.

TO ——

Percy Bysshe Shelley

> Music, when soft voices die,
> Vibrates in the memory—
> Odours, when sweet violets sicken,
> Live within the sense they quicken.
> Rose leaves, when the rose is dead,
> Are heaped for the belovèd's bed;
> And so thy thoughts, when thou art gone,
> Love itself shall slumber on.

(1821)

When you begin to read a new poem, one of the first things that you are likely to do is to try to catch on to *the way it goes,* the particular swing that will at once carry you along and at the same time take account of the normal accenting and stressing of the words. Sometimes, after reading a few verses, you discover that you were off on the wrong foot, as it were, and then you start over again. It's not just a question of where to place the stress; there's a second question—how the unstressed elements are related to the stresses. For our nervous systems are organizing devices: we tend to group things by twos or threes, as duples or triples. The *tick tick tick tick tick tick* of a clock becomes *tockTICK tockTICK tock-*

TICK, or perhaps *TICKtock TICKtock TICKtock,* or even *TICKtocktock TICKtocktock.* So it is that we tend to group unstressed syllables either with the following stresses or with the preceding stresses.

Some readers will have made a false start in reading the above poem, trying the following placement of the stresses:

> MUSic, when SOFT voices DIE,
> VIbrates in THE mem-o-RY.

And this reading, in which the rhythm is conceived as *triple,* may satisfy a few readers, except that the unimportant "the" is accented quite unnaturally several times. But most readers who first try this triple swing, will back up and make a fresh start:

> MUSic, WHEN soft VOICes DIE,
> VIbrates IN the MEM-o-RY.

For them, this *duple* reading, stressing the alternate syllables, will seem to follow more nearly the "natural" stressing of the words, though there is still some wrenching of the stress, as is often the case in such trial flights.

But that second question now arises. How does the reader tend to "organize" or group the stressed and unstressed syllables in this duple reading? He will probably feel that the music of the poem "goes" either this way—

> MU- sicWHEN softVOIC- esDIE,
> VI- bratesIN theMEM- o-RY—

or this way—

> MUsic WHENsoft VOICes DI-e,
> VIbrates INthe MEM-o- RY-e.

The first of these two rhythmic groupings will give the reader a *rising* feeling; for the voice, heard or imagined, slides from the unstressed syllable, normally lower in pitch, up to the stressed syllable, normally higher in pitch. The second of these two readings

will give him a descending or *falling* feeling; for his voice will
slide from the stressed syllable down to the unstressed. By the time
the reader comes to the line—

ODours, WHENsweet VIolets SICKen,

he is likely to feel more certain that the poem "goes" with this
falling duple rhythm.

But *after discovering how the poem goes, the reader makes the
further discovery that it doesn't go exactly that way after all—it
only* TENDS *to go that way.*

For the poetic rhythm, the most conspicuous feature of the music
of a poem, is a complex phenomenon. It is a sort of compromise
between two different factors operating upon the reader at one and
the same time. One of these factors is the *metrical pattern;* the
other one is the meaning or *sense pattern.* How a poem goes, its
gait, is its metrical pattern; what puts you on to this metrical pattern, yet keeps the poem from following it exactly, is its sense pattern. The metrical pattern of a poem, once it is grasped, will set
up an *expectancy* in the reader, an expectancy that the rhythmic
flow will continue to be falling duple, if that's how the poem goes.
But the sense of the words, as the reader thinks of their meaning,
will set up a relationship of stressed and unstressed elements at
times contrary to this expectancy. If the reader is at all sensitive
to the metrical pattern and to the sense pattern, he will feel these
two psychological pulls contending for his attention. And the poetic
rhythm that he feels, and which may be evidenced when he reads
the poem out loud, will show many *deviations* from the strict
metrical pattern. These deviations from the metrical expectancy,
which are a characteristic of the poetic rhythm, will result from
the influence of the sense pattern.

Let us illustrate. The metrical pattern of the short poem last presented was seen to be falling duple—at least, that is how it "goes"
for this reader:

DUMMde DUMMde DUMMde DUMMde,
DUMMde DUMMde DUMMde DUMMde.

But as the pairs of lines have similar end-sounds, which we shall call *rime,* we may objectify the underlying metrical sing-song of the poem in this way:

DUMMde DUMMde DUMMde DAEde,
DUMMde DUMMde DUMMde DAEde;
DUMMde DUMMde DUMMde DOEde,
DUMMde DUMMde DUMMde DOEde.

And so on. This represents the metrical pattern. It is utterly mechanical. Like what the second fiddles or the pianist's left hand may play as an accompaniment, there is no melody to it.

But now look at the sense pattern, wherein the disposition of the stresses is hardly more regular than for typical prose:

MUsic, when SOFT VOICes DIE, VI-BRATES in the MEM-o-ry. ODours, when SWEET VI-o-lets SICKen, LIVE within the SENSE they QUICKen. ROSE LEAVES, when the ROSE is DEAD, are HEAPED for the beLOV'D'S BED. . . .

If you read aloud, and listen closely, you will see how much more melodious this is than the sing-song of the

DUMMde DUMMde DUMMde DUMMde.

The reader will be like Launcelot Gobbo, in Shakespeare's *The Merchant of Venice,* who was torn between his Conscience and the Fiend. The metrical pattern counsels the reader to say:

MUsic WHENsoft VOICes DIEa,

but the sense pattern tempts him to say:

MUsic when SOFT VOICes DIE( ).

Each reader will resolve these contrary pulls, these points of tension, in his own way. The metrical pattern bids him stress the "when" and leave the "soft" unstressed; the sense pattern may urge him to place less stress on the "when," but to stress "soft" by all means. The metrical pattern leads him to expect an unstressed syllable at the end of "die"; the sense pattern says that there is no syllable there. Some readers will heed one demand, some the other; but many readers find a balance in their poetic rhythm, and will read "when" and "soft" with what is often called a hovering accent:

MUsic, WHEN SOFT VOICes DIEE,

and with perhaps a slight lingering on the last word. No reader, I believe, will really make "die" into two syllables, though the metrical pattern invites him to do so.

For the next line, little arrows are used to indicate the points of tension between the two patterns, and the empty parentheses indicate the absence of a syllable:

Metrical pattern: VIbrates IN the MEM-o-RY-a
                         ↑   ↑   ↑ ⋮
                         ↓   ↓   ↓ ⋮
Sense pattern: VIBRATES in the MEM-o-ry (˙)

The poetic rhythm, for many readers, will be a sort of compromise, then, with half stress on the "in" and on the final syllable of "memory," and with the second syllable of "vibrates" perhaps losing its stress:[5]

Poetic rhythm: VIbrates ɪɴ the MEM-o-ʀʏ ( ).

But there is one more deviation from the established metrical pattern. After one catches on to how this poem "goes," one expects the lines to rime in pairs. But "die" and the last syllable in "memory," as the two words are regularly pronounced, are not as similar in sound as we expect for rime. The metrical pattern tempts one to say "MEM-o-RIE-a"; but few readers will yield to the temptation, and most of them will find enjoyment in the deviation.

Perhaps analogy will make the phenomenon of the so-called *poetic rhythm* somewhat clearer. Think again of Launcelot Gobbo, subjected to the contending pulls of Conscience and Fiend within him. Think again of the pianist who, while hammering out a 1-2-3 1-2-3 1-2-3 accompaniment with the left hand, plays a free flowing melody with the right hand. Now think of the equestrian sport—

---

[5] The word "vibrate" is shown in dictionaries as having the accent on the first syllable; but in the speech of many persons the syllables seem to be almost equally stressed. Contrast this, however, with your own pronunciation of "vibrant."

you may have seen it at the circus, or in newsreels of cavalry ma-
neuvers—in which a rider is mounted with one foot on the back
of each of two horses. The rhythmic motion of the rider's body is
a sort of compromise between the slightly different motions of each
of his two horses. While maintaining a balance, he will be in
rhythmic motion, on-going and exciting. Such may well be the
sensation which the sensitive reader has as he rides down the wind
upon his two chargers, the steady-going metrical pattern and that
fractious filly, the sense pattern.

The music of poetry, then, which vibrates in the mind's-ear and
which can be felt on the mind's-tongue, is based upon a rhythmic
flow of unuttered and unheard sounds, whose melodic undulations
follow and deviate from the expectancy of a metrical pattern.

4. THE SORTS OF METRICAL PATTERN

It is important, therefore, that the reader discover what the
metrical pattern of a poem is, for it is "from" this pattern that
the poetic rhythm will deviate in some obvious and in many very
subtle ways. Following an introductory illustration, we shall consider in some detail *the chief features that distinguish various sorts
of metrical pattern.*

THE HUNTSMEN

Walter de la Mare

Three jolly gentlemen,
    In coats of red,
Rode their horses
    Up to bed.

Three jolly gentlemen
    Snored till morn,
Their horses champing
    The golden corn.

Three jolly gentlemen,
    At break of day,
Came clitter-clatter down the stairs
    And galloped away.

(1913)

The reader who starts out—

> Three JOLly GENTlemen
> In COATS of RED, . . .

will probably find himself in trouble, and may make another try:

> THREEjolly GENTlemen
> INcoats of RED( )( ). . . .

The expectancy of "falling triple" is established, though the deviations are indeed numerous and amusing, "CAME clitter-clatter."
    But to proceed. *The chief features of a metrical pattern are three:*
foot, meter, and line-scheme. By taking note of these three features,
a metrical pattern may be described easily and clearly.
    The word *foot* names the rhythmic unit, both as regards the
number of syllables in each group, and as regards the organization
of the syllables within it. Since, as was earlier said, we tend to
group things in twos or threes, there can be only a few possible
sorts of metrical feet. In fact, only five types are regularly to be
found in the metrical patterns of English poetry, and the first one,
in the list below, is by far the most common. Here they are given
in the *deDUMM* notation that we have been using, together with
their usual names, borrowed inaccurately from the Greek, and a
descriptive phrase for each:

> deDUMM   —ī′ămb, the ĭām′bĭc foot; or, rising-duple
> dedeDUMM—ăn′ăpĕst, the ănăpĕs′tic foot; rising-triple
> DUMMde   —trō′chee, the trōchā′ic foot; falling-duple
> DUMMdede—dăc′tўl, the dăctўl′ic foot; falling-triple
> deDUMMde—ăm′phĭbrăch, the unusual "rocking" triple.[6]

The iambic foot is by far the commonest type found in the metrical
patterns of English poetry; most metrical patterns are based on it,

---

[6] It will be convenient to know the names of these five sorts of metrical foot—
even their pronunciations (note the *k* sound in "trochee" and "amphibrach").
There is no very easy way to learn them; but the following jingle, inspired by one
the poet Coleridge wrote for his son, may be of some help:

> Iambic feet are rising twos,
>   Anapestic is rising and three;
> Trochee is in falling duple,
>   Dactyl is falling like—Tripoli;
> And lastly, remember the amphibrach's rocking, dear pupil.

and comparatively seldom are the others to be found. Yet some of the best-loved among the shorter poems make use of anapestic and trochaic metrical patterns. Dactylic poems are unusual in English, though not in the classical languages; and the use of amphibrach is extremely rare.[7]

The word *meter* is here used to name the number of rhythmic units, feet, in the verse or line. There may be any number, from one to eight. Two different systems are commonly used in naming verse length. One of them simply gives the number of stresses normally found in the line, and that is the same as the number of feet; so one finds the term "three-stress" or "five-stress." The commoner system makes use of terms taken, again inaccurately, from the Greek—the root word *meter* (measure) with a prefix indicating number. Neither terminology is difficult to remember:

mōnŏm'ētĕr—one-stress verse; that is, one foot to the line.

> Thus I
> Pass by
> And die . . .
> (See p. 72 for the poem.)

dĭm'ēter—two-stress. This and the above are very rare.

> Three jolly gentlemen,
> In coats of red,
> Rode their horses
> Up to bed.
> (p. 105)

trĭm'eter—three-stress; used in many shorter poems.

> We swing ungirded hips,
> And lighted are our eyes,
> The rain is on our lips,
> We do not run for prize.
> (p. 57)

[7] Parts of Browning's "The Glove" may supply an illustration:

> The sentence no sooner was uttered,
> Than over the rails a glove fluttered,
> Fell close to the lion, and rested:
> The dame 't was, who flung it and jested. . . .

tĕtrăm′eter—four-stress; found very frequently.

> Tell me not, in mournful numbers,
> "Life is but an empty dream!"
>   (p. 85)

pĕntăm′eter—five-stress; the commonest of them all.

> It little profits that an idle king,
> By this still hearth, among these barren crags,
> Match'd with an aged wife, I mete and dole
> Unequal laws unto a savage race . . .
>   (p. 83)

hĕxăm′eter—six-stress; often in classical poetry.

> I will arise and go now, and go to Innisfree,
> And a small cabin build there, of clay and wattles made . . .
>   (p. 122)

hĕptăm′eter—seven-stress; the long "septenarius."

> I must go down to the seas again, to the lonely sea and the sky,
> And all I ask is a tall ship and a star to steer her by . . .
>   (p. 21)

ŏctăm′eter—eight-stress. This and the above are unusual.

> Once upon a midnight dreary, while I pondered, weak and weary,
> Over many a quaint and curious volume of forgotten lore . . .
>   (p. 345)

Notice that the pentameter is by far the most common of all English meters, as the iamb is the commonest foot. In fact, about 90 per cent of all English poetry is iambic pentameter. Neither the very short nor the very long verse-lengths are frequent. Many poems use a single meter throughout; others make use of various line-lengths.

The phrase *line-scheme* is here used to name one aspect of poetic "form," the way in which the lines of the poem are grouped and related; and we considered it briefly in the text and the supplement of the last chapter. In some poems the lines follow each other continuously with only occasional paragraphing as in prose; and this was called *continuous form*. In other poems, however, the lines are arranged in similar groups called stanzas, usually with some pattern of rime that is repeated in successive stanzas; and this was called *stanzaic form*. In still other cases the poem (like a sonnet) is fashioned as a unit, with the line-scheme often involving an elaborate pattern of rime; and this was called *special form*.[8]

But we must proceed to a consideration of rime, which is often the distinguishing feature of a line-scheme.

Rime—or "rhyme," as it is also spelled—names that repetition of sound which is often found at the end, and occasionally in the middle, of adjacent verses. The similarity in the end-sounds of the riming verses strikes the ear, or the mind's-ear, at once. But often the words also look somewhat similar, owing to their spelling. Rime normally involves words at the ends of lines (*end rime*), words ending with stressed syllables (*masculine rime*), and words that are identical in their stressed vowels and any following consonants, but with differing sounds preceding the stressed vowels (*perfect rime*). This is what one tends to expect: "go—so," "break—lake," "invent—consent" (*at the ends of lines*).[9]

The usual method of describing the arrangement of rimes in a line-scheme is to use small italic letters, *a b c,* etc., each letter representing a different end-sound as found in the successive verses. The letter is repeated each time the end-sound is repeated; that is, when there is rime. For instance, a four-line stanzaic form with the second and fourth lines riming, would be symbolized in this way: *abcb*. A six-line stanzaic form with the lines riming in pairs would be: *aabbcc*.

Let us now illustrate this discussion by describing the metrical pattern—foot, meter, line-scheme—of the poems so far encountered in this chapter. Here is the opening stanza of Shakespeare's "Spring":

> When daisies pied and violets blue
> And lady-smocks all silver-white
> And cuckoo-buds of yellow hue
> Do paint the meadows with delight,

[8] See the previous discussion, pp. 74-79 and pp. 83-86, citing illustrations.
[9] For a further consideration of *rime* see the Glossarial Handbook.

> The cuckoo then, on every tree,
> Mocks married men; for thus sings he,
> Cuckoo;
> Cuckoo, cuckoo: O, word of fear,
> Unpleasing to a married ear!

The foot is rising-duple (or *iambic*). The meter is four-stress (or *tetrameter*) for all but the ninth line ("Cuckoo"), which is one-stress (or *monometer*). The line-scheme is a stanzaic form, riming *ababccdee*. The last three lines are repeated at the end of each of the two stanzas. So, with small superior numerals to indicate the meter of the lines and capital letters to indicate the repetition of the whole lines, we might describe the entire metrical pattern thus: (*iambic*) $ababcc^4D^1EE^4$.

Look at the metrical pattern of the first stanza of Housman's poem:

> The lads in their hundreds to Ludlow come in for the fair,
> There's men from the barn and the forge and the mill and the fold,
> The lads for the girls and the lads for the liquor are there,
> And there with the rest are the lads that will never be old.

The foot is rising-triple (*anapestic*); the meter is five-stress (*pentameter*); the line-scheme is a four-line stanzaic form (a quatrain) with crossed rimes. The metrical pattern may be described simply as: (*anapestic*) $abab^5$.

Now look at Shelley's lyric:

> Music, when soft voices die,
> Vibrates in the memory—
> Odours, when sweet violets sicken,
> Live within the sense they quicken.
> Rose leaves, when the rose is dead,
> Are heaped for the belovèd's bed;
> And so thy thoughts, when thou art gone,
> Love itself shall slumber on.

This is falling-duple (*trochaic*); four-stress (*tetrameter*); the line-scheme is one of the continuous forms, riming in couplets. The metrical pattern may be described as: (*trochaic*) $aabb^4$, *etc.*

Here are the opening lines of de la Mare's "The Huntsmen":

> Three jolly gentlemen,
>   In coats of red,
> Rode their horses
>   Up to bed.

This is falling-triple (*dactylic*), two-stress (*dimeter*), in a stanzaic form riming *abcb*. Or simply (*dactylic*) *abcb*².

So much, then, for the chief features of the metrical pattern. But there are in addition three or four minor features of a metrical pattern: *pitch, intensity, tempo,* and *voice quality.* As readers vary so widely in observing them, these features will, for the sake of simplicity, be no more than mentioned here; but with one comment: When the reader discovers for himself how a poem "goes," he will probably have decided that a generally high, middle, or low voice is appropriate; that soft, medium, or loud speech sounds are called for; that rapid, moderate, or slow articulation is in order; that sweet, acid, or rough tones will be "right." Once having made such judgments, the reader will probably expect the poem to continue in this way. An illustration will be provided for the reader if he will turn back to stanzas just quoted and give consideration to "appropriate" pitch, intensity, tempo, and voice quality.

5. THE SORTS OF DEVIATION

Once the reader catches on to how a poem "goes"—that is, the metrical pattern—this basic pattern does not usually change. The reader will expect the poem to continue to be iambic, if that is what it starts out to be; he will expect it to continue to be tetrameter-trimeter in alternate lines, if those are the meters in the first stanza; he will expect the line-scheme to continue to be stanzaic, riming *abcb*. And he will also expect it to continue to be low-pitched, soft-voiced, slow-moving, and sweet-toned, if that is how, for him, it begins.

But the *deviations* from this established expectancy are in many cases numerous; and they may be gross as well as subtle. Sometimes, but not often, they succeed in altering the expectancy itself.

A number of phenomena described in the next paragraphs as deviations may, if somewhat regularly used in a poem, become a part of the metrical pattern itself. For instance, in "The Huntsmen" we expect, after the metrical pattern is established in the first stanza, that the second and fourth lines of the other stanzas will also end upon stressed syllables, will also omit the unstressed syllables of the final falling-triple.

Let us turn now to a closer examination of these deviations.

Remember that these anti-metrical elements in the poetic rhythm result from the pull of the sense pattern. Remember also that, whereas most readers will usually be conscious of the same metrical pattern as they read a poem (at least as regards its chief features), they will often differ widely in their feeling for the stresses that make up the sense pattern. Consequently the deviations from the metrical pattern are likely to be highly individual.

The following anonymous lyric was first printed in John Wilbye's *Second Set of Madrigals.*

LOVE NOT ME FOR COMELY GRACE

Anonymous

Love not me for comely grace,
For my pleasing eye or face,
Nor for any outward part,
No, nor for my constant heart:
  For those may fail or turn to ill,
    So thou and I shall sever.
Keep therefore a true woman's eye,
And love me still, but know not why,
  So hast thou the same reason still
    To dote upon me ever!

(1609)

This poem is written in one of the "special forms," a variety of madrigal, a love lyric for unaccompanied singing in five or six parts. Its metrical pattern is (*iambic*) *aabbc⁴d³eec⁴d³*, with the *d*-rime a double or feminine rime: "sever—ever." For this particular

reader the expectancy that establishes itself is, furthermore, tenor
in pitch, rather soft, moderate in tempo, and sweet-toned.

As the deviations will depend upon the sense pattern (the stresses
set up by the reader's interpretation of the poem), it will be necessary to look closely at the meaning. The following paraphrase will
serve to indicate my own understanding of the sense of it:

Give me your love, but *not* because of my pleasing ways, or because
of my good looks, or because of anything physical—no, not even because my love for you is true! For all these things may undergo a
change; then your reason for loving me would be gone, and we might
come to a parting of the ways.

In place of this, be guided by your woman's quick eye and impulse.
Go on loving me, but without questioning; then, come what may, you
will for ever have the same reason for being in love with me.

It is our business now to look back at the poem and observe the
deviations of the poetic rhythm from the metrical expectancy. Some
of these deviations are obvious enough; some are more subtle. In
the following representation of my own reading, vertical lines are
used to separate the feet, and double and triple lines to mark brief
and longer pauses.

( ) LOVE | NOT ME | for COME | ly GRACE ||
( ) FOR | my PLEAS | ing EYE | or FACE ||
( ) NOR | for AN | y OUT | ward PART ||
( ) NO || NOR for | my CON | stant HEART ||
For THOSE | may FAIL | or TURN | to ILL ||
SO THOU | and I | shall SEV | er |||

There is only one of these first six lines that completely fulfills
the expectancy, the fifth: "For THOSE may FAIL or TURN to
ILL." Notice that each of the first four lines lacks the initial unstressed syllable to be expected in iambic verse. (This is *initial truncation*.) [10] In the first verse I stress the "NOT" as well as the "ME,"
because it is so important to my understanding of the meaning.
(The "NOT ME" in place of the expected iambic foot, "not ME,"
is called a *spondaic substitution;* a *spondee* is a foot consisting of two

[10] The technical vocabulary used in naming the various sorts of deviation is
treated with some detail in the Glossarial Handbook of the Appendix.

stressed syllables.) Certain words here—"COME | ly," "PLEAS | -
ing," "OUT | ward," etc.—break over from one foot to the next;
they are "falling" words in a "rising" rhythm; the effect is not unlike musical tied-notes, or the melody moving off the beat; or
like rising waves and diving dolphin. (There is no generally recognized term to describe this *dolphin effect*.) After the "NO" in line
four there is a definite pause. (The within-the-line pause is called
a *caesura*.) In the next foot of that line "NOR for," as I read it,
has the stress on the first rather than on the second syllable. (This
is a *trochaic substitution;* it is an *inversion* of the expected iamb.)
The sixth line begins with an unexpected foot of two stresses
(*spondaic substitution*), and ends with an extra-metrical syllable
(called a *feminine ending*). Note that the sense calls for a brief
pause at the end of each one of these lines. (They are called *end-
stopped lines*.)

But let us go on and look at the remaining four lines:

> KEEP THERE | fore a | TRUE WOM | an's EYE ||
> And LOVE | me STILL || but KNOW | not WHY ||
> SO HAST | THOU the | SAME REAS ¹ on STILL
> To DOTE | upon | me EV | er |||

In the first verse here I stress the "KEEP" and "TRUE" because
of their importance to the meaning, though the metrical pattern
calls for unstressed syllables. (Again this results in *spondaic substitutions*.) In the second foot of the line I seem to read with about
half stress on both the "fore" and "a"—the sense pattern suggesting
some emphasis for the one and the metrical pattern for the other.
(A comparable phenomenon was earlier called *hovering accent,*
p. 104.) Note the mid-line pause in the second line after "STILL"
(*caesura*). My reading of the next to the last line involves a succession of three deviations: the first foot with two stresses; the next
with the stressed and unstressed syllables inverted; the third with
two stresses again—"SO HAST | THOU the | SAME REA | son
STILL." (The first and third are *spondaic substitutions;* the second
a *trochaic substitution*.) And there is no pause, as expected, at the
end of this line, the sense being carried right on into the next
line. (It is therefore called a *run-on line*.) In the last line the second
foot is without a stressed syllable. (It is called a *pyrrhic substitution*

—*pyrrhic* being used to name a foot consisting of two unstressed syllables.) And the last line concludes with an extra syllable (*feminine ending*).

Such an enumeration of the gross deviations from the metrical expectancy gives, alas, too crude a notion of the poetic rhythm of this (for me) comely and graceful Elizabethan lyric. It is still a two- or three-valued analysis, taking no account of the many different degrees of stress, of the larger movements in pitch of the melody, of the subtle rushing and lingering, of the notable changes in voice quality. But this description may at least have suggested that *it is the departures from the expectancy that give the poetic rhythm of a particular poem its unique character;* and that the only way the reader may become conscious of them is by discovering how the poem "goes"—what its metrical pattern is—and then observing the independent pulling and hauling of the sense pattern.

6. SUBSIDIARY RHYTHMS AND SOUND PATTERN

Early in this chapter it was said that the poetic rhythm, with which we have been dealing in some detail, is only one of the rhythms of poetry. It is now time to consider two other sorts of rhythm which are a part of the "music" of a poem.

Rhythm, you will recall, was defined as the feeling that may accompany the apperception of repeated points of interest. Word stress and syllabic accent are repeated points of interest that, forced upon the attention of the reader and organized by his nervous system into twos or threes, give rise to that certain feeling which we call the poetic rhythm. If this poetic rhythm is thought of as the ripple on the surface of the ocean, the recurrence of rime-scheme may be likened to the chop of small waves; and the recurrence of stanzaic endings may be compared to the periodic breakers in the surf. But there will be yet larger movements in the logical or narrative structure of longer poems that may give the reader a sense of recurrence like the great movement of the tides. These larger rhythmic feelings, slower in their time scheme, are also a very important part of the "music" of a poem, though less conspicuous than what we have called the poetic rhythm.

Another sort of rhythm is set up by the repetition of particular sounds. The entire complex of such repetitions will here be called the *sound pattern* of a poem. Rime is one of the two obvious forms of this repetition; but as its occurrence is marked with some regularity, usually at the ends of verses, we have considered it as a feature of the metrical pattern. The other quite obvious form of sound pattern is alliteration.

Alliteration is the use of the same consonant sounds at the beginnings of adjacent words; it is sometimes called "initial rime." In very early poetry it occurred quite regularly and was one of the features of the accentual pattern of Old English verse. But in modern poetry alliteration is not a part of the regular expectancy, yet in many poems it does give rise to subsidiary rhythms that appear and disappear as the verses flow along. Several such rhythms are often delicately interlaced with the so-called poetic rhythm.

To serve as an illustration, let us take one of Shelley's other poems. This "Sonnet: England in 1819" was written when King George III, of American Revolutionary infamy, was old, blind, and insane. The Prince Regent and the other sons of the King, so brilliantly characterized in the opening pages of Lytton Strachey's *Queen Victoria,* were notorious profligates. Oppression by a standing army, exploitation of the working people, the enclosure of common lands, corruption in high place, intolerable Parliamentary abuses, the decay of religion—against these Shelley and many of his fellow countrymen spoke out. When Shelley heard of the Manchester massacre, in which troops attacked a crowd of assembled workers, his indignation stirred him to write this sonnet, which was to have been part of a volume of poems dedicated to human freedom. Revolutionary activity during these years did find some success in the Reform Bill passed in 1832 and in other such liberal measures.

SONNET: ENGLAND IN 1819

Percy Bysshe Shelley

An old, mad, blind, despised, and dying king,—
Princes, the dregs of their dull race, who flow
Through public scorn,—mud from a muddy spring,—
Rulers who neither see, nor feel, nor know,

But leech-like to their fainting country cling,
Till they drop, blind in blood, without a blow,—
A people starved and stabbed in the untilled field,—
An army, which liberticide and prey
Makes as a two-edged sword to all who wield
Golden and sanguine laws which tempt and slay;
Religion Christless, Godless—a book sealed;
A Senate,—Time's worst statute unrepealed,—
Are graves, from which a glorious Phantom may
Burst, to illumine our tempestuous day.

(*1819,* 1839)

Certain pairs of words, bound together by alliteration, at once stand out in this poem: "despised and dying," "mud from a muddy," "leech-like," "blind in blood," "starved and stabbed," among others. But this alliteration may be looked upon as a more obvious aspect of the complex *sound pattern* involving the repetition of consonant sounds wherever they may fall within the word, and involving the vowel sounds as well.

But let us look more closely at the sonnet. Notice first that the *d* alliteration is preceded by the *d* sound at the ends of words:

an olD, maD, blinD, DespiseD, anD Dying king,—
princes, the Dregs of their Dull race, who flow
through public scorn—muD from a muDDy spring,—

and the *d* pattern, absent for two verses, recurs in the sixth:

till they Drop, blinD in blooD, without a blow.

You may observe an increased distinctness in your articulatory tied-imagery, even accompanied by vocalization, as you come to the *d* sounds. But at the same time there are other consonant recurrences, the less frequent *p* sounds, for instance:

an old, mad, blind, desPised and dying king,—
Princes, the dregs of their dull race, who flow
through Public scorn—mud from a muddy sPring.

The *m* and *n* sounds, introduced in the first two lines, come into prominence in the next two:

> through public scorN—Mud froM a Muddy spring,—
> rulers who Neither see, Nor feel, Nor kNow.

And *b* and *l,* also initiated in the opening lines, become prominent in the fifth and sixth lines:

> But Leech-Like to their fainting country cLing,
> tiLL they drop, BLind in BLood, without a BLow.

But we have not yet mentioned the alliteration of "Race" and "Rulers"; the minor recurrence of the *k* sound, announced boldly in the "King" of the first line, hidden in the publiK sKorn" of the third and "liKe" of the fifth, and alliterating in the "Kountry Kling" of that line; and the repetition of the *ng* sound, especially prominent in the rime-scheme.

The recurrences of these consonant sounds are not felt separately of course. They are superimposed one upon the other, and the resulting complexity may be suggested by the following typography:

> aN olD, maD, BliND, DesPiseD aND Dying King,—
>
> PriNces, the Dregs of their Dull race, who flow
>
> through PuBliK sKorN—muD from a muDDy sPring,—
>
> rulers who Neither see, Nor feel, Nor kNow,
>
> But leech-liKe to thier fainting Kountry Kling,
>
> till they DroP BliND iN BlooD, without a Blow,—

The effect is that of a juggler manipulating a ball, a cube, a bracelet, a paste jar, and an alarm clock, in a complicated aerial pattern!

No mention, however, has yet been made of the recurrence of vowel sounds, or of the effect of related vowel sounds in the "music" of a poem. The word *assonance* is used to name the recurrence of vowel sounds followed by different consonant sounds. It is prominent in some poetry in place of end-rime. The repetition of vowel sounds, whether strictly assonance or not, may be observed throughout a poem. In noting this phenomenon, the reader should be cautioned to listen to the sounds and not be misled by the letters, for English is not a phonetic language in its spelling.

In Shelley's sonnet, the short *u* sound, announced in "dull" of line two, recurs thrice in line three:

> through pUblic scorn, mUd from a mUddy spring.

So the *oo* sound recurs in "who," "through," "rulers," and "who" again. The short *i*, already noted in the *ing* endings, recurs in other near-by words. But we shall not detail these recurrences further.

Just as important is the relationship of different vowel sounds to each other. Look at those of the accented syllables in the first line:

> an Old, mÆd, blAInd, despAIsed, and dAIing kIng.

There is here an unbroken progression from the back diphthong, long *o*, up to the high front vowel, short *i*, which may give the reader a feeling of rising protest in the poet's cry. And the short *i* is repeated in "princes," beginning the next line, before the vowel sequence descends:

> prInces the drEgs of thEIr dUll rAce, who flO
> thrOO pUblic scOrn. . . .

And this degradation may give the reader a feeling appropriate to the meaning of the lines. The special relationship of vowels to one another may, as for this reader in this instance, form a part of the sound pattern of the poem.

The more prominent features of the sound pattern—close alliteration, for example, certain instances of assonance, and any striking relationship of vowels—these will easily engage the reader's attention. But the less obvious consonant recurrences buried within words or alliterating at a distance, and less obvious vowel relationships, are likely to go unnoticed. Yet they may operate subtly upon the reader, giving him a general feeling of richness of oral texture.

It is from two other arts, music and painting, that the word *tone-color* comes. It will here serve to name, not so much the complicated pattern of recurrent consonants and vowels, as the qualities of these sounds themselves in relationship to the full meaning of the words.

Sometimes there is an obvious relationship between sound and sense. The sound of some words is imitative of the things that they name. This is called *onomatopoeia,* and examples are not hard to find: "pop," "bang," "buzz," and so on. Indeed one theory of the origin of language held that all words were originally of this imitative sort, bow-wow words. But though these words will be found occasionally in poetry, as in all language, a much more important place is occupied by the very numerous class of words of which, in one way or another, it can be said that *the sound suggests some aspect of the sense,* or stirs the imagination, or arouses some special feeling.

Certain consonant sounds—such as the sibilant *s,* for instance, the lingering liquid *l,* the plosive *p,* the murmuring *m,* the guttural *g,* and combinations of these—are said to have certain rather special effects upon the reader. So, too, the high front vowels, such as the short *i,* which for some people is bright in tone-color, and the low back vowels like *aw,* which for some is dark, will be subtly different in their effect upon the reader. Generally pleasing combinations of sound are called *euphonious;* and harsh and unpleasant combinations, *cacophonous.* But what in tone-color is one man's meat turns out to be another man's poison; for individuals will react with marked difference, depending upon their particular temperaments and their cultural environment. To a Scot, a bagpipe is sweet music; many others find it intolerable.

This matter of the affective influence of word sounds will be referred to again in the chapter on "The Emotional Response to Poetry." At this point it will be enough to say, in the words of Pope the poet, "The sound must seem an echo of the sense." And it is well to emphasize the fact that the amazing variety of tone-color in the flow of speech sounds, either heard or imagined, is one of the most remarkable aspects of the "music" of poetry.

So, while the reader is enjoying the principal poetic rhythm, that tug of war between metrical and sense patterns, and while he is conscious of those fleeting recurrences of various vowels and consonants interwoven in the sound pattern, he will enjoy the full flavor of the sounds themselves heard in the mind's-ear and felt along the mind's-tongue, these sounds at times suggesting the sense and effecting a stir of his feelings.

7. THE INEFFABLE MUSIC OF POETRY

Before introducing a culminating illustration for this chapter, "The Music of Poetry," a few words of counsel should be given both to the enthusiastic and to the discouraged reader:

First, remember that the "music" of poetry is not an aspect of the printed verses but of the poem-experience. The metrical pattern and deviations, the sound pattern and tone-color, are not an aspect of the poem on the page; they are to be found only in the individual human consciousness, first of the poet and then, with differences, in each particular reader.

Second, the rich "music" of a certain poem-experience, the full effect in the mind's-ear, is such a complex phenomenon that, even with careful analysis, its essential character will often remain ineffable, defying description. Certainly the mere foot, meter, line-scheme; the minor features of the metrical pattern; the gross and even more subtle deviations; the sound pattern and tone-color—the verbal or graphic representation of these will often fail to catch the throbbing pulse or unspeakable languor, the celestial radiance or the humanitarian passion that may characterize the "music" of a particular poem-experience.

Third, the person who has no knowledge of the analytical techniques and vocabulary of prosody, the science of versification, may actually have a very rich experience of the "music" of a poem, enjoy what he hears in his mind's-ear and what he feels on his mind's-tongue; he may also be able to read well aloud, giving much pleasure to others—all without benefit of prosodic learning. Nor is the knowledge of foot, meter, line-scheme, deviations, etc., any guarantee at all that the reader will be able to realize the full musical potentialities of a poem.

BUT *fourth*, some knowledge of these things—of the contending psychological pulls, of the expectancy and deviations, patterns and variations; of the chief rhythms and subsidiary rhythms—some knowledge of these things *may* increase and enrich the "music" of the poem-experience. The reader *may* become more sensitive to the stimulative creative possibilities in printed verses; he *may* also become more discerning and discriminating in listening to the sounds in his mind's-ear and in feeling the sounds on his mind's-tongue, or in reading aloud to others and in hearing them as they read to him.

Without thought of the more or less technical considerations of this chapter, read the following lyric—aloud at first, and then silently. Let yourself go, and enjoy to the fullest the "music" of the poem.

THE LAKE ISLE OF INNISFREE
William Butler Yeats

I will arise and go now, and go to Innisfree,
And a small cabin build there, of clay and wattles made;
Nine bean rows will I have there, a hive for the honey bee,
And live alone in the bee-loud glade.

And I shall have some peace there, for peace comes dropping slow,
Dropping from the veils of the morning to where the cricket sings;
There midnight's all a glimmer, and noon a purple glow,
And evening full of the linnet's wings.

I will arise and go now, for always night and day
I hear lake water lapping with low sounds by the shore;
While I stand on the roadway, or on the pavements gray,
I hear it in the deep heart's core.

(1890)

Do not read the next paragraphs until you are satisfied that you have had as rich a musical experience with these verses as possible. . . .

I cannot tell you what the goings-on have been in *your* consciousness, what articulatory sensations you have had on your mind's-tongue, what complex sound sequences you have heard in your mind's-ear. To the extent that I am skilled in the oral interpretation of poetry, I might communicate to you something of the music of *my own* experience by reading the poem aloud to you.

But that would be impracticable, though it would be possible through the making of a recording.[11]

Much less successful will be my efforts to communicate to you through written and graphic symbols the musical richness of my inner experience of Yeats' poem. Yet the attempt may be worth while in helping the reader to consider the perhaps quite different "music" of his own experience.

First, let me tell you how the poem "goes" as I read it. The metrical pattern is one of the stanzaic forms: (*iambic*) aba^6b^4—a quatrain of three hexameter lines and one tetrameter with crossed rimes. The sense pattern pulls me away from what might otherwise be a singsongy poetic rhythm: several of the lines begin with inversions; and there are a number of anapestic, pyrrhic, and spondaic substitutions.[12] The amphibrachic substitution in the third foot of each of the long lines and the strong caesura that follows it in all but one such line become (for me) a part of the metrical pattern itself. The lines are notably end-stopped, with only one run-on line in the poem. The sound pattern, superimposed upon this strongly marked poetic rhythm, is not distinguished by the more crowded sort of consonant and vowel patterns; but the simple crossed rimes, and the less obvious assonance and alliteration, seem to be bound up with a generally rich tone-color. . . . But this paragraph does not seem likely to communicate the uniqueness of the music of "The Lake Isle of Innisfree" as I experience it.

Let me make a *second* effort to do so, and employ a number of graphic devices as shown on the next page. . . . But this, too, though it may call attention to many of the phenomena of the music of the poem-experience, will by no means fully communicate its essential character.

A *third* attempt may prove only relatively more successful, for the recesses of consciousness are filled with ineffable secrets:

The most conspicuous feature of the music of "The Lake Isle

[11] Such a recording was indeed made by W. B. Yeats himself of "The Lake Isle of Innisfree," though it is not generally available. He is described by John Holmes as reading the poem "rather rapidly, and almost gutturally, though he dwells on the long sounds. . . . He by no means makes a dreamy nostalgic thing of it."

[12] These terms were explained and used on pp. 113-15.

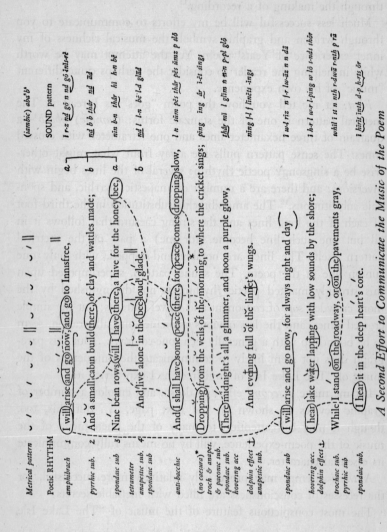

A Second Effort to Communicate the Music of the Poem

of Innisfree" is (for me) the long six-stress line with its marked
mid-pause following an extra syllable.

deDUMM deDUMM deDUMMde || deDUMM deDUMM deDUMM ||

The effect is not unlike a line from Masefield's "Sea-Fever," a poem
bespeaking another one of Man's deep yearnings:

> And all I ask is a tall ship and a star to steer her by. . . .

But the "tall ship" has a strong double beat found only once (for
me) in Yeats' poem. The expectancy of this verse pattern, once
established, is a firm underpinning for the free-flowing poetic
rhythm, a melody which, with its "and go now" and "build now,"
carries me on with a springy step.

But the stanza here is no common quatrain with crossed rimes,
as I hear it. The four-stress line closing each stanza is not broken
by a mid-line pause; and though it is shorter than the preceding
six-stress lines, it is longer than the preceding *half*-lines, and therefore gives the effect of slowing down the melody, terminating each
stanza with a thoughtful note.

Against the movement of this poetic rhythm there is another
voice (as it were) in counterpoint; and it is singing an insistent
alto; "and go now, and go" . . . and "build there" . . . and "have
there" . . . "And live alone" . . . and "have some peace there, for
peace comes dropping slow,/ Dropping from the veils of morning"
. . . "I will arise and go now." . . .

Indeed it is impossible to think further of the "music" of "The
Lake Isle of Innisfree" without considering all of the other aspects
of this poem-experience; for it is, above all, a complex unity. Even
the eye-movement in reading and the general retinal image of the
poem, are related to the music; for the four fixations per line (for
me) accompany the metrical pattern with a "two against three" in
the half-line; and the long stretch of the full lines on the page puts
the realization of this Utopian dream afar off.

Indeed the music here seems to spring from the deep heart's core.
For the hunger of man to possess a plot of ground and the peace
that may come with it, is a universal hunger of the heart. As the
poet stands by the roadway and walks the city pavements, he hears,

from the depth of his longing, the gentle lapping of the lake; and he again resolves to go now to "the lake isle of Innisfree," where he will build him a cabin and plant a patch, and hive some bees— and he will have some peace there. For peace will descend upon him from morning till night, and he will be surrounded by the beauties of nature. So this deep desire comes upon the poet again and again. But, though he may have his dream, he does not really arise and go; he is still walking the pavements. Yet, in the deep heart's core, he hears the lake and sees the midnight stars upon it.

And Yeats the man, who loved his native Ireland and helped to establish its modern literature, spent much of his mature life in London and Paris and on the Italian Riviera. He was honored with the Nobel Prize, and was markedly successful. Dying at Nice, he was duly buried in his homeland. But before the years of his success, he had walked the streets of London in poverty. This dream, then, is his dream; this yearning.

So, for me, the music of this poem is richly colored by its meaning, by the pictures that flash and the feelings that are stirred within me.

8. THE POETIC RHYTHM OF FREE VERSE

Earlier in this chapter, prose was distinguished from verse both as regards its appearance on the page and its rhythmic effect upon the reader. And it was said about language, "All is prose that is not verse, and all is verse that is not prose"—all, that is, except *free verse,* which, in some ways, stands between verse (of the usual sort) and prose. Stated most simply: free verse looks like verse, but sounds like prose.

This chapter has so far ignored free verse, and has dealt principally with the musical phenomena of so-called "bound" verse. It will conclude with a brief note on the music of free verse, which music is radically different.

The *poetic rhythm of free verse* is no delicate balance between the contending psychological pulls of metrical pattern and sense pattern, for the reader of free verse does not become conscious of a metrical pattern. He may not realize at first that he is reading free verse, and make a futile effort to scan it, to find an underlying pattern of rhythmic regularity. With no underlying metrical pattern, there will be no expectancy of regularity for the sense pattern to pull against. So in reading free verse the reader will discover no gross or subtle deviations.

This is not to say that free verse does not have any "music." But, rather, that the "music" of free verse is of a different sort. The melodic undulations of its poetic rhythm are those of the sense pattern, the phrase and cadence somewhat controlled by the pattern of eye-movements. And this more natural poetic rhythm of free verse is often fortified by a sound pattern rich in tone color and using alliteration and assonance, phrasal repetition and sometimes rime.

Free verse is the gift of Modern Poetry, but it is as old as David. Decried a generation ago, when it sounded strange to ears accustomed only to bound verse, it is in our day recognized for what it is: a kind of poetry providing its own sort of experience for the reader, its own sort of "music."

There have been a number of poems in free verse included so far in this volume. One will be added here to serve as an immediate illustration. It will also serve another purpose: it will be balm from Gilead for those who have found the technical analysis of the music of poetry to be stultifying and destructive of the beauty that they sense intuitively and feel to be indescribable.

WHEN I HEARD THE LEARN'D ASTRONOMER
Walt Whitman

When I heard the learn'd astronomer;
When the proofs, the figures, were ranged in columns before me;
When I was shown the charts and the diagrams, to add, divide, and
    measure them;
When I, sitting, heard the astronomer, where he lectured with much
    applause in the lecture-room,
How soon, unaccountable, I became tired and sick;
Till rising and gliding out, I wander'd off by myself,
In the mystical moist night-air, and from time to time,
Look'd up in perfect silence at the stars.
        (1865)

SUGGESTIONS FOR STUDY

1. *Review.* Glance back through this long and complex chapter, and jot down the section headings. Take note also of the subordinate points made in each section. Now work these notes into a formal (complete sentence) outline of the substance of the chapter. It may help you in determining the more important things to be remembered.

2. *Articulatory Tied-Imagery.* To increase your consciousness of the vocal and articulatory activity involved in reading poetry aloud, and the articulatory tied-imagery that will be a part of the "music" of silent reading, the following exercise is suggested:

(a) Resting your elbows upon a table or the arms of a chair, put the thumb and forefinger of your *left* hand firmly up under your jaw, just forward of the points of the jaw, and place your other fingers of this left hand lightly along the side of your Adam's apple. Put your *right* forefinger up under your nose, your middle finger under your lower lip, your third finger under your chin, and your thumb up by your right ear. This wrestler's hold may seem ridiculous to you, but it will make you more conscious of the amazingly complex activity of spoken language than descriptive paragraphs and diagrams.

When your tactile and kinesthetic receptors are thus in adjustment, read the following stanza *out loud* as clearly and articulately as you can:

> 'Twas brillig, and the slithy toves
> Did gyre and gimble in the wabe;
> All mimsy were the borogoves,
> And the mome raths outgrabe.

The lower fingers of your left hand must have made you acutely aware both of the muscular activity around the voice box and of the vibration of the entire throat. The forefinger and thumb up under the jaw made you conscious, not so much of the movements of the jaw, as of the muscles at the base of the tongue. The fingers of the right hand called your attention to the work done by the lips and jaw. And it must be added that the tip of the tongue and the soft palate at the back of the roof of the mouth also are active in the formation of speech sounds.

Still in the same posture, read the second stanza. But only *whisper* this time, forming the sounds but without giving full voice to them.

> "Beware the Jabberwock, my son!
> The jaws that bite, the claws that catch!
> Beware the Jubjub bird, and shun
> The frumious Bandersnatch!"

You notice at once that the vibration of the neck has stopped, but that the jaw, lips, and tongue are still active.

As a final experiment, with the same grip, read *silently:*

> He took his vorpal sword in hand:
>   Long time the manxome foe he sought—
> So rested he by the Tumtum tree,
>   And stood awhile in thought.

This time you may have felt no more than the pulsing of your facial arteries, though perhaps you felt in the tip of your tongue a sort of titillation. There is indeed no sharp line between fully vocalized and silent reading. But during this silent reading you may have been more conscious of some goings-on in the mind that we have called "tied imagery"—the *feel* of the words upon "the mind's-tongue" and the *sound* of the words in "the mind's-ear."

(b) Without the encumbrance of experimental receptors, read the entire poem, which comes from *Through the Looking-Glass, and What Alice Found There,* by Lewis Carroll, the pen name of Charles Lutwidge Dodgson. Read slowly and silently, but with zest and relish, for this is no common nonsense. Give particular attention to your experience of articulatory tied-imagery.

JABBERWOCKY
Lewis Carroll

> 'Twas brillig, and the slithy toves
>   Did gyre and gimble in the wabe:
> All mimsy were the borogoves,
>   And the mome raths outgrabe.

> "Beware the Jabberwock, my son!
>   The jaws that bite, the claws that catch!
> Beware the Jubjub bird, and shun
>   The frumious Bandersnatch!"

> He took his vorpal sword in hand:
>   Long time the manxome foe he sought—
> So rested he by the Tumtum tree,
>   And stood awhile in thought.

> And, as in uffish thought he stood,
>   The Jabberwock, with eyes of flame,
> Came whiffling through the tulgey wood,
>   And burbled as it came!

One, two! One, two! And through and through
  The vorpal blade went snicker-snack!
He left it dead, and with its head
  He went galumphing back.

"And hast thou slain the Jabberwock?
  Come to my arms, my beamish boy!
O frabjous day! Callooh! Callay!"
  He chortled in his joy.

'Twas brillig, and the slithy toves
  Did gyre and gimble in the wabe:
All mimsy were the borogoves,
  And the mome raths outgrabe.

(1872)

3. *Metrical Pattern.* Turn back through the first four chapters of this book and examine each of the poems, rereading at least a part of it. (a) Determine first whether it is "bound" verse or "free" verse; that is, whether or not an underlying metrical pattern is a part of your poem-experience. (b) If there is such an expectancy established, determine what the metrical pattern is—its foot, meter, and line-scheme.

4. *Metrical Variations.* Read the following short lyric; it is sometimes entitled "Simplex Munditiis" (of simple neatness), a quotation from Horace's *Ode,* I, 5, to which Jonson owed his inspiration.

CLERIMONT'S SONG

from EPICOENE; OR THE SILENT WOMAN, I, i

Ben Jonson

Still to be neat, still to be drest,
As you were going to a feast;
Still to be powder'd, still perfum'd:
Lady, it is to be presum'd,
Though Art's hid causes are not found,
All is not sweet, all is not sound.

Give me a look, give me a face,
That makes simplicity a grace;

> Robes loosely flowing, hair as free:
> Such sweet neglect more taketh me,
> Than all the adulteries of Art;
> They strike mine eyes, but not my heart.
>
> (1609)

(a) Let us say that the metrical pattern is (*iambic*) *aabbcc*[4].
(b) Let us accept the following paraphrase of the sense of it:

> If you are for ever dressed up as if you were going out,—if you are for ever powdered and perfumed,—then, my good woman, men will say that you are covering up bad breath or that you are not healthy.
>
> Give me the girl with a face that is simple but pleasing,—loose dress and free-hanging hair,—for I am more taken by natural good-looks than by all the tricks of dressing; they may have some attraction for my eye, but not for my heart.

(c) Reread the poem until you feel satisfied that the poetic rhythm is for you an entirely satisfying compromise between the metrical pattern and the sense pattern.

(d) Now note, as you consider the poetic rhythm, what deviations there are from the metrical pattern. Copy the poem out so as to mark it up. Then provide explanatory marginalia.

5. *Sound Pattern and Tone-Color.* "The Destruction of Sennacherib," Lord Byron's well-known narrative poem, will provide the basis for some further study of sound pattern and tone-color. Sennacherib was King of Assyria (ancient Ashur), and he invaded Palestine in the 7th century B.C. The Biblical background is found in *II Kings,* 18:13-19:37, which describes how Sennacherib descended upon the cities of Judah; his conflicts with Hezekiah, king of Judah; the intercession of Isaiah with the Lord, and the amazing result.

> And it came to pass that night, that the angel of the Lord went out, and smote in the camp of the Assyrians an hundred fourscore and five thousand: and when they arose early in the morning, behold, they were all dead corpses.

As a matter of fact Sennacherib himself is not reported to have been killed at this time; but his power was destroyed and he was shortly murdered by his sons.

THE DESTRUCTION OF SENNACHERIB
George Gordon, Lord Byron

The Assyrian came down like the wolf on the fold,
And his cohorts were gleaming in purple and gold;
And the sheen of their spears was like stars on the sea,
When the blue wave rolls nightly on deep Galilee.

Like the leaves of the forest when Summer is green,
That host with their banners at sunset were seen:
Like the leaves of the forest when Autumn hath blown,
That host on the morrow lay wither'd and strown.

For the Angel of Death spread his wings on the blast,
And breathed in the face of the foe as he pass'd;
And the eyes of the sleepers wax'd deadly and chill,
And their hearts but once heaved, and for ever grew still!

And there lay the steed with his nostril all wide,
But through it there roll'd not the breath of his pride:
And the foam of his gasping lay white on the turf,
And cold as the spray of the rock-beating surf.

And there lay the rider distorted and pale,
With the dew on his brow and the rust on his mail;
And the tents were all silent, the banners alone,
The lances unlifted, the trumpet unblown.

And the widows of Ashur are loud in their wail,
And the idols are broke in the temple of Baal;
And the might of the Gentile, unsmote by the sword,
Hath melted like snow in the glance of the Lord!

(1815)

(a) How would you characterize the poetic rhythm of this poem?
What is the metrical pattern? What is the nature of the principal deviations from it?

(b) Turn your attention to the *sound pattern,* the alliteration and
other consonant recurrences, the assonance and relationship of vowel
sounds. Make some notations to objectify your observations, such as the
following for the first two lines:

i n k*a*m d*ou*n l k *oo*f *o*n f*o*ld [*descending vowels*
k*o* *o*r *e*r gl*ea*m *i*n p*er*pl nd g*o*ld; [*tone-color*

(c) Observe now the *tone-color*. Make marginal note of particular words, the sound of which seems especially to suggest some aspect of the meaning.

6. *The Music of the West Wind*. Without thought of technical analysis, read Shelley's "Ode to the West Wind."

(a) Read it aloud or silently at your pleasure, but read it slowly enough to savor fully the words as they flow by. When you are through with the reading, give some quiet thought to the phenomena of the "music" in relation to the other aspects of the whole poem-experience— the imagery, the meaning, the stir of your feelings. Try to work out a non-technical description of the music that might communicate this aspect of it to another person.

(b) An ode, by the way, is a poem of somewhat formal praise, sometimes honoring a person, sometimes a thing. Shelley writes,

> This poem was conceived and chiefly written in a wood that skirts the Arno, near Florence, and on a day when that tempestuous wind, whose temperature is at once mild and animating, was collecting the vapours which pour down the autumnal rains. They began, as I foresaw, at sunset with a violent tempest of hail and rain, attended by that magnificent thunder and lightning peculiar to the Cisalpine regions.

Shelley had observed that marine vegetation is influenced by the winds that announce seasonal changes. This poem was written in the same autumn as the scathing denunciation of "Sonnet: England in 1819" (p. 116), when Shelley, a rebel at heart, was fighting for Liberty and hoping that the Spirit of Freedom might burst, like a glorious Phantom, from the graves of the dead and corrupt institutions of his time. Now, walking through the woods in the wind that was blowing off the Mediterranean, he likened himself to the autumn leaf, to the stormy cloud, to the waves of the sea, and he asked to be uplifted, inspired, and heartened.

ODE TO THE WEST WIND

Percy Bysshe Shelley

I

O wild West Wind, thou breath of Autumn's being,
Thou, from whose unseen presence the leaves dead
Are driven, like ghosts from an enchanter fleeing,

Yellow, and black, and pale, and hectic red,
Pestilence-stricken multitudes: O thou,
Who chariotest to their dark wintry bed

The wingèd seeds, where they lie cold and low,
Each like a corpse within its grave, until
Thine azure sister of the spring shall blow

Her clarion o'er the dreaming earth, and fill
(Driving sweet buds like flocks to feed in air)
With living hues and odours plain and hill:

Wild Spirit, which art moving everywhere;
Destroyer and preserver; hear, Oh hear!

2

Thou on whose stream, 'mid the steep sky's commotion,
Loose clouds like earth's decaying leaves are shed,
Shook from the tangled boughs of Heaven and Ocean,

Angels of rain and lightning: there are spread
On the blue surface of thine airy surge,
Like the bright hair uplifted from the head

Of some fierce Maenad, even from the dim verge
Of the horizon to the zenith's height
The locks of the approaching storm. Thou dirge

Of the dying year, to which this closing night
Will be the dome of a vast sepulchre,
Vaulted with all thy congregated might

Of vapours, from whose solid atmosphere
Black rain, and fire, and hail will burst: Oh hear!

3

Thou who didst waken from his summer dreams
The blue Mediterranean, where he lay,
Lulled by the coil of his crystàlline streams,

Beside a pumice isle in Baiae's bay,
And saw in sleep old palaces and towers
Quivering within the wave's intenser day,

All overgrown with azure moss and flowers
So sweet, the sense faints picturing them! Thou
For whose path the Atlantic's level powers

Cleave themselves into chasms, while far below
The sea-blooms and the oozy woods which wear
The sapless foliage of the ocean, know

Thy voice, and suddenly grow gray with fear,
And tremble and despoil themselves: Oh hear!

4

If I were a dead leaf thou mightest bear;
If I were a swift cloud to fly with thee;
A wave to pant beneath thy power, and share

The impulse of thy strength, only less free
Than thou, O uncontrollable! If even
I were as in my boyhood, and could be

The comrade of thy wanderings over heaven,
As then, when to outstrip thy skiey speed
Scarce seemed a vision; I would ne'er have striven

As thus with thee in prayer in my sore need.
Oh lift me as a wave, a leaf, a cloud!
I fall upon the thorns of life! I bleed!

A heavy weight of hours has chained and bowed
One too like thee: tameless, and swift, and proud.

5

Make me thy lyre, even as the forest is:
What if my leaves are falling like its own!
The tumult of thy mighty harmonies

Will take from both a deep, autumnal tone,
Sweet though in sadness. Be thou, spirit fierce,
My spirit! Be thou me, impetuous one!

Drive my dead thoughts over the universe
Like withered leaves to quicken a new birth!
And, by the incantation of this verse,

Scatter, as from an unextinguished hearth
Ashes and sparks, my words among mankind!
Be through my lips to unawakened earth

The trumpet of a prophecy! O, wind, ·
If Winter comes, can Spring be far behind?

(1819)

7. *The Music of Poetry on Records*. (a) Although a detailed account of the study of poetry with records will be reserved for Chapter 22, it may well be first suggested as a part of the present consideration of the Music of Poetry. Listening to poetry as read skillfully by others may sharpen the reader's interest in his own articulatory and auditory tied-imagery, and it will increase his store of auditory experiences from which a wide range of voice qualities and speech patterns may be recalled to form new patterns in his mind's-ear at the time of future silent reading. (b) Recordings are available for a number of the poems so far included in this book. Two British actors may be heard reading Shelley's "Ode to the West Wind"—John Gielgud (in Columbia set M-419) and Basil Rathbone (in Columbia set E-11). Norman Corwin has recorded "When I Heard the Learn'd Astronomer" (in Columbia set E-5); and "Jabberwocky" has also been recorded. The most complete listing of poetry and other speech records is the catalogue of Linguaphone Institute, 30 Rockefeller Plaza, New York City 20. (c) Listen to the recordings of a number of poems for which you have not the printed verses in hand, and fix your attention upon various phases of the music. Do you catch the underlying metrical pattern in each case? Are you conscious of deviations from the established expectancy? Are subsidiary rhythms and sound pattern discernible?

6

VISUAL AND OTHER
FREE-IMAGERY

This anatomizing of the poem-reading-experience began with a chapter entitled "Seeing the Poem on the Page," which dealt with the *retinal image* (the sensory link with the printed verses) and its relation to the conscious seeing of the poem in the mind. Then we turned to a discussion of "The Music of Poetry," the articulatory and auditory *tied-imagery,* the effect of the words on the mind's-tongue and in the mind's-ear. We come now to a consideration of "Visual and Other Free-Imagery," in which we shall take up those fragmentary imitations of sensory experience, those bits of daydream, those pictures in the mind's-eye, those *free images,* as Dr. Richards calls them, that are for many people such an important part of the reading-experience.[1]

The first sort of imagery may be illustrated by the form "W e s t W i n d" in a white field of stimulated rods and cones in the retina of the eye. The second sort of imagery would be the sounds "wɛst wınd," which in silent reading are immediately associated or tied-up with the retinal image "W e s t W i n d." But the third sort of imagery suggested in the above paragraph is quite different: *the free images of the things for which the words stand.* They are the mind pictures of what the retinal image of "W e s t W i n d" on the page and the tied image of "wɛst wınd" as if sounded and heard, call up from the storehouse of experience—tall trees that I myself have seen tossed and torn by that unseen presence, autumn leaves scudding along the street, racing clouds, chopping waves, the

<hr>

[1] I. A. Richards, *Science and Poetry,* London, 1935, p. 18; I. A. Richards, *Principles of Literary Criticism,* Harcourt, Brace, 1930, pp. 121-24.

swell of a sloop's sail, the brace of my body against the sudden gust, the cooled feel of my skin. As with tied imagery, there is no outside sensory stimulation; the sights and feels of the moment are not "real"; the consciousness of them is but the recalling of sights and feels associated with the retinal image and the tied image of the words in the past.

For Mrs. Wordsworth, the recollection of the brilliant daffodils blossoming by the lake was a vivid and pleasurable experience, and she said to her husband,

> They flash upon that inward eye
> Which is the bliss of solitude.

And William Wordsworth incorporated these lines in the poem, "I Wandered Lonely as a Cloud," which you read in connection with Chapter 3.

I. INDIVIDUAL DIFFERENCES IN FREE IMAGERY

It must be pointed out at once that readers differ widely as regards this free imagery. Some people say that they don't "see" any pictures at all when they read a poem. Other people catch but fleeting, out-of-focus glimpses, momentary pictures on the screen of the mind. For many people, however, scenes and action will flash upon the inward eye, clear and bright. A few people find such experiences as vivid as things actually seen; and an occasional unfortunate individual loses the power to distinguish the events of the two worlds, the real and fancied.

To focus our attention upon this aspect of the poem-reading-experience, let us read "The Listeners" by Walter de la Mare, a modern British poet whose verses are unusually stimulative of free imagery for many people. Read the poem silently at first, so that you may illustrate from this exercise what has just been said about the three different sorts of image. Then read the poem a second time—aloud or not, at your pleasure—and concentrate your attention upon the pictures in your mind's-eye.

THE LISTENERS
Walter de la Mare

"Is there anybody there?" said the Traveler,
  Knocking on the moonlit door;
And his horse in the silence champed the grasses
  Of the forest's ferny floor.
And a bird flew up out of the turret,
  Above the Traveler's head:
And he smote upon the door again a second time;
  "Is there anybody there?" he said.
But no one descended to the Traveler;
  No head from the leaf-fringed sill
Leaned over and looked into his gray eyes,
  Where he stood perplexed and still.
But only a host of phantom listeners
  That dwelt in the lone house then
Stood listening in the quiet of the moonlight
  To that voice from the world of men:
Stood thronging the faint moonbeams on the dark stair
  That goes down to the empty hall,
Hearkening in an air stirred and shaken
  By the lonely Traveler's call.
And he felt in his heart their strangeness,
  Their stillness answering his cry,
While his horse moved, cropping the dark turf,
  'Neath the starred and leafy sky;
For he suddenly smote on the door, even
  Louder, and lifted his head:—
"Tell them I came, and no one answered,
  That I kept my word," he said.
Never the least stir made the listeners,
  Though every word he spake
Fell echoing through the shadowiness of the still house
  From the one man left awake:
Aye, they heard his foot upon the stirrup,
  And the sound of iron on stone,
And how the silence surged softly backward,
  When the plunging hoofs were gone.

(1912)

What were the pictures that you "saw"? Was there one principal view? Were there others? Were they vague or vivid? Were they dull in color or bright? Were they stationary or moving? Were there sound effects? Take a moment to make such graphic or verbal notes as will fix this free imagery in your mind. . . .

If we were to compare notes, we should see how completely individual our experiences have been in this regard. *My* Traveler, for instance, is dressed in a sort of composite early nineteenth century costume—yours may be American Revolutionary or Victorian or modern or nondescript or indefinite. *My* surrounding forest has thick underbrush, and the clearing is overgrown with rank grasses. There are wisps of river mist; the trees, with trailing vines and mistletoe, are dripping. And it is all made dimly luminous by the greenish moonlight. That's *my* scenery—yours may be a forest of tall clean-limbed firs, or of ragged eucalyptus, or of live oak, or of some entirely different sort. *My* phantom listeners are three wispy translucent women, like double exposure photography, in a dusty and cobwebby haunted house, as in the movies—yours may be white-sheeted Halloween ghosts or mysterious beams of light.

2. THREE QUESTIONS ABOUT IMAGERY

We could go on with our comparison, but let us rather ask a question: Where do these "pictures" come from?

They are reminiscent tidbits of sensory experience pieced together in a sort of montage, as a composite of many small pieces of photography is called. The reader's visual imagery will be compounded of recalled scraps of things that he has seen. Today we are living in a time when most people have seen, through travelogue and newsreel, tropical jungles, distant deserts, ocean storms, overgrown forests, Tudor mansions, and what not. And this has greatly supplemented our store of scenery gathered at first hand. So, too, we have seen movies of innumerable individual and type characters, all appropriately costumed and made-up, which increases the assortment of persons waiting in our "casting offices" all ready to be called for a rôle. But the storehouse of memory will contain other things too: scraps of dream-stuff and vivid images evoked as a part of previous reading; but these too go back, in one way or another, to live visual and other sensory experience. In each of us, then, the free images that come with our reading will be pieced together from the old curiosity attics of our remembrance.

A second question may now be asked: What is the form of such pictures in the mind's-eye? Let us seek the answer while reading another poem.

There is a group of modern poets, who called themselves imagists, for whom the activating of the imagination was a principal objective. Amy Lowell, one of the most important American poets of this group, wrote a short poem, "Night Clouds," that may be of interest in this connection.

NIGHT CLOUDS
Amy Lowell

The white mares of the moon rush along the sky
Beating their golden hoofs upon the glass Heavens;
The white mares of the moon are all standing on their hind legs
Pawing at the green porcelain doors of the remote Heavens.
Fly, mares!
Strain your utmost,
Scatter the milky dust of stars,
Or the tiger sun will leap upon you and destroy you
With one lick of his vermilion tongue.

(1925)

The "picture" that these verses stimulate in my own imagination is in no sense a single definite thing like a full-page illustration. In its form it is a *moving* picture; it is a *developing* picture; it is a *fluctuating* picture; it is *dream-like*. More than that, there is a whole series of *marginal* pictures that come and go fleetingly with the senses of the words.

It's almost as though I started, from the title "Night Clouds," with a dim background photograph of fleecy moonlit clouds against a night sky, covering the entire "page" of my inner vision. Then the curved forms of some of the clouds become the flying manes and curved backs and haunches of white horses, galloping along—

the effect of wind-blown clouds passing across the moon. In the margin of my vision, I see momentarily the white galloping legs. Personally I do *not* see "golden hoofs"; and, though I get the sense of "glass Heavens," the allusion to Ptolemy's concentric crystalline spheres and to the great glassy domes of the heavens, I do not *see* anything of it in my vision. Then my four or five white mares rear up, pawing the air—and, for an instant, I see in the margin a high sandstone wall with jade-enameled iron grates—more like Beverly Hills, alas, than Heaven! Now my ramping mares charge on, a whole herd of them, as part of the clouds against the moonlit sky. I do *not* see "The milky dust of stars" at all; I *see* only a fleeting marginal image of a crouching tiger, which turns into the sun with its rays, and back again into the tiger licking his chops. During the brief moments of these so-called marginal images, the main image becomes dim but does not fade clear out, and there is something dream-like in the way one thing *becomes,* or suddenly *is,* another.[2]

At best such verbal descriptions of visual imagery—of line, form, chiaroscuro, color, movement—are bound to be crude. They will serve, however, to emphasize the highly individual character of this aspect of the poem-reading-experience. But if readers differ in the nature and extent of their free imagery stimulated by the same printed poem, it must also be said that poems differ too; for some are more likely than others to provide colorful and clear pictures for the mind's-eye.

And this leads to a third question: What causes this imaginative activity?

We are not yet able to say why we dream dreams when asleep; why we dream dreams when awake; what causes the magic flashings above and beyond our eyes; what the reason is for those sudden insights and intuitions. As theories are advanced, the real causes may escape. But one or two negative suggestions may here be made. *First,* so-called descriptive language does not necessarily activate the imagination, for the so-called concrete details and qualifying adjectives and figures of speech may be realized in a purely

[2] Of "Night Clouds" another reader writes: ". . . I get a definitely concrete picture from the poem—an imaginative, colorful, but flat, Edmund Dulac."

rational way by the recognition of the mere sense of the words without visual imagery at all. Many a reader confesses to having skipped the descriptive passages in Scott's novels; and many a patient reader plods stone-blind through descriptions in some narrative poetry. Concrete details may, but do not necessarily, come alive in the inner vision. *Second,* the will to see, likewise, does not necessarily activate the imagination. The effort to visualize may succeed in bringing pictures to mind, but they may prove to be incongruous or inappropriate. However, a *willingness* to see is a different matter, and may be helpful.

Perhaps the causes of this inward seeing with the mind's-eye may be found in a combination of circumstances. The disposition to active imagining may be in part innate; but it may also be partly induced. Some people will readily *see* things; but the readiness to *see* things may be brought about in a person by various means. Everyone has heard of the abnormal effects of various drugs in this regard; and we use the phrase "pipe dreams." Music also may serve as an inducement to reverie; and for many listeners, the musical experience includes very active visual imagery. The "music" of poetry itself may act in very much the same way, whether it is actually heard or imagined; and a great deal has been made of the hypnotic effect of the poetic rhythm and tone-color. So, the sound of the words in the mind's-ear will at times soothe and entrance the reader, and awaken his imagination. The feelings stirred in the reader by the poem will also induce imaginative activity. But it is the meaning of the poem, the sense of the words as one interprets them, that will supply the immediate stimulus and that will serve to guide the process. Here again we should remind ourselves that the poem-experience is a totality of which the various aspects are intimately interrelated parts.

3. TWO EXAMPLES OF VISUAL IMAGERY

We must turn aside from this abstract discussion to observe the imagery in two more poems.

LORD RANDAL

Anonymous

"O where hae ye been, Lord Randal, my son?
O where hae ye been, my handsome young man?"
   "I hae been to the wild wood; mother, make my bed soon,
   For I'm weary wi hunting, and fain wald lie down."

"Where gat ye your dinner, Lord Randal, my son?
Where gat ye your dinner, my handsome young man?"
   "I dined wi my true love; mother, make my bed soon,
   For I'm weary wi hunting, and fain wald lie down."

"What gat ye to your dinner, Lord Randal, my son?
What gat ye to your dinner, my handsome young man?"
   "I gat eels boiled in broo; mother, make my bed soon,
   For I'm weary wi hunting, and fain wald lie down."

"What became of your bloodhounds, Lord Randal, my son?
What became of your bloodhounds, my handsome young man?"
   "O they swelld and they died; mother, make my bed soon,
   For I'm weary wi hunting, and fain wald lie down."

"O I fear ye are poisond, Lord Randal, my son!
O I fear ye are poisond, my handsome young man!"
   "O yes! I am poisond; mother, make my bed soon,
   For I'm sick at the heart, and I fain wald lie down."

                    (*?c. 1450;* 1802-3)

If the reader experiences any notable visual imagery while reading this old English folk ballad, it will certainly not be caused by
very elaborate description. There are no concrete details of the
youth's appearance (except that he is handsome), of the hunt (except that it was in the wildwood), of the dinner (except the presence of his true-love and the eels boiled in brew), of the return
home (except the death of the hounds), of his feelings (except that
he is weary wi' hunting—and poisoned). Yet, as the dramatic situation unfolds, *some* readers will have a clear picture of the tragic
homecoming and of the several preceding scenes.

Now turn to the second of this pair of poems.

ODE

William Collins

How sleep the brave who sink to rest
By all their country's wishes bless'd!
When Spring, with dewy fingers cold,
Returns to deck their hallow'd mould,
She there shall dress a sweeter sod
Than Fancy's feet have ever trod.

By fairy hands their knell is rung;
By forms unseen their dirge is sung;
There Honour comes, a pilgrim gray,
To bless the turf that wraps their clay;
And Freedom shall awhile repair,
To dwell a weeping hermit there!

(1747)

The language here is in some ways more descriptive than in "Lord Randal." Note the concreteness of *deck* and *dress, knell* and *turf*. Note the qualifying adjectives: the *sweeter* sod, the *fairy* hands, the *unseen* forms, the *gray* pilgrim, the *weeping* hermit. Note the personification of *Spring* and *Fancy, Honour* and *Freedom*. This would seem to be highly descriptive language; yet (for me) clean-cut pictures do not come alive as I read. For the poem-experience as a whole is abstract, and vivid imagery does not seem to be an appropriate accompaniment to its meaning.

But let me communicate to you the sense of my reading of the poem as a step toward making clear what I mean about its imagery. Writing early in 1746, Collins said:

The war dead of the past year are sleeping in peace, happy in the praise of their countrymen. By spring time, with the rain, flowers will come up from the earth made holy by their bodies. Their death bell is sounded by angels; their death song, by voices from heaven. All honour is theirs; and the Spirit of Free Men, out of respect for their noble works, is with them.

As long as I content myself with a few general and simple visual images—the tomb of the Unknown Soldier, or the veterans' graves in a country cemetery—I find that I have no difficulty. But when I exert my "will to see," the visual imagery becomes inappropriate and even ridiculous. When I force myself to "see" Miss Blossom-time, with dewy fingers cold, coming back to strew flowers on the mouldy remains of the dead! when I push myself to "see" Miss Imagination dancing airily amongst the dandelions! when pixies pull the bell ropes! when old Mister Honour, in the habit of pilgrim gray, limps along to sprinkle the turfs that wrap round the heroes' bodies! when old Mister Freedom also hobbles in to live a hermit's life in the churchyard—then I am shocked by the sequence of incongruous pictures. Imagery at best is difficult to control; forced imagery most easily gets out of hand. But when I read this poem without obtrusive imagery, it provides me with a solemn and stately experience.

4. AUDITORY AND OTHER SORTS OF IMAGERY

So far we have dealt chiefly with visual imagery. But there are comparable images of all manner of sensory experience. Very often *auditory imagery* accompanies the pictures seen in the mind's-eye. While reading "The Listeners" and enjoying my view of the pictorial scene, I was also aware of numerous sound effects: the knocking at the door, the horse's champing of the grass, the flutter of bird wings, the repeated knocking, the voice of the traveler, etc.[3] While reading "Night Clouds," I not only "saw" the white mares, I "heard" their clatter and whinny. I also "heard" the plaintive voice of Lord Randal's mother, and the suppressed agony of the son's reply.

It is important to distinguish between auditory tied-imagery, the sound in the mind's-ear of the word itself, and *auditory free-imagery,* the sound in the mind's-ear of what the word stands for. The two are usually quite unrelated, except for those onomatopoetic words mentioned in the last chapter.

[3] Another and much fuller discussion of auditory imagery stimulated by "The Listeners" will be found in the Suggestions for Study, pp. 159-60.

Nowadays, we may have an unusually rich store of auditory experiences. Through microphone and celluloid we have heard the sound of lapping water, the crackling of twigs in the forest, the rushing of trains, the stampeding of cattle, the veritable din of battle—or, if not reproductions of the actual sounds, at least reasonable facsimiles. And the fullness of our auditory free-imagery will probably be proportionate to the wealth of our past auditory experiences.

The following poem may serve as an example of auditory free-imagery. It is one of John Dryden's two stately odes written in praise of music for performance in celebration of the Feast of St. Cecilia. The poem opens with a description of the creation of the universe, called into being by the musical voice of God, beginning with the ordering of the four elements and carrying through the entire range (dīapā'son) of creation to man himself. And among mankind it was Jubal, descendant of Cain, who was "the father of all such as handle harp and organ." So the poem goes on to cite the various emotions that may be evoked by the several instruments. After Orpheus, who in Greek legend invented the lyre and who pied-pipered the creatures and even the trees, came St. Cecilia, the martyred virgin who is said to have invented the organ, most heavenly of instruments. As the world began with God's Word and the music of the spheres, so, concludes the poem, it will be brought to an end by the musical sound of Gabriel's trumpet. This irregular ode is one of the few great poems in which the rhythmic unit of the metrical pattern changes, here to stimulate the auditory free-imagery of the different musical instruments.

A SONG FOR ST. CECILIA'S DAY

1687

John Dryden

I

From harmony, from heav'nly harmony,
    This universal frame began:
    When Nature underneath a heap

Of jarring atoms lay,
And could not heave her head,
The tuneful voice was heard from high:
"Arise, ye more than dead."
Then cold, and hot, and moist, and dry,
In order to their stations leap,
And Music's pow'r obey.
From harmony, from heav'nly harmony,
This universal frame began:
From harmony to harmony
Through all the compass of the notes it ran
The diapason closing full in Man.

2

What passion cannot Music raise and quell!
When Jubal struck the corded shell,
His list'ning brethren stood around,
And, wond'ring, on their faces fell
To worship that celestial sound.
Less than a god they thought there could not dwell
Within the hollow of that shell
That spoke so sweetly and so well.
What passion cannot Music raise and quell!

3

The Trumpet's loud clangour
Excites us to arms,
With shrill notes of anger,
And mortal alarms.
The double double double beat
Of the thund'ring Drum
Cries: "Hark! the foes come;
Charge, charge, 'tis too late to retreat."

4

The soft complaining Flute
In dying notes discovers
The woes of hopeless lovers,
Whose dirge is whisper'd by the warbling Lute.

5

Sharp Violins proclaim
Their jealous pangs, and desperation,
Fury, frantic indignation,
Depth of pains, and height of passion,
  For the fair, disdainful dame.

6

But oh! what art can teach,
What human voice can reach,
The sacred Organ's praise?
  Notes inspiring holy love,
Notes that wing their heav'nly ways
  To mend the choirs above.

7

Orpheus could lead the savage race;
And trees unrooted left their place,
  Sequacious [4] of the lyre;
But bright Cecilia rais'd the wonder high'r:
When to her Organ vocal breath was giv'n,
An angel heard, and straight appear'd,
  Mistaking earth for heav'n.

GRAND CHORUS

As from the pow'r of sacred lays
  The spheres began to move,
And sung the great Creator's praise
  To all the blest above;
So, when the last and dreadful hour
This crumbling pageant shall devour,
The Trumpet shall be heard on high,
The dead shall live, the living die,
And Music shall untune the sky.
  (1687)

But let us turn from this poem, which may have stimulated strong and varied auditory free-imagery in some readers, to a con-

[4] following.

sideration of the other sorts of free-imagery: gustatory and olfactory imagery—the fancied taste and smell of things; tactile and thermal imagery—the fancied feel of things to the sense of touch and the sensation of heat and cold; kinesthetic and equilibrial imagery—the fancied heft of things in the muscular sensation and the sense of balance; pain and visceral imagery—the fancied hurt and internal sensations; sensual and erotic imagery—the fancied nakedness and sexual sensations.

For the most part, imagery of these kinds is less frequent and less vivid than are visual and auditory free-imagery. But the "Odours, when sweet violets sicken" and the "flowers/So sweet, the sense faints picturing them" of Shelley's lyrics (pp. 100 and 135) may have stimulated strong olfactory imagery. Shakespeare's "Winter" (p. 93), with its icicles and cold fingers, frozen milk and nipped blood, probably brought imagined feelings of cold. Denney's "The Hammer-Throw" (p. 8) and Sorley's "The Song of the Ungirt Runners" (p. 57) doubtless suggested muscular sensations of pivot-and-release and of running. Robert Frost's "Out, Out—" (p. 30) may have brought to mind an even-too-vivid recollection of pain sensations, as also Ulysses gashed and torn in his fight to come in through the surf (p. 37). And Wallace Stevens' "Peter Quince at the Clavier" (p. 60) suggests Susanna's bathing and the Elders' erotism.

The following selection from a somewhat longer poem will serve for present illustration of gustatory imagery; but note while you are reading it that many of the so-called tastes really come to us through the sense of smell.

from FOOD AND DRINK
Louis Untermeyer

. . . Let us give thanks before we turn
To other things of less concern
For all the poetry of the table:
Clams that parade their silent fable;
Lobsters that have a rock for stable;
Red-faced tomatoes ample as

A countryman's full-bosomed lass;
Plain-spoken turnips; honest beets;
The carnal gusto of red meats;
The wood-fire pungence of smoked ham;
The insipidity of lamb;
Young veal that's smooth as natural silk;
The lavish motherliness of milk;
Sweet-sour carp, beloved by Jews;
Pot luck simplicity of stews;
Crabs, juiciest of Nature's jokes;
The deep reserve of artichokes;
Mushrooms, whose taste is texture, loath
To tell of their mysterious growth;
Quick, mealy comfort glowing in
A baked potato's crackled skin;
The morning promise, hailed by man,
Of bacon crisping in the pan;
The sage compound of *Hasenpfeffer*
With dumplings born of flour and zephyr;
Spinach whose spirit is the soil;
Anchovies glorified in oil;
Corn that is roasted in the ash;
The eternal compromise of hash;
The slow-gold nectar maples yield;
Pale honey tasting of the field
Where every clover is Hymettus;
The cooling sanity of lettuce,
And every other herbal green
Whose touch is calm, whose heart is clean;
Succulent bean-sprouts; bamboo-shoots;
The sapid catalogue of fruits:
Plebeian apple; caustic grape;
Quinces that have no gift for shape;
Dull plums that mind their own affairs;
Incurably bland and blunted pears;
Fantastic passion-fruit; frank lemons
With acid tongues as sharp as women's;
Exotic loquats; sly persimmons;
White currants; amber-fleshed sultanas
(Miniature and sweetened mannas);

Expansive peaches; suave bananas;
Oranges ripening in crates;
Tight-bodied figs; sun-wrinkled dates;
Melons that have their own vagaries;
The bright astringency of berries;
Pepper, whose satire stings and cuts;
The pointless persiflage of nuts;
Sauces of complex mysteries;
Proverbial parsnips; muscular cheese;
Innocent eggs that scorn disguises;
Languid molasses; burning spices
In kitchen-oracles to Isis;
Thick sauerkraut's fat-bellied savor;
Anything with a chocolate flavor;
Deep generosity of pies;
Rich puddings bursting to surprise;
The smug monotony of rice. . . .

(1932)

5. A FINAL ILLUSTRATION

John Keats' "Ode on a Grecian Urn" will serve as a final illustration for this chapter. The reader is invited to pay close attention
to the various sorts of free imagery that may be a part of his
experience.

ODE ON A GRECIAN URN
John Keats

I

Thou still unravish'd bride of quietness,
    Thou foster-child of silence and slow time,
Sylvan historian, who canst thus express
    A flowery tale more sweetly than our rhyme:
What leaf-fring'd legend haunts about thy shape
    Of deities or mortals, or of both,
        In Tempe or the dales of Arcady?
    What men or gods are these? What maidens loth?
What mad pursuit? What struggle to escape?
        What pipes and timbrels? What wild ecstasy?

2

Heard melodies are sweet, but those unheard
  Are sweeter; therefore, ye soft pipes, play on;
Not to the sensual ear, but, more endear'd,
  Pipe to the spirit ditties of no tone:
Fair youth, beneath the trees, thou canst not leave
  Thy song, nor ever can those trees be bare;
  Bold Lover, never, never canst thou kiss,
Though winning near the goal—yet, do not grieve;
  She cannot fade, though thou hast not thy bliss,
  For ever wilt thou love, and she be fair!

3

Ah, happy, happy boughs! that cannot shed
  Your leaves, nor ever bid the Spring adieu;
And, happy melodist, unwearièd,
  For ever piping songs for ever new;
More happy love! more happy, happy love!
  For ever warm and still to be enjoy'd,
    For ever panting, and for ever young;
All breathing human passion far above,
  That leaves a heart high-sorrowful and cloy'd,
    A burning forehead, and a parching tongue.

4

Who are these coming to the sacrifice?
  To what green altar, O mysterious priest,
Lead'st thou that heifer lowing at the skies,
  And all her silken flanks with garlands drest?
What little town by river or sea shore,
  Or mountain-built with peaceful citadel,
    Is emptied of this folk, this pious morn?
And, little town, thy streets for evermore
  Will silent be; and not a soul to tell
    Why thou art desolate, can e'er return.

5

O Attic shape! Fair attitude! with brede
  Of marble men and maidens overwrought,

With forest branches and the trodden weed;
   Thou, silent form, dost tease us out of thought
As doth eternity: Cold Pastoral!
   When old age shall this generation waste,
   Thou shalt remain, in midst of other woe
Than ours, a friend to man, to whom thou say'st,
   "Beauty is truth, truth beauty,"—that is all
   Ye know on earth, and all ye need to know.
              (*1819;* 1820)

SUGGESTIONS FOR STUDY

1. *The Imagery of Keats' Ode.* The following suggestions are intended to focus your attention upon certain specific aspects of your imagery in experiencing "Ode on a Grecian Urn."

(a) Reread the poem thoughtfully, making use of these notes relative to the sense of it: Why is the urn addressed as a "still unravished bride of quietness"? Why "foster-child of silence and slow time"? This Greek vase has survived the centuries. It cannot speak; yet, because of its pictorial decorations, it is a *sylvan* (woodland) *historian* (story teller). *Timbrels:* tambourines; *sensual:* sensory; *Attic:* Athenian, Greek; *Fair attitude:* beautiful form; *brede:* braid, embroidery; *Cold Pastoral:* shepherd story told by the cold vase.

(b) Now, without looking back again to the poem, draw a rough sketch of the vase, two views if you wish. Where your graphic skill breaks down, supplement with verbal notes tied into the drawing with connecting arrows. What do you do with the little town? the peaceful citadel?

(c) Go back to the poem and bring your visual images once more into focus. Improve upon your sketch. At best it is likely to be a very crude representation of only one aspect of your visual imagery, and will completely miss the moving, developing, fluctuating, and dreamlike character of your experience. Compare your work nevertheless with the sketches of other readers. It may reveal the marked individuality of your mind-pictures.

(d) Give careful consideration to the other sorts of sensory imagery that you may have had as a part of your reading. Did you experience auditory free-imagery of actual music with the "Heard melodies are sweet, but those unheard/ Are sweeter"? Did you experience that strange thing—the image of silence? What thermal and organic sensations were re-created in your mind as you read? Do you "feel" that the surface of the vase is glazed, or rough?

(e) Pay attention now to the "music" of the poem—to the unheard melodies of the auditory tied-imagery. Characterize briefly the music of your experience. Does it seem to you that the poetic rhythm helps to activate your imagination? Does the stanzaic form seem to you to bear any relation to the visual imagery?

(f) Consider now the last lines of this "Ode on a Grecian Urn," and its over-all meaning. Turn back to those other poems on Art and Beauty in chapters 3 and 4.

2. *Visual Imagery of Motion.* The central image of Keats' ode is static; the urn does not in itself change, but remains constant. The following very different poem describes a moving object—a swimmer diving. Give particular attention to your experience of the visual imagery of motion as you read.

THE DIVE
Ted Robins

Like a strong bow bent forcefully,
His body curves; then, like the bow released,
His body straightens and becomes the shaft
Which plugs the center of the amber targe,
The eye from which the rapid wavelets spread
In silver rings. Under their largening,
Under their lacy froth, their bubbling spume,
His body melts into the liquid mass,
Foreshortens, gleams with an unnatural light—
Half, green-and-amber water, half, smooth flesh.
Each hair gives up its tiny crystal globe,
Which buoyant rises. Other bubbles join
To weave together in the fretted plan,
The elusive pattern of the growing wake.
Urged by an otter twist, up the incline
Of the translucency his body glides,
The muscles rippling. Soon the surface breaks.
Dark as sleek seal the shining head appears;
The strong, tanned shoulders, glistening, arise.
And from the phantom plane, the phantom being,
Fabulous merman, issues now the man.

(1934)

3. *Kinesthetic Imagery of Motion.* But the reader of "The Dive" will probably not only "see" the motion of the diver in his mind's-eye, but also apperceive the motion through his recollection of muscular sensa-

tions. Other recent poems, "High Flight" by John Magee and "P-51" by John Ciardi, will provide many with kinesthetic and equilibrial imagery of the sort experienced in air flight and in observing it. These are indeed twentieth century songs for those who find new and shaking beauty in the perilous dip of a plane's wing and the roar of its engine. (a) After reading the poems several times, consider this question: From what experiences that you have had do the bits of sensation come that are woven together as the principal imagery of these poems? (b) Write a short paper in which you describe the imagery and its sources in your past experience.

HIGH FLIGHT [5]

John Gillespie Magee, Jr.

Oh! I have slipped the surly bonds of Earth
   And danced the skies on laughter-silvered wings;
Sunward I've climbed, and joined the tumbling mirth
   Of sun-split clouds,—and done a hundred things
You have not dreamed of—wheeled and soared and swung
   High in the sunlit silence. Hov'ring there,
I've chased the shouting wind along, and flung
   My eager craft through footless halls of air. . . .

Up, up the long, delirious, burning blue
   I've topped the wind-swept heights with easy grace,
Where never lark, or even eagle flew—
   And, while with silent, lifting mind I've trod
   The high untrespassed sanctity of space,
Put out my hand and touched the face of God.

                    (1942)

P-51

John Ciardi

It fills the sky like wind made visible
   And given voice like drums through amplifiers,
Too great a terror to be lost on death
   Remembering that all our dreams are fliers.

This terror, cannoned as the hawk is billed,
   Taloned with lusty boys who love their toy,

[5] See Hermann Hagedorn, *Sunward I've Climbed,* Macmillan, 1942.

Mounts on the living energy of grace
Whose passing cracks on burning lathes of joy.

Piston by piston the made fumes of flight
Frenzy the startled air her passing sears.
Fast as a head can turn from East to West
She summons distances and disappears.

That moment only—glancing up and gone—
And see, her boy outburns the burning year.
And we are clod and pasture fixed upon
Her birth above the hills like a crowd's cheer.

(1945)

4. *Verbal Portraiture.* The description of a personality may take the
form of a verbal portrait enlivened by characterizing incident and by
the revelation of the subject's thoughts. Stephen Vincent Benét's *John
Brown's Body* contains portraits of many historic as well as fictional
characters. Note, as you read this sketch of Abraham Lincoln, how your
attention is turned from a central image of the appearance of the man
to thoughts about his personality, but with quick glimpses at a wide
variety of mind-pictures.

from JOHN BROWN'S BODY

LINCOLN

Stephen Vincent Benét

Lincoln, six feet one in his stocking feet,
The lank man, knotty and tough as a hickory rail,
Whose hands were always too big for white-kid gloves,
Whose wit was a coonskin sack of dry, tall tales,
Whose weathered face was homely as a plowed field—
Abraham Lincoln, who padded up and down
The sacred White House in nightshirt and carpet-slippers,
And yet could strike young hero-worshipping Hay
As dignified past any neat, balanced, fine
Plutarchan sentences carved in a Latin bronze;
The low clown out of the prairies, the ape-buffoon,
The small-town lawyer, the crude small-time politician,
State-character but comparative failure at forty

In spite of ambition enough for twenty Caesars,
Honesty rare as a man without self-pity,
Kindness as large and plain as a prairie wind,
And a self-confidence like an iron bar:
This Lincoln, President now by the grace of luck,
Disunion, politics, Douglas and a few speeches
Which make the monumental booming of Webster
Sound empty as the belly of a burst drum,
Lincoln shambled in to the Cabinet meeting
And sat, ungainly and awkward. Seated so
He did not seem so tall nor quite so strange
Though he was strange enough. His new broadcloth suit
Felt tight and formal across his big shoulders still
And his new shiny top-hat was not yet battered
To the bulging shape of the old familiar hat
He'd worn at Springfield, stuffed with its hoard of papers.
He was pretty tired. All week the office-seekers
Had plagued him as the flies in fly-time plague
A gaunt-headed, patient horse. The children weren't well
And Mollie was worried about them so sharp with her tongue.
But he knew Mollie and tried to let it go by.
Men tracked dirt in the house and women liked carpets.
Each had a piece of the right, that was all most people could stand.

(1928)

5. *Imagery and Meaning*. Read this one of Shakespeare's sonnets with a special "willingness to see" and to experience rich and varied imagery.

(a) Write a simple and clear paraphrase of the sense of this poem. (b) Take note of the typographical form of the poem as here reprinted (the retinal image of the poem on the page). (c) Consider briefly its "music" (the auditory tied-imagery): the metrical pattern and variations, the rime-scheme of this special form, the sound pattern and tone-color. (d) Give particular thought to the free imagery. What are the principal images? How do they change and develop? From what source in your experience do their elements come? What sorts of nonvisual imagery do you note? (e) What relation do the retinal image, the articulatory tied-imagery, and the free imagery bear to the over-all meaning of the poem?

THAT TIME OF YEAR THOU MAYST IN ME BEHOLD

from SONNETS, LXXIII

William Shakespeare

That time of year thou mayst in me behold
When yellow leaves, or none, or few, do hang
Upon those boughs which shake against the cold,
Bare ruin'd choirs, where late the sweet birds sang.
In me thou see'st the twilight of such day
As after sunset fadeth in the west;
Which by and by black night doth take away,
Death's second self, that seals up all in rest.
In me thou see'st the glowing of such fire,
That on the ashes of his youth doth lie,
As the death-bed whereon it must expire,
Consùm'd with that which it was nourish'd by.
   This thou perceiv'st, which makes thy love more strong,
   To love that well which thou must leave ere long.

                               (c. 1598, 1609)

6. *The Listeners Again.* (a) Study carefully the following comment on de la Mare's "The Listeners" prepared for this book by John Holmes. Distinguish the auditory *tied*-imagery and the auditory *free*-imagery and their relation to each other as he records his experience:

The suggestive auditory images in "The Listeners" are to be known best by frequent reading aloud. In the opening question we hear the bold cry in the silence; the force of the knocking is in the NOCK and MOON and DOOR, rather tentative at first. Then the Traveller waits. He looks about, he looks up—and the succession of vowels, light, reaching, and almost lost, in the line "And a bird flew up out of the turret," begins the moonlit suspense. He breaks that suspense abruptly, half in fear, half in a rough impatience. But as auditory image we certainly hear a more rapid and a longer, sharper knocking in "He *smote* upon the *door* a*gain* a *sec*ond *time*." Not an even knock; but excited. Then ever so slight a pause—the subtlety of the semicolon—and the call again, and we know it is much louder, rising to a shout at the last word—"Is there anybody THERE?" he said. The word "sill" comes as the best word imaginable for a high edge to lean over; and there is long, strange waiting in the "leaned over and looked," and again that slowness and silence in the combination of this with "grey eyes." If there had not been the word "perplexed," de la Mare would have invented it, in the next line. As auditory image no sound could be as meaningful of helplessness, puzzlement, and lack of will and purpose to motion. What a vivid image is packed into the short clenched syllable, "plexed." Then come the quiet lines of hollow mystery, during which we feel the Traveller's raptness. It is broken by the short, blunt sounds of "While his horse moved, cropping the dark turf." The consonants suggest and imitate the nervous biting of the horse with head lowered. This natural sound rouses the Traveller, who beats on the door, and calls his real message; but there is a crescendo of his emotion in "For he suddenly smote on the door even" and an auditory image of heightened tension, with the dramatic effect of the word "even" at the line's end. This pulls the line high and tight—then the word "Louder" beginning the next line comes with violent effect, like a rumble of drums, and makes possible the climax fortissimo, "Tell them I came, and no one answered,/ That I kept my word." The whole poem, auditorily, has built up, retarded, and built again to this high point. What it means we must think about, but what it sounds to our ears we know. From this climax there is a diminuendo of action and meaning: silence and departure. But what skill in sounding it! First the shadowy listening, then the hurried leap into the saddle, and the ring of the n's in "And the sound of iron on stone." Iron was never so iron or so hard on stony stony stone in the dark of night. Then the slow, soft s's as "the silence surged softly backward," smothering the dead secret, the old doors and turrets in night again. The last echo of the n's in "the plunging hoofs were gone," and then nothing. The interrupted silence resumes. The whole experience of the poem has been richly auditory.

(b) Reread "The Listeners" yet again, and note carefully the changes in your own auditory experience as it has been affected by the study of Holmes' comment.

7. *Lord Randal on Record.* (a) The ballad "Lord Randal" has come down to us in a number of different versions, three of which, from the numerous gathering of Francis J. Child, are reprinted in George L. Kittredge, ed., *English and Scottish Popular Ballads,* Houghton Mifflin, 1904. (b) One of the other versions has been recorded by Richard Dyer-Bennet (Harvard Vocarium record). If this record is available, play it repeatedly and study the imagery developed in this experience. (c) Reconsider the imagery that was stimulated by reading the version included in the text, and compare the two.

7

THE MEANING OF POETRY

We come now to the fourth aspect of the poem-reading-experience, *the sense of it,* but more than that: *the full meaning.* It would
be a mistake to assume that seeing the poem on the page, the
"music," the free imagery, and the meaning occur in a neat one-
two-three-four order; and that the emotional response and the residuum are five and six in the sequence. Except for the initial
seeing and the final residuum, which obviously come first and last,
the central four aspects occur more or less simultaneously. At least,
they do not exist in any set order, as the chapter sequence would
lead one to believe, but are so closely interrelated that it may seem
quite artificial to separate them. On one occasion, the tied image
of the sound of a word will suggest its sense; at another time,
thoughts about the meaning will indicate how the word should be
pronounced.

By and large, however, *the sense phase of the poem-experience
will lead the way.* It will dictate the placement of stress and accent
that lets the reader know how the poem "goes," the metrical pattern; and then it will set up its own pattern of varying degrees and
sequences of stress that pulls the poetic rhythm away from the
metrical expectancy. The sense of the words will call up from the
vaults of memory the colored slides to be flashed as pictures upon
the mind's screen. The sense of the words and other aspects of the
full meaning will contribute to that stir of feeling most characteristic of the art experience. But if the sense of a poem is thus central,
touching and affecting all of the other aspects, leading the way and
guiding the whole experience, it must at once be pointed out that
the *mere* sense of it is usually not the most important part of a

poem. Other phases of the full meaning, and other aspects than the meaning—the "music" or free imagery or emotional response—may provide more immediate pleasure, and the subtle adjustment in his attitudes may long outlast the reader's running-fire thoughts of the sense.

As the present chapter will carry on the discussion initiated in the introductory chapter on "Language and Art," it may be worth while to summarize the points made at that time:[1] First, language has three somewhat distinct functions—communication, problem-solving, and the art function; but it does not necessarily serve these functions separately. Second, words have meaning only when they are put to work by speaker or hearer, by writer or reader; they acquire meaning from their context, the surroundings and the circumstances of their use. Third, words may acquire more than one meaning in a given utterance, and this ambiguity may be either confusing or enriching. Fourth, the full meaning of an utterance or of an interpretation will consist of feeling, tone, and intention as well as the mere sense of it.

These points and several others will occupy us further as we now approach the problem of the *meaning* in poetry.

I. THE FUNCTIONS OF LANGUAGE IN POETRY

In poetry, language does not serve a single function, but a variable combination of three functions: communication, problem-solving, and what we have called the art function, personality adjustment.

The writing of an ode, for instance, may give the poet a certain emotional satisfaction; it may effect for him a needed personality adjustment; it may restore in him the essential integration and balance of his interests. Keats—to take an example—Keats may have felt, as he completed "Ode on a Grecian Urn," that the turbulence of his own emotional life—his brother's death, his own ill health, his financial worries, his frustrated love—was somehow stilled and brought into focus by his contemplation of enduring

[1] See particularly pp. 43-51.

Beauty. This is one phase of the art function of language as it is put to use by the poet. But there may also be a certain amount of problem-solving going on at the same time. For Keats there was not only the philosophical problem, the thought of the poem and its structural development, but also the exacting stanzaic form that he set for himself and from which he consciously departed. So he must have sketched out the rime-scheme or held it firmly in mind as he created the verses and stanza. But at the same time Keats was using language with the purpose of communication. While he was writing, he may have had in mind particular readers or groups of readers, hoping that he might somehow transmit to them the thoughts and feelings, the music and the imagery, that were a part of his growing experience. And Keats did publish the poem in his 1820 volume. Such, then, are the several functions of language as used by the poet.

Now, when a reader takes up the poem, he too will find language functioning in all three ways in varying proportions. The printed verses will be a work of art and also a sort of personal letter from the poet. The reader will complete the communication by interpreting the language; he may also puzzle some philosophical problem while he is doing this; and he may realize that peculiar sort of experience of which esthetic significance and personal integration are a part.

Thoughtful reading of the following poem may serve to illustrate this point.

THE PRAYING MANTIS VISITS A PENTHOUSE
Oscar Williams

The praying Mantis with its length of straw
Out of the nowhere's forehead born full armed
Engages the century at my terrace door.
Focused at inches the dinosaur insect sends
Broadsides of epic stillness at my eye,
Above the deafening projects of the age.
My wife, who fears the thunder of its poise,
Has seen it and cries out. The clouds like curls

Fall in my faith as I seize a stick to stop
This Martian raid distilled to a straw with legs,
To wisps of prowess. Bristling with motionlessness
The Mantis prays to the Stick twice armed with Man.

I strike, the stick whistles, shearing off two legs
Which run off by themselves beneath some boards.
The Mantis spreads out tints of batlike wing,
The many colored pennants of its blood,
And hugs my weapon; the frantic greens come out,
The reds and yellows blurt out from the straw,
All sinews doubtless screaming insect death.
Against the railing's edge I knock the stick
Sending that gay mad body into the gulf.
Such noisy trappings in defeat wake doubts.
I search my mind for possible wounds and feel
The victim's body heavy on the victor's heart.

(1945)

The reader of this poem may observe language fulfilling a composite function; but it will be difficult to separate communication from problem-solving, and problem-solving from personality adjustment. There is the immediate question of interpretation—to complete the communication, to surmise the poet's thought, to get the sense of it: *The praying Mantis* (a dictionary will help the reader who is short on entomology) is a grotesque insect whose front legs are held in a position that suggests praying hands. It was Minerva (Pallas Athena) who was *born full armed,* mature and complete with armor, from the forehead of her father Jupiter. The *century* may be the twentieth century, or the skyscraper civilization, or modern man. Note that the primordial insect is only *focused at inches,* yet, because of its size and appearance, is fearsome at a distance of feet; and that, though it is silent and does not move, its attack seems to scream above the city's din. Storm *clouds* of fear descend upon the poet in the same way that Orson Welles' broadcast of attacking men from Mars spread panic through the hearts of many. The Mantis seems now to pray to the stick, which is grasped epicwise in the poet-hero's two hands. . . . And so the reader begins to piece together the meaning, the narrative thread of which may be summarized as follows: The poet's wife discovered a strange insect at the doorsill of their apartment terrace high above the city, and cried out to her husband, who came and killed it. But knocking the lifeless Mantis from his stick into the street below set the poet to thinking—he had not been injured by this strange creature which at first seemed so menacing, but now so beautiful in color, and he regrets his action.

But to complete the communication by ferreting out the poet's meaning is only one function of language in the process of reading. For some readers certainly will have puzzled the implications and the over-all meaning. Was the poet thinking of other causes of private fear and impulsive defensive assault? Or was he thinking of social or national fears? So the language of the poem may raise questions in the reader's mind or may seem to answer questions already asked. And who shall say what changes in personal attitude—interest in strange insect life harmless and beautiful, control of sudden and preposterous fears, realization of guilt for innocent victims—may have resulted in particular readers through the interpretation of this poem.

2. CONTEXT AND COMMUNICATION

It has been said that words have meaning only in context. The *words* of a poem bear a certain objective relation to each other in the verses on the page, and these surrounding words may be thought of as "the literary or verbal context." They also bear a certain relation to the life experiences of the *poet* who set them down and to his thoughts and feelings, which may be said to be "the vital context of utterance." But it is the *reader's* experience of words and things that provides "the vital context of interpretation."

The reading of another poem, a relatively self-sufficient selection from one of William Blake's so-called Prophetic Books, may serve to illustrate this point.

from MILTON
William Blake

And did those feet in ancient time
   Walk upon England's mountains green?
And was the holy Lamb of God
   On England's pleasant pastures seen?

And did the Countenance Divine
   Shine forth upon our clouded hills?
And was Jerusalem builded here
   Among these dark Satanic mills?

Bring me my bow of burning gold!
   Bring me my arrows of desire!
Bring me my spear! O clouds, unfold!
   Bring me my chariot of fire!

I will not cease from mental fight,
   Nor shall my sword sleep in my hand,
Till we have built Jerusalem
   In England's green and pleasant land.

(1804)

Though these four stanzas have been wrenched from their larger context, they will here be considered as an independent poem. There may seem to be no difficulties of interpretation for the reader of this poem: the relationship of the words to each other in the literary context seems to pose no serious problems. And once it is realized that the poet is operating in the religious universe of discourse, *those feet* suggest a reference to Jesus, as does the *Lamb of God*. But what can be meant by the apparent assertion, in the form of a rhetorical question, that Jesus walked upon the meadows and hills of England? Does England here mean simply *this Earth*? And what of *Jerusalem*? Is the reference here to the ancient city? or to the New Jerusalem? the City or the Kingdom of God? Were the *dark Satanic mills* here on earth when the ancient Jerusalem was built? Or, where once there was ancient glory, now there is sordid industry? And what of the *Jerusalem* in the next to the last line?

and of the fight to bring it about on this earth? . . . These questions, and the reader's effort to answer them, may have suggested the way in which meaning is dependent upon context, both verbal and vital.

The process of communicating thought is indeed more complex than it may at first seem. It would be so easy if the poet could put his *thought* into an "envelope of language," as it has been said, and send it to the reader for him to open and take out the thought. But this is not possible. It is only words, and not thoughts, that can be thus directly transmitted. The poet chooses and arranges WORDS to *stand for* his THOUGHTS that *point to* certain THINGS in his experience—"things" in the broadest sense, including other thoughts as well as external objects and events perceived through the senses. For each individual reader of the poem these same WORDS will *stimulate* related but at least slightly *DIFFERENT THOUGHTS* that will *point to* what certainly must be *DIFFERENT THINGS* in each particular reader's unique body of experience.

For the reader of a poem, then, the *sense* of it will be *the stream of his thoughts*—the darting, splashing, eddying stream of thoughts —stimulated by the words on the page, *the thoughts of what the words stand for*. And the *sense* of it, what the words stand for in the reading of a particular reader, will depend upon his experience with them.

At best, language is an imperfect instrument of communication. The thought stimulated in the reader can never be identical with the thought in the mind of the poet, for their verbal and vital experiences are bound to be different. And the interpretation of an utterance, whether poem or letter, is always a sort of elaborate surmise, some might even say guessing game, in which the reader tries his best to determine the meaning of the poet or of his correspondent.

However, it would be a mistake to assume that, since words do not have absolute and objectively determinable meanings, therefore one man's guess is as good as another's; that the poem says whatever the reader wants it to say; that everyone is free to read into it whatever he likes. For success in reading comes only when the reader's experience turns out to be similar to the poet's, when the sequence of thoughts stimulated in the interpreter is comparable to the thoughts which the poet tried to express through the words of the poem. But we shall return to this point in a later paragraph.

3. TONE, FEELING, AND INTENTION

The meaning of a poem is very much more than the mere sense of it, as we have already suggested. A full meaning may be thought of as having at least three components besides the sense—the intention, feeling, and tone. In oral discourse we are likely to be more conscious of these other aspects of a full meaning, for many signs and clues are supplied by the speaker's gestures, facial expression, and qualities of voice. But if the reader of written discourse—of a poem, for instance—is alert, he may catch somewhat comparable clues to these other phases of the full meaning.

Intention, as a separate phase of meaning, is the reason why the utterer says what he does, as distinguished from the sense, feeling, or tone of what he may wish to communicate. We are accustomed to noting "deceit" or "currying favor" or "malice" as special sorts of intention; and the phrases "speaking carefully," "evasively," "mysteriously," and "ambiguously" also describe particular kinds of intention that may be a part of a full meaning. *Feeling,* as another phase of meaning, is the indication of the speaker's affective response to the thing of which he is speaking. It is to be distinguished from *tone* as a phase of meaning, for "tone" will be used to name the attitude of the speaker toward the hearer or reader. The phrases, "in a friendly tone," "sarcastically," "tolerantly," "ironically," "contemptuously," "insolently," suggest the *tone* phase of meaning, which is more readily apparent in oral discourse, but which may be detected in written discourse from sometimes rather subtle clues.

An utterance will hardly ever be pure sense ("This is a $\frac{3}{8}''$ x $1''$ stove bolt"), or almost pure intention ("Stop!"), or almost pure feeling ("Just too darling!"), or almost pure tone ("You dirty so-and-so!"). The meaning will usually be made up of these components in various proportions. In poetry especially the full meaning will certainly be more than the mere sense, and is likely to be rich in feeling and intention, and sometimes in tone also.

When the following quatrain was first uttered in the presence of the very much alive Charles II, that Merry Monarch (as the dark-skinned king with the spaniels and the mistresses was called) must have caught something of its full meaning.

EPITAPH ON CHARLES II [2]

John Wilmot, Earl of Rochester

Here lies our Sovereign Lord the King,
    Whose word no man relies on;
Who never said a foolish thing,
    Nor ever did a wise one.

                    (*c. 1675, 1707*)

There could have been little doubt about the mere sense of it. To the gay court there was a rich context for interpretation. Gossip had circulated many instances of the King's word not being kept; everyone could think of innumerable instances of his brilliance in repartee; there were secret differences of opinion regarding his wisdom in political action. But the tone, feeling, and intention? Just how much in jest, how much in earnest, was it intended to be? Was it really a compliment—"Better to be witty than wise"? Or was there underlying hatred and rancor on the part of Wilmot because of His Majesty's failure to keep his promises to him? Or was there a deep contempt for the King? Since the subject of the verses (the King) may also have been the intended hearer, feeling and tone merged, and the possible contempt for the subject became one with the impudence toward the hearer. And was it indeed contempt? Or was it no more than the flippant insincerity of current raillery? Was it a brazen trial of the King's ability to take a lingual scourging in the same good spirit with which he lashed out at others?

Such questions must have buzzed as this satirical quatrain made the rounds. The King himself, upon hearing it, said that indeed he

[2] The quatrain is sometimes entitled: "Written on the Bedchamber Door of Charles II."

had never said a foolish thing or done a wise one—since his words were his own, and his acts were the acts of his ministers! Thus he parried the thrust. But he certainly realized how much more than mere sense is the full meaning of an utterance.

4. AMBIGUITY IN POETRY

Before carrying our discussion further, let us undertake the interpretation of another poem, "The Racer" by John Masefield. Do not work too hard as you read it. Enjoy the effect of the full body of the words in the mind's-ear and along the mind's-tongue, and the succession of images that may flash before you. Yet, in a second or third reading, try to keep your attention focused upon the sense of it, the stream of thoughts of the things for which the words stand.

THE RACER

John Masefield

I saw the racer coming to the jump,
    Staring with fiery eyeballs as he rusht,
I heard the blood within his body thump,
    I saw him launch, I heard the toppings crusht.
And as he landed I beheld his soul
    Kindle, because, in front, he saw the Straight
With all its thousands roaring at the goal;
    He laughed, he took the moment for his mate.
Would that the passionate moods on which we ride
    Might kindle thus to oneness with the will;
Would we might see the end to which we stride,
    And feel, not strain in struggle, only thrill,
And laugh like him and know in all our nerves
Beauty, the spirit, scattering dust and turves.

(1923)

I think you will say that this is not a difficult poem, that the sense of it and the over-all meaning are reasonably clear. There are really no unusual words or phrases, except for several sports terms—like "jump" and "toppings." And the meaning of these you may feel to be self-evident.

Yet, just exactly *what is the sense of it?* To what does your thought point in response to the word "racer"? Is the racer a horse? or the horseman? or a sprinter? or a hurdler? or a whippet? Is the "jump" an obstacle at the end of a steeplechase? or the start for such a race? or the start for a foot-race? or the final hurdle in a hurdle or handicap race? Are the "toppings" the top of a stiff hedge, or the brush attached to the top bar of an obstacle? or the cinders or other special covering for a race course? or the natural dust and turves? or the top bar of a hurdle? What is the "Straight"? And who is it who laughs in line 8: the horse? the rider? the sprinter? the hurdler?

If the racer is the horse, what do you make of these lines?

> Would that the passionate moods on which we ride
> Might kindle thus to oneness with the will. . . .

Are the "passionate moods" likened to the horse, and is the "will" that of the rider? or are the "moods" and "will" both those of the horse? or of the sprinter? or hurdler? In line 11, is our "striding" likened to the striding of horse? rider? sprinter? hurdler? If it's the rider who laughs, is it not the horse who scatters the dust and turves?

These questions may prove irritating to you. You may respond, "Of course I know what it's all about!" . . . "No one but an idiot would think *that!*" . . . "How can you *prove* what he means?!" . . . You see, there is a human tendency to maintain one's position.

The point that must be made is this: if, when you see the title of the poem, the word *racer* stimulates a *thought* that points or refers to your past experience of *horses,* then you will go ahead and try to adjust what comes to that initial thought. If *racer* stimulates a *thought* that points to *rider,* you will try to make the stream of further thoughts accord with that. And if *racer* evokes a *thought* that points to *hurdler,* you will fairly break your neck to keep the following thoughts consistent with that.

But which interpretation of "The Racer" is correct? "Certainly," many people will say, "there is a right answer, the true meaning, and other readings of the poem must then be wrong!"

What the poet meant is the true meaning, as the word "true" is here used. And we may never know for certain just what that was, unless we ask the poet himself.[3] But he may have forgotten just what he meant when he wrote the poem, or his explanation may turn out to be an utterance equally difficult to interpret. Or the poet may not be at hand to answer the question, and he may never have written a note of explanation. What then?

Well, interpretation is not merely a guessing game. It is a game of skill and judgment. Where several interpretations of a poem seem possible, the question becomes this: Which interpretation takes account of all the available clues and leaves the fewest unanswered questions? which is most self-consistent and makes use of the richest background of relevant knowledge and experience? And such an interpretation, arrived at with skill and judgment, will probably come reasonably close to the poet's meaning.

Taking account of such clues as the "fiery eyeballs" and the phrase "on which we ride," and accepting the "laugh" as naming a particular sound made by the horse (not quite a whinny or neigh, nicker or squeal, as here used), the writer presents the following prose paraphrase of the sense of Masefield's poem, with some confidence that it is essentially what the poet meant.

Having seen a group of horses in competition, Masefield says in effect: I saw one horse running up to the last brushwood jump, with fixed hot eyeballs and blood pumping violently in his body. I saw him take off with a spring, get clear of the top; and as he came down safely, I saw that his soul was on fire with a sort of joy, because in front of him was the straight road and the end of his run, with the noise of thousands waiting for him. He gave a cry, almost a laugh; his mind and heart and body became one in the event.

If only *we* were able in this same way to make our hearts one with our minds! If only *we* were able to see clearly the end to which we are moving; to have the feeling, not of hard work, but of pleasure, crying out like that horse because all of our forces are acting together as one beautiful unit!

The reader may wish to turn back to the poem—especially if he began by giving it a horseman, sprinter, or hurdler interpretation—

[3] The curious student will find an extended note at the end of this chapter.

in order to re-examine the clues that might have saved him from misunderstanding.

This capacity of words to stimulate several quite different streams of thought, any one of which seems to make sense, was earlier referred to as *ambiguity*. At times it gets in our way. At other times, as perhaps in the interpretation of "The Racer," the rejected streams of thought never completely dry up and disappear, but remain as damp and verdant old channels in an enriched valley of experience.

5. METAPHOR, SIMILE, AND PERSONIFICATION

There is an important device of language, somewhat related to ambiguity, that consciously makes use of this capacity of words to stimulate two parallel streams of thought. We saw it at work in Keats' "Ode on a Grecian Urn" (p. 152), where the poet addresses the vase as a "still unravished bride of quietness," as "a foster-child of silence and slow time," as a "sylvan historian." Of course the vase is utterly unlike all of these three things—unlike, that is, except in some particulars. There is *something* about the urn that is like *something* about the "unravished bride of quietness." This unknown something is sought out by the reader. And this linguistic phenomenon is called *metaphor*.

In Amy Lowell's short poem in the last chapter (p. 141), "the white mares of the moon" is a metaphor. We are prepared to interpret it easily, for the title is "Night Clouds." Now, night clouds and white mares are utterly unlike one another, except in one or two features. It is the discovery of these few similarities that serves to communicate the poet's thought. We commonly speak of fleecy white clouds with a vague thought of sheep. "No," the poet seems to say, "think of the arched necks and flying manes of white horses, the pawing, ramping, and charging, and you'll get some notion of how the night clouds look to me." The description of the white mares is merely the *vehicle* for conveying to us the *tenor,* the general drift or sense, of what Amy Lowell has to say about night clouds.

You may have observed the device of metaphor in "The Racer," not only in the larger structure of the poem, but in the phrase "The passionate moods on which we ride." Whatever your original interpretation of the earlier lines of this sonnet, you were probably conscious at this point of the linguistic equation:

$$\frac{we}{moods} = \frac{rider}{horse}$$

We are not riders, of course; our moods are not horses. It is the *relationship* that is the same.

$$we : moods :: rider : horse$$
$$x_R \qquad = \qquad y_R$$

The symbol y_R stands for the Known Relationship: the relation of rider to horse in the equestrian universe of discourse; that is, the riding relationship—the rider is carried along by his horse. But the poet says that the relation of the "we" to "moods," the Unknown Relationship (x_R), is the same as this well-known $\frac{rider}{horse}$ relationship (y_R)—that is, we are carried along by them.

One of the great religious metaphors is the basis for the "Twenty-third Psalm" of David (p. 68):

> The Lord is my shepherd; I shall not want.
> He maketh me to lie down in green pastures:
> he leadeth me beside the still waters. . . .

God is not a shepherd, of course. Indeed He is no more like a sheep herder than like men of other vocations or trades. And I am certainly not a sheep; I am not anything like a sheep. . . . But we have missed the point.

$$God : me :: shepherd : sheep$$

It is God's relationship to me that, the poet says, is like a shepherd's relation to his sheep. Everyone in the pastoral Judaic society knew that the shepherd tended his flock, looking after the needs of each ewe and lamb. The x_R, the Unknown Relationship, is like that; that is the way God cares for us His creatures.

So, when language is used metaphorically, a quality or relationship from one universe of discourse or field of experience is made use of to suggest a quality or relationship in another universe of discourse.

There are a number of different kinds of metaphor—using the word now in a broad sense to name a group of comparable devices of language and including several of the so-called figures of speech. One of these is the *simile*. It is easily distinguished, for in it the vehicle is introduced by the words *like* or *as*. Wordsworth wandered "lonely as a cloud" (p. 59); and we are led to understand the manner and mood of his afternoon walk by thinking out the implied equation. When Keats came across Chapman's translation of Homer (p. 25), he felt "like some watcher of the skies" discovering a new planet; he felt "like stout Cortez" discovering the Pacific! If we can appreciate the special quality of *their* emotional experiences, then we can determine the Unknown Quality (x_Q) of Keats' emotion. And we have also encountered similes in Burns' lyric (p. 11):

> O, my luve is like a red, red rose,
>   That's newly sprung in June.
> O, my luve is like the melodie,
>   That's sweetly played in tune.

Whether the "luve" is his sweetheart or his emotion, we can deduce the x_Q by observing closely the equation implied in the two similes.

Personification is another form of metaphor in this wider sense. In it an inanimate thing or abstract idea is given the attributes of a person, and the tenor is conveyed by a human vehicle. Again we have already met instances of this linguistic device. Donne challenges Death in his "Holy Sonnet X" (p. 12). Edna St. Vincent Millay says that "Euclid alone has looked on Beauty bare" (p. 46), and the rest of us are fortunate to have heard no more than her distant footfall! And we commented in the last chapter on Collins' use of personification in his "Ode, Written in . . . 1746" (p. 145).

> When Spring, with dewy fingers cold,
> Returns to deck their hallow'd mould,
> She there shall dress a sweeter sod
> Than Fancy's feet have ever trod.

We shall not extend further the list of various sorts of metaphor, but point out how important it is, when interpreting this kind of poetic language, to catch on to the linguistic equation, to grasp the tenor as distinct from the vehicle, in order to get the sense of it.

The following early seventeenth century lyric supplies a number of examples both of metaphor in the restricted sense and of simile.

THERE IS A GARDEN IN HER FACE
Thomas Campion

There is a garden in her face,
    Where roses and white lilies grow,
A heavenly paradise is that place,
    Wherein all pleasant fruits do flow.
There cherries grow, which none may buy
Till "Cherry ripe!" themselves do cry.

Those cherries fairly do enclose
    Of orient pearl a double row;
Which when her lovely laughter shows,
    They look like rose-buds filled with snow.
Yet them nor peer nor prince can buy,
Till "Cherry ripe!" themselves do cry.

Her eyes like angels watch them still;
    Her brows like bended bows do stand,
Threatening with piercing frowns to kill
    All that attempt with eye or hand
Those sacred cherries to come nigh,
Till "Cherry ripe!" themselves do cry.

                       (1618)

6. THE OVER-ALL MEANING

Let us, however, take a more serious poem, and use our reading-experience of it to carry further our discussion of the meaning of poetry. Read carefully and slowly, and give particular attention to the stream of your thoughts about the sense phase of the meaning.

SAY NOT THE STRUGGLE NOUGHT AVAILETH

Arthur Hugh Clough

Say not the struggle nought availeth,
    The labor and the wounds are vain,
The enemy faints not, nor faileth,
    And as things have been they remain.

If hopes were dupes, fears may be liars;
    It may be, in yon smoke concealed,
Your comrades chase e'en now the fliers,
    And, but for you, possess the field.

For while the tired waves, vainly breaking,
    Seem here no painful inch to gain,
Far back, through creeks and inlets making,
    Comes silent, flooding in, the main.

And not by eastern windows only,
    When daylight comes, comes in the light,
In front, the sun climbs slow, how slowly,
    But westward, look, the land is bright.

(*1849*, 1862)

To illustrate what I mean by the stream of thoughts that form one aspect of the poem-experience, let me present a prose paraphrase in Basic English of my reading of the poem.[4] You will probably discover that "the real poetry of it" has escaped capture, which will but emphasize the fact that a poem is a *whole* experience of which we are now investigating only one part.

[4] The other paraphrases included in this book are also in Basic English, which is a special language consisting of about 1000 words, including the special list used in writing about verse. It provides a highly controlled medium for this sort of exercise. Basic English was invented by C. K. Ogden more than a decade ago, and has attracted wide attention as an international language and as a linguistic tool. For a comprehensive discussion of it, see C. K. Ogden, *The System of Basic English,* Harcourt, Brace, 1934, and I. A. Richards, *Basic English and Its Uses,* W. W. Norton, 1943. The student who wishes to learn Basic English may need C. K. Ogden, *The Basic Words,* London, 1932, and *The General Basic English Dictionary,* W. W. Norton, 1942; and I. A. Richards and Christine Gibson, *Learning Basic English,* W. W. Norton, 1945.

THE SENSE OF CLOUGH'S *SAY NOT THE STRUGGLE NOUGHT AVAILETH* PUT INTO BASIC ENGLISH

Clough seems to say (or is it a Voice that says to him?): "Do not say that the fighting you are now doing is not getting you anywhere; that the hard work and wounds are all for nothing; that those whom you are fighting are becoming stronger and are not giving up; and that everything is as it was before!

"If it is true that your hopes were false, it may as well be true that your fears are equally false. It may be that, over there out of view in the smoke from the guns, your friends are at this very time going after those in flight; and that, if you had given them help, they would have full control of the field.

"Looking at the thing differently: the waves of the sea, tired from smashing without effect against the land, do not seem to get anywhere at all right here; but, far inland, in the small rivers and inlets, you will see the water slowly getting higher, the effect of the great in-coming of the sea.

"And again: in the early morning, it is not from the east windows only that the first light of day is seen. There the sun comes up very slowly; but, turning round to the west, you will see that the view of the country is even now clear and bright."

In presenting this paraphrase, no account has been given of those ambiguous phrases that suggest two or three possible interpretations. Does "as things have been they remain" mean that the struggle will be never-ending? Or that, the struggle being lost, the situation will be exactly what it was before the fight began? Does "but for you" mean that your comrades have completely evicted the enemy and your side *with the exception of you* is in possession of the field? or that your comrades have not chased the enemy clear off, but should have done so *if you had helped*?

We shall not puzzle these questions, but shall encourage the reader to do so. Nor shall we consider the sequence of metaphors implicit in the first two, the third, and the fourth stanzas. Instead, we shall ask some other questions: What struggle is the poet talking about? or what kind of struggle? and who or what are the combatants? . . . Was it war? then, what war? . . . Or was it the fight for freedom of an oppressed people? or the Class Struggle? . . . And who is this man Clough? . . .

But is it right to ask such questions as these? That is, does it make any difference *who* the poet was, or *what* circumstances in his life may have prompted his writing? Shouldn't a poem, or any work of art, stand on its own feet?

It has already been pointed out that words have no meaning in themselves, but only such meaning as they acquire by being put to use in a context, either by writer or by reader. A poem cannot be interpreted in a vacuum; a reader, dispossessed of all experiential memory, would not to able to interpret those strange marks at all! So, the ordinary reader will make use of what background he has in reading a poem. If he happens to know who the poet is, what the general outline of his personality seems to have been, what his environment was, under what circumstances he wrote the poem, *then* the reader will have a context for interpretation that is rich in these particular data. If he doesn't know anything about who wrote the poem and the circumstances of its composition, then the reader will have a context for interpretation that is poor in these particular data.

What difference does it make?

For one type of person the object of the game of reading a poem is simply to make use of the printed verses as the stimulus for *composing his own poem,* enjoying his own independent stream of thoughts on the subject. Now, *if* it makes no difference what direction the stream of the reader's thoughts and feelings takes—as long as it goes places!—then careful interpretation is of no consequence, and reading a poem is in no sense the completion of a communication from the poet.

But there are persons of another type for whom the object of the game of reading a poem is *to achieve an experience as much like that of the poet as possible,* following along *his* stream of thoughts and feelings as nearly as possible. For this sort of reader, careful interpretation of the sense of a poem and the full use of all the available data as part of the context of interpretation are the rules of his game, and they increase markedly the pleasure of his sport. A poem, or any other work of art, is something of a communication from the poet or other artist. And like many a good letter, it takes much reading between the lines and knowledge of the situation and human understanding to get its full message.

Then who is this Clough? And what is the struggle?

Arthur Hugh Clough was an English university student a hundred years ago, a time when many of the ideas that we take for granted in modern thought were just being born. Clough excelled in football and swimming and attained scholastic honors while a student at Rugby, but at Oxford he was caught up in the strong currents of thought and spiritual feeling that were a part of the Oxford Movement which, under John Henry Newman, was bringing a new vitality to the Church of England. Clough failed to fulfill his early promise of intellectual achievement; but, at the age of twenty-four, he was appointed tutor at Oriel College, Oxford. His skepticism, coupled with a life of stern self-discipline, made for a certain aloofness, which covered over the intellectual struggles and emotional conflicts that were shaping his life. He resigned his tutorship and taught in London; spent a year in Cambridge, Massachusetts; returned to England, where he spent the remainder of his short life working in the Education Office. Little did those who were disappointed in this failure to attain eminence realize the extent to which this minor "poet of doubt" really "had conquered the world," as his American friend, Charles Eliot Norton, put it. He had refused to give in to the conventionality and complacency of the early Victorian period; he had thrown overboard his comfortable university connection when it hindered his freedom of thought and expression; he had carried on the struggle as head of University Hall in London. It was following his resignation at Oxford that he wrote "Say Not the Struggle Nought Availeth."

Does not this brief note on the poet make the general meaning of the poem clearer? To answer the question you may wish to turn back to the printed verses and reinterpret them in the light of your enriched context for interpretation. . . .

Have you really reread and reinterpreted Clough's poem? Then let me add one more bit of relevant information: "Say Not the Struggle Nought Availeth" was written in 1849, the year after the Revolutions of 1848, which affected almost every state in Europe, and in which the liberal parties gained control of their governments and began to carry out their programs of reform. By the end of that year and the beginning of the year 1849, however, the forces of reaction were again largely in control, and the revolutionary efforts seemed to have been of no avail. . . . What does this do to your earlier interpretation?

A final word should now be said about the *over-all meaning* of Clough's poem. This will be based upon the running-fire interpretation of the sense of the verses, plus the special thoughts regarding the intention, feeling, and tone phases of the meaning. The overall meaning of the poem will not be the same for any two persons, as the following statements of it will make clear. Two competent critics phrase their general interpretation in this way: "Life is to be faced, not in disillusioned hopelessness, but in courageous endurance, and with a sense of the *whole* human struggle, of which our individual efforts form part." Another pair speak of that note "of confidence in life and in the spirit of man, sounded most buoyantly" in the poem. To one, it is "Clough's 'everlasting yea' to the devil of pessimism and despair." To a second, it conveys "that spirit of doubt, of dismay, and yet of resolution to go forward and endure the struggle which was felt by many of the finer souls of the time." To a third, an English critic writing during the First World War, it gave special "consolation and hope" for that time. *Courageous endurance—confidence—"everlasting yea"—doubt and dismay—consolation and hope!* These quotations suggest notable variations in the general meaning that Clough's poem has had for different experienced readers, professional literary historians. And this may encourage the average reader in his own interpretation.

7. COMMUNICATION OF THE POET'S MEANING

As a final illustration for this chapter, let us undertake a pair of short poems by Robert Browning. They were originally published as one poem called "Night and Morning," the first part headed "I. Night," and the second "II. Morning." [5]

[5] Later they were designated two poems, separately headed but printed in sequence. The headings used for this reprinting are a combination of the original and revised titles.

NIGHT AND MORNING
Robert Browning

MEETING AT NIGHT

1

The grey sea and the long black land;
And the yellow half-moon large and low;
And the startled little waves that leap
In fiery ringlets from their sleep,
As I gain the cove with pushing prow,
And quench its speed i' the slushy sand.

2

Then a mile of warm sea-scented beach;
Three fields to cross till a farm appears;
A tap at the pane, the quick sharp scratch
And blue spurt of a lighted match,
And a voice less loud, thro' its joys and fears,
Than the two hearts beating each to each!

PARTING AT MORNING

Round the cape of a sudden came the sea,
And the sun looked over the mountain's rim:
And straight was a path of gold for him,
And the need of a world of men for me.

(1845)

One question had better be answered at once. The point of view of the first poem is that of the Man, I think most readers will agree. But from whose point of view is the second poem written? From the Woman's, as the "him" in its third line would demand? or from the Man's, as the logic of its relation to the first poem would suggest? To an enquiry about this puzzling line, Browning himself wrote a reply that makes clear his intention: the Man is the speaker in "Parting at Morning"; the "him" (in line 3) refers to the sun. Now reread this second poem and straighten out your thoughts about the sense of it—and then, about the over-all meaning.

Notice that it is only in the titles to the separate poems that the reader is given the "meeting" and "parting" clue to the story thread. A Man (secret lover or husband?) comes, *meets* his beloved, spends the night with her, *parts* from her in the morning, and goes back to "the world of men." The title of a poem will often guide the reader toward its general meaning. The readers of Browning's poems as originally printed and titled surely must have had more trouble with them than we are having now.

Instead of presenting a number of different interpretations of the over-all meaning of this poem (and they *would be* different, make no mistake about that), I shall present Browning's own comment. Only occasionally is such a statement available. In 1889 the members of the Day's End Club of Exeter, studying contemporary literature, were interested in an evening's program on the work of Robert Browning, whose shorter poems were read, paraphrased, and discussed. Several questions of interpretation, raised in this group, were communicated to the poet by one member of the club who had known him. One of the queries concerned the last line of "Parting at Morning"—

> And the need of a world of men for me.

The question was, "Is this an expression by her of her sense of loss of him, or the despairing cry of a ruined woman?"

Browning answered, "Neither: it is *his* confession of how fleeting is the belief (implied in the first part) that such raptures are self-sufficient and enduring—as for the time they appear."

And this is, in the poet's own words, the meaning!

A general question implied earlier in this chapter must finally be asked again: How important *is* it to get the sense of a poem? And some persons might question further, "Doesn't this over-emphasis upon the interpretation of the meaning of a poem destroy the precious thing that it contains?! Surely this intellectual quibbling about the senses of the words stultifies and desiccates what should be essentially an emotional experience!?!"

The question becomes heated and expands in the very asking.

And the cool answer that will be given here is not likely to be accepted by the persons who feel most strongly about it. But, *as I see it,* and as has been said in this and the last two chapters, sense leads the way in the poem-reading-experience. It guides or directs the rest of the psychological activity that makes up the whole poem. On the one hand, it conditions the music and conjures the imagery; on the other hand, it evokes the emotions and develops the residual attitudes, the two final aspects of the poem-experience that will form the substance of the next two chapters.

If the reader gets the "wrong" sense, he will go off in the wrong direction in his experience; and if he can't make any sense of it all, which sometimes happens, he will not go anywhere!

SUGGESTIONS FOR STUDY

1. *Sense Leads the Way.* Restudy the Browning pair of poems, making a special effort to visualize the dramatic scene and incidents.

(a) Draw a map that will objectify the geography. The following questions may help you in reaching certain decisions: At what time of night is the "half moon" low in the eastern sky? in the western sky? at what time in the lunar month? Where must the moon be in relation to the land to make the land seem "black"? Where must the moon be in relation to the boatman if he is to see "the startled little waves"? Where do you imagine the cove to be in relation to the open sea and the mile of sea-scented beach? Does your map allow for the relationship of morning sun and the mountain's rim and open sea requisite for the second poem of the pair?

(b) Do you think that the poet really thought of these things when he was writing the poem? Or that he intuitively "saw" things in proper relation to each other? Or that he recalled scenic relationships from a particular past experience? Or that he was just lucky in not making mistakes? Or that he did trip up on details? Or that he didn't bother about such matter-of-fact things?

2. *A Comparable Problem.* Read the following poem thoughtfully. Let your understanding of the sense of it guide your visual imagery.

MOVE EASTWARD, HAPPY EARTH
Alfred, Lord Tennyson

Move eastward, happy earth, and leave
Yon orange sunset waning slow:

From fringes of the faded eve,
  O, happy planet, eastward go;
Till over thy dark shoulder glow
  Thy silver sister-world, and rise
  To glass herself in dewy eyes
That watch me from the glen below.

Ah, bear me with thee, smoothly borne,
  Dip forward under starry light,
And move me to my marriage-morn,
  And round again to happy night.

                    (1842)

(a) As an aid to your study, answer the following multiple-choice questions. (If no one of the suggested responses seems to you to be satisfactory, jot down what you think would be appropriate.)

1. After first reading the poem, is the *meaning:* (a) perfectly clear to you, (b) clear as to its general idea, (c) obscure at certain points, (d) not clear at all?
2. What direction does the *earth actually rotate:* (a) from west to east, (b) from east to west, or (c) does it actually stand still, as it is the sun which revolves?
3. Does *shoulder* in line 5 suggest (a) that the Sun-god is brawny, (b) that the poet, viewing the rotating earth as from a distance, sees the moonlight creep over the earth's rounded edge or "shoulder," (c) that all is shrouded in darkness until the sun rises again?
4. What is the *silver sister-world:* (a) the planets or one of them, (b) the earth steeped in moonshine, (c) the world of fancy and imagination, (d) the moon?
5. Does *to glass herself in dewy eyes* mean: (a) that the moonlight is mirrored in the tearful or sparkling eyes of the beloved, (b) that the starlight is reflected by the dewdrops of the grass, (c) that the earth is sheathed in the sparkling moonlight?
6. Is a *glen:* (a) a hill, (b) a field, (c) a village, (d) a small valley?
7. Why does the poet want the earth to *bear* him along with it: (a) because he loves the moonlight, (b) because he can't bear to bring tears to the eyes of his beloved, (c) because he is impatient as he awaits his marriage-morn, (d) because he can't get to sleep?
8. What is the *time of day* as the poet writes: (a) afternoon, (b) evening, (c) night, (d) dawn?
9. What is the poem all *about:* (a) the happy anticipation of mar-

riage, (b) the beauties of early morning, (c) the splendor of the moonlight, (d) the glories of the sunset?

10. Which phrase best suggests the poet's *tone* and *feeling:* (a) mocking cynicism, (b) somber reverie; (c) eager love, (d) starry-eyed wonderment?

(b) Give some thought to this poem in relation to your interpretation of "Night and Morning."

3. *Ambiguous Enrichment.* By definition an epigram is a poem both concise and compact. Ben Jonson's "Of Life and Death" was printed with his *Epigrams.* As you read it, observe closely your thoughts of the several senses with which certain of the words may be operating. (a) Make helpful use of appropriate dictionaries, and list the crucial words and various likely senses. The *New English Dictionary* (the so-called Oxford Dictionary) will give you the senses of words in use at a given date. (b) Give some account of those words that you interpret as ambiguous. (c) Take note of any words that may be operating metaphorically. (d) Consider the over-all meaning of the poem.

OF LIFE AND DEATH
Ben Jonson

The ports of death are sins; of life, good deeds;
Through which our merit leads us to our meeds.
How wilful blind is he, then, that would stray,
And hath it in his powers to make his way!
This world death's region is, the other life's;
And here, it should be one of our first strifes,
So to front death, as men might judge us past it:
For good men but see death, the wicked taste it.

(1616)

4. *The Last Word.* In reading Matthew Arnold's "The Last Word," interpret the metaphors with particular care.

THE LAST WORD
Matthew Arnold

Creep into thy narrow bed,
Creep, and let no more be said!
Vain thy onset! all stands fast.
Thou thyself must break at last.

> Let the long contention cease!
> Geese are swans, and swans are geese.
> Let them have it how they will!
> Thou art tired; best be still.
>
> They out-talk'd thee, hiss'd thee, tore thee?
> Better men fared thus before thee;
> Fired their ringing shot and pass'd,
> Hotly charged—and sank at last.
>
> Charge once more, then, and be dumb!
> Let the victors, when they come,
> When the forts of folly fall,
> Find thy body by the wall!

                                            (1867)

(a) Answering the following questions will focus your attention upon certain points in your interpretation.

1. What is the sense of *narrow bed* in line 1: (a) shelter, (b) retirement, (c) grave, (d) the bed you made for yourself—now you can lie in it!?

2. What is the sense of *vain thy onset* in line 3: (a) your attack is futile; (b) it is conceited in you to set yourself above others; (c) your beginning has been worthless?

3. Between whom is *the long contention:* (a) the geese and swans, (b) the "thou" of line 4 and the "them" of line 7, (c) the "better men" of line 10 and the "victors" of line 14?

4. What is the relation of *Geese are swans, and swans are geese* to the line that precedes it: (a) it suggests the futility of "the long contention"; (b) that's what they're arguing about; (c) "they" will continue to confuse geese and swans no matter how you may try to enlighten them; (d) the ugly ducking became a beautiful swan?

5. To whom does the *they* of line 9 refer: (a) the geese and swans, (b) the "better men" of line 10, (c) the "victors" of line 14, (d) the persons contending with "thee"?

6. Who are the *better men:* (a) the persons contending against "thee," (b) men better than "thee," who have lost in other fights, (c) other men better than those who have beaten them, (d) the "victors"?

7. What is the sense of *charged* in line 12: (a) the "better men" charged their foes; (b) the "better men" were charged upon by

their foes; (c) the shot had been rammed into hot muskets or guns; (d) the "better men" were roundly accused during the hot contention?

8. What is the sense of *dumb:* (a) dead, (b) stupid, (c) silent, (d) unreasonable?

9. Who are the *victors:* (a) the ones defending "the forts of folly" against your charge, (b) the "better men" who "fared thus before thee," (c) the persons who, in line 13, are told to "charge," (d) the men who will finally succeed where you have failed?

10. What is the *sense of the title,* "The Last Word": (a) the last straw, (b) the utterance before the fatal charge, (c) a parting word of advice, (d) the final word in the argument, (e) a word from dying lips?

(b) Compare the over-all meaning of "The Last Word" and of Jonson's "Of Life and Death."

5. *Prose Paraphrase.* Interpretation of the following poem by John Donne will call for close application.

LOVE'S DEITY

John Donne

I long to talk with some old lover's ghost,
    Who died before the god of Love was born:
I cannot think that he, who then lov'd most,
    Sunk so low, as to love one which did scorn.
But since this god produc'd a destiny,
And that vice-nature, custom, lets it be;
    I must love her, that loves not me.

Sure, they which made him god, meant not so much,
    Nor he, in his young godhead practis'd it.
But when an even flame two hearts did touch,
    His office was indulgently to fit
Actives to passives. Correspondency
Only his subject was; it cannot be
    Love, till I love her, that loves me.

But every modern god will now extend
    His vast prerogative, as far as Jove.
To rage, to lust, to write to, to commend,
    All is the purlieu of the God of Love.
Oh were we waken'd by this Tyranny

To ungod this child again, it could not be
I should love her, who loves not me.

Rebel and Atheist too, why murmur I,
As though I felt the worst that love could do?
Love might make me leave loving, or might try
A deeper plague, to make her love me too,
Which, since she loves before, I'm loth to see;
Falsehood is worse than hate; and that must be,
If she whom I love, should love me.

(*c. 1595*, 1633)

(a) As an aid to understanding "Love's Deity," study this prose paraphrase of the first stanza in Basic English made by John L. Sweeney.[6]

It would give me great pleasure and comfort to have a talk with some old-time lover whose death took place before the birth of that power which is now ruling over our ways of love. I am certain that he, who in those days was most deeply in love, would not have put such a low value on his love as to give it to someone who had no respect for it—and let his love be laughed at and looked down upon. A man has a very low opinion of himself who puts such a low value on his love. The old-time lover would not have come to this. But because this new government has given us a fixed design controlling the ways of love and because something unnatural in man lets it be so—something which has taken the place of natural impulses and keeps them in its grip—I have to go on loving a woman who has no love for me.

A verse paraphrase, also in Basic English, has been prepared by the same hand:

Talk with some old lover
Dead before Love came to be
Would do my poor heart good. For he
As full of love when living as I am now
Would not have done what I have done,
Have given love to an unkind, unloving one.
But as this ruler Love has made things so,
And ways of men have not till now said "no,"

---

[6] From "Basic in Reading," *Kenyon Review*, winter 1943, p. 56. This article on the use of Basic English as a device for teaching reading, also includes a more complete interpretation of the stanza in the form of an "argument."

No other way I see
But give my love to one
Who has no love for me.

Study these paraphrases carefully, comparing them with the first stanza
of the poem.

(b) Now proceed with a thoughtful interpretation of the second,
third, and fourth stanzas. Jot down the several senses of the possibly
ambiguous words and phrases. As you conclude each stanza, look back
to the final lines of the preceding stanzas.

(c) Write a simple and clear prose or verse paraphrase of the fourth
stanza.

6. *Background for Interpretation.* Words have meaning only in a
context; that is, the surrounding words and the user's vital and verbal
past experiences combine to give meaning to a particular word-symbol.
If the reader's experiences with a certain word are notably different
from the poet's, he will go astray in his interpretation. Archibald Mac-
Leish's poem "The Too-Late Born" will not have much meaning to
the reader whose verbal experience has not included certain reading.
(a) Read this poem and spy out and list the words and phrases for
which you feel your interpretation is not satisfactory. (b) Make such
use of appropriate reference works in the Library as to provide you
with a sufficiently enriched background for interpretation of the poem.
(c) Write a prose paraphrase of "The Too-Late Born," followed by a
discussion of its over-all meaning.

THE TOO-LATE BORN
Archibald MacLeish

We too, we too, descending once again
The hills of our own land, we too have heard
Far off—Ah, que ce cor a longue haleine—
The horn of Roland in the passages of Spain,
The first, the second blast, the failing third,
And with the third turned back and climbed once more
The steep road southward, and heard faint the sound
Of swords, of horses, the disastrous war,
And crossed the dark defile at last, and found
At Roncevaux upon the darkening plain
The dead against the dead and on the silent ground
The silent slain—

(1926)

7. *Meaning, Music, and Imagery.* Again we must remind ourselves that a poem-experience is an integrated whole. Concentration upon one aspect or another (such as the sense phase of the meaning) is valueless unless it finally brings us to a fuller comprehension and appreciation of this unified whole. With such unity in mind, study Edna St. Vincent Millay's "When It Is Over," written during the dark days of 1940. Think of the music and the imagery and the meaning—separately and in relation to each other, and in relation to the whole poem.

WHEN IT IS OVER
Edna St. Vincent Millay

When it is over—for it will be over,
Though we who watched it be gone, watched it and with it died—
Will there be none the less the yellow melilot, the white, the high
    sweet clover,
Close to the dusty, fragrant, hot roadside?
Oh, yes, there will!—
Escaped from fields of fodder, for there must be fodder still.

Ah, yes, but nothing will escape. . . .

Yet sweet, perhaps, in fields of fodder still.

When it is over—for it will be over—
Will there be none the less, will there be still
In April on the southern slope of an orchard, apple orchard hill,
Red-and-white buds already fragrant, intent upon blossoming?—
There will; I know there will.

But for whom will they blossom?—
             They will blossom for what, not whom,
I think:—the streakèd bloom
Red-and-white, and the hardy fragrance, strong, all but visible, almost
    but not quite in sight,
Long, long before its pretty petals in a May wind fall,
Will be the finished apple in the eyes of all beholding it;

I see him well: the human creature studying the only good
A tree can be—stout wood
For building or for pulp whereon to print the expedient thing,
Or, if not that, food.

He walks through the apple orchard just now blossoming,
Dismissing to the necessary, the developing, past
The present beauty and the fragrance enfolding it.

(1941)

8. *Note on "The Racer."* (a) To the writer's enquiry in 1943 about
the meaning of the poem John Masefield graciously responded: "I refer
to the horse, which as it happens was not a race-horse, proper, but a
fine black hunter, running in what we call a Hunt Steeplechase, that
is a gallop over a course of country, for horses which have been ridden
during the season in the local fox-hunt. I was standing near the last
jump of the course, which was a pretty grim thorn-fence, and beyond
it the horses had the Straight running slightly uphill to the winning
post, where a great crowd had gathered; there were, I think, five horses
finishing, and this one I shall never forget. The creature was like a
beast inspired by the sight of the crowd; he cried aloud at it, and
would have won hands down if the worse beast riding him had not
flogged him and made him shut up like a telescope." (b) Masefield
wrote a long narrative poem, entitled "Right Royal," concerning a
steeplechase. It is to be found in Part II of the 1925 edition of his *Poems*.
After reading "Right Royal," consider its relationship to "The Racer."
(c) In the Introduction to Part II of his *Poems,* Masefield wrote: "In
the poem about a steeplechase I was concerned mainly with the idea of
the subtle relation between horse and rider which in moments of excitement, in the race, the hunt, or even the panic, makes them curiously one.
I was also interested in the spiritual nature of contests, in which the
individual souls of the competitors must be swayed, not only by their
own feelings, but by the intensely excited feelings and desires of many
thousands of partisans close by. Sometimes, in watching contests at
which many thousands of spectators have been present, I have felt that
the competing emotions of the partisans almost took spiritual shape
and fought above the competitors." (d) Is it clear to you whether Masefield is here writing about "The Racer" or about "Right Royal"? What
statement in his comment is applicable especially to "Right Royal" and
not to "The Racer"?

8

THE EMOTIONAL RESPONSE
TO POETRY

Regarding the meaning of poetry, it was pointed out that, in addition to the sense of it, there are also tone, feeling, and intention. In the interpretation of a poem, then, one may have thoughts about the feeling or any other separate phase of the full meaning. But pointing out the fact that the poet seems to be wrought-up about his subject is one thing; becoming wrought-up about it oneself is quite another. We have, so far, spoken only of this recognition of feeling as a phase of meaning; we now come to that stir of feeling within the reader, his emotional response, which is, in the opinion of many, the most important part of the poem-experience.

I. COMMUNICATION AND THE POET'S EMOTION

Indeed it may be said—it has already been suggested—that the chief business of all the arts is the communication of emotion. But we shall need to recall what was said in the preceding chapter about the nature of communication (p. 167). Emotion is not something that can be passed from one person to another by means of a poem or a picture or a sonata. There is no *thing* carried across. The poet or other artist is possessed of an emotion; it may be a deep, consuming feeling about some person or thing. Perhaps as a part of his personality adjustment, the poet writes some verses. When his writing is done and he reads over what he has written, he may see in his poem a perfect expression of his thoughts and feelings; and when years later he rereads the lines, he may have that moving experience vividly recalled to him with much of its original anguish or rapture.

But when some other person reads the poem, he may not have an emotional experience in any way comparable to the poet's. He may enjoy the "music" and imagery that are stimulated by it; he may get the sense of it quite completely, and recognize the feeling phase of the meaning; but he may not himself experience any *stir of feeling* within his own being. If this is so, then certainly no communication of emotion has taken place.

However, another particular reader, even though he may be less understanding of the sense of the poem, may experience a very definite *stir of feeling*. If these feelings are somewhat like those of the poet, then communication of emotion may be said to have taken place. But if the reader's feelings are of quite a different sort from the poet's, then certainly the poem has stimulated emotion, but it has not (in our sense) communicated it.

For *the only way in which a printed poem may be said to communicate emotion is by stimulating in the reader an emotional state somewhat akin to that of the poet*. The reader never feels the poet's emotion; he only feels his own emotion, which, according to his temperament and conditioning, may be in some degree comparable to the poet's.

But who shall say just what *the emotional state of the poet* really was? There is not likely to be any clearer record of this than the poem itself, though occasionally, as with the Browning and Masefield poems in the preceding chapter, there may be some data outside of the poem that will provide clues to the feeling phase of the poet's full meaning. As said earlier, however, the reader must be both skillful and sensitive as he undertakes the interpretation of the printed verses.

To illustrate this central problem in the communication of emotion, read the following selection from George Crabbe's long poem *The Village,* and give particular attention to the recognition of the poet's emotion as a phase of the meaning.

from THE VILLAGE
George Crabbe

Thus groan the old, till, by disease oppress'd,
They taste a final wo, and then they rest.
  Theirs is yon house that holds the parish-poor,
Whose walls of mud scarce bear the broken door;
There, where the putrid vapors, flagging, play,
And the dull wheel hums doleful through the day;—
There children dwell who know no parents' care;
Parents who know no children's love, dwell there!
Heartbroken matrons on their joyless bed,
Forsaken wives, and mothers never wed,
Dejected widows with unheeded tears,
And crippled age with more than childhood fears;
The lame, the blind, and, far the happiest they!
The moping idiot and the madman gay.
  Here too the sick their final doom receive,
Here brought, amid the scenes of grief, to grieve,
Where the loud groans from some sad chamber flow,
Mix'd with the clamors of the crowd below;
Here, sorrowing, they each kindred sorrow scan,
And the cold charities of man to man:
Whose laws indeed for ruin'd age provide,
And strong compulsion plucks the scrap from pride;
But still that scrap is bought with many a sigh,
And pride embitters what it can't deny.
  Say ye, oppress'd by some fantastic woes,
Some jarring nerve that baffles your repose;
Who press the downy couch, while slaves advance
With timid eye, to read the distant glance;
Who with sad prayers the weary doctor tease,
To name the nameless ever-new disease;
Who with mock patience dire complaints endure,
Which real pain and that alone can cure;
How would ye bear in real pain to lie,
Despised, neglected, left alone to die?
How would ye bear to draw your latest breath,
Where all that's wretched paves the way for death?

(1783)

There can hardly be any question about how George Crabbe felt in regard to the poorhouse and the miserable creatures there inhabiting. Readers are likely to be in pretty general agreement interpreting the feeling phase of the full meaning of *The Village:* pity for the aged, indigent, and orphans, the crippled, handicapped, and insane—half starved and fully humiliated by the scraps of cold charity forced from the idle rich by the poor laws! The pity, ah, the pity of it! Nor are most readers likely to miss the tone in which Crabbe addresses himself to his intended readers, the comfortable gentry and those of wealth who, in contrast to the destitute, can afford the luxury of hypochondria and enjoy their imaginary ills. With what scorn and contempt he addresses them! What would they do if, like the miserable poor, they had something to cry about? Certainly there are few readers who would say that Crabbe's feeling toward the charity cases is one of indifference or reproach or blame, though such may be the feelings of some of the readers themselves toward the undeserving poor.

But how does the reader come to an understanding of the poet's emotion, the feeling phase of the full meaning? Just as the over-all meaning of a poem was said to be based upon the running-fire interpretation of the sense of the verses, so the over-all emotion attributed to the poet may be thought of as based upon the running-fire interpretation of the feeling phase of the meaning of the verses. Some words are more definitely emotive than others; that is, they carry, for many persons, a charge of emotional meaning. Certain words, also, are used in referring to feeling states or their expression.

> Thus *groan* the old, till, by disease *oppress'd,*
> They *taste* a final *wo,* and then they rest.

The word *groan* here refers to an outward expression of distress or pain, and *wo* refers to a feeling state of affliction, sorrow, or misery. *Oppress'd* does not name an emotional expression or state, but for this reader refers to the condition of being weighted down, brought low, rendered helpless—with an emotional surcharge, however, of desolation. And *taste,* which is here used to convey the idea of experiencing, is loaded in this context with the feeling of bitterness. Nor are the other words—*old, disease, final, rest*—without their share of feeling, all of which is gathered up into the over-all feeling of the poem.

Two further observations, however, must be made about the poet's use of the word *taste:* First, it is somewhat metaphorical, though for many readers perhaps it is a dead metaphor of whose essential equation they are not conscious. Yet the vehicle (for this reader) is "to apperceive by sensations from the taste buds," and the tenor is "to experience and be keenly aware of." Metaphor is often of great importance in the poet's expression of emotion, though not particularly so in this case; and Dr. Richards has said that "the poet's task is constantly (though not only) that of finding ways and means of controlling feeling through metaphor."[1] A second observation about *taste* in this passage: it evokes (in this reader) a strongly gustatory image—the thick brown taste of sickness. And certainly the free-imagery, visual or of whatever other sense, that is evoked by the poet's words will often be a principal means of communicating the poet's feeling.

The reader should look back through the first two dozen lines of the selection, and note the words and phrases that serve in one way or another as clues to the feeling phase of the meaning. Notice the description of the poorhouse suggested by two or three visual details, the smell, the sound, and an enumeration of the sorts of occupant. For each of them there is an essentially emotive comment— the *broken* door, the *putrid* vapor, the *doleful* hum, the *heartbroken* matron, etc.; and together they build up the reader's interpretation of the poet's emotion. How different it is, though, when the poet addresses the pampered rich, "oppress'd by some fantastic [that is, imaginary] woes"! and what a surcharge of feeling is suggested by these lines, which parallel the opening couplet of the selection! For most readers will agree that Crabbe's sympathy with the underprivileged of his day was complemented by his denunciation of complacency among the gentry, the rich, the influential.

[1] I. A. Richards, *Practical Criticism,* Harcourt, Brace, 1930, p. 223.

2. THE EMOTION OF FICTIONAL CHARACTERS

The matter of interpretation becomes more complex when the poem is dramatic rather than lyric. It is assumed that the lyric poet gives expression to his own emotion; whereas the dramatic poet gives expression to the emotions of his fictional characters. Robert Browning in his "Night and Morning" (p. 182) has created, if ever so sketchily, two fictional characters, the Man and the Woman, with a certain relationship to each other, to the time and place, and to the "world of men." Even though the emotions expressed are ultimately based in the poet's knowledge of his own emotional nature, we recognize the feelings of the Man and of the Woman as being those of the dramatic characters, not of the poet himself.

It might be well at this point for us to read another one of Browning's poems, one of his *Dramatic Lyrics,* as a further illustration. Study out the meaning thoughtfully.[2] Then read it aloud in an effort to catch the tones of voice and the feeling of the soliloquizing monk.

SOLILOQUY OF THE SPANISH CLOISTER

Robert Browning

I

Gr-r-r—there go, my heart's abhorrence!
    Water your damned flower-pots, do!
If hate killed men, Brother Lawrence,
    God's blood, would not mine kill you!
What? your myrtle-bush wants trimming?
    Oh, that rose has prior claims—
Needs its leaden vase filled brimming?
    Hell dry you up with its flames!

---

[2] Before you begin to read, look up the following words in your dictionary: *gall, Barbary, corsair, Arian, Manichee, scrofulous, Belial, greengage.* Here are a few notes. *Salve tibi:* Hail to thee, *Text in Galatians:* 5:19-21. *Plena gratiâ, Ave, Virgo:* Hail, Mary, full of grace (an Angelus prayer).

2

At the meal we sit together:
   Salve tibi! I must hear
Wise talk of the kind of weather,
   Sort of season, time of year:
Not a plenteous cork-crop: scarcely
   Dare we hope oak-galls, I doubt:
What's the Latin name for "parsley"?
   What's the Greek name for Swine's Snout?

3

Whew! We'll have our platter burnished,
   Laid with care on our own shelf!
With a fire-new spoon we're furnished,
   And a goblet for ourself,
Rinsed like something sacrificial
   Ere 't is fit to touch our chaps—
Marked with L. for our initial!
   (He-he! There his lily snaps!)

4

Saint, forsooth! While brown Dolores
   Squats outside the Convent bank
With Sanchicha, telling stories,
   Steeping tresses in the tank,
Blue-black, lustrous, thick like horsehairs,
   —Can't I see his dead eye glow,
Bright as 't were a Barbary corsair's?
   (That is, if he'd let it show!)

5

When he finishes refection,
   Knife and fork he never lays
Cross-wise, to my recollection,
   As do I, in Jesu's praise.
I the Trinity illustrate,
   Drinking watered orange-pulp—
In three sips the Arian frustrate;
   While he drains his at one gulp.

6

Oh, those melons? If he's able
  We're to have a feast! so nice!
One goes to the Abbot's table,
  All of us get each a slice.
How go on your flowers? None double?
  Not one fruit-sort can you spy?
Strange!—And I, too, at such trouble,
  Keep them close-nipped on the sly!

7

There's a great text in Galatians,
  Once you trip on it, entails
Twenty-nine distinct damnations,
  One sure, if another fails:
If I trip him just a-dying,
  Sure of heaven as sure as can be,
Spin him round and send him flying
  Off to hell, a Manichee?

8

Or, my scrofulous French novel
  On grey paper with blunt type!
Simply glance at it, you grovel
  Hand and foot in Belial's gripe:
If I double down its pages
  At the woeful sixteenth print,
When he gathers his greengages,
  Ope a sieve and slip it in 't?

9

Or, there's Satan!—one might venture
  Pledge one's soul to him, yet leave
Such a flaw in the indenture
  As he'd miss till, past retrieve,
Blasted lay that rose-acacia
  We're so proud of! *Hy, Zy, Hine*
'St, there's Vespers! *Plena gratiâ
  Ave, Virgo!* Gr-r-r—you swine!

(1842)

There will probably be no great difference among most readers as regards their interpretation of the emotion of the central character of this dramatic monologue: consuming if not actually psychopathic hatred of Brother Lawrence. Yet, as one reader has described it more fully, "the character's words, while they show entire self-approval, at the same time damn him in our eyes as a sly, treacherous, pharisaical, envious, dirty-minded dog." His emotion, as suggested by the poem, is indeed complex, especially when compared to the simplicity of his genial fellow monk, who loves his garden and delights in all good things.

But what is Browning's own emotion, the feeling phase of the full meaning? Does he join with the soliloquizing speaker of this monologue in his detestation? Certainly not, most of us will say. For many readers, Browning stands in the background, as dramatists usually do, and presents his characters objectively, without personal comment. But other readers will interpret the poem as expressing Browning's "dislike and distrust of asceticism," to use DeVane's phrase.[3] Certainly the very choice of subject is a most important clue to Browning's own emotion. Yet perhaps the poet's feeling toward his protagonist is not so much one of hatred or even dislike as it is one of curious interest, the feeling that these strangely different monks are both explicable creatures, both molded by the restrictive environment of monastic life, the one embittered and with gnawing incertitude, the other happily adjusted and with a comforting faith.

Whether this is so or not, and no letter or comment by the poet comes to hand that would verify either interpretation of the poet's feeling, it can certainly be said with assurance that Browning's own emotion in writing "Soliloquy of the Spanish Cloister" was markedly different from that which he attributed to either one of his fictional characters.

3. THE READER'S EMOTIONAL RESPONSE

But let us turn from the recognition of the poet's emotion as a part of the meaning of the poem, to the actual stir of feeling within

[3] William Clyde DeVane, *A Browning Handbook*, Crofts, 1935, p. 103.

the reader. Very often, of course, the reader of a poem simply experiences no feeling at all. He may interpret the full meaning expertly, and identify the poet's feelings as distinct from those which the poet attributes to his fictional characters, but remain unmoved himself. Emotional response to a poem will not come by patient analysis; it will result, if at all, from a different body-chemistry, over which one's critical thought may only, at best, exert some guidance.

In reading Shelley's "Ozymandias" slowly and silently, focus your attention first upon the sense of it, then upon the other phases of the full meaning.

OZYMANDIAS

Percy Bysshe Shelley

I met a traveller from an antique land
Who said: "Two vast and trunkless legs of stone
Stand in the desert. Near them, on the sand,
Half sunk, a shattered visage lies, whose frown,
And wrinkled lip, and sneer of cold command,
Tell that its sculptor well those passions read
Which yet survive, stamped on these lifeless things,
The hand that mocked them and the heart that fed;
And on the pedestal these words appear:
'My name is Ozymandias, king of kings;
Look on my works, ye Mighty, and despair!'
Nothing beside remains. Round the decay
Of that colossal wreck, boundless and bare
The lone and level sands stretch far away."

(1817)

Sometimes this poem is printed under the title "Ozymandias of Egypt." Indeed there was an Egyptian tyrant named Ozymandias; and his colossal statue, bearing a boastful inscription, was reputed to be the largest in the land. Although the general idea of the poem may be clear to you, the central lines are ambiguous and (for some readers) obscure. The following paraphrase may help the reader in developing his own interpretation of the meaning of the poem.

A man, back from a journey to Egypt, said: "In that hot wasteland I saw two stone legs, upright but without body. Near them, half out of view in the sand, I saw the broken face, whose eyes of anger, twisted lip, and smile of cruel authority, were a sign that the stonecutter was fully conscious of the man's evil desires and feelings—which, as they were fixed in this work of art, are still in existence, though the stonecutter whose hand made the copy of them and the king whose heart gave them food are long dead.

"On the stone base are these words: 'My name is Ozymandias; I am King over all kings! You others, take a look at my public buildings—and give up!' Nothing more is to be seen. Round the broken bits of that great stone work, the level sands go off in every direction as far as the eye can see."

Now turn back to the poem itself, and reread it aloud trying to distinguish the voices of the three different speakers: the poet, the traveler, and the ancient tyrant. . . . Are you clear in distinguishing also the feelings of the three characters: the traveler, the sculptor, and the king? What about the feeling phase of the full meaning, the poet's emotion as you surmise it? Glance back for a quick review of Shelley's "Sonnet: England in 1819" (p. 116) and his "Ode to the West Wind" (p. 133). How does Shelley feel about the tyranny of his own time and the cause of human freedom? In what way does reference to these other poems help you to interpret the feeling phase of the meaning of "Ozymandias"? With which of the characters in the poem does the poet identify his own feelings? Reread the poem yet again. . . .

But we have not yet come to the reader's own emotional response to the poem. Was there any stir of your own feelings as you reread it? Or did it leave you cold? And if you did respond emotionally as a part of your reading-experience, what was the nature of your feelings? *Pleasure* in the wide expanse of desert country? or in the thought of heroic sculpture? *Superiority* in recognizing the irony of the tyrant's boast? or in catching the modern parallel of Mussolini and his North African empire? *Humility* in the thought that things temporal will all pass away? that only things spiritual will survive? *Comfort* in the thought that *all* tyrannies finally crumble? that *all* totalitarian dictators are finally overcome by death? *De-*

fiance in taunting contemporary imperialists and monopolists? Or did you feel weariness? boredom? or disgust?

If the stir of feeling within the reader is somewhat comparable to the feeling phase of the full meaning of the poem, as he interprets it, he will judge that communication of emotion has taken place, and the poem-reading-experience may be thought of as most successful in this regard. But if the reader says, "Shelley was in revolt against the tyranny of his day; but that's all been settled, and I'm bored with these radicals," then emotion has not been communicated, and the reading experience has been unsuccessful in this regard.

4. CAUSES OF THE READER'S EMOTION

We come now to the important question: *What causes the stir of feeling within the reader?* But to this question there is no simple answer.

The full meaning of the poem as the reader interprets it, the "music" as it sounds in his mind's-ear, and the visual and other free-imagery that flashes before him—these combine in effecting the reader's emotional response to the poem. Let it again be said that the sense of it, the running-fire thoughts of what the words stand for, leads the way, guiding and informing the whole process; the interpretation of the tone and intention also contributes its share; but it is the feeling phase of the meaning, the recognition of the poet's emotion, that is most important. If the reader not only recognizes but also *understands* the way the poet felt (that is, if it seems right that under the circumstances he should have felt that way), then indeed a responsive chord may be struck in the reader. But another musical analogy is better yet: the string on a musical instrument may be set in vibration directly by bow or hammer stroke, but it will also vibrate sympathetically in the presence of a strong sound of the same wave length to which it is tuned. So man is likely to feel joy in the presence of laughter, and to sorrow where others grieve. And the recognition and understanding of the poet's emotion is likely to stir the sympathetic vibration of the reader's own feelings.

This understanding of the poet's emotion will be dependent upon the reader's emotional experiences and nature. The reader's own past and present desires and ambitions and longings, whether ultimately frustrated or fulfilled, his own body and actions and thoughts, provide the basis for understanding the emotional experiences of the poet. However, the reader is likely to be most deeply stirred when the poet's feelings, as he understands them, closely parallel or recall his own especially poignant experiences of heightened emotion, which are thereupon revived, often with something of their earlier pain or piquancy.

Trailing along with the senses of words will come the reader's affective response to them, for verbal experiences of each reader provide words not only with certain senses but also with certain feelings. These fleeting feelings that tag along are sometimes called the connotation of words, as opposed to their denotations, and they are often a part of what we called tone-color, the relationship of the sounds of words to their sense in a particular utterance. This suggestive power of particular words has a cumulative effect in developing the emotional response of the reader to a poem.

But other phases of the "music" of a poem will also play a part in stirring the reader's feelings. The poetic rhythm, that subtle interplay of metrical expectancy and semantic insistency,—the melody and its tempo, its rushing and lingering,—is not only affected by the reader's feelings, but also affects them, as does the sound pattern, alliteration and assonance.

Certainly one of the most powerful stimuli of emotion will be the free imagery, not only the pictures in the mind's-eye but the tastes and smells and sounds stimulated in the reader's consciousness. But the causes of an individual reader's emotional response to a particular poem are likely to be highly complex, as the reader's close study of his own experience of the following sonnet will doubtless show.

LONDON, 1802

William Wordsworth

Milton! thou shouldst be living at this hour:
England hath need of thee: she is a fen
Of stagnant waters: altar, sword, and pen,
Fireside, the heroic wealth of hall and bower,

Have forfeited their ancient English dower
Of inward happiness. We are selfish men;
O, raise us up, return to us again;
And give us manners, virtue, freedom, power!
Thy soul was like a Star, and dwelt apart:
Thou hadst a voice whose sound was like the sea:
Pure as the naked heavens, majestic, free,
So didst thou travel on life's common way,
In cheerful godliness; and yet thy heart
The lowliest duties on herself did lay.

(*1802*, 1807)

Each person can only speak at firsthand of his own experience; and it must by now be clear to the reader that the communication of emotion is by no means sure or simple, which is quite as true of the critic's explanation as of the poem itself. Yet a brief description of this particular reader's emotional response to "London, 1802" may serve to illustrate the above paragraphs.

My own efforts to understand the poem may be suggested by the following paraphrase, in which I have tried to symbolize the sense of the poem, my thoughts of what the words stand for:

Wordsworth, writing in London in the year 1802, said, as though to the spirit of the dead Milton: If you were but living again, in this very hour! England has need of you, for things are in a bad way. England is like a stretch of quiet water topped with dirty green and with the smell of death. Church and army, arts and letters, fireside and landed families—they have all given up their English birthright, the spirit of holy joy. We are men of self-interest. Oh, give us a needed lift; come back to us again. Give us once more our old ways, gentle and noble; good hearts, free lives, strong minds. Your soul was like a star, off by itself. You had a voice whose sound was like the sea. Clean as the unclouded sky, great and free, you went through life a good and happy man; but at the same time you undertook the common work at hand.

So this close attention to the sense of it leads me to a consideration of Wordsworth's feeling. He seems to me to be discouraged about his homeland, its spirit and tone. Life about him seems corrupt and lethargic. People are selfish, complacent, indifferent. He thinks of other times when Englishmen were strong and true, noble and courageous; and he thinks of John Milton, poet and patriot, who spoke out fearlessly and clearly for human freedom, who acted wisely and cheerfully, who turned his hand to common work dutifully and unselfishly. If only, the poet feels, Milton were now alive to rally them, to raise them up from the morass of their stagnation, to restore the virtues that Englishmen should rightly inherit from their stalwart forebears!

And my understanding of Wordsworth's feeling is furthered by a note which I find for his preceding sonnet "Written in London, September, 1802," a note in which he describes how, when he returned from a visit to France, he was struck by "the vanity and parade of our own country, especially in the great towns and cities, as contrasted with the quiet, and I may say the desolation, that the revolution had produced in France." And he goes on: ". . . with what depth of feeling I entered into the struggle carried on by the Spaniards for their deliverance from the usurped power of the French." So the poet's feeling was one of discouragement that his own inherently freedom-loving people should stand idly by without regard for, let alone help for, the desolate and the oppressed peoples on the continent.

If these paragraphs present my interpretation of the feeling phase of Wordsworth's meaning, what of my own emotional response?

I too am stirred by a feeling of deep gloom, not for a stagnant England in 1802, but for my own complacent land in this hour, unscathed by the immediate ravages of war, enjoying a full larder and undiminished creature comfort with little regard for a world laid waste, a world whose millions are still desolate and oppressed! And I too am stirred by the feeling that great men, great voices of other ages might, if they were now with us, speak out bold and clear, to rouse us to our own duty to these times.

It is clear from this description of my own emotional response that my feelings are by no means identical with those that I attribute to Wordsworth. For one thing, I am apparently not so deeply stirred by Milton's work at this moment, and my feelings are obviously the outgrowth of a markedly different experience— I have not just come from France in 1802, but I have lived through the years of World War II. Yet I believe that it would be agreed that my emotional response is somewhat akin to what I judge to have been the poet's feeling, and that communication of emotion has taken place.

It still remains, however, to speak briefly of the *causes* of my emotional response to this poem. My interpretation of the meaning, of course, is the primary cause, and sense led the way together with my understanding of the poet's feeling. His feeling of discouragement at the surrounding complacency struck a responsive chord; or, to vary the metaphor, the strings of my own heart, attuned by comparable experiences, were set in sympathetic vibration by the sounding of his emotion. But there were other immediate stimuli of my feelings: the striking metaphor implicit in the assertion that England is a *fen,* the strong olfactory imagery stimulated by *stagnant,* the rich connotation of *hall and bower,* the tone-color of the *voice whose sound was like the sea,* even the stately Miltonic "music" of the poetic rhythm, suggesting the power of the great poets of the past.

Having illustrated the various causes of my own emotional response to this poem, it is not necessary to particularize them further, but only to add that no matter how careful the reader's introspection may be, he is not likely to uncover all of the hidden causes of his emotional response.

5. THE PROBLEM OF COMMUNICATION

The problem of communication of emotion is relatively easy to deal with in regard to Wordsworth's sonnet, whose meaning is in no sense really obscure. But sometimes difficulties of interpretation stand in the way. The sense of a poem, which at first glance may look clear enough, often eludes the reader when he begins to interpret it closely. As sense is rather expected to lead the way, the reader may flounder in his interpretation of the poet's feeling if and when the sense is or seems to be a bit obscure.

Read this next poem thoughtfully a number of times.

THE ROAD NOT TAKEN
Robert Frost

Two roads diverged in a yellow wood,
And sorry I could not travel both
And be one traveler, long I stood
And looked down one as far as I could
To where it bent in the undergrowth;

Then took the other, as just as fair,
And having perhaps the better claim,
Because it was grassy and wanted wear;
Though as for that the passing there
Had worn them really about the same,

And both that morning equally lay
In leaves no step had trodden black.
Oh, I kept the first for another day!
Yet knowing how way leads on to way,
I doubted if I should ever come back.

I shall be telling this with a sigh
Somewhere ages and ages hence:
Two roads diverged in a wood, and I—
I took the one less traveled by,
And that has made all the difference.

(1915)

Do you believe that the poet's feeling was one of self-reproach
at having made a wrong choice, at having taken the "low road'
of life? Or is the poet sad because he chose the unpopular course,
less traveled by man, and is now lonely? Or is he troubled because
all choices are irrevocable, and man can never go back to the moment of past decision? Or is he heavy of heart because he realizes
that, as "way leads on to way," we can't see ahead or tell where our
choices may lead us? Or is he wistful, wondering where he would
now be, and what experiences he would have had, if he had traveled "the road not taken"?

This series of questions suggests that, though many readers will attribute to Robert Frost somewhat different emotions, a number of them will take a cue from the poet's "telling this with a sigh," interpreting the poet's feeling as being some sort of regret regarding "the road not taken."

Of this "much-quoted and much-misunderstood poem," Louis Untermeyer writes the following commentary:[4]

Once while traveling alone, Frost tells us, he stood at a fork in the road, undecided which path to take. Finally, he chose one because it seemed a little less frequented, though actually there was no such difference, for "the passing there had worn them really about the same." Yet, even at the moment of choice, the poet quizzically imagined that the choice was important, that he would someday tell himself he took the less traveled road:

> And this had made all the difference.

The poet's "difference" is in him from the beginning, long before he sets out on his career. The road that Robert Frost took was not only the "different" road, the right road for him, but the only road he could have taken.

But Robert Frost may not have drawn upon his first-hand experience at all, as this interpretation assumes. John Holmes writes me: "I have it from Frost personally that 'The Road Not Taken' was not written about himself—he is not like that. It is a description of his friend Edward Thomas, a poet whom he knew in England about 1915 or a little earlier."

Certainly Louis Untermeyer in his discussion of "The Road Not Taken" (an authorized commentary, issued by the poet's regular publishers) was unaware of the poet's expressed remark that the poem was not written about himself. Recognizing that the poem is much misunderstood, the critic proceeded to misunderstand it yet again and in yet another way, and attributes to the poet personal feelings that are inconsistent with what is now known about the poem's origin, the poet's observation of another person. It can thus be seen how difficult it is for the reader to be sure that he is really

[4] Louis Untermeyer, ed., Robert Frost's *Come In and Other Poems,* Henry Holt, 1943, p. 162.

interpreting the poet's feeling correctly. He will need to take into account all of the clues within the poem itself, and make use of all other relevant data; he will need to couple shrewdness with sensitiveness, skill with insight, and then hope with humility that his interpretation has not gone astray.

And if the poet's feeling is at times thus difficult to ascertain, what a problem it is to determine whether communication of emotion has actually taken place; that is, whether the reader's emotion is actually comparable to the poet's.

6. STOCK RESPONSE AND SENTIMENTALITY

Reading the next poem will carry us a step further.

MAKE BELIEVE
Alice Cary

Kiss me, though you make believe;
  Kiss me, though I almost know
You are kissing to deceive:
  Let the tide one moment flow
Backward ere it rise and break,
Only for poor pity's sake!

Give me of your flowers one leaf,
  Give me of your smiles one smile,
Backward roll this tide of grief
  Just a moment, though, the while,
I should feel and almost know
You are trifling with my woe.

Whisper to me sweet and low;
  Tell me how you sit and weave
Dreams about me, though I know
  It is only make believe!
Just a moment, though 'tis plain
You are jesting with my pain.

(1850)

The reading of this poem may well raise two questions about emotional response. The first concerns the reader's feelings; and the second, the poet's.

If, when you began reading—"Kiss me . . . kiss me . . . Give me of your flowers . . . Give me of your smiles . . . Whisper to me . . . Tell me how you sit and weave/ Dreams about me . . . Just a moment . . ."—if as you read the phrases, you felt that deep stirring of desire for affection that is such a universal human emotion, yours is what we shall call a *stock response* to the poem. The opening words, "Kiss me," are sufficient stimulus for some readers, prompting them to make a ready-to-wear response to the poem; they turn on the emotional tap, to change the metaphor, and let the water run hot. Indeed it may be hard not to be carried away upon a flood of such emotion, for all the world loves a lover. If the reader makes a stock response to a poem, he will be responding to only one factor of a complicated stimulus without regard to the other factors. He will then proceed to *create his own poem,* often with utter disregard for the sense of what he is reading. "Make Believe," then, will elicit a stock response from some readers.

But others will respond quite differently, and feel genuine longing for past affections, or desire for love that is true and lasting, or smug superiority toward Victorian sentimentality, or disdain for the weak who cannot command constancy, or disgust at such craven display of emotional inadequacy! Or the reader may feel no emotional response at all to this poem.

There is a second question, concerning the feeling that the reader attributes to the poet. As you read "Make Believe," did you think that Alice Cary really meant what her words seem to say? The sense of it will be clear enough for most readers: "Give me your kisses, even though you have no more love for me." Does she really want the husks of love? deceptive tenderness? false kisses? For this is what she leads me, at any rate, to believe. Or does she really mean, "Backward, turn backward, O Time, in your flight," so that she may once more enjoy the real love now past? And who has not looked back over his shoulder for a wistful glance at past pleasures, friendships, love? to some fork, some road not taken? But that would be a different poem. "Make Believe" seems to me to be essentially *insincere;* the poet's feeling is not genuine; it does not ring true. It is not only false, however, it is (as I interpret it) excessive. If she really wants an empty kiss only to remind her of past moments of real affection, then her rhapsodizing of the means seems disproportionate. "Kiss me though you make believe," though you deceive, trifle, jest! Such overabundance of feeling on the part of the poet we shall call *sentimentality,* but the word is just as applicable to excessive emotion on the part of the reader.

Some readers, of course, will prefer their ready-made stock responses, or excessively sentimental responses, to the poems that they read. But their pleasure and profit from reading will be limited by the narrow range of their habitual feelings and by an undiscriminating intensity; and all poem-experiences are likely to have, for them, the same brown gravy or vanilla flavor.

But the reader who wants to get the most out of poetry, will want to have communicated to him, in the only way that can be done, the particular emotion of the poet. It is the sense of the poem that must lead the way, so that the feelings that are spontaneously stirred may be transmuted and shaped, becoming feelings that are something like those of the poet. And this will take careful and sensitive interpretation.

7. SUMMARY AND ILLUSTRATION

Let us summarize briefly the chief points of this chapter before presenting a final poem:

1. *Communication of emotion* takes place in reading poetry when the emotional state or feeling evoked in the reader is somewhat like that of the poet.

2. The *feelings of the poet* can only be deduced by thoughtful interpretation of the poem, and must be distinguished from the feelings that he may attribute to fictional characters. The poet's feelings may be (a) either genuine or insincere, and (b) either restrained or sentimental.

3. The *feelings stirred in the reader* may be
   (a) *inappropriate* because they are either
      (1) a stock response to the poem, or

(2) a sentimental response to the poem; or they may be

(b) *appropriate* because they are either

(1) akin to the poet's feelings [*communication of emotion has taken place*], or

(2) not like, but in harmony with, the poet's.

And now for the poem.

TO AN ATHLETE DYING YOUNG

A. E. Housman

The time you won your town the race
We chaired you through the market-place;
Man and boy stood cheering by,
And home we brought you shoulder-high.

Today, the road all runners come,
Shoulder-high we bring you home,
And set you at your threshold down,
Townsman of a stiller town.

Smart lad, to slip betimes away
From fields where glory does not stay,
And early though the laurel grows
It withers quicker than the rose.

Eyes the shady night has shut
Cannot see the record cut,
And silence sounds no worse than cheers
After earth has stopped the ears:

Now you will not swell the rout
Of lads that wore their honors out,
Runners whom renown outran
And the name died before the man.

So set, before its echoes fade,
The fleet foot on the sill of shade,
And hold to the low lintel up
The still-defended challenge-cup.

And round that early-laureled head
Will flock to gaze the strengthless dead,
And find unwithered on its curls
The garland briefer than a girl's.

(1896)

SUGGESTIONS FOR STUDY

1. *Meaning and Emotion*. What was your emotional response to A. E. Housman's poem, "To an Athlete Dying Young"?

(a) The untimely death, from whatever cause, of young people is likely to stir feelings in each one of us. We have all had friends or acquaintances—just coming into the fullness of life, with everything ahead of them, strong in body, alert of mind, pleasing as to person—whose lives have been cut short by fatal sickness, accident, or war. Why, we ask, should this be? Why should the freshness of his glance, the friendly warmth of his smile, his powerful symmetry, his activity, courage, drive, and all those things that make a man of him—why should this life, not half spent yet, be wasted? . . .

If your emotional response has been something like that suggested in this paragraph, it would be called a stock response because you are reading a meaning into the poem that is contrary to the poet's intention as more carefully interpreted.

(b) Whatever the nature of your response, turn back to the poem, and reinterpret it carefully, stanza by stanza, line by line. (1) Does the first stanza evoke a clear image? (2) Is the contrast between the first and second stanza clear? *Today:* take a cue from the title. *The road:* try another metaphor, "the course of life." *Home:* his parents' home? his grave? or the Land of the Dead? *Threshold:* doorstep of his home? edge of the grave? doorsill to the gate of Hades? *Town:* home town again? or Hades? *Stiller:* out of respect for the dead? or out of indifference, as he is not now a winner? or because the dead cannot speak? (3) Note the *smart lad* in direct address, a transition to the next stanzas. *Betimes:* early? swiftly? *Fields:* athletic competition? all life? *The laurel:* a foliage used to crown winning athletes in ancient Greece? symbol of fame and honor? *Withers:* laurel blossoms wither readily? athletic honors are soon forgotten? *The rose:* symbol of physical freshness? youth? beauty? (4) *The shady night:* death. *Silence:* of the dead? of the living who cheered him when he was winning? (5) *Swell:* increase. *Rout:* confused retreat? uproar? crowd? *To wear out:* outlast. (6) *Its echoes:* of his name? of his reputation? of his footfall? *Sill of shade:* edge of the grave? threshold of Hades? *Lintel:* beam over a doorway. *Low* lintel: to suggest entrance to the

Underworld? the athlete's height? the depth of the grave? (7) *Strengthless* dead: because the dead athletes who greet him outlived their prime? because all the dead are without strength? *Garland:* the crown of laurel. *Briefer* than a girl's: the laurel normally withers sooner than the rose which a girl might twine in her hair? fame usually fades before beauty?

(c) What, after careful rereading, do you consider to be Housman's feeling? Does he really feel that the athlete was lucky to have died young while he was still at the top—lucky that he, who had been acclaimed by his home town, didn't live to be an athletic has-been? Or is it possible that this is merely Housman's ironic way of expressing his very real feeling of loss and misfortune? Or is it an elaborate rationalization, an acceptance of things as they are?

(d) Reconsider your own emotional response to the poem. To what extent is it appropriate? To what extent do you think that the poet's emotion has been communicated?

(e) Turn back to A. E. Housman's "The Lads in Their Hundreds" (p. 98). Reread it carefully. Then write a short paper in which you compare the emotional aspect of your experience of the two Housman poems.

2. *The Causes of Emotional Response.* The poem here presented for close study is in marked contrast to others in this chapter.

CHICAGO
Carl Sandburg

Hog Butcher for the World,
Tool Maker, Stacker of Wheat,
Player with Railroads and the Nation's Freight Handler;
Stormy, husky, brawling,
City of the Big Shoulders:

They tell me you are wicked and I believe them, for I have seen your
    painted women under the gas lamps luring the farm boys.
And they tell me you are crooked and I answer: Yes, it is true I have
    seen the gunman kill and go free to kill again.
And they tell me you are brutal and my reply is: On the faces of
    women and children I have seen the marks of wanton hunger.
And having answered so I turn once more to those who sneer at this
    my city, and I give them back the sneer and say to them:
Come and show me another city with lifted head singing so proud to
    be alive and coarse and strong and cunning.

Flinging magnetic curses amid the toil of piling job on job, here is a
    tall bold slugger set vivid against the little soft cities;
Fierce as a dog with tongue lapping for action, cunning as a savage
    pitted against the wilderness,
        Bareheaded,
        Shoveling,
        Wrecking,
        Planning,
        Building, breaking, rebuilding,
Under the smoke, dust all over his mouth, laughing with white teeth,
Under the terrible burden of destiny laughing as a young man laughs,
Laughing even as an ignorant fighter laughs who has never lost a
    battle,
Bragging and laughing that under his wrist is the pulse, and under
    his ribs the heart of the people,
                                    Laughing!
Laughing the stormy, husky, brawling laughter of Youth, half-naked,
    sweating, proud to be Hog Butcher, Tool Maker, Stacker of
    Wheat, Player with Railroads and Freight Handler to the Nation.
                                                            (1914)

(a) Review the paragraphs in the text on the causes of the reader's
emotion.

(b) Reread "Chicago" giving particular attention to those fleeting
feelings that tag along with the senses of the words. To what extent
does the connotation of the words contribute to your emotional response as an aspect of the whole poem?

(c) Read the poem aloud and slowly, savoring the verses for their
"music"—the poetic rhythm and the sound pattern. To what extent
does the sound of the poem in the mind's-ear condition the stir of your
feelings?

(d) Glance through the poem yet again attending to the free
imagery. What various sorts of sensory imagery do you note? To what
extent are the successive images responsible for your affective response
to "Chicago"?

(e) At last consider the over-all meaning as you interpret it. Have
you lived in the Windy City? or visited it, or read about it? Or do
you know some other great metropolis? What feelings do you attribute
to Sandburg—that is, what is the feeling phase of the full meaning?
To what extent do these seem to cause your own stir of feeling?

3. *A Garner of Rosebuds.* A. E. Housman juxtaposed the symbols
of "laurel" and "rose." Burns likened his love or beloved to a "red,

red rose." Here is another well-known poem that uses the rose as a symbol.

TO THE VIRGINS, TO MAKE MUCH OF TIME
Robert Herrick

Gather ye rosebuds while ye may,
　　Old Time is still a-flying;
And this same flower that smiles today
　　Tomorrow will be dying.

The glorious lamp of heaven, the Sun,
　　The higher he's a-getting,
The sooner will his race be run,
　　And nearer he's to setting.

That age is best which is the first,
　　When youth and blood are warmer;
But being spent, the worse and worst
　　Times still succeed the former.

Then be not coy, but use your time;
　　And while ye may, go marry;
For having lost but once your prime,
　　You may forever tarry.

(1648)

(a) There are few difficulties here as regards the sense for most readers. Have you noted the analogies of the first three stanzas: the rose *bud,* morning, youth? What is a *worse* time than youth? the *worst* time of all? What is the sense of *coy* for you here? And surely the over-all meaning, also, will be rather similar for most readers— the sense, intention, tone, and feeling.

(b) Turn to a standard reference work, preferably the *Dictionary of National Biography,* for an account of the life of Robert Herrick (1591-1674). Reread the poem, and note how your interpretation of it changes —particularly the intention, tone, and feeling phases of the meaning.

(c) Many poets have given expression to comparable feelings, using the rose to symbolize youthful love. The following stanza comes from Edmund Spenser's *The Faerie Queene* (II, xii, 75).

So passeth, in the passing of a day,
　　Of mortal life the leaf, the bud, the flower;

No more doth flourish after first decay
That erst was sought to deck both bed and bower
Of many a lady and many a paramour.
Gather therefore the rose whilst yet is prime,
For soon comes age that will her pride deflower;
Gather the rose of love whilst yet is time,
Whilst loving thou mayst lovèd be with equal crime.

(1590)

And Pierre de Ronsard (into whose mouth Browning put his version of "The Glove") sang a somewhat similar refrain. Perhaps you can read the French, and may wish to make a translation for those who can't.[5]

QUAND VOUS SEREZ BIEN VIEILLE
Pierre de Ronsard

Quand vous serez bien vieille, au soir, à la chandelle,
Assise auprès du feu, dévidant et filant,
Direz, chantant mes vers, en vous émerveillant:
    «Ronsard me célébrait du temps que j'étais belle.»
Lors vous n'aurez servante oyant telle nouvelle,
Déjà sous le labeur à demi sommeillant,
Qui au bruit de Ronsard ne s'aille réveillant,
Bénissant votre nom de louange immortelle.
Je serai sous la terre, et fantôme sans os;
Par les ombres myrteux je prendrai mon repos;
Vous serez au foyer une vieille accroupie,
    Regrettant mon amour et votre fier dédain.
Vivez, si m'en croyez, n'attendez à demain;
Cueillez dès aujourd'hui les roses de la vie.

(1578)

4. *Dramatic Emotions.* Amy Lowell's "Patterns" is somewhat like the dramatic monologues of Robert Browning; it reveals the thoughts and feelings of a character in a dramatic situation.

[5] Translations of this sonnet, addressed to Hélène de Surgères, have been made by Andrew Lang, William A. Drake, William Butler Yeats, Morris Bishop, and others.

PATTERNS

Amy Lowell

I walk down the garden-paths,
And all the daffodils
Are blowing, and the bright blue squills.
I walk down the patterned garden-paths
In my stiff, brocaded gown.
With my powdered hair and jeweled fan,
I too am a rare
Pattern. As I wander down
The garden-paths.

My dress is richly figured,
And the train
Makes a pink and silver stain
On the gravel, and the thrift
Of the borders.
Just a plate of current fashion,
Tripping by in high-heeled, ribboned shoes.
Not a softness anywhere about me,
Only whalebone and brocade.
And I sink on a seat in the shade
Of a lime tree. For my passion
Wars against the stiff brocade.
The daffodils and squills
Flutter in the breeze
As they please.
And I weep;
For the lime tree is in blossom
And one small flower has dropped upon my bosom.

And the plashing of waterdrops
In the marble fountain
Comes down the garden-paths.
The dripping never stops.
Underneath my stiffened gown
Is the softness of a woman bathing in a marble basin,
A basin in the midst of hedges grown

So thick, she cannot see her lover hiding,
But she guesses he is near,
And the sliding of the water
Seems the stroking of a dear
Hand upon her.
What is Summer in a fine brocaded gown!
I should like to see it lying in a heap upon the ground.
All the pink and silver crumpled up on the ground.

I would be the pink and silver as I ran along the paths,
And he would stumble after,
Bewildered by my laughter.
I should see the sun flashing from his sword-hilt and the buckles
    on his shoes.
I would choose
To lead him in a maze along the patterned paths,
A bright and laughing maze for my heavy-booted lover.
Till he caught me in the shade,
And the buttons of his waistcoat bruised my body as he clasped me,
Aching, melting, unafraid.
With the shadows of the leaves and the sundrops,
And the plopping of the waterdrops,
All about us in the open afternoon—
I am very like to swoon
With the weight of this brocade,
For the sun sifts through the shade.

Underneath the fallen blossom
In my bosom
Is a letter I have hid.
It was brought to me this morning by a rider from the Duke.
"Madam, we regret to inform you that Lord Hartwell
Died in action Thursday se'nnight."
As I read it in the white, morning sunlight,
The letters squirmed like snakes.
"Any answer, Madam?" said my footman.
"No," I told him.
"See that the messenger takes some refreshment.
No, no answer."
And I walked into the garden,

Up and down the patterned paths,
In my stiff, correct brocade.
The blue and yellow flowers stood up proudly in the sun,
Each one.
I stood upright too,
Held rigid to the pattern
By the stiffness of my gown;
Up and down I walked,
Up and down.

In a month he would have been my husband.
In a month, here, underneath this lime,
We would have broke the pattern;
He for me, and I for him,
He as Colonel, I as Lady,
On this shady seat.
He had a whim
That sunlight carried blessing.
And I answered, "It shall be as you have said."
Now he is dead.

In Summer and in Winter I shall walk
Up and down
The patterned garden-paths
In my stiff, brocaded gown.
The squills and daffodils
Will give place to pillared roses, and to asters, and to snow.
I shall go
Up and down
In my gown.
Gorgeously arrayed,
Boned and stayed.
And the softness of my body will be guarded from embrace
By each button, hook, and lace.
For the man who should loose me is dead,
Fighting with the Duke in Flanders,
In a pattern called a war.
Christ! What are patterns for?

(1916)

(a) In a first reading of "Patterns" try to straighten out your thoughts of the sense of it. If necessary, look these words up in your dictionary: *squill, brocade, whalebone, maze, boned, stayed*. Who is the *Duke:* Marlborough (1650-1722) or Wellington (1769-1852)? The former was victorious at Audenarde in Flanders in 1708; the latter at Waterloo near Flanders in 1815. What are some clues within the poem that may help you to decide which Duke, and therefore the historic period? Does the historic period make any difference in your understanding of the character and her feelings?

(b) Consider the dramatic situation: the Lady who thinks the stream of thoughts that form the substance of the poem, her relation to Lord Hartwell (the Colonel), their love and engagement, the news of his death, her physical and emotional response to it.

(c) The poem is entitled "Patterns." What is the relation of the title to the Lady's emotion? What are the poet's feelings as you distinguish them from the Lady's? What do you consider to be the over-all meaning of the poem?

(d) Do you experience any stirring of your own feelings as you read the poem? If so, how would you describe it?

5. *Emotional Response.* While reading "The Pulley" by George Herbert, try to keep the central image clear and distinct.

THE PULLEY
George Herbert

When God at first made man,
Having a glass of blessings standing by,
"Let us," said He, "pour on him all we can;
Let the world's riches, which dispersèd lie,
    Contract into a span."

So strength first made a way,
Then beauty flowed, then wisdom, honor, pleasure;
When almost all was out, God made a stay,
Perceiving that, alone of all His treasure,
    Rest in the bottom lay.

"For if I should," said He,
"Bestow this jewel also on My creature,
He would adore My gifts instead of Me,
And rest in Nature, not the God of Nature;
    So both should losers be.

"Yet let him keep the rest,
But keep them with repining restlessness;
Let him be rich and weary, that at least
If goodness lead him not, yet weariness
May toss him to My breast."

(1633)

(a) Note the shifting sense of *rest* as the word is used in three places. One sense of *toss* is "to be restless when trying to sleep"; another is "to fling, lift up, or raise with a sudden sharp motion." *Span:* limited space, the glass beaker. *Made a way:* moved, poured out. *Stay:* a stop. *Repining:* languishing, discontented. Notice the opposition of *Nature* and *God of nature.*

(b) What is the over-all meaning of the poem as you interpret it? What, specifically, seems to you to be the feeling of the poet? Do you experience any emotional response as part of the poem? If so, what is its nature and intensity? Do you consider it an appropriate response? closely akin to the poet's feeling, or merely harmonious with it?

(c) Write a two-page paper in which you give consideration to the music, imagery, meaning, and emotion of this poem.

9

RESIDUUM OF THE
POEM-EXPERIENCE

We are the product, not alone of our heritage, but of our experiences. We are what we are, in large measure, because of what we have been through. There is no such thing as traveling life's road unchanged. Having taken one fork, rather than another, does make "all. the difference." Each of us is constantly being affected, in one way or another, by all the events of which we are a part, by the things we do, by the thoughts we think, by the emotions we feel. Not least important of these events are the art-experiences we enjoy. We shall never be quite the same after standing in awe before the Lincoln Memorial, or after contemplating the powerful frescoes of Rockefeller Center, or after sweeping along with Tschaikowsky's *Fourth Symphony*. We will never look with the same eyes upon our fellow creatures if we have watched Iago's villainy and Othello's tragic downfall, if we have read the character of Becky Sharp out of *Vanity Fair,* if we have been moved to suffer with the Lady of "Patterns."

But if you think back, you may actually not *recall* more than a handful of the poems of your childhood; and the poems of your school days may be buried out of sight and out of mind. And what you do recall may be no more than mere *scraps of remembrance:* the lilt and go of some nursery rime, a single image that may come back on occasion, a faintly lingering feeling, a phrase or verse, a title and author, a neat moral pointed by parent or pedagogue, and perhaps some single whole poem once committed to memory.

He who would consciously prod about in the recesses of his mind may soon discover how devious are the mnemonic avenues of association that may bring back to him other remnants of past events that have apparently been forgotten. For poems are filed away in the vaults of remembrance, or pressed within one's book of precious memories, or crumpled up in the hidden wastebasket of the brain—some never to be found even when rummaged for.

Perhaps the poem-reading-experiences that leave the greatest residue are those that have been rich and full. The weak poems that result from a casual reading, from an indifferent perusal of the verses, will leave only unnoticeable traces. On the other hand, that poem which has resulted from open-hearted, full-throated, wide-awake, sensitive reading by a person who is curious to taste life and eager to share in the significant thoughts and emotions of others— that poem in which communication of meaning and emotion has taken place and which has somehow spoken directly to the needs of the reader—that poem may well deposit its riches where they will remain at work and on demand in the counting-house of the mind.

I. RESIDUAL ATTITUDES

This chapter, called "Residuum of the Poem-Experience" and discussing the sixth aspect of the poem, will have to distinguish the more easily discernible residue, the things that may consciously be pulled out of the mind for a quiz or literary small-talk, from the subtle changes that the poem-experience may effect in the unconscious reaches of the reader's personality. These changes, remaining long after the poem has been forgotten, may be thought of in terms of personal *attitudes*.

We do not react fully to all of the stimuli present to our sensory systems. We should go mad, for instance, were we even to be sensible of all the patterns of light coming into our eyes, all the sound waves striking our ears, all the smells, all the feels! (1) To a few of these things we give our attention consciously, and respond. (2) To certain of them we respond somewhat automatically and sub-consciously—scratch an itch or bat an eye. (3) To other ones we subconsciously assume an *attitude,* a readiness to respond if need arises. (4) To yet other stimuli we do not respond at all, nor do we make any preparation to respond; indeed we simply ignore them, and perhaps should not call them stimuli but, rather, potential stimuli—the pinched nerve ends as I hold this pen, the peripheral vision as I look at this page, the bookish smell of my study—I only note them at this moment by giving special attention to them.

Now an *attitude,* for our purposes, will be this *readiness to respond,* the third category above—the disposition to act in a certain way. We speak of a person's assuming a belligerent attitude—he does no fighting at the moment, but he is apparently ready to do so; he will fight, we say, at the drop of a hat. The man with a kindly attitude is disposed to perform acts of kindness, though at the moment no action at all seems called for. We often assert that it is not enough to do the right thing; it is desirable to have the right attitude. For having a certain attitude, or psychological posture, is the same as being *pointed in a certain direction;* and when the stimulus to act *does* come, suddenly as it often does, the person will move off in the direction that he is headed.

Perhaps the most important part of the poem-reading-experience will be the *residual attitude* that may be developed during the reading and as a part of it. This will long outlast the momentary pleasure of the music and the imagery, and it may long outlast the memory of the mere sense of it or the stir of feeling. Upon some personalities ineradicable traces have been left by the world's so-called great poems—poems such as A. E. Housman's "To an Athlete Dying Young," Walt Whitman's "Song of Myself," Tennyson's "Ulysses," Keats' "Ode on a Grecian Urn," George Herbert's "The Pulley," David's "Twenty-third Psalm." For other people, fundamental attitudes have been shaped by poems as various in substance and reputation as Longfellow's "Psalm of Life," Alice Cary's "Make Believe," Felicia Hemans' "Casabianca," Burns' "Red, Red Rose" which you have read in this book, and others that you may have read elsewhere, such as Edgar Guest's "You are the fellow who has to decide," Kilmer's "Trees," Kipling's "If," and Henley's "Invictus." For weal or woe, most persons have at some time had the experience of the Wedding Guest in Coleridge's poem, who was held by the eye of the Ancient Mariner; they have stayed to hear his tale, and have departed from him a sadder if not always a truly wiser man.

The following poem by Ralph Waldo Emerson, called "Forbearance," may serve the reader as a possible illustration. Read it slowly and thoughtfully.[1]

FORBEARANCE
Ralph Waldo Emerson

Hast thou named all the birds without a gun?
Loved the wood-rose, and left it on the stalk?
At rich men's tables eaten bread and pulse?
Unarmed, faced danger with a heart of trust?
And loved so well a high behavior,
In man or maid, that thou from speech refrained,
Nobility more nobly to repay?
O, be my friend, and teach me to be thine!

(1847)

May I suggest one or two readings of the, for me, troublesome verses before commenting upon possible residual attitudes? The third line seems to me to be clear, and I might paraphrase it in this way: "Have you, while at the table of persons who are well off, taken bread and common things only, without touching the better-tasting foods?" But how about the "high behavior" lines? Is a person showing high behavior when he is deep in thought, or doing good work, or when he has "the right point of view"? And just how would refraining from speech repay "nobility more nobly"? Is it desired reward to keep quiet so that the high-minded person may go on with his thoughts? Or is it good to keep from making suggestions to the person who is working things out in his own mind? Or is the highest approval given in other ways than by words? Is this the rough sense of the lines: "And is your love for serious thought in others such that you give your best approval without using words"?

Taking the whole poem, I interpret Emerson as saying:

If you are the sort of person who, in learning about birds, keeps himself from doing them damage; who, loving the flowers, lets them be there on the stem; who, with good foods before him, takes only

---

[1] The word *pulse* in line 3: beans, thick pea soup, or homely fare.

bread and soup; who, no gun in hand, is without fear in facing danger; who has such a good opinion of high-minded persons that he lets them be, and gives his approval without using cheap words—if you are *this* sort of person, be my friend and, by teaching me these things, make me good enough to be your friend as well.

It is quite impossible, of course, to read a poem and then say what subtle shifts in one's attitudes have taken place that will remain long after the poem is forgotten. But we may surmise that, for a particular reader, after the friendly emotion stirred by this poem has passed away, after the sense of the lines has been forgotten, there might yet remain an attitude predisposing him to value forbearance in those others whom he would call friend, and predisposing him to that same forbearance.

2. ATTITUDES OF VARIOUS SORTS

There is always some danger that we may equate "attitudes" with "solemnity," and hold to the mistaken notion that it is only the poems dealing with God's love, Pride humbled, and Death defied that leave their marks upon us. This, of course, is not so. Our personalities are bundles of attitudes toward all manner of things, trivial as well as serious, light and gay as well as somber. Perhaps George Wither's lyric may serve to represent here this less formidable sort of poetry.

SHALL I, WASTING IN DESPAIR?

George Wither

Shall I, wasting in despair,
Die because a woman's fair!
Or make pale my cheeks with care
'Cause another's rosy are?
Be she fairer than the day
Or the flowery meads in May,
    If she think not well of me,
    What care I how fair she be?

Shall my silly heart be pined
'Cause I see a woman kind?

Or a well disposèd nature
Joinèd with a lovely feature?
Be she meeker, kinder than
Turtle-dove or pelican,
   If she be not so to me,
    What care I how kind she be?

Shall a woman's virtues move
Me to perish for her love?
Or her well-deservings known
Make me quite forget mine own?
Be she with that goodness blest
Which may merit name of Best,
   If she be not such to me,
    What care I how good she be?

'Cause her fortune seems too high
Shall I play the fool and die?
She that bears a noble mind,
If not outward helps she find,
Thinks what with them he would do,
That without them dares her woo:
   And unless that mind I see,
    What care I how great she be?

Great, or good, or kind, or fair,
I will ne'er the more despair:
If she love me, this believe,
I will die ere she shall grieve;
If she slight me when I woo,
I can scorn and let her go;
   For if she be not for me,
    What care I for whom she be?

               (1619)

This poem might, without his knowing it, influence the reader's attitudes toward his relations to others, and make him the more likely to accept philosophically their rejection of his affections.

A poem of a very different sort is John Milton's sonnet "On His Blindness." It was written in 1655, while he was serving as Latin Secretary to Oliver Cromwell. Milton the poet had turned to political pamphleteering and from that to the exacting responsibilities of the secretaryship. Then at the age of forty-four he became totally blind. He carried on for Cromwell, however, dictating the Latin state documents to an amanuensis; but he must have felt like the unprofitable servant in the Parable of the Talents (*Matthew,* 25:14-30) who was cast "into outer darkness." You may recall the parable: a man, about to undertake a long journey, called in his servants and divided his property amongst them according to their merits. To the first he gave five talents, about $10,000; to the second, two; to the third, one. Then he went away. The first servant invested his five talents, and made five more; the second did likewise, doubling his money also; but the third "went and digged in the earth, and hid his lord's money." After a long time, the man returned and "reckoned" with them. The first servant, who had doubled his money, he commended, "Thou hast been faithful over a few things, I will make thee ruler over many things." So, also, with the second. But the third came whining, "Lord, I knew thee that thou art an hard man, reaping where thou hast not sown"; and he confessed that he had been afraid, and had buried his talent. The master rebuked him, called him wicked and slothful, blamed him for not putting the money to use, and ordered the one talent taken away from him to be given to the servant who had originally been given five. "For unto every one that hath shall be given . . . ; but from him that hath not shall be taken away even that which he hath," said the master. "And cast ye the unprofitable servant into outer darkness. . . ."

ON HIS BLINDNESS
John Milton

When I consider how my light is spent
　　Ere half my days in this dark world and wide,
　　And that one talent, which is death to hide,
Lodged with me useless, though my soul more bent
To serve therewith my Maker, and present
　　My true account, lest He returning chide;
　　"Doth God exact day-labor, light denied?"
I fondly ask. But Patience, to prevent

That murmur, soon replies, "God doth not need
    Either man's work or his own gifts. Who best
        Bear His mild yoke, they serve Him best. His state
Is kingly. Thousands at His bidding speed
And post o'er land and ocean without rest.
    They also serve who only stand and wait.

$(c.\ 1655)$

It does not seem possible to consider the residual attitude that might possibly result from reading this well-known sonnet without considering the poem-experience as a whole made up of closely interrelated parts.

I see at a glance that this short poem is a sonnet; its width and length on the page and the indentations as it is here reprinted make it look like a sonnet. So at once I expect its music to "go" sonnet-wise: iambic pentameter with a fairly complex rime-scheme. And I find as my eyes explore further and as they then proceed to skip along the lines, that this indeed is so. But there are many subtle deviations from the metrical expectancy: notable spondaic substitutions and hovering accents, a preponderance of run-on lines and great freedom in the caesural pauses within the verses, the thought division within the eighth line rather than after it, etc. And the music of this sonnet is (for me) made sonorous by the unusual richness of the sound pattern with its dark tone-color, its pervasively low vowels and consonant pattern. I hear a stately organ quality, *vox humana* with pedal bass; and I am moved by its solemnity.

Here indeed come pictures into my mind's-eye: the blind Milton, in somber dress, seated amongst his books (after the manner of the old print) with his daughter beside him on the floor; and God enthroned in a sunburst (a bit like Blake), with a wingèd angel as Patience, speaking down to the poet; and then God again, upon an elaborate throne surrounded by hosts of angels (after Doré now), messengers arriving and departing—and the blind poet, still in black, standing to one side, waiting to do His bidding.

While this music has been ringing in my mind's-ear, and while these scenes have flashed before me, I have been giving a good bit of my attention to the sense of it, to what the poet seems to be thinking:

It comes to me (he says) that, with my days on earth less than half done, the use of my eyes is gone! Because of this, I am not able to make use of that special power in writing which, like the money given the servants in the Bible story, will be taken from me if it is not used—even though it is my great desire to be writing in God's name and for His profit, for fear He may come back and put me to shame. So I put the simple and foolish question, "Does God, the Maker, keep a man at work needing daylight when that man is not able to see?"

But Quiet Waiting puts a stop to such talk, answering, "God has no need of man's work or of the things that he rightly gives to Him. Those men who, without protest, do whatever God says—they are His best servants. God's way of living is that of a great king. He has thousands of servants who, at His order, go quickly and without resting, over land and sea to do His work. But those other persons are as much His servants who quietly keep their places, waiting for His orders."

But my thoughts haven't run as smoothly as this paraphrase would make it appear. I have taken quick glances down the side streets of ambiguity and metaphor: *my light:* sight, means of working, inspiration; *talent:* money, special gift, aptitude; *day-labor:* work by daylight, work by the day, manual labor; *fondly:* affectionately, foolishly, like a fool; *prevent:* forestall, anticipate; *his* (His) *own* (owed) *gifts:* man's gifts to God, or the gifts man owes to God, or God's gifts to man; *bear:* endure, carry; *His* (his) *mild yoke:* the burden placed on him by God, man's own burden; *mild yoke:* light load, the burden could easily have been heavier, the patient ox (see *Matthew,* 11:30); *state:* Kingdom of Heaven, throne, condition; *stand and wait:* attend, remain in readiness.

It is the over-all meaning, rather than the interpretative darting of my thoughts, that begins to catch up the fullness of this poem. For Milton seems to say to me: "God does not expect the impossible; the man who does his best and whose attitude is one of readiness, serves God as much as does the man of spectacular action." And I believe that Milton's own feeling was one of philosophical resignation to his blindness, or that he achieved such a psychological adjustment as a part of his writing the poem. His whining complaints were silenced by the realization that, though he could no longer serve what he thought of as God's Cause in the Latin Secretaryship, he would stand ready to serve God when and where he could. And out of his blind years came *Paradise Lost*.

So I am myself stirred as I come to recognize Milton's feelings. I am not myself blind, nor have I ever suffered a comparable affliction, though my grandmother was blind; but I am humanly conscious of my limitations in other ways, and I too wonder what accounting I may be able to give for my talent. My emotional response, then, seems to be an appropriate one. Perhaps my feelings are not sufficiently akin to Milton's to say that emotional communication has taken place; but surely my feelings are harmonious with his.

Who shall say what of this poem-experience will remain with me? Perhaps the foolish question: "Shall God exact day-labor, light denied?" The final line: "They also serve who only stand and wait." The music of other sonnets may be colored by the solemnity of this one. I may glimpse again the poet-statesman, blind in the prime of his life. But there may be a subconscious residuum to this poem-experience in the form of reshaped and reinforced attitudes, a readiness to accept the yoke as mild when it may be placed upon my own shoulders.

Such is my experience of Milton's sonnet "On His Blindness." [2]

3. CONCLUDING EXAMPLE

Through a full experiencing of the great poems and other works of art, man enlarges his mind and spirit; he increases in knowledge and tolerance of his fellow beings; he comes to an understanding of Life.

---

[2] There will be other readers who, after conscientious interpretation, may be left perfectly cold by the poem, or who may feel antagonistic to the idea of the poem as they understand it, and say, in effect: "That's what Milton thinks, but I don't feel that way; I don't believe it's true! No patient bearing of the yoke for me! The world is moved forward by the man of action, not by the man who stands and waits!!"

I believe that Robert Frost's "Mending Wall" will provide many a reader with an experience that will leave him a significant residuum.

MENDING WALL
Robert Frost

Something there is that doesn't love a wall,
That sends the frozen-ground-swell under it,
And spills the upper boulders in the sun;
And makes gaps even two can pass abreast.
The work of hunters is another thing:
I have come after them and made repair
Where they have left not one stone on a stone,
But they would have the rabbit out of hiding,
To please the yelping dogs. The gaps I mean,
No one has seen them made or heard them made,
But at spring mending-time we find them there.
I let my neighbor know beyond the hill;
And on a day we meet to walk the line
And set the wall between us once again.
We keep the wall between us as we go.
To each the boulders that have fallen to each.
And some are loaves and some so nearly balls
We have to use a spell to make them balance:
"Stay where you are until our backs are turned!"
We wear our fingers rough with handling them.
Oh, just another kind of out-door game,
One on a side. It comes to little more:
There where it is we do not need the wall:
He is all pine and I am apple-orchard.
My apple trees will never get across
And eat the cones under his pines, I tell him.
He only says, "Good fences make good neighbors."
Spring is the mischief in me, and I wonder
If I could put a notion in his head:
"*Why* do they make good neighbors? Isn't it
Where there are cows? But here there are no cows.
Before I built a wall I'd ask to know
What I was walling in or walling out,
And to whom I was like to give offense.

Something there is that doesn't love a wall,
That wants it down." I could say "elves" to him,
But it's not elves exactly, and I'd rather
He said it for himself. I see him there
Bringing a stone grasped firmly by the top
In each hand, like an old-stone savage armed.
He moves in darkness as it seems to me,
Not of woods only and the shade of trees.
He will not go behind his father's saying,
And he likes having thought of it so well
He says again, "Good fences make good neighbors."

(1914)

Someone asked Robert Frost to give his interpretation of "Mending Wall." He is reported to have replied, "The poem means what it says to *you*." That was a good reply, though it did not answer the question.

So we bring this chapter and "The Anatomy of the Poem-Experience" to a close.

SUGGESTIONS FOR STUDY

1. *Walls About What*. Reread Robert Frost's "Mending Wall" in order to sharpen your understanding of the different attitudes of the poet and his neighbor.

(a) Louis Untermeyer has written: "Although Frost is not arguing for anything in particular, one senses here something more than the enemies of walls. In 'Mending Wall,' we see two elemental and opposed forces. 'Something there is that doesn't love a wall,' insists the seeker after causes; 'Good fences make good neighbors,' doggedly replies the literal-minded lover of tradition. Here, beneath the whimsical turns and pungency of expression, we have the essence of nationalism versus the internationalist: the struggle, though the poet would be the last to prod the point, between blind obedience to custom and questioning iconoclasm." [3]

(b) With this interpretation in mind, turn back to Robert Frost's poem. What are the walls that separate nations? Should they be kept up? What is the history of the long unfortified border between the United States and Canada? What are some other sorts of wall that

[3] Louis Untermeyer, *Modern American Poetry*, Harcourt, Brace, 1942, p. 206.

separate people? Do you think that it is "legitimate" to apply Frost's central idea in this way?

2. *Remembrance and Residuum.* There have been some eighty poems so far included in this book. Certain ones you have studied in great detail; others you have read more casually.

(a) *Without looking back,* make a list of the poems that you recall. Give title and author, if you remember them. In any case, note down some phrase of identification, and indicate briefly what aspects of the poem-experience you remember. List them in the order that they occur to you. Don't work too hard at it, and don't reproach yourself with loss of memory.

(b) Glance down your list and star the titles of those poems that you *think* may have left some notable residuum in your subconscious, serving to shape, alter, or reinforce certain of your fundamental attitudes.

3. *For the Vaults.* (a) Glance back through these first nine chapters and select some poetry that you would like to keep with you for long remembrance—one or more poems, say about thirty lines in all. (b) Commit this poetry to memory, not as a task, but as a treasured acquisition. Just read it aloud, time and time again, noting the interplay of sound and sense in the poetic rhythm, watching the flickering images, following along the sense of it, allowing yourself the luxury of emotion. Do not make hard work of it; just take it easy. Some people are slow in memorization, but such persons often are tenacious of what they once learn. Gradually take your eyes off the book for more and more time while you read aloud, and glance down at the book only when necessary. Before you know it, the poem will be yours to keep.

4. *Three Attitudes Toward Life.* Three sonnets entitled "The Choice" come from Dante Gabriel Rossetti's *House of Life,* and suggest three very different ways of life.

from THE HOUSE OF LIFE

THE CHOICE

Dante Gabriel Rossetti

I

Eat thou and drink; tomorrow thou shalt die.
Surely the earth, that's wise (being very old),
Needs not our help. Then loose me, love, and hold
Thy sultry hair up from my face; that I

May pour for thee this golden wine, brim-high,
Till round the glass thy fingers glow like gold.
We'll drown all hours; thy song, while hours are tolled,
Shall leap, as fountains veil the changing sky.
Now kiss, and think that there are really those,
My own high-bosomed beauty, who increase
Vain gold, vain lore, and yet might choose our way!
Through many years they toil; then on a day
They die not,—for their life was death,—but cease;
And round their narrow lips the mold falls close.

2

Watch thou and fear; tomorrow thou shalt die.
Or art thou sure thou shalt have time for death?
Is not the day which God's word promiseth
To come man knows not when? In yonder sky,
Now while we speak, the sun speeds forth; can I
Or thou assure him of his goal? God's breath
Even at this moment haply quickeneth
The air to a flame; till spirits, always nigh
Though screened and hid, shall walk the daylight here.
And dost thou prate of all that man shall do?
Canst thou, who hast but plagues, presume to be
Glad in his gladness that comes after thee?
Will *his* strength slay *thy* worm in hell? Go to:
Cover thy countenance, and watch, and fear.

3

Think thou and act; tomorrow thou shalt die.
Outstretched in the sun's warmth upon the shore,
Thou say'st: "Man's measured path is all gone o'er;
Up all his years, steeply, with strain and sigh,
Man clomb until he touched the truth; and I,
Even I, am he whom it was destined for."
How should this be? Art thou then so much more
Than they who sowed, that thou shouldst reap thereby?
Nay, come up hither. From this wave-washed mound
Unto the furthest flood-brim look with me;
Then reach on with thy thought till it be drowned.

Miles and miles distant though the gray line be,
And though thy soul sail leagues and leagues beyond,—
Still, leagues beyond those leagues, there is more sea.

(1847, 1869)

(a) Can you think of any other expressions in poetry of the three attitudes presented by Rossetti's "The Choice"? Do you know what names are commonly applied to these philosophies of life? Which one of them do you feel to be Rossetti's own view?

(b) Write a short paper considering the meaning of these sonnets and their relation to your own fundamental attitudes.

5. *Differences in Love.* "Reconciliation" is a short lyric in which two characters are presented in a dramatic situation.

RECONCILIATION

Frank M. Towne

Turning to go, she feels her hand in his,
And then her fingers clutch the withered rose,
And all between what might have been and is
Burns in her bitter aspect as she goes,
Feeling the stone baluster, up the stair
To the highest pavement, where she turns to wait,
Her fingers toying with a wisp of hair.
He catches at the last tag-ends of fate,
Finding in her regret a thing to do,
And mounts the pavements of the stairway too.

(1935)

(a) To what extent do you fill in the details as you read "Reconciliation"? Do you *see* the setting? What is it? The time of day? Do you visualize the characters? Have you some grasp of their personalities? What are their attitudes toward each other? What is the background story? What has gone before? What has just happened? What now happens?

(b) Give some thought to Frank Towne's "Reconciliation" in relation to George Wither's "Shall I, Wasting in Despair?" and Alice Cary's "Make Believe." What do they have in common? How do the poets' attitudes seem to differ?

6. *The Complete Poem.* As a summary exercise for Part Two of this book, read Coleridge's "Kubla Khan."

KUBLA KHAN;

OR, A VISION IN A DREAM

Samuel Taylor Coleridge

In Xanadu did Kubla Khan
A stately pleasure-dome decree:
Where Alph, the sacred river, ran
Through caverns measureless to man
   Down to a sunless sea.
So twice five miles of fertile ground
With walls and towers were girdled round:
And here were gardens bright with sinuous rills,
Where blossomed many an incense-bearing tree;
And here were forests ancient as the hills,
Enfolding sunny spots of greenery.

But oh! that deep romantic chasm which slanted
Down the green hill athwart a cedarn cover!
A savage place! as holy and enchanted
As e'er beneath a waning moon was haunted
By woman wailing for her demon-lover!
And from this chasm, with ceaseless turmoil seething,
As if this earth in fast thick pants were breathing,
A mighty fountain momently was forced;
Amid whose swift half-intermitted burst
Huge fragments vaulted like rebounding hail,
Or chaffy grain beneath the thresher's flail:
And 'mid these dancing rocks at once and ever
It flung up momently the sacred river.
Five miles meandering with a mazy motion
Through wood and dale the sacred river ran,
Then reached the caverns measureless to man,
And sank in tumult to a lifeless ocean:
And 'mid this tumult Kubla heard from far
Ancestral voices prophesying war!

   The shadow of the dome of pleasure
   Floated midway on the waves;
   Where was heard the mingled measure
   From the fountain and the caves.

It was a miracle of rare device,
A sunny pleasure-dome with caves of ice!

A damsel with a dulcimer
In a vision once I saw:
It was an Abyssinian maid,
And on her dulcimer she played,
Singing of Mount Abora.
Could I revive within me
Her symphony and song,
To such a deep delight 'twould win me,
That with music loud and long,
I would build that dome in air,
That sunny dome! those caves of ice!
And all who heard should see them there,
And all should cry, Beware! Beware!
His flashing eyes, his floating hair!
Weave a circle round him thrice,
And close your eyes with holy dread,
For he on honey-dew hath fed,
And drunk the milk of Paradise.

(*1797,* 1816)

(a) Consider "Kubla Khan" in some detail as regards each of its separate aspects and their interrelation in the unity of the complete poem-reading-experience. Make such notes as you think may be helpful.

(b) Write an extended essay upon your own experience in reading "Kubla Khan."

(c) Now find out what you can about Coleridge's composition of this famous poem by consulting standard reference works of literary history. (The curious student may find time to read John Livingston Lowes' *The Road to Xanadu*.) Then proceed to seek out critical comment and interpretation of this poem to compare with your own. (Many such will be found gathered together in Moulton's *Library of Literary Criticism*.)

PART THREE

The Evaluation of Poetry

10

GOOD POEMS AND BAD

So far we have considered what "a poem" *is* (or may be) and of what the poem-reading-experience consists. We have said little if anything about individual preferences, and have only hinted that some poems are worth less than others. Yet this study of Poetry, as a part of one of the Fine Arts, must ultimately concern itself with the evaluation of poetry. And it is hoped that the reader will learn how to tell a good poem from a bad one, and that his taste will undergo a gradual cultivation.

Literary criticism has developed from ancient times as the art and/or science of the interpretation and/or evaluation of poetry and other works of literature. The elasticity of such a definition is warranted by the wide diversity of aims and methods of those who have devoted themselves to this branch of belletristic study. No attempt will be made here to pass the great critics in review, to sketch the history of their achievements, or to classify them according to schools. But a number of the general methods of evaluating poetry will be suggested briefly.

I. FIVE CRITICAL METHODS

The *first* of these is *judicial,* the judging of poems according to the so-called laws or rules of poetry. At its best this method tries to discover the broad principles or fundamental "laws" of human nature as they relate to the art experience, and to apply them to particular works; at its worst this method merely promulgates nuisance rules to invoke against the strangers in town. Judicial criticism stems from the *Poetics,* those incomplete student notes of Aristotle's brilliant analysis of Greek tragedy and epic poetry. It, and its various interpretations and extensions, became Law to periodic generations of critics. The Rules prevailed, for the most part, during the later seventeenth and the eighteenth centuries. During this time most poems were written upon *appropriate* themes, in the *approved* meters, in the *accepted* poetic diction.

The evaluation of poetry by the Rules may be illuminated by reading the following selections from Alexander Pope's celebrated *Essay on Criticism.* Written when the poet was only twenty-one, it gave liberal and elegant expression to many of the critical ideas of his time, and has supplied successive generations with a score of apt quotations.

from AN ESSAY ON CRITICISM
Alexander Pope

> Those RULES of old discover'd, not devis'd,
> Are Nature still, but Nature methodiz'd;
> Nature, like liberty, is but restrain'd
> By the same laws which first herself ordain'd.
> Hear how learn'd Greece her useful rules indites,
> When to repress, and when indulge our flights:
> High on Parnassus' top her sons she show'd,
> And pointed out those arduous paths they trod;
> Held from afar, aloft, th' immortal prize,
> And urg'd the rest by equal steps to rise.
> Just precepts thus from great examples giv'n,
> She drew from them what they deriv'd from Heav'n. . . .
>   When first young [Virgil] in his boundless mind
> A work t' outlast immortal Rome design'd,
> Perhaps he seem'd above the critic's law,
> And but from Nature's fountains scorn'd to draw:
> But when t' examine ev'ry part he came,
> Nature and Homer were, he found, the same.
> Convinc'd, amaz'd, he checks the bold design;
> And rules as strict his labour'd work confine,
> As if [Aristotle] o'erlook'd each line.

Learn hence for ancient rules a just esteem;
To copy nature is to copy them. . . .
    A perfect Judge will read each work of Wit
With the same spirit that its author writ:
Survey the Whole, nor seek slight faults to find
Where nature moves, and rapture warms the mind;
Nor lose, for that malignant dull delight,
The gen'rous pleasure to be charm'd with wit.
But in such lays as neither ebb, nor flow,
Correctly cold, and regularly low,
That shunning faults, one quiet tenour keep,
We cannot blame indeed—but we may sleep. . . .
In every work regard the writer's End,
Since none can compass more than they intend;
And if the means be just, the conduct true,
Applause, in spite of trivial faults, is due. . . .
    Some to *conceit* alone their taste confine,
And glitt'ring thoughts struck out at ev'ry line; . . .
True Wit is Nature to advantage dress'd,
What oft was thought, but ne'er so well expressed. . . .
    Others for *language* all their care express,
And value books, as women men, for Dress:
Their praise is still,—the Style is excellent:
The Sense, they humbly take upon content. . . .
Some by old words to fame have made pretence,
Ancients in phrase, mere moderns in their sense;
Such labour'd nothings, in so strange a style,
Amaze th' unlearn'd, and make the learned smile. . . .
In words, as fashions, the same rule will hold;
Alike fantastic, if too new, or old:
Be not the first by whom the new are try'd,
Nor yet the last to lay the old aside.
    But most by Numbers judge a Poet's song;
And smooth or rough, with them is right or wrong. . . .
Who haunt Parnassus but to please their ear,
Not mend their minds; as some to Church repair,
Not for the doctrine, but the music there. . . .
True ease in writing comes from art, not chance,
As those move easiest who have learn'd to dance.

'Tis not enough no harshness gives offence,
The sound must seem an Echo to the sense.

(1711)

But with the opening of the nineteenth century, and even before, a number of young poets defied the established neo-classical rules— rules that to them seemed artificial and stultifying. The conservative critic of the time judged their work according to the old rules, and cried, "This will never do!" But what began as a revolt against stuffy tradition settled down into its own conventions, with its own principles and rules; and against these now younger men in their turn revolted.[1] But despite the fact that we now know how swift may be the changes in literary fashion, there is still a tendency on the part of many persons to distinguish good poetry from bad by citing precedent and principle, the laws of letters and the rules of rime. Someone says, "You can't write a serious poem in anapests, because the anapest is a light airy foot!" . . . "This sonnet is bad; it confuses the rime-scheme of the Shakespearean form and the thought-division of the Petrarchan!" . . . "This is not good: 'every' is never trisyllabic, and 'stallion' not 'stud' is the poetic word!" . . . "City slums are no fit subject for poetry!" . . . Alas, what are one man's prejudices turn out to be another man's principles; what is license in one land is the law in another; what is ridiculed in one age is the rule for the next. It would be so easy to evaluate poems, to distinguish the good from the bad, if rules of thumb were eternal laws!

The *second* method of evaluating poetry is *intuitive*. It is a method without method, inexplicable insight rather than reason. At its best it is the functioning of cultivated taste; at its worst, the vagary of irresponsible whimsey. The intuitive critic may say quite frankly, "I know what I like. And what I like is good poetry; what I don't like, is bad." Or else he may talk in high abstraction about "Poetic Truth" and "Beauty," covering the subject with a fabric woven of verbal magic. But whether he avoids explanation of his choice or rationalizes it at length, the person who uses this method

---

[1] See John Livingston Lowes, *Convention and Revolt in Poetry,* Houghton Mifflin, 1919.

just *knows* good poetry when he sees it. He may be candid in admitting the very personal nature of his evaluation, and recognizing that others may legitimately differ from him; or he may be dogmatic and assume that, of course, other persons of taste agree. He may say, "I don't know why, but I certainly think this is good." Or he may thunder: "Obviously a bad sonnet, as anyone can see who has a good ear!"

The best practitioners of the judicial and the intuitive methods of criticism may really not be so far apart. For the first will search for broad underlying principles by observing and generalizing upon the phenomena of recognized literary masterpieces, and will then be guided by these cautious generalizations in evaluating new works. And the second, the more conscientious intuitive critic, will consciously discipline his taste by an expanding acquaintance with the acknowledged "best." They may both be humble and tolerant. But the carping rule-monger and capricious impressionist, who also have something in common, are likely to be smug and arrogant.

A *third* method of evaluating poetry is *comparative*. This may take the form of pairing two poems and then proceeding either judicially or intuitively to a choice of the better. Leigh Hunt's "The Glove and the Lions" and Browning's "The Glove" were thus juxtaposed (pp. 13-14) as an exercise in preference. And Herrick's "To the Virgins—," the stanza from Spenser, and Ronsard's sonnet were similarly grouped (pp. 218-19), but with no explicit suggestion to compare and judge them.

A special form of this comparative criticism is the *touchstone* method proposed by Matthew Arnold, critic and poet of the later nineteenth century. "Indeed," says he, "there can be no more useful help for discovering what poetry belongs to the class of the truly excellent, and can therefore do us most good, than to have always in one's mind lines and expressions of the great masters, and to apply them as a touchstone to other poetry. Of course we are not to require this other poetry to resemble them; it may be very dissimilar. But if we have any tact we shall find them, when we have lodged them well in our minds, an infallible touchstone for detecting the presence or absence of high poetic quality, and also the degree of this quality, in all other poetry which we may place beside them." [2] Citing some single lines and short passages from Homer and Dante, Matthew Arnold then suggests two touch-stones from Shakespeare: Henry the Fourth's soliloquy upon sleep,

> Wilt thou upon the high and giddy mast
> Seel up the ship-boy's eyes, and rock his brains
> In cradle of the rude imperious surge, . . .

and Hamlet's dying words to Horatio,

> If thou didst ever hold me in thy heart,
> Absent thee from felicity awhile,
> And in this harsh world draw thy breath in pain,
> To tell my story. . . . [3]

Rub your untried verse against such sure hard poetry as these and the Miltonic lines Arnold quotes, and you will (he says) see its true worth. And each reader might well have ready in mind famous quotations from the great masterpieces for this and other uses. But one trouble with this method of evaluation is that *no* "new" poetry is likely to seem as rich as the old gems worn smooth by frequent handling.

A *fourth* method of evaluation is *authoritarian*. At its best the reader withholds his independent judgment until he has assured himself that it is not erratic, to prevent which he may consult the opinions of others or enlist the support of recognized critics. At its worst, the reader simply accepts the judgment of others as his own; he follows the crowd with his eyes shut or quotes (without marks!) the current reviews. Pope describes the method and its practitioners in his *Essay on Criticism*:

> Some ne'er advance a Judgment of their own,
> But catch the spreading notion of the Town;
> They reason and conclude by precedent,
> And own stale nonsense which they ne'er invent.

[2] Matthew Arnold, "Introduction" ["The Study of Poetry"], *The English Poets*, T. W. Ward., ed., third ed., Macmillan, 1885, pp. xxv-xxvi.
[3] *Henry the Fourth, Part Two*, III, i, 18-21; *Hamlet*, V, ii, 346-49.

And he adds an important variation of the method:

> Some judge of author's names, not works, and then
> Nor praise nor blame the writings, but the men.

Those who use this method, in any of its forms, are either timorous souls fearful of being caught in a mistaken judgment, or indolent readers unwilling to bestir themselves to independent thought.

A *fifth* method of evaluating poetry may be called *historical*. It is more concerned with interpreting the poem in relation to the poet, his age, his sources, and literary tradition, than it is in judging its "real worth." At its best, it may illuminate the poem and show its value as a biographical, sociological, or historical document. It may proceed by the comparative method and pronounce the poem the best of a then popular sort, or the most representative of a then current attitude. It may proceed by the authoritarian method to judge of its value in the age that produced it. At its worst, this method may merely recite anecdotes about the poem's authorship, publication, and reception. But the great usefulness of historical criticism must not be overlooked simply because it descends at times to literary small-talk. It must also be remembered, however, that a work of art may have very real value for many persons in one age, and no immediate value at all for most of the persons of another age, and that many "representative" and "revealing" poems of the past are not poems at all for modern readers.

It is of value, however, to view a poem in its original environment and to square one's judgment of it with that of other persons, just as it is worth while to seek for the universal in human nature, to cultivate a sensitive and refined taste, and to measure one thing against another. But there are no critical authorities on poetry; there are no enduring touchstones for poetry; there are no eternal verities about poetry; there are no ultimate laws of poetry! The favored poems of one period are quite often neglected in the next; the divining-rod of one master discovers fool's gold in the hands of another; the absolute truths of an older generation seem trite or false to the youngsters; what once were principles are now viewed as preconceptions. . . . How disconcerting to the reader who really wants to know what is what!

2. BARROOM, BOWER, AND BARGE

Before going forward to a sixth method of evaluating poetry, the reader should be given the opportunity to exercise his skill in judgment, using whatever methods he may wish.

DON'T GO IN
Mrs. Kidder

It is lighted, we know, like a palace,
    That fair, gilded temple of sin;
It has signs on the walls; let us read them:
    "The best of wine, brandy, and gin."
(As if human stomachs could need them!)
    My son, oh, my son, don't go in.

Though it giveth its beautiful color,
    Though it gleams in the cup like a rose,
Though it seeks like a serpent to charm you,
    And glitters and glimmers and glows,
Like the bright, wily serpent 'twill harm you
    And rob you of earthly repose.

It will tarnish your glorious manhood
    And sow the vile seeds of disgrace.
Then, why deal with this terrible danger?
    Why enter this crime-haunted place?
Much better to pass it a stranger
    Than God's whole image deface.

Much better to gird on the armor
    To fight life's great battle and win,
Than to lay down your all on the altar
    That burns in this temple of sin.
So, strike for the right and not falter—
    My son, oh, my son, don't go in.

                  (*?c. 1880*)

from THE FAERIE QUEENE, II, v, 26 ff.

CYMOCHLES IN THE BOWER OF BLISS

Edmund Spenser

26

He was a man of rare redoubted might,
Famous throughout the world for warlike prayse,
And glorious spoiles, purchast in perilous fight:
Full many doughtie knights he in his dayes
Had doen to death, subdewde in equall frayes,
Whose carkases, for terrour of his name,
Of fowles and beastes he made the piteous prayes,
And hong their conquered armes for more defame
On gallow trees, in honour of his dearest Dame.

27

His dearest Dame is that Enchaunteresse,
The vile *Acrasia,* that with vaine delightes,
And idle pleasures in her *Bowre* of *Blisse,*
Does charme her louers, and the feeble sprightes
Can call out of the bodies of fraile wightes:
Whom then she does transforme to monstrous hewes,
And horribly misshapes with vgly sightes,
Captiu'd eternally in yron mewes,
And darksom dens, where *Titan* his face neuer shewes.

28

There *Atin* found *Cymochles* soiourning,
To serue his Lemans loue: for he, by kind,
Was giuen all to lust and loose liuing,
When euer his fiers hands he free mote find:
And now he has pourd out his idle mind
In daintie delices, and lauish ioyes,
Hauing his warlike weapons cast behind,
And flowes in pleasures, and vaine pleasing toyes,
Mingled emongst loose Ladies and lasciuious boyes.

29

And ouer him, art striuing to compaire
With nature, did an Arber greene dispred,
Framed of wanton Yuie, flouring faire,
Through which the fragrant Eglantine did spred
His pricking armes, entrayld with roses red,
Which daintie odours round about them threw,
And all within with flowres was garnishèd,
That when myld *Zephyrus* emongst them blew,
Did breath out bounteous smels, and painted colors shew.

30

And fast beside, there trickled softly downe
A gentle streame, whose murmuring waue did play
Emongst the pumy stones, and made a sowne,
To lull him soft a sleepe, that by it lay;
The wearie Traueiler, wandring that way,
Therein did often quench his thristy heat,
And then by it his wearie limbes display,
Whiles creeping slomber made him to forget
His former paine, and wypt away his toylsom sweat.

31

And on the other side a pleasaunt groue
Was shot vp high, full of the stately tree,
That dedicated is t' *Olympicke Ioue,*
And to his sonne *Alcides,* whenas hee
Gaynd in *Nemea* goodly victoree;
Therein the mery birds of euery sort
Chaunted alowd their chearefull harmonie:
And made emongst them selues a sweet consort,
That quickned the dull spright with musicall comfort.

32

There he him found all carelesly displayd,
In secret shadow from the sunny ray,
On a sweet bed of lillies softly layd,
Amidst a flocke of Damzels fresh and gay,

That round about him dissolute did play
Their wanton follies, and light meriment;
Euery of which did loosely disaray
Her vpper parts of meet habiliments,
And shewd them naked, deckt with many ornaments.

33

And euery of them stroue, with most delights,
Him to aggrate, and greatest pleasures shew;
Some framd faire lookes, glancing like euening lights,
Others sweet words, dropping like honny dew;
Some bathèd kisses, and did soft embrew
The sugred licour through his melting lips:
One boastes her beautie, and does yeeld to vew
Her daintie limbes aboue her tender hips;
Another her out boastes, and all for tryall strips.

34

He, like an Adder, lurking in the weeds,
His wandring thought in deepe desire does steepe,
And his fraile eye with spoyle of beautie feedes;
Sometimes he falsely faines himselfe to sleepe,
Whiles through their lids his wanton eies do peepe,
To steale a snatch of amorous conceipt,
Whereby close fire into his heart does creepe:
So, them deceiues, deceiu'd in his deceipt,
Made drunke with drugs of deare voluptuous receipt.

35

Atin arriuing there, when him he spide,
Thus in still waues of deepe delight to wade,
Fiercely approching, to him lowdly cride,
Cymochles; oh no, but Cymochles shade,
In which that manly person late did fade,
What is become of great Acrates sonne?
Or where hath he hong vp his mortall blade,
That hath so many haughtie conquests wonne?
Is all his force forlorne, and all his glory donne? . . .

(1590)

from ANTONY AND CLEOPATRA, II, ii, 196 ff.

ENOBARBUS' DESCRIPTION OF CLEOPATRA

William Shakespeare

The barge she sat in, like a burnish'd throne,
Burn'd on the water; the poop was beaten gold,
Purple the sails, and so perfumed that
The winds were love-sick with them, the oars were silver,
Which to the tune of flutes kept stroke, and made
The water which they beat to follow faster,
As amorous of their strokes. For her own person,
It beggar'd all description; she did lie
In her pavilion,—cloth-of-gold of tissue,—
O'er-picturing that Venus where we see
The fancy outwork nature; on each side her
Stood pretty-dimpled boys, like smiling Cupids,
With divers-colour'd fans, whose wind did seem
To glow the delicate cheeks which they did cool,
And what they undid did.
                                        (O! rare for Antony.) [4]
Her gentlewomen, like the Nereides,
So many mermaids, tended her i' the eyes,
And made their bends adornings; at the helm
A seeming mermaid steers; the silken tackle
Swell with the touches of those flower-soft hands,
That yarely frame the office. From the barge
A strange invisible perfume hits the sense
Of the adjacent wharfs. The city cast
Her people out upon her, and Antony,
Enthron'd i' the market-place, did sit alone,
Whistling to the air; which, but for vacancy,
Had gone to gaze on Cleopatra too
And made a gap in nature.
                                        (Rare Egyptian!)
Upon her landing, Antony sent to her,
Invited her to supper; she replied
It should be better he became her guest,

[4] The parenthesized exclamations are those of Agrippa and Mecaenas to whom Enobarbus is speaking.

Which she entreated. Our courteous Antony,
Whom ne'er the word of "No" woman heard speak,
Being barber'd ten times o'er, goes to the feast,
And, for his ordinary pays his heart
For what his eyes eat only.
                                                    (Royal wench!
She made great Caesar lay his sword to bed;
He plough'd her, and she cropp'd.)
                                                            I saw her once
Hop forty paces through the public street;
And having lost her breath, she spoke, and panted,
That she did make defect perfection,
And, breathless, power breathe forth.
                (Now Antony must leave her utterly.)
                                        Never; he will not:
Age cannot wither her, nor custom stale
Her infinite variety; other women cloy
The appetites they feed, but she makes hungry
Where most she satisfies; for vilest things
Become themselves in her, that the holy priests
Bless her when she is riggish. . . .
                                        (*1607, 1623*)

3. JUDGMENT OF A BAD POEM

We shall not take time here to evaluate all three of these selections, but shall confine our comments to the first one. Reactions to
Mrs. Kidder's "Don't Go In" will vary widely: "Spoken in a good
Cause!" . . . "The worst poem imaginable!" . . . "The funniest
poem I've ever read!" With side comments on whether that was
really her name, and whether it's intended to be taken seriously.

The *judicial* critic will call up his generalization of poetic principles or his formulation of the rules of rime, and set to work in
considering the "fair, gilded temple of sin" in accordance with
them. If he is judicious as well as judicial he will try to read Mrs.
Kidder's poem "With the same spirit that its author writ," and
then come (for instance) to questions of versification: the elephan-
tine kittenishness of the anapestic rhythm in relation to the subject
matter, the heavy-footed use of anti-bacchic substitutions, the ama-

zons amongst the feminine endings, the failure to deviate sufficiently from the insistent metrical pattern, the use of easily antici-
pated rimes. And such a judgment might consider the theme in
relation to preconceptions regarding what is proper to poetry (Is
propaganda, however well intentioned, within the province of
poetry?); the logic of its thought development (the grammatical
reference of the "it" of stanza 2 and of the "it" of stanza 3 is not
at once evident); the reader is left in doubt about the sense at certain points ("repose" is ambiguous without enrichment; refraining
from "going in" is not clearly related to fighting "for the right");
the metaphors are mixed and confused ("it gleams in the cup like
the rose"; it will at once "tarnish" and "sow seeds"). This judicial
critic may comment further upon the poet's failure to evoke a clear
view of the old-time saloon, either from within or without (the
swinging half-doors, the sawdust floor and brass rail, the long bar
and plate glass mirror, the cheap music and stale air, the alcoholic
sensations both gustatory and systemic). And such a judge would
also remark upon the poet's emotional stock responses ("temple of
sin") and sentimentality ("My son, oh, my son," addressed to all
young men). Of whatever variety, the judicial critic will probably
pronounce the verdict, after studying the evidence and the Law
during the court hearing: "Don't Go In" is guilty of being an
extremely bad poem!

But the *intuitive* critic will say, "Such a procedure is a waste of
time and effort. I can tell at a glance that 'Don't Go In' is worthless." He may even say that the application of the so-called rules is,
after all, a matter of cultivated taste. Turning from his quarrel
with the judicial, he may say, "It's bad because I don't like it.
I don't like to be preached at. Besides, there's no danger of my
going in if the 'fair, gilded temple of sin' is no more enticing than
the poet depicts it; and I really don't think that the color and
clarity of wines and liquors are their chief attraction to those who
enjoy them." But the evaluation of this poem intuitively by a person of cultivated taste is likely to involve the feeling that "there is
really no 'poetry' here," that it possesses many of the outer characteristics of verse without the inner qualities of art, that it fails to
come alive within him, that it is somehow "indescribably bad."

The *comparative* critic will measure up Mrs. Kidder's "temple of sin" against Spenser's "Bower of Bliss" and Shakespeare's "barge" of Cleopatra, and will probably come to the conclusion that "Don't Go In" is inferior to both of them. He will probably note that the first is a "temperance piece" addressed directly to presumably susceptible youths; that "the Bower of Bliss" is but a subordinate incident in Spenser's "The Second Booke of *The Faerie Queene,* contayning, the Legend of Sir Guyon, or Of Temperance," an elaborate and systematic allegory; and that Shakespeare's description is a part of the early exposition setting the stage for Mark Antony's tragic intemperance as he succumbs to the charms of Cleopatra. This comparative critic might then proceed either judicially or intuitively to a consideration of details. The *touchstone* critic will approach "Don't Go In" in a somewhat similar way, but using his well-worn quotations from recognized masterpieces as he tests for true gold in "That fair, gilded temple of sin." He will match up

> Like the bright, wily serpent 'twill harm you
> And rob you of earthly repose,

against Iago's aside upon the entrance of Othello (III, iii, 331 ff.),

> Not poppy, nor mandragora,
> Nor all the drowsy syrups of the world,
> Shall ever medicine thee to that sweet sleep
> Which thou owedst yesterday.

He will juxtapose Mrs. Kidder's

> It will tarnish your glorious manhood
> And sow the vile seeds of disgrace,

and the sobered Cassio's cry of despair (*Othello,* II, iii, 286 ff.),

> . . . O God! that men should put an enemy in their mouths to steal away their brains; that we should, with joy, pleasance, revel, and applause, transform ourselves into beasts.

And this touchstone critic will probably conclude, in assaying "Don't Go In," that it is not pay dirt, that its temple of sin is indeed gilded with fool's gold; and that, tarnished!

The *authoritative* critic who relies for guidance upon recorded opinion will be at a loss in his evaluation of Mrs. Kidder's poem. No reviews of it have come to light, and it is not dignified by inclusion in reputable anthologies or by discussion in critical histories of American literature. "But since the above paragraphs say that the judicial, intuitive, and comparative critics say that it's bad, why I guess it's bad all right!"

But let us play out the play: there is yet something to say in the behalf of this same "temple of sin." The *historical* critic may find some good in it; for it is, at least, a very good example of bad poetry! Moreover, it belongs to a very considerable body of temperance verse, and may be looked upon as a good representative of the type. Mid-nineteenth century humanitarianism was concerned with various Causes, all directed toward human betterment. The spread of foreign missions, to enlighten the benighted; the movement to abolish bond slavery; the crusade against the saloon and the liquor traffic, against organized vice, against the sweatshops, against political corruption and greed—these developed in the evangelistic climate of the last century; and the historian, while pointing out that these causes are not yet won and that the crusaders were often mistaken, will recognize the salutary effect of that vast body of pamphlet and journalistic writing, the *Ten Nights in a Barroom* and *Uncle Tom's Cabin,* the hortative verse and schoolroom declamation, that shaped public opinion toward laudible social ends.

Surely, now, we may leave Mrs. Kidder's "Don't Go In," and move forward.

4. ORTHOLOGICAL CRITICISM

There is a *sixth* method of evaluating poetry, which will here be called *orthological*. It proceeds from the point of view so far advanced in this Preface to Poetry, and says unhesitatingly that one can evaluate a printed poem only by evaluating poem-experiences; that the good poem, for a particular reader, is the one that provides him with a valuable experience, and that there are many sorts and degrees of goodness in human experience.

Many of the practitioners of the previously named methods of evaluation seem (at least) to seek to find "value" as a property of the poem on the page, rather than as a quality attributed to it by various readers. Judicial critics may quarrel, even when they agree upon the rules, because they are not applying the rules to the printed verses (as they may suppose) but to two different experiences stimulated by them. The intuitive critics, also, may assume that they discern certain values in the printed poem rather than in their individual poem-experiences; or their hot contentions and charges of "bad taste" may result from the false assumption that the poem-experience is the same for all competent readers. The comparative critic, too, may fasten his attention upon the two pages, without realizing that he is really comparing two reading-experiences. The authoritarian critic, as well, may overlook the fact that what another says about the poem is really said about his particular interpretation of it; and that of course the critics don't agree, for they are always talking about different things! And even the most patient and conscientious historical critic is likely to impute to the poet ideas and attitudes which are entirely his own.

Except for this one radical difference, however, the orthological evaluation of a poem may not differ markedly in method from the other methods at their best. Indeed the orthological method is in many ways eclectic. The critic using this method may also seek for the broad literary principles by generalizing upon the language and art behavior of human beings, and will bring these "laws" to bear in considering particular poems. He too may cultivate a refined taste and sensitive discernment. He too may find profit in comparisons and the discriminating application of touchstones. He too may be alert to the evaluation of others. He too may study the biographical, sociological, and historical environment, and the problems of authorship, source material, literary tradition, text, publication, and reception. For orthological evaluation of a poem will rest upon a judgment of the poem-reading-experience, and this judgment will be withheld until the poem is completely realized in all of its aspects and as a unified whole.

"Poetic experiences are valuable (when they are)," writes Dr. Richards, "in the same ways as any other experiences. They are to be judged by the same standards." [5] And he proceeds to set up *a psychological theory of value.* The best life, he suggests, "would be the opposite of torpor, that is to say, the fullest, keenest, most active and completest kind of life. Such a life is one which brings into play as many as possible of the *positive* interests . . . with as little conflict among themselves as possible." The best life for a man, then, "will be one in which as much as possible of himself is engaged. And this with as little conflict, as little frustrating interference between different sub-systems of his activities as there can be. The more he lives and the less he thwarts himself the better." But Dr. Richards adds that the good experience "must not only be full of life and free from conflict, but it must be likely to lead to other experiences . . . also full of life and free from conflict."

The *good poem*—that is, the good poem-experience—will be crowded with a rich and varied "music" and/or with vivid and sensuous imagery and/or with unusual and provocative thought and/or with a deep and enduring stir of feeling; it will be free from dissonant notes and incongruous pictures, inappropriate thoughts and contrary emotions. Someone has written of the way in which the thought of a poem is "crushed into a small space," like gunpowder, ready to explode into the reader's mind.[6] Indeed the good poem is one that bursts upon the reader as he experiences it—delights, titillates, surprises, dazzles, stimulates, engages, puzzles, provokes, rewards, challenges, satisfies!

Not so the *bad poem.* It will be one in which the musical effects and images are few and uninteresting, or in which they seem to be in conflict with the rest of the experience; in which the thoughts and feelings evoked are less cogent or perhaps inappropriate. The bad poem does not explode as one reads it; there is no subtle interplay of tensions within the music, no over-sounding of enriching patterns, no kaleidoscopic visions of strange beauty, no sudden disclosure of rare thought, no unspeakable stirring of the human depths.

[5] I. A. Richards, *Science and Poetry,* London, 1935, pp. 33-42. For a more extended treatment see I. A. Richards, *Principles of Literary Criticism,* Harcourt, Brace, 1930.
[6] William Empson in "Basic and Poetry," *Kenyon Review,* autumn, 1940.

But let us turn back and reread Enobarbus' description of Cleopatra and "the barge she sat in." . . .

This poem, as I am conscious of it, is of high value, though perhaps not of the highest. Each time I reread the poem and revive the experience, there comes that magical explosion of its gunpowder, as vivid and varied images flash upon my inward eye and senses, as rich and ornate music bursts in upon me, as the aptness of phrase and fullness of meaning crackle in my thoughts, as the alluring beauty at once sensual and cloying stirs within me. And the whole experience, so full of life and bringing into play so many facets of my person, is bound into a complex unity around the central moving picture: the barge resplendent in the sunlight, its purple sails and silver oars, the canopy of lustrous cloth-of-gold—the heavy perfume and the flute song timing the oar strokes—the Queen herself, who "beggar'd all description," in a setting of oriental splendor, attendant boys with cooling colored fans, and decorative maids in waiting. The crowded wharfs, and Antony in the emptied market place. His invitation sent, and hers sent in return; his acceptance and personal preparation. The side pictures of Caesar conquered, and Cleopatra charming though breathless—her eternal charm, her infinite variety which "Age cannot wither . . . nor custom stale!"

And everything in my experience seems to pull one way; it is "full of life and free from conflict," with "as little frustrating interference . . . as there can be." The blank verse is extremely fluid, with many run-on lines and variety of caesural pauses, great freedom in the metrical variations, and appropriate enrichment by an elaborate sound pattern. The imagery is sensuous and decorative, with pervading odors and flute and oar sounds, the feel of hot and cool and moving air and silk ropes, as well as the ornateness of form and texture and brilliant color, and the overabundance of physical attractiveness. And how directly this music and imagery are related to the mere sense of it, the human situation that is described, the dramatic incident that is narrated! Nor are the side comments, of those who listen to Enobarbus, wasted; for in their exclamations of response are caught up the feelings of my own reading. Except that my feeling is piteous, too, for I cannot refrain from looking beyond the dramatic moment to the full sweep of the tragedy. For Mark Antony, who gave "All for Love" (as Dryden called his play on the same theme, and subtitled it "The World Well Lost")—Mark Antony was caught in a fatal passion, and for abandonment to love for Cleopatra he paid in power and possession, prestige and self-esteem, life itself. But my ethical judgment of Antony's intemperance does not (for me) seem to be in conflict with the abundance of life that, "crushed" within the verses, bursts upon me as I read. Perhaps, in realizing the overmastering passion of Antony, I have come, as a part of my experience, to a broader tolerance of my fellow men, to a deeper understanding of life.

5. A CLOSING PAIR

Let us turn from this orthological evaluation of Enobarbus' description of Cleopatra—not that all is said that might be said—and conclude the chapter by presenting a pair of poems without comment, except to say that they are not in this place and in juxtaposition without design.

KEEP A-GOIN'
Frank L. Stanton

If you strike a thorn or rose,
    Keep a-goin'!
If it hails or if it snows,
    Keep a-goin'!
'Tain't no use to sit an' whine
When the fish ain't on your line;
Bait your hook an' keep a-tryin'—
    Keep a-goin'!

When the weather kills your crop,
    Keep a-goin'!
Though 'tis work to reach the top,
    Keep a-goin'!
S'pose you're out o' ev'ry dime,
Gittin' broke ain't any crime;

Tell the world you're feelin' *prime*—
    Keep a-goin'!

When it looks like all is up,
    Keep a-goin'!
Drain the sweetness from the cup,
    Keep a-goin'!
See the wild birds on the wing,
Hear the bells that sweetly ring,
When you feel like singin', sing—
    Keep a-goin'!

              (*c.* 1898)

SOME THINGS THERE ARE

Margaret Yale

Some things there are that were not meant for sharing:
The sea at dawn, grey gulls against grey sky,
A lonely wind, the rain. I should be caring
For things that might be yours and mine: the shy
And gentle laughter of a child; a nest
Of humming-birds, hid in the trumpet-vine
Where none but we shall know; pigeons abreast
And telling secrets; quail walking in a line
Like children bound for church:—all these may be
Spoken of safely, shared, recalled. But I,
I have been stung by salt spray of the sea,
I have been bound within the seagull's cry.
Before these things I could not have you say,
"How nice," and take my hand, and turn away.

              (1943)

SUGGESTIONS FOR STUDY

1. *Gathering Touchstones.* Glance back at the poems so far included in this volume, and pick out the verses and short passages that seem to you to be of the highest poetic value, ones that might serve you as touchstones in assaying new and untried poems. (a) Copy these touchstones, for ready reference, in your notebook or commonplace book. (b) Commit them to memory, if you have not already done so. (c) Put them to use in an evaluation of Margaret Yale's "Some Things There

Are." (d) Compare your touchstones and your judgments with those of other readers.

2. *Principles and Rules.* Give some thought to the matter of judicial criticism. (a) Work out a statement of what you consider some broad principles that might well be applied in the evaluation of particular poems. (b) If you wish to do so, devise some specific rules subordinate to the general principles. (c) Compare your statements of principle and your rules with the selection from Pope's *Essay on Criticism.*

3. *The Bower of Bliss.* Turn back to "Cymochles in the Bower of Bliss" from Spenser's *The Faerie Queene,* and reread it. Note that Spenser wrote in Shakespeare's time, but that he was consciously archaic. Shakespeare (as here reprinted) is slightly modernized in typography, as in standard texts; but Spenser is here reprinted in the original spelling.

(a) How do you like it? What is your intuitive judgment of its worth?

(b) Consider it in relation to the selection from Shakespeare's *Antony and Cleopatra,* proceeding with your comparison intuitively rather than judicially.

(c) Use Moulton's *Library of Literary Criticism* in making an authoritarian evaluation of *The Faerie Queene.* Read the comments of recognized critics, and take note of specific points of agreement and disagreement with your intuitive judgments.

(d) Now make an historical evaluation of *The Faerie Queene* by reading the pertinent passages in three different one-volume histories of English Literature, and take note of the judgments passed upon this work by these literary historians.

(e) Write a two-page paper in which you discuss these four evaluations of different sorts.

4. *Comparative Cheer.* Reread Stanton's "Keep a-Goin'" and Clough's "Say Not the Struggle Nought Availeth" (p. 177) or Arnold's "The Last Word" (p. 186). (a) Proceed somewhat judicially with your comparative evaluation; try to bring to bear the principles and rules that you have already formulated. (b) Make a list in three parallel columns of the principle or rule involved and of your pertinent comments upon each of the two poems.

5. *Four Poems.* The poems here presented in a group are all love poems, variations upon a universal theme, but they are widely different in many ways.

(a) In reading them, try to experience each one fully and fairly, richly and completely. Do not move on to the second poem until you have read and reread the first one slowly and aloud, alert of mind and with an open heart.

TO CELIA
Ben Jonson

Drink to me, only, with thine eyes,
   And I will pledge with mine;
Or leave a kiss but in the cup,
   And I'll not look for wine.
The thirst that from the soul doth rise,
   Doth ask a drink divine:
But might I of Jove's nectar sup,
   I would not change for thine.

I sent thee, late, a rosy wreath,
   Not so much honoring thee,
As giving it a hope, that there
   It could not wither'd be.
But thou thereon didst only breathe,
   And sent'st it back to me:
Since when it grows, and smells, I swear,
   Not of itself, but thee.

                (1616)

BELIEVE ME, IF ALL THOSE ENDEARING YOUNG CHARMS
Thomas Moore

Believe me, if all those endearing young charms,
   Which I gaze on so fondly today,
Were to change by tomorrow, and fleet in my arms,
   Like fairy-gifts fading away,
Thou wouldst still be adored, as this moment thou art,
   Let thy loveliness fade as it will,
And around the dear ruin each wish of my heart
   Would entwine itself verdantly still.

It is not while beauty and youth are thine own,
   And thy cheeks unprofaned by a tear,
That the fervor and faith of a soul can be known,
   To which time will but make thee more dear;
No, the heart that has truly loved never forgets,
   But as truly loves on to the close,

As the sun-flower turns on her god, when he sets,
The same look which she turned when he rose.
(1808)

I LOVE TO LOVE
Marion Ward

"I love to *love*," said a darling pet,
Whose soul looked out through her eyes of jet,
And she nestled down like a fondled dove,
And lisped, "Dear Mamma, how I love to *love!*"

"I love to *love*," said a new-made bride,
As she gazed on the loved one by her side,
And she clung to his arm in the star-lit grove,
And breathed on his lips, "How I love to *love!*"

"I love to *love*," said a mother blest,
As her first-born lay like a rose on her breast,
And she thought as she smoothed down its silken hair,
That nothing on earth *could* be half so fair.

And thus, as we sail o'er the ocean of life,
Love pours out the oil on the desert of strife,
And swiftly our bark nears the haven above,
While we've something to hope for, *something to love*.
(?c. 1880)

THUMBPRINT
Celeste Turner Wright

Almost reluctant, we approach the block
Cleft from a stout sequoia; calculate
By arches, loops, concentric rings the date
Of Hastings, Plymouth, Gettysburg. The shock
Darkens our eyes; as dying men a clock,
We read the scornful summary of fate—
Elizabeth an inch—and estimate
How such curtailment at our love shall mock.
Redwood has fingerprinted Time, the seams

Of his gigantic thumb: this circlet grew
While Heloise yet laughed; these whorls define
Dante's "new life"; and when this curve was new,
John Keats could hope for mercy. Shall our dreams
Shrink to a millimeter, half a line?

(1942)

(b) Now consider these four poems comparatively, and rank them in the following two ways: (1) according to your purely personal preference, using the symbols *A* (for the best) through *D* (for the worst); (2) according to your judgment of what a person of cultivated taste ought to prefer, using the symbols *1* (for the best) through *4*.

(c) Are the two ratings the same in each case? If not, what is the basis for the difference in your judgment of "what you actually prefer" and "what you think you should prefer"?

6. *Critical Queries.* The following questions may be of help in an orthological evaluation of a poem. Turn back to one of the poems in the earlier chapters, one that you have forgotten, and reread it thoughtfully. Then ask yourself—and answer—these critical questions:

Has the poem-experience been *musical?* Did you enjoy the feel of the words along the mind's-tongue? Has the "music" in your mind's-ear been rich in its poetic rhythm, with a happy accompaniment of interlacing subsidiary rhythms? Have the melody and tone-color been in themselves interesting to you and appropriate to the rest of the poem-experience?

Has the poem been *pictorial?* Has the visual imagery been vivid and appropriate? Has the imagery included other sorts of sensation?

Has the poem been *meaningful?* Have the thoughts compacted within the words burst upon you, full and clear, with the darting sparks of metaphor and ambiguous enrichment? Or is there something haunting, or suggestive, or puzzling, or disturbingly ambiguous, or enigmatic about its over-all meaning that keeps you wondering?

Has the poem been *emotional?* Did you recognize and understand the feelings of the poet? Did you also have your own emotions stirred by your reading? and was this response appropriate?

Has the poem as a whole been *worth while?* Has the experience been an integrated whole? Has it had a positive relation to past experiences? Do you feel that it has furthered your understanding of yourself? of other persons? of Life? Do you feel that something has been left with you that will outlast remembrance of the poem, or that your fundamental attitudes may have been somehow affected by it?

7. *All the Difference.* After reading T. S. Eliot's "La Figlia Che Piange," turn back to reread Frank Towne's "Reconciliation," (p. 239).

LA FIGLIA CHE PIANGE

T. S. Eliot

O QUAM TE MEMOREM VIRGO . . .

Stand on the highest pavement of the stair—
Lean on a garden urn—
Weave, weave the sunlight in your hair—
Clasp your flowers to you with a pained surprise—
Fling them to the ground and turn
With a fugitive resentment in your eyes:
But weave, weave the sunlight in your hair.

So I would have had him leave,
So I would have had her stand and grieve,
So he would have left
As the soul leaves the body torn and bruised,
As the mind deserts the body it has used.
I should find
Some way incomparably light and deft,
Some way we both should understand,
Simple and faithless as a smile and shake of the hand.

She turned away, but with the autumn weather
Compelled my imagination many days,
Many days and many hours:
Her hair over her arms and her arms full of flowers.
And I wonder how they should have been together!
I should have lost a gesture and a pose.
Sometimes these cogitations still amaze
The troubled midnight and the noon's repose.

(1917)

11

GREAT POETRY AND TRUE

The last chapter may have left the reader with the suspicion that there really is no such thing as good, unequivocally *good,* poetry; for each individual will, by whatsoever means, make his own evaluations of the poems he reads, and of course people will not agree in their value-judgments. But there indeed is a sense in which it can be said that Milton's sonnet "On His Blindness" and Keats' "Ode on a Grecian Urn" are really and truly good, even though for certain individuals they may fail to evoke good poem-experiences. And we shall call poems of this sort the *great* poems of our literature.

How can such a statement be harmonized with the tenor of the last chapter?

I. A DEFINITION OF "GREAT" POETRY

Let us begin by setting up a working definition: *The great poems* (as the phrase is here used) *are those of the past that have provided many of the better readers of most of the subsequent periods with good poem-reading-experiences.*

Does this mean that no modern poetry is great? . . . The question is belligerent in tone, and the answer is calmly this: The test of time is an aspect of greatness (*in this sense*), and no one can say for certain which of the strictly contemporary works will survive the buffeting storms of fashion. Comparatively few poems are reprinted beyond a possible collected works; many seem dated by the end of a decade. Perhaps it would not be too much to say that the great poems are those that have outlived their generation.

And who are these so-called better readers of most of the subsequent periods? . . . They are the people who love poetry, who read widely and thoughtfully the poems of their own time and of the past; the scholars who devote themselves to the history and the principles of this art; the students, teachers, critics; the poets themselves. Poems that are vindicated by such a jury, not once only, but repeatedly in the successive periods since their first publication, certainly merit our respect and consideration.

But who is to say whether the poem-reading-experiences have been good for all these so-called better readers? . . . It is true that studies in literary reputation are more difficult to control than the somewhat more scientific polls of public opinion. But sometimes such studies can now be successfully made with the aid of modern bibliographies, critical studies, and literary histories. Books are reprinted in order to sell; they are bought to be read; they are read to satisfy certain interests or desires. The story of a poem's publication is some measure of its value to readers.[1] Another measure, and in some ways a more important one, is the body of recorded criticism.[2] At best this will be but a scattered sampling of the innumerable evaluations made by discriminating readers. Evaluating the evaluations in order to determine whether the poem really provided these numerous, successive better readers with good poem-experiences will, of course, require nice judgment.

Such by definition are the *great poems,* and quite a number of them have been set forth in the preceding pages of this book. Not only are Milton's sonnet "On His Blindness" and Keats' "Ode on a Grecian Urn" great, but also Browning's "The Glove," Shakespeare's "Spring and Winter," Housman's "To an Athlete Dying Young" and Landor's "Rose Aylmer," David's "Twenty-third

[1] *The Cambridge Bibliography of English Literature* and the bibliographies in *The Cambridge History of American Literature* record the publication of the successive editions of works by English and American poets—book-length poems and collections of poems, but without listing the separate poems in such collections. Special bibliographies have been compiled for many individual poets. *The United States Catalog* and *The Cumulative Book Index* list the editions recently published or in print. *Granger's Index to Poetry and Recitations* will serve as some measure of the reprinting of particular poems in anthologies.

[2] Moulton's *Library of Literary Criticism* is a valuable collection of critical comments upon individual literary words and authors, both English and American, though it was published more than a generation ago and therefore does not include contemporary estimates.

Psalm" and Whitman's "Song of Myself." Perhaps half of the poems in the chapters read so far have been in some degree *great poems* as we are using the term. However, most of the others have provided many readers with "good" reading-experiences. Some are too recent to have passed the test of time; some others have not been widely published or read; yet others, among the older poems, have come and gone and come again into favor. Certain ones, of course, are examples of "mediocre" or "bad" poetry—though there are many persons who would not have us call "bad verse" poetry at all.

Now, certain of these so-called "great poems" may fail to provide *you* with poem-experiences that *you* consider valuable. Everyone, honestly, has found this to be true. But if *none* or few only of the "great poems," of those that you have read, have been found by you to be "good," then may not the trouble be with you rather than with Poetry? Unhappy will be the man who is so completely out of touch with his fellows and his human ancestry that he can find no pleasure in the things that have pleasured them!

2. DEGREES OF GREATNESS

But just as there are degrees of goodness, so we may say that there are degrees of greatness. That is, if one poem has been valued "highly" by *many* of the "better" readers in *most* of the subsequent periods, another poem may have been valued yet "more highly" by *more* of the "best" readers in *all* of the subsequent periods. It is futile to debate at length such questions as these: Is Keats greater than Shelley? Is "Ode on a Grecian Urn" greater than "Ode to the West Wind"? And yet it is not hard to demonstrate that Shelley is greater than Leigh Hunt, and that "Ode to the West Wind" is greater than "The Glove and the Lions"; for there are a good many who say that Leigh Hunt is not great at all.

Take the four lyrics, for instance, given in Suggestions for Study #5 in the preceding chapter. Of these, Ben Jonson's song "To Celia" is a great poem. It not only provides me repeatedly with a good poem-experience; it has provided more than three centuries of readers and hearers, both critical and popular, with good poem-experiences. One has only to turn to the anthologies and song books and histories of literature to see that this is true. On the other hand, Tom Moore's "Believe Me, If All Those Endearing Young Charms" is not, in my opinion, a great poem. Written something over a century ago, it enjoyed and has continued to enjoy a certain popularity as a song. And, though this poem may be one of your favorites, I find it mediocre. There have not been many of the "better" readers of poetry in these latter times who have turned back again and again to this lyric for repeatedly valuable poem-experiences. As for Marion Ward's "I Love to Love," I judge it to be neither good nor great. It provides me, and the "better" readers of our time (if I know them), with thoroughly bad poem-experiences; nor has it made a place for itself among the poems greatly beloved by an earlier generation. But how shall we evaluate Celeste Turner Wright's "Thumbprint"? It certainly gives me a very good poem-experience, as it has other recent readers of *Wings,* that contemporary quarterly of verse in which it first appeared. But it cannot be called great in the sense that Ben Jonson's song is great, for it has not as yet reached a wide enough group of readers of this generation through frequent republication (that may still await it), nor has it yet been fired in the slow kiln of Time. And these are hallmarks of greatness as we are here using the word.

So, of the four lyrics, one is bad, one is mediocre, one is good, and one is great. . . . But let us come up into the wind on another tack, and examine a great poem at closer range.

3. A "GREAT" POEM

John Keats' "Ode to a Nightingale" is a great poem, according to our working definition. That fact does not insure your having a valuable experience reading it, but it may prompt you to give the poem a thoughtful, sensitive reading and evaluation.

ODE TO A NIGHTINGALE
John Keats

1

My heart aches, and a drowsy numbness pains
　My sense, as though of hemlock I had drunk,
Or emptied some dull opiate to the drains
　One minute past, and Lethe-wards had sunk:
'Tis not through envy of thy happy lot,
　But being too happy in thine happiness,—
　　That thou, light-wingèd Dryad of the trees,
　　　In some melodious plot
　Of beechen green, and shadows numberless,
　　Singest of summer in full-throated ease.

2

O, for a draught of vintage! that hath been
　Cool'd a long age in the deep-delved earth,
Tasting of Flora and the country green,
　Dance, and Provençal song, and sunburnt mirth!
O for a beaker full of the warm South,
　Full of the true, the blushful Hippocrene,
　　With beaded bubbles winking at the brim,
　　　And purple-stained mouth;
　That I might drink, and leave the world unseen,
　　And with thee fade away into the forest dim:

3

Fade far away, dissolve, and quite forget
　What thou among the leaves hast never known,
The weariness, the fever, and the fret
　Here, where men sit and hear each other groan;
Where palsy shakes a few, sad, last gray hairs,
　Where youth grows pale, and spectre-thin, and dies;
　　Where but to think is to be full of sorrow
　　　And leaden-eyed despairs,
　Where Beauty cannot keep her lustrous eyes,
　　Or new Love pine at them beyond tomorrow.

4

Away! away! for I will fly to thee,
  Not charioted by Bacchus and his pards,
But on the viewless wings of Poesy,
  Though the dull brain perplexes and retards:
Already with thee! tender is the night,
    And haply the Queen-Moon is on her throne,
      Cluster'd around by all her starry Fays;
        But here there is no light,
    Save what from heaven is with the breezes blown
      Through verdurous glooms and winding mossy ways.

5

I cannot see what flowers are at my feet,
  Nor what soft incense hangs upon the boughs,
But, in embalmèd darkness, guess each sweet
  Wherewith the seasonable month endows
The grass, the thicket, and the fruit-tree wild;
    White hawthorn, and the pastoral eglantine;
      Fast fading violets cover'd up in leaves;
        And mid-May's eldest child,
    The coming musk-rose, full of dewy wine,
      The murmurous haunt of flies on summer eves.

6

Darkling I listen; and, for many a time
  I have been half in love with easeful Death,
Call'd him soft names in many a musèd rhyme,
  To take into the air my quiet breath;
    Now more than ever seems it rich to die,
To cease upon the midnight with no pain,
    While thou art pouring forth thy soul abroad
      In such an ecstasy!
  Still wouldst thou sing, and I have ears in vain—
    To thy high requiem become a sod.

7

Thou wast not born for death, immortal Bird!
  No hungry generations tread thee down;

The voice I hear this passing night was heard
In ancient days by emperor and clown:
Perhaps the self-same song that found a path
Through the sad heart of Ruth, when, sick for home,
She stood in tears amid the alien corn;
The same that oft-times hath
.Charm'd magic casements, opening on the foam
Of perilous seas, in faery lands forlorn.

8

Forlorn! the very word is like a bell
To toll me back from thee to my sole self!
Adieu! the fancy cannot cheat so well
As she is fam'd to do, deceiving elf.
Adieu! adieu! thy plaintive anthem fades
Past the near meadows, over the still stream,
Up the hill-side; and now 'tis buried deep
In the next valley-glades:
Was it a vision, or a waking dream?
Fled is that music:—Do I wake or sleep?

(*1819,* 1820)

This poem has survived not only its decade but its century. It has been reprinted in countless hundreds of thousands of copies. I find it in every one of the first twelve recent anthologies that I reach down from my book shelves. It is listed in *Granger's Index* as appearing in 63 of some 400 miscellaneous collections that it indexes. The *Cambridge Bibliography* records 39 different editions of Keats' complete works, selections, and separate editions of this "Ode" that appeared between 1820 and 1928, and many of these editions have had many printings. *The United States Catalog: Books in Print January 1, 1928,* lists some 40 editions of Keats' works; *The Cumulative Book Index* (the volumes covering the years 1928-1945) lists some 34 more editions! There is no way to discover the total number of separate reprintings of the poem, for, as it is out of copyright, anyone may reprint it who wishes.

It is easy to determine the evaluation of the poem by certain ones of the better readers. The taste of poetry lovers as appraised by editors and anthologists determines the selection of a poem for inclusion in the general collections. The taste of teachers and students as appraised by textbook makers determines its inclusion in school texts. The judgment of critics and literary historians determines its place and inclusion in a variety of critical and historical works and anthologies. In four out of five recent books about poetry that I reach down from my shelves, Keats' "Ode to a Nightingale" is singled out for lengthy consideration as a great, if not perfect, poem.

Kipling wrote in special praise of the lines,

> Charm'd magic casements, opening on the foam
> Of perilous seas, in faery lands forlorn.

Of these, together with three lines from "Kubla Khan," he said: "These are the magic. These are the vision. The rest is only poetry." For the poet Swinburne it was "one of the finest masterpieces of human work in all time and for all ages." For the critic Stedman it was "of our shorter English lyrics . . . the nearest to perfection, the one I would surrender last of all." For Bryant, too, "there is scarce a word we should be willing to part with" in this one of Keats' odes. A contemporary review in the *Edinburgh Magazine* preferred it to the other poems in its volume; and a century later Robert Bridges also preferred it. Matthew Arnold felt that it had "the power of natural magic"; and Tennyson used to recite lines from it as expressive of "the innermost soul of poetry." [3]

Here is evidence that Keats' "Ode to a Nightingale" has provided successive "better" readers with good poem-reading-experiences— evidence sufficient to warrant our judgment that it is an undeniably *great poem*.

But let us turn from greatness in poetry to the question of Truth.

[3] These quotations are taken from Charles W. Moulton, ed., *Library of Literary Criticism*, Moulton, 1904, IV, 673-77; George B. Wood, ed., *English Poetry and Prose of the Romantic Movement*, Scott Foresman, 1916, p. 1291; and Dorothy Hewlett, *Adonais, A Life of John Keats*, Bobbs-Merrill, 1938, p. 327-46.

4. THE PROBLEM OF TRUTH

The *good,* the *true,* and the *beautiful.* These are famous words in the history of thought, and they are household words as well. We have already made cautious use of the word *beautiful* in the early chapter on "Language and Art," and of the word *good* in the last chapter; now for the word *true.*

There are many persons who hold that poems should be read *as poems*—not as historical or biographical documents, not as technical or formal exercises, not as exhortations on morals or conduct—but as poems. Above all the reader must avoid message-hunting (so they tell us) and eschew ethical considerations. And the implication seems to be that in poetry falsehood is as good as truth. This critical attitude is widespread, and is a modern development of the "art for art's sake" reaction in the last century to certain aspects of mid-Victorianism. However, it is difficult, if not impossible, for some other persons to read a poem richly and fully without considering its *truth*—its relationship to their experience of fact and belief.[4]

Let us turn our attention to a particular poem and then to our thoughts about its truth.

John Henry Newman was a leader in that spiritual revival within the Church of England known as the Oxford Movement. As vicar of St. Mary's, Oxford, from 1828-43, he influenced many younger men of his day, both through his preaching and his writing; but he was repudiated by his church superiors and resigned his vicarage. Two years later he became a Roman Catholic. As priest, then rector at the Catholic University in Dublin, and finally cardinal, he continued a deeply spiritual and influential life. "The Pillar of the Cloud," his best-known poem, was written when Newman, as a young man, was on a sea trip in the Mediterranean. The allusion in the title is to an incident in Moses' leading the Israelites out of Egypt:

[4] See I. A. Richards, *Basic Rules of Reason,* London, 1933, for a systematic application of the language machine to the theory of knowledge, with special consideration of the chief senses of such words as *fact, knowledge, belief,* and *true.*

And the Lord went before them by day in a pillar of a cloud, to lead them the way; and by night in a pillar of fire, to give them light; to go by day and night. He took not away the pillar of the cloud by day, nor the pillar of fire by night, from before the people.[5]

THE PILLAR OF THE CLOUD

John Henry Newman

Lead, Kindly Light, amid the encircling gloom,
    Lead Thou me on!
The night is dark, and I am far from home—
    Lead Thou me on!
Keep Thou my feet; I do not ask to see
The distant scene—one step enough for me.

I was not ever thus, nor prayed that Thou
    Shouldst lead me on.
I loved to choose and see my path; but now
    Lead Thou me on!
I loved the garish day, and, spite of fears,
Pride ruled my will; remember not past years.

So long Thy power hath blessed me, sure it still
    Will lead me on,
O'er moor and fen, o'er crag and torrent, till
    The night is gone;
And with the morn those angel faces smile
Which I have loved long since, and lost awhile.

                     (*1833, 1836*)

Simple as this hymn is in so many ways, it may still raise a number of interesting questions. Its title, as here given (for it is often called "Lead, Kindly Light"), is "The Pillar of the Cloud." But it was "a pillar of *fire*" that led Moses by night; and Newman says of his scene, "The night was dark." Or is the title intended merely to be allusive, sending the reader back to re-examine the two verses from *Exodus* so as to make his own application? Note also that, written on a sea voyage and suggested by the return of the Israel-

[5] *Exodus,* 13:22 and 14:25.

ites out of Egypt, the scene described suggests a very English path "o'er moor and fen, o'er crag and torrent." The following paraphrase may serve to stimulate the reader's closer attention to the poem itself and to his own experience of it.

O God of Light and Love, go before me now and make clear the road. The night is dark, and I am far away from friends and fireside. Keep me from falling; I have no need to see far—one step at a time is enough.

But I have not been of this mind in other times—in prayer for Your pointing the way. Before, I was pleased to make decisions for myself and to see the road far off in front of me; but now, will You be my guide. In the past I took pleasure in the bright daytime and, without thought of fears, I was self-important in my purposes. Do not keep this in Your mind against me!

You have given me so much in the past; certainly You will still give me light on my journey—across the waste lands and wet lands, across sharp mountains and rough rivers—till the night is gone and morning comes in which I will see the smiling of angels whom I have not seen for this long time.

Without considering here certain phrases that invite special attention—"kindly Light," "far from home," "the distant scene," "the garish day," "spite of fears," "Pride ruled my will," "Thy power hath blessed me," "those angel faces"—I should like to direct the reader's attention to three different general interpretations of the poem as a whole, hypothetical interpretations that may bring us around to the problem of poetry and Truth.

A Catholic reader (let us assume) might read "The Pillar of the Cloud" with the realization that Newman, who in this poem prays for Divine guidance, was subsequently led to the Church; that his errant years and venial sins were forgiven him; that, from the night of encircling gloom and confusion of spirit, he came into the cheerful morning of clear vision, into the presence of the angelic host; that he who had been lost awhile was at last brought home to God by His earthly Vicar.

A Protestant reader (it may be) might read "The Pillar of the Cloud" with the realization that it gave expression to that great spiritual revival within Anglican Protestantism known as the Oxford Movement; that Newman, who was indeed far from home when he wrote it, turned directly to Jesus Christ, the Light of the world, for personal guidance; that his sins were washed away by the acceptance of his Savior; that the way was made light in this closer walk with God; and that at last, Salvation and Glory!

A Jewish reader (to illustrate a different reading) might at once catch the Mosaic allusion in "The Pillar of the Cloud," and with Jehovah as the guiding Light in the pillar of fire, experience once again the liberation of the ancient Israelites from Egyptian bondage, and their escape through the Wilderness and the Red Sea; he might think of the Zionist prayer for guidance in returning Judaism to its ancient homeland; and of the millions of refugees wandering the wastelands of our own time.

There will, of course, be many other readings of Newman's poem: some persons may scorn his sentimental resort to prayer, mock his recourse to a fictitious god, discredit his taking refuge in a superstitious church. Others may interpret the guiding Light as that spark of God in each personality. But we shall confine ourselves to the three suggested above, and make one or two general remarks:

To Catholic, Protestant, and Jew as here represented "The Pillar of the Cloud" is a good poem, *good* (partly at least) *because it is true*. And yet how very different the truth is for each of these readers! It cannot be said that they are all three equally valid readings, if we hold that to be successful the reading experience should be comparable to the poet's; but for this "Pillar of the Cloud" we might not be in very close agreement regarding what the poet's experience really was. The truth is that *Truth*—when we take a broad view—the absolute Truth is, at best, seen by man as "through a glass, darkly"; and that, if we are not indeed blind as the six Hindus of fable who examined different parts of the elephant and then disputed its nature, at least our eyes are not yet opened to all that may be true.

"And ye shall know the truth, and the truth shall make you free." [6] These words, like so many of the great utterances—in

---

[6] *John*, 8:32.

poetry, in polity, and in philosophy—these words are rich in the possibility of meanings that are at once complex and simple, ambiguous and absolute, enigmatic and clear, obscure and obvious, the riddle and the answer. And in the arts, as in religion, there are those who definitely say they know the truth and who feel free therefore; and there are those who earnestly seek to know the truth and who feel free to follow the truth, as they see it, wherever it may lead them. But there are yet others who, with jesting Pilate, will ask, "What is truth?" and will not stay for an answer,[7] scorning the dogmatic and scoffing the seeker.

We have suggested three different interpretations of one poem, in which the readers' experiences have been measured against three different structures of religious truth, and have said that for each of these hypothetical readers the poem-experience was both good and true. Let us now proceed to some other and quite different poetry as the basis for our continuing discussion—two poems which logically and historically form a complementary pair.

5. TWO VIEWS OF LIFE

The *Rubáiyát of Omar Khayyám* has been an extremely popular poem for nearly a century. These quatrains of Omar the Tent-Maker, written by the Persian astronomer in the twelfth century, were loosely translated and paraphrased by Edward Fitzgerald. The present selection is made from the final version in which there are one hundred and one stanzas.[8]

from RUBÁIYÁT OF OMAR KHAYYÁM
Edward Fitzgerald

I

Awake! for Morning in the Bowl of Night
Has flung the Stone that puts the Stars to Flight:
    And Lo! the Hunter of the East has caught
The Sultan's Turret in a Noose of Light.

[7] See Francis Bacon's "Of Truth," *Essays*, I; and *John*, 18:38.
[8] Except that the first quatrain as here given is from Fitzgerald's first version.

7

Come, fill the Cup, and in the fire of Spring
Your Winter-garment of Repentance fling:
  The Bird of Time has but a little way
To flutter—and the Bird is on the Wing.

9

Each Morn a thousand Roses brings, you say;
Yes, but where leaves the Rose of Yesterday?
  And this first Summer month that brings the Rose
Shall take Jamshyd and Kaikobád away.

12

A Book of Verses underneath the Bough,
A Jug of Wine, a Loaf of Bread—and Thou
  Beside me singing in the Wilderness—
Oh, Wilderness were Paradise enow!

13

Some for the Glories of This World; and some
Sigh for the Prophet's Paradise to come;
  Ah, take the Cash, and let the Credit go,
Nor heed the rumble of a distant Drum!

21

Ah, my Belovéd, fill the Cup that clears
Today of past Regrets and future Fears:
  Tomorrow!—Why, Tomorrow I may be
Myself with Yesterday's Sev'n Thousand Years.

54

Waste not your Hour, nor in the vain pursuit
Of This and That endeavor and dispute;
  Better be jocund with the fruitful Grape
Than sadden after none, or bitter, Fruit.

63

Oh threats of Hell and Hopes of Paradise!
One thing at least is certain—*This* Life flies;

One thing is certain and the rest is Lies—
The Flower that once has blown for ever dies.

64

Strange, is it not? that of the myriads who
Before us pass'd the door of Darkness through,
 Not one returns to tell us of the Road,
Which to discover we must travel too.

66

I sent my Soul through the Invisible,
Some letter of that After-life to spell:
 And by and by my Soul return'd to me,
And answer'd "I Myself am Heav'n and Hell:"

67

Heav'n but the Vision of fulfill'd Desire,
And Hell the Shadow from a Soul on fire,
 Cast on the Darkness into which Ourselves,
So late emerged from, shall so soon expire.

74

YESTERDAY *This* Day's Madness did prepare;
TOMORROW's Silence, Triumph, or Despair:
 Drink! for you know not whence you came, nor why:
Drink! for you know not why you go, nor where.

82

As under cover of departing Day
Slunk hunger-stricken Ramàzan away,
 Once more within the Potter's house alone
I stood, surrounded by the Shapes of Clay.

83

Shapes of all Sorts and Sizes, great and small,
That stood along the floor and by the wall;
 And some loquacious Vessels were; and some
Listen'd perhaps, but never talk'd at all.

84

Said one among them—"Surely not in vain
My substance of the common Earth was ta'en
   And to this Figure moulded, to be broke,
Or trampled back to shapeless Earth again."

85

Then said a Second—"Ne'er a peevish Boy
Would break the Bowl from which he drank in joy;
   And He that with his hand the Vessel made
Will surely not in after Wrath destroy."

86

After a momentary silence spake
Some Vessel of a more ungainly Make:
   "They sneer at me for leaning all awry:
What! did the Hand then of the Potter shake?"

87

Whereat some one of the loquacious Lot—
I think a Sufi pipkin—waxing hot—
   "All this of Pot and Potter—Tell me then,
Who is the Potter, pray, and who the Pot?"

88

"Why," said another, "Some there are who tell
Of one who threatens he will toss to Hell
   The luckless Pots he marr'd in making—Pish!
He's a Good Fellow, and 'twill all be well."

89

"Well," murmur'd one, "Let whoso make or buy,
My Clay with long Oblivion is gone dry:
   But fill me with the old familiar Juice,
Methinks I might recover by and by."

90

So while the Vessels one by one were speaking,
The little Moon look'd in that all were seeking:

And then they jogg'd each other, "Brother! Brother!
Now for the Porter's shoulder-knot a-creaking!"

96

Yet Ah, that Spring should vanish with the Rose!
That Youth's sweet-scented manuscript should close!
  The Nightingale that in the branches sang,
Ah whence, and whither flown again, who knows!

99

Ah Love! could you and I with Him conspire
To grasp this sorry Scheme of Things Entire,
  Would not we shatter it to bits—and then
Re-mould it nearer to the Heart's desire!
                              (1859-79)

The second poem of this pair is "Rabbi Ben Ezra," from which
again only selected stanzas will be given so as to bring some of
Browning's ideas into more immediate contrast to Fitzgerald's.
Robert Browning, who was fond of rabbinical lore, knew the writ-
ings of Ibn Ezra, the twelfth century Jewish scholar and theologian
who was born in Spain, traveled in Arabia and Palestine, and died
in Rome. In his dramatic monologue, Browning imagines the
Rabbi as addressing himself to a youth.

from RABBI BEN EZRA
Robert Browning

1

Grow old along with me!
  The best is yet to be,
The last of life, for which the first was made:
  Our times are in His hand
  Who saith "A whole I planned,
Youth shows but half; trust God: see all nor be afraid!"

5

Rejoice we are allied
To That which doth provide

And not partake, effect and not receive!
  A spark disturbs our clod;
  Nearer we hold of God
Who gives, than of His tribes that take, I must believe.

6

  Then, welcome each rebuff
  That turns earth's smoothness rough,
Each sting that bids nor sit nor stand but go!
  Be our joys three-parts pain!
  Strive, and hold cheap the strain;
Learn, nor account the pang; dare, never grudge the throe!

7

  For thence,—a paradox
  Which comforts while it mocks,—
Shall life succeed in that it seems to fail:
  What I aspired to be,
  And was not, comforts me:
A brute I might have been, but would not sink i' the scale.

8

  What is he but a brute
  Whose flesh has soul to suit,
Whose spirit works lest arms and legs want play?
  To man, propose this test—
  Thy body at its best,
How far can that project thy soul on its lone way?

12

  Let us not always say
  "Spite of this flesh today
I strove, made head, gained ground upon the whole!"
  As the bird wings and sings,
  Let us cry "All good things
Are ours, nor soul helps flesh more, now, than flesh helps soul!"

13

  Therefore I summon age
  To grant youth's heritage,

Life's struggle having so far reached its term:
    Thence shall I pass, approved
    A man, for aye removed
From the developed brute; a god though in the germ.

15

    Youth ended, I shall try
    My gain or loss thereby;
Leave the fire ashes, what survives is gold:
    And I shall weigh the same,
    Give life its praise or blame:
Young, all lay in dispute; I shall know, being old.

19

    As it was better, youth
    Should strive, through acts uncouth,
Toward making, than repose on aught found made:
    So, better, age, exempt
    From strife, should know, than tempt
Further. Thou waitest age: wait death nor be afraid!

23

    Not on the vulgar mass
    Called "work," must sentence pass,
Things done, that took the eye and had the price;
    O'er which, from level stand,
    The low world laid its hand,
Found straightway to its mind, could value in a trice:

24

    But all, the world's coarse thumb
    And finger failed to plumb,
So passed in making up the main account;
    All instincts immature,
    All purposes unsure,
That weighed not as his work, yet swelled the man's amount:

25

    Thoughts hardly to be packed
    Into a narrow act,

Fancies that broke through language and escaped;
    All I could never be,
    All, men ignored in me,
This, I was worth to God, whose wheel the pitcher shaped.

26

    Ay, note that Potter's wheel,
    That metaphor! and feel
Why time spins fast, why passive lies our clay,—
    Thou, to whom fools propound,
    When the wine makes its round,
"Since life fleets, all is change; the Past gone, seize today!"

27

    Fool! All that is, at all,
    Lasts ever, past recall;
Earth changes, but thy soul and God stand sure:
    What entered into thee,
    That was, is, and shall be:
Time's wheel runs back or stops: Potter and clay endure.

30

    Look not thou down but up!
    To uses of a cup,
The festal board, lamp's flash and trumpet's peal,
    The new wine's foaming flow,
    The Master's lips a-glow!
Thou, heaven's consummate cup, what need'st thou
    with earth's wheel?

31

    But I need, now as then,
    Thee, God, who mouldest men;
And since, not even while the whirl was worst,
    Did I,—to the wheel of life
    With shapes and colours rife,
Bound dizzily,—mistake my end, to slake Thy thirst:

32

So, take and use Thy work:
Amend what flaws may lurk,
What strain o' the stuff, what warpings past the aim!
My times be in Thy hand!
Perfect the cup as planned!
Let age approve of youth, and death complete the same!

(1864)

6. BELIEF AND SUSPENSION OF DISBELIEF

The reader of these two poems may note at once that they con-
tradict each other. Indeed it is generally agreed that Browning read
the early edition of Fitzgerald's *Rubáiyát* and answered him by
making use of Ibn Ezra. "Ay, note that Potter's wheel,/ That
metaphor," [9] writes Browning, and then launches into a direct re-
futation of the *carpe diem* philosophy of Omar Khayyám. As was
the case with the three different philosophies suggested by Rossetti
in "The Choice" (p. 237), the Fitzgerald-Khayyám hedonism and
the Browning-Ezra Judeo-Christianity cannot *both* be true. At
least, they cannot both be true at the same time for the same person,
who must either believe in the doctrine of immortality, as he understands it, or not believe in it.

And yet . . . millions of readers who have not been hedonists
or epicureans, who have been temperate and circumspect, who have
not seriously doubted spiritual survival, have read the *Rubáiyát,*
have carried it with them and quoted it in love, have found it good
and valued it highly! . . . "But how can a person like it if he
doesn't believe it? how can it be good if it isn't true? if it's really
a pack of lies—?!" The friction of ideas generates a certain amount
of heat, if not always light.

It is true that (1) some persons read the *Rubáiyát* without having very clear or connected thoughts about its meaning, and they
enjoy the "Book of Verses underneath the Bough . . . and Thou/
Beside me singing in the Wilderness," with an enthusiasm gener-

[9] The metaphor is from *Isaiah,* 64:8, and *Jeremiah,* 18:2-6. Browning, by the
way, seems to have read Ibn Ezra's commentary on *Isaiah.*

ated by the dashing typography, the flowing stanzas, the senten-
tious style, and the oriental scenery, but without worrying themselves about the philosophical implications; for them it is really
neither true nor untrue. (2) Certain readers, interpreting it more
closely, find it gives expression to their own views of life, and they
like it because for them it is *true.* (3) Certain others who also read
it critically, are annoyed by the facility and flippancy with which
it advances thoughts that for them are *untrue,* and they dislike and
reject it. (4) Yet others there are who read it and understand its
implications, but play a sort of game with themselves, accepting
the thought of the poem *as if it were true,* pretending to believe
what they really don't believe, assuming the truth of what they
really hold to be false, enjoying the make-believe. And about this
last hoodwinking of Truth and dallying with Falsehood (as some
would denounce it), something more must be said.

Coleridge, the early nineteenth century critic and poet, spoke of
"that willing suspension of disbelief for the moment, which con-
stitutes poetic faith," and which he expected from the readers of
his poems of the supernatural and the romantic.[10] And his friend
Charles Lamb explained, in a whimsical essay "On the Artificial
Comedy of the Last Century," that he left his everyday morality
behind him, "glad for a season to take an airing beyond the diocese
of the strict conscience," when he entered "the land . . . of cuck-
oldry" of Congreve's Restoration gallants, faithless wives, and duped
husbands.[11] We are accustomed in our own time to various "es-
capist" theories of fiction and cinema. And this may bring us to
the suggestion that *poetic* truth might be distinguished by the reader
from what he would consider the *real* truth that guides his life.
For the purposes of the poem-experience, he may be satisfied to
accept the poetic truth *as if it were* the real truth.

And so the pessimist, who doesn't believe in Browning's so-called
philosophy of the imperfect (the paradox: "Shall life succeed in
that it seems to fail")—the hedonist, unsympathetic to Browning's
Christian optimism ("wait death nor be afraid!" for "All that is,

[10] Samuel Taylor Coleridge, *Biographia Literaria,* chap. xiv.
[11] Many disagreed with him, and Macaulay answered him in the *Edinburgh
Review* a score of years later (July, 1841).

at all,/ Lasts ever, past recall")—such a person may be *willing to play the game* of Browning's system of ideas; and he may actually judge his experience of "Rabbi Ben Ezra" to be very good indeed and rich in *poetic truth*.

In the last chapter it was said that the good experience will be "full of life and free from conflict." If the hedonist is able willingly to suspend disbelief, there will be no conflict as he reads "Rabbi Ben Ezra," and his experience will be good or not depending upon how "full of life" the poem-experience is; but if he is unable to leave his disbelief behind him, his reading will be "full of conflict," and the poem-experience will not be good.

Happily, most persons can operate with poetic truth in this way. Protestants can read Francis Thompson, Catholics can read William Cowper, both can read Heinrich Heine and David. Modern Naturalists cannot only read T. S. Eliot, but also Matthew Arnold, and Tennyson, and Wordsworth, and Milton. And though they may keep their tongue in cheek, and willingly suspend disbelief, their reading of "Dover Beach" (for instance) may increase their understanding of Matthew Arnold and their tolerance of persons quite unlike themselves.

So, in reading the *great* poems, various as they are and giving expression to diverse philosophies, Truth may quietly be served for those willing to glimpse the Light reflected from Its multifarious facets.

SUGGESTIONS FOR STUDY

1. *The Nightingale Again*. Make a further study of Keats' "Ode to a Nightingale."

(a) Read it again and again, giving attention separately to the several aspects of the poem-experience. The following brief notes may be of some help: In December 1818 John Keats' brother Tom died of consumption, and the poet (who had already contracted the disease) nursed him tenderly and tirelessly. John Keats fell passionately in love with Fanny Brawne, but realized that, without means and in poor health, he could never hope to marry her. In the spring of 1819, a nightingale built her nest near the house where John Keats was living. He "took great pleasure in her song," wrote Lord Houghton, "and one morning took his chair from the breakfast-table to the grass plot under a plum tree, where he remained between two and three hours. He then reached the house with some scraps of paper in his hand, which he soon put together in the form of this Ode." For the story of Ruth, who "stood in tears amid the alien corn," see the *Book of Ruth*, 2:2 ff. Of the following words, all of which are to be found in *Webster's Collegiate Dictionary* (fifth edition), some may be strange to you, and others may be used in senses with which you are not familiar: *hemlock* (the drug made from it), *Lethe, Dryad, draught* (pronunciation), *vintage, Flora, Provençal, beaker, Hippocrene, spectre, pards, viewless, Fays, embalmed, pastoral, eglantine, requiem, clown, corn.* Now reread "Ode to a Nightingale" so as to see the interrelationship of the several aspects of your experience of the poem. (By the way, do *not* reread the evaluative comments quoted in the text.)

(b) Write a carefully-thought-out paper, say two pages long, in which you try to give as full an account of your experience as you can within the limits of that space.

(c) Now find an extended critical discussion of "Ode to a Nightingale." The following are likely places to look: a biography or critical study of John Keats, a critical study of the literature or the poetry of the Romantic Movement or of the Nineteenth Century, or more general discussions of poetry. In recent books of this last sort, the following include analyses of interest: Blair and Chandler, *Approaches to Poetry,* D. Appleton-Century, 1935 (pp. 552-56); Brooks and Warren, *Understanding Poetry,* Holt, 1938 (pp. 407-15); Thomas and Brown, *Reading Poems,* Oxford Press, 1941 (pp. 658-60); Earl Daniels, *The Art of Reading Poetry,* Farrar & Rinehart, 1941 (pp. 366-72).

(d) In what ways and at what points does your account differ from that of the critic you have just read? Make a few specific comparative notes.

2. *The Greatness of the Rubáiyát.* In what degree is Edward Fitzgerald's *Rubáiyát of Omar Khayyám* a great poem? Study the history of its publication and of its evaluation by the so-called better readers. Glance back to the first half of this chapter and to the footnotes for suggestions as to bibliographical tools. Take notes on your findings, and work out a statement of your conclusions regarding the greatness of the *Rubáiyát.*

3. *Rationalism and "Enthusiasm."* The following two hymns, from the early and late eighteenth century, represent two very different approaches to religious truth. You may have sung them at one time or another without giving much thought to them. Study them closely. What is the relation of one to the other? What is the relation of each to the system of ideas in which you yourself place belief?

THE SPACIOUS FIRMAMENT ON HIGH

from THE SPECTATOR, no. 465

Joseph Addison

The spacious firmament on high,
With all the blue ethereal sky,
And spangled heavens, a shining frame,
Their great Original proclaim.
The unwearied Sun, from day to day,
Does his Creator's power display;
And publishes to every land
The work of an Almighty hand.

Soon as the evening shades prevail,
The Moon takes up the wondrous tale;
And nightly to the listening Earth
Repeats the story of her birth:
Whilst all the stars that round her burn,
And all the planets in their turn,
Confirm the tidings as they roll
And spread the truth from pole to pole.

What though, in solemn silence, all
Move round the dark terrestrial ball?
What though nor real voice nor sound
Amidst their radiant orbs be found?
In Reason's ear they all rejoice,
And utter forth a glorious voice;
For ever singing as they shine,
"The Hand that made us is divine."

(1712)

WALKING WITH GOD [12]

from OLNEY HYMNS

William Cowper

Oh! for a closer walk with God,
A calm and heavenly frame;

[12] An allusion to *Genesis*, 5:24.

A light to shine upon the road
That leads me to the Lamb!

Where is the blessedness I knew
When first I saw the Lord?
Where is the soul-refreshing view
Of Jesus and his word?

What peaceful hours I once enjoyed!
How sweet their memory still!
But they have left an aching void
The world can never fill.

Return, O holy Dove, return,
Sweet messenger of rest!
I hate the sins that made thee mourn
And drove thee from my breast.

The dearest idol I have known,
Whate'er that idol be,
Help me to tear it from thy throne,
And worship only thee.

So shall my walk be close with God,
Calm and serene my frame;
So purer light shall mark the road
That leads me to the Lamb.

(1779)

4. *Faith and Doubt*. The two poems here paired were written by an American poet and an English poet during the nineteenth century, and represent quite different interpretations of religious truth.

(a) The first of these is by John Greenleaf Whittier, the Quaker poet and Abolitionist. The background of the poem is the so-called unprogrammed worship still characteristic of the First-Day (Sunday) meetings among certain groups of Friends, where, without priest or preacher, men and women sit in quiet meditation waiting upon "the still small voice" that will direct their steps, and reading God's commandment from their hearts, as Moses read the tablets on Mount Sinai.

FIRST-DAY THOUGHTS
John Greenleaf Whittier

In calm and cool and silence, once again
  I find my old accustomed place among
  My brethren, where, perchance, no human tongue
  Shall utter words; where never hymn is sung,
  Nor deep-toned organ blown, nor censer swung,
Nor dim light falling through the pictured pane!
There, syllabled by silence, let me hear
The still small voice which reached the prophet's ear;
Read in my heart a still diviner law
Than Israel's leader on his tables saw!
There let me strive with each besetting sin,
  Recall my wandering fancies, and restrain
  The sore disquiet of a restless brain;
  And, as the path of duty is made plain,
May grace be given that I may walk therein,
  Not like the hireling, for his selfish gain,
With backward glances and reluctant tread,
Making a merit of his coward dread,—
  But, cheerful, in the light around me thrown,
  Walking as one to pleasant service led;
  Doing God's will as if it were my own,
Yet trusting not in mine, but in His strength alone!
                            (1853)

(b) The second poem in this pair grows out of a different background. Matthew Arnold, son of Thomas Arnold, Anglican headmaster of Rugby School, was himself a teacher, inspector of schools, and professor of poetry at Oxford. He was deeply sensitive to the critical and religious ideas of his time, to the disturbing effects of scientific thought, to the doubts that plagued the faith of many of his contemporaries.

DOVER BEACH
Matthew Arnold

The sea is calm tonight.
The tide is full, the moon lies fair

Upon the straits;—on the French coast the light
Gleams and is gone; the cliffs of England stand,
Glimmering and vast, out in the tranquil bay.
Come to the window, sweet is the night-air!
Only, from the long line of spray
Where the sea meets the moon-blanch'd land,
Listen! you hear the grating roar
Of pebbles which the waves draw back, and fling,
At their return, up the high strand,
Begin, and cease, and then again begin,
With tremulous cadence slow, and bring
The eternal note of sadness in.

Sophocles long ago
Heard it on the Aegean, and it brought
Into his mind the turbid ebb and flow
Of human misery; we
Find also in the sound a thought,
Hearing it by this distant northern sea.

The Sea of Faith
Was once, too, at the full, and round earth's shore
Lay like the folds of a bright girdle furl'd.
But now I only hear
Its melancholy, long, withdrawing roar,
Retreating, to the breath
Of the night-wind, down the vast edges drear
And naked shingles of the world.

Ah, love, let us be true
To one another! for the world, which seems
To lie before us like a land of dreams,
So various, so beautiful, so new,
Hath really neither joy, nor love, nor light,
Nor certitude, nor peace, nor help for pain;
And we are here as on a darkling plain
Swept with confused alarms of struggle and flight,
Where ignorant armies clash by night.

(1867)

5. *"Long Pursuit"* or *"Unweeting Way."* [13] The two poems of this
third pair are a part of what we call Modern Poetry. Again the poets
have given expression to their deepest conceptions of religious truth.

THE HOUND OF HEAVEN
Francis Thompson

I fled Him, down the nights and down the days;
  I fled Him, down the arches of the years;
I fled Him, down the labyrinthine ways
  Of my own mind; and in the mist of tears
 I hid from Him, and under running laughter.
      Up vistaed hopes I sped;
      And shot, precipitated,
Adown Titanic glooms of chasmèd fears,
  From those strong Feet that followed, followed after.
      But with unhurrying chase,
      And unperturbèd pace,
  Deliberate speed, majestic instancy,
      They beat—and a Voice beat
      More instant than the Feet—
"All things betray thee, who betrayest Me."

      I pleaded, outlaw-wise,
By many a hearted casement, curtained red,
  Trellised with intertwining charities
(For, though I knew His love Who followèd,
      Yet was I sore adread
Lest, having Him, I must have naught beside);
But, if one little casement parted wide,
  The gust of His approach would clash it to:
  Fear wist not to evade, as Love wist to pursue.
Across the margent of the world I fled,
  And troubled the gold gateways of the stars,
  Smiting for shelter on their clangèd bars;
      Fretted to dulcet jars
And silvern chatter the pale ports o' the moon.
I said to Dawn: Be sudden—to Eve: Be soon;

[13] *Unweeting* is a negative form of the participle of the archaic verb *wit,* which
means "to know, or have knowledge of, to learn, to be or become aware of." The
past tense of this verb is *wist.*

With thy young skiey blossoms heap me over
  From this tremendous Lover—
Float thy vague veil about me, lest He see!
  I tempted all His servitors, but to find
My own betrayal in their constancy,
In faith to Him their fickleness to me,
  Their traitorous trueness, and their loyal deceit.
To all swift things for swiftness did I sue;
  Clung to the whistling mane of every wind.
    But whether they swept, smoothly fleet,
    The long savannahs of the blue;
      Or whether, Thunder-driven,
      They clanged his chariot 'thwart a heaven,
Plashy with flying lightnings round the spurn o' their feet:—
  Fear wist not to evade as Love wist to pursue.
      Still with unhurrying chase,
      And unperturbèd pace,
    Deliberate speed, majestic instancy,
      Came on the following Feet,
      And a Voice above their beat—
  "Naught shelters thee, who wilt not shelter Me."

I sought no more that after which I strayed
      In face of man or maid;
But still within the little children's eyes
      Seems something, something that replies,
They at least are for me, surely for me!
I turned me to them very wistfully;
But just as their young eyes grew sudden fair
      With dawning answers there,
Their angel plucked them from me by the hair.
"Come then, ye other children, Nature's—share
With me" (said I) "your delicate fellowship;
      Let me greet you lip to lip,
      Let me twine with you caresses,
        Wantoning
      With our Lady-Mother's vagrant tresses,
        Banqueting
      With her in her wind-walled palace,
      Underneath her azured daïs,

Quaffing, as your taintless way is,
>   From a chalice
Lucent-weeping out of the dayspring."
>   So it was done:
I in their delicate fellowship was one—
Drew the bolt of Nature's secrecies.
>   *I* knew all the swift importings
>   On the willful face of skies;
>   I knew how the clouds arise
>   Spumèd of the wild sea-snortings;
>   All that's born or dies
>   Rose and drooped with; made them shapers
Of mine own moods, or wailful or divine;
>   With them joyed and was bereaven.
>   I was heavy with the even,
>   When she lit her glimmering tapers
>   Round the day's dead sanctities.
>   I laughed in the morning's eyes.
I triumphed and I saddened with all weather,
>   Heaven and I wept together,
And its sweet tears were salt with mortal mine;

Against the red throb of its sunset-heart
>   I laid my own to beat,
>   And share commingling heat;
But not by that, by that, was eased my human smart.
In vain my tears were wet on Heaven's gray cheek.
For ah! we know not what each other says,
>   These things and I; in sound *I* speak—
Their sound is but their stir, they speak by silences.
Nature, poor stepdame, cannot slake my drouth;
>   Let her, if she would owe me,
Drop yon blue bosom-veil of sky, and show me
>   The breasts o' her tenderness:
Never did any milk of hers once bless
>   My thirsting mouth.
>   Nigh and nigh draws the chase,
>   With unperturbèd pace,
>   Deliberate speed, majestic instancy;
>   And past those noisèd Feet

A Voice comes yet more fleet—
"Lo! naught contents thee, who content'st not Me."

Naked I wait Thy love's uplifted stroke!
My harness piece by piece Thou hast hewn from me,
    And smitten me to my knee;
    I am defenseless utterly.
    I slept, methinks, and woke,
And, slowly gazing, find me stripped in sleep.
In the rash lustihead of my young powers,
    I shook the pillaring hours
And pulled my life upon me; grimed with smears,
I stand amid the dust o' the mounded years—
My mangled youth lies dead beneath the heap.
My days have crackled and gone up in smoke,
Have puffed and burst as sun-starts on a stream.
    Yea, faileth now even dream
The dreamer, and the lute the lutanist;
Even the linked fantasies, in whose blossomy twist
I swung the earth a trinket at my wrist,
Are yielding; cords of all too weak account
For earth with heavy griefs so overplused.
    Ah! is Thy love indeed
A weed, albeit an amaranthine weed,
Suffering no flowers except its own to mount?
    Ah! must—
    Designer infinite!—
Ah! must Thou char the wood ere Thou canst limn with it?
My freshness spent its wavering shower i' the dust;
And now my heart is as a broken fount,
Wherein tear-dripping stagnate, spilt down ever
    From the dank thoughts that shiver
Upon the sighful branches of my mind.
    Such is; what is to be?
The pulp so bitter, how shall taste the rind?
I dimly guess what Time in mists confounds;
Yet ever and anon a trumpet sounds
From the hid battlements of Eternity;
Those shaken mists a space unsettle, then

Round the half-glimpsèd turrets slowly wash again.
    But not ere him who summoneth
    I first have seen, enwound
With glooming robes purpureal, cypress-crowned;
His name I know, and what his trumpet saith.
Whether man's heart or life it be which yields
    Thee harvest, must Thy harvest-fields
    Be dunged with rotten death?

    Now of that long pursuit
    Comes on at hand the bruit;
    That Voice is round me like a bursting sea:
    "And is thy earth so marred,
    Shattered in shard on shard?
    Lo, all things fly thee, for thou fliest Me!
    Strange, piteous, futile thing!
Wherefore should any set thee love apart?
Seeing none but I makes much of naught" (He said),
"And human love needs human meriting:
    How hast thou merited—
Of all man's clotted clay the dingiest clot?
    Alack, thou knowest not
How little worthy of any love thou art!
Whom wilt thou find to love ignoble thee
    Save Me, save only Me?
All which I took from thee I did but take,
    Not for thy harms,
But just that thou might'st seek it in My arms.
    All which thy child's mistake
Fancies as lost, I have stored for thee at home:
    Rise, clasp My hand, and come!"

    Halts by me that footfall:
    Is my gloom, after all,
Shade of His hand, outstretched caressingly?
    "Ah, fondest, blindest, weakest,
    I am He Whom thou seekest!
Thou dravest love from thee, who dravest Me."
            (*1891, 1893*)

NEW YEAR'S EVE
Thomas Hardy

"I have finished another year," said God,
    "In gray, green, white and brown;
I have strewn the leaf upon the sod,
Sealed up the worm within the clod,
    And let the last sun down."

"And what's the good of it?" I said,
    "What reasons made you call
From formless void this earth we tread,
When nine-and-ninety can be read
    Why nought should be at all?

"Yea, Sire; why shaped you us, 'who in
    This tabernacle groan'—
If ever a joy be found herein,
Such joy no man had wished to win
    If he had never known!"

Then he: "My labors—logicless—
    You may explain; not I:
Sense-sealed I have wrought, without a guess
That I evolved a Consciousness
    To ask for reasons why.

"Strange that ephemeral creatures who
    By my own ordering are,
Should see the shortness of my view,
Use ethic tests I never knew,
    Or made provision for!"

He sank to raptness as of yore,
    And opening New Year's Day
Wove it by rote as theretofore,
And went on working evermore
    In his unweeting way.

                              (*1906*)

(a) Find brief accounts of the lives of Francis Thompson and Thomas Hardy. Short biographical notes on recent poets are to be found in Louis Untermeyer's *Modern British Poetry* and *Modern American Poetry,* Harcourt, Brace, 1942. A useful reference work is Kunitz and Haycraft's *Twentieth Century Authors,* H. W. Wilson Co., 1942. *The Dictionary of American Biography* and the supplementary volumes of *The Dictionary of National Biography* (British) give comprehensive but compressed articles upon modern poets, but only for those already deceased.

(b) Put this biographical data to work in a careful reinterpretation of the two poems.

(c) Contrast the two poets' conceptions of God in His relationship to Man.

6. *Belief and the Suspension of Disbelief.* Glance back over the six poems presented in the three pairs. Read them carefully once again, with a sincere effort to understand the several poets' religious attitudes, specifically their attitudes toward God. The systems of religious belief here illustrated may be called (*for our present purposes*): 1. Rational deism, 2. Evangelicalism, 3. Quakerism, 4. Agnosticism, 5. Catholicism, 6. Naturalism.

(a) To which one or ones of these poems can you say, "This is what I believe to be true"?

(b) In reading which one or ones of the poems were you conscious of a willing suspension of disbelief that allowed you to enjoy the poem quite as though you believed it to be true?

(c) Which one or ones of the poems were bad (for you) because the experience, though perhaps full of life, was not free from conflict? That is, did you keep saying, "I don't believe this!" "It's not so!" "That's all superstition!" as you were reading any one or ones of the poems?

(d) Make this the occasion for setting down, in the form of an essay, your own conceptions of religious truth.

12

POETIC IMMEDIACY—AND SO FORTH

The reading of poetry is worth while—it may give you pleasure, make you happy, keep you sane. In an early chapter it was pointed out that in poetry language is primarily serving its art function of emotional adjustment. And a later chapter was devoted to the discussion of the changes in personal attitude that may result as a part of the reader's poem-experience. Poetry—other literature, too, and works in the other arts—poetry may indeed "minister to a mind diseas'd"; it may indeed bring peace to "that noble and most sovereign reason" when "like sweet bells jangled" it is "out of tune and harsh"; it may indeed be "the balm from Gilead."

I. POETIC THERAPY

Not that the readers of poetry are out of their minds! But each and every personality is in constant need of at least minor repair and adjustment: the healing of inner hurts, the resolution of doubts, the regulation of desires, the deflation of egocentricity, the restoration of ideals. Perhaps the deepest of human ills, those of the spirit, find their remedy in the widely various practices of religion. Some such maladjustments are in this day the concern of psychiatry. Many, very many, however, of the lesser maladies of the mind respond to the ministrations of art.

One man, too tired and tense to rest, turns on the radio, listens to the César Franck *Symphony,* and finds himself relaxed and refreshed. Another person, torn by conflicting interests, attends a performance of Shakespeare's *The Tempest,* and, moved by the spectacle of its storm and contending creatures, comes away with a feeling of integration and peace within. For some persons, the reading of poetry effects the same almost miraculous personality adjustments; and this is widely recognized. Robert Haven Schauffler has entitled one of his anthologies *The Poetry Cure: a Pocket Medicine Chest of Verse,* arranging his selections to encourage home doctoring of the inner man. And Robert Graves, in his *On Reading Poetry,* writes: "A well-chosen anthology is a complete dispensary of medicine for the more common mental disorders, and may be used as much for prevention as cure."

Such is poetic therapy.

Is there anyone who has not, at some time, felt the terrific instancy, the overwhelming impact, of a particular drama or novel or poem at some particular moment in his life? The sailor who during the forlorn anchor watch reconciled himself to his fate by turning to his pocket *Rubáiyát*—the girl in a restrictive environment to whom *Walt Whitman* opened the window upon a new and fresh world—the city youth who, upon first looking into Chapman's *Homer,* suddenly felt the thrill of discovery and adventuresome exploration! A particular poem, in each of these three cases, "spoke to the condition" of the reader (to use a phrase from George Fox), satisfying his unique emotional needs, readjusting his attitudes, restoring a balance amongst his various interests.

2. SPEAKING TO THE READER'S CONDITION

A poem which illustrates the way the reader's unique condition may thus be spoken to, is Browning's "Saul." This is a long, and in some ways difficult, dramatic monologue, well worth study in its entirety. But to hasten its application to this discussion of poetic immediacy, it will be presented here in summary and condensation.

According to the Biblical account, when King Saul was at strife with a spirit, his servants asked permission "to seek out a man who is a cunning player on an harp: and it shall come to pass, when the evil spirit from God is upon thee, that he shall play with his hand, and thou shalt be well." [1] It is the boy David, the psalmist, whom the poet here conceives as relating the incident.

[1] *I Samuel,* 16:14-23.

from SAUL

Robert Browning

[King Saul, agonizing in spiritual conflict, summoned the shepherd boy David to come and sing for him. David arrived, was greeted by Saul's cousin Abner, and went into the inner tent where, in the dark, stood Saul, erect against the tent-prop, with arms outstretched along the cross support.]

5

Then I tuned my harp,—took off the lilies we twine round its chords
Lest they snap 'neath the stress of the noontide—those sunbeams like swords!
And I first played the tune all our sheep know, as, one after one,
So docile they come to the pen-door till folding be done.
They are white and untorn by the bushes, for lo, they have fed
Where the long grasses stifle the water within the stream's bed;
And now one after one seeks its lodging, as star follows star
Into eve and the blue far above us,—so blue and so far!

6

—Then the tune, for which quails on the cornland will each leave his mate
To fly after the player; then, what makes the crickets elate
Till for boldness they fight one another: and then, what has weight
To set the quick jerboa a-musing outside his sand house—
There are none such as he for a wonder, half bird and half mouse!
God made all the creatures and gave them our love and our fear,
To give sign, we and they are his children, one family here.

7

Then I played the help-tune of our reapers, their wine-song, when hand
Grasps at hand, eye lights eye in good friendship, and great hearts expand
And grow one in the sense of this world's life.—And then, the last song
When the dead man is praised on his journey—"Bear, bear him along
With his few faults shut up like dead flowerets! Are balm-seeds not here
To console us? The land has none left such as he on the bier.
Oh, would we might keep thee, my brother!"—And then, the glad chaunt
Of the marriage,—first go the young maidens, next, she whom we vaunt
As the beauty, the pride of our dwelling.—And then, the great march
Wherein man runs to man to assist him and buttress an arch
Nought can break; who shall harm them, our friends?—Then, the chorus in
    toned
As the Levites go up to the altar in glory enthroned.
But I stopped here: for here in the darkness Saul groaned.

[Having played and sung these nine different songs, David paused. Saul, unresponsive as yet, shuddered and moved his head. And the boy bent once more to his harp, and sang the joy of life and mortal pleasures:]

9

"Oh, our manhood's prime vigour! No spirit feels waste,
Not a muscle is stopped in its playing nor sinew unbraced.
Oh, the wild joys of living! the leaping from rock up to rock,
The strong rending of boughs from the fir-tree, the cool silver shock
Of the plunge in a pool's living water, the hunt of the bear,
And the sultriness showing the lion is couched in his lair.
And the meal, the rich dates yellowed over with gold dust divine,
And the locust-flesh steeped in the pitcher, the full draught of wine,
And the sleep in the dried river-channel where bulrushes tell
That the water was wont to go warbling so softly and well.
How good is man's life, the mere living! how fit to employ
All the heart and the soul and the senses for ever in joy!
Hast thou loved the white locks of thy father, whose sword thou didst guard
When he trusted thee forth with the armies, for glorious reward?
Didst thou see the thin hands of thy mother, held up as men sung
The low song of the nearly-departed, and hear her faint tongue
Joining in while it could to the witness, 'Let one more attest,
I have lived, seen God's hand thro' a lifetime, and all was for best'?
Then they sung thro' their tears in strong triumph, not much, but the rest.
And thy brothers, the help and the contest, the working whence grew
Such result as, from seething grape-bundles, the spirit strained true:
And the friends of thy boyhood—that boyhood of wonder and hope,
Present promise and wealth of the future beyond the eye's scope,—
Till lo, thou art grown to a monarch; a people is thine;
And all gifts, which the world offers singly, on one head combine!
On one head, all the beauty and strength, love and rage (like the throe
That, a-work in the rock, helps its labour and lets the gold go)
High ambition and deeds which surpass it, fame crowning them,—all
Brought to blaze on the head of one creature—King Saul!"

[Now Saul, hearing his name, shuddered again, and relaxed. Holding his brow, he looked about, then folded his arms. David felt that though Saul let him praise life, yet he would have none of it. So, musing upon his shepherd days spent in dreaming, David again struck his harp, and sang of the spirit and of immortal deeds:]

13

"Yea, my King,"
I began—"thou dost well in rejecting mere comforts that spring
From the mere mortal life held in common by man and by brute:
In our flesh grows the branch of this life, in our soul it bears fruit.

Thou hast marked the slow rise of the tree,—how its stem trembled first
Till it passed the kid's lip, the stag's antler; then safely outburst
The fan-branches all round; and thou mindest when these too, in turn
Broke a-bloom and the palm-tree seemed perfect: Yet more was to learn,
E'en the good that comes in with the palm-fruit. Our dates shall we slight,
When their juice brings a cure for all sorrow? or care for the plight
Of the palm's self whose slow growth produced them? Not so! stem and branch
Shall decay, nor be known in their place, while the palm-wine shall staunch
Every wound of man's spirit in winter. I pour thee such wine.
Leave the flesh to the fate it was fit for! the spirit be thine!
By the spirit, when age shall o'ercome thee, thou still shalt enjoy
More indeed, than at first when inconscious, the life of a boy.
Crush that life, and behold its wine running! Each deed thou hast done
Dies, revives, goes to work in the world; until e'en as the sun
Looking down on the earth, though clouds spoil him, though tempests efface,
Can find nothing his own deed produced not, must everywhere trace
The results of his past summer-prime,—so, each ray of thy will,
Every flash of thy passion and prowess, long over, shall thrill
Thy whole people, the countless, with ardour, till they too give forth
A like cheer to their sons, who in turn fill the South and the North
With the radiance thy deed was the germ of. Carouse in the past!
But the license of age has its limit; thou diest at last:
As the lion when age dims his eyeball, the rose at her height
So with man—so his power and his beauty for ever take flight.
No! Again a long draught of my soul-wine! Look forth o'er the years!
Thou hast done now with eyes for the actual; begin with the seer's!
Is Saul dead? In the depth of the vale make his tomb—bid arise
A grey mountain of marble heaped four-square till, built to the skies,
Let it mark where the great First King slumbers: whose fame would ye know?
Up above see the rock's naked face, where the record shall go
In great characters cut by the scribe,—Such was Saul, so he did;
With the sages directing the work, by the populace chid,—
For not half, they'll affirm, is comprised there! Which fault to amend,
In the grove with his kind grows the cedar, whereon they shall spend
(See, in tablets 't is level before them) their praise, and record
With the gold of the graver, Saul's story,—the statesman's great word
Side by side with the poet's sweet comment. The river's a-wave
With smooth paper-reeds grazing each other when prophet-winds rave:
So the pen gives unborn generations their due and their part
In thy being! Then, first of the mighty, thank God that thou art!"

[As David sang, Saul gradually came to life, adjusted his turban,
wiped his brow, girded his loins; then sank down to a seated posture
to listen to David. Saul laid his hand upon David's head, and looked
with kindness upon him; and David returned his affection. And in
love for King Saul, David burst forth in rhapsody:]

17

"I have gone the whole round of creation: I saw and I spoke:
I, a work of God's hand for that purpose, received in my brain
And pronounced on the rest of his handwork—returned him again
His creation's approval or censure: I spoke as I saw:
I report, as a man may of God's work—all's love, yet all's law.
Now I lay down the judgeship he lent me. Each faculty tasked
To perceive him, has gained an abyss, where a dewdrop was asked.
Have I knowledge? confounded it shrivels at Wisdom laid bare.
Have I forethought? how purblind, how blank, to the Infinite Care!
Do I task any faculty highest, to image success?
I but open my eyes,—and perfection, no more and no less,
In the kind I imagined, full-fronts me, and God is seen God
In the star, in the stone, in the flesh, in the soul and the clod.
And thus looking within and around me, I ever renew
(With that stoop of the soul which in bending upraises it too)
The submission of man's nothing-perfect to God's all-complete,
As by each new obeisance in spirit, I climb to his feet.
Yet with all this abounding experience, this deity known,
I shall dare to discover some province, some gift of my own.
There's a faculty pleasant to exercise, hard to hoodwink,
I am fain to keep still in abeyance, (I laugh as I think)
Lest, insisting to claim and parade in it, wot ye, I worst
E'en the Giver in one gift.—Behold! I could love if I durst!
But I sink the pretension as fearing a man may o'ertake
God's own speed in the one way of love: I abstain for love's sake. . . .

18

"I believe it! 'T is thou, God, that givest, 't is I who receive:
In the first is the last, in thy will is my power to believe.
All's one gift: thou canst grant it moreover, as prompt to my prayer
As I breathe out this breath, as I open these arms to the air.
From thy will, stream the worlds, life and nature, thy dread Sabaoth:
I will?—the mere atoms despise me! Why am I not loth
To look that, even that in the face too? Why is it I dare
Think but lightly of such impuissance? What stops my despair?
This;—'t is not what man Does which exalts him, but what man Would do!
See the King—I would help him but cannot, the wishes fall through.
Could I wrestle to raise him from sorrow, grow poor to enrich,
To fill up his life, starve my own out, I would—knowing which,
I know that my service is perfect. Oh, speak through me now!
Would I suffer for him that I love? So wouldst thou—so wilt thou!
So shall crown thee the topmost, ineffablest, uttermost crown—

And thy love fill infinitude wholly, nor leave up nor down
One spot for the creature to stand in! It is by no breath,
Turn of eye, wave of hand, that salvation joins issue with death!
As thy Love is discovered almighty, almighty be proved
Thy power, that exists with and for it, of being Beloved!
He who did most, shall bear most; the strongest shall stand the most weak.
'T is the weakness in strength, that I cry for! my flesh, that I seek
In the Godhead! I seek and I find it. O Saul, it shall be
A Face like my face that receives thee; a Man like to me,
Thou shalt love and be loved by, for ever: a Hand like this hand
Shall throw open the gates of new life to thee! See the Christ stand!"

[And David, realizing that he had ministered to Saul's need, was
uplifted by his own inspiration. As he went home, he saw that all life
witnessed to "the new law" of God's infinite love.]

(1855)

After singing many different songs, and by an amazing intuition,
the boy David finally spoke to Saul's spiritual condition. Of the
twelve songs, the first nine were clearly of no interest to Saul, who
took no notice of them; the song of mortal pleasures he heard and
understood, but without satisfaction; the song of man's spirit and
the immortality of man's deeds came closer home to Saul, and he
listened and was moved to wonderment by it; but the rhapsody on
God's love spoke directly to him.

So each reader, at strife with a different spirit, will read a dozen
poems, or a score or a hundred, before finding the particular one
that will speak to his condition, that will strike home, restoring
his inner harmony and essential integration. It is in the crises of
life that one is tested; it is at these times that some one of the great
poems may be most valuable, may seem most apt and pat.

But it would be a mistake to assume that it is only the so-called
great poems that on occasion affect the reader thus, or that it is
only the solemn poetry on God and Death and the Conduct of
Life that will be valuable to the reader in this way. Poems of grace
and gayety and wit will also speak to our conditions at certain
times and fulfill our psychological needs and shape our attitudes.
And the popular poems, often considered by the critical to be bad,
have been valuable to the many in just this way, possessing a cer-

tain poetic immediacy and striking a timely response in many readers of the day.

And it would also be a mistake to assume that the poem which fails to speak immediately to the condition of the reader is therefore and necessarily valueless to him. For it may have something to say to him at another and more crucial time. Phrases from it, images or feelings, may be recalled by him in an hour of need, and he may then go back to reread the whole poem. Or attitudes shaped subconsciously as a part of the reading process may stand him in stead. So it would be folly to say that reading a particular poem will be useless unless one is in the mood for it.

3. CONDITIONING THE READER

But if some poems speak immediately to the reader's condition—or, understood and appreciated now, leave residual attitudes, readinesses to respond in time of future need—other poems may be able to speak to the reader only when his condition has been made ready for them. And some of the truly great poems, as we have seen, may have comparatively little to say to the reader who has an inadequate background for understanding them. It is worth noting, then, that the reader may put himself into a condition to be spoken to by some of the great poems that might not otherwise be opened to him.

The discussion of Clough's "Say Not the Struggle—" and of Milton's "On His Blindness" in earlier chapters may have illustrated this point for the reader. But another and final illustration will be given.

"The Collar" by George Herbert, like a good many of the great poems, is not an easy one to read. It may not speak to the condition of many readers simply because it does not speak, for them, at all! But the reader may be *conditioned* (to shift the sense of the word) for this poem; he may be provided with an adequate background, enriching the context for interpretation so that the poem-experience will be more meaningful. And this special conditioning for the poem will take the form of—

A PREFATORY ESSAY ON GEORGE HERBERT

FOR READERS OF "THE COLLAR"

The personality and life of George Herbert are full of conflicts and contradictions. He grew up a courtier and died a "saint."

He was born of a noble English family during the last years of Queen Elizabeth's reign, when Shakespeare was beginning his career. And he was one of the five sons in a large family which included a number of distinguished members: poets, philosophers, adventurers, courtiers. It was his mother, Magdalen Herbert, who exerted a more than usually strong influence upon her son George. A woman of great personal charm and fervent piety, she was herself a minor poet and patroness of John Donne, a leading poet and preacher of his day. Widowed, she took her family up to Oxford so as to superintend the education of her eldest son, Edward.

So George Herbert, of courtly family, grew up in a university atmosphere under the intellectual and dominant eye of a mother who early determined that his life and "lines" should be directed toward the Church. But this did not suit well with George's temperament. Both at Westminster School and at Trinity College, Cambridge, he distinguished himself as a scholar. He loved modern as well as classic languages, he wrote occasional poetry, he was proud and ambitious, he liked good clothes and gay times. Though not ever robust in health, he had healthy passions and a temper.

He took his B.A. at twenty, and was appointed Public Orator to the University. Although he wanted to travel, his mother kept him at his work, and he took his M.A. at the age of twenty-four. His oratorship brought him to the notice of King James I, who liked to have him "in suit" (in attendance at Court). He liked the courtly pleasures, and was ambitious for further honors, aspiring to become Secretary of State and thus come into "a land of corn and wine, a land of bread and vineyards." The King did reward him, not with "bays" (to crown him as a poet), but with a religious benefice (the income from a church position that he might fill with an inexpensive substitute).

But King James I soon died. Herbert was only 32, and his office-seeking plans were "blasted" (or withered). His disappointment, and probably the renewed exhortations of his pious mother, turned his thoughts to the Church. He was given another religious sinecure, but this time he went to work with enthusiasm in directing the rebuilding of the church at Leighton Bromswold.

Then his mother died quite suddenly. Her death was a serious blow to him. It affected his health, and he had to resign his oratorship. His life was very unsettled for a period of three years; it was a time of doubts and irresolution. Then quite suddenly he married; and his influential cousin, the Earl of Pembroke, secured another church appointment for him.

So he was ordained at the age of 37, and undertook the active duties of the "pitiful little chapel" of Bemerton, which would have seemed a mere "cage" (or prison) to him in more ambitious days, but which now seemed to him "as large as store," providing him with abundant opportunity. He devoted himself "only" (that is, wholly) to the task of repairing the chapel at his own expense, ministering to his small flock, and living happily that "saintly" life of consecration that earned him his name, Holy George Herbert.

It was during these years that he wrote the poems for which he is remembered. Certain factors in Herbert's life, some of which have already been mentioned, may have determined the kind of poetry he wrote: the personal influence of John Donne, the university intellectualism of his day, the wit of courtly life, his continued interest in music, the dedication of these last years to the service of God. So, now, he was "in suit" to the Church—both as to dress and attendance—as he had earlier been "in suit" to the Court.

When these three years closed and he saw "the death's-head" (that skull symbolic of death) before him, he did not "wink" (closing his eyes to it), but accepted his approaching end. He sent his MS of Sacred Poems to a religious friend, saying that he would "find in it a picture of the many spiritual conflicts that have passed betwixt God and my soul, before I could subject mine to the will of Jesus my master; in whose service I have now found perfect freedom." The poems were published under the title of *The Temple: Sacred Poems and Private Ejaculations*. They are indeed personal outcries in which the poet, as Izaak Walton put it, "by declaring his own spiritual conflicts, . . . hath comforted and raised many a dejected and discomposed soul and charmed them with sweet and quiet thoughts." So it was in the mid-Seventeenth Century for Crashaw (the Catholic poet), for Baxter (the Nonconformist preacher), for Vaughan (the Welsh mystic), for Charles I (the King awaiting the ax). So it was for Cowper in the next century, and Coleridge in the next, and for many in our own time who have found something that speaks to their condition in the poetry of

Holy George Herbert, the sophisticated courtier and "saint" of Bemerton.

Now let us turn to the poem itself, for which we have been thus conditioned:

THE COLLAR
George Herbert

I struck the board, and cried, "No more;
        I will abroad."
What, shall I ever sigh and pine? ·
My lines and life are free; free as the road,
    Loose as the wind, as large as store.
        Shall I be still in suit?
Have I no harvest but a thorn
To let me blood, and not restore
What I have lost with cordial fruit?
        Sure there was wine
Before my sighs did dry it; there was corn
    Before my tears did drown it;
    Is the year only lost to me?
        Have I no bays to crown it,
No flowers, no garlands gay? all blasted,
        All wasted?
Not so, my heart; but there is fruit,
        And thou hast hands.
Recover all thy sigh-blown age
On double pleasures; leave thy cold dispute
Of what is fit and not; forsake thy cage,
        Thy rope of sands
Which petty thoughts have made; and made to thee
    Good cable, to enforce and draw,
        And be thy law,
While thou didst wink and wouldst not see.
        Away! take heed;
        I will abroad.
Call in thy death's-head there, tie up thy fears;
        He that forbears

> To suit and serve his need
>   Deserves his load.
> But as I raved and grew more fierce and wild
>   At every word,
> Methought I heard one calling, "Child";
>   And I replied, "My Lord."

(1633)

Conditioned by the prefatory essay on George Herbert (which may require a second reading in connection with the poem), the reader may find "The Collar" increasingly meaningful. It is indeed a *great poem,* as we have used the phrase. And whether the central tenet of the poem is accepted by the reader as truth, or (with a willing suspension of disbelief) as poetic truth, it is for many modern readers a *good poem,* full of life and free from conflict. And there are some readers to whose condition "The Collar" will speak out loud and bold, with signal *poetic immediacy.* And these will be the readers who are in rebellious mood, who are tired of the self-imposed task, who chafe under the restrictions demanded by long-range goals, who want to have their cake and eat it too! And, like George Herbert, they too may hear the Voice that calls them to obedience.

4. CONCLUSION AND SO FORTH

And so, let us bring this book to a conclusion. It should not be phrased as an end but as another beginning. Like the traditional commencement oratory, it affirms that *this* is but the threshold of a wider adventure. You are invited to go forth, to hunt out particular collections of poetry garnered to suit your own special tastes and needs. You already know which certain poems have provided you with experiences that are good. Now find other poems of these sorts or by these poets.

And so, forth, reader—whosoever ye be—the world of poetry, with its realms of gold, is yours to explore; and you may claim what you will as your own, to have and to hold, for ever.

SUGGESTIONS FOR STUDY

1. *Poetic Immediacy.* Have any of the poems read thus far delivered their meaning to you with an especial impact? If so, list them, and in a short essay describe your experience with one of them.

2. *The Player Speaks to Hamlet.* (a) When the strolling players come to the Castle at Elsinore, they are welcomed by Hamlet, Prince of Denmark. Though deeply affected by the death of his father, by the burden laid upon him by his father's Ghost, and by the circumstances of his uncle's guilt and his mother's remarriage, Hamlet has not been able, or has not found occasion during the past weeks, to avenge his father's murder. Greeting his old friends the players, he asks one of them to deliver a certain speech from a play which included "Aeneas' tale to Dido" of Priam's slaughter during the Greek sack of Troy. This the First Player does with such a display of emotion that old Polonius is moved to say: "Look! wh'er he has not turned his colour and has tears in 's eyes." After Hamlet arranges with the First Player to perform a particular play before the Court the next day, and to insert a speech of Hamlet's contriving, the players are ushered out by the Lord Chamberlain, and Hamlet is left alone with his thoughts as revealed through this well-known soliloquy.

from HAMLET, II, ii, 555 ff.

William Shakespeare

O! what a rogue and peasant slave am I:
Is it not monstrous that this player here,
But in a fiction, in a dream of passion,
Could force his soul so to his own conceit
That from her working all his visage wann'd,
Tears in his eyes, distraction in 's aspect,
A broken voice, and his whole function suiting
With forms to his conceit? and all for nothing!
For Hecuba!
What's Hecuba to him or he to Hecuba
That he should weep for her? What would he do
Had he the motive and the cue for passion
That I have? He would drown the stage with tears,
And cleave the general ear with horrid speech,
Make mad the guilty and appall the free,
Confound the ignorant, and amaze indeed

The very faculties of eyes and ears.
Yet I,
A dull and muddy-mettled rascal, peak,
Like John-a-dreams, unpregnant of my cause,
And can say nothing; no, not for a king,
Upon whose property and most dear life
A damn'd defeat was made. Am I a coward?
Who calls me villain? breaks my pate across?
Plucks off my beard and blows it in my face?
Tweaks me by the nose? gives me the lie i' the throat,
As deep as to the lungs? Who does me this?
Ha!
'Swounds, I should take it, for it cannot be
But I am pigeon-liver'd, and lack gall
To make oppression bitter, or ere this
I should have fatted all the region kites
With this slave's offal. Bloody, bawdy villain!
Remorseless, treacherous, lecherous, kindless villain!
O! vengeance!
Why, what an ass am I! This is most brave
That I, the son of a dear father murder'd,
Prompted to my revenge by heaven and hell,
Must, like a whore, unpack my heart with words,
And fall a-cursing, like a very drab,
A scullion!
Fie upon't! foh! About, my brain! I have heard,
That guilty creatures sitting at a play
Have by the very cunning of the scene
Been struck so to the soul that presently
They have proclaim'd their malefactions;
For murder, though it have no tongue, will speak
With most miraculous organ. I'll have these players
Play something like the murder of my father
Before mine uncle; I'll observe his looks;
I'll tent him to the quick: if he but blench
I know my course. The spirit that I have seen
May be the devil: and the devil hath power
To assume a pleasing shape; yea, and perhaps
Out of my weakness and my melancholy—
As he is very potent with such spirits—

Abuses me to damn me. I'll have grounds
More relative than this: the play's the thing
Wherein I'll catch the conscience of the king.

(1604)

(b) In what way can it be said that the First Player spoke to Hamlet's condition? Consider further the dramatic situation; turn to a copy of the complete drama for a fuller understanding of the scene. Note that Hamlet himself suggests the speech that he particularly wants to hear; that it is not the substance alone but the histrionic vehemence that strikes him with such immediacy; that his attitudes seem to be affected, and that a plan for action results.

(c) Several recordings of this speech have been made by famous actors of the rôle of Hamlet: John Barrymore (Victor record 6827), John Gielgud (in Linguaphone set 12, or single record 33-34), Maurice Evans (in Columbia set M-340).

3. *Prufrock Not a Hamlet.* (a) "The Love Song of J. Alfred Prufrock," by the American poet T. S. Eliot who became a British subject, is a peculiarly modern poem depicting a sort of Hamlet character who declares that he is not Hamlet, "nor was meant to be." This poem has been called "a minor masterpiece; . . . nothing in English since the seventeenth century metaphysicals, has communicated so great a sense of ambiguous hurt and general frustration." [2]

THE LOVE SONG OF J. ALFRED PRUFROCK
T. S. Eliot

S'io credesse che mia risposta fosse
A persona che mai tornasse al mondo,
Questa fiamma staria senza piu scosse.
Ma perciocche giammai di questo fondo
Non torno vivo alcun, s'i'odo il vero,
Senza tema d'infamia ti rispondo.

Let us go then, you and I,
When the evening is spread out against the sky
Like a patient etherized upon a table;
Let us go, through certain half-deserted streets,
The muttering retreats
Of restless nights in one-night cheap hotels
And sawdust restaurants with oyster-shells:
Streets that follow like a tedious argument

[2] Louis Untermeyer, *Modern American Poetry,* Harcourt, Brace, 1942, p. 421.

Of insidious intent
To lead you to an overwhelming question . . .
Oh, do not ask, "What is it?"
Let us go and make our visit.

In the room the women come and go
Talking of Michelangelo.

The yellow fog that rubs its back upon the window-panes,
The yellow smoke that rubs its muzzle on the window-panes
Licked its tongue into the corners of the evening,
Lingered upon the pools that stand in drains,
Let fall upon its back the soot that falls from chimneys,
Slipped by the terrace, made a sudden leap,
And seeing that it was a soft October night,
Curled once about the house, and fell asleep.

And indeed there will be time
For the yellow smoke that slides along the street,
Rubbing its back upon the window-panes;
There will be time, there will be time
To prepare a face to meet the faces that you meet;
There will be time to murder and create,
And time for all the works and days of hands
That lift and drop a question on your plate;
Time for you and time for me,
And time yet for a hundred indecisions,
And for a hundred visions and revisions,
Before the taking of a toast and tea.

In the room the women come and go
Talking of Michelangelo.

And indeed there will be time
To wonder, "Do I dare?" and, "Do I dare?"
Time to turn back and descend the stair,
With a bald spot in the middle of my hair—
[They will say: "How his hair is growing thin!"]
My morning coat, my collar mounting firmly to the chin,
My necktie rich and modest, but asserted by a simple pin—
[They will say: "But how his arms and legs are thin!"]
Do I dare

Disturb the universe?
In a minute there is time
For decisions and revisions which a minute will reverse.

For I have known them all already, known them all:—
Have known the evenings, mornings, afternoons,
I have measured out my life with coffee spoons;
I know the voices dying with a dying fall
Beneath the music from a farther room.
      So how should I presume?

And I have known the eyes already, known them all—
The eyes that fix you in a formulated phrase,
And when I am formulated, sprawling on a pin,
When I am pinned and wriggling on the wall,
Then how should I begin
To spit out all the butt-ends of my days and ways?
      And how should I presume?

And I have known the arms already, known them all—
Arms that are braceleted and white and bare
[But in the lamplight, downed with light brown hair!]
Is it perfume from a dress
That makes me so digress?
Arms that lie along a table, or wrap about a shawl.
      And should I then presume?
      And how should I begin?

✦

Shall I say, I have gone at dusk through narrow streets
And watched the smoke that rises from the pipes
Of lonely men in shirt-sleeves, leaning out of windows? . . .

I should have been a pair of ragged claws
Scuttling across the floors of silent seas.

✦

And the afternoon, the evening, sleeps so peacefully!
Smoothed by long fingers,
Asleep . . . tired . . . or it malingers,
Stretched on the floor, here beside you and me.
Should I, after tea and cakes and ices,

Have the strength to force the moment to its crisis?
But though I have wept and fasted, wept and prayed,
Though I have seen my head [grown slightly bald] brought in upon a
        platter,
I am no prophet—and here's no great matter;
I have seen the moment of my greatness flicker,
And I have seen the eternal Footman hold my coat, and snicker,
And in short, I was afraid.

And would it have been worth it, after all,
After the cups, the marmalade, the tea,
Among the porcelain, among some talk of you and me,
Would it have been worth while,
To have bitten off the matter with a smile,
To have squeezed the universe into a ball
To roll it toward some overwhelming question,
To say: "I am Lazarus, come from the dead,
Come back to tell you all, I shall tell you all"—
If one, settling a pillow by her head,
        Should say: "That is not what I meant at all.
        That is not it, at all."

And would it have been worth it, after all,
Would it have been worth while,
After the sunsets and the dooryards and the sprinkled streets,
After the novels, after the teacups, after the skirts that trail along the
        floor—
And this, and so much more?—
It is impossible to say just what I mean!
But as if a magic lantern threw the nerves in patterns on a screen:
Would it have been worth while
If one, settling a pillow or throwing off a shawl,
And turning toward the window, should say:
        "That is not it at all,
        That is not what I meant, at all."

✦

No! I am not Prince Hamlet, nor was meant to be;
Am an attendant lord, one that will do
To swell a progress, start a scene or two,
Advise the prince; no doubt, an easy tool,

Deferential, glad to be of use,
Politic, cautious, and meticulous;
Full of high sentence, but a bit obtuse;
At times, indeed, almost ridiculous—
Almost, at times, the Fool.

I grow old . . . I grow old . . .
I shall wear the bottoms of my trousers rolled.

Shall I part my hair behind? Do I dare to eat a peach?
I shall wear white flannel trousers, and walk upon the beach.
I have heard the mermaids singing, each to each.

I do not think that they will sing to me.

I have seen them riding seaward on the waves
Combing the white hair of the waves blown back
When the wind blows the water white and black.

We have lingered in the chambers of the sea
By sea-girls wreathed with seaweed red and brown
Till human voices wake us, and we drown.

(1917)

(b) The following notes may be of some help in a second reading of the above "Love Song." The Italian quotation that heads the poem is from Dante's *Inferno*, 27:61-6, and is translated by Henry F. Carey:

> If I did think my answer were to one
> Who ever could return unto the world,
> This flame should rest unshaken. But since ne'er,
> If true be told me, any from this depth
> Has found his upward way, I answer thee,
> Nor fear lest infamy record the words.

A dying fall: the phrase, meaning "a diminishing and falling cadence," is an allusion to Shakespeare's *Twelfth Night*, I, i, 4. *My head . . . brought in upon a platter:* the allusion is to Salome's request for the head of John the Baptist (*Matthew*, 14:8). *Lazarus:* the brother of Mary and Martha, whom Jesus raised from the dead (*John*, 11:1 ff.). *An attendant lord:* the allusion may be to Polonius who in *Hamlet* is indeed "full of high sentence, but a bit obtuse . . . almost ridiculous— almost . . . the Fool." (There is no Fool, in the type-character sense, in *Hamlet;* the Gravediggers are "clowns," in the early sense of that word.) Interesting discussions of the poem are to be found in Brooks and Warren, *Understanding Poetry,* Holt, 1938, pp. 589-96; and Thomas and Brown, *Reading Poems,* Oxford Press, 1941, pp. 698-701, 707.

(c) Now give detailed consideration to Prince Hamlet and J. Alfred Prufrock as revealed in the above soliloquy and dramatic monologue— their personalities, their psychological attitudes, their problems.

4. *A Book of Verses Underneath the Bough.* (a) Spend some time browsing in library or bookshop, and hunt out a collection of poems garnered to suit your special taste and/or purse. Perhaps Schauffler's *Manthology* or Grover's *Nature Lover's Knapsack* will catch your interest. Or Hill's *World's Great Religious Poetry* or Walsh's *Catholic Anthology* or Morris's *Poems of Inspiration.* You may find your pleasure in the *Oxford Book of Light Verse* or in Lewis and Lee's *Stuffed Owl: an Anthology of Bad Verse.* You may wish to own a comprehensive anthology like the *Viking Book of Poetry* or the *Treasury of Great Poems English and American,* or a slim volume like the *College Book of Verse* or the inexpensive *Pocket Book of Verse.* You may find what you want in the mammoth *Home Book of Verse,* in which the poems are classified by theme, or in the *Anthology of World Poetry,* where they are classified by country, or in the *Modern American Poetry* and *Modern British Poetry,* where the work of recent poets is arranged chronologically.

(b) Borrow or buy the book—and make use of it, reading such poetry as you like for the sheer pleasure of it—skimming and skipping, rushing and lingering, pausing and rereading—and (if you own the book) marking your finds and staking out your claims for future digging.

5. *On a Subject of Your Interest.* It might now be well to start work upon the study of some subject of your interest that will be appropriate for a so-called term paper in the general field of Poetry. Such a subject might be (a) a single poem (preferably one of at least moderate length, and one that invites intensive study and that poses provocative questions of interpretation), or (b) a group of poems by a single poet (preferably one whose life is reasonably open to study, and whose poems seem to bear a close relation to his personality and to the events of his life), or (c) a group of poems by various poets but upon some general theme, or upon the same subject, or of the same type, or in the same style, or in the same form. In any case the poems you read should be ones that genuinely stir your interest, and that will be able to hold your interest in repeated rereadings as your study progresses.

BOOK TWO

The Poetry

In every volume of poems something good may be found. —SAMUEL JOHNSON

PART FOUR
Poems for Oral Interpretation

13

READING ALOUD

Throughout ancient times, and up until the invention of printing, bards and minstrels held an honored position in society, for theirs was a highly developed, traditional art. In earlier American times, too, elocution (as it was called), public reading and recitation, was held in high esteem. And there was much reading aloud and reciting in the schoolroom and in the homes of our grandparents. In many families, Scripture in the morning was balanced by *St. Nicholas* or the *Atlantic Monthly* at night, read aloud by the oldster or youngster with the clearest voice, while the family circle was busy with sedentary chores, mending, and handwork.

But now, each one reads his own book or magazine, not in silence, but to the accompaniment of assorted radiotonics. And all, young and old, learn the facile tricks of half-listening with one ear and half-reading with the other. Few families nowadays spend their evenings in oral reading of novels and narrative verse; so it is small wonder that as a people we today have small skill in reading poetry aloud.

I. LEARNING TO READ POETRY ALOUD

It is the point of view of this book that until you have learned the art of oral reading, together with the art of listening to poetry, you will miss much of the potential richness of poem-experiences. Not until you can utter the great verses with the living voice, can you hear their expressive melodies and harmonies with the inner ear.

The art of reading poetry aloud is no native skill. It can, indeed it must, be learned. It is within the reach not only of a gifted few; it may be cultivated by all persons who really desire to come into the more abundant life, the peace and plenty of the world of books, the milk and honey of great poetry.

The beginning of this self-cultivation in oral reading may be made through attentive and discriminating listening, taking note of vocal range and speech melody. And then, of course, it will call for practice, conscious and persistent effort, welcoming every opportunity to read aloud and being prepared to do so.

As your ability to read poetry aloud develops, your enjoyment of the "music" of poetry will doubtless increase. You will, when reading silently, realize more fully the auditory potential of great poetry. For printed verses are like musical score. It takes a skilled musician to pick up a *familiar* score and re-create the symphony in his mind's-ear, revivifying the full complexity of, let us say, Tschaikovsky's *Fourth Symphony*. But it takes a more unusual talent, plus the close study and practice of live music, to pick up a *new* symphonic score and to create in the auditory imagination the full effect of the work as it would be heard when actually performed! Most of us can do no more than follow a simple melody-line, and even then we resort to humming or a whispered whistle.

Yet—when it comes to poetry—many readers, who have never cultivated the art of reading aloud or of listening to poetry, who indeed scorn "oral interpretation," feel quite confident that they are getting, in their silent reading, the fullest realization of the "music" of a poem. They may be satisfied with a thin-toned, narrow-ranged poem, not aware of the wealth of experience that lies within their grasp.

From the first pages of this book you have been urged to read aloud to yourself. No matter how badly you have read, no matter how much you have stumbled, it has not really mattered; no one else has been affected. But when you undertake to read *to another person, you have an obligation to read well*—or, at least, your best. And this will take special preparation.

The following four steps may guide you in preparing to read

poetry to others. First, read the poem silently, and *study out the full meaning of the poem,* not only the sense of it, but the tone, feeling, and intention as well. Mark your book generously; underline the key verses or star them in the margin. Look up strange words or familiar words used strangely—pronunciations, too, while you are at it. Second, *turn your attention to the "music" of the poem.* Is the poetic rhythm that of free verse or of bound verse? [1] If it has a metrical pattern, what is it? Read the poem aloud, sensitive to the interplay of metrical pattern and sense pattern. Read it aloud so as to savor its tone-color and to catch the various subsidiary rhythms. Third, again silently, read it focusing upon the free imagery and your emotional response, and *relishing the poem-experience as a complex unity.* Fourth, think of *the problem of communication.* Read the poem aloud in what you think will be appropriate voice tones, pitch, volume, tempo, and speech tune to give such expression to your poem-experience as may communicate it to your intended listeners. And practice to perfect this oral interpretation of your poem.

So prepared, you are ready to read to others. Let your actual reading to them be vitalized by *your earnest desire to share with them something rich and valuable.* You will seek to communicate to the listeners the music of the poem and its full meaning; you will seek to stir their imaginations and their emotions even as yours have been stirred. You will watch their reactions closely, adjusting your rate to their comprehension and their responses. Remember, you are not reading aloud to yourself, but to them—for their enjoyment, not your own.

2. SOME FURTHER SUGGESTIONS

Those with less formal speech training may be helped by a few additional *hints.* Articulate clearly, activate your lips and tongue, so that the listeners need not reach for and guess at the words you utter. Loosen your jaw so that your mouth may open and let out

---

[1] These and other terms are defined in the Glossarial Handbook with references to earlier chapters in the text.

the tone. "Think" your speech sounds forward in the mouth so as to project the words to your hearers. Energize your speech by full and deep breathing. Try to relax your body generally, and more especially shoulders, neck, and throat. If you are reading aloud to more than a few persons, stand before them, rather than sit, for a seated posture crowds the breathing. Good reading aloud of poetry will be based upon generally good speech habits.

Certain other hints apply particularly to the oral reading of verse. Almost everyone will read poetry in a tone of voice at least slightly different from that used in the reading of prose. The complex "music" of a poem, its relation to the other aspects of the full poem-experience, and the desire to communicate this to others—these are likely to stimulate the use of wider than usual ranges of pitch and volume, of tempos and qualities of voice.

The mid-line and end-line pauses will call for careful timing, not only to make clear the meaning, but to vary the poetic rhythm. A special problem is presented by the run-on lines, at the end of which (usually indicated by the absence of punctuation) the sense carries the reader over into the next line. It must be remembered that *verse* consists of *verses;* that the line of poetry is not only a unit to the eye, but to the ear; and that the poetic rhythm (as described earlier, pp. 102-05) may be thought of as a compromise between the at times contrary pulls of the metrical pattern and the sense pattern. Some readers, to avoid the hurried effect of dashing on where no punctuation stays them, make an ever-so-slight pause, holding up the voice at the ends of such lines before running on with the thought. An ever-so-slight weighting of the final word of the run-on line may achieve the same effect. In the reading of so-called "open couplets" (such as those in Chapman's translation of *The Odyssey,* pp. 35-38), the recurring rime words at the ends of run-on lines serve automatically to preserve the integrity of the verses. In reading blank verse, however, cultivated skill will be required to keep the line from being completely lost. But there is wide difference, both in theory and practice, as regards the oral reading of blank verse, especially in Shakespearean drama.

And now for common *faults* to be avoided in the oral reading of poetry. One is that monotonous, narrow-ranged, dead-pan reading without any expression whatsoever, a mere mumbling of the bare words. A second is the stumbling and faltering that indicate either that the reader is tired or unprepared, or that his eye-movements and comprehension are not keeping ahead of his speaking. A third fault is found in the reading of those who have failed to catch the metrical pattern or who, having discovered it, jounce along, deDUMM deDUMM deDUMM, beating the life out of the poor verses. A fourth fault is yet more painful: the artificial rhapsody of the older elocution and the coy cuteness of kittenish kiddies! And fifth, worst fault of all, the drooling "poetic" tone heard all too often on the radio, against a mortuary background of musical sentimentality.

A person who is honest and forthright in tone, clear and articulate in speech, earnest in the desire to share a rich experience with others, willing to work at the problems of interpretation and communication—such a person will avoid many of the common faults in oral reading.

Success in reading to others will be dependent in large measure upon the appropriateness of the poetry for the occasion. It has been pointed out that sometimes a poem speaks directly to the reader's condition. Every effort should be made to choose a poem that will somehow strike home to the listeners, or so to prepare the listeners (with a few, but only a few, introductory comments) that they will be in a receptive mood.

Appropriateness to the occasion is, however, only one consideration in choosing poems to read aloud. Generally speaking, the simple, objective, impersonal poems are best for reading to others. Narrative poems—ballads and tales, idyls and epic episodes—make the best oral reading, as the story thread ties the experience together, and persons and places and actions are readily projected in the listeners' imaginations. Furthermore, such poems are long enough to provide a listening experience of some duration. But the simple and more familiar lyrics, too, may be read successfully to others—though it may be helpful for the listener to hear each one of them at least twice. And it is often desirable to read a group of such lyrics upon related themes or by a single poet. Yet another sort of poetry may well be read to others, poems of folk or national sentiment, and poems of social significance. The most difficult to real aloud will be the knotty and gnarled poems, those filled with learned allusions, the enigmatic moderns and the metaphysicals, with their conceits, and the more delicate and intensely personal poems. It will take unusual skill to communicate one's experience of these difficult poems to other persons without resorting to undesirably lengthy paraphrase and commentary.

The poems that form the body of this chapter are all by American poets. They represent a wide range in subject matter, form, and period of composition; but each of them, in one way or another, reflects an aspect of American life and culture. And each of them, in its own fashion, is a good poem to read aloud.

Modern American Poems

I HEAR AMERICA SINGING
Walt Whitman

I hear America singing, the varied carols I hear,
Those of mechanics, each one singing his as it should be blithe and
    strong,
The carpenter singing his as he measures his plank or beam,
The mason singing his as he makes ready for work, or leaves off work,
The boatman singing what belongs to him in his boat, the deckhand
    singing on the steamboat deck,
The shoemaker singing as he sits on his bench, the hatter singing as he
    stands,
The wood-cutter's song, the plowboy's on his way in the morning, or
    at the noon intermission or at sundown,
The delicious singing of the mother, or of the young wife at work, or
    of the girl sewing or washing,

Each singing what belongs to him or her and to none else,
The day what belongs to the day—at night the party of young fellows,
     robust, friendly,
Singing with open mouths their strong melodious songs.

(1860)

from THE PEOPLE, YES, section 45
Carl Sandburg

     They have yarns
Of a skyscraper so tall they had to put hinges
On the two top stories so to let the moon go by,
Of one corn crop in Missouri when the roots
Went so deep and drew off so much water
The Mississippi riverbed that year was dry,
Of pancakes so thin they had only one side,
Of "a fog so thick we shingled the barn and six feet out on the fog,"
Of Pecos Pete straddling a cyclone in Texas and riding it to the west
     coast where "it rained out under him,"
Of the man who drove a swarm of bees across the Rocky Mountains
     and the Desert "and didn't lose a bee,"
Of a mountain railroad curve where the engineer in his cab can touch
     the caboose and spit in the conductor's eye,
Of the boy who climbed a cornstalk growing so fast he would have
     starved to death if they hadn't shot biscuits up to him,
Of the old man's whiskers: "When the wind was with him his whis-
     kers arrived a day before he did,"
Of the hen laying a square egg and cackling, "Ouch!" and of hens
     laying eggs with the dates printed on them,
Of the ship captain's shadow: it froze to the deck one cold winter
     night,
Of mutineers on that same ship put to chipping rust with rubber
     hammers,
Of the sheep counter who was fast and accurate: "I just count their
     feet and divide by four,"
Of the man so tall he must climb a ladder to shave himself,
Of the runt so teeny-weeny it takes two men and a boy to see him,
Of mosquitoes: one can kill a dog, two of them a man,

Of a cyclone that sucked cookstoves out of the kitchen, up the chimney
    flue, and on to the next town,

Of the same cyclone picking up wagon-tracks in Nebraska and drop-
    ping them over in the Dakotas,

Of the hook-and-eye snake unlocking itself into forty pieces, each piece
    two inches long, then in nine seconds flat snapping itself together
    again,

Of the watch swallowed by the cow—when they butchered her a year
    later the watch was running and had the correct time,

Of horned snakes, hoop snakes that roll themselves where they want
    to go, and rattlesnakes carrying bells instead of rattles on their tails,

Of the herd of cattle in California getting lost in a giant redwood tree
    that had hollowed out,

Of the man who killed a snake by putting its tail in its mouth so it
    swallowed itself,

Of railroad trains whizzing along so fast they reached the station before
    the whistle,

Of pigs so thin the farmer had to tie knots in their tails to keep them
    from crawling through the cracks in their pens,

Of Paul Bunyan's big blue ox, Babe, measuring between the eyes forty-
    two ax-handles and a plug of Star tobacco exactly,

Of John Henry's hammer and the curve of its swing and his singing
    of it as "a rainbow round my shoulder."

> "Do tell!"
> "I want to know!"
> "You don't say so!"
> "For the land's sake!"
> "Gosh all fish-hooks!"
> "Tell me some more. . . ."

(1936)

POLO GROUNDS

Rolfe Humphries

Time is of the essence. This is a highly skilled
And beautiful mystery. Three or four seconds only
From the time that Riggs connects till he reaches first,

And in those seconds Jurges goes to his right,
Comes up with the ball, tosses to Witek at second
For the force on Reese, Witek to Mize at first,
In time for the out—a double play.

(Red Barber crescendo. Crowd noises, obbligato;
Scattered staccatos from the peanut boys,
Loud in the lull, as the teams are changing sides) . . .

Hubbell takes the sign, nods, pumps, delivers—
A foul into the stands. Dunn takes a new ball out,
Hands it to Danning, who throws it down to Werber;
Werber takes off his glove, rubs the ball briefly,
Tosses it over to Hub, who goes to the rosin bag,
Takes the sign from Danning, pumps, delivers—
Low, outside, ball three. Danning goes to the mound,
Says something to Hub, Dunn brushes off the plate,
Adams starts throwing in the Giant bullpen,
Hub takes the sign from Danning, pumps, delivers,
Camilli gets hold of it, a *long* fly to the outfield,
Ott goes back, back, back, against the wall, gets under it,
Pounds his glove, and takes it for the out.
That's all for the Dodgers. . . .

Time is of the essence. The rhythms break,
More varied and subtle than any kind of dance;
Movement speeds up or lags. The ball goes out
In sharp and angular drives, or long, slow arcs,
Comes in again controlled and under aim;
The players wheel or spurt, race, stoop, slide, halt,
Shift imperceptibly to new positions,
Watching the signs, according to the batter,
The score, the inning. Time is of the essence.

Time is of the essence. Remember Terry?
Remember Stonewall Jackson, Lindstrom, Frisch,
When they were good? Remember Long George Kelly?
Remember John McGraw and Benny Kauff?
Remember Bridwell, Tenney, Merkel, Youngs,
Chief Meyers, Big Jeff Tesreau, Shufflin' Phil?
Remember Matthewson, and Ames, and Donlin,

Buck Ewing, Rusie, Smiling Mickey Welch?
Remember a left-handed catcher named Jack Humphries,
Who sometimes played the outfield, in '83?

Time is of the essence. The shadow moves
From the plate to the box, from the box to second base,
From second to the outfield, to the bleachers.
Time is of the essence. The crowd and players
Are the same age always, but the man in the crowd
Is older every season. Come on, play ball!

(1944)

SHINE, PERISHING REPUBLIC
Robinson Jeffers

While this America settles in the mold of its vulgarity, heavily thicken-
    ing to empire,
And protest, only a bubble in the molten mass, pops and sighs out, and
    the mass hardens,

I sadly smiling remember that the flower fades to make fruit, the fruit
    rots to make earth.
Out of the mother; and through the spring exultances, ripeness and de-
    cadence; and home to the mother.

You making haste haste on decay: not blameworthy; life is good, be it
    stubbornly long or suddenly
A mortal splendor: meteors are not needed less than mountains: shine,
    perishing republic.

But for my children, I would have them keep their distance from the
    thickening center; corruption
Never has been compulsory, when the cities lie at the monster's feet
    there are left the mountains.

And boys, be in nothing so moderate as in love of man, a clever servant,
    insufferable master.
There is the trap that catches noblest spirits, that caught—they say.—
    God, when he walked on earth.

(1924)

THE BALLAD OF WILLIAM SYCAMORE (1790-1871)
Stephen Vincent Benét

My father, he was a mountaineer,
His fist was a knotty hammer;
He was quick on his feet as a running deer,
And he spoke with a Yankee stammer.

My mother, she was merry and brave,
And so she came to her labor,
With a tall green fir for her doctor grave
And a stream for her comforting neighbor.

And some are wrapped in the linen fine,
And some like a godling's scion;
But I was cradled on twigs of pine
In the skin of a mountain lion.

And some remember a white, starched lap
And a ewer with silver handles;
But I remember a coonskin cap
And the smell of bayberry candles.

The cabin logs, with the bark still rough,
And my mother who laughed at trifles,
And the tall, lank visitors, brown as snuff,
With their long, straight squirrel-rifles.

I can hear them dance, like a foggy song,
Through the deepest one of my slumbers,
The fiddle squeaking the boots along
And my father calling the numbers.

The quick feet shaking the puncheon-floor,
And the fiddle squealing and squealing,
Till the dried herbs rattled above the door
And the dust went up to the ceiling.

There are children lucky from dawn till dusk,
But never a child so lucky!
For I cut my teeth on "Money Musk"
In the Bloody Ground of Kentucky!

When I grew tall as the Indian corn,
My father had little to lend me,
But he gave me his great, old powder-horn
And his woodsman's skill to befriend me.

With a leather shirt to cover my back,
And a redskin nose to unravel
Each forest sign, I carried my pack
As far as a scout could travel.

Till I lost my boyhood and found my wife,
A girl like a Salem clipper!
A woman straight as a hunting-knife
With eyes as bright as the Dipper!

We cleared our camp where the buffalo feed,
Unheard-of streams were our flagons;
And I sowed my sons like the apple-seed
On the trail of the Western wagons.

They were right, tight boys, never sulky or slow,
A fruitful, a goodly muster.
The eldest died at the Alamo.
The youngest fell with Custer.

The letter that told it burned my hand.
Yet we smiled and said, "So be it!"
But I could not live when they fenced the land,
For it broke my heart to see it.

I saddled a red, unbroken colt
And rode him into the day there;
And he threw me down like a thunderbolt
And rolled on me as I lay there.

The hunter's whistle hummed in my ear
As the city-men tried to move me,
And I died in my boots like a pioneer
With the whole wide sky above me.

Now I lie in the heart of the fat, black soil,
Like the seed of a prairie-thistle;
It has washed my bones with honey and oil
And picked them clean as a whistle.

And my youth returns, like the rains of Spring,
And my sons, like the wild-geese flying;
And I lie and hear the meadow-lark sing
And have much content in my dying.

Go play with the towns you have built of blocks,
The towns where you would have bound me!
I sleep in my earth like a tired fox,
And my buffalo have found me.

(1923)

MR. FLOOD'S PARTY

Edwin Arlington Robinson

Old Eben Flood, climbing alone one night
Over the hill between the town below
And the forsaken upland hermitage
That held as much as he should ever know
On earth again of home, paused warily.
The road was his with not a native near;
And Eben, having leisure, said aloud,
For no man else in Tilbury Town to hear:

"Well, Mr. Flood, we have the harvest moon
Again, and we may not have many more;
The bird is on the wing, the poet says,
And you and I have said it here before.
Drink to the bird." He raised up to the light
The jug that he had gone so far to fill,
And answered huskily: "Well, Mr. Flood,
Since you propose it, I believe I will."

Alone, as if enduring to the end
A valiant armor of scarred hopes outworn,

He stood there in the middle of the road
Like Roland's ghost winding a silent horn.
Below him, in the town among the trees,
Where friends of other days had honored him,
A phantom salutation of the dead
Rang thinly till old Eben's eyes were dim.

Then, as a mother lays her sleeping child
Down tenderly, fearing it may awake,
He set the jug down slowly at his feet
With trembling care, knowing that most things break;
And only when assured that on firm earth
It stood, as the uncertain lives of men
Assuredly did not, he paced away,
And with his hand extended paused again:

"Well, Mr. Flood, we have not met like this
In a long time; and many a change has come
To both of us, I fear, since last it was
We had a drop together. Welcome home!"
Convivially returning with himself,
Again he raised the jug up to the light;
And with an acquiescent quaver said:
"Well, Mr. Flood, if you insist, I might.

"Only a very little, Mr. Flood—
For auld lang syne. No more, sir; that will do."
So, for the time, apparently it did,
And Eben evidently thought so too;
For soon amid the silver loneliness
Of night he lifted up his voice and sang,
Secure, with only two moons listening,
Until the whole harmonious landscape rang—

"For auld lang syne." The weary throat gave out,
The last word wavered; and the song being done,
He raised again the jug regretfully
And shook his head, and was again alone.
There was not much that was ahead of him,
And there was nothing in the town below—
Where strangers would have shut the many doors
That many friends had opened long ago.

(1921)

SPEECH TO THOSE WHO SAY COMRADE
Archibald MacLeish

The brotherhood is not by the blood certainly:
But neither are men brothers by speech—by saying so:
Men are brothers by life lived and are hurt for it:

Hunger and hurt are the great begetters of brotherhood:
Humiliation has gotten much love:
Danger I say is the nobler father and mother:

Those are as brothers whose bodies have shared fear
Or shared harm or shared hurt or indignity.
Why are the old soldiers brothers and nearest?

For this: with their minds they go over the sea a little
And find themselves in their youth again as they were in
Soissons and Meaux and at Ypres and those cities:

A French loaf and the girls with their eyelids painted
Bring back to aging and lonely men
Their twentieth year and the metal odor of danger:

It is this in life which of all things is tenderest—
To remember together with unknown men the days
Common also to them and perils ended:

It is this which makes of many a generation—
A wave of men who having the same years
Have in common the same dead and the changes.

The solitary and unshared experience
Dies of itself like the violations of love
Or lives on as the dead live eerily:

The unshared and single man must cover his
Loneliness as a girl her shame for the way of
Life is neither by one man nor by suffering.

Who are the born brothers in truth? The puddlers
Scorched by the same flame in the same foundries:
Those who have spit on the same boards with the blood in it:

Ridden the same rivers with green logs:
Fought the police in the parks of the same cities:
Grinned for the same blows: the same flogging:

Veterans out of the same ships—factories—
Expeditions for fame: the founders of continents:
Those that hid in Geneva a time back:

Those that have hidden and hunted and all such—
Fought together: labored together: they carry the
Common look like a card and they pass touching.

Brotherhood! No word said can make you brothers!
Brotherhood only the brave earn and by danger or
Harm or by bearing hurt and by no other.

Brotherhood here in the strange world is the rich and
Rarest giving of life and the most valued:
Not to be had for a word or a week's wishing.

(1936)

PROEM and EPILOGUE
Langston Hughes

PROEM

I am a Negro:
    Black as the night is black,
    Black like the depths of my Africa.

I've been a slave:
    Caesar told me to keep his door-steps clean.
    I brushed the boots of Washington.

I've been a worker:
    Under my hand the pyramids arose.
    I made mortar for the Woolworth Building.

I've been a singer:
　All the way from Africa to Georgia
　I carried my sorrow songs.
　I made ragtime.

I've been a victim:
　The Belgians cut off my hands in the Congo.
　They lynch me now in Texas.

I am a Negro:
　Black as the night is black,
　Black like the depths of my Africa.

EPILOGUE

I, too, sing America.

I am the darker brother.
They send me to eat in the kitchen
When company comes,
But I laugh,
And eat well,
And grow strong.

Tomorrow,
I'll sit at the table
When company comes.
Nobody'll dare
Say to me,
"Eat in the kitchen,"
Then.

Besides,
They'll see how beautiful I am
And be ashamed,—

I, too, am America.

(1926)

Earlier American Poems

SONG

Francis Hopkinson

My gen'rous heart disdains
   The slave of love to be,
I scorn his servile chains,
   And boast my liberty.
     This whining
      And pining
And wasting with care,
Are not to my taste, be she ever so fair.

I

Shall a girl's capricious frown
Sink my noble spirits down?
Shall a face of white and red
Make me droop my silly head?
Shall I set me down and sigh
For an eye-brow or an eye?
For a braided lock of hair,
Curse my fortune and despair?
   Refrain: My gen'rous heart disdains, &c.

2

Still uncertain is tomorrow,
Not quite certain is today—
Shall I waste my time in sorrow?
Shall I languish life away?
All because a cruel maid,
Hath not Love with Love repaid.
   Refrain: My gen'rous heart disdains, &c.

(1792)

THE RAVEN
Edgar Allan Poe

Once upon a midnight dreary, while I pondered, weak and weary,
Over many a quaint and curious volume of forgotten lore,
While I nodded, nearly napping, suddenly there came a tapping,
As of someone gently rapping, rapping at my chamber door.
" 'Tis some visitor," I muttered, "tapping at my chamber door—
       Only this and nothing more."

Ah, distinctly I remember it was in the bleak December,
And each separate dying ember wrought its ghost upon the floor.
Eagerly I wished the morrow; vainly I had sought to borrow
From my books surcease of sorrow—sorrow for the lost Lenore,
For the rare and radiant maiden whom the angels name Lenore—
       Nameless *here* for evermore.

And the silken, sad, uncertain rustling of each purple curtain
Thrilled me—filled me with fantastic terrors never felt before;
So that now, to still the beating of my heart, I stood repeating,
" 'Tis some visitor entreating entrance at my chamber door—
Some late visitor entreating entrance at my chamber door—
       This it is and nothing more."

Presently my soul grew stronger: hesitating then no longer,
"Sir," said I, "or Madam, truly your forgiveness I implore;
But the fact is I was napping, and so gently you came rapping,
And so faintly you came tapping, tapping at my chamber door,
That I scarce was sure I heard you"—here I opened wide the door—
       Darkness there and nothing more.

Deep into the darkness peering, long I stood there, wondering, fearing,
Doubting, dreaming dreams no mortal ever dared to dream before;
But the silence was unbroken, and the stillness gave no token,
And the only word there spoken was the whispered word "Lenore!"
This I whispered, and an echo murmured back the word "Lenore!"
       Merely this and nothing more.

Back into the chamber turning, all my soul within me burning,
Soon again I heard a tapping, somewhat louder than before.
"Surely," said I, "surely that is something at my window lattice;
Let me see, then, what thereat is, and this mystery explore,—
Let my heart be still a moment and this mystery explore—
'Tis the wind and nothing more."

Open here I flung the shutter, when, with many a flirt and flutter,
In there stepped a stately Raven of the saintly days of yore.
Not the least obeisance made he, not a minute stopped or stayed he,
But with mien of lord or lady perched above my chamber door—
Perched upon a bust of Pallas just above my chamber door—
Perched and sat, and nothing more.

Then, this ebony bird beguiling my sad fancy into smiling
By the grave and stern decorum of the countenance it wore,
"Though thy crest be shorn and shaven, thou," I said, "art sure no
craven,
Ghastly, grim, and ancient Raven, wandering from the nightly shore:
Tell me what thy lordly name is on the night's Plutonian shore!"
Quoth the Raven, "Nevermore."

Much I marveled this ungainly fowl to hear discourse so plainly,
Though its answer little meaning, little relevancy bore;
For we cannot help agreeing that no living human being
Ever yet was blessed with seeing bird above his chamber door—
Bird or beast upon the sculptured bust above his chamber door—
With such name as "Nevermore."

But the Raven, sitting lonely on the placid bust, spoke only
That one word, as if his soul in that one word he did outpour.
Nothing farther then he uttered, not a feather then he fluttered;
Till I scarcely more than muttered, "Other friends have flown before:
On the morrow *he* will leave me, as my hopes have flown before."
Then the bird said, "Nevermore."

Startled at the stillness broken by reply so aptly spoken,
"Doubtless," said I, "what it utters is its only stock and store,
Caught from some unhappy master whom unmerciful Disaster

Followed fast and followed faster till his songs one burden bore,
Till the dirges of his hope that melancholy burden bore
    Of 'Never—nevermore.'"

But the Raven still beguiling my sad fancy into smiling,
Straight I wheeled a cushioned seat in front of bird and bust and door;
Then, upon the velvet sinking, I betook myself to linking
Fancy unto fancy, thinking what this ominous bird of yore,
What this grim, ungainly, ghastly, gaunt, and ominous bird of yore
            Meant in croaking "Nevermore."

This I sat engaged in guessing, but no syllable expressing
To the fowl, whose fiery eyes now burned into my "bosom's" core;
This and more I sat divining, with my head at ease reclining
On the cushion's velvet lining that the lamp-light gloated o'er,
But whose velvet violet lining with the lamp-light gloating o'er,
        She shall press, ah, nevermore!

Then, methought, the air grew denser, perfumed from an unseen censer
Swung by seraphim whose foot-falls tinkled on the tufted floor.
"Wretch," I cried, "thy God hath lent thee—by these angels he hath
    sent thee
Respite—respite and nepenthe from thy memories of Lenore!
Quaff, oh quaff this kind nepenthe, and forget this lost Lenore!"
            Quoth the Raven, "Nevermore."

"Prophet!" said I, "thing of evil! prophet still, if bird or devil!
Whether Tempter sent, or whether tempest tossed thee here ashore,
Desolate yet all undaunted, on this desert land enchanted—
On this home by Horror haunted—tell me truly, I implore:
Is there—*is* there balm in Gilead?—tell me—tell me, I implore!"
            Quoth the Raven, "Nevermore."

"Prophet!" said I, "thing of evil—prophet still, if bird or devil!
By that Heaven that bends above us, by that God we both adore,
Tell this soul with sorrow laden if, within the distant Aidenn,
It shall clasp a sainted maiden whom the angels name Lenore:
Clasp a rare and radiant maiden whom the angels name Lenore!"
            Quoth the Raven, "Nevermore."

"Be that word our sign of parting, bird or fiend!" I shrieked, up-
  starting:
"Get thee back into the tempest and the Night's Plutonian shore!
Leave no black plume as a token of that lie thy soul hath spoken!
Leave my loneliness unbroken! quit the bust above my door!
Take thy beak from out my heart, and take thy form from off my
  door!"
          Quoth the Raven, "Nevermore."

And the Raven, never flitting, still is sitting, still is sitting
On the pallid bust of Pallas just above my chamber door;
And his eyes have all the seeming of a demon's that is dreaming,
And the lamp-light o'er him streaming throws his shadow on the floor;
And my soul from out that shadow that lies floating on the floor
          Shall be lifted—nevermore!

                                                    (1845)

SHERIDAN AT CEDAR CREEK
(OCTOBER 1864)

Herman Melville

Shoe the steed with silver
  That bore him to the fray,
When he heard the guns at dawning—
  Miles away;
When he heard them calling, calling—
  Mount! nor stay:
      Quick, or all is lost;
      They've surprised and stormed the post,
      They push your routed host—
  Gallop! retrieve the day.

House the horse in ermine—
  For the foam-flake blew
White through the red October;
  He thundered into view;
They cheered him in the looming,

Horseman and horse they knew.
The turn of the tide began,
The rally of bugles ran,
He swung his hat in the van;
The electric hoof-spark flew.

Wreathe the steed and lead him—
For the charge he led
Touched and turned the cypress
Into amaranths for the head
Of Philip, king of riders,
Who raised them from the dead.
The camp (at dawning lost),
By eve, recovered—forced,
Rang with laughter of the host
At belated Early fled.

Shroud the horse in sable—
For the mounds they heap!
There is firing in the Valley,
And yet no strife they keep;
It is the parting volley,
It is the pathos deep.
There is glory for the brave
Who lead, and nobly save,
But no knowledge in the grave
Where the nameless followers sleep.

(1866)

THE DAY IS DONE
Henry Wadsworth Longfellow

The day is done, and the darkness
Falls from the wings of Night,
As a feather is wafted downward
From an eagle in his flight.

I see the lights of the village
Gleam through the rain and the mist,

And a feeling of sadness comes o'er me
  That my soul cannot resist:

A feeling of sadness and longing,
  That is not akin to pain,
And resembles sorrow only
  As the mist resembles the rain.

Come, read to me some poem,
  Some simple and heartfelt lay,
That shall soothe this restless feeling,
  And banish the thoughts of day.

Not from the grand old masters,
  Not from the bards sublime,
Whose distant footsteps echo
  Through the corridors of Time.

For, like strains of martial music,
  Their mighty thoughts suggest
Life's endless toil and endeavor;
  And tonight I long for rest.

Read from some humbler poet,
  Whose songs gushed from his heart,
As showers from the clouds of summer,
  Or tears from the eyelids start;

Who, through long days of labor,
  And nights devoid of ease,
Still heard in his soul the music
  Of wonderful melodies.

Such songs have power to quiet
  The restless pulse of care,
And come like the benediction
  That follows after prayer.

Then read from the treasured volume
  The poem of thy choice,

And lend to the rhyme of the poet
The beauty of thy voice.

And the night shall be filled with music,
And the cares, that infest the day,
Shall fold their tents, like the Arabs,
And as silently steal away.

(1844)

SUGGESTIONS FOR STUDY

1. *A Musical Review.* Turn to the Glossarial Handbook and then back to Chapter 5, and make sure that you are still clear as to the distinction between free verse and bound verse; that you understand the relation of metrical pattern and sense pattern to the poetic rhythm, expectancy and deviation; that you remember what the chief features of a metrical pattern are, and what sorts of foot and meter and line-scheme may be encountered; that you recall the sorts of deviation, metrical variations; that you are alert to the phenomena of sound pattern and tone-color; that you are still aware of the complexity of the "music" of poetry and its relation to the other constituents of the poem-experience.

2. *Aloud and Alone.* (a) Get acquainted with the above poems by reading them silently. (b) Read at least part of each one of them out loud to determine the nature of its "music." (c) Do you recall other poems by the same poets? other poems on similar themes? Which ones give rise to the most valuable experiences? (d) Read several of the poems in this chapter time and time again, both silently and aloud, following the directions and hints given in the text.

3. *Mutual Reading.* (a) Arrange to read some of the poems with another person. (b) Take turn about, reading and listening. (c) Be as helpful as possible in coaching the other reader, and insist upon his frankness in commenting upon your own reading. (d) Make use of the suggestions given you, and practice to improve your capacity to communicate to others your experience of poems that you like.

4. *Off the Record.* (a) One can learn much about reading poetry aloud by listening to the reading of others. For a good many poems phonograph recordings are available. Some of them record the reading of the poets themselves; some, the reading of professional readers or actors. Such recordings are by no means of equal value or interest, for some of the poets are not skilled in the oral communication of their poetic experiences, and some of the professional readers sound (to many

listeners) insincere and artificial. (b) Stephen Vincent Benét has recorded his own "Ballad of William Sycamore," and Carl Sandburg has recorded long selections from *The People, Yes,* though not the one reprinted in this book. There is a recording of Longfellow's "The Day Is Done" by Lowell Cartwright. (c) Some libraries now have record collections and listening rooms, and many individuals have collections of speech as well as musical records. A comprehensive listing of poetry records will be found in the catalogue of Linguaphone Institute (30 Rockefeller Plaza, New York City 20), from which the recordings of many manufacturers may be purchased.

5. *To Hear Ourselves.* (a) If recording equipment is available for use with inexpensive discs and low service cost, the student may wish to record his prepared reading of one of the poems from this chapter. Speech departments often have the necessary equipment, and many radio shops are equipped to make speech records. Good results are often obtained with home recorders. (b) The careful study of such a poetry recording may serve a useful purpose in the improvement of one's oral reading.

6. *The American Muse.* (a) Prepare a half-hour program of American poetry, using several of the poems given in this chapter. (b) Choose poems that will illustrate a general statement that you might make about American poetry. Work out some sort of a framework for your program, a few sentences of introduction and of conclusion, and appropriate transitions. You may wish to read certain poems two times in order to communicate their full meaning. (c) Cast about for a possible audience, in a situation that will not be too obviously artificial. Prevail upon your family to listen to you; or call in a dormitory group, or read to a small club, or to a Sunday School class. (d) Strive earnestly to communicate your full experience of the poems you read. Watch your auditors, and try to adjust your reading to their evident ability to follow you. (e) Make some estimate of your success in this venture.

7. *The Poem of Your Choice.* (a) Find a book-length poem that you think will hold your interest, and begin reading it—aloud and alone, or (if you know someone with similar tastes) turn and turn about with another reader. (b) The following are long poems of widely different sorts: Masefield's sea yarn, *Dauber;* Benét's poem of the Civil War, *John Brown's Body;* Robinson's version of the medieval romance, *Tristram;* MacLeish's narrative of Spanish conquerors, *Conquistador;* Masters' collection of American sketches, *Spoon River Anthology;* Sandburg's gathering of our folklore, *The People, Yes;* Tennyson's knights of the Round Table, *Idylls of the King;* Whitman's personal

and philosophical rhapsody, *Song of Myself;* Bryant's translation of *The Odyssey.* These are but a few suggestions.

8. *For the Vaults.* It will be no trick at all to memorize one of the poems in this chapter, as you will already know it quite well. Simply read it a few more times, looking up from the book more and more of the time as you read it aloud. Or perhaps you are one who may enjoy memorizing while off on a walk with book under your arm. Or a daily bus or car ride may be the occasion for learning one or more of them by heart.

14

CHORAL READING

Within the past generation there has been a revival of the ancient practice of choral speech. Dramatic choruses, refrains in ballads, sea chanties, and liturgical responses—all remain as evidences of a time when poetry was a group function and belonged to the people.

The renewed interest in choral speech stems largely from the work begun in England by Marjorie Gullan and Mona Swann, and carried on in this country by many enthusiastic teachers under various names: verse speaking, choral speaking, choral reading, choral verse speaking, etc. Adults have found pleasure in it, as have children, and it has been useful in speech training and in cultivating an appreciation of poetry.

I. VALUES OF GROUP READING

Many persons discover, when they begin to read poetry aloud, that their speech is limited in range; that they command only a narrow pitch-band, only one tone of voice, one rate of speed, one degree of volume; that their phrasal patterns are monotonously repetitive. Much may be done to increase speech range by the patient practice of rather dull exercises. But perhaps much more may be done by the zestful participation in choral speaking. Vocal inhibitions are relaxed as the individual becomes one with the group. The others in the group pull him along or slow him down; the others encourage his inflections and cadences; the others keep him with them in their phrasing; and together with others he will develop voice tones suitable to express a variety of attitudes and moods.

354

Those who have not themselves practiced choral speech, or who have not observed the results of its training, are often skeptical of its value. But, among speech teachers, it has now become an accepted technique for trying "to pull out a few more stops in that powerful but at present somewhat narrow-toned organ," the American student, to turn Matthew Arnold's phrase to a new purpose.

He who would enjoy the full flavor of poetry when reading it silently must (it is the contention of this book) develop at least adequacy in oral interpretation. Choral reading will help him to attain this adequacy. But it will profit him in other ways as well.

Those poems that have been studied thoughtfully in group rehearsals may remain with the individual as prized possessions, keys that will unlock the meaning of other poems at a future time. Certainly the old ballads and other folk poetry are better understood as a result of one's joining into the choric utterance of their refrains. So, too, the ancient drama, and the liturgical forms of worship.

No more than a brief description of choral reading can be given here. Those who would organize and direct speech choirs are referred to the works of Marjorie Gullan, Mona Swann, Elizabeth Keppie, and others, readily available in libraries. But a beginning in choral reading may be made by interested persons without extended exploration of theory or technique.

A speech choir consists of a group of from ten to twenty interested persons who meet repeatedly with a choirmaster, director, or leader for the purpose of reading poetry in unison and in parts. Groups smaller than ten may work successfully without formal leadership, and larger groups may be managed by a skilled director.

It is desirable to group the choristers according to the weight or color of their voices, which is not quite the same thing as their pitch. For in the reading of some poems, the light voices will be used antiphonally (responsively, turn and turn about) with the dark voices, or the men's voices against the women's. It will be necessary at times to divide into more numerous groups. During the first meetings, when the individuals are becoming accustomed to working with each other, only easier forms of choral reading should be attempted, and the individuals should be discovered who are already capable of taking the solo parts.

Individual study and oral reading of the poem to be rehearsed may well precede group discussion of its meaning and "music." Small groups may wish to practice together between rehearsals. It is in the rehearsals, of course, that the most valuable work will take place. And these should be so organized and conducted as to accomplish much without unnecessary loss of time.

There are a number of different sorts of "chorustration" possible for the group speaking of poetry—solo voice with choral refrain, two semichoruses in antiphony, more complex arrangements of solo voices and variable groups, and unison reading. The ballads and lyrics with refrains are the simplest forms, and the extended unison lyrics are the most difficult. The arrangement of a poem for choral reading should, of course, be appropriate to the development of its thought, and no merely whimsical division into various parts; and it will call for sensitive interpretation on the part of the director.

2. POINTERS, PROBLEMS, PITFALLS

Good choral reading will be, first of all, good oral reading. And the suggestions given in the preceding chapter would bear repetition here. But there is added the problem of speaking with others, with definiteness of attack, with perfect concurrence of phrase, conforming to predetermined inflectional patterns, and closing the cadences with precision. Then, there is the matter of ensemble, merging the one voice with the many and fitting the several parts into a smoothly articulated whole. These, however, are the negative virtues of good choral speech.

The positive virtues are more difficult of attainment. Good choral reading should be measured in terms of *communication* and *interpretation*. The first question is whether the choirmaster and choristers have succeeded in giving such "expression" to the thoughts and feeling of the poem (as they have experienced it) as to "communicate" these thoughts and feelings to the listeners—that is, so as to arouse in the listeners comparable thoughts and feelings. The second question is whether the choirmaster and choristers have made a satisfactory interpretation of the printed verses, realizing a full and vivid poem-experience that takes into account all the clues in the literary context and that is consistent with all the relevant critical and historical data. Sensitiveness to the implications of the printed poem and zestfulness in sharing an interpretation of it with others—these are requisite to good choral reading.

But there will be some difference of opinion, among practitioners of verse choir, about several matters. Should the chorus intone or chant the poem? or should the chorus speak it using a modification of normal speech melody? Should the individual voices be brought into pitch unison or into harmonious intervals? or should the effect be one of atonality—not discordant, but without reference to pitch harmony? Should the poems, typed off for each chorister's notebook, have the "choristration" already fully indicated? or should this be dictated by the choirmaster? or should it be worked out by the group in rehearsal? Should the director conduct the speech choir with hand movements, standing in front of the group? or should he stand in with the other speakers? Should a verse choir recite without book in hand? or should the activity be choral reading? Should the speech choir set public performance or contests as its goal? or should it rehearse for the sheer love of reading together, to develop the capacity to enjoy great poetry yet more fully? Should the speech choir confine itself to choral reading? or should it co-ordinate its work with such other arts as music, drama, and dance?

No answers will be suggested here, but a closing word must warn the reader of special pitfalls that lie ahead: Again, the dangers that choral speech is heir to, will be the same as those that beset individual oral reading—expressionlessness, stumbling and faltering, rhythmic singsong, artificiality of expression, sentimentality of "poetic" tone. But there are other dangers: emphasis upon speech melody irrespective of meaning, the performance of nonsense and children's verse in dead earnestness for an adult audience, the selection of essentially effeminate poetry for mixed groups, the dull dragging tempo, the use of an artificial diction rather than the accepted standard of the region.

Let it not be forgotten that choral speech is deeply rooted in our culture. The Pledge of Allegiance, the Apostles' Creed and Lord's Prayer, lodge rituals and fraternity initiations—these are but instances of group speech as it is widely practiced in our most serious moments. But the "Hip, hip, *hurrah!* . . . hip, hip, *hurrah!*" of an earlier generation, and the organized rooting at football games in our own, are other sorts of comparable group behavior. And who has not, in youthful reading of *Treasure Island,* roared out with the best of pirates:

> Fifteen men on the dead man's chest—
> Yo-ho-ho, and a bottle of rum!
> Drink and the devil had done for the rest—
> Yo-ho-ho, and a bottle of rum!

Poems for Solo Voice and Chorus

[The "arrangement" of the poems by Browning and Herbert was in each case indicated by the poet.]

CAVALIER TUNES
Robert Browning

I. MARCHING ALONG

> Kentish Sir Byng stood for his King,
> Bidding the crop-headed Parliament swing:
> And, pressing a troop unable to stoop
> And see the rogues flourish and honest folk droop,
> Marched them along, fifty-score strong,
> Great-hearted gentlemen, singing this song:
>
> God for King Charles! Pym and such carles
> To the Devil that prompts 'em their treasonous parles!
> Cavaliers, up! Lips from the cup,
> Hands from the pasty, nor bite take nor sup
> Till you're—

Chorus.—*Marching along, fifty-score strong,*
       Great-hearted gentlemen, singing this song.

Hampden to hell, and his obsequies' knell.
Serve Hazelrig, Fiennes, and young Harry as well!
England, good cheer! Rupert is near!
Kentish and loyalists, keep we not here,
   Chorus.—*Marching along, fifty-score strong,*
          Great-hearted gentlemen, singing this song?

Then, God for King Charles! Pym and his snarls
To the Devil that pricks on such pestilent carles!
Hold by the right, you double your might;
So, onward to Nottingham, fresh for the fight,
   Chorus.—*March we along, fifty-score strong,*
          Great-hearted gentlemen, singing this song!

II. GIVE A ROUSE

King Charles, and who'll do him right now?
King Charles, and who's ripe for fight now?
Give a rouse: here's, in hell's despite now,
King Charles!

Who gave me the goods that went since?
Who raised me the house that sank once?
Who helped me to gold I spent since?
Who found me in wine you drank once?
   Chorus.—*King Charles, and who'll do him right now?*
          King Charles, and who's ripe for fight now?
          Give a rouse: here's, in hell's despite now,
          King Charles!

To whom used my boy George quaff else,
By the old fool's side that begot him?
For whom did he cheer and laugh else,
While Noll's damned troopers shot him?
   Chorus.—*King Charles, and who'll do him right now?*
          King Charles, and who's ripe for fight now?
          Give a rouse: here's, in hell's despite now,
          King Charles!

III. BOOT AND SADDLE

Boot, saddle, to horse, and away!
Rescue my castle before the hot day
Brightens to blue from its silvery gray.
   CHORUS.—*Boot, saddle, to horse, and away!*

Ride past the suburbs, asleep as you'd say;
Many's the friend there, will listen and pray
"God's luck to gallants that strike up the lay—
   CHORUS.—*"Boot, saddle, to horse, and away!"*

Forty miles off, like a roebuck at bay,
Flouts Castle Brancepeth the Roundheads' array:
Who laughs, "Good fellows ere this, by my fay,
   CHORUS.—*"Boot, saddle, to horse, and away!"*

Who? My wife Gertrude; that, honest and gay,
Laughs when you talk of surrendering, "Nay!
I've better counselors; what counsel they?
   CHORUS.—*"Boot, saddle, to horse, and away!"*

                       (1842)

ANTIPHON

George Herbert

  Chorus. Let all the world in ev'ry corner sing,
            "My God and King."
    Verse. The heav'ns are not too high,
        His praise may thither fly;
        The earth is not too low,
        His praises there may grow.
  Chorus. Let all the world in ev'ry corner sing,
            "My God and King."
    Verse. The Church with psalms must shout,
        No door can keep them out;
        But, above all, the heart
        Must bear the longest part.
  Chorus. Let all the world in ev'ry corner sing,
            "My God and King."

                       (1633)

ROBIN-A-THRUSH

ENGLISH BALLAD

Anonymous

Old Robin-a-thrush he married a wife
With a hoppitty moppitty mow now.
She proved to be the plague of his life.
With a hig jig jiggitty, ruffetty petticoat,
Robin-a-thrush cries mow now.

She never gets up till twelve o'clock
With a hoppitty moppitty mow now.
Puts on her gown and above it her smock.
With a hig jig jiggitty, ruffetty petticoat,
Robin-a-thrush cries mow now.

Her butter she made in an old man's boot
With a hoppitty moppitty mow now.
And to churn it well she put in her foot.
With a hig jig jiggitty, ruffetty petticoat,
Robin-a-thrush cries mow now.

Her cheese when made was put on the shelf
With a hoppitty moppitty mow now.
And it never was turned till it turned itself.
With a hig jig jiggitty, ruffetty petticoat,
Robin-a-thrush cries mow now.

This song it was made for gentlemen
With a hoppitty moppitty mow now.
If you want any more you must sing it again.
With a hig jig jiggitty, ruffetty petticoat,
Robin-a-thrush cries mow now.

(?c. 1400)

Poems for Two-part Reading

[The first two of these poems fall very easily into two-part arrangements for choral reading. The third has been arranged for antiphonal reading by chorus and two semichoruses.]

UP-HILL

Christina Rossetti

Does the road wind up-hill all the way?
 Yes, to the very end.
Will the day's journey take the whole long day?
 From morn to night, my friend.

But is there for the night a resting-place?
 A roof for when the slow, dark hours begin.
May not the darkness hide it from my face?
 You cannot miss that inn.

Shall I meet other wayfarers at night?
 Those who have gone before.
Then must I knock, or call when just in sight?
 They will not keep you standing at that door.

Shall I find comfort, travel-sore and weak?
 Of labor you shall find the sum.
Will there be beds for me and all who seek?
 Yea, beds for all who come.

        (1861)

AH, ARE YOU DIGGING ON MY GRAVE?

Thomas Hardy

"Ah, are you digging on my grave
 My loved one?—planting rue?"

> —*"No: yesterday he went to wed*
> *One of the brightest wealth has bred.*
> *'It cannot hurt her now,' he said,*
> *'That I should not be true.'"*

"Then who is digging on my grave?
  My nearest, dearest kin?"
    —*"Ah, no: they sit and think, 'What use!*
    What good will planting flowers produce?
    No tendance of her mound can loose
    Her spirit from Death's gin.'"

"But someone digs upon my grave?
  My enemy?—prodding sly?"
    —*"Nay: when she heard you had passed the Gate*
    That shuts on all flesh soon or late,
    She thought you no more worth her hate,
    And cares not where you lie."

"Then, who is digging on my grave?
  Say—since I have not guessed!"
    —*"O it is I, my mistress dear,*
    Your little dog, who still lives near,
    And much I hope my movements here
    Have not disturbed your rest?"

"Ah, yes! *You* dig upon my grave. . . .
  Why flashed it not on me
That one true heart was left behind!
What feeling do we ever find
To equal among human kind
  A dog's fidelity!"

> *"Mistress, I dug upon your grave*
>   *To bury a bone, in case*
> *I should be hungry near this spot*
> *When passing on my daily trot.*
> *I am sorry, but I quite forgot*
>   *It was your resting-place."*

(1914)

THE TWENTY-FOURTH PSALM
David

Chorus The earth is the Lord's, and the fulness thereof;
     The world, and they that dwell therein.
     For He hath founded it upon the seas,
     And established it upon the floods.

I.   WHO SHALL ASCEND INTO THE HILL OF THE LORD?
     OR WHO SHALL STAND IN HIS HOLY PLACE?

II.   *He that hath clean hands, and a pure heart;*
     Who hath not lifted up his soul unto vanity,
      nor sworn deceitfully.
     He shall receive the blessing from the Lord,
     And righteousness from the God of his salvation.
     This is the generation of them that seek Him,
      that seek thy face, O Jacob.

Chorus Lift up your heads, O ye gates;
     And be ye lift[ed] up, ye everlasting doors;
     And the King of glory shall come in.

I.   WHO IS THIS KING OF GLORY?

II.   *The Lord strong and mighty,*
     The Lord mighty in battle.

Chorus Lift up your heads, O ye gates;
     Even lift them up, ye everlasting doors;
     And the King of glory shall come in.

I.   WHO IS THIS KING OF GLORY?

II.   *The Lord of Hosts,*

Chorus He is the King of glory.

           (*bef. 150* B.C., tr. 1611 A.D.)

Poems for Complex "Chorustration"

[The first of these poems, an American Negro spiritual, is here arranged for complex, cumulative and sequential group reading by five solo voices and three choral groups. The First Voice might well be rich and deep; the Second, light; the Third, medium; the Fourth and Fifth, contrasting in quality. The chorus might well be divided into light, medium, and dark voice groups. An imaginative effort should be made to realize in voice quality and articulation the full flavor of this folk ballad.]

JOSHUA FIT DE BATTLE OB JERICO

AMERICAN SPIRITUAL

Anonymous

First V. Joshua fit de battle ob Jerico—
"   Jerico—   *Light Gp.*
"   Jerico—   *Dark Gp.*
"   Joshua fit de battle ob Jerico,   *Medium Gp.*
"   And de walls came a-tumblin' down.   *Full Ch.*

Second   "Good mornin', Brother Pilgrim,
           Pray tell me where you boun';
           O tell me where you travelin' to
           'Cause dis enchanted groun'."

Third   "My name it is Poor Pilgrim,
           To Canaan I am boun';
           Travelin' through dis wilderness
           'Cause dis enchanted groun'."

Fourth   You may talk about yo' King ob Gideon,
Fifth   You may talk about yo' man ob Saul,
First   Dere's none like good ole Joshua,
           At de battle ob Jerico.

           Up to de walls ob Jerico
           He marched wid spear in han',
           "Go blow dem ram horns," Joshua cried,
           "Kase de battle am in my han'."

Third   Den de lam' ram sheep-horns begin to
"   blow,   *Medium Gp.*

Second Trumpets begin to
   "   soun',   *Light Gp.*
First   Joshua commanded de chillun to
   "   shout,   *Dark Gp.*
   "   An' de walls came a-tumblin' down.   *Full Ch.*

First [*solus and slowly*] Dat mornin'—
   "   [*faster*] Joshua fit de battle ob Jerico—
                   Jerico—   *Light Gp.*
                   Jerico—   plus *Dark*
   "   Joshua fit de battle ob Jerico,   *Full Ch.*
   "   An' de walls came a-tumblin' down.   "

(*?bef. 1800*)

from THE FROGS

Aristophanes, translated by *J. Hookham Frere*

[This selection and the next poem, "The Ghosts of the Buffaloes," may be arranged in a variety of ways for choral reading. This Chorus from *The Frogs* is the first one in the comedy. Bacchus (Dionysus), the Greek god in whose honor were held the dramatic festivals, is represented in the play as undertaking a trip to the Underworld to bring back one of the great dramatists to adorn once more the Athenian stage. Seated in Charon's boat, Bacchus is crossing the River Styx and is himself put to plying the oars, and he hears "A chorus of Frogs—uncommon musical Frogs," as Charon describes them.]

CHORUS

Brekeke-kesh, koash, koash,
Shall the Choral Quiristers of the Marsh
Be censured and rejected as hoarse and harsh;
   And their Cromatic essays
     Deprived of praise?
No, let us raise afresh
Our obstreperous Brekeke-kesh;
The customary croak and cry
   Of the creatures
     At the theatres,

In their yearly revelry,
Brekeke-kesh, koash, koash.

Bac. (*rowing in great misery*).
How I'm maul'd,
How I'm gall'd;
Worn and mangled to a mash—
There they go! *"Koash, koash!"*—

Frogs. Brekeke-kesh, koash, koash.

Bac. Oh, beshrew,
All your crew . . .
—Have you nothing else to say?
"Brekeke-kesh, koash" all day!

Frogs. We've a right,
We've a right;
And we croak at ye for spite.
We've a right,
We've a right;
Day and night,
Day and night;
Night and day,
Still to creak and croak away.

Phoebus and every Grace
Admire and approve of the croaking race;
And the egregious guttural notes
That are gargled and warbled in their lyrical throats.
In reproof
Of your scorn
Mighty Pan
Nods his horn;
Beating time
To the rhyme
With his hoof,
With his hoof.
Persisting in our plan,
We proceed as we began,
Breke-kesh, Breke-kesh,
Kooash, kooash. . . .

Bac. Hold your tongues, you tuneful creatures. . . .

Frogs. Silence is against our natures. . . .
Our aquatic crew repair

From their periodic sleep,
In the dark and chilly deep,
To the cheerful upper air;
Then we frolic here and there
All amidst the meadows fair, . . .
All the livelong summer hours,
Till the sudden gusty showers
Send us headlong, helter, skelter,
To the pool to seek for shelter;
Meager, eager, leaping, lunging,
From the sedgy wharfage plunging
To the tranquil depth below,
There we muster all a-row;
Where, secure from toil and trouble,
With a tuneful hubble-bubble,
Our symphonious accents flow.
Brekeke-kesh, koash, koash.

Bac. I forbid you to proceed.

Frogs. That would be severe indeed;
Arbitrary, bold, and rash—
Brekeke-kesh, koash, koash.

Bac. I command you to desist—
—Oh, my back, there! oh, my wrist!
What a twist!
What a sprain!

Frogs. Once again—
We renew the tuneful strain.
Brekeke-kesh, koash, koash.

Bac. I disdain—(Hang the pain!)
All your nonsense, noise, and trash.
Oh, my blister! Oh, my sprain!

Frogs. Brekeke-kesh, koash, koash.
Friends and Frogs, we must display
All our powers of voice today;
Suffer not this stranger here,
With fastidious foreign ear,
To confound us and abash.
Brekeke-kesh, koash, koash.

Bac. Well, my spirit is not broke.

If it's only for the joke,
I'll outdo you with a croak.
Here it goes—(*very loud*) "Koash, koash."
Frogs. Now for a glorious croaking crash,   [*Still louder.*—
Brekeke-kesh, koash, koash.

(*405* B.C., tr. *c.* 1820)

THE GHOSTS OF THE BUFFALOES
Vachel Lindsay

Last night at black midnight I woke with a cry,
The windows were shaking, there was thunder on high,
The floor was atremble, the door was ajar,
White fires, crimson fires, shone from afar.
I rushed to the dooryard. The city was gone.
My home was a hut without orchard or lawn.
It was mud-smear and logs near a whispering stream,
Nothing else built by man could I see in my dream . . .

Then . . .
Ghost-kings came headlong, row upon row,
Gods of the Indians, torches aglow.
They mounted the bear and the elk and the deer,
And eagles gigantic, agèd and sere,
They rode long-horn cattle, they cried "A-la-la."
They lifted the knife, the bow, and the spear,
They lifted ghost-torches from dead fires below,
The midnight made grand with the cry "A-la-la."
The midnight made grand with a red-god charge,
A red-god show,
A red-god show,
"A-la-la, a-la-la, a-la-la, a-la-la."

With bodies like bronze, and terrible eyes
Came the rank and the file, with catamount cries,
Gibbering, yipping, with hollow-skull clacks,
Riding white bronchos with skeleton backs,
Scalp-hunters, beaded and spangled and bad,

Naked and lustful and foaming and mad,
Flashing primeval demoniac scorn,
Blood-thirst and pomp amid darkness reborn,
Power and glory that sleep in the grass
While the winds and the snows and the great rains pass.
They crossed the gray river, thousands abreast,
They rode out in infinite lines to the west,
Tide upon tide of strange fury and foam,
Spirits and wraiths, the blue was their home,
The sky was their goal where the star-flags are furled,
And on past those far golden splendors they whirled.
They burned to dim meteors, lost in the deep,
And I turned in dazed wonder, thinking of sleep.

And the wind crept by
Alone, unkempt, unsatisfied,
The wind cried and cried—
Muttered of massacres long past,
Buffaloes in shambles vast . . .
An owl said, "Hark, what is a-wing?"
I heard a cricket caroling,
I heard a cricket caroling,
I heard a cricket caroling.

Then . . .
Snuffing the lightning that crashed from on high
Rose royal old buffaloes, row upon row.
The lords of the prairie came galloping by.
And I cried in my heart "A-la-la, a-la-la.
A red-god show,
A red-god show,
A-la-la, a-la-la, a-la-la."
Buffaloes, buffaloes, thousands abreast,
A scourge and amazement, they swept to the west.
With black bobbing noses, with red rolling tongues,
Coughing forth steam from their leather-wrapped lungs,
Cows with their calves, bulls big and vain,
Goring the laggards, shaking the mane,
Stamping flint feet, flashing moon eyes,
Pompous and owlish, shaggy and wise.

Like sea-cliffs and caves resounded their ranks
With shoulders like waves, and undulant flanks.
Tide upon tide of strange fury and foam,
Spirits and wraiths, the blue was their home,
The sky was their goal where the star-flags are furled,
And on past those far golden splendors they whirled.
They burned to dim meteors, lost in the deep,
And I turned in dazed wonder, thinking of sleep.

I heard a cricket's cymbals play,
A scarecrow lightly flapped his rags,
And a pan that hung by his shoulder rang,
Rattled and thumped in a listless way,
And now the wind in the chimney sang,
The wind in the chimney,
The wind in the chimney,
The wind in the chimney,
Seemed to say:—
"Dream, boy, dream,
If you anywise can.
To dream is the work
Of beast or man.
Life is the west-going dream-storm's breath,
Life is a dream, the sigh of the skies,
The breath of the stars, that nod on their pillows
With their golden hair mussed over their eyes."
The locust played on his musical wing,
Sang to his mate of love's delight.
I heard the whippoorwill's soft fret.
I heard a cricket caroling,
I heard a cricket caroling,
I heard a cricket say: "Good-night, good-night,
Good-night, good-night, . . . good-night."

(1917)

Poems for Choral Reading in Unison

from ANTIGONE

CHORAL ODE

Sophocles, translated into prose by *Richard C. Jebb*

[Polyneices, who marched against Thebes with an army to seize the throne from his brother, killed him and was killed by him in single combat. So their uncle Creon, now king, buried the one with honor, but dishonored the body of Polyneices by ordering it left unburied. But someone has defied his edict, and has secretly performed the burial rites as required by their religion. "Can this deed," asks the Chorus of Theban Elders, "be e'en the work of gods?" Creon, angered by the suggestion, orders the culprit found.]

CHORUS

str. 1.[1]   Wonders are many, and none is more wonderful than man; the power that crosses the white sea, driven by the stormy south-wind, making a path under surges that threaten to engulf him; and Earth, the eldest of the gods, the immortal, the unwearied, doth he wear, turning the soil with the offspring of horses, as the ploughs go to and fro from year to year.

ant. 1.   And the light-hearted race of birds, and the tribes of savage beasts, and the sea-brood of the deep, he snares in the meshes of his woven toils, he leads captive, man excellent in wit. And he masters by his arts the beast whose lair is in the wilds, who roams the hills; he tames the horse of shaggy mane, he puts the yoke upon its neck, he tames the tireless mountain bull.

str. 2.   And speech, and wind-swift thought, and all the moods that mould a state, hath he taught himself; and how to flee the arrows of the frost, when 'tis hard lodging under the clear sky,

---

[1] For the words "strophe" and "antistrophe," see the Glossarial Handbook.

and the arrows of the rushing rain; yea, he hath resource for all; without resource he meets nothing that must come: only against Death shall he call for aid in vain; but from baffling maladies he hath devised escapes.

ant. 2.   Cunning beyond fancy's dream is the fertile skill which brings him, now to evil, now to good. When he honours the laws of the land, and that justice which he hath sworn by the gods to uphold, proudly stands his city: no city hath he who, for his rashness, dwells with sin. Never may he share my hearth, never think my thoughts, who doth these things!

(441 B.C., tr. 1904 A.D.)

from ATALANTA IN CALYDON

CHORUS

Algernon Charles Swinburne

Before the beginning of years,
    There came to the making of man
Time, with a gift of tears;
    Grief, with a glass that ran;
Pleasure, with pain for leaven;
    Summer, with flowers that fell;
Remembrance fallen from heaven,
    And madness risen from hell;
Strength without hands to smite;
    Love that endures for a breath;
Night, the shadow of light,
    And life, the shadow of death.

And the high gods took in hand
    Fire, and the falling of tears,
And a measure of sliding sand
    From under the feet of the years;
And froth and drift of the sea;
    And dust of the laboring earth;
And bodies of things to be
    In the houses of death and of birth;

And wrought with weeping and laughter,
　　And fashioned with loathing and love,
With life before and after
　　And death beneath and above,
For a day and a night and a morrow,
　　That his strength might endure for a span
With travail and heavy sorrow,
　　The holy spirit of man.

From the winds of the north and the south
　　They gathered as unto strife;
They breathed upon his mouth,
　　They filled his body with life;
Eyesight and speech they wrought
　　For the veils of the soul therein,
A time for labor and thought,
　　A time to serve and to sin;
They gave him light in his ways,
　　And love, and a space for delight,
And beauty and length of days,
　　And night, and sleep in the night.
His speech is a burning fire;
　　With his lips he travaileth;
In his heart is a blind desire,
　　In his eyes foreknowledge of death;
He weaves, and is clothed with derision;
　　Sows, and he shall not reap;
His life is a watch or a vision
　　Between a sleep and a sleep.

　　　　　　　　　　　　(1856)

from ODE
Arthur O'Shaughnessy

We are the music-makers,
　　And we are the dreamers of dreams,
Wandering by lone sea-breakers,
　　And sitting by desolate streams;
World-losers and world-forsakers,

On whom the pale moon gleams:
Yet we are the movers and shakers
Of the world for ever, it seems.

With wonderful deathless ditties
We build up the world's great cities,
  And out of a fabulous story
  We fashion an empire's glory:
One man with a dream, at pleasure,
  Shall go forth and conquer a crown;
And three with a new song's measure
  Can trample an empire down.

We, in the ages lying
  In the buried past of the earth,
Built Nineveh with our sighing,
  And Babel itself with our mirth;
And o'erthrew them with prophesying
  To the old of the new world's worth;
For each age is a dream that is dying,
  Or one that is coming to birth.

(1874)

SUGGESTIONS FOR STUDY

1. *Get Acquainted.* (a) Read the above poems, first with the purpose of getting acquainted with them, silently studying out their meanings, and then aloud, sensitive to their poetic rhythms and tone-coloring. (b) Now read them aloud with your attention upon their possible use for choral reading. (c) Practice reading the choral refrains of each of the poems in the first group, in what you believe to be an appropriate speech tune, tone of voice, pitch, volume, and tempo.

2. *Double Talk.* Prepare to read aloud Christina Rossetti's "Up-hill" and Thomas Hardy's "Ah, Are You Digging on My Grave," making a special effort to distinguish question and answer by differences in voice quality and pitch, and to achieve inflectional variety in asking the repeated questions. Such practice may help to extend the range of your voice available for ordinary uses.

3. *Ensemble Reading.* (a) Find three or four congenial persons who can meet with you occasionally for group reading of poetry. (b) Do not confine your reading to the poems in this chapter, but look back

through the preceding chapters to find other poems too that lend themselves to various sorts of group reading.

4. *Choric Records*. (a) Of the poems included in this chapter, recordings of choral reading are available for the following: "The Twenty-fourth Psalm" and O'Shaughnessy's "Ode" ('We are the music-makers'), spoken by the London Verse Speaking Choir under the direction of Marjorie Gullan; and selections from *The Frogs* spoken by the Channing School Verse Speaking Choirs, directed by Hilda Brettell. A solo reading of Christina Rossetti's "Up-hill" by Cornelia Otis Skinner has been recorded; and the Hall-Johnson Choir has been recorded singing (not speaking) "Joshua Fit de Battle of Jericho" (Victor, 4460). (b) Recordings of other verse speaking choirs are also available: English choirs directed by Mona Swann and E. L. Laming; American choirs directed by John Laurie and Miriam D. Gow. (Again, see the catalogue of Linguaphone Institute.) (c) In studying the recordings of choral reading, give thoughtful consideration to the questions raised in the last four paragraphs of the text; but do not forget that the English choirs were reading for English audiences.

5. *"Chorustration."* (a) Work out a complex arrangement of the Chorus from *The Frogs,* using several solo voices and smaller choral groups as well as full chorus. Mark your book clearly, or type out your "chorustration" with several carbons. Then try it out in ensemble reading. (b) Now prepare a complex arrangement of Lindsay's "The Ghosts of the Buffaloes." And try it out also with a smaller group of readers.

6. *Choir Practice*. (a) Organize a verse choir consisting of those in your class who honestly wish to participate. (b) Determine upon a time and place convenient for a series of regular rehearsals, and select a group leader and manager and steering committee. (c) Rehearse frequently, but for short periods of time, and strive to make notable progress during each practice period. (d) Do not become discouraged; do not expect too much too soon. Few people really astound their friends by learning to play the piano in six easy lessons. It will take time for the individual to change life-long speech habits; it will take time to develop perfect team-work within a speech choir.

7. *Class Recital*. (a) Prepare for the presentation of a class recital at the end of the term. (b) Invite as guests those persons whom you think will be interested in what you are doing. (c) Let the program be skill-fully introduced and concluded, with appropriate brief transitions from one poem to the next; and let the recital be made up of a variety of choral readings, yet so arranged as to provide an adequately unified performance. (d) If recording equipment is available, it will be of interest

to make a recording of some parts or all of the verse choir recital. If this is done during the period of final rehearsals, it will serve a valuable purpose in letting the chorus study its work objectively.

8. *Communal Creation.* (a) Two or three persons in a verse choir might well undertake the writing, in collaboration, of a poem especially suited to the needs and the interests of the group. (b) Trying this out in rehearsal, and welcoming suggestions from the choristers, may stimulate successive revisions in this creative work. (c) The choir is likely to take great pride in achievement of such a communal poem, and doubtless will enjoy giving it in recital.

15

POEMS WITH MUSIC

Much poetry has been written to be sung or chanted. From earliest times, indeed, and among primitive peoples today, poetry and music have been intimately related. The ancient Greek bards and medieval troubadours recited or sang their verses to the accompaniment of lyre or vielle. And in Shakespeare's tuneful day, young men whiled away an hour in the barber shop by strumming the lute and singing ballads and rounds, madrigals and popular show songs.

I. RELATION OF MUSIC TO POETRY

It is worth noting that, with minor exceptions, there is *no* vocal music without words. And these words for music are almost always verse—in fact, the stanzas of a song, as opposed to the "chorus," are called "verses." This close interrelationship of poetry and music is further illustrated by their common use of such words as *lyric, song, chanson, ballad,* and *chorus,* with somewhat different though related meanings. To a musician *lyric* usually means simply the words for a song. To the reader of poetry, *lyric* may refer to any short poem that is not primarily narrative or expository, or to a short poem expressive of a single emotion or mood, or to a somewhat song-like poem. And although the composer may write a song that is music without words, the poet even more often writes a song that is words without music. Yet both of them will be suggesting the kinship of these two arts.

It is important that the reader recognize this kinship of music and poetry. For unless he does so, he will fail to catch the song-like character of many lyric poems. Consciousness of the air will strangely affect the "music" of a poem-reading-experience; it may influence syllabic length, govern the pace of reading and the pauses.

378

Awareness of the musical "setting" of a lyric may determine the reader's emotional response and stimulate his free imagery. It may even play a part in his interpretation of the full meaning of the poem. Yet anthologies of poetry and books about poetry almost never include the tunes when reprinting the lyrics of songs, with the implication that a song-lyric is a poem in spite of the fact that it was written to or for music.

The poems forming the body of this chapter are presented with musical notation of their tunes, or of later musical settings, so that the reader may sing them aloud if he wishes to do so—and that was, with two or three exceptions, the intention of the poet—or he may "sing" them silently; or, having hummed the tune, he may read the lyric with the melody still "running in his head." For those songs that he knows well, harmony as well as melody may become a part of the singing or the reading experience.

The wealth of song literature may be suggested by naming a few of the well-established categories.

Among what have been called *folk songs* will be found some of the old English ballads and many of the native American ballads, various work songs and sea chanties, cowboy songs and Negro spirituals. Many of them will be found in such a book as Carl Sandburg's *The American Songbag*. Folk songs often appear in differing versions, for they are characteristically anonymous and passed along by word of mouth until noted down by an attentive ballad collector.

The folk songs are *popular songs* in one sense, but we are now more likely to reserve that name for the productions of Tin Pan Alley—the dance tunes, juke box ballads, and radio song hits of the day. They are characteristically short-lived; few survive the year. Yet their tunes are on every whistle, and phrases from their lyrics flow briefly through the currents of popular speech. A few of the songs popular in other generations have survived, and remain in the songbooks of Old Favorites. Among these are our national anthem, our state songs, and some of the war songs. Such also are Ben Jonson's "To Celia" ('Drink to me only with thine eyes') and Tom Moore's "Believe Me if All Those Endearing Young Charms."

Church songs—chants, hymns, anthems, oratorios—form another category. Some are as old as the first Pope Gregory. Many of the great hymns come from the eighteenth and nineteenth centuries, as exemplified by the poems of Addison, Cowper, and Newman included in Chapter 11.

Yet another group of songs might be called *theater songs*. They range from current show tunes through grand opera, with a good many varieties in between. Some become the popular songs of their day; others become the recital songs of generations to come. There were many incidental songs in the plays of Shakespeare, Ben Jonson, and their contemporaries; and a good many English poets of light verse have written song-lyrics for the stage.

Art songs—one might call them *recital* songs—may also be distinguished as a separate class. They are often more self-consciously artful than the others. Some of them are the great lyric poems, not originally intended to be sung, but provided with musical settings by recognized composers of that or a later day.

But songs are of great variety from another point of view. There are songs for solo voice (accompanied or unaccompanied), solos with chorus, part-songs (like rounds, canons, madrigals), harmonized duets, trios, quartets, songs for chorus or choir (with or without piano or organ accompaniment, with or without solo parts).

So rich and varied is this song literature that it is difficult to generalize about song-lyrics as poetry, or about the relationship of lyric to air.

2. INTERPRETATION OF SONG-LYRICS

Song-lyrics are generally simple, uncomplex poems. Apart from their tunes, they usually do not provide especially rich reading experiences. Sometimes the "music" of the unsung song-lyric will leave the reader uncertain as to the metrical pattern. Usually there will be no great difficulties of interpretation; traditional symbols and trite metaphors abound; and often the meaning, as a separable aspect of the experience, will seem to be of small importance. Imagery of a commonplace or facile sort may seem to be quite appropriate to the rest of the poem. In the mind of many readers, the song-lyric is almost characteristically sentimental, and calls for emotional stock responses.

If this is so, are not song-lyrics generally bad poetry?

Not necessarily, for poems written as song-lyrics are *intended to be sung,* and the reading experience may be enriched by a consciousness of the melody (or by a consciousness that it goes to music). Indeed, the song-lyric should be simple enough so that the hearer may catch the essential meaning of the verses while giving much of his attention to the music.

The relation of verse to air presents an interesting contrast between poetry and music. Most English poetry is in what we have called "rising rhythm"; that is, the unaccented syllables precede the accented syllables in the metrical feet—deDUMM deDUMM deDUMM, or dedeDUMM dedeDUMM dedeDUMM. But in music the beat is on the first of the measure—ONEtwo ONEtwo ONEtwo, or ONEtwothree ONEtwothree ONEtwothree. Since the metrical accent and the musical beat will tend to coincide, there is a tendency for songs to begin on the up-beat; that is, with a pick-up note.

Then there is the question of quantity (syllabic length) in relation to musical time. In an early chapter "accent" was defined in terms of rise in pitch, greater volume, and increased duration. The melodies written for lyrics will usually take account of this, and the stressed words and accented syllables will often be given longer notes than those that are unaccented. A simple example is to be seen in the $\frac{6}{8}$ time of "Sumer is icumen in" (p. 383), wherein the ( )DUMM deDUMM deDUMM deDUMM of the verse and the ( ) 𝄞𝄽𝄽𝄽 of the music neatly coincide. So, too, the poetic verse (or two verses) and the musical phrase coincide in length.

But usually there is a certain amount of pulling and pushing amongst the *meter* and the *meaning* and the *music,* just as there is between the metrical pattern and the sense pattern in the poetic rhythm of the "music" of poetry as it was earlier pointed out. Everyone has had some experience in fitting the words to the music so that verse and musical phrase come out right.[1] Sometimes

[1] A special instance is to be noted in the singing of hymn-lyrics to hymn-tunes other than those with which they are printed. Both the lyrics and tunes are an-

the syllables give way to the demands of the tune, and one sings "heav'n" for "heaven." But often the music must give way to the demands of the verse, and allow for a pick-up note to begin the second stanza, or for doubling up the notes to take account of extra syllables.

Singing is one form of the oral or vocal interpretation of poetry. It "belongs" to poetry as much as it does to music, and need not be left to musicians alone. All people might well be encouraged to sing with attentive enthusiasm, to follow the tune or harmonize with it, to think of the meaning of the lyric. Sing out lustily and enjoy it, not only about the campfire but on the trail, not only at rallies but around the piano, not only in church but at club meetings.

Through such practice of singing will come greater vocal skill, for the speaking as well as for the singing voice. Through singing, students of poetry will not only find individual and group pleasure, but they will also come to an appreciation of the "musical" potentialities of song-lyrics, and of much lyric poetry that has never been set to music.

Song-Lyrics with Airs

SUMER IS ICUMEN IN
Lyric and music by (or copied by) John of Fornsete

[This early English art-song is a four-part round with a two-part "ground bass." The lyric, as here given with the air, is a modern translation.]

---

alyzed on the basis of syllabic count, and are classified in the metrical index to be found in many hymnals. It is possible to interchange the tunes and lyrics that belong to the same group, *if the metrical accents and musical beats coincide*—that is, if a lyric beginning with an unstressed syllable is fitted to a tune that opens with a pick-up note.

CUCKOO SONG

Sumer is icumen in:
  Lhude sing cuccu!
Groweth sed, and bloweth med,
  And springth the wude nu.
    Sing cuccu!
Awe bleteth after lomb;
  Lhouth after calve cu;
Bulluc sterteth, bucke verteth.
  Murie sing cuccu!
Cuccu, cuccu, well singes thu, cuccu:
  Ne swike thu naver nu.

  Sing cuccu, nu, sing cuccu,
  Sing cuccu, nu, sing cuccu!
          (*c. 1226*)

A MIGHTY FORTRESS IS OUR GOD

Lyric and music by Martin Luther

Translation by Frederick H. Hedge

[The music for this famous hymn is perhaps best known as harmonized and arranged for organ by John Sebastian Bach in the early eighteenth century.]

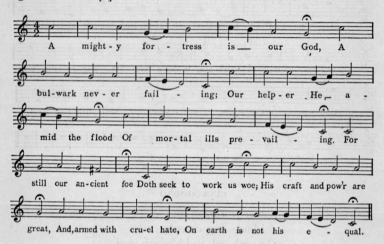

A might-y for-tress is our God, A bul-wark nev-er fail-ing; Our help-er He a-mid the flood Of mor-tal ills pre-vail-ing. For still our an-cient foe Doth seek to work us woe; His craft and pow'r are great, And, armed with cru-el hate, On earth is not his e-qual.

EIN FESTE BURG	A MIGHTY FORTRESS IS OUR GOD
Ein feste Burg ist unser Gott,	A mighty fortress is our God,
Ein gute Wehr und Waffen,	A bulwark never failing;
Er hilft uns frei aus aller Not,	Our helper He amid the flood
Die uns jetzt hat betroffen.	Of mortal ills prevailing.
Der alt böse Feind	For still our ancient foe
Mit Ernst ers jetzt meint,	Doth seek to work us woe;
Gross Macht und viel List	His craft and power are great,
Sein grausam Rüstung ist,	And, armed with cruel hate,
Auf Erd ist nicht seins Gleichen.	On earth is not his equal.
Mit unsrer Macht ist nichts getan,	Did we in our own strength confide
Wir sind gar bald verloren;	Our striving would be losing,—
Es streit für uns der rechte Mann,	Were not the right man on our side,
Den Gott hat selbst erkoren.	The man of God's own choosing.

Fragst du, wer der ist!
Er heisst Jesus Christ,
Der Herr Zebaoth,
Und ist kein andrer Gott,
    Das Feld muss er behalten.

Und wenn die Welt voll Teufel
    wär
  Und wollt uns gar verschlingen,
So fürchten wir uns nicht so sehr,
  Es soll uns doch gelingen.
    Der Fürst dieser Welt,
    Wie saur er sich stellt,
    Tut er uns doch nicht;
Das macht, er ist gericht,
    Ein Wörtlein kann ihn fällen.

Das Wort sie sollen lassen stan
  Und kein Dank dazu haben.
Er ist bei uns wohl auf dem Plan
  Mit seinem Geist und Gaben.
    Nehmen sie den Leib,
    Gut, Ehr, Kind und Weib,
    Lass fahren dahin,
Sie habens kein Gewinn:
    Das Reich muss uns doch
      bleiben.   (1529)

Dost ask who that may be?
Christ Jesus, it is He,
Lord Sabaoth His name,
From age to age the same,
And He must win the battle.

And though this world, with devils
    filled,
  Should threaten to undo us,
We will not fear, for God hath willed
  His truth to triumph through us.
    The Prince of Darkness grim,—
    We tremble not for him;
    His rage we can endure,
    For lo! his doom is sure:
  One little word shall fell him.

That word above all earthly powers,
  No thanks to them, abideth;
The spirit and the gifts are ours
  Through Him who with us sideth.
    Let goods and kindred go,
    This mortal life also;
    The body they may kill,
    God's truth abideth still,
  His Kingdom is forever.
                        (tr. 1853)

O MISTRESS MINE

from TWELFTH NIGHT, II, iii

Lyric by William Shakespeare (?), Music by Thomas Morley (?)

[This song appeared in Morley's *First Booke of Consort Lessons
made by divers exquisite Authors . . .* in 1599. The next year Shakespeare included it in his comedy *Twelfth Night*. There is less certainty
that Morley wrote the music than there is that Shakespeare wrote the
lyric.]

O MISTRESS MINE

O mistress mine, where are you roaming?
O, stay and hear; your true love's coming,
  That can sing both high and low:
Trip no further, pretty sweeting;
Journeys end in lovers meeting,
  Every wise man's son doth know.

What is love? 'tis not hereafter;
Present mirth hath present laughter;
  What's to come is still unsure:
In delay there lies no plenty;
Then come kiss me, sweet and twenty,
  Youth's a stuff will not endure.

(1599)

WHO IS SILVIA?

from TWO GENTLEMEN OF VERONA, IV, ii

Lyric by William Shakespeare, Music by Franz Schubert

[This musical setting is, of course, not the original one, but was composed for a German translation early in the nineteenth century. The
lyric as commonly printed with the music is altered in the last line of
the first stanza to sing: "That adorèd she might be."]

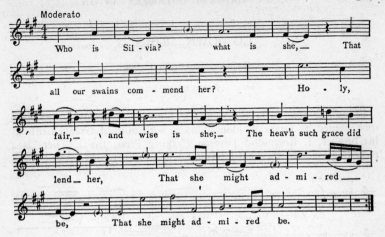

SONG

Who is Silvia? what is she?
    That all our swains commend her?
Holy, fair, and wise is she;
    The heaven such grace did lend her,
That she might admirèd be.

Is she kind as she is fair?
    For beauty lives with kindness:
Love doth to her eyes repair,
    To help him of his blindness;
And, being help'd, inhabits there.

Then to Silvia let us sing,
    That Silvia is excelling;
She excels each mortal thing
    Upon the dull earth dwelling;
To her let us garlands bring.
        (c. 1590)

GO DOWN, MOSES

AMERICAN NEGRO SPIRITUAL

Anonymous

[This folk song is taken from *The Book of American Negro Spirituals* edited by James Weldon Johnson, with musical arrangements by his brother, J. Rosamond Johnson (Viking Press, 1925). There is a recording made by the Hall-Johnson Choir (Victor record 4553).]

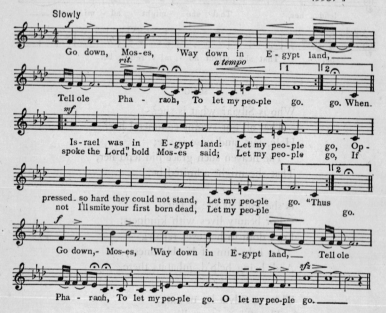

GO DOWN, MOSES

Go down, Moses,
'Way down in Egypt land,
Tell ole Pharaoh,
To let my people go.

When Israel was in Egypt land:
Let my people go,

Oppressed so hard they could not stand,
    Let my people go.

"Thus spoke the Lord," bold Moses said;
    Let my people go,
If not I'll smite your first born dead,
    Let my people go.

    Go down, Moses,
    'Way down in Egypt land,
    Tell ole Pharaoh,
    To let my people go.
        (? *bef. 1800*)

AULD LANG SYNE

Lyric by Robert Burns, Scottish Folk Tune

[There are occasional variations in the published versions of this popular old song: ". . . And days of auld lang syne./ For auld lang syne we meet tonight . . ." (fourth line of the verse, and first line of the chorus). *Auld lang syne* means "old times"; *be your pint-stowp:* "pay for your own drink"; *braes:* "hillsides"; *gowans:* "daisies"; *burn:* "brook"; *dine:* "dinner-time"; *fiere:* "friend"; *waught:* "draught."]

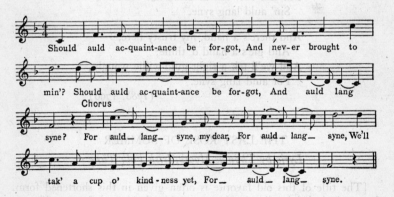

Should auld ac-quaint-ance be for-got, And nev-er brought to min'? Should auld ac-quaint-ance be for-got, And auld lang syne? *Chorus* For auld— lang— syne, my dear, For auld— lang— syne, We'll tak' a cup o' kind-ness yet, For— auld— lang— syne.

AULD LANG SYNE

Should auld acquaintance be forgot,
    And never brought to min'?
Should auld acquaintance be forgot,
    And auld lang syne?

CHORUS

    For auld lang syne, my dear,
    For auld lang syne,
    We'll tak a cup o' kindness yet,
    For auld lang syne.

And surely ye'll be your pint-stowp,
    And surely I'll be mine;
And we'll tak a cup o' kindness yet
    For auld lang syne.

We twa hae run about the braes,
    And pu'd the gowans fine;
But we've wandered mony a weary foot
    Sin' auld lang syne.

We twa hae paidled i' the burn,
    From morning sun till dine;
But seas between us braid hae roared
    Sin' auld lang syne.

And there's a hand, my trusty fiere,
    And gie's a hand o' thine;
And we'll tak a right guid-willie waught,
    For auld lang syne.

                        (*1788,* 1796)

THE LAST ROSE OF SUMMER

Lyric by Thomas Moore, Irish Folk Tune

[The title of this old favorite is often given in this shortened form.
It was included in the popular opera *Martha* (1847) by von Flotow.
The Irish tune is "The Groves of Blarney."]

'Tis the last rose of summer Left blooming alone; All her lovely companions Are faded and gone; No flow'r of her kindred, No rosebud, is nigh, To reflect back her blushes, Or give sigh for sigh.

'TIS THE LAST ROSE OF SUMMER

'Tis the last rose of summer
    Left blooming alone;
All her lovely companions
    Are faded and gone;
No flower of her kindred,
    No rosebud, is nigh,
To reflect back her blushes,
    Or give sigh for sigh.

I'll not leave thee, thou lone one,
    To pine on the stem;
Since the lovely are sleeping,
    Go, sleep thou with them.
Thus kindly I scatter
    Thy leaves o'er the bed,
Where thy mates of the garden
    Lie scentless and dead.

So soon may *I* follow
    When friendships decay,
And from Love's shining circle
    The gems drop away!
When true hearts lie wither'd,
    And fond ones are flown,
Oh! who would inhabit
    This bleak world alone?

                (1808)

DEAR LORD AND FATHER OF MANKIND
Lyric by John Greenleaf Whittier, Music by Frederick C. Maker

[This hymn-lyric is not a separate poem, but the final stanzas of "The Brewing of Soma." Many hymnals print: "Forgive our *feverish* ways."]

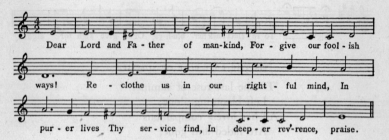

Dear Lord and Father of mankind, Forgive our foolish ways! Reclothe us in our rightful mind, In purer lives Thy service find, In deeper reverence, praise.

from "THE BREWING OF SOMA"

Dear Lord and Father of mankind,
    Forgive our foolish ways!
Reclothe us in our rightful mind,
In purer lives Thy service find,
    In deeper reverence, praise.

In simple trust like theirs who heard
    Beside the Syrian sea
The gracious calling of the Lord,
Let us, like them, without a word,
    Rise up and follow Thee.

O Sabbath rest by Galilee!
    O calm of hills above,
Where Jesus knelt to share with Thee
The silence of eternity
    Interpreted by love!

With that deep hush subduing all
    Our words and works that drown

The tender whisper of Thy call,
As noiseless let Thy blessing fall
  As fell Thy manna down.

Drop Thy still dews of quietness,
  Till all our strivings cease;
Take from our souls the strain and stress,
And let our ordered lives confess
  The beauty of Thy peace.

Breathe through the heats of our desire
  Thy coolness and Thy balm;
Let sense be dumb, let flesh retire;
Speak through the earthquake, wind, and fire,
  O still, small voice of calm!

                    (1872, music 1887)

THE OLD CHISHOLM TRAIL

Lyric and tune by unknown cowboy singers

[There are a number of quite different versions of this American cowboy ballad, of which this one is a composite adaptation.[2] Jesse Chisholm, Scotch and Cherokee, was a government interpreter and traveled in his work from Wichita to San Antonio as early as the 1830's. After the Civil War, Texans drove longhorn cattle over the "ol' Chizzum Trail," up from the Texas plains to shipping points on the railroads.]

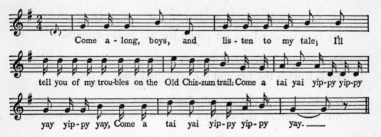

Come a-long, boys, and lis-ten to my tale; I'll tell you of my trou-bles on the Old Chiz-zum trail: Come a tai yai yip-py yip-py yay yip-py yay, Come a tai yai yip-py yip-py yay.

[2] Another tune, for instance, is given in Frank Luther's *Americans and Their Songs* (Harper, 1942). John A. Lomax and Alan Lomax, *American Ballads and Folk Songs* (Macmillan, 1934) also give another tune and many additional stanzas. One version of the tune here given is to be found in Olin Downes and Elie Siegmeister, *A Treasury of American Songs* (Howell, Soskin, 1940). A slightly different version was sung in the production of *Green Grow the Lilacs*.

THE OLD CHISHOLM TRAIL

Come along, boys, and listen to my tale;
I'll tell you of my troubles on the old Chisholm Trail—
  CHORUS: *Come a tai yai yippy, yippy yay, yippy yay,*
          Come a tai yai yippy yippy yay.

Goin' back west on the old Chisholm Trail,
Ribbon on a heifer and a bull by the tail—CHORUS.

I started up the trail October twenty-third
I started up the trail with the 2U herd—CHORUS.

On a ten dollar hoss an' a forty dollar saddle
An' I'm goin' to punchin' Texas cattle—CHORUS.

Foot in the stirrup, hand on the horn,
Best durn cowboy that ever was born—CHORUS.

I woke up one morning on the old Chisholm Trail,
Rope in my hand an' a cow by the tail—CHORUS.

I'm up in the morning afore day-light,
An' afore I sleep the moon shines bright—CHORUS.

Old Ben Bolt was a blamed good boss,
But he'd go t' see his gal on a sore back hoss—CHORUS.

I herded and I hollered and I done very well
Till the boss says, "Boys, just let 'em go to hell—CHORUS.

My hoss throwed me off at the creek called Mud,
My hoss throwed me off round the 2U herd—CHORUS.

Haven't got a rope and I cain't ketch a horse,
To hell with the job and the cock-eyed boss!—CHORUS.

It's cloudy in the west an' a-lookin' like rain,
An' my durned old slicker's in the wagon again—CHORUS.

Stray in the herd an' the boss says kill it,
So I shot 'im in the rump with the handle of a skillet—CHORUS.

Oh, it's bacon an' beans 'most every day;
I'd just as soon be eatin' prairie hay—CHORUS.

We rounded 'em up an' put 'em in the cars,
An' that was the last of the old two bars—CHORUS.

I went to the boss to draw my roll,
He had me figgered out seven dollars in the hole—CHORUS.

I'll sell my out-fit soon as I can;
I won't punch cattle fer no durned man—CHORUS.

So I'm goin' to Oklahoma, gonna marry me a squaw,
And raise papooses for my paw-in-law—CHORUS.

Goin' back to town to draw my money,
Goin' back home to see my honey—CHORUS.

With my knees in the saddle an' my seat in the sky,
I'll quit punchin' cows in the sweet by and by—CHORUS.

(c. 1870)

WHEN I WAS A LAD

from H.M.S. PINAFORE

Lyric by William S. Gilbert, Music by Arthur Sullivan

[This song is sung by the Rt. Hon. Sir Joseph Porter, K.C.B., First Lord of the Admiralty. The Chorus consists of "His sisters and his cousins,/ Whom he reckons up by dozens,/ And his aunts." Also, the gallant captain and the gallant crew of *H.M.S. Pinafore*.]

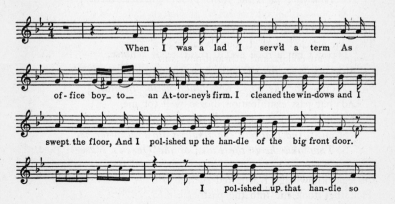

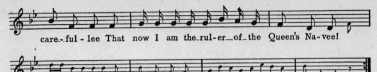

care.-ful - lee That now I am the.-rul-er_of_the Queen's Na-vee!

SONG—SIR JOSEPH

When I was a lad I served a term
As office boy to an Attorney's firm.
I cleaned the windows and I swept the floor,
And I polished up the handle on the big front door.
    [CHORUS—*He polished up the handle of the big front door.*]
  I polished up that handle so carefullee
That now I am the Ruler of the Queen's Navee!
    [CH.—*He polished up that handle so carefullee*
      That now he is the Ruler of the Queen's Navee!]

As office boy I made such a mark
That they gave me the post of a junior clerk.
I served the writs with a smile so bland,
And I copied all the letters in a big round hand—
    [CH.—*He copied all the letters in a big round hand.*]
  I copied all the letters in a hand so free,
That now I am the Ruler of the Queen's Navee!
    [CH.—*He copied all the letters in a hand so free,*
      That now he is the Ruler of the Queen's Navee!]

In serving writs I made such a name
That an articled clerk I soon became;
I wore clean collars and a brand-new suit
For the pass examination at the Institute,
    [CH.—*For the pass examination at the Institute.*]
  And that pass examination did so well for me,
That now I am the Ruler of the Queen's Navee!
    [CH.—*And that pass examination did so well for he,*
      That now he is the Ruler of the Queen's Navee!]

Of legal knowledge I acquired such a grip
That they took me into the partnership.

And that junior partnership, I ween,
Was the only ship that I ever had seen.
    [CH.—*Was the only ship that he had ever seen.*]
  But that kind of ship so suited me,
That now I am the Ruler of the Queen's Navee!
    [CH.—*But that kind of ship so suited he,*
      That now he is the Ruler of the Queen's Navee!]

I grew so rich that I was sent
By a pocket borough into Parliament.
I always voted at my party's call,
And I never thought of thinking for myself at all.
    [CH.—*He never thought of thinking for himself at all.*]
  I thought so little, they rewarded me
By making me the Ruler of the Queen's Navee!
    [CH.—*He thought so little, they rewarded he*
      By making him the Ruler of the Queen's Navee!]

Now landsmen all, whoever you may be,
If you want to rise to the top of the tree,
If your soul isn't fettered to an office stool,
Be careful to be guided by this golden rule—
    [CH.—*Be careful to be guided by this golden rule—*]
  Stick close to your desks and never go to sea,
And you all may be Rulers of the Queen's Navee!
    [CH.—*Stick close to your desks and never go to sea,*
      And you all may be Rulers of the Queen's Navee!]
                            (1878)

THE DAISIES

Lyric by James Stephens, Music by Samuel Barber

[This is a recent musical setting by an American composer of a lyric written some years earlier by an Irish poet. The complete musical setting by Samuel Barber may be obtained from G. Schirmer, Inc. Copyright, 1936, by G. Schirmer, Inc.]

THE DAISIES

In the scented bud of the morning O,
When the windy grass went rippling far!
I saw my dear one walking slow
In the field where the daisies are.

We did not laugh, and we did not speak,
As we wandered happily, to and fro,
I kissed my dear on either cheek,
In the bud of the morning O!

A lark sang up, from the breezy land;
A lark sang down, from a cloud afar;
As she and I went, hand in hand,
In the field where the daisies are.

                          (1926, music 1936)

BEGIN THE BEGUINE [8]

Cole Porter

[The music for this popular song, which is also by Cole Porter, is readily available in sheet music. "Beguine," pronounced *begeen,* is here used to name a current dance.]

When they begin the Beguine
  It brings back the sound of music so tender,
  It brings back a night of tropical splendour,
It brings back a memory ever green.
I'm with you once more under the stars
  And down by the shore an orchestra's playing,
  And even the palms seem to be swaying
When they begin the Beguine.

To live it again is past all endeavour,
  Except when that tune clutches my heart,
  And there we are, swearing to love forever,
And promising never, never to part.
What moments divine, what rapture serene,
  Till clouds came along to disperse the joys we had tasted,
  And now when I hear people curse the chance that was wasted,
I know but too well what they mean;

So don't let them begin the Beguine,
  Let the love that was once afire remain an ember;
  Let it sleep like the dead desire I only remember
When they begin the Beguine:
Oh yes, let them begin the Beguine, make them play
  Till the stars that were there before return above you,
  Till you whisper to me once more, "Darling, I love you!"
And we suddenly know what heaven we're in,

  When they begin the Beguine,
  When they begin the Beguine.

(1935)

ALMA MATER

Lyric by Robert Dye, Music by Guy Frank

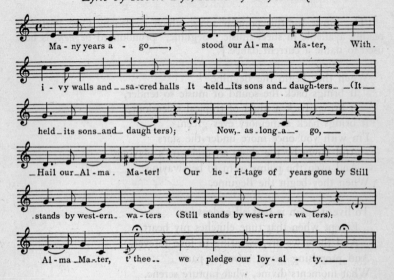

ALMA MATER

Many years ago, stood our Alma Mater,
   With ivy walls and sacred halls
   It held its sons and daughters
     (It held its sons and daughters);
Now, as long ago, hail our Alma Mater!
   Our heritage of years gone by
   Still stands by western waters
     (Still stands by western waters):
Alma Mater, t' thee—we pledge our loyalty.

                      (1942)

ENVOY

Francis Thompson

Go, songs, for ended is our brief, sweet play;
   Go, children of swift joy and tardy sorrow:

And some are sung, and that was yesterday,
 And some unsung, and that may be tomorrow.

Go forth; and if it be o'er stony way,
 Old joy can lend what newer grief must borrow:
And it was sweet, and that was yesterday,
 And sweet is sweet, though purchasèd with sorrow.

Go, songs, and come not back from your far way:
 And if men ask you why ye smile and sorrow,
Tell them ye grieve, for your hearts know Today,
 Tell them ye smile, for your eyes know Tomorrow.

           (1897)

SUGGESTIONS FOR STUDY

1. *With Accompaniment.* (a) Some of the songs, here presented with airs only, will be found with four-part harmony, for quartet or piano, in many song books and hymnals. Others will be more difficult to find. The *Song Index* (H. W. Wilson Co., 1926) and its *Supplement* (1934) will be of help. Copies of the piano score for *H.M.S. Pinafore* are readily available in libraries. Stephens-Barber's "The Daisies" is included in the *A New Anthology of American Song* (G. Schirmer, 1942). (b) If you play the piano, you may wish to find copies of some of these songs, and play an accompaniment while you and/or others sing. Schubert's "Who Is Silvia?" and the Bach arrangement of "Ein Feste Burg" are of unusual musical artistry. (c) Or perhaps you have some skill in the use of one of the popular instruments for accompaniment, accordion or guitar.

2. *With Phonograph.* (a) Most of these songs may be studied by means of recordings. A handy reference work listing available records is *The Gramophone Shop Encyclopedia of Recorded Music* (Simon and Schuster, 1942). (b) Several recordings have been made of "Sumer is icumen in" (Columbia 5715 [in Columbia History of Music set M-231]; Columbia D40119 [International Education Society]; Roycroft 157; Victor 4316), Shakespeare's "O Mistress Mine" (Gramophone [HMV] B4201), Shakespeare-Schubert's "Who Is Silvia?" (Victor 1306), Burns' "Auld Lang Syne" (Victor 22082), "The Old Chisholm Trail" (Keystone, set 104), Gilbert-Sullivan's "When I Was a Lad" (Columbia 4273M [in set M440]).

3. *Vocal Solo.* (a) If you are able to sight-sing, work out and practice Shakespeare's "O Mistress Mine." It may take you a while to catch

on to the peculiar relation of meter, meaning, and music that gives this song its individual character. (b) In order to fix the musical intervals accurately in mind, you may need to sit at the piano; and a tapping foot may help you with the musical beat. (c) Notice that, though the air strikes our ears as mournful, the lyric is not so. The Elizabethans were accustomed to somewhat different musical modes. (d) Now study the melody of Samuel Barber's setting for "The Daisies," giving particular attention to the free changing of the time and to the relation of the melodic line to the thought and feeling of the lyric.

4. *Close Harmony*. (a) Find three congenial persons who can and will sing with you in a male, mixed, or woman's quartet. (b) Without finding a quartet arrangement, sing "Auld Lang Syne," and try to work out two-, three-, or four-part harmonizations. (c) Don't be afraid to "try things"—in the bass, in the separate movement of the middle parts, in the placing of a high tenor above the melody, etc.—and have fun singing together.

5. *The Music Goes Round and Round*. (a) Now learn to sing the "Cuckoo Song" ('Sumer is icumen in'). It is a four-part round with a two-part bass. It is best sung by four tenors and two basses, or by four sopranos and two altos; but it can be sung by a mixed group. (b) The four who will sing the air in succession (as in "Three Blind Mice") may well learn the tune by singing it in unison; and those singing the bass may learn their part together in the same way. Then the bass might split up, singing their two-part bass while the melodists perfect their work in unison. (c) In singing this canon, the singers enter two measures apart (one tenor and one bass starting off together), and they continue until the last one to enter has sung the entire song. Though a piano may help in the learning process, this round is properly sung unaccompanied. Not until it flows smoothly, will the singers gain the full effect of its polyphony. (d) Interesting comments on "Sumer is icumen in" will be found in *Grove's Dictionary of Music*. Shakespeare's "cuckoo song" ("Spring and Winter," p. 93) may be recalled in this connection.

6. *The Back Numbers*. (a) Glance back through the chapters thus far, and you will find a number of song-lyrics and poems that have been set to music. You will also find a number of poems called songs that are obviously not intended to be sung. (b) *The Song Index* and *Supplement* list the contents of many collections of songs. You may wish to find the music for some of the lyrics in this book.

7. *More Verses*. (a) "The Old Chisholm Trail" is the sort of folk song that, since its beginning, has been changing and growing. Anyone is free to tell of further troubles on the old Chisholm Trail, or on any

trail for that matter, with or without horses and cattle. (b) With the tune and the folk style well in mind, you may be able to think up some more verses for this song. Refinements in diction and sentiment are not requisite. (c) Now look once more at the song from *H.M.S. Pinafore*. Again this is a tune with a firm beat and a way of accommodating itself to a variable number of syllables in the lyric. (d) Perhaps you may wish to contrive an additional verse or two for this song, in the spirit and style of the original, or you may be able to work out a parody, adapting the lyric to a different situation.

8. *"Thinking" the Music.* (a) Study over the melody of one of the two hymns given above until you can hum it silently without looking at the musical notation. You may need to pick it out on the piano, or whistle or hum it aloud while you are studying it. (b) Now read the hymn-lyric silently with the tune running in your head, and note the relation of the poetic rhythm to the auditory imagery of the music. (c) If you can find a four-part arrangement of the music, ask someone to play it over for you on a piano, or pick it out yourself. Repeat this several times, until you can hum it over silently with the full harmony ringing in your mind's-ear. (d) Now, again, read the hymn-lyric, and note what the effect of the richer music may be upon the poem-experience. (e) Perform a similar experiment with "Who Is Silvia?"

PART FIVE

Poems Approached in Various Ways

16

THE BROAD TYPES— NARRATIVE AND LYRIC

A poem-experience—like anything else—may be seen from different points of view. Just as a dog may be contemplated as a domestic animal, or as a zoological specimen, or as a vicious whelp, or as a blooded terrier, or as a seeing-eye dog, or simply as Jocko—so "The Old Chisholm Trail" (p. 394) may be viewed as a narrative poem, or as a poem in one of the ballad forms, or as a poem upon the theme of human woes, or as a poem in a light mood, or as a realistic folk poem of no conscious "school," or as a poem unrelated to any literary personality. In the same way, the reader may look at "Ah, Are You Digging on My Grave?" (p. 362) from several angles, through divers vistas. And he may report these observations: It is a lyric, and in an original stanzaic form. Its theme is the transience of love, and its mood is mocking or ironic. It belongs to the early modern realistic school, and is an expression of the personality of Thomas Hardy.

Each of these assertions about a poem suggests that the poem-experience has been approached from various directions. Each of them also indicates that the reader, ever on the alert for similarities and differences, ever comparing the new with the known, has been automatically sorting poems as he has experienced them. Approaching poems in various ways, he will sort them out according to a number of schemes of classification.

It is the purpose of the half-dozen chapters that make up Part

Five of this book, to consider briefly a number of these approaches and their corresponding classifications. But, for the sake of simplicity, each will be illustrated by poems falling into two only of the often numerous categories, and most of the technical details will be relegated to the Glossarial Handbook.

I. THE BROAD TYPES

The first of these approaches is from the viewpoint of the so-called broad *types of poetry*. Just as Literature is commonly divided into three great branches—Poetry, Prose Literature, and Dramatic Literature—so Poetry itself (all poems) may be divided into three groups, three broad types: narrative poetry, lyric poetry, and reflective poetry. This three-broad-type division of poetry may be said to parallel the well-known hand-heart-head triangle of man's nature. *Narrative* poetry, the hand, tells the story of man's actions. *Lyric* poetry, the heart, is a verbal outpouring of man's emotive thoughts. *Reflective* poetry, the head, gives expression to man's critical thoughts.

At once it must be said that no such scheme of classification will prove to be generally satisfactory. One critic will say that the third category should (of course) be dramatic poetry. (But in the above classification dramatic poetry would fall within Dramatic Literature, and separate passages from poetic dramas would be classified as narrative, lyric, or reflective poetry as the case might be.) And another critic will say that "reflective" is the wrong word to label the third category; it might better be "expository" or "didactic." But yet another critic might retort that the verse that would fall into this third class isn't really poetry at all—but mere verse!

A much more serious objection would be that "in-between" pigeonholes seem to be needed, and one might indeed propose a five-fold classification: (1) narrative, (2) dramatic-lyric, (3) pure lyric, (4) reflective-lyric, and (5) expository. Such a grouping of poems would suggest the important observation that a good three-fifths of all poetry is more or less lyrical, the expression of primarily emotive thought in rhythmical and artful language. Such a grouping may further suggest that there are fewer purely narrative poems, and very few purely expository poems.

It is not easy to choose representative illustrations of these five sorts of poetry that will be agreeable to all readers. For each person's experience of a given poem will be unique, and definitions of the categories will also be somewhat different. But for many persons Leigh Hunt's "The Glove and the Lions" (p. 13) is a narrative poem, Walter de la Mare's "The Listeners" (p. 139) is a sort of dramatic lyric, Rupert Brooke's "The Soldier" (p. 78) is a pure lyric, William Wordsworth's "I Wandered Lonely as a Cloud" is a reflective lyric, and Alexander Pope's *Essay on Criticism* is an expository poem.

2. NARRATIVE AND LYRIC POETRY

A *narrative poem* is one that tells a story. Such a poem may either relate a story directly or merely suggest it. For the purpose of this discussion, a *story* is a representation of human beings in a sequence of significant happenings. A story puts one in mind of people doing things. The reader of a narrative poem will be conscious of some kind of setting; of one or more characters, often with definite desires or drives; of a describable situation, the relationship of characters to each other and to past events; of incidents, often causally related to each other; of significance or meaning or application. It is of these elements that a story may be fashioned.

There are a number of well-recognized sub-types of narrative poetry: The *ballad* is characteristically a simple folk story in simple verse form. The old English and Scottish popular ballads like "Lord Randal" (p. 144) are anonymous, as are American ballads like "The Dying Cowboy" (p. 55). However, there have been many ballads, such as "The Ballad of William Sycamore" (p. 337), written by literary men who have tried to catch something of the spirit of the folk ballads. Many ballads are written in the so-called ballad meter, but some of them are written in other stanzaic forms with refrains.

The *epic* is characteristically a long poem upon a great national theme, involving heroic characters in momentous actions, conceived and narrated in an elevated style, and making use of a number of special story-telling devices. *The Odyssey* (p. 35) is one of the two great epics of Ancient Greece; and many of the western peoples have their own folk epics, extended narrative poems on one of their own traditional heroes. A good many poets have turned their hands to the writing of literary epics. *John Brown's Body* (p. 157) by Stephen Vincent Benét may in many ways be considered a modern American epic.

The *metrical romance* is usually a poem of moderate length relating the amorous or valorous adventures of knights and ladies, often in a metrical form of some intricacy. It is characteristically more sophisticated than the ballad, and less extended and elevated than the epic. *The Faerie Queene* (p. 251) by Edmund Spenser is sometimes called a romantic epic; in substance and form its episodes are much like the metrical romances.

The *dramatic monologue* is a narrative poem in which the story is revealed by the speech of a single character, sometimes soliloquizing, as in Browning's "Soliloquy of the Spanish Cloister" (p. 198), and sometimes addressing other characters, as in Tennyson's "Ulysses" (p. 83).

The *tale* will for our purposes name a wide variety of narrative poems, characteristically more artful than the ballad and less ornate than the metrical romance. Some would call Byron's "Destruction of Sennacherib" (p. 132) and Robert Frost's "Out, Out—" (p. 30) tales, though neither is as long as are more typical examples.

With this very brief discussion of narrative poetry and its subtypes, let us turn to the lyric.

Lyric poems—and we shall here include the dramatic lyrics and the reflective lyrics as well as the so-called pure lyrics—are often quite short as compared to narrative poems. Instead of representing a group of characters in a sequence of significant happenings, a lyric usually gives expression to a single feeling, mood, or thoughtful emotion. Most of the poems so far presented in this book have been lyrics of one sort or another.

Of the sub-types of lyric, we have already encountered the *song-lyric,* which is distinguished by its actual or implied relation to

music. All song-lyrics—notably the song-ballads—are not lyrics in
the sense in which we are here using it. But most of them are; and,
as suggested in the preceding chapter, they are indeed of wide
variety: from the art songs of this and other days, through the
sentimental popular songs and show songs, to the more reflective
hymns. So, too, through examples and comment in earlier chapters,
attention has been called to the *sonnet,* a sub-type of lyric distinguished by its form, which will be discussed further in the next
chapter. These sonnets, so much alike in form, have yet been widely
various in theme and mood, and in dramatic, purely lyrical, or reflective character. Milton's sonnet "On His Blindness" (p. 231),
Shelley's "Ozymandias" (p. 202), and Margaret Yale's "Some
Things There Are" (p. 263) will serve as present examples. The
ode, as a sub-type of lyric, is also partly distinguished by its form,
and it too will be considered at some length in the next chapter;
but such quite different lyrics as Keats' "Ode on a Grecian Urn"
(p. 152), Collins' "Ode Written in . . . 1746" (p. 145) and Sophocles' choral ode from *Antigone* (p. 372) may suggest some of its
varieties.

The *idyl,* the *elegy,* the *epithalamion*—these are but some of the
further sub-types of lyric, only to be named here, though defined
in the Glossarial Handbook in the Appendix. And there are others,
also, many of them, such as the so-called French forms, distinguished by their metrical form; and one of these is the *rondel.*
A word, however, will be added about the epigram and about the
free lyric. The *epigram* is a poem characterized by its brevity, its
conciseness of statement, its surcharge of feeling. Often it is no
more than a quatrain. The *free lyric,* as the phrase is here used,
names that great number of lyrics that do not fall conveniently into
any of the above suggested classes; and in modern poetry it is indeed a distinguished group, free from obligation to the established
sub-types and forms of the past.

So great are the riches of lyric poetry as a type that no one classification into sub-types will begin to reveal their infinite variety.

Narrative Poems

THE TWA BROTHERS

OLD SCOTTISH BALLAD

Anonymous

There were twa brethren in the north,
   They went to school thegithar;
The one unto the other said,
   Will you try a warsle afore?

They wrestled up, they wrestled down,
   Till Sir John fell to the ground,
And there was a knife in Sir Willie's pouch,
   Gied him a deadlie wound.

"Oh brither dear, take me on your back,
   Carry me to yon burn clear,
And wash the blood from off my wound,
   And it will bleed nae mair."

He took him up upon his back,
   Carried him to yon burn clear,
And washd the blood from off his wound,
   And aye it bled the mair.

"Oh brother dear, take me on your back,
   Carry me to yon kirk-yard,
And dig a grave baith wide and deep,
   And lay my body there."

He's taen him up upon his back,
   Carried him to yon kirk-yard,
And dug a grave both deep and wide,
   And laid his body there.

"But what will I say to my father dear,
  Should he chance to say, Willie, whar's John?"
"Oh say that he's to England gone,
  To buy him a cask of wine."

"And what shall I say to my mother dear,
  Should she chance to say, Willie, whar's John?"
"Oh say that he's to England gone,
  To buy her a new silk gown."

"And what will I say to my sister dear,
  Should she chance to say, Willie, whar's John?"
"Oh say that he's to England gone,
  To buy her a wedding ring."

"What will I say to her you loe dear,
  Should she cry, Why tarries my John?"
"Oh tell her I lie in fair Kirk-land,
  And home will never come."

                    (*c. 1250-1450*)

from PARADISE LOST Book IV

John Milton

[Satan to revenge himself upon God has made his way to the newly created world, where he expects to do what mischief he can by a subtle assault upon Man.]

So on he fares, and to the border comes
Of Eden, where delicious Paradise,
Now nearer, crowns with her inclosure green,
As with a rural mound, the champaign head
Of a steep wilderness, whose hairy sides
With thicket overgrown, grotesque and wild,
Access deny'd; and over head up grew,
Insuperable height of loftiest shade,
Cedar, and pine, and fir, and branching palm;
A sylvan scene; and as the ranks ascend

Shade above shade, a woody theatre
Of stateliest view. Yet higher than their tops
The verdurous wall of Paradise up sprung;
Which to our gen'ral sire gave prospect large
Into his nether empire neighb'ring round:
And higher than that wall a circling row
Of goodliest trees loaden with fairest fruit,
Blossoms and fruits at once of golden hue,
Appear'd with gay enamel'd colours mix'd:
On which the Sun more glad impress'd his beams
Than in fair ev'ning cloud, or humid bow,
When God hath show'r'd the earth: so lovely seem'd
That landskip: and of pure now purer air
Meets his approach, and to the heart inspires
Vernal delight and joy, able to drive
All sadness but despair: now gentle gales,
Fanning their odorif'rous wings, dispense
Native perfumes, and whisper whence they stole
Those balmy spoils. . . .

Beneath him, with new wonder, now he views
To all delight of human sense exposed
In narrow room Nature's whole wealth, yea more,
A Heav'n on Earth: for blissful Paradise
Of God the garden was, by him in th' east
Of Eden planted; Eden stretch'd her line
From Auran eastward to the royal tow'rs
Of great Seleucia, built by Grecian kings,
Or where the sons of Eden long before
Dwelt in Telassar. In this pleasant soil
His far more pleasant garden God ordain'd;
Out of the fertile ground he caused to grow
All trees of noblest kind for sight, smell, taste;
And all amid them stood the tree of life,
High eminent, blooming ambrosial fruit
Of vegetable gold; and next to life,
Our death, the tree of knowledge, grew fast by,
Knowledge of good bought dear by knowing ill. . . .

Thus was this place
A happy rural seat of various view;

Groves whose rich trees wept od'rous gums and balm,
Others whose fruit burnish'd with golden rind
Hung amiable, Hesperian fables true,
If true, here only, and of delicious taste;
Betwixt them lawns, or level downs, and flocks
Grazing the tender herb, were interposed,
Or palmy hillock; or the flow'ry lap
Of some irriguous valley spread her store,
Flow'rs of all hue, and without thorn the rose:
Another side, umbrageous grots and caves
Of cool recess, o'er which the mantling vine
Lays forth her purple grape, and gently creeps
Luxuriant: mean while murm'ring waters fall
Down the slope hills, dispersed, or in a lake,
That to the fringed bank with myrtle crown'd
Her crystal mirror holds, unite their streams.
The birds their choir apply; airs, vernal airs,
Breathing the smell of field and grove, attune
The trembling leaves, while universal Pan,
Knit with the Graces and the Hours in dance,
Led on th' eternal spring.

(1667)

THE EVE OF ST. AGNES

John Keats

[There was a belief in medieval times that on St. Agnes' Eve, January 20th, a girl, with proper preparation, might dream of her future husband, who would appear to her as in a vision and kiss her and feast with her.]

I

St. Agnes' Eve—Ah, bitter chill it was!
The owl, for all his feathers, was a-cold;
The hare limped trembling through the frozen grass,
And silent was the flock in woolly fold:
Numb were the Beadsman's fingers while he told
His rosary, and while his frosted breath,

Like pious incense from a censer old,
Seemed taking flight for heaven, without a death,
Past the sweet Virgin's picture, while his prayer he saith.

2

His prayer he saith, this patient, holy man;
Then takes his lamp, and riseth from his knees,
And back returneth, meager, barefoot, wan,
Along the chapel aisle by slow degrees:
The sculptured dead, on each side, seem to freeze,
Imprisoned in black, purgatorial rails:
Knights, ladies, praying in dumb orat'ries,
He passeth by, and his weak spirit fails
To think how they may ache in icy hoods and mails.

3

Northward he turneth through a little door,
And scarce three steps, ere Music's golden tongue
Flattered to tears this aged man and poor;
But no—already had his death-bell rung:
The joys of all his life were said and sung:
His was harsh penance on St. Agnes' Eve:
Another way he went, and soon among
Rough ashes sat he for his soul's reprieve,
And all night kept awake, for sinners' sake to grieve.

4

That ancient Beadsman heard the prelude soft;
And so it chanced, for many a door was wide,
From hurry to and fro. Soon, up aloft,
The silver, snarling trumpets 'gan to chide:
The level chambers, ready with their pride,
Were glowing to receive a thousand guests.
The carved angels, ever eager-eyed,
Stared, where upon their heads the cornice rests,
With hair blown back, and wings put crosswise on their
      breasts.

5

At length burst in the argent revelry,
With plume, tiara, and all rich array,
Numerous as shadows haunting faerily
The brain new-stuffed, in youth, with triumphs gay
Of old romance. These let us wish away,
And turn, sole-thoughted, to one Lady there,
Whose heart had brooded, all that wintry day,
On love, and winged St. Agnes' saintly care,
As she had heard old dames full many times declare.

6

They told her how, upon St. Agnes' Eve,
Young virgins might have visions of delight,
And soft adorings from their loves receive
Upon the honeyed middle of the night,
If ceremonies due they did aright;
As, supperless to bed they must retire,
And couch supine their beauties, lily white;
Nor look behind, nor sideways, but require
Of Heaven with upward eyes for all that they desire.

7

Full of this whim was thoughtful Madeline:
The music, yearning like a God in pain,
She scarcely heard: her maiden eyes divine,
Fixed on the floor, saw many a sweeping train
Pass by—she heeded not at all: in vain
Came many a tiptoe, amorous cavalier,
And back retired; not cooled by high disdain,
But she saw not: her heart was otherwhere;
She sighed for Agnes' dreams, the sweetest of the year.

8

She danced along with vague, regardless eyes,
Anxious her lips, her breathing quick and short:
The hallowed hour was near at hand: she sighs
Amid the timbrels, and the thronged resort
Of whisperers in anger or in sport;

'Mid looks of love, defiance, hate, and scorn,
Hoodwinked with faery fancy; all amort,
Save to St. Agnes and her lambs unshorn,
And all the bliss to be before tomorrow morn.

9

So, purposing each moment to retire,
She lingered still. Meantime, across the moors,
Had come young Porphyro, with heart on fire
For Madeline. Beside the portal doors,
Buttressed from moonlight, stands he, and implores
All saints to give him sight of Madeline,
But for one moment in the tedious hours,
That he might gaze and worship all unseen;
Perchance speak, kneel, touch, kiss—in sooth such things
    have been.

10

He ventures in: let no buzzed whisper tell,
All eyes be muffled, or a hundred swords
Will storm his heart, Love's feverous citadel:
For him, those chambers held barbarian hordes,
Hyena foemen, and hot-blooded lords,
Whose very dogs would execrations howl
Against his lineage; not one breast affords
Him any mercy in that mansion foul,
Save one old beldame, weak in body and in soul.

11

Ah, happy chance! the aged creature came,
Shuffling along with ivory-headed wand,
To where he stood, hid from the torch's flame,
Behind a broad hall pillar, far beyond
The sound of merriment and chorus bland.
He startled her: but soon she knew his face,
And grasped his fingers in her palsied hand,
Saying, "Mercy, Porphyro! hie thee from this place;
They are all here tonight, the whole blood-thirsty race!

12

"Get hence! get hence! there's dwarfish Hildebrand:
He had a fever late, and in the fit
He cursed thee and thine, both house and land:
Then there's that old Lord Maurice, not a whit
More tame for his gray hairs—Alas me! flit!
Flit like a ghost away."—"Ah, Gossip dear,
We're safe enough; here in this arm-chair sit,
And tell me how—" "Good saints! not here, not here!
Follow me, child, or else these stones will be thy bier."

13

He followed through a lowly arched way,
Brushing the cobwebs with his lofty plume;
And as she muttered "Well-a—well-a-day!"
He found him in a little moonlight room,
Pale, latticed, chill, and silent as a tomb.
"Now tell me where is Madeline," said he,
"O tell me, Angela, by the holy loom
Which none but secret sisterhood may see,
When they St. Agnes' wool are weaving piously."

14

"St. Agnes! Ah! it is St. Agnes' Eve—
Yet men will murder upon holy days.
Thou must hold water in a witch's sieve,
And be liege-lord of all the Elves and Fays
To venture so: it fills me with amaze
To see thee, Porphyro!—St. Agnes' Eve!
God's help! my lady fair the conjurer plays
This very night: good angels her deceive!
But let me laugh awhile,—I've mickle time to grieve."

15

Feebly she laugheth in the languid moon,
While Porphyro upon her face doth look,
Like puzzled urchin on an aged crone
Who keepeth closed a wondrous riddle-book,
As spectacled she sits in chimney nook.

But soon his eyes grew brilliant, when she told
His lady's purpose; and he scarce could brook
Tears, at the thought of those enchantments cold,
And Madeline asleep in lap of legends old.

16

Sudden a thought came like a full-blown rose,
Flushing his brow, and in his pained heart
Made purple riot: then doth he propose
A stratagem, that makes the beldame start:
"A cruel man and impious thou art!
Sweet lady, let her pray, and sleep and dream
Alone with her good angels, far apart
From wicked men like thee. Go, go! I deem
Thou canst not surely be the same that thou didst seem."

17

"I will not harm her, by all saints I swear!"
Quoth Porphyro: "O may I ne'er find grace
When my weak voice shall whisper its last prayer,
If one of her soft ringlets I displace,
Or look with ruffian passion in her face.
Good Angela, believe me, by these tears;
Or I will, even in a moment's space,
Awake, with horrid shout, my foemen's ears,
And beard them, though they be more fanged than wolves
    and bears."

18

"Ah! why wilt thou affright a feeble soul?
A poor, weak, palsy-stricken, churchyard thing,
Whose passing-bell may ere the midnight toll;
Whose prayers for thee, each morn and evening,
Were never missed." Thus plaining, doth she bring
A gentler speech from burning Porphyro;
So woeful, and of such deep sorrowing,
That Angela gives promise she will do
Whatever he shall wish, betide her weal or woe.

19

Which was, to lead him, in close secrecy,
Even to Madeline's chamber, and there hide
Him in a closet, of such privacy
That he might see her beauty unespied,
And win perhaps that night a peerless bride,
While legioned fairies paced the coverlet,
And pale enchantment held her sleepy-eyed.
Never on such a night have lovers met,
Since Merlin paid his Demon all the monstrous debt.

20

"It shall be as thou wishest," said the Dame:
"All cates and dainties shall be stored there
Quickly on this feast-night: by the tambour frame
Her own lute thou wilt see: no time to spare,
For I am slow and feeble, and scarce dare
On such a catering trust my dizzy head.
Wait here, my child, with patience; kneel in prayer
The while. Ah! thou must needs the lady wed,
Or may I never leave my grave among the dead."

21

So saying she hobbled off with busy fear.
The lover's endless minutes slowly passed;
The dame returned, and whispered in his ear
To follow her; with aged eyes aghast
From fright of dim espial. Safe at last
Through many a dusky gallery, they gain
The maiden's chamber, silken, hushed and chaste;
Where Porphyro took covert, pleased amain.
His poor guide hurried back with agues in her brain.

22

Her faltering hand upon the balustrade,
Old Angela was feeling for the stair,
When Madeline, St. Agnes' charmed maid,
Rose, like a missioned spirit, unaware:
With silver taper's light, and pious care,

She turned, and down the aged gossip led
To a safe level matting. Now prepare,
Young Porphyro, for gazing on that bed;
She comes, she comes again, like ring-dove frayed and fled.

23

Out went the taper as she hurried in;
Its little smoke, in pallid moonshine, died:
She closed the door, she panted, all akin
To spirits of the air, and visions wide:
No uttered syllable, or, woe betide!
But to her heart, her heart was voluble,
Paining with eloquence her balmy side;
As though a tongueless nightingale should swell
Her throat in vain, and die, heart-stifled, in her dell.

24

A casement high and triple-arched there was,
All garlanded with carven imageries,
Of fruits, and flowers, and bunches of knot-grass,
And diamonded with panes of quaint device,
Innumerable of stains and splendid dyes,
As are the tiger-moth's deep-damasked wings;
And in the midst, 'mong thousand heraldries,
And twilight saints, and dim emblazonings,
A shielded scutcheon blushed with blood of queens and
    kings.

25

Full on this casement shone the wintry moon,
And threw warm gules on Madeline's fair breast,
As down she knelt for Heaven's grace and boon;
Rose-bloom fell on her hands, together prest,
And on her silver cross soft amethyst,
And on her hair a glory, like a saint:
She seemed a splendid angel, newly drest,
Save wings, for heaven:—Porphyro grew faint:
She knelt, so pure a thing, so free from mortal taint.

26

Anon his heart revives: her vespers done,
Of all its wreathed pearls her hair she frees;
Unclasps her warmed jewels one by one;
Loosens her fragrant bodice; by degrees
Her rich attire creeps rustling to her knees:
Half-hidden, like a mermaid in sea-weed,
Pensive awhile she dreams awake, and sees,
In fancy, fair St. Agnes in her bed,
But dares not look behind, or all the charm is fled.

27

Soon, trembling in her soft and chilly nest,
In sort of wakeful swoon, perplexed she lay,
Until the poppied warmth of sleep oppressed
Her soothed limbs, and soul fatigued away;
Flown, like a thought, until the morrow-day;
Blissfully havened both from joy and pain;
Clasped like a missal where swart Paynims pray;
Blinded alike from sunshine and from rain,
As though a rose should shut, and be a bud again.

28

Stolen to this paradise, and so entranced,
Porphyro gazed upon her empty dress,
And listened to her breathing, if it chanced
To wake into a slumberous tenderness;
Which when he heard, that minute did he bless,
And breathed himself: then from the closet crept,
Noiseless as fear in a wide wilderness,
And over the hushed carpet, silent, stept,
And 'tween the curtains peeped, where, lo!—how fast she
    slept.

29

Then by the bed-side, where the faded moon
Made a dim, silver twilight, soft he set
A table, and, half anguished, threw thereon
A cloth of woven crimson, gold, and jet:—
O for some drowsy Morphean amulet!

The boisterous, midnight, festive clarion,
The kettle-drum, and far-heard clarinet,
Affray his ears, though but in dying tone:—
The hall-door shuts again, and all the noise is gone.

30

And still she slept an azure-lidded sleep,
In blanched linen, smooth, and lavendered,
While he from forth the closet brought a heap
Of candied apple, quince, and plum, and gourd;
With jellies soother than the creamy curd,
And lucent syrops, tinct with cinnamon;
Manna and dates, in argosy transferred
From Fez; and spiced dainties, every one,
From silken Samarcand to cedared Lebanon.

31

These delicates he heaped with glowing hand
On golden dishes and in baskets bright
Of wreathed silver: sumptuous they stand
In the retired quiet of the night,
Filling the chilly room with perfume light.—
"And now, my love, my seraph fair, awake!
Thou art my heaven, and I thine eremite:
Open thine eyes, for meek St. Agnes' sake,
Or I shall drowse beside thee, so my soul doth ache."

32

Thus whispering, his warm, unnerved arm
Sank in her pillow. Shaded was her dream
By the dusk curtains:—'twas a midnight charm
Impossible to melt as iced stream:
The lustrous salvers in the moonlight gleam;
Broad golden fringe upon the carpet lies:
It seemed he never, never could redeem
From such a stedfast spell his lady's eyes;
So mused awhile, entoiled in woofed phantasies.

33

Awakening up, he took her hollow lute,—
Tumultuous,—and, in chords that tenderest be,
He played an ancient ditty, long since mute,
In Provence called, "La belle dame sans mercy:"
Close to her ear touching the melody;—
Wherewith disturbed, she uttered a soft moan:
He ceased—she panted quick—and suddenly
Her blue affrayed eyes wide open shone:
Upon his knees he sank, pale as smooth-sculptured stone.

34

Her eyes were open, but she still beheld,
Now wide awake, the vision of her sleep:
There was a painful change, that nigh expelled
The blisses of her dream so pure and deep
At which fair Madeline began to weep,
And moan forth witless words with many a sigh,
While still her gaze on Porphyro would keep;
Who knelt, with joined hands and piteous eye,
Fearing to move or speak, she looked so dreamingly.

35

"Ah, Porphyro!" said she, "but even now
Thy voice was at sweet tremble in mine ear,
Made tuneable with every sweetest vow;
And those sad eyes were spiritual and clear:
How changed thou art! how pallid, chill, and drear!
Give me that voice again, my Porphyro,
Those looks immortal, those complainings dear!
Oh, leave me not in this eternal woe,
For if thou diest, my Love, I know not where to go."

36

Beyond a mortal man impassioned far
At these voluptuous accents, he arose,
Ethereal, flushed, and like a throbbing star
Seen 'mid the sapphire heaven's deep repose;
Into her dream he melted, as the rose

Blendeth its odor with the violet,—
Solution sweet: meantime the frost-wind blows
Like Love's alarum, pattering the sharp sleet
Against the window-panes; St. Agnes' moon hath set.

37

'Tis dark: quick pattereth the flaw-blown sleet.
"This is no dream, my bride, my Madeline!"
'Tis dark: the iced gusts still rave and beat:
"No dream, alas! alas! and woe is mine!
Porphyro will leave me here to fade and pine.
Cruel! what traitor could thee hither bring?
I curse not, for my heart is lost in thine,
Though thou forsakest a deceived thing;—
A dove forlorn and lost with sick unpruned wing."

38

"My Madeline! sweet dreamer! lovely bride!
Say, may I be for aye thy vassal blest?
Thy beauty's shield, heart-shaped and vermeil-dyed?
Ah, silver shrine, here will I take my rest
After so many hours of toil and quest,
A famished pilgrim,—saved by miracle.
Though I have found, I will not rob thy nest,
Saving of thy sweet self; if thou think'st well
To trust, fair Madeline, to no rude infidel.

39

"Hark! 'tis an elfin-storm from faery land,
Of haggard seeming, but a boon indeed:
Arise—arise! the morning is at hand;—
The bloated wassailers will never heed;—
Let us away, my love, with happy speed;
There are no ears to hear, or eyes to see,—
Drowned all in Rhenish and the sleepy mead:
Awake! arise! my love, and fearless be,
For o'er the southern moors I have a home for thee."

40

She hurried at his words, beset with fears,
For there were sleeping dragons all around,
At glaring watch, perhaps, with ready spears—
Down the wide stairs a darkling way they found;
In all the house was heard no human sound.
A chain-drooped lamp was flickering by each door;
The arras, rich with horseman, hawk, and hound,
Fluttered in the besieging wind's uproar;
And the long carpets rose along the gusty floor.

41

They glide, like phantoms, into the wide hall;
Like phantoms, to the iron porch they glide,
Where lay the Porter, in uneasy sprawl,
With a huge empty flagon by his side:
The wakeful bloodhound rose, and shook his hide,
But his sagacious eye an inmate owns:
By one, and one, the bolts full easy slide:—
The chains lie silent on the footworn stones;
The key turns, and the door upon its hinges groans.

42

And they are gone: aye, ages long ago
These lovers fled away into the storm.
That night the Baron dreamt of many a woe,
And all his warrior-guests with shade and form
Of witch, and demon, and large coffin-worm,
Were long be-nightmared. Angela the old
Died palsy-twitched, with meager face deform;
The Beadsman, after thousand aves told,
For aye unsought-for slept among his ashes cold.

(1819, 1820)

THE DEATH OF OENONE

Alfred, Lord Tennyson

[It was prophesied that infant Paris, son of Priam, King of Troy, would bring great woe upon his people; so he was abandoned, but was found and raised by shepherds. He grew to manhood and married the lovely Oenone; and they were happy until, as a shepherd youth, he was chosen to judge which of three goddesses was fairest. He chose Venus, and she rewarded him with the promise of the most beautiful woman in the world—Helen, wife of Menelaus, King of Sparta. He wooed and won, and carried her off to Troy, where he was now accepted as one of the Princes. The Trojan War followed, as Menelaus and other Greeks came for Helen. After ten years, Troy fell, and Helen was taken back by her husband. In one of the closing conflicts, Paris was wounded by one of the poisoned arrows of Hercules, which was given to the Greeks by Philoctetes. At this point in the story, Tennyson's narrative begins.]

Oenone sat within the cave from out
Whose ivy-matted mouth she used to gaze
Down at the Troad; but the goodly view
Was now one blank, and all the serpent vines
Which on the touch of heavenly feet had risen,
And gliding thro' the branches over-bower'd
The naked Three, were wither'd long ago,
And thro' the sunless winter morning-mist
In silence wept upon the flowerless earth.
  And while she stared at those dead cords that ran
Dark thro' the mist, and linking tree to tree,
But once were gayer than a dawning sky
With many a pendent bell and fragrant star,
Her Past became her Present, and she saw
Him, climbing toward her with the golden fruit,
Him, happy to be chosen Judge of Gods,
Her husband in the flush of youth and dawn,
Paris, himself as beauteous as a God.
  Anon from out the long ravine below,
She heard a wailing cry, that seem'd at first
Thin as the batlike shrillings of the Dead
When driven to Hades, but, in coming near,

Across the downward thunder of the brook
Sounded "Oenone"; and on a sudden he,
Paris, no longer beauteous as a God,
Struck by a poison'd arrow in the fight,
Lame, crooked, reeling, livid, thro' the mist
Rose, like the wraith of his dead self, and moan'd
    "Oenone, *my* Oenone, while we dwelt
Together in this valley—happy then—
Too happy had I died within thine arms,
Before the feud of Gods had marr'd our peace,
And sunder'd each from each. I am dying now
Pierced by a poison'd dart. Save me. Thou knowest,
Taught by some God, whatever herb or balm
May clear the blood from poison, and thy fame
Is blown thro' all the Troad, and to thee
The shepherd brings his adder-bitten lamb,
The wounded warrior climbs from Troy to thee.
My life and death are in thy hand. The Gods
Avenge on stony hearts a fruitless prayer
For pity. Let me owe my life to thee.
I wrought thee bitter wrong, but thou forgive,
Forget it. Man is but the slave of Fate.
Oenone, by thy love which once was mine,
Help, heal me. I am poison'd to the heart."
"And I to mine," she said, "Adulterer,
Go back to thine adulteress and die!"
    He groan'd, he turn'd, and in the mist at once
Became a shadow, sank and disappear'd,
But, ere the mountain rolls into the plain,
Fell headlong dead; and of the shepherds one
Their oldest, and the same who first had found
Paris, a naked babe, among the woods
Of Ida, following lighted on him there,
And shouted, and the shepherds heard and came.
    One raised the Prince, one sleek'd the squalid hair,
One kiss'd his hand, another closed his eyes,
And then, remembering the gay playmate rear'd
Among them, and forgetful of the man,
Whose crime had half unpeopled Ilion, these
All that day long labour'd, hewing the pines,

And built their shepherd-prince a funeral pile;
And, while the star of eve was drawing light
From the dead sun, kindled the pyre, and all
Stood round it, hush'd, or calling on his name.

But when the white fog vanish'd like a ghost
Before the day, and every topmost pine
Spired into bluest heaven, still in her cave,
Amazed, and ever seeming stared upon
By ghastlier than the Gorgon head, a face,—
His face deform'd by lurid blotch and blain—
There, like a creature frozen to the heart
Beyond all hope of warmth, Oenone sat
Not moving, till in front of that ravine
Which drowsed in gloom, self-darken'd from the west,
The sunset blazed along the wall of Troy.

Then her head sank, she slept, and thro' her dream
A ghostly murmur floated, "Come to me,
Oenone! I can wrong thee now no more,
Oenone, my Oenone," and the dream
Wail'd in her, when she woke beneath the stars.

What star could burn so low? not Ilion yet.
What light was there? She rose and slowly down,
By the long torrent's ever-deepen'd roar,
Paced, following, as in trance, the silent cry.
She waked a bird of prey that scream'd and past;
She roused a snake that hissing writhed away;
A panther sprang across her path, she heard
The shriek of some lost life among the pines,
But when she gain'd the broader vale, and saw
The ring of faces redden'd by the flames
Enfolding that dark body which had lain
Of old in her embrace, paused—and then ask'd
Falteringly, "Who lies on yonder pyre?"
But every man was mute for reverence.
Then moving quickly forward till the heat
Smote on her brow, she lifted up a voice
Of shrill command, "Who burns upon the pyre?"
Whereon their oldest and their boldest said,
"He, whom thou wouldst not heal!" and all at once
The morning light of happy marriage broke

Thro' all the clouded years of widowhood,
And muffling up her comely head, and crying
"Husband!" she leapt upon the funeral pile,
And mixt herself with *him* and past in fire.

(1892)

JESSE JAMES: AMERICAN MYTH

A DESIGN IN RED AND YELLOW FOR A NICKEL LIBRARY

William Rose Benét

Jesse James was a two-gun man,
    (*Roll on, Missouri!*)
Strong-arm chief of an outlaw clan.
    (*From Kansas to Illinois!*)
He twirled an old Colt forty-five,
    (*Roll on, Missouri!*)
They never took Jesse James alive.
    (*Roll, Missouri, roll!*)
Jesse James was King of the Wes';
    (*Cataracks in the Missouri!*)
He'd a di'mon' heart in his lef' breas';
    (*Brown Missouri rolls!*)
He'd a fire in his heart no hurt could stifle;
    (*Thunder, Missouri!*)
Lion eyes an' a Winchester rifle.
    (*Missouri, roll down!*)

Jesse James rode a pinto hawse;
Come at night to a water-cawse;
Tetched with the rowel that pinto's flank;
She sprung the torrent from bank to bank.

Jesse rode through a sleepin' town;
Looked the moonlit street both up an' down;
Crack-crack-crack, the street ran flames
An' a great voice cried, "I'm Jesse James!"

Hawse an' afoot they're after Jess!
    (*Roll on, Missouri!*)

Spurrin' an' spurrin'—but he's gone Wes'.
  (*Brown Missouri rolls!*)
He was ten foot tall when he stood in his boots;
  (*Lightnin' light the Missouri!*)
More'n a match fer sich galoots.
  (*Roll, Missouri, roll!*)

Jesse James rode outa the sage;
Roun' the rocks come the swayin' stage;
Straddlin' the road a giant stan's
An' a great voice bellers, "Throw up yer han's!"

Jesse raked in the di'mon' rings,
The big gold watches an' the yuther things;
Jesse divvied 'em then an' thar
With a cryin' child had lost her mar.

The U. S. Troopers is after Jess;
  (*Roll on, Missouri!*)
Their hawses sweat foam, but he's gone Wes';
  (*Hear Missouri roar!*)
He was broad as a b'ar, he'd a ches' like a drum,
  (*Wind an' rain through Missouri!*)
An' his red hair flamed like Kingdom Come.
  (*Missouri down to the sea!*)

Jesse James all alone in the rain
Stopped an' stuck up the Eas'-boun' train;
Swayed through the coaches with horns an' a tail,
Lit out with the bullion an' the registered mail.

Jess made 'em all turn green with fright,
Quakin' in the aisles in the pitch-black night;
An' he give all the bullion to a pore ole tramp
Campin' nigh the cuttin' in the dirt an' damp.

The whole U. S. is after Jess;
  (*Roll on, Missouri!*)
The son-of-a-gun, if he ain't gone Wes';
  (*Missouri to the sea!*)

He could chaw cold iron an' spit blue flame;
  (*Cataracks down the Missouri!*)
He rode on a catamount he'd larned to tame.
   (*Hear that Missouri roll!*)

Jesse James rode into a bank;
Give his pinto a tetch on the flank;
Jumped the teller's window with an awful crash;
Heaved up the safe an' twirled his mustache;

He said, "So long, boys!" He yelped, "So long!
Feelin' porely today—I ain't feelin' strong!"
Rode right through the wall agoin' crack-crack-crack,—
Took the safe home to Mother in a gunny-sack.

They're creepin', they're crawlin', they're stalkin' Jess;
  (*Roll on, Missouri!*)
They's a rumor he's gone much further Wes';
  (*Roll, Missouri, roll!*)
They's word of a cayuse hitched to the bars
  (*Ruddy clouds on Missouri!*)
Of a golden sunset that busts into stars.
  (*Missouri, roll down!*)

Jesse James rode hell fer leather;
He was a hawse an' a man together;
In a cave in a mountain high up in air
He lived with a rattlesnake, a wolf, an' a bear.

Jesse's heart was as sof' as a woman;
Fer guts an' stren'th he was sooper-human;
He could put six shots through a woodpecker's eye
And take in one swaller a gallon o' rye.

They sought him here an' they sought him there,
  (*Roll on, Missouri!*)
But he strides by night through the ways of the air,
  (*Brown Missouri rolls!*)
They say he was took an' they say he is dead;
  (*Thunder, Missouri!*)

But he ain't—he's sunset overhead!
    (*Missouri down to the sea!*)

Jesse James was a Hercules.
When he went through the woods he tore up the trees.
When he went on the plains he smoked the groun'
An' the hull lan' shuddered fer miles aroun'.

Jesse James wore a red bandanner
That waved on the breeze like the Star Spangled Banner;
In seven states he cut up dadoes.
He's gone with the buffler an' the desperadoes.

Yes, Jesse James was a two-gun man
        (*Roll on, Missouri!*)
The same as when this song began;
        (*From Kansas to Illinois!*)
An' when you see a sunset bust into flames
        (*Lightin' light the Missouri!*)
Or a thunderstorm blaze—that's Jesse James!
        (*Hear that Missouri roll!*)

                                        (1927)

AN AFTERNOON IN ARTILLERY WALK

MARY MILTON LOQUITUR

Leonard Bacon

I think it is his blindness makes him so
He is so angry, and so querulous.
Yes, Father! I will look in Scaliger.
Yes, Cousin Phillips took the notes—I think—
May all the evil angels fly away
With Cousin Phillips to the Serbonian Bog,
Wherever that may be. And here am I
Locked in with him the livelong afternoon.
There's Anne gone limping with that love of hers,
Her master-carpenter, and Deborah

Stolen away. Yes, Father, 'tis an aleph
But the Greek glose on't in the Septuagint
Is something that I cannot quite make out.
The letter's rubbed.

Oh, thus to wear away
My soul and body with this dry-as-dust
This tearer-up of words, this plaguey seeker
After the things that no man understands.
'Tis April. I am seventeen years old,
And Abram Clark will come a-courting me.
Oh what a Hell a midday house can be!
Dusty and bright and dumb and shadowless,
Full of this sunshot dryness, like the soul
Of this old pedant here. I will not bear
Longer this tyranny of death in life
That drains my spirit like a succubus.
I am too full of blood and life for this—
This dull soul-gnawing discipline he sets
Upon our shoulders, the sad characters.
Chapter on chapter, blank and meaningless.
Now by the May-pole merry-makers run,
And the music throbs and pulses in light limbs,
And the girls' kirtles are lifted to the knee.
Ah would that I were blowsy with the heat,
Being bussed by some tall fellow, and kissing him
On his hot red lips—some bully royalist
With gold in's purse and lace about his throat
And a long rapier for the Puritans.
Or I would wander by some cool yew-hedge,
Dallying with my lover all the afternoon,
And then to cards and supper—cinnamon,
Some delicate pastry, and an amber wine
Burning on these lips that know a year-long lent.
Then to the theatre, and Mistress Nell
That the king's fond of. Mayhap gentlemen
About would praise me, and I should hear them buzz,
And feel my cheek grow warm beneath my mask,
And glance most kindly—

I was in a muse
I have the paper, Father, and the pens.
Now for the damnable dictation. So!
"High—on a throne—of royal state—which far
Outshone—the wealth of 'Ormus'—S or Z?
How should I know the letter?—*"and of Ind.*
Or where—the gorgeous East—with richest hand
Showers—on her kings—barbaric—pearl and gold,
Satan exalted sate."

(1927)

THE U. S. SAILOR WITH THE JAPANESE SKULL
Winfield Townley Scott

Bald-bare, bone-bare, and ivory-yellow: skull
Carried by a thus two-headed U. S. sailor
Who got it from a Japanese soldier killed
At Guadalcanal in the ever-present war: our

Bluejacket, I mean, aged 20, in August strolled
Among the little bodies on the sand and hunted
Souvenirs: teeth, tags, diaries, boots; but bolder still
Hacked off this head and under a leopard tree skinned it:

Peeled with a lifting knife the jaw and cheeks, bared
The nose, ripped off the black-haired scalp and gutted
The dead eyes to these thoughtful hollows: a scarred
But bloodless job, unless it be said brains bleed.

Then, his ship under weigh, dragged this aft in a net
Many days and nights—the cold bone tumbling
Beneath the foaming wake, weed-worn and salt-cut
Rolling safe among fish and washed with Pacific;

Till on a warm and level-keeled day hauled in
Held to the sun and the sailor, back to a gun-rest,
Scrubbed the cured skull with lye, perfecting this:
Not foreign as he saw it first: death's familiar cast.

Bodiless, fleshless, nameless, it and the sun
Offend each other in strange fascination
As though one of the two were mocked; but nothing is in
This head, or it fills with what another imagines

As: here were love and hate and the will to deal
Death or to kneel before it, death emperor,
Recorded orders without reasons, bomb-blast, still
A child's morning, remembered moonlight on Fujiyama:

All scoured out now by the keeper of this skull
Made elemental, historic, parentless by our
Sailor boy who thinks of home, voyages laden, will
Not say "Alas! I did not know him at all."

                                        (*1944*)

Lyric Poems

FIGHTING SOUTH OF THE CASTLE

Anonymous, translated from the Chinese by *Arthur Waley*

> They fought south of the Castle,
> They died north of the wall.
> They died in the moors and were not buried.
> Their flesh was the food of crows.
> "Tell the crows we are not afraid;
> We have died in the moors and cannot be buried.
> Crows, how can our bodies escape you?"
> The waters flowed deep
> And the rushes in the pool were dark.
> The riders fought and were slain:
> Their horses wander neighing.
> By the bridge there was a house.
> Was it south, was it north?
> The harvest was never gathered.

How can we give you your offerings?
You served your Prince faithfully,
Though all in vain.
I think of you, faithful soldiers;
Your service shall not be forgotten.
For in the morning you went out to battle
And at night you did not return.

           (*c. 124* B.C., *tr.* 1919)

ALONS AU BOIS LE MAY CUEILLIR

A RONDEL FROM THE OLD FRENCH

Charles d'Orleans, translated by *W. E. Henley*

We'll to the woods and gather may
Fresh from the footprints of the rain;
  We'll to the woods, at every vein
To drink the spirit of the day.
The winds of the spring are out at play,
  The needs of spring in heart and brain.
We'll to the woods and gather may
  Fresh from the footprints of the rain.

The world's too near her end, you say?—
  Hark to the blackbird's mad refrain.
  It waits for her, the 'vast Inane?—
Then, girls, to help her on the way
We'll to the woods and gather may.

           (*c. 1420,* tr. 1888)

VOLPONE'S SONG: TO CELIA

from VOLPONE; OR, THE FOX, III, V

Ben Jonson

Come, my Celia, let us prove,
While we can, the sports of love.

Time will not be ours for ever;
He, at length, our good will sever;
Spend not then his gifts in vain.
Suns that set may rise again;
But if once we lose this light,
'T is with us perpetual night.
Why should we defer our joys?
Fame and rumor are but toys.
Cannot we delude the eyes
Of a few poor household spies?
Or his easier ears beguile,
Thus removèd by our wile?
'T is no sin love's fruits to steal;
But the sweet thefts to reveal,
To be taken, to be seen,
These have crimes accounted been.

(1605)

AN ODE FOR BEN JONSON

Robert Herrick

Ah, Ben!
Say how or when
Shall we, thy guests,
Meet at those lyric feasts
Made at the Sun,
The Dog, the Triple Tun?
Where we such clusters had
As made us nobly wild, not mad;
And yet each verse of thine
Out-did the meat, out-did the frolic wine.

My Ben!
Or come again,
Or send to us
Thy wit's great overplus;
But teach us yet
Wisely to husband it,

Lest we that talent spend;
And, having once brought to an end
That precious stock, the store
Of such a wit the world should have no more.
(*c. 1640, 1648*)

A POISON TREE
William Blake

I was angry with my friend:
I told my wrath, my wrath did end.
I was angry with my foe:
I told it not, my wrath did grow.

And I watered it in fears
Night and morning with my tears,
And I sunnèd it with smiles
And with soft deceitful wiles.

And it grew both day and night,
Till it bore an apple bright,
And my foe beheld it shine,
And he knew that it was mine—

And into my garden stole
When the night had veiled the pole;
In the morning, glad, I see
My foe outstretched beneath the tree.
(1794)

ON HIS SEVENTY-FIFTH BIRTHDAY
Walter Savage Landor

I strove with none, for none was worth my strife;
    Nature I loved, and next to Nature, Art;
I warmed both hands before the fire of life,
    It sinks, and I am ready to depart.
(*1850, 1853*)

COMPOSED UPON WESTMINSTER BRIDGE

SEPTEMBER 3, 1802

William Wordsworth

Earth has not anything to show more fair;
Dull would he be of soul who could pass by
A sight so touching in its majesty:
This City now doth, like a garment, wear
The beauty of the morning; silent, bare,
Ships, towers, domes, theaters, and temples lie
Open unto the fields, and to the sky;
All bright and glittering in the smokeless air.
Never did sun more beautifully steep
In his first splendor, valley, rock, or hill;
Ne'er saw I, never felt, a calm so deep!
The river glideth at his own sweet will:
Dear God! the very houses seem asleep;
And all that mighty heart is lying still!

(1807)

SONG

Christina Rossetti

When I am dead, my dearest,
  Sing no sad songs for me;
Plant thou no roses at my head,
  Nor shady cypress tree.
Be the green grass above me
  With showers and dewdrops wet;
And if thou wilt, remember,
  And if thou wilt, forget.

I shall not see the shadows,
  I shall not feel the rain;
I shall not hear the nightingale

    Sing on as if in pain.
And dreaming through the twilight
    That doth not rise nor set,
Haply I may remember,
    And haply may forget.

                   (1862)

OUTWITTED

Edwin Markham

He drew a circle that shut me out—
Heretic, rebel, a thing to flout.
But Love and I had the wit to win:
We drew a circle that took him in!

                   (1913)

HELEN

H. D.

All Greece hates
the still eyes in the white face,
the luster as of olives
where she stands,
and the white hands.

All Greece reviles
the wan face when she smiles,
hating it deeper still
when it grows wan and white,
remembering past enchantments
and past ills.

Greece sees unmoved,
God's daughter, born of love,
the beauty of cool feet
and slenderest knees,
could love indeed the maid,

only if she were laid,
white ash amid funereal cypresses.
(*c. 1922*)

ONE STAR FELL AND ANOTHER

from PRELUDES FOR MEMNON

Conrad Aiken

One star fell and another as we walked.
Lifting his hand toward the west, he said—
—How prodigal that sky is of its stars!
They fall and fall, and still the sky is sky.
Two more have gone, but heaven is heaven still.

Then let us not be precious of our thought,
Nor of our words, nor hoard them up as though
We thought our minds a heaven which might change
And lose its virtue when the word had fallen.
Let us be prodigal, as heaven is;
Lose what we lose, and give what we may give,—
Ourselves are still the same. Lost you a planet—?
Is Saturn gone? Then let him take his rings
Into the Limbo of forgotten things.

O little foplings of the pride of mind,
Who wrap the phrase in lavender, and keep it
In order to display it: and you, who save your loves
As if we had not worlds of love enough—!

Let us be reckless of our words and worlds,
And spend them freely as the tree his leaves;
And give them where the giving is most blest.
What should we save them for,—a night of frost? . . .
All lost for nothing, and ourselves a ghost.

(1931)

OH YOUNG MEN OH YOUNG COMRADES
Stephen Spender

oh young men oh young comrades
it is too late now to stay in those houses
your fathers built where they built you to build to breed
money on money   it is too late
to make or even to count what has been made
Count rather those fabulous possessions
which begin with your body and your fiery soul:—
the hairs on your head the muscles extending
in ranges with their lakes across your limbs
Count your eyes as jewels and your valued sex
then count the sun and the innumerable coined light
sparkling on waves and spangled under trees
It is too late to stay in great houses where the ghosts are prisoned
—those ladies like flies perfect in amber
those financiers like fossils of bones in coal.
Oh comrades, step beautifully from the solid wall
advance to rebuild and sleep with friend on hill
advance to rebel and remember what you have
no ghost ever had, immured in his hall.

(1933)

DAEMON & LECTERN & A LIFE-SIZE MIRROR
Horace Gregory

For God's sake, do not explain that picture
of the bright-haired girl on a diamond black horse,
nor the stilled eyes of imperishable Greek ladies
carefully undressing before a life-size mirror.

Let us be glad that we cannot discover
daemon or child who made them, that these realities
of delight and beauty at their imperfect source
are indiscreet, if not indecent, subjects for any lecture.

(1940)

MONOLOGUE AT MIDNIGHT
Robert Penn Warren

Among the pines we ran and called
In joy and innocence, and still
Our voices doubled in the high
Green groining our simplicity.

And we have heard the windward hound
Bell in the frosty vault of dark.
(Then what pursuit?) How soundlessly
The maple shed its pollen in the sun.

Season by season from the skein
Unwound, of earth and of our pleasure;
And always at the side, like guilt,
Our shadows over the grasses moved,

Or moved across the moonlit snow;
And move across the grass or snow.
Or was it guilt? Philosophers
Loll in their disputatious ease.

The match flame sudden in the gloom
Is lensed within each watching eye
Less intricate, less small, than in
One heart the other's image is.

The hound, the echo, flame, or shadow . . .
And which am I and which are you?
And are we Time who flee so fast,
Or stone who stand, and thus endure?

Our mathematic yet has use
For the integers of blessedness:
Listen! the poor deluded cock
Salutes the coldness of no dawn.

(1944)

SUGGESTIONS FOR STUDY

1. *Story Elements.* (a) Read "The Eve of St. Agnes" giving close attention to the story elements—setting, characters, situation, incidents, meaning. (b) Read and read "The Twa Brothers," "The Death of Oenone," and "An Afternoon in Artillery Walk," and prepare to discuss the methods used in story telling.

2. *Lyric Emotion.* (a) Read the group of lyrics presented in this chapter, not once but repeatedly, until you feel that your reading-experience for each of them has been rich and meaningful. (b) Now give your thought to the question of the poet's emotion—the feeling-phase of the full meaning, as you understand it—and to your own emotional response to the poem. (c) You may find it useful to turn back to Chapter 8 (pp. 193-97, 200-03) for a brief review.

3. *Poems of Sorts.* (a) The above poems are already sorted into two main piles, narrative and lyric. Now proceed to classify them according to the scheme of sub-types suggested in the chapter. (b) Turn back to the poems in the first three chapters of the book. Revive your experience of these poems sufficiently to classify them as to type and sub-type.

4. *Paradise and Bower.* (a) Read the selections from Milton's epic, *Paradise Lost,* giving your attention to the description of the setting. (b) Turn back to the selection from Spenser's romantic epic, *The Faerie Queene* (pp. 251-53), and reread the description of the Bower of Bliss. (c) Write a one-page paper comparing the techniques used by the two poets in describing the setting for these parts of the narrative poems.

5. *A Turner in Words.* (a) J. M. W. Turner, a contemporary of Wordsworth, was a landscape and seascape painter. Colored reproductions of his paintings will be found in many art histories. Look for some examples of his later and more impressionistic work. (b) Then return to a rereading of Wordsworth's sonnet, "Composed upon Westminster Bridge," giving particular attention to your visual imagery. In this poem, description is not used as a narrative element, but as the basis for communicating the poet's emotion. (c) Find some means of expressing your experience in comparing the two: Write a short essay comparing the sonnet with a particular Turner picture. Or sketch the Wordsworth scene in any medium you wish. Or describe the Turner in words, in verse if you will, in sonnet form if you care to.

6. *Ballads.* (a) Ten ballads, as here classified, have been included thus far in this volume. Hunt them out and reread them. (b) They are

of the three sorts: old English and Scottish popular ballads, American folk ballads, and literary ballads. Assign them to their proper categories. (c) Investigate the ballad further by using the *Encyclopaedia Britannica,* other standard reference work, or available books on the ballad or types of poetry. (d) What are some of the devices of story telling employed by the writers of ballads?

7. *Storycraft.* Try your hand at *one* of the following narrative problems. (a) Rewrite "An Afternoon in Artillery Walk" in the form of a one-act play, describing the scene and characters, filling out the implied dialogue, and supplying stage-directions. Or (b) work out in screen-story or scenario form the scene in Madeline's chamber from "The Eve of St. Agnes," describing in detail each camera angle and shot, and supplying dialogue and sound effects. Or (c) retell, in common ballad meter, the story of Oenone's death.

8. *Poetcraft.* (a) He who would really understand and appreciate a tool must not only pick it up and examine it, and watch the skilled craftsmen using it, but he must in truth try it out in his own hand. If this is generally true of language, man's master tool, it is yet more particularly true of poetry. (b) Perhaps you already keep a commonplace book in which you jot down good ideas that come to you, or into which you poke notes that you have taken on stray scraps of paper. Why not include bits of verse as they may occur to you? (c) Does a reading of the lyrics in this chapter give you any poetic ideas? Have you some deep feeling about particular boys who have fallen in the Pacific or in North Africa or in Normandy? Have you some advice for young comrades? Have you some thoughts on your twentieth or twenty-fifth birthday that come to you in response to Landor's reflections on his seventy-fifth? What could you sing to Celia? or to rare Ben? Such emotions and thoughts are the impulses from which poems spring—or are evolved. (d) You may wish to do some scribbling or some riming, some fashioning of verses, in any of the many sub-types of the lyric, in any of the forms, on any of the themes, in any of the moods, in any of the historic styles—getting something off your chest, giving vent to some strong feeling, working out some thoughtful problem, expressing a definite attitude—showing in words some facet of your personality.

17

POETIC FORMS—SONNET AND ODE

All poems, as we saw in the last chapter, may be sorted into three groups conventionally called the types of poetry—narrative, lyric, and reflective—though all readers will not quite agree as to what the third of these types is, or how they should be defined, or which group is the right one for some particular poem. Nevertheless, the ascription of the term "narrative" or "lyric" to a poem indicates that the reader has approached that poem from one certain point of view.

I. POETIC FORM AND FORMS

In the enumeration of the so-called sub-types, it was pointed out that certain ones, such as the sonnet and the ode, were distinguished at least in part by their form. And it is the purpose of the present chapter to clarify this statement, to define and discuss *poetic form,* to particularize by commenting on two special forms, and to present two groups of illustrative poems. This consideration will be a second of several approaches to poetry; it will view the poem from a somewhat different angle; it will provide the basis of another classification of poem-experiences.

The concept of *poetic form* is complex, but not difficult to grasp. Consideration has already been given to two of its components.[1] Poetic form consists, in part, of the typographical form on the page; rather, the visual pattern of this in the process of seeing the poem on the page. The poetic form also consists, in part, of the rhythmic form, whether it is metrical or free. A third part of the poetic form may be the thought structure, which often bears a special relation to the rhythmic form and the typographical form. A poem, then,

[1] See Chapter 4, "Seeing the Poem on the Page" (pp. 76-79, 86, 89), and Chapter 5, "The Music of Poetry" (pp. 105 ff.).

may have form to the eye, form to the ear, and form to the mind; and the *poetic form* may be thought of as a complex of the three.

To one who is acquainted with poetic forms, "The Death of Oenone" *looks* like blank verse (continuing down the page without stanzaic spacing; no visual clues for riming; lines of about the same width, two-thirds page width). It *sounds* like blank verse (a metrical poetic rhythm, but free flowing and without rime). Its *thought structure,* too, suggests blank verse; for, outside of a certain measured pace, it seems unrestricted by the metrical pattern. And that is in fact what it is, blank verse. This particular form accommodates itself to reflective or expository poetry and to poetic drama quite as easily as to narrative poetry; and even some few lyrics are to be found in this form.

Or take, for example, "Jesse James: American Myth" by William Rose Benét. It *looks* like a ballad to the experienced eye. (Note the italicized and parenthesized refrains; the successive quatrains; the length of the whole poem.) It *sounds* like a ballad. (Note the refrains again; the rugged four-stress rhythmic beat; the four-line stanzas.) [2] And its *thought structure* is like that of a ballad. (Note the leaping and lingering, and what is called "incremental repetition.") It is these together that constitute the ballad form, which distinguishes the ballad as a sub-type of narrative poetry.

To the reader who has come thus far in this book, surely Wordsworth's "Composed upon Westminster Bridge" *looks* like a sonnet (two-thirds page width in this book and about as long as wide; heavy end-line punctuation and rimes-to-the-eye). It also *sounds* like a sonnet (the measured five-stress, rising tread; the riming pattern of recurring end-sounds; the ebb and flow of its larger rhythm). Its *thought structure* also is one of those found amongst sonnets (the developing picture of the first and larger half; and the comparison and reflective comment in the second and smaller half). And indeed it is a sonnet of one of the several somewhat similar forms. Most poems in sonnet form are lyrics, but sometimes this poetic form is used for an almost purely narrative or expository poem. And on occasion the sonnet form is used stanzaically in a

---

[2] The so-called "ballad meter," however, is a slightly different metrical pattern: $a^4b^3c^4b^3$.

longer narrative, or even imbedded in the dialogue of a poetic drama.

Such, then, is the general concept of *poetic form,* illustrated by three particular poems, each in a different form. The very numerous and varied poetic forms—many of which have had a long literary history—are of three principal sorts, for which the above cited poems may again serve as examples: the *continuous* forms, as illustrated in the blank verse of "The Death of Oenone"; the *stanzaic* forms, of which the ballad is one, as exemplified in "Jesse James"; the *special* forms, one being the sonnet, and "Westminster Bridge" an instance.

But blank verse (unrimed iambic pentameter) is only one of *continuous forms,* which, as a group, are distinguished by the fact that the lines follow each other continuously with only occasional paragraphing as in prose, or with indentations and spacing arbitrarily determined upon by the poet. In addition to blank verse (further illustrated by *Paradise Lost,* p. 411, and Frost's "Mending Wall," p. 235), the continuous forms include heroic couplet (exemplified by Chapman's translation of *The Odyssey,* p. 35, and Pope's *Essay on Criticism,* p. 244), short couplet (used in Jonson's "Volpone's Song: to Celia," p. 436, and Vaughan's "The Retreat," p. 645), irregular metrical form (such as Arnold's "Dover Beach," p. 295, and Thompson's "The Hound of Heaven," p. 297), and free verse (as Spender's "oh young men oh young comrades," p. 442, and Waley's translation of "Fighting South of the Castle," p. 435).[3]

The *stanzaic forms* are of another sort. The various stanzaic forms are distinguished by their metrical patterns, which may be described in terms of foot, meter, line-scheme—really "rime-scheme" here, as (with few exceptions) stanzas are groups of verses spaced off and bound together by an arrangement of rime. A very few poems are written in couplet stanzas, and not many in triplets (as Herrick's "Upon His Departure Hence," p. 72) or in terza rima (like Shelley's "Ode to the West Wind," p. 133). The four-line stanza, or quatrain, is common, and with several different metrical patterns: the ballad meter (of "The Ballad of William Sycamore," p. 337), the special quatrain of *The Rubáiyát of Omar Khayyám*

---

[3] For definitions of these terms and those in the following paragraphs, see the Glossarial Handbook.

(p. 281), the quatrain riming in couplets (as in Blake's "A Poison Tree," p. 438), and many others. Of the other stanzaic forms, the most notable are the rime royal, the ottava rima (as in Byron's *Don Juan,* p. 529), and the Spenserian stanza (used first in *The Faerie Queene,* p. 251, and later in "The Eve of St. Agnes," p. 413). But many poets, like Spenser, have invented stanzaic forms or adapted existing stanzaic forms to their own purposes.

Of the *special forms,* two—the sonnet and the ode—are to be particularized in this chapter; but there are a number of other special forms that should at least be mentioned. As a group they are distinguished by a more or less complex unitary form; that is, the metrical pattern is set for the poem as a whole. Unlike the continuous and stanzaic forms, the special forms are usually restricted in length and complex in structure. One group of these is known as the French forms, for they originated with the medieval Provençal poets: the ballade (as Villon's "Ballade des dames du temps jadis," p. 563), the rondel (d'Orlean's "Alons au bois le may cueillir," p. 436), the triolet (Dobson's "Urceus Exit," p. 517), and the rondeau, villanelle, and sestina. These French forms are characterized by the limited number of rime-sounds and the recurrence of entire lines as a part of the intricate set pattern. Other special forms, with a particular relation to music, are the madrigal (such as "Love Not Me for Comely Grace," p. 112), and the round ("Sumer is icumen in," p. 383). Other simple special forms are the limerick and various forms of the epitaph and epigram, which will be illustrated in one of the next chapters.

These are the various poetic forms, of which two in the last group will supply the illustrative poems for the present chapter.

2. THE SONNET AND THE ODE

By far the most widely practiced of the special forms is the *sonnet,* of which a good bit has already been said. The word "sonnet" is used to name any one of several related poetic forms, each of which consists of fourteen lines of iambic pentameter with a more or less complex rime-scheme.[4] This form developed in the

---

[4] With just enough exceptions to prove the rule. For the term has been applied to a rare twelve-line or sixteen-line poem; to a poem in tetrameter and another in hexameter; to a poem without measured rhythm and another without rime!

early Italian Renaissance and was practiced by many men of that time, notably Dante, whose sonnets were addressed to his beloved Beatrice, and by Petrarch, to his Laura. The Petrarchan or *Italian form* of the sonnet is characteristically divided into two parts, the octave, as the first eight lines are called, and the sestet, the final six lines. The octave usually rimes *abbaabba;* but any of several rime-schemes is to be found in the sestet. The division into octave and sestet usually marks a division in the thought structure of the sonnet in Italian form; the second part may complement the first, or be a response to or an application of it. A number of sonnets of this kind have been included in the earlier pages of this book; among them, Ronsard's "Quand vous serez bien vieille" (p. 219), Donne's "Holy Sonnet: X" (p. 12), Wordsworth's "Composed upon Westminster Bridge," (p. 439), and Wright's "Thumbprint" (p. 266).

The second of the principal forms is the so-called Shakespearean or *Elizabethan form*. Composed of three quatrains with crossed rimes (*abab*) and concluding with a rimed couplet, it is much more easily managed in English, a language with comparatively fewer riming words than Italian. Sometimes the thought structure follows the division into quatrains and couplet; sometimes it develops through the first twelve lines to the concluding couplet. Shakespeare's "That Time of Year—" (p. 159), Masefield's "The Racer" (p. 170), and Margaret Yale's "Some Things There Are" (p. 263) will serve to illustrate this form.

There are several other sonnet forms: the Spenserian, with a unique linking of the rimes; [5] the Miltonic, which follows the Petrarchan rime-scheme, but avoids the thought division (as in the sonnet "On His Blindness," p. 231); the composite forms, combining features of the Italian and Elizabethan forms (as in Rupert Brooke's "The Soldier," p. 78); and the irregular sonnets, which are a law unto themselves (such as Shelley's "Ozymandias," p. 202). A special instance of this latter sort is the so-called American sonnet, freely rhythmed and rimed (as Merrill Moore's "And to the Young Men," p. 458).

This brief description has given little notion of the wealth of

[5] The rime scheme is *abab bcbc cdcd ee*[5].

poetry written in the various sonnet forms during the early Renaissance and again in the nineteenth and twentieth centuries—the many sonnet sequences, groups of as many as a hundred sonnets often addressed to a single person, and the wide range of separate poems, occasional and reflective, narrative and purely lyrical, that are cast in this poetic form.

But we must turn now to a brief consideration of the ode.

The word *ode* again is used to name any one of several somewhat different poetic forms, only some of which are special forms as we have defined the term. But most of them, whether they are entitled odes or not, would fall within the following descriptive definition: the ode is ordinarily a poem of *moderate length,* usually expressing the poet's *exalted praise* of some person or thing or idea, and often bearing some conscious relation to *classical tradition.* Thus Housman's "To an Athlete Dying Young" (though not including the word "ode" in its title) might well be considered as belonging to this special form: it is a poem of some twenty-eight lines; it is ironically in praise of the smart lad who slipped betimes away; it is related in spirit and stanzaic form to certain of the classical odes of the past.

The various sorts of ode written by modern poets must be viewed in relation to their ancient forebears. Later poets have derived inspiration from three sorts of ode to be found in classical literature: the various odes of *Pindar,* some of which were written in exalted praise of Greek heroes and athletic victors (p. 461); the *choral odes* in the Greek dramas, also sometimes poems of praise, such as the one earlier quoted from the tragedy by Sophocles (p. 372); and the quite different odes, sophisticated stanzaic lyrics by the Roman poet *Horace* (p. 547). The Pindaric odes and the choral odes were in form related to the movements of the stately dance of that time, and were divided into parts (or long stanzas) called strophes, antistrophes, and epodes—corresponding to the movement, countermovement, and pause of the dance. Each part of these odes, which were written for oral interpretation, was complex in structure and characterized by verses of varying length; and such features in them were later imitated.

There are also three kinds of ode in English poetry: the so-called *regular* Pindaric ode with strophe, antistrophe, and epode (there are comparatively few of these, and none is widely read today); the so-called *irregular* ode (which tries to suggest the structure of Pindar's strophes by the use of varying line lengths and free use of rime); and the so-called *stanzaic* ode (which substitutes any of the stanzaic forms for Pindar's complicated strophes, but is still characterized by exaltation and praise). From the purely metrical point of view, odes in this third group might be classified, not as poems in one of the special forms, but as poems in stanzaic form; and the odes in the second group might be placed in the continuous-form category. But their relation (even though remote) to the traditional strophic form of Pindar might justify their inclusion here among the poems of special form.

Of the poems earlier included in this book, Dryden's "Song for St. Cecilia's Day" (p. 147) and Thompson's "The Hound of Heaven" (p. 297) will serve as examples of the irregular ode; and Collins' "Ode Written in . . . 1746" (p. 145) and Keats' "Ode on a Grecian Urn" (p. 152) will serve to illustrate the stanzaic ode. Amongst the great poems there is a goodly handful making use of one or another of these related poetic forms.

Sonnets

I FELT A SPIRIT OF LOVE BEGIN TO STIR [6]

from LA VITA NUOVA, XXIV

Dante Alighieri, translated by *Dante Gabriel Rossetti*

I felt a spirit of love begin to stir
    Within my heart, long time unfelt till then;
    And saw Love coming towards me fair and fain,
(That I scarce knew him for his joyful cheer),

[6] Dante's sonnet in Italian is reprinted on p. 76.

Saying, "Be now indeed my worshiper!"
  And in his speech he laugh'd and laugh'd again.
  Then, while it was his pleasure to remain,
I chanced to look the way he had drawn near
And saw the Ladies Joan and Beatrice
  Approach me, this the other following,
    One and a second marvel instantly.
And even as now my memory speaketh this,
  Love spake it then: "The first is christen'd Spring;
    The second Love, she is so like to me."

                                    (*1290*, tr. 1861)

LOVE'S INCONSISTENCY

Francesco Petrarca, translated by *Sir Thomas Wyatt*

I find no peace, and all my war is done;
  I fear and hope, I burn and freeze likewise;
  I fly above the wind, yet cannot rise;
  And nought I have, yet all the world I seize on;
That looseth, nor locketh, holdeth me in prison,
  And holds me not, yet can I 'scape no wise;
  Nor lets me live, nor die, at my devise,
  And yet of death it giveth none occasion.
Without eyes I see, and without tongue I plain;
  I wish to perish, yet I ask for health;
  I love another, and yet I hate myself;
I feed in sorrow, and laugh in all my pain;
  Lo, thus displeaseth me both death and life,
  And my delight is causer of my grief.

                                    (*c. 1350*, tr. 1557)

ONE DAY I WROTE HER NAME UPON THE STRAND

from AMORETTI, LXXV

Edmund Spenser

One day I wrote her name upon the strand,
  But came the waves and wash'ed it away;

Again I wrote it, with a second hand,
But came the tide and made my pains his prey.

"Vain man," said she, "that dost in vain essay
A mortal thing so to immortalize;
For I myself shall like to this decay,
And eke my name be wipèd out likewise."

"Not so," quoth I, "let baser things devise
To die in dust, but you shall live by fame:
My verse your virtues rare shall eternize,
And in the heavens write your glorious name,

Where, whenas death shall all the world subdue,
Our love shall live and, later, life renew."

(1595)

LET ME NOT TO THE MARRIAGE OF TRUE MINDS

from SONNETS, CXVI

William Shakespeare

Let me not to the marriage of true minds
Admit impediments. Love is not love
Which alters when it alteration finds,
Or bends with the remover to remove:
O, no! it is an ever-fixèd mark,
That looks on tempests and is never shaken;
It is the star to every wand'ring bark,
Whose worth's unknown, although his height be taken.
Love's not Time's fool, though rosy lips and cheeks
Within his bending sickle's compass come;
Love alters not with his brief hours and weeks,
But bears it out even to the edge of doom:—
   If this be error and upon me proved,
   I never writ, nor no man ever loved.

(c. 1598, 1609)

ON HIS BEING ARRIVED AT THE AGE OF
TWENTY-THREE
John Milton

How soon hath Time, the subtle thief of youth,
Stolen on his wing my three and twentieth year!
My hasting days fly on with full career,
But my late spring no bud or blossom shew'th.
Perhaps my semblance might deceive the truth
That I to manhood am arrived so near;
And inward ripeness doth much less appear,
That some more timely-happy spirits endu'th.
Yet be it less or more, or soon or slow,
It shall be still in strictest measure even
To that same lot, however mean or high,
Toward which Time leads me, and the will of Heaven;
All is, if I have grace to use it so,
As ever in my great Task-Master's eye.

(*1631*, 1645)

WHEN I HAVE FEARS THAT I MAY CEASE TO BE
John Keats

When I have fears that I may cease to be
  Before my pen has glean'd my teeming brain,
Before high pilèd books, in charact'ry,
  Hold like rich garners the full-ripen'd grain;
When I behold, upon the night's starr'd face,
  Huge cloudy symbols of a high romance,
And think that I may never live to trace
  Their shadows, with the magic hand of chance;
And when I feel, fair creature of an hour!
  That I shall never look upon thee more,
Never have relish in the faery power
  Of unreflecting love!—then on the shore

Of the wide world I stand alone, and think,
Till Love and Fame to nothingness do sink.

(1818, 1848)

HOW DO I LOVE THEE

from SONNETS FROM THE PORTUGUESE, XLIII

Elizabeth Barrett Browning

How do I love thee? Let me count the ways.
I love thee to the depth and breadth and height
My soul can reach, when feeling out of sight
For the ends of Being and Ideal Grace.
I love thee to the level of every day's
Most quiet need, by sun and candle-light.
I love thee freely, as men strive for right;
I love thee purely, as they turn from praise.
I love thee with the passion put to use
In my old griefs; and with my childhood's faith.
I love thee with a love I seemed to lose
With my lost saints. I love thee with the breath,
Smiles, tears, of all my life!—and, if God choose,
I shall but love thee better after death.

(1846, 1850)

TO ROBERT BROWNING

Walter Savage Landor

There is delight in singing, though none hear
Beside the singer; and there is delight
In praising, though the praiser sit alone
And see the prais'd far off him, far above.
Shakespeare is not our poet, but the world's,
Therefore on him no speech! and brief for thee,
Browning! Since Chaucer was alive and hale,
No man hath walked along our roads with step
So active, so inquiring eye, or tongue
So varied in discourse. But warmer climes

Give brighter plumage, stronger wing: the breeze
Of Alpine heights thou playest with, borne on
Beyond Sorrento and Amalfi, where
The Siren waits thee, singing song for song.

(1846)

NON PAX—EXPECTATIO
Francis Thompson

Hush! 'tis the gap between two lightnings. Room
Is none for peace in this thou callest peace,
This breathing-while wherein the breathings cease.
The pulses sicken, hearkening through the gloom.
Afar the thunders of a coming doom
Ramp on the cowering winds. Lo! at the dread,
Thy heart's tomb yawns and renders up its dead,—
The hopes 'gainst hope embalmèd in its womb.

Canst thou endure, if the pent flood o'erflows?
Who is estated heir to constancy?
Behold, I hardly know if I outlast
The minute underneath whose heel I lie;
Yet I endure, have stayed the minute passed,
Perchance may stay the next. Who knows, who knows?

(*bef. 1907*)

WHAT LIPS MY LIPS HAVE KISSED
Edna St. Vincent Millay

What lips my lips have kissed, and where, and why,
I have forgotten, and what arms have lain
Under my head till morning; but the rain
Is full of ghosts tonight, that tap and sigh
Upon the glass and listen for reply;
And in my heart there stirs a quiet pain
For unremembered lads that not again
Will turn to me at midnight with a cry.

Thus in the winter stands the lonely tree,
Nor knows what birds have vanished one by one,
Yet knows its boughs more silent than before:
I cannot say what loves have come and gone;
I only know that summer sang in me
A little while, that in me sings no more.

(1923)

AND TO THE YOUNG MEN

Merrill Moore

And to the young men awaiting their sacrifice
You brought water in an invisible pail
And promised them the plans would surely fail
That were written against them, recorded in the stars.
And you brought straw and padded the cold bars
Of the prison beds whereon the young men lay,
And sung to some at night and fanned by day
Those who were fevering into paradise.

But even then you did not do enough.
For you remember a boy, the silent one?
With a silent eye, who scarcely loved the sun,
And felt too keenly the winter wind's dry sough?
Well, you should have brought him cresses from a far stream
Over which nymphs and under which naiads dream.

(1935)

HERESY FOR A CLASS ROOM

Rolfe Humphries

Green willows are for girls to study under
When that green lady, Spring, strolls down the street:
Look out the window, Jean, look out and wonder
About their unseen earth-embedded feet.
Under the dark uncolored mouldy clay
Where willow roots are thrust, their life is drawn

Up through the limbs, to burst in bud, and sway
Slow-shaken green festoons above the lawn.

So never doubt that gloom turns into light
As winter into April, or as bloom
Breaks on the barren branches over-night—
Little enough is learned in any room
With blackboard walls, on afternoons like these,—
O Jean, look out the window at the trees!

(1942)

AGAIN THE NATIVE HOUR LETS DOWN THE LOCKS

from MORE SONNETS AT CHRISTMAS

Allen Tate

Again the native hour lets down the locks
Uncombed and black, but gray the bobbing beard;
Ten years ago His eyes, fierce shuttlecocks,
Pierced the close net of what I failed: I feared
The belly-cold, the grave-clout, that betrayed
Me slithering in the rift of cordial seas;
Ten years is time enough to be dismayed
By mummy Christ, head crammed between his knees.

Suppose I take an arrogant bomber, stroke
By stroke, up to the frazzled sun to hear
Sun-ghostlings whisper: Yes, the capital yoke—
Remove it and there's not a ghost to fear
This crucial day, whose decapitate joke
Languidly winds into the inner ear.

(1943)

SONNET

William Empson

Not wrongly moved by this dismaying scene
    The thinkers like the nations getting caught

Joined in the organizing that they fought
To scorch all earth of all but one machine.

It can be swung, is what these hopers mean,
  For all the loony hooters can be bought
    On the small ball. It can then all be taught
And reconverted to be kind and clean.

A more heartening fact about the cultures of man
  Is their appalling stubbornness. The sea
    Is always calm three fathoms down. The gigan-

tic anthropological circus riotously
  Holds open all its booths. The pigmy plan
    Is one note each and the tune goes out free.

                    (1945)

SCORN NOT THE SONNET
William Wordsworth

Scorn not the Sonnet; Critic, you have frowned,
Mindless of its just honors; with this key
Shakespeare unlocked his heart; the melody
Of this small lute gave ease to Petrarch's wound;
A thousand times this pipe did Tasso sound;
With it Camöens soothed an exile's grief;
The Sonnet glittered a gay myrtle leaf
Amid the cypress with which Dante crowned
His visionary brow: a glowworm lamp,
It cheered mild Spenser, called from Faery-land
To struggle through dark ways; and, when a damp
Fell round the path of Milton, in his hand
The Thing became a trumpet; whence he blew
Soul-animating strains,—alas! too few.

                    (1827)

Odes

ISTHMIAN ODE III

TO MELISSUS OF THEBES, VICTOR IN THE HORSE-RACE

Pindar, translated by *Abraham Moore*

STROPHE

The man, by fortune raised, that holds
  Unflush'd with pride his blameless course,
Though glory's wreath his front enfolds,
  Or wealth with power hath bless'd his stores,
His country's praise to deathless fame shall give.
  Yet but from thee th' exalted virtues flow,
  All-bounteous Jove! and they that know,
And fear thy laws, rejoice and live;
  While he that walks sin's wandering way,
  Ends not in bliss the changeful day.

ANTISTROPHE

Reward awaits the virtuous deed;
  The brave command the grateful lyre;
For them th' applauding Graces lead,
  And swell the loud triumphal choir.
Fortune on proud Melissus hath bestow'd
  The twofold boon, that glads his manly breast;—
  First in the cirque his waving crest
With Isthmian wreaths exulting glow'd;
  Now through the Lion's vale the name
  Of Thebes his herald's shouts proclaim—

EPODE

Him master of the equestrian race
Proclaim; his deeds no kindred name disgrace:
His grandsire's fame, 'mong charioteers of old,
Cleonymus, all tongues have told;
Told how from Labdacus, with affluence crown'd,
His mother's sires in happier days
The car quadrigal proudly drove.
But Time, as rolling seasons onward move,
His altering hand on all things lays:
The sons of gods alone nor chance nor change can wound.

(*c. 475* B.C.)

ALEXANDER'S FEAST

OR, THE POWER OF MUSIC

John Dryden

AN ODE IN HONOR OF ST. CECILIA'S DAY

[Alexander the Great, son of Philip of Macedon, conquered the
Persians under Darius III in 331 B.C. He celebrated the victory with
Thaïs, an Athenian courtesan who accompanied him, and Timotheus,
his favorite musician. This is the second of the two comparable odes
written by Dryden.]

I

'T was at the royal feast, for Persia won
By Philip's warlike son.
Aloft in awful state
The godlike hero sate
On his imperial throne:
His valiant peers were placed around;
Their brows with roses and with myrtles bound
(So should desert in arms be crowned).
The lovely Thais, by his side,
Sate like a blooming Eastern bride
In flow'r of youth and beauty's pride.

Happy, happy, happy pair!
None but the brave,
None but the brave,
None but the brave deserves the fair.

CHORUS

> *Happy, happy, happy pair!*
> *None but the brave,*
> *None but the brave,*
> *None but the brave deserves the fair.*

2

Timotheus, plac'd on high
    Amid the tuneful choir,
      With flying fingers touch'd the lyre:
The trembling notes ascend the sky,
      And heav'nly joys inspire.
The song began from Jove,
Who left his blissful seats above,
(Such is the pow'r of mighty love.)
A dragon's fiery form belied the god:
Sublime on radiant spires he rode,
    When he to fair Olympia press'd;
    And while he sought her snowy breast:
Then, round her slender waist he curl'd,
And stamp'd an image of himself, a sov'reign of the world.
The list'ning crowd admire the lofty sound;
"A present deity," they shout around;
"A present deity," the vaulted roofs rebound:
    With ravish'd ears
    The monarch hears,
    Assumes the god,
    Affects to nod,
  And seems to shake the spheres.

CHORUS

> *With ravish'd ears,*
> *The monarch hears,*

Assumes the god,
Affects to nod,
And seems to shake the spheres.

3

The praise of Bacchus then the sweet musician sung,
  Of Bacchus ever fair and ever young:
    The jolly god in triumph comes;
    Sound the trumpets; beat the drums;
      Flush'd with a purple grace
      He shews his honest face:
Now give the hautboys breath: he comes, he comes.
    Bacchus, ever fair and young,
      Drinking joys did first ordain;
    Bacchus' blessings are a treasure,
    Drinking is the soldier's pleasure:
        Rich the treasure,
        Sweet the pleasure,
    Sweet is pleasure after pain.

CHORUS

Bacchus' blessings are a treasure,
Drinking is the soldier's pleasure:
    Rich the treasure,
    Sweet the pleasure,
    Sweet is pleasure after pain.

4

Sooth'd with the sound, the king grew vain;
  Fought all his battles o'er again;
And thrice he routed all his foes; and thrice he slew the slain.
The master saw the madness rise;
His glowing cheeks, his ardent eyes;
And, while he heav'n and earth defied,
Chang'd his hand, and check'd his pride.
    He chose a mournful Muse,
      Soft pity to infuse:
He sung Darius great and good,
    By too severe a fate,

Fallen, fallen, fallen, fallen,
    Fallen from his high estate,
        And welt'ring in his blood;
Deserted, at his utmost need,
By those his former bounty fed;
On the bare earth expos'd he lies,
With not a friend to close his eyes.

With downcast looks the joyless victor sate,
    Revolving in his alter'd soul
        The various turns of chance below;
    And, now and then, a sigh he stole;
        And tears began to flow.

CHORUS

Revolving in his alter'd soul
    The various turns of chance below;
And, now and then, a sigh he stole;
    And tears began to flow.

5

The mighty master smil'd, to see
That love was in the next degree:
'T was but a kindred sound to move,
For pity melts the mind to love.
    Softly sweet, in Lydian measures,
    Soon he sooth'd his soul to pleasures.
    "War," he sung, "is toil and trouble;
    Honor, but an empty bubble;
        Never ending, still beginning,
    Fighting still, and still destroying:
        If the world be worth thy winning,
    Think, O think it worth enjoying;
        Lovely Thais sits beside thee,
        Take the good the gods provide thee."

The many rend the skies with loud applause;
So Love was crown'd, but Music won the cause.
    The prince, unable to conceal his pain,
        Gaz'd on the fair

Who caus'd his care,
And sigh'd and look'd, sigh'd and look'd,
Sigh'd and look'd, and sigh'd again:
At length, with love and wine at once oppress'd,
The vanquish'd victor sunk upon her breast.

CHORUS

The prince, unable to conceal his pain,
     Gaz'd on the fair
     Who caus'd his care,
And sigh'd and look'd, sigh'd and look'd,
Sigh'd and look'd, and sigh'd again:
At length, with love and wine at once oppress'd,
The vanquish'd victor sunk upon her breast.

6

Now strike the golden lyre again:
A louder yet, and yet a louder strain.
Break his bands of sleep asunder,
And rouse him, like a rattling peal of thunder.
     Hark, hark, the horrid sound
          Has rais'd up his head:
          As awak'd from the dead,
          And amaz'd, he stares around.
"Revenge, revenge!" Timotheus cries,
     "See the Furies arise!
     See the snakes that they rear,
     How they hiss in their hair,
And the sparkles that flash from their eyes!
     Behold a ghastly band,
     Each a torch in his hand!
Those are Grecian ghosts, that in battle were slain,
          And unburied remain
          Inglorious on the plain:
          Give the vengeance due
          To the valiant crew.
Behold how they toss their torches on high,
          How they point to the Persian abodes,
And glitt'ring temples of their hostile gods!"

The princes applaud, with a furious joy;
And the king seiz'd a flambeau with zeal to destroy;
    Thais led the way,
    To light him to his prey,
And, like another Helen, fir'd another Troy.

CHORUS

And the king seiz'd a flambeau with zeal to destroy;
    Thais led the way,
    To light him to his prey,
And, like another Helen, fir'd another Troy.

7

    Thus, long ago,
Ere heaving bellows learn'd to blow,
    While organs yet were mute;
Timotheus, to his breathing flute,
    And sounding lyre,
Could swell the soul to rage, or kindle soft desire.
    At last, divine Cecilia came,
    Inventress of the vocal frame;
The sweet enthusiast, from her sacred store,
    Enlarg'd the former narrow bounds,
    And added length to solemn sounds,
With nature's mother wit, and arts unknown before.
    Let old Timotheus yield the prize,
    Or both divide the crown;
He rais'd a mortal to the skies;
    She drew an angel down.

GRAND CHORUS

    At last, divine Cecilia came,
    Inventress of the vocal frame;
The sweet enthusiast, from her sacred store,
    Enlarg'd the former narrow bounds,
    And added length to solemn sounds,
With nature's mother wit, and arts unknown before.
    Let old Timotheus yield the prize,
    Or both divide the crown;

He rais'd a mortal to the skies;
She drew an angel down.

(1697)

ODE TO EVENING

William Collins

If aught of oaten stop, or pastoral song,
May hope, chaste Eve, to soothe thy modest ear,
    Like thy own solemn springs,
    Thy springs and dying gales,

O nymph reserved, while now the bright-haired sun
Sits in yon western tent, whose cloudy skirts,
    With brede ethereal wove,
    O'erhang his wavy bed:

Now air is hushed, save where the weak-eyed bat,
With short shrill shriek, flits by on leathern wing,
    Or where the beetle winds
    His small but sullen horn,

As oft he rises 'midst the twilight path,
Against the pilgrim borne in heedless hum:
    Now teach me, maid composed,
    To breathe some softened strain,

Whose numbers, stealing through thy dark'ning vale,
May not unseemly with its stillness suit,
    As, musing slow, I hail
    Thy genial loved return!

For when thy folding-star arising shows
His paly circlet, at his warning lamp
    The fragrant Hours, and elves
    Who slept in flowers the day,

And many a nymph who wreaths her brows with sedge,
And sheds the fresh'ning dew, and, lovelier still,
    The pensive Pleasures sweet,
    Prepare thy shadowy car.

Then lead, calm vot'ress, where some sheety lake
Cheers the lone heath, or some time-hallowed pile
 Or upland fallows gray
 Reflect its last cool gleam.

But when chill blust'ring winds, or driving rain,
Forbid my willing feet, be mine the hut
 That from the mountain's side
 Views wilds, and swelling floods,

And hamlets brown, and dim-discovered spires,
And hears their simple bell, and marks o'er all
 Thy dewy fingers draw
 The gradual dusky veil.

While Spring shall pour his show'rs, as oft he wont,
And bathe thy breathing tresses, meekest Eve;
 While Summer loves to sport
 Beneath thy ling'ring light;

While sallow Autumn fills thy lap with leaves;
Or Winter, yelling through the troublous air,
 Affrights thy shrinking train,
 And rudely rends thy robes;

So long, sure-found beneath the sylvan shed,
Shall Fancy, Friendship, Science, rose-lipped Health,
 Thy gentlest influence own,
 And hymn thy fav'rite name!

         (1746)

ODE

John Keats

[This ode is addressed to Beaumont and Fletcher, dramatists contemporary with Shakespeare.]

  Bards of Passion and of Mirth,
  Ye have left your souls on earth!

Have ye souls in heaven too,
Double-lived in regions new?
Yes, and those of heaven commune
With the spheres of sun and moon;
With the noise of fountains wond'rous,
And the parle of voices thund'rous;
With the whisper of heaven's trees
And one another, in soft ease
Seated on Elysian lawns
Browsed by none but Dian's fawns;
Underneath large blue-bells tented,
Where the daisies are rose-scented,
And the rose herself has got
Perfume which on earth is not;
Where the nightingale doth sing
Not a senseless, tranced thing,
But divine, melodious truth;
Philosophic numbers smooth;
Tales and golden histories
Of heaven and its mysteries.

Thus ye live on high, and then
On the earth ye live again;
And the souls ye left behind you
Teach us, here, the way to find you,
Where your other souls are joying
Never slumber'd, never cloying.
Here, your earth-born souls still speak
To mortals, of their little week;
Of their sorrows and delights;
Of their passions and their spites;
Of their glory and their shame;
What doth strengthen and what maim.
Thus ye teach us, every day,
Wisdom, though fled far away.

Bards of Passion and of Mirth,
Ye have left your souls on earth!
Ye have souls in heaven too,
Double-lived in regions new!

(1820)

E. P. ODE POUR L'ELECTION DE SON SEPULCHRE

from HUGH SELWYN MAUBERLEY

Ezra Pound

[The title translated: "Ezra Pound—an ode on the choice of his tomb."]

For three years, out of key with his time,
He strove to resuscitate the dead art
Of poetry; to maintain "the sublime"
In the old sense. Wrong from the start—

No, hardly, but seeing he had been born
In a half-savage country, out of date;
Bent resolutely on wringing lilies from the acorn;
Capaneus; trout for factitious bait;

Ἴδμεν γάρ τοι πάνθ', ὅσ' ἐνὶ Τροίη [7]
Caught in the unstopped ear;
Giving the rocks small lee-way
The chopped seas held him, therefore, that year.

His true Penelope was Flaubert,
He fished by obstinate isles;
Observed the elegance of Circe's hair
Rather than the mottoes on sun-dials.

Unaffected by "the march of events,"
He passed from men's memory in *l'an trentiesme
De son eage;* [8] the case presents
No adjunct to the Muses' diadem.

(1920)

[7] Translated: "For we know all the things which are in Troy."
[8] Altered from Villon: "In the thirtieth year of my life"; used to suggest the beginning of a reminiscence.

SUGGESTIONS FOR STUDY

1. *Formal Review*. (a) Turn back and reread pp. 76 and 86 from Chapter 4, and pp. 105-11 from Chapter 5. (b) Check over the poems in Chapters 4–6, and consider them as regards their poetic form. (c) Work out, in the form of an outline, a classification of the thirty-three poems in these three chapters.

2. *Sonnets of Sorts*. (a) Read the above sonnets without special regard to their poetic form, but in order to experience them as fully and richly as you can. (b) After rereading pp. 449-51 in the text, turn your attention more particularly to the poetic form of each of them—to the eye, to the ear, to the mind. (c) Sort them out, and then prepare a classified list of these sonnets under three headings: (1) Italian form, (2) Elizabethan form, (3) Other forms—noting the particular form of each of those in the last group.

3. *Form and Substance*. (a) Reread the sonnet by Francis Thompson thoughtfully. (b) Write a simple and unambiguous prose paraphrase of the meaning as you understand it. Add notes exploring various interpretations of the possibly ambiguous phrases. (c) Now study the relation of the thought structure to the metrical form of this sonnet.

4. *Scorn Not the Thought*. (a) Study Milton's sonnet "On His Being Arrived at the Age of Twenty-Three" and Keats' "When I Have Fears That I May Cease to Be," which, by the way, was written in his twenty-third year. (b) Note the poetic form of each and the relation of the thought structure to the metrical form. (c) Write a clear prose paraphrase of each of the two sonnets, and then proceed to a comparison of the attitudes of the two men.

5. *Gather Ye Odes*. All odes, of course, are not so entitled; and, as explained in the text, poems of different sorts have been called "odes." (a) Nevertheless, hunt out the odes in this volume with the help of the Title Index. (b) Sort them out according to the suggestions given earlier in this chapter (pp. 451-52). (c) Prepare an outline classification of these odes.

6. *Ode to Music*. (a) Study Dryden's "Alexander's Feast," and prepare to read it according to the directions given in Chapter 13. Or (b) prepare a "chorustration" of it and rehearse it with a verse choir. Or (c) read and reread the above odes by Collins and Keats, giving particular attention to the "music" of your poem-experiences.

7. *Praise in Our Time*. (a) Reconsider the occasional nature of Pindar's odes—each of them was written to honor a person or event—and

make a list of those occasions within the range of your own experience for which the choral reading of a specially composed ode would be appropriate. (b) If an idea comes to you for an ode that would befit some future occasion, you may wish to sketch it out. Perhaps you might work with one or two others in the preparation of such a poem with a view to its being presented by a verse choir.

8. *French Forms.* (a) Make a study of one of the so-called French forms mentioned in the text. (b) For the one chosen, look up the poetic form in the Glossarial Handbook. (c) Refer to standard encyclopedias and reference books on prosody to investigate the form further. (d) Find examples of the form in comprehensive anthologies. (e) Write a two-page paper on the subject.

9. *Sonneteering.* (a) As a controlled exercise in riming, the following Elizabethan sonnet has been printed with multiple-choice line endings. One of the bracketed words is the poet's; the others are not. In making your choices, be guided by the necessities of meter and thought as well as rime. (For the rime-scheme of the Elizabethan sonnet, see p. 450 in the text, or the Glossarial Handbook.) Work on scratch paper, and then copy off the completed sonnet.

DOWN IN A VALLEY—

William Browne

Down in a valley, by a forest's [*edge, side, flank,* or *path*],
  Near where the crystal Thames rolls on her [*way, course, waves, bank*],
I saw a mushroom stand in haughty [*wrath, mien, sedge, pride*],
  As if the lilies grew to be his [*slaves, prey, thanks, queen*].
The gentle daisy, with her silver [*leaves, trim, wreath, crown*],
  Worn in the breast of many a shepherd's [*hat, lass, smock, shirt*];
The humble violet, that lowly [*down, leaf, grieves, cried*]
  Salutes the gay nymphs as they trimly [*sat, pass, walk, flirt*];
These with a many more, methought, [*observed, forbid, complained, sighed*]
  That nature should those needless things [*produce, endear, deny, provide*],
Which not alone, the sun from others [*hid, gave, reserved, gained*],
  But turn it wholly to their proper [*sphere, grave, place, use*].
    I could not choose but grieve that nature [*said, 'lowed, made, say*]
    So glorious flowers to live in such a [*way, shade, bed, cloud*].

                                                              (*c. 1614*)

Or (b) choose one of the lyrics from the last chapter, or from an earlier chapter in the book—a lyric the thought of which you think would lend itself to treatment in the sonnet form. Then try your hand at writing a sonnet, in any one of the sonnet forms, that preserves the essential thought of the original lyric.

Or (c) take any one of the sonnets from this chapter and try to rewrite it in another one of the sonnet forms. Save as many of the lines as you can, and try to hold on to the poet's thought as you understand it. Much of the "poetry" of it will, of course, evaporate through this transformation; but you may come to a deeper appreciation of that which has been lost.

Or (d) you may now wish to undertake a translation of Ronsard's sonnet given on p. 219 or of another one of his sonnets, if you read French, or of a Petrarch sonnet if you read Italian. Or you may wish to make a Basic English version, in the form of an American sonnet, of one of the great sonnets of Milton or Wordsworth not given in this book.

Or (e) you may wish to write an original sonnet in one of the several sonnet forms, upon some poetic theme that comes to mind. Perhaps one of the sonnets in this chapter has struck in you a responsive chord, and has stirred your thoughtful feelings in such a way as to suggest another sonnet awaiting within you. Be patient as you work at it; sonneteering is a craft as well as an art.

18

RECURRENT THEMES—
THE ARTS AND SOCIAL JUSTICE

Call in the poems again; dump them from the formal pigeon-holes into a heap once more upon the table. For we shall now approach them from another point of view, look at them in a different light. As we sort them this time, with attention upon the *theme* of each poem, we shall find them falling into quite different groupings; and our understanding and appreciation of the separate poems will increase as we note what company they keep through the shifting hands of the game.

This matter of classification is by no means a purely academic one. It is one of our means of gaining control of the complex environment in which we live. We are constantly sorting over our experiences: "typing" our acquaintances, compartmentizing our notebooks, categorizing the widely assorted data of our daily reading. Consciously or unconsciously, the readers of poetry have always compared new poem-experiences with past ones, remembering the notably good (and the execrably bad!), comparing and contrasting divers works of the same broad type, various uses of the same particular form, different treatments of the same general theme. And the poets themselves, as well as their editors and the anthologists, have spent much headache upon the problem of classifying the poems that they are going to publish.

We are pretty well accustomed to the omnibus of poetry in which the arrangement is roughly chronological, but with the works of each poet kept together and the poets arranged in order of their birth. A few minutes in the library stacks, however, will unearth many collections in which the poems are differently classified—anthologies in which the poems are grouped according to the broad types, or limited to examples of one of them; or grouped with regard to the poetic forms, or restricted to certain of them; or grouped as to poetic themes, or some one of them; or grouped as to mood, literary period, historic style, or so as to illustrate the personality of the poets, or confined to one of them.

I. RECURRENT POETIC THEMES

The present chapter will concern itself with the sorting of poems according to their *themes*. And this would present no difficulty at all if there were more general agreement in the use of the term, or even if the categories were as well fixed in literary history as the so-called poetic forms. For what is one man's War poem, is another man's Immortality poem, and a third man's Consolation; but a poem in sonnet form is likely to be identified as a sonnet by most of those readers who have given some attention to poetic form. It is even more evident, however, when we start to classify poems in regard to their themes, that we are not really sorting printed-poems at all, but poem-experiences; and that with one "Ode to Evening" on the page, there will be as many different "Ode-to-Evening" experiences as there are readers.

The word *theme* is here used to name the particular subject-matter of the poem in relationship to the reader's previous observation of the life about him and within him. *Theme,* then, here refers to those broad generalizations and high-order abstractions which each person develops in dealing with the common experiences of life. Each of us was born, and each of us will die. And, though no one of us can report his own birth or his own death, everyone has had some personal observation at first or second hand of these elemental and universal facts of life, Birth and Death. So, too, every mature person has had some experience of what we shall call Body and of Mind, of Friendship and of Love, of Youth and of Age, of Nature and of Art, of Work and of Play, of War and of Justice, of Doubt and of Terror, of the Values of Life and of the Conduct of Life, of human Character and Actions; and most persons would add that they have had some experience of Faith and of God. This is not a complete list of *universal experiences,* but it will do to suggest the possible range of poetic themes.

But each of us has had *particular* experiences of many or most of these sorts. The birth of a particular niece or brother, and the death of sister or parent; the consciousness of one's own anatomy or physiology, and of the ability to solve quadratic equations; a special comradeship, and the mysterious pull of love; the song of a morning meadowlark, and the inspiration of the Lincoln Memorial; the grinding sweat at a lathe, and the thrill of a perfect serve at tennis; the shock of war deaths or atrocities, and the championing of the underprivileged; the unquenchable faith that things will be better, and the awesome reality of something beyond ourselves that makes for righteousness, etc. But each person has lived his own life only, though his knowledge of Life has been greatly increased through observation and listening to others, and through reading.

Now, the poet is a person gifted to an unusual degree with the capacity to give verbal expression to his unique experiences of life. But the only reason his verses are able to communicate these unique experiences to others is that they are not utterly unique experiences after all: they are in some measure like the experiences of each and every single reader. And the ease or difficulty that the reader may encounter in the reading of a particular poem will result from the obviousness or obscurity of the connection between the poet's experiences and his own.

The poet's experience, as interpreted by the reader, must prove to be similar enough to the reader's previous experience of life to be comprehended, and yet different enough to engage his attention. It is indeed a paradox: we understand a poem because it is universal, but we are interested in it because it is unique.

No set of thematic categories will satisfy very many readers of poetry. There will be pleasant disagreements in the process of sorting, and there will usually have to be a good-sized cubbyhole labeled Miscellaneous. But for most readers "What Lips My Lips Have Kissed" (p. 457) is a Love poem, and "Ode to Evening" (p. 468) is a Nature poem, and "A Poison Tree" (p. 438) is a poem on the Conduct of Life; "Fighting South of the Castle" (p. 435) is a War poem, and "Alexander's Feast" (p. 462) is an Art poem.

Nor is that sufficient, for of Love poems there are many subspecies, which will again be variously differentiated and named; and of the subspecies, a number of varieties. We have thus far encountered poems on the transience of love and on its permanence, on the inconstancy of lovers and on their faithfulness, on the sensual in love and its transcendence, and so on. Not that we would necessarily agree in phrasing the more particular theme of, say, Jonson's "Volpone's Song: to Celia" (p. 436) or of Spenser's "One Day I Wrote Her Name upon the Strand" (p. 453)!

To illustrate this approach to poetry, two general themes will be introduced and then illustrated by groups of poems.

2. TWO THEMES: THE ARTS AND SOCIAL JUSTICE

The first of these general themes is here called *the Arts*.[1] A good many artists—and amongst them poets—have turned their thoughts to the problems of their own and the other arts. In Chapter 3 several poems were presented which touch, in one way or another, the central problem of Beauty: Edna St. Vincent Millay's sonnet "Euclid alone has looked on Beauty bare" (p. 46) and Elsa Gidlow's "Twentieth Century Songs" (p. 52). Wallace Stevens' "Peter Quince at the Clavier" (p. 60) and Wordsworth's "I Wandered Lonely as a Cloud" (p. 59) also suggested definite notions of Beauty. But no one of these poems is as definitely upon the general theme of the Arts (or one of the arts) as are MacLeish's "Ars Poetica" (p. 89) and Wordsworth's "Nuns Fret Not—" (p. 87), which are both upon Poetry, and Dryden's "Song for St. Cecilia's Day" (p. 147) and Keats' "Ode on a Grecian Urn" (p. 152) which, each in its own way, are upon the arts of Music and Ceramics. And the last chapter contains some half dozen very different poems upon one aspect or another of the Arts. A closer study of these, and of the poems on this general theme that follow, will reveal a number of notable subspecies: poems upon Beauty and Truth, upon Intuition and Conscious Craft, upon the Master Artists, and upon many other more particular themes, such as the relation of Art to Life.

[1] See John Holmes, ed., *The Poet's Work*, Oxford Press, 1939, for a collection of the poets' own utterances upon their art.

This last has been the concern of many poets. The conflict between "art for art's sake" and "art for man's sake" as guiding philosophies for poets and other artists, belongs as much to our own time as it does to the nineteenth century; and, like most such controversies, it thrives best when the crucial terms remain undefined. If many poets have written poems about poetry, many others have turned their pens to the pleading of human causes.

Social Justice is a second general theme, then, that will be illustrated in the poems of this chapter. In addition to Clough's "Say Not the Struggle Nought Availeth" (p. 177) and Arnold's "The Last Word" (p. 186)—which may be interpreted as encouragement for the perennial and often downcast liberals—Shelley's "Sonnet: England in 1819" (p. 116) and Langston Hughes' "Proem" and "Epilogue" (p. 342) have given expression to particular aspects of this theme. Amongst the poems on the general theme of Social Justice, there are a good many subspecies: the Rights of Farmer and Worker, Child and Woman Labor, Wage and Bond Slavery, Discrimination and Degradation, etc. No inconsiderable number of the poets of the past two centuries have felt that, for them, art must be enlisted in the great causes of humanity, and they have written in behalf of human freedom and social justice.

The Arts

ANDREA DEL SARTO

CALLED "THE FAULTLESS PAINTER"

Robert Browning

[The scene is Andrea del Sarto's studio in Fiesole, a few miles from Florence and not far from Mount Morello. Other artists referred to are Raphael (the Urbinate), Michelangelo, and Leonardo da Vinci. Andrea had earlier painted for King Francis at his palace near Paris.]

But do not let us quarrel any more,
No, my Lucrezia; bear with me for once:
Sit down and all shall happen as you wish.
You turn your face, but does it bring your heart?
I'll work then for your friend's friend, never fear,
Treat his own subject after his own way,
Fix his own time, accept too his own price,
And shut the money into this small hand
When next it takes mine. Will it? tenderly?
Oh, I'll content him,—but tomorrow, Love!
I often am much wearier than you think,
This evening more than usual, and it seems
As if—forgive now—should you let me sit
Here by the window with your hand in mine
And look a half-hour forth on Fiesole,
Both of one mind, as married people use,
Quietly, quietly the evening through,
I might get up tomorrow to my work
Cheerful and fresh as ever. Let us try.
Tomorrow, how you shall be glad for this!
Your soft hand is a woman of itself,
And mine the man's bared breast she curls inside.
Don't count the time lost, neither; you must serve
For each of the five pictures we require:
It saves a model. So! keep looking so—
My serpentining beauty, rounds on rounds!
—How could you ever prick those perfect ears,
Even to put the pearl there! oh, so sweet—
My face, my moon, my everybody's moon,
Which everybody looks on and calls his,
And, I suppose, is looked on by in turn,
While she looks—no one's: very dear, no less.
You smile? why, there's my picture ready made,
There's what we painters call our harmony!
A common grayness silvers everything,—
All in a twilight, you and I alike
—You, at the point of your first pride in me
(That's gone you know),—but I, at every point;
My youth, my hope, my art, being all toned down
To yonder sober pleasant Fiesole.

There's the bell clinking from the chapel-top;
That length of convent-wall across the way
Holds the trees safer, huddled more inside;
The last monk leaves the garden; days decrease,
And autumn grows, autumn in everything.
Eh? the whole seems to fall into a shape
As if I saw alike my work and self
And all that I was born to be and do,
A twilight-piece. Love, we are in God's hand.
How strange now looks the life he makes us lead;
So free we seem, so fettered fast we are!
I feel he laid the fetter: let it lie!
This chamber for example—turn your head—
All that's behind us! You don't understand
Nor care to understand about my art,
But you can hear at least when people speak:
And that cartoon, the second from the door
—It is the thing, Love! so such thing should be—
Behold Madonna!—I am bold to say.
I can do with my pencil what I know,
What I see, what at bottom of my heart
I wish for, if I ever wish so deep—
Do easily, too—when I say, perfectly,
I do not boast, perhaps: yourself are judge,
Who listened to the Legate's talk last week,
And just as much they used to say in France.
At any rate 'tis easy, all of it!
No sketches first, no studies, that's long past:
I do what many dream of all their lives,
—Dream? strive to do, and agonize to do,
And fail in doing. I could count twenty such
On twice your fingers, and not leave this town,
Who strive—you don't know how the others strive
To paint a little thing like that you smeared
Carelessly passing with your robes afloat,—
Yet do much less, so much less, Someone says,
(I know his name, no matter)—so much less!
Well, less is more, Lucrezia: I am judged.
There burns a truer light of God in them,
In their vexed beating stuffed and stopped-up brain,

Heart, or whate'er else, than goes on to prompt
This low-pulsed forthright craftsman's hand of mine.
Their works drop groundward, but themselves, I know,
Reach many a time a heaven that's shut to me,
Enter and take their place there sure enough,
Though they come back and cannot tell the world.
My works are nearer heaven, but I sit here.
The sudden blood of these men! at a word—
Praise them, it boils, or blame them, it boils too.
I, painting from myself and to myself,
Know what I do, am unmoved by men's blame
Or their praise either. Somebody remarks
Morello's outline there is wrongly traced,
His hue mistaken; what of that? or else,
Rightly traced and well ordered; what of that?
Speak as they please, what does the mountain care?
Ah, but a man's reach should exceed his grasp,
Or what's a heaven for? All is silver-gray
Placid and perfect with my art: the worse!
I know both what I want and what might gain,
And yet how profitless to know, to sigh
"Had I been two, another and myself,
Our head would have o'erlooked the world!" No doubt.
Yonder's a work now, of that famous youth
The Urbinate who died five years ago.
('Tis copied, George Vasari sent it me.)
Well, I can fancy how he did it all,
Pouring his soul, with kings and popes to see,
Reaching, that heaven might so replenish him,
Above and through his art—for it gives way;
That arm is wrongly put—and there again—
A fault to pardon in the drawing's lines,
Its body, so to speak: its soul is right,
He means right—that, a child may understand.
Still, what an arm! and I could alter it:
But all the play, the insight and the stretch—
Out of me, out of me! And wherefore out?
Had you enjoined them on me, given me soul,
We might have risen to Rafael, I and you!
Nay, Love, you did give all I asked, I think—

More than I merit, yes, by many times.
But had you—oh, with the same perfect brow,
And perfect eyes, and more than perfect mouth,
And the low voice my soul hears, as a bird
The fowler's pipe, and follows to the snare—
Had you, with these the same, but brought a mind!
Some women do so. Had the mouth there urged
"God and the glory! never care for gain.
The present by the future, what is that?
Live for fame, side by side with Agnolo!
Rafael is waiting: up to God, all three!"
I might have done it for you. So it seems:
Perhaps not. All is as God overrules.
Beside, incentives come from the soul's self;
The rest avail not. Why do I need you?
What wife had Rafael, or has Agnolo?
In this world, who can do a thing, will not;
And who would do it, cannot, I perceive:
Yet the will's somewhat,—somewhat, too, the power—
And thus we half-men struggle. At the end,
God, I conclude, compensates, punishes.
'T is safer for me, if the award be strict,
That I am something underrated here,
Poor this long while, despised, to speak the truth.
I dared not, do you know, leave home all day,
For fear of chancing on the Paris lords.
The best is when they pass and look aside;
But they speak sometimes; I must bear it all.
Well may they speak! That Francis, that first time,
And that long festal year at Fontainebleau!
I surely then could sometimes leave the ground,
Put on the glory, Rafael's daily wear,
In that humane great monarch's golden look,—
One finger in his beard or twisted curl
Over his mouth's good mark that made the smile,
One arm about my shoulder, round my neck,
The jingle of his gold chain in my ear,
I painting proudly with his breath on me,
All his court round him, seeing with his eyes,
Such frank French eyes, and such a fire of souls

Profuse, my hand kept plying by those hearts,—
And, best of all, this, this, this face beyond,
This in the background, waiting on my work,
To crown the issue with a last reward!
A good time, was it not, my kingly days?
And had you not grown restless . . . but I know—
'T is done and past; 't was right, my instinct said;
Too live the life grew, golden and not gray,
And I'm the weak-eyed bat no sun should tempt
Out of the grange whose four walls make his world.
How could it end in any other way?
You called me, and I came home to your heart.
The triumph was—to reach and stay there; since
I reached it ere the triumph, what is lost?
Let my hands frame your face in your hair's gold,
You beautiful Lucrezia that are mine!
"Rafael did this, Andrea painted that;
The Roman's is the better when you pray,
But still the other's Virgin was his wife"—
Men will excuse me. I am glad to judge
Both pictures in your presence; clearer grows
My better fortune, I resolve to think.
For, do you know, Lucrezia, as God lives,
Said one day Agnolo, his very self,
To Rafael . . . I have known it all these years . . .
(When the young man was flaming out his thoughts
Upon a palace-wall for Rome to see,
Too lifted up in heart because of it)
"Friend, there's a certain sorry little scrub
Goes up and down our Florence, none cares how,
Who, were he set to plan and execute
As you are, pricked on by your popes and kings,
Would bring the sweat into that brow of yours!"
To Rafael's!—And indeed the arm is wrong.
I hardly dare . . . yet, only you to see,
Give the chalk here—quick, thus the line should go!
Ay, but the soul! he's Rafael! rub it out!
Still, all I care for, if he spoke the truth,
(What he? why, who but Michel Agnolo?
Do you forget already words like those?)

If really there was such a chance, so lost,—
Is, whether you're—not grateful—but more pleased.
Well, let me think so. And you smile indeed!
This hour has been an hour! Another smile?
If you would sit thus by me every night
I should work better, do you comprehend?
I mean that I should earn more, give you more.
See it is settled dusk now; there's a star;
Morello's gone, the watch-lights show the wall,
The cue-owls speak the name we call them by.
Come from the window, love,—come in, at last,
Inside the melancholy little house
We built to be so gay with. God is just.
King Francis may forgive me: oft at nights
When I look up from painting, eyes tired out,
The walls become illumined, brick from brick
Distinct, instead of mortar, fierce bright gold,
That gold of his I did cement them with!
Let us but love each other. Must you go?
That Cousin here again? he waits outside?
Must see you—you, and not with me? Those loans?
More gaming debts to pay? you smiled for that?
Well, let smiles buy me! have you more to spend?
While hand and eye and something of a heart
Are left me, work's my ware, and what's it worth?
I'll pay my fancy. Only let me sit
The gray remainder of the evening out,
Idle, you call it, and muse perfectly
How I could paint, were I but back in France,
One picture, just one more—the Virgin's face,
Not yours this time! I want you at my side
To hear them—that is, Michel Agnolo—
Judge all I do and tell you of its worth.
Will you? Tomorrow, satisfy your friend.
I take the subjects for his corridor,
Finish the portrait out of hand—there, there,
And throw him in another thing or two
If he demurs; the whole should prove enough
To pay for this same Cousin's freak. Beside,
What's better and what's all I care about,

Get you the thirteen scudi for the ruff!
Love, does that please you? Ah, but what does he,
The Cousin! what does he to please you more?

I am grown peaceful as old age tonight.
I regret little, I would change still less.
Since there my past life lies, why alter it?
The very wrong to Francis!—it is true
I took his coin, was tempted and complied,
And built this house and sinned, and all is said.
My father and my mother died of want.
Well, had I riches of my own? you see
How one gets rich! Let each one bear his lot.
They were born poor, lived poor, and poor they died:
And I have labored somewhat in my time
And not been paid profusely. Some good son
Paint my two hundred pictures—let him try!
No doubt, there's something strikes a balance. Yes,
You loved me quite enough, it seems tonight.
This must suffice me here. What would one have?
In heaven, perhaps, new chances, one more chance—
Four great walls in the New Jerusalem,
Meted on each side by the angel's reed,
For Leonard, Rafael, Agnolo and me
To cover—the three first without a wife,
While I have mine! So—still they overcome
Because there's still Lucrezia,—as I choose.

Again the Cousin's whistle! Go, my Love.
(1855)

ARS VICTRIX

IMITATED FROM THÉOPHILE GAUTIER
Austin Dobson

[The Latin title translated: "Art triumphant," or "craftsmanship en-
dures." Gautier's poem referred to is called "L'Art."]

Yes; when the ways oppose—
When the hard means rebel,

Fairer the work out-grows,—
   More potent far the spell.

O POET, then, forbear
   The loosely-sandalled verse,
Choose rather thou to wear
   The buskin—strait and terse;

Leave to the tyro's hand
   The limp and shapeless style;
See that thy form demand
   The labor of the file.

SCULPTOR, do thou discard
   The yielding clay,—consign
To Paros marble hard
   The beauty of thy line;—

Model thy Satyr's face
   For bronze of Syracuse;
In the veined agate trace
   The profile of thy Muse.

PAINTER, that still must mix
   But transient tints anew,
Thou in the furnace fix
   The firm enamel's hue;

Let the smooth tile receive
   Thy dove-drawn Erycine;
Thy Sirens blue at eve
   Coiled in a wash of wine.

All passes. ART alone
   Enduring stays to us;
The Bust out-lasts the throne,—
   The Coin, Tiberius;

Even the gods must go;
   Only the lofty Rhyme

Not countless years o'erthrow,—
Not long array of time.

Paint, chisel, then, or write;
But, that the work surpass,
With the hard fashion fight,—
With the resisting mass.

(*1876*)

ACCIDENT IN ART
Richard Hovey

What painter has not with a careless smutch
Accomplished his despair?—one touch revealing
All he had put of life, thought, vigor, feeling,
Into the canvas that without that touch
Showed of his love and labor just so much
Raw pigment, scarce a scrap of soul concealing!
What poet has not found his spirit kneeling
A-sudden at the sound of such or such
Strange verses staring from his manuscript,
Written he knows not how, but which will sound
Like trumpets down the years? So Accident
Itself unmasks the likeness of Intent,
And even in blind Chance's darkest crypt
The shrine-lamp of God's purposing is found.

(*bef. 1900*)

ISRAFEL
Edgar Allan Poe

AND THE ANGEL ISRAFEL, WHOSE HEART-STRINGS ARE A LUTE,
AND WHO HAS THE SWEETEST VOICE OF ALL GOD'S CREATURES.
—KORAN.

In Heaven a spirit doth dwell
    "Whose heart-strings are a lute;"

None sing so wildly well
As the angel Israfel,
And the giddy stars (so legends tell)
Ceasing their hymns, attend the spell
  Of his voice, all mute.

Tottering above
  In her highest noon,
  The enamoured moon
Blushes with love,
  While, to listen, the red levin
  (With the rapid Pleiads, even,
  Which were seven,)
  Pauses in Heaven.

And they say (the starry choir
  And the other listening things)
That Israfeli's fire
Is owing to that lyre
  By which he sits and sings—
The trembling living wire
  Of those unusual strings.

But the skies that angel trod,
  Where deep thoughts are a duty—
Where Love's a grown-up God—
  Where the Houri glances are
Imbued with all the beauty
  Which we worship in a star.

Therefore thou art not wrong,
  Israfeli, who despisest
An unimpassioned song;
To thee the laurels belong,
  Best bard, because the wisest!
Merrily live, and long!

The ecstasies above
  With thy burning measures suit—
Thy grief, thy joy, thy hate, thy love,

With the fervour of thy lute—
Well may the stars be mute!

Yes, Heaven is thine; but this
　Is a world of sweets and sours;
　　Our flowers are merely—flowers,
And the shadow of thy perfect bliss
　Is the sunshine of ours.

If I could dwell
Where Israfel
　Hath dwelt, and he where I,
He might not sing so wildly well
　A mortal melody,
While a bolder note than this might swell
　From my lyre within the sky.

(1831)

I DIED FOR BEAUTY

Emily Dickinson

I died for beauty, but was scarce
　Adjusted in the tomb,
When one who died for truth was lain
　In an adjoining room.

He questioned softly why I failed?
　"For beauty," I replied.
"And I for truth,—the two are one;
　We brethren are," he said.

And so, as kinsmen met a night,
　We talked between the rooms,
Until the moss had reached our lips
　And covered up our names.

(*c.* 1890)

POETRY

Marianne Moore

I too, dislike it: there are things that are important
        beyond all this fiddle.
  Reading it, however, with a perfect contempt for it, one
      discovers in
  it after all, a place for the genuine.
     Hands that can grasp, eyes
     that can dilate, hair that can rise
       if it must, these things are important not because a

high sounding interpretation can be put upon them
        but because they are
  useful. When they become so derivative
    as to become unintelligible,
  the same thing may be said for all of us, that we
    do not admire what
    we cannot understand: the bat,
      holding on upside down or in quest of something to

eat, elephants pushing, a wild horse taking a roll,
        a tireless wolf under
  a tree, the immovable critic twitching his skin
     like a horse that feels a flea, the base-
  ball fan, the statistician—
    nor is it valid
      to discriminate against "business documents and

school-books"; all these phenomena are important.
       One must make a distinction
  however: when dragged into prominence by half-poets,
     the result is not poetry,
  nor till the poets among us can be
    "literalists of
    the imagination"—above
      insolence and triviality and can present

for inspection, imaginary gardens with real toads in
  them, shall we have
 it. In the meantime, if you demand on the one hand,
 the raw material of poetry in
  all its rawness and
  that which is on the other hand
   genuine, then you are interested in poetry.
           (1921)

Social Justice

from THE DESERTED VILLAGE
Oliver Goldsmith

[The Enclosure Acts of the later eighteenth century were depriving
the British peasants of their means of livelihood, driving them to the
cities and to emigration. The deserted village that Goldsmith had in
mind, and which he called "sweet Auburn," may have been the Irish
village in which he lived as a youth.]

 Sweet smiling village, loveliest of the lawn,
 Thy sports are fled, and all thy charms withdrawn;
 Amidst thy bowers the tyrant's hand is seen,
 And Desolation saddens all thy green:
 One only master grasps the whole domain,
 And half a tillage stints thy smiling plain.
 No more thy glassy brook reflects the day,
 But, choked with sedges, works its weedy way;
 Along thy glades, a solitary guest,
 The hollow-sounding bittern guards its nest:
 Amidst thy desert walks the lapwing flies,
 And tires their echoes with unvaried cries:
 Sunk are thy bowers in shapeless ruin all,
 And the long grass o'ertops the moldering wall;

And, trembling, shrinking from the spoiler's hand,
Far, far away thy children leave the land.
    Ill fares the land, to hastening ills a prey,
Where wealth accumulates, and men decay.
Princes and lords may flourish, or may fade;
A breath can make them, as a breath has made:
But a bold peasantry, their country's pride,
When once destroyed, can never be supplied.
    A time there was, ere England's griefs began,
When every rood of ground maintained its man;
For him light Labor spread her wholesome store,
Just gave what life required, but gave no more:
His best companions, Innocence and Health;
And his best riches, ignorance of wealth.
    But times are altered: Trade's unfeeling train
Usurp the land, and dispossess the swain;
Along the lawn, where scattered hamlets rose,
Unwieldy wealth and cumbrous pomp repose;
And every want to opulence allied,
And every pang that folly pays to pride.
Those gentle hours that plenty bade to bloom,
Those calm desires that asked but little room,
Those healthful sports that graced the peaceful scene,
Lived in each look, and brightened all the green—
These, far departing, seek a kinder shore,
And rural mirth and manners are no more. . . .
    Ye friends to truth, ye statesmen, who survey
The rich man's joys increase, the poor's decay,
'Tis yours to judge how wide the limits stand
Between a splendid and a happy land.
Proud swells the tide with loads of freighted ore,
And shouting Folly hails them from her shore;
Hoards, e'en beyond the miser's wish, abound,
And rich men flock from all the world around.
Yet count our gains. This wealth is but a name
That leaves our useful products still the same.
Not so the loss. The man of wealth and pride
Takes up a space that many poor supplied;
Space for his lake, his park's extended bounds,
Space for his horses, equipage, and hounds;

The robe that wraps his limbs in silken sloth,
Has robbed the neighboring fields of half their growth;
His seat, where solitary sports are seen,
Indignant spurns the cottage from the green;
Around the world each needful product flies,
For all the luxuries the world supplies;
While thus the land, adorned for pleasure all,
In barren splendor feebly waits the fall. . . .

Thus fares the land by luxury betrayed;
In nature's simplest charms at first arrayed;—
But verging to decline, its splendors rise,
Its vistas strike, its palaces surprise;
While, scourged by famine, from the smiling land
The mournful peasant leads his humble band;
And while he sinks, without one arm to save,
The country blooms—a garden and a grave!

Where, then, ah! where shall poverty reside,
To 'scape the pressure of contiguous pride?
If to some common's fenceless limits strayed,
He drives his flock to pick the scanty blade,
Those fenceless fields the sons of wealth divide,
And e'en the bare-worn common is denied.

If to the city sped—what waits him there?
To see profusion that he must not share;
To see ten thousand baneful arts combined
To pamper luxury and thin mankind;
To see those joys the sons of pleasure know
Extorted from his fellow-creature's woe:
Here while the courtier glitters in brocade,
There the pale artist plies the sickly trade;
Here while the proud their long-drawn pomps display,
There the black gibbet glooms beside the way:
The dome where Pleasure holds her midnight reign,
Here, richly decked, admits the gorgeous train;
Tumultuous grandeur crowds the blazing square,
The rattling chariots clash, the torches glare.
Sure scenes like these no troubles e'er annoy!
Sure these denote one universal joy!— . . .

E'en now the devastation is begun,
And half the business of destruction done;

E'en now, methinks, as pondering here I stand,
I see the rural Virtues leave the land.
Down where yon anchoring vessel spreads the sail
That idly waiting flaps with every gale,
Downward they move, a melancholy band,
Pass from the shore, and darken all the strand;
Contented Toil, and hospitable Care,
And kind connubial Tenderness are there;
And Piety with wishes placed above,
And steady Loyalty, and faithful Love.

(1770)

THE SONG OF THE SHIRT
Thomas Hood

[This was published in the same year as Elizabeth Barrett Browning's humanitarian poem, "The Cry of the Children."]

With fingers weary and worn,
  With eyelids heavy and red,
A woman sat, in unwomanly rags,
  Plying her needle and thread—
Stitch! stitch! stitch!
  In poverty, hunger, and dirt,
And still with a voice of dolorous pitch
  She sang the "Song of the Shirt."

"Work! work! work!
  While the cock is crowing aloof!
And work—work—work,
  Till the stars shine through the roof!
It's Oh! to be a slave
  Along with the barbarous Turk,
Where woman has never a soul to save,
  If this is Christian work.

"Work—work—work,
  Till the brain begins to swim;
Work—work—work,

Till the eyes are heavy and dim!
Seam, and gusset, and band,
   Band, and gusset, and seam,
Till over the buttons I fall asleep,
   And sew them on in a dream!

"Oh, Men, with Sisters dear!
   Oh, Men, with Mothers and Wives!
It is not linen you're wearing out
   But human creatures' lives!
Stitch—stitch—stitch,
   In poverty, hunger, and dirt,
Sewing at once, with a double thread,
   A Shroud as well as a Shirt.

"But why do I talk of Death?
   That Phantom of grisly bone,
I hardly fear its terrible shape,
   It seems so like my own—
It seems so like my own,
   Because of the fasts I keep;
Oh, God, that bread should be so dear,
   And flesh and blood so cheap!

"Work—work—work!
   My labor never flags;
And what are its wages? A bed of straw,
   A crust of bread—and rags.
That shattered roof—this naked floor—
   A table—a broken chair—
And a wall so blank, my shadow I thank
   For sometimes falling there!

"Work—work—work!
   From weary chime to chime,
Work—work—work,
   As prisoners work for crime!
Band, and gusset, and seam,
   Seam, and gusset, and band,
Till the heart is sick, and the brain benumbed,
   As well as the weary hand.

"Work—work—work,
  In the dull December light,
And work—work—work,
  When the weather is warm and bright—
While underneath the eaves
  The brooding swallows cling
As if to show me their sunny backs
  And twit me with the spring.

"Oh! but to breathe the breath
  Of the cowslip and primrose sweet—
With the sky above my head,
  And the grass beneath my feet;
For only one short hour
  To feel as I used to feel,
Before I knew the woes of want
  And the walk that costs a meal.

"Oh! but for one short hour!
  A respite however brief!
No blessèd leisure for Love or Hope,
  But only time for Grief!
A little weeping would ease my heart,
  But in their briny bed
My tears must stop, for every drop
  Hinders needle and thread!"

With fingers weary and worn,
  With eyelids heavy and red,
A woman sat, in unwomanly rags,
  Plying her needle and thread—
Stitch! stitch! stitch!
  In poverty, hunger, and dirt,
And still with a voice of dolorous pitch,—
  Would that its tone could reach the Rich!—
  She sang this "Song of the Shirt!"

                              (1843)

THE CHRISTIAN SLAVE

John Greenleaf Whittier

[This abolitionist poem was inspired by "a description of a slave auction at New Orleans, at which the auctioneer recommended the woman on the stand as *'a good Christian!'* "]

A CHRISTIAN! going, gone!
Who bids for God's own image?—for his grace,
Which that poor victim of the marketplace
    Hath in her suffering won?

My God! can such things be?
Hast thou not said that whatsoe'er is done
Unto thy weakest and thy humblest one
    Is even done to thee?

In that sad victim, then,
Child of thy pitying love, I see thee stand,—
Once more the jest-word of a mocking band,
    Bound, sold, and scourged again!

A Christian up for sale!
Wet with her blood your whips, o'ertask her frame,
Make her life loathsome with your wrong and shame,
    Her patience shall not fail!

A heathen hand might deal
Back on your heads the gathered wrong of years:
But her low, broken prayer and nightly tears,
    Ye neither heed nor feel.

Con well thy lesson o'er,
Thou *prudent* teacher,—tell the toiling slave
No dangerous tale of Him who came to save
    The outcast and the poor.

But wisely shut the ray
Of God's free Gospel from her simple heart,

And to her darkened mind alone impart
One stern command,—OBEY!

So shalt thou deftly raise
The market price of human flesh; and while
On thee, their pampered guest, the planters smile,
Thy church shall praise.

Grave, reverend men shall tell
From Northern pulpits how thy work was blest,
While in that vile South Sodom first and best,
Thy poor disciples sell.

O, shame! the Moslem thrall,
Who, with his master, to the Prophet kneels,
While turning to the sacred Kebla feels
His fetters break and fall.

Cheers for the turbaned Bey
Of robber-peopled Tunis! he hath torn
The dark slave-dungeons open, and hath borne
Their inmates into day:

But our poor slave in vain
Turns to the Christian shrine his aching eyes,—
Its rites will only swell his market price,
And rivet on his chain.

God of all right! how long
Shall priestly robbers at thine altar stand,
Lifting in prayer to thee, the bloody hand
And haughty brow of wrong?

O, from the fields of cane,
From the low rice-swamp, from the trader's cell,—
From the black slave-ship's foul and loathsome hell,
And coffle's weary chain,—

Hoarse, horrible, and strong,
Rises to Heaven that agonizing cry,
Filling the arches of the hollow sky,
How LONG, O GOD, HOW LONG?

(1846)

BROTHERS
James Weldon Johnson

See! There he stands; not brave, but with an air
Of sullen stupor. Mark him well! Is he
Not more like brute than man? Look in his eye!
No light is there; none, save the glint that shines
In the now glaring, and now shifting orbs
Of some wild animal caught in the hunter's trap.

How came this beast in human shape and form?
Speak, man!—We call you man because you wear
His shape—How are you thus? Are you not from
That docile, child-like, tender-hearted race
Which we have known three centuries? Not from
That more than faithful race which through three wars
Fed our dear wives and nursed our helpless babes
Without a single breach of trust? Speak out!

I am, and am not.

Then who, why are you?

I am a thing not new, I am as old
As human nature. I am that which lurks,
Ready to spring whenever a bar is loosed;
The ancient trait which fights incessantly
Against restraint, balks at the upward climb;
The weight forever seeking to obey
The law of downward pull—and I am more:
The bitter fruit am I of planted seed;
The resultant, the inevitable end
Of evil forces and the powers of wrong.

Lessons in degradation, taught and learned,
The memories of cruel sights and deeds,
The pent-up bitterness, the unspent hate
Filtered through fifteen generations have

Sprung up and found in me sporadic life.
In me the muttered curse of dying men,
On me the stain of conquered women, and
Consuming me the fearful fires of lust,
Lit long ago, by other hands than mine.
In me the down-crushed spirit, the hurled-back prayers
Of wretches now long dead—their dire bequests—
In me the echo of the stifled cry
Of children for their bartered mothers' breasts.

    I claim no race, no race claims me; I am
No more than human dregs; degenerate;
The monstrous offspring of the monster, Sin;
I am—just what I am. . . . The race that fed
Your wives and nursed your babes would do the same
Today, but I—

                Enough, the brute must die!
Quick! Chain him to that oak! It will resist
The fire much longer than this slender pine.
Now bring the fuel! Pile it 'round him! Wait!
Pile not so fast or high! or we shall lose
The agony and terror in his face.

And now the torch! Good fuel that! the flames
Already leap head-high. Ha! hear that shriek!
And there's another! Wilder than the first.
Fetch water! Water! Pour a little on
The fire, lest it should burn too fast. Hold so!
Now let it slowly blaze again. See there!
He squirms! He groans! His eyes bulge wildly out,
Searching around in vain appeal for help!
Another shriek, the last! Watch how the flesh
Grows crisp and hangs till, turned to ash, it sifts
Down through the coils of chain that hold erect
The ghastly frame against the bark-scorched tree.

    Stop! to each man no more than one man's share.
You take that bone, and you this tooth; the chain—

Let us divide its links; this skull, of course,
In fair division, to the leader comes.

And now his fiendish crime has been avenged;
Let us back to our wives and children.—Say,
What did he mean by those last muttered words,
"Brothers in spirit, brothers in deed are we"?

(1935)

TOM MOONEY
William Ellery Leonard

[Thomas Mooney, a San Francisco labor leader, was indicted, tried, and convicted for the Preparedness Parade bombing of July 22, 1916, which killed six people. His defense, and the efforts to secure his reprieve and then pardon, became one of the notable liberal causes for a generation. Following the election of Culbert L. Olsen as governor of California in 1938, Tom Mooney was pardoned.]

1

Tom Mooney sits behind a grating,
Beside a corridor. (He's waiting.)
Long since he picked or peeled or bit away
The last white callus from his palms, they say.
The crick is gone from out his back;
And all the grease and grime
Gone from each finger-nail and every knuckle-crack.
(And that took time.)

2

Tom Mooney breathes behind a grating,
Beside a corridor. (He's waiting.)
The Gold-men from ten cities hear in sleep
Tom Mooney breathing—for he breathes so deep.
The Gold-men from ten cities rise from bed
To make a brass crown for Tom Mooney's head;
They gather round great oaken desks—each twists
Two copper bracelets for Tom Mooney's wrists.

And down sky-scraper basements (all their own)
They forge the spikes for his galvanic throne.
The Gold-men love the jests of old Misrule—
At ease at last, they'll laugh their fill;
They'll deck Tom Mooney king, they will—
King over knave and fool.
And from enameled doors of rearward office-vaults,
Lettered in gold with names that never crock,
They will draw back the triple iron bolts,
Then scatter from the ridges of their roofs
The affidavits of their paper-proofs
Of pallid Tomfool's low and lubber stock.

3

Tom Mooney thinks behind a grating,
Beside a corridor. (He's waiting.)
(Tom Mooney free was but a laboring man;
Tom Mooney jailed's the Thinker of Rodin.)
The Workers in ten nations now have caught
The roll and rhythm of Tom Mooney's thought—
By that earth-girdling S.O.S.,
The subtle and immortal wireless
Of Man's strong justice in distress.
The Workers in ten nations think and plan:
The pick-ax little Naples man,
The rice-swamp coolies in Japan
(No longer mere embroidery on a screen),
The crowds that swarm from factory gates,
At yellow dusks with all their hates,
In Ireland, Austria, Argentine,
In England, France, and Russia far
(That slew a Czar),—
Or where the Teutons lately rent
The Iron Cross (on finding what it meant);
At yellow dusks with all their hates
From fiery shops or gas-choked mines,
From round-house, mill, or lumber-pines,
In the broad belt of these United States.
The Workers, like the Gold-men, plan and wake,—
What bodes their waking?

The Workers, like the Gold-men, something make,—
What are they making?—
The Gold-men answer often—
"They make Tom Mooney's coffin."

4

Tom Mooney talks behind a grating,
Beside a corridor. (He's waiting.)
You cannot get quite near
Against the bars to lay your ear;
You find the light too dim
To spell the lips of him.
But, like a beast's within a zoo
(That was of old a god to savage clans),
His body shakes at you—
A beast's, a god's, a man's!
And from its ponderous, ancient rhythmic shaking
Ye'll guess what 'tis the workers now are making.
They make for times to come
From times of old—how old!—
From sweat, from blood, from hunger, and from tears,
From scraps of hope (conserved through bitter years
Despite the might and mockery of gold),
They make, these haggard men, a bomb,—
These haggard men with shawl-wives dumb
And pinched-faced children cold,
Descendants of the oldest, earth-born stock,
Gnarled brothers of the surf, the ice, the fire, the rock,
Gray wolf and gaunt storm-bird.
They make a bomb more fierce than dynamite,—
They weld a Word.
And on the awful night
The Gold-men set Tom Mooney grinning
(If such an hour shall be in truth's despite)
They'll loose the places of much underpinning
In more than ten big cities, left and right.

(1920)

CHICAGO IDYLL

E. Merrill Root

A knife within his hand he stood
   And struck his blow by rote:
All day, for six days in the week,
   He waded blood, and smote
Again . . . again . . . his knife into
   A tied hog's squealing throat.

Bare to the waist, with clot and clog
   Of steaming sweat and blood,
He watched the line of chain-caught hogs
   Flow by in screaming flood;
And slit their red life out, that caked
   His shoes like crimson mud.

Strange flies within an iron web,
   The writhing hogs clicked by—
One after one, in clockwork hell,
   Across a plaster sky—
Their blood-shot, little, bulging eyes
   Aware that they must die.

One hind leg noosed within a loop
   Of chain, head down they hung;
They writhed and squealed, they squealed and writhed,
   As down the room they swung,
Their damp snouts wrinkling at the smell
   Of blood from slit throats flung . . .

Of blood from throats wherein he thrust
   His blade like frozen fire . . .
He slit the soft and heavy flesh
   All day, and did not tire—
A wooden executioner
   Whose arms were twitched by wire.

He thrust the blade into their flesh
  And when he drew it out
The life came with it, choked and thick
  As from a gutter-spout;
Screams spattered into gasps, his hands
  Were red with froth and gout . . .

Thus for ten bloody years he stood
  And slaughtered hogs by rote:
Ten years—ten crimson stolid years—
  He waded blood, and smote
(Each day for six days in the week)
  His blade into a throat.

    .   .   .   .   .   .

And then one day a something clicked
  Within his heavy brain:
The Life that is not a machine,
  From every sullen vein
And artery, rose to wreak abroad
  On others its own pain.

The clockwork nightmare flood of hogs
  Still clicked its shrieking way;
The river of blood dashed on the stones
  Its steaming froth and spray:
The slaughtering went on, but he
  Took ghastly holiday.

He stood beside a struggling hog—
  His knife was at its neck;
But there the razor-whetted blade
  Found strange and sudden check;
And the tied hog went squealing by,
  Its throat without a fleck.

He stood, the knife within his hand,
  He stood and seemed to brood;
And then he turned—still knife in hand—
  From death's mere interlude . . .
And his knife (still hot with blood of hogs)
  Found fit vicissitude.

He thrust it with a practised ease
   And a swift blow's soft jar
Straight thru a fellow-workman's throat
   And slit the jugular
And watched him sob his red life out
   In ways familiar.

Then knife in hand he ran amok . . .
   Slit, slit . . . before they knew,
Men felt the hot steel in their flesh,
   And then the blood was thru . . .
And then they stiffened on the floor—
   Heads hideously askew . . .

Before the dazed and cursing men
   Could scatter from his rush,
He struck three times and from three throats
   He saw the hot life gush . . .
And then an axe beat in his skull
   Against the brain's grey plush . . .

Even in that place of blood and doom,
   Where death was a cliché,
Men turned aside—and "Jesus Christ!"
   Was all that they could say.
And then the hogs moved on once more
   Upon their screaming way.

(1929)

SUGGESTIONS FOR STUDY

1. *Faultless Art.* (a) Study Browning's "Andrea del Sarto" silently, and then read it aloud a time or two. (To what broad type of poetry does it belong? to what sub-type? What is its poetic form?) (b) Draw a floor-plan or sketch of Andrea's studio, indicating the relative position of the objects to which he refers. (c) Write a summary of Andrea's life-story, narrating the incidents in chronological order. (d) According to his own witness, what are his artistic skills and limitations? What do you think was his theory of creative excellence?

2. *Craft or Chance.* (a) Read Dobson's "Ars Victrix" and Hovey's "Accident in Art" thoughtfully. (To what type and sub-type does each

belong? What is the poetic form of each?) (b) Consider in detail the contrast in art theory and the relation of the thought of these two poems to "Andrea del Sarto."

3. *Poetry for the Sake of What?* (a) Read Edgar Allan Poe's "Israfel," Emily Dickinson's "I Died for Beauty," and Marianne Moore's "Poetry." (b) What do you think is the over-all thought of each of these poems? (c) Consider these three thoughts about poetry in relation to each other, and in relation to the general thought of the Browning, Dobson, and Hovey poems. (d) Now reread MacLeish's "Ars Poetica" (p. 89) and Wordsworth's "Nuns Fret Not—" (p. 87) and "Scorn Not the Sonnet—" (p. 460); and compare their over-all meanings, as you interpret them, with those of the poems in this chapter.

4. *The Arts Theme.* (a) Glance back over all the poems on the general theme of "the Arts" that are listed in the text as being included so far in this book. (b) Work out a classification of them, setting up no more than six subspecies. (c) Present your sorting of them in the form of an outline.

5. *Liberal Causes.* (a) Read the half-dozen poems above printed under the heading "Social Justice." (b) What particular social problem is presented by each of them? (c) To what extent are the liberal social causes partly or completely won to which these poems give expression?

6. *Propaganda and/or poetry.* (a) Develop a working definition of the term "propaganda" that might be useful in considering the above poems. (The word "poetry" has been used in this book to name "a poem, or poems, or part of a poem"—*poem* in the sense of "printed-poem and/or poem-experience"—and all poems taken collectively are here called *Poetry,* which was defined as that branch of Literature consisting of non-dramatic literary works in verse; and *Literature* was defined as that one of the Fine Arts whose medium is written language.) (b) Do you feel that poetry and propaganda are incompatible? If so, why? If not, why not? (c) Which ones of the above six works provide you with what you consider "good" poem-experiences? Are any of them poems that you would consider to be, or to have been, propaganda in a social cause? (d) How about "Don't Go In" (p. 250) and "The Bower of Bliss" from *The Faerie Queene* (p. 251)? Shelley's "Sonnet: England in 1819" (p. 116) and "Ode to the West Wind" (p. 133)?

7. *The Cause Before the Art.* (a) Investigate the stir that was caused in 1933 by the murals of the eminent Mexican painter Diego Rivera commissioned for Rockefeller Center, and then removed by the owners

because of their social philosophy. Artists, poets, journalists joined in the critical fray that ensued. Find several accounts of the murals and the discussion of them in the magazines of the time. (b) Now find a copy of Archibald MacLeish's poem *Frescoes for Mr. Rockefeller's City* (it has been reprinted a number of times, and there is a recording of it), and study its bearing on the controversy. (c) Consider further the relationship of the Arts and the Social Cause.

8. *Thematic Variation.* (a) Work out a six-category scheme for sorting poems from the viewpoint of their themes—that is, a statement of six general and all-inclusive poetic themes. (b) Now proceed to review the poems in Chapters 7–9, and to sort them out according to this six-fold scheme; and present your classification in the form of an outline. (c) For which ones of your categories do you not find examples in the designated chapters?

9. *Prose-poem.* (a) The poems on the theme of Social Justice are trumpet calls that rally men and women to the colors either of the Cause or of the Status-Quo. You may feel stirred rather violently one way or another by one of the poems in this chapter, and you might give expression to your thoughts and feelings by writing some sort of a poem in verse or in free verse or in the form of a prose-poem. (b) Or you may wish to read up on one of the *causes célèbres* of recent decades—the Mooney Case (1916-1939), the Sacco-Vanzetti Case (1919-1927), the Scottsboro Case (1931-37). Perhaps you may find in your reaction to one of these cases, and the Causes they came to symbolize, the inspiration for writing some sort of a comment in verse or prose. (c) Or you may have some strong feeling about art, or the art and/or craft of poetry, that will get you under way in the writing of a poem.

19

DIVERS MOODS—COMIC AND SATIRIC

This chapter, discussing and illustrating divers poetic *moods,* is sufficiently related to the preceding chapter on the recurring poetic *themes* to warrant some comparisons and contrasts in an opening paragraph. They both represent approaches to poetry that are less well-defined than, for instance, poetic form; and for neither of them is there a systematic classification fixed by critical sanction with a generally recognized vocabulary. Yet they both name points of view that are common enough, and important to any fully rounded consideration of Poetry.

The word *theme* has been used to refer to the general subject-matter of the poem; the word *mood* will be used to name the general attitude toward the subject-matter. In determining the *theme* of a poem, the reader pursues particularly the sense phase of the meaning; in determining the *mood,* he gives especial attention to the tone, feeling, and intention.[1] The theme of "The Christian Slave" (p. 498), for instance, was said to be Social Justice—more particularly, the injustice of bond slavery. The mood—the poet's temper of mind and feeling—is that of invective, of bitter denunciation, of devastating irony! The theme of "Israfel" (p. 488), to take another example, was said to be the Arts—more specifically, the source of poetic inspiration. The mood is that of ecstasy, of rhapsody and rapture.

I. VARIETY OF POETIC MOODS

Poems on the same general theme may illustrate a wide variety of poetic moods. We have, for instance, encountered thus far a

[1] See pp. 50 f. and 168 ff.

good number of poems upon the theme of Death, but how different have been the attitudes of the poets toward this universal life experience! John Donne's mood, in his sonnet "Death, Be Not Proud—" (p. 12), is one of noble defiance. Robert Frost's is a tragic mood (the very title suggests it) as he narrates the boy's death in "Out, Out—" (p. 30). A. E. Housman's mood is that of a special irony in his poem "To an Athlete Dying Young" (p. 214). And Rupert Brooke faces death in a mood of high seriousness in "The Soldier" (p. 78). But these interpretations will probably not satisfy all readers, for, let it be said yet once more, they represent the classification, not of printed-poems, but of one individual's unique poem-experiences.

It should also be noted once again that the *mood* stimulated in the reader may be quite different from the *mood* which the reader may judge to have been that of the poet.[2] Felicia Hemans, let us charitably suppose, conceived the poem "Casabianca" ('The boy stood on the burning deck,' p. 29) in an heroic mood. But today many readers of this poem upon the theme of Death will not be put into an heroic mood at all, and may variously find in themselves a critical or comic mood, and condemn the poem as sentimental or ridiculous. But there are few readers, I believe, for whom Landor's quatrain "On His Seventy-fifth Birthday" (p. 438) does not stimulate an experience the mood of which is some sort of manly resignation or acceptance of Death, in whatever words it may be phrased.

Some *moods* are more dominantly emotional and others are more dominantly intellectual. At the same time, some are dominantly serious, and others humorous or gay. The majority of poems are of the *serious-emotional* mood. But we have met a number of poems that might be called *serious-intellectual* in mood, and this has been a poetic mood characteristic of our own time as it was of the early seventeenth century. Marianne Moore's "Poetry" (p. 491) is of this kind, and Ezra Pound's "E. P. Ode pour l'election de son sepulchre" (p. 471) and Allen Tate's "Again the Native Hour—" (p. 459). And there are the earlier poems of so-called serious wit, such as John Donne's "Love's Deity" (p. 188), Ben Jonson's "Of

---

[2] See the discussion of the "communication of emotion" on pp. 193 f.

Life and Death" (p. 186), and George Herbert's "Easter Wings" (p. 75).

Another divergence from the usual serious-emotional mood is the poetry of the *light-emotional* sort, and this has been found with recurrent favor from time to time throughout the centuries. Charles d'Orleans' "Alons au bois le may cueillir" ('We'll to the woods and gather may,' p. 436) and Herrick's "To the Virgins" (p. 218) are of this sort, as are Tom Moore's "Believe Me If All Those Endearing Young Charms" (p. 265), like many of the song-lyrics, and James Stephens' "The Daisies" (p. 398).

2. LIGHT VERSE: COMIC AND SATIRIC

A third divergence from the serious-emotional mood is that yet smaller body of *light-intellectual* verse, some of it purely witty, some of it comic; some with the edge of satire, some softened with the balm of humor. Walter de la Mare's "The Huntsmen" ('Three jolly gentlemen,' p. 105) is such a comic poem, light-intellectual in mood; W. S. Gilbert's song "When I Was a Lad" (p. 395) is barbed with satire; and the old ballad "Robin-a-Thrush" (p. 361) is in the mood of light good humor.

The variety of poetic moods to be found in the great bulk of serious-emotional poetry is, of course, too great to be more than suggested here: the mood of reverence and of praise, of hope and of rapture, of desolation and of degradation, of wonderment and of contemplation, of high seriousness and of high tragedy, and so on. Nor will it be possible to do more than mention several of the special moods of serious-intellectual poetry: philosophical reflection, irony, cynicism, etc. For the purpose of this chapter is to limit the discussion and the illustrations to what is often called Light Verse, that poetry whose mood, whether emotional or intellectual, is gay or whimsical, flippant or frolicsome, witty or satirical.

Taken by and large, Poetry tends to be a more uniformly serious part of Literature than Dramatic Literature (in which Comedy is such an important type) and Prose Literature (with its Informal Essay and Light Fiction). Yet some twenty-five to thirty of the approximately two hundred poems so far included in this volume are, in one way or another, *light verse*. And in the category of today's magazine verse, poetry in this mood holds its own. But the Comic Spirit has a way of playing about the current foibles and follies of life; it touches upon the fashions of the day and the slang of the hour. Its contemporaneity is its undoing, and it passes with the passing of the day. So, amongst the many comic and satirical poems of the past, there are comparatively few that have survived, and many of them can only be read to the somber accompaniment of footnotes.

The comic element in literature seems to depend upon two factors: the recognition of incongruity and the judgment of superiority. The sudden discovery of what one does not expect, or of the disparity between promise and performance, or of the deception of appearances—when it does no discredit to the observer, or actually redounds to his advantage—gives rise to a pleasant feeling that may find expression in mirth, whether in the mere disposition to smile or in an outburst of laughter. From the physical incompatabilities, the slapstick and horseplay of farce, to the psychological *jeu de mots* and higher forms of wit in the most spirited light verse, there may be seen the same pair of factors, incongruity and superiority, lightening with risibility the serious-emotional mood with which life is so often faced.

The satirical element in literature has been defined as risible criticism. It is, then, like the comic except that its laughter is directed by the utterer's purpose, the purpose of reforming or of abusing the subject of mirth. From the time of Roman Literature, the gentler and more urbane satire, after the manner of Horace, has been distinguished from the vituperative satire and invective of Juvenal. Only satire of the former sort belongs within the category of Light Verse; for the latter is often bitter denunciation quite devoid of risibility.

The light verse that follows is presented under a number of separate headings: epigrams, comic epitaphs, limericks, triolets, light amorous verse, comic incidents, parodies, and satire.[3] These are

---

[3] Most of these terms are defined in the Glossarial Handbook.

divisions of convenience rather than of logic, and they are by no means comprehensive. Nonsense verse, such as Lewis Carroll's "Jabberwocky" (p. 129), must not be forgotten, nor that considerable body of unconsciously-humorous "bad" verse like Mrs. Kidder's "Don't Go In" (p. 250) and Marion Ward's "I Love to Love" (p. 266).

Epigrams

NON AMO TE—
Martial

Non amo te, Sabidi, nec possum dicere quare;
Hoc tantum possum dicere, non amo te.
(*bef. 100* A.D.)

[A French version of the same, by Comte de Bussy Rabutin.]

Je ne vous aime pas, Hylas;
Je n'en saurois dire la cause,
Je sais seulement une chose;
C'est que je ne vous aime pas.
(*c. 1650*)

[An English version by Tom Brown and addressed to the Dean of the College, is entitled "Written While a Student at Christ Church, Oxford."]

I do not love thee, Doctor Fell,
The reason why I cannot tell;
But this alone I know full well,
I do not love thee, Doctor Fell.
(*c. 1685*)

WHAT IS AN EPIGRAM
Samuel Taylor Coleridge

What is an epigram? a dwarfish whole,
Its body brevity, and wit its soul.

(*c. 1825*)

LINES
ON THE ANTIQUITY OF MICROBES

Strickland Gillilan

Adam
Had 'em.

(*c. 1910*)

Epitaphs

EPITAPH INTENDED FOR HIS WIFE
John Dryden

Here lies my wife: here let her lie!
Now she's at rest—and so am I.

(*c. 1675*)

HIS OWN EPITAPH
John Gay

[John Gay was buried in Westminster Abbey under this epitaph.]

Life is a jest, and all things show it;
I thought so once, and now I know it.

(*bef.* 1732)

EPITAPH FOR CIMANTHA PROCTOR

Anonymous

Here lies the late Cimantha Proctor;
She ketched a cold and wouldn't doctor;
She couldn't stay, she had to go;
Praise God from whom all blessings flow.

(*?c. 1750*)

Limericks

THERE WAS A FAITH-HEALER OF DEAL

Anonymous

There was a faith-healer of Deal
Who said, "Although pain isn't real,
   If I sit on a pin
   And I puncture my skin
I dislike what I *fancy* I feel!"

(*?c. 1900*)

THERE ONCE WAS AN OLD MAN OF LYME

Edward Lear

There once was an Old Man of Lyme
Who married three wives at a time.
   When asked, "Why the third?"
   He replied, "One's absurd,
And bigamy, sir, is a crime!"

(*bef. 1888*)

THERE WAS A YOUNG FELLOW NAMED TATE
Carolyn Wells

There was a young fellow named Tate
Who dined with his girl at 8:08,
    But I'd hate to relate
    What that person named Tate
And his tête-à-tête ate at 8:08.
                (*?c.* 1920)

Triolets

EASY IS THE TRIOLET
William Ernest Henley

Easy is the Triolet,
    If you really learn to make it!
Once a neat refrain you get,
Easy is the Triolet.
As you see!—I pay my debt
    With another rhyme. Deuce take it,
Easy is the Triolet,
    If you really learn to make it!
                (1888)

URCEUS EXIT
Austin Dobson

[In another version, the refrain "turned to a Sonnet"—with Rose crossing the road "In her latest new bonnet"!]

I intended an Ode,
   And it turned into Triolets.
It began *à la mode,*
I intended an Ode;
But Rose crossed the road
   With a bunch of fresh violets.
I intended an Ode,
   And it turned into Triolets.
            (1874)

A LITTLE KISS WHEN NO ONE SEES
Samuel Minturn Peck

A little kiss when no one sees,
   Where is the impropriety?
How sweet amid the birds and bees
A little kiss when no one sees!
Nor is it wrong, the world agrees,
   If taken with sobriety.
A little kiss when no one sees,
   Where is the impropriety?
           (c. 1900)

Light Amorous Verse

MAIDS AND WIDOWS
Anonymous

If ever I marry, I'll marry a maid;
To marry a widow, I am sore afraid;
For maids they are simple, and never will grutch,
But widows full oft, as they say, know too much.

A maid is so sweet, and so gentle of kind,
That a maid is the wife I will choose to my mind.
A widow is froward, and never will yield;
Or if such there be, you will meet them but seeld.

A maid ne'er complaineth, do what so you will;
But what you mean well, a widow takes ill.
A widow will make you a drudge and a slave,
And, cost ne'er so much, she will ever go brave.

A maid is so modest, she seemeth a rose
When it first beginneth the bud to unclose;
But a widow full-blowen full often deceives,
And the next wind that bloweth shakes down all her leaves.

The widows be lovely, I never gainsay,
But too well all their beauty they know to display;
But a maid hath so great hidden beauty in store,
She can spare to a widow, yet never be poor.

Then, if ever I marry, give me a fresh maid,
If to marry with any I be not afraid;
But to marry with any, it asketh much care;
And some bachelors hold they are best as they are.
                                        (*bef. 1600*)

CORINNA GOES A-MAYING
Robert Herrick

Get up, get up for shame, the blooming morn
Upon her wings presents the god unshorn.
　　See how Aurora throws her fair
　　Fresh-quilted colors through the air:
　　Get up, sweet slug-a-bed, and see
　　The dew bespangling herb and tree.
Each flower has wept and bowèd toward the east
Above an hour since: yet you not dressed;
　　Nay! not so much as out of bed?

When all the birds have matins said
And sung their thankful hymns, 'tis sin,
Nay, profanation, to keep in,
Whenas a thousand virgins on this day
Spring, sooner than the lark, to fetch in May.

Rise, and put on your foliage, and be seen
To come forth, like the spring-time, fresh and green,
    And sweet as Flora. Take no care
    For jewels for your gown or hair:
    Fear not; the leaves will strew
    Gems in abundance upon you:
Besides, the childhood of the day has kept,
Against you come, some orient pearls unwept;
    Come and receive them while the light
    Hangs on the dew-locks of the night:
    And Titan on the eastern hill
    Retires himself, or else stands still
Till you come forth. Wash, dress, be brief in praying:
Few beads are best when once we go a-Maying.

Come, my Corinna, come; and, coming mark
How each field turns a street, each street a park
    Made green and trimmed with trees; see how
    Devotion gives each house a bough
    Or branch: each porch, each door ere this
    An ark, a tabernacle is,
Made up of white-thorn, neatly interwove;
As if here were those cooler shades of love.
    Can such delights be in the street
    And open fields and we not see 't?
    Come, we'll abroad; and let's obey
    The proclamation made for May:
And sin no more, as we have done, by staying;
But, my Corinna, come, let's go a-Maying.

There's not a budding boy or girl this day
But is got up, and gone to bring in May.
    A deal of youth, ere this, is come
    Back, and with white-thorn laden home.

Some have dispatched their cakes and cream
Before that we have left to dream:
And some have wept, and wooed, and plighted troth,
And chose their priest, ere we can cast off sloth:
Many a green-gown has been given;
Many a kiss, both odd and even:
Many a glance too has been sent
From out the eye, love's firmament;
Many a jest told of the keys betraying
This night, and locks picked, yet we're not a-Maying.

Come, let us go while we are in our prime;
And take the harmless folly of the time.
We shall grow old apace, and die
Before we know our liberty.
Our life is short, and our days run
As fast away as does the sun;
And, as a vapor or a drop of rain,
Once lost, can ne'er be found again,
So when or you or I are made
A fable, song, or fleeting shade,
All love, all liking, all delight
Lies drowned with us in endless night.
Then while time serves, and we are but decaying,
Come, my Corinna, come let's go a-Maying.

(1648)

SONG

John Wilmot, Earl of Rochester

All my past life is mine no more,
The flying hours are gone,
Like transitory dreams giv'n o'er,
Whose images are kept in store
By memory alone.

Whatever is to come, is not;
How can it then be mine?
The present moment's all my lot,

And that, as fast as it is got,
   Phyllis, is wholly thine.

Then talk not of inconstancy,
   False hearts, and broken vows;
If I, by miracle, can be
This live-long minute true to thee,
   'Tis all that Heav'n allows.

                 (1680)

Comic Incidents

CASEY AT THE BAT
Ernest Lawrence Thayer

It looked extremely rocky for the Mudville nine that day,
The score stood four to six with but an inning left to play.
And so, when Cooney died at first, and Burrows did the same,
A pallor wreathed the features of the patrons of the game.

A straggling few got up to go, leaving there the rest,
With that hope which springs eternal within the human breast.
For they thought if only Casey could get a whack at that,
They'd put up even money with Casey at the bat.

But Flynn preceded Casey, and likewise so did Blake,
And the former was a pudding and the latter was a fake;
So on that stricken multitude a death-like silence sat,
For there seemed but little chance of Casey's getting to the bat.

But Flynn let drive a single to the wonderment of all,
And the much despisèd Blakey tore the cover off the ball,
And when the dust had lifted and they saw what had occurred,
There was Blakey safe on second, and Flynn a-hugging third.

Then from the gladdened multitude went up a joyous yell,
It bounded from the mountain top and rattled in the dell,
It struck upon the hillside, and rebounded on the flat,
For Casey, mighty Casey, was advancing to the bat.

There was ease in Casey's manner as he stepped into his place,
There was pride in Casey's bearing and a smile on Casey's face,
And when responding to the cheers he lightly doffed his hat,
No stranger in the crowd could doubt, 'twas Casey at the bat.

Ten thousand eyes were on him as he rubbed his hands with dirt,
Five thousand tongues applauded as he wiped them on his shirt;
And while the writhing pitcher ground the ball into his hip—
Defiance gleamed from Casey's eye—a sneer curled Casey's lip.

And now the leather-covered sphere came hurtling through the air,
And Casey stood a-watching it in haughty grandeur there;
Close by the sturdy batsman the ball unheeded sped—
"That hain't my style," said Casey—"Strike one," the Umpire said.

From the bleachers black with people there rose a sullen roar,
Like the beating of the storm waves on a stern and distant shore,
"Kill him! kill the Umpire!" shouted someone from the stand—
And it's likely they'd have done it had not Casey raised his hand.

With a smile of Christian charity great Casey's visage shone,
He stilled the rising tumult and he bade the game go on;
He signalled to the pitcher and again the spheroid flew,
But Casey still ignored it and the Umpire said "Strike two."

"Fraud!" yelled the maddened thousands, and the echo answered
    "Fraud,"
But one scornful look from Casey and the audience was awed;
They saw his face grow stern and cold; they saw his muscles strain,
And they knew that Casey would not let that ball go by again.

The sneer is gone from Casey's lip; his teeth are clenched with hate,
He pounds with cruel violence his bat upon the plate;
And now the pitcher holds the ball, and now he lets it go,
And now the air is shattered by the force of Casey's blow.

Oh! somewhere in this favored land the sun is shining bright,
The band is playing somewhere, and somewhere hearts are light,
And somewhere men are laughing, and somewhere children shout;
But there is no joy in Mudville—mighty Casey has "Struck Out."

(1888)

THE BLIND MEN AND THE ELEPHANT

A HINDOO FABLE

John Godfrey Saxe

It was six men of Indostan
  To learning much inclined,
Who went to see the Elephant
  (Though all of them were blind),
That each by observation
  Might satisfy his mind.

The *First* approached the Elephant,
  And happening to fall
Against his broad and sturdy side,
  At once began to bawl:
"God bless me! but the Elephant
  Is very like a wall!"

The *Second,* feeling of the tusk,
  Cried, "Ho! what have we here
So very round and smooth and sharp?
  To me 'tis mighty clear
This wonder of an Elephant
  Is very like a spear!"

The *Third* approached the animal,
  And happening to take
The squirming trunk within his hands,
  Thus boldly up and spake:
"I see," quoth he, "the Elephant
  Is very like a snake!"

The *Fourth* reached out an eager hand,
 And felt about the knee.
"What most this wondrous beast is like
 Is mighty plain," quoth he;
"'Tis clear enough the Elephant
 Is very like a tree!"

The *Fifth* who chanced to touch the ear,
 Said: "E'en the blindest man
Can tell what this resembles most;
 Deny the fact who can,
This marvel of an Elephant
 Is very like a fan!"

The *Sixth* no sooner had begun
 About the beast to grope,
Than, seizing on the swinging tail
 That fell within his scope,
"I see," quoth he, "the Elephant
 Is very like a rope!"

And so these men of Indostan
 Disputed loud and long,
Each in his own opinion
 Exceeding stiff and strong,
Though each was partly in the right,
 And all were in the wrong!

MORAL

So oft in theologic wars,
 The disputants, I ween,
Rail on in utter ignorance
 Of what each other mean,
And prate about an Elephant
Not one of them has seen!
   (*bef.* 1887)

THE PURIST

Ogden Nash

I give you now Professor Twist,
A conscientious scientist.
Trustees exclaimed, "He never bungles!"
And sent him off to distant jungles.
Camped on a tropic riverside,
One day he missed his loving bride.
She had, the guide informed him later,
Been eaten by an alligator.
Professor Twist could not but smile.
"You mean," he said, "a crocodile."

(1938)

Parodies

HOW DOTH THE LITTLE CROCODILE

from ALICE'S ADVENTURES IN WONDERLAND

Charles L. Dodgson ("Lewis Carroll")

[This is a parody of the opening stanzas of Isaac Watts' early
eighteenth-century poem:

How doth the little busy bee
  Improve each shining hour,
And gather honey all the day
  From every opening flower!

How skilfully she builds her cell!
  How neat she spreads the wax!
And labors hard to store it well
  With the sweet food she makes. . . .]

Alice, puzzling her identity, said:

" 'I must have been changed for Mabel! I'll try and say *"How doth the little—"* ' and she crossed her hands on her lap, as if she were saying lessons, and began to repeat it, but her voice sounded hoarse and strange, and the words did not come the same as they used to do:—

> "How doth the little crocodile
>   Improve his shining tail,
> And pour the waters of the Nile
>   On every golden scale!
>
> "How cheerfully he seems to grin,
>   How neatly spreads his claws,
> And welcomes little fishes in
>   With gently smiling jaws!"

" 'I'm sure those are not the right words,' said poor Alice, and her eyes filled with tears again as she went on, 'I must be Mabel after all. . . .' "

(1865)

THE AMATEUR BOTANIST
Franklin P. Adams

[William Wordsworth's "Peter Bell," a long and rather uninspiring narrative poem written in 1819, contains the following stanza:

> "In vain, through every changeful year,
>   Did Nature lead him as before;
> A primrose by a river's brim
> A yellow primrose was to him,
>   And it was nothing more."]

A primrose by a river's brim
Primula vulgaris was to him,
   And it was nothing more;
A pansy, delicately reared,
Viola tricolor appeared
   In true botanic lore.

That which a pink the layman deems
Dianthus caryophyllus seems

To any flower-fan; or
A sunflower, in that talk of his,
Annuus helianthus is,
And it is nothing more.

(1911)

EDGAR A. GUEST

SYNDICATES THE OLD WOMAN WHO LIVED IN A SHOE

Louis Untermeyer

[This parody from *Mother Goose Up-to-date* is a double ricochet, glancing off the old nursery rime as well as Edgar Guest's poem, "Home," with its well-known line: "It takes a heap o' livin' in a house t' make it home."]

It takes a heap o' children to make a home that's true,
And home can be a palace grand, or just a plain, old shoe;
But if it has a mother dear, and a good old dad or two,
Why, that's the sort of good old home for good old me and you.

Of all the institutions this side the Vale o' Rest
Howe'er it be, it seems to me a good old mother's best;
And fathers are a blessing, too, they give the place a tone;
In fact each child should try and have some parents of its own.

The food can be quite simple; just a sop of milk and bread
Are plenty when the kiddies know it's time to go to bed.
And every little sleepy-head will dream about the day
When he can go to work because a Man's Work is his Play.

And, oh, how sweet his life will seem, with nought to make him cross;
And he will never watch the clock and always mind the boss.
And when he thinks (as may occur), this thought will please him best:
That ninety million think the same—including   *Eddie Guest.*

(1926)

Satires

from DON JUAN, Canto I

George Gordon, Lord Byron

1

I want a hero: an uncommon want,
    When every year and month sends forth a new one,
Till, after cloying the gazettes with cant,
    The age discovers he is not the true one:
Of such as these I should not care to vaunt,
    I'll therefore take our ancient friend Don Juan—
We all have seen him, in the pantomime,
Sent to the devil somewhat ere his time. . . .

6

Most epic poets plunge "in medias res"
    (Horace makes this the heroic turnpike road),
And then your hero tells, whene'er you please,
    What went before—by way of episode,
While seated after dinner at his ease,
    Beside his mistress in some soft abode,
Palace, or garden, paradise, or cavern,
Which serves the happy couple for a tavern.

7

That is the usual method, but not mine—
    My way is to begin with the beginning;
The regularity of my design
    Forbids all wandering as the worst of sinning,
And therefore I shall open with a line
    (Although it cost me half an hour in spinning)

Narrating somewhat of Don Juan's father,
And also of his mother, if you'd rather.

8

In Seville was he born, a pleasant city,
   Famous for oranges and women—he
Who has not seen it will be much to pity,
   So says the proverb—and I quite agree;
Of all the Spanish towns is none more pretty,
   Cadiz, perhaps—but that you soon may see;
Don Juan's parents lived beside the river,
A noble stream, and call'd the Guadalquivir.

9

His father's name was Jóse—*Don,* of course,—
   A true Hidalgo, free from every stain
Of Moor or Hebrew blood, he traced his source
   Through the most Gothic gentlemen of Spain;
A better cavalier ne'er mounted horse,
   Or, being mounted, e'er got down again,
Than Jóse, who begot our hero, who
Begot—but that's to come—Well, to renew:

10

His mother was a learned lady, famed
   For every branch of every science known
In every Christian language ever named,
   With virtues equall'd by her wit alone:
She made the cleverest people quite ashamed,
   And even the good with inward envy groan,
Finding themselves so very much exceeded
In their own way by all the things that she did.

11

Her memory was a mine: she knew by heart
   All Calderon and greater part of Lopé,
So that if any actor miss'd his part
   She could have served him for the prompter's copy;
For her Feinagle's were an useless art,

And he himself obliged to shut up shop—he
Could never make a memory so fine as
That which adorn'd the brain of Donna Inez.

12

Her favorite science was the mathematical,
    Her noblest virtue was the magnanimity;
Her wit (she sometimes tried at wit) was Attic all,
    Her serious sayings darken'd to sublimity;
In short, in all things she was fairly what I call
    A prodigy—her morning dress was dimity,
Her evening silk, or, in the summer, muslin,
And other stuffs, with which I won't stay puzzling. . . .

15

Some women use their tongues—she *look'd* a lecture,
    Each eye a sermon, and her brow a homily,
An all-in-all sufficient self-director,
    Like the lamented late Sir Samuel Romilly,
The Law's expounder, and the State's corrector,
    Whose suicide was almost an anomaly—
One sad example more, that "All is vanity,"—
(The jury brought their verdict in "Insanity"). . . .

18

Perfect she was, but as perfection is
    Insipid in this naughty world of ours,
Where our first parents never learn'd to kiss
    Till they were exiled from their earlier bowers,
Where all was peace, and innocence, and bliss
    (I wonder how they got through the twelve hours),
Don Jóse, like a lineal son of Eve,
Went plucking various fruit without her leave.

19

He was a mortal of the careless kind,
    With no great love for learning, or the learn'd,
Who chose to go where'er he had a mind,
    And never dream'd his lady was concern'd;

The world, as usual, wickedly inclined
   To see a kingdom or a house o'erturn'd,
Whisper'd he had a mistress, some said *two*—
But for domestic quarrels *one* will do.

20

Now Donna Inez had, with all her merit,
   A great opinion of her own good qualities;
Neglect, indeed, requires a saint to bear it,
   And such, indeed, she was in her moralities;
But then she had a devil of a spirit,
   And sometimes mix'd up fancies with realities,
And let few opportunities escape
Of getting her liege lord into a scrape. . . .

23

Don José and his lady quarrell'd—*why*,
   Not any of the many could divine,
Though several thousand people chose to try,
   'Twas surely no concern of theirs nor mine;
I loathe that low vice—curiosity;
   But if there's anything in which I shine,
'Tis in arranging all my friends' affairs,
Not having, of my own, domestic cares. . . .

26

Don José and the Donna Inez led
   For some time an unhappy sort of life,
Wishing each other, not divorced, but dead;
   They lived respectably as man and wife,
Their conduct was exceedingly well-bred,
   And gave no outward signs of inward strife,
Until at length the smother'd fire broke out,
And put the business past all kind of doubt. . . .

32

Their friends had tried at reconciliation,
   Then their relations, who made matters worse,
('Twere hard to tell upon a like occasion

To whom it may be best to have recourse—
I can't say much for friend or yet relation):
    The lawyers did their utmost for divorce,
But scarce a fee was paid on either side
Before, unluckily, Don Jóse died. . . .

37

Dying intestate, Juan was sole heir
    To a chancery suit, and messuages and lands,
Which with a long minority and care,
    Promised to turn out well in proper hands:
Inez became sole guardian, which was fair,
    And answer'd but to nature's just demands;
An only son left with an only mother
Is brought up much more wisely than another.

38

Sagest of women, even of widows, she
    Resolved that Juan should be quite a paragon,
And worthy of the noblest pedigree:
    (His sire was of Castile, his dam from Aragon).
Then for accomplishments of chivalry,
    In case our lord the king should go to war again,
He learn'd the arts of riding, fencing, gunnery,
And how to scale a fortress—or a nunnery.

39

But that which Donna Inez most desired,
    And saw into herself each day before all
The learned tutors whom for him she hired,
    Was, that his breeding should be strictly moral:
Much into all his studies she inquired,
    And so they were submitted first to her, all,
Arts, sciences, no branch was made a mystery
To Juan's eyes, excepting natural history.

40

The languages, especially the dead,
    The sciences, and most of all the abstruse,

The arts, at least all such as could be said
   To be the most remote from common use,
In all these he was much and deeply read:
   But not a page of anything that's loose,
Or hints continuation of the species,
Was ever suffer'd, lest he should grow vicious.

41

His classic studies made a little puzzle,
   Because of filthy loves of gods and goddesses,
Who in the earlier ages raised a bustle,
   But never put on pantaloons or bodices;
His reverend tutors had at times a tussle,
   And for their Aeneids, Iliads, and Odysseys,
Were forced to make an odd sort of apology,
For Donna Inez dreaded the Mythology.

42

Ovid's a rake, as half his verses show him,
   Anacreon's morals are a still worse sample,
Catullus scarcely has a decent poem,
   I don't think Sappho's Ode a good example,
Although Longinus tells us there is no hymn
   Where the sublime soars forth on wings more ample;
But Virgil's songs are pure, except that horrid one
Beginning with "Formosum Pastor Corydon."

43

Lucretius' irreligion is too strong,
   For early stomachs, to prove wholesome food;
I can't help thinking Juvenal was wrong,
   Although no doubt his real intent was good,
For speaking out so plainly in his song,
   So much indeed as to be downright rude;
And then what proper person can be partial
To all those nauseous epigrams of Martial?

44

Juan was taught from out the best edition,
   Expurgated by learned men, who place,

Judiciously, from out the schoolboy's vision,
   The grosser parts; but, fearful to deface
Too much their modest bard by this omission,
   And pitying sore his mutilated case,
They only add them all in an appendix,
Which saves, in fact, the trouble of an index;

45

For there we have them all "at one fell swoop,"
   Instead of being scatter'd through the pages;
They stand forth marshall'd in a handsome troop,
   To meet the ingenuous youth of future ages,
Till some less rigid editor shall stoop
   To call them back into their separate cages,
Instead of standing staring all together,
Like garden gods—and not so decent either. . . .

49

Young Juan wax'd in godliness and grace;
   At six a charming child, and at eleven
With all the promise of as fine a face
   As e'er to man's maturer growth was given.
He studied steadily, and grew apace,
   And seem'd, at least, in the right road to heaven,
For half his days were pass'd at church, the other
Between his tutors, confessor, and mother.

50

At six, I said, he was a charming child,
   At twelve he was a fine, but quiet boy;
Although in infancy a little wild,
   They tamed him down amongst them: to destroy
His natural spirit not in vain they toil'd,
   At least it seem'd so; and his mother's joy
Was to declare how sage, and still, and steady,
Her young philosopher was grown already. . . .

52

For my part I say nothing—nothing—but
   This I will say—my reasons are my own—

That if I had an only son to put
   To school (as God be praised that I have none),
'Tis not with Donna Inez I would shut
   Him up to learn his catechism alone,
No—no—I'd send him out betimes to college,
For there it was I pick'd up my own knowledge.

53

For there one learns—'tis not for me to boast,
   Though I acquired—but I pass over *that,*
As well as all the Greek I since have lost:
   I say that there's the place—but *"Verbum sat,"*
I think I pick'd up too, as well as most,
   Knowledge of matters—but no matter *what*—
I never married—but, I think, I know
That sons should not be educated so. . . .

(1819)

THE LATEST DECALOGUE
Arthur Hugh Clough

Thou shalt have one God only; who
Would be at the expense of two?
No graven images may be
Worshipped, except the currency.
Swear not at all; for, for thy curse
Thine enemy is none the worse.
At church on Sunday to attend
Will serve to keep the world thy friend.
Honor thy parents; that is, all
From whom advancement may befall.
Thou shalt not kill; but need'st not strive
Officiously to keep alive.
Do not adultery commit;
Advantage rarely comes of it.
Thou shalt not steal; an empty feat,
When it's so lucrative to cheat.
Bear not false witness; let the lie

Have time on its own wings to fly.
Thou shalt not covet, but tradition
Approves all forms of competition.

(1862)

THE V-A-S-E

James Jeffrey Roche

From the madding crowd they stand apart,
The maidens four and the Work of Art;

And none might tell from sight alone
In which had Culture ripest grown,—

The Gotham Million fair to see,
The Philadelphia Pedigree,

The Boston Mind of azure hue,
Or the soulful Soul from Kalamazoo,—

For all loved Art in a seemly way,
With an earnest soul and a capital A.

. . . .

Long they worshipped; but no one broke
The sacred stillness, until up spoke

The Western one from the nameless place,
Who blushing said: "What a lovely vace!"

Over three faces a sad smile flew,
And they edged away from Kalamazoo.

But Gotham's haughty soul was stirred
To crush the stranger with one small word.

Deftly hiding reproof in praise,
She cries: " 'Tis, indeed, a lovely vaze!"

But brief her unworthy triumph when
The lofty one from the home of Penn,

With the consciousness of two grandpapas,
Exclaims: "It is quite a lovely vahs!"

And glances round with an anxious thrill,
Awaiting the word of Beacon Hill.

But the Boston maid smiles courteouslee,
And gently murmurs: "Oh pardon me!

"I did not catch your remark, because
I was so entranced with that charming vaws!"

> *Dies erit praegelida*
> *Sinistra quum Bostonia.*

(*bef.* 1908)

SIR, I ADMIT YOUR GENERAL RULE

Matthew Prior or *Alexander Pope*

Sir, I admit your general rule,
That every poet is a fool:
But you yourself may serve to show it,
That every fool is not a poet.

(*c.* 1700)

SUGGESTIONS FOR STUDY

1. *Divers Moods.* (a) Turn back to Chapters 10–12. Review the poems, and sort them out according to what you consider their moods. (b) Designate the categories, and list the poems in an outline. (c) The poems for these chapters were chosen, not to illustrate the diversity of poetic moods, but to further the discussion of the subjects of the chapters. What are a few of the poetic moods that are not found in this group of poems?

2. *Sorts of Light Verse.* The poems in this chapter have been sorted and are presented in groups of three, each of which has been named— "epigrams," "epitaphs," etc. (a) As you read each group, work out a tentative definition of the designating group-name; and write this out on scratch paper. (b) Turn to the Glossarial Handbook, and study the

definitions there given, improving your own definitions when that seems possible.

3. *Sense and Nonsense.* (a) Reread Lewis Carroll's "Jabberwocky" (p. 129) and the nonsense refrains to "The Old Chisholm Trail" (p. 393), the old ballad "Robin-a-Thrush" (p. 361), and the chorus from *The Frogs* by Aristophanes (p. 366). (b) "In no one of these poems is the nonsense really meaningless." Consider what might be meant by *nonsense* and *meaningless* in this sentence in connection with the poems themselves. Think once more of the so-called four phases of meaning (see pp. 50, 168). (c) Work out statements of what you think is the meaning for you of "Jabberwocky" and of the nonsense refrains.

4. *Life's Ironies.* (a) Review the following three poems, each of which in its way may be said to be ironic: Hardy's "Ah, Are You Digging on My Grave?" (p. 362), Housman's "To an Athlete Dying Young" (p. 214), and Whittier's "The Christian Slave" (p. 498). Note that they are not equally *light* verse. (b) Try to work out a tentative definition of *irony,* and then consult the Glossarial Handbook in revising your statement. (c) Reread the discussion of *ambiguity* (pp. 49 f. and 170 ff.), and consider its relation to irony.

5. *Parodies Lost.* You have already (Suggestion 2, above) given some thought to the matter of parody. (a) Now re-examine the three parodies in this chapter. Which ones of them seem to be satirical—risibly critical of something? At what is the criticism directed: at the poet or poem parodied, or at something else? (b) Note the particular methods used by the parodists.

6. *The Butt of Satire.* Satire, here defined as risible criticism, is always satire *of* something. (a) Reread the selections from Byron's mock-epic, *Don Juan,* and take note of the things against which he is throwing his darts. Jot down a list of Byron's specific points of social criticism. (b) Study Clough's "The Latest Decalogue" with particular reference to the ironic method of his satire.

7. *To Ween and to Wit.* Three poems in this group may be read with special reference to the psychology of language-behavior: "The Blind Men and the Elephant," "The Purist," and "The V-a-s-e." (a) Review the statements of the contextual theory of meaning (pp. 49, 162, 165-68) and of the relativism of truth (p. 290). Then reread "The Blind Men and the Elephant," and consider the language problem that is there suggested. (b) The doctrines of the "right" word and of the "right" pronunciation are satirically illustrated in "The Purist" and in "The V-a-s-e." Read them and prepare to comment upon the language problems involved.

8. *A Twist of the Pen.* Perhaps light verse is most enjoyable to those who have experimented in writing it. It calls forth the spirit of fun and mockery, and is sometimes at its best when there is a certain straining for effect, double rime and false rime. (a) The simplest exercise of this kind is the writing of cynical *epitaphs* for the benefit of one's friends: "Here lies the body of John Bevin—"; or a fatal note on somebody Bell, or on the "wild O'Gradys"; or less obvious names, which will call for more ingenuity. (b) Anyone can catch the swing of the *limerick*. One of the following first lines may get you started: "There was a young fellow [or 'woman'] from [or 'named']—[any name with accent on the first syllable]"; or "There was a professor of [any subject you may choose]"; or "A stout-hearted sergeant named—." Now jot down a list of words riming with the name chosen; a riming dictionary may be of help (there's one in the *Webster's Collegiate Dictionary*); but remember that bad and original rimes are good for a smile. Now, with the jingling pattern in mind, scratch head and pen, twisting and turning the words to your trifling purpose. (c) Or you may wish to try your hand at the pleasant art of *parody.* Nursery rimes, sentimental and popular poems, and the poets whose personal style is most distinctive are all meat for the smart perversions of parody. (d) Even the *triolet* is not beyond the amateur rimester.

20

HISTORIC STYLES—
CLASSIC AND ROMANTIC

We turn now from these divers moods to the consideration of a group of related classifications of poetry, one of which, the *historic styles,* will provide the substance for this chapter. But, first, the group as a whole must be described briefly.

I. PERIODS, SCHOOLS, MOVEMENTS, STYLES

Courses in poetry, and books about poetry, are most frequently organized chronologically with regard to literary *periods*. These periods are blocks of time ordinarily bounded by reasonably fixed dates (1558-1603 or 1590-1610), and are often named for the reigning sovereign (the Elizabethan Period) or for an outstanding literary figure (the Age of Shakespeare). This is the convenient arrangement of histories of poetry and literature; and it makes for indisputable classification of the poems, except when the poet's dates and/or the dates of composition or publication are unknown. But there is a tendency for the period boundaries, arbitrary and artificial at best, to cause difficulties. Certain poems seem really to belong on the other side of the line, and such poets as Ben Jonson and John Donne are caught astraddle the fence between the Elizabethan and the Jacobean-Caroline periods. And a second difficulty results from the easy assumption that all the poetry of a given period will possess the so-called characteristics of the age.

A second classification of this kind, avoiding some of the problems of period divisions, sorts poetry according to literary *schools,* though the word "school" is not widely used to name, for instance,

the Sons of Ben (as the young followers of Ben Jonson called themselves) [1] or the Cavalier Poets. Such groupings, often based upon
the personal association of the poets, are quite natural ones, though
they also run into difficulties: the sorting of poets rather than
poems, and the presumption that all of a group of friends or acquaintances will be much alike.

The grouping of poems according to their place in broad literary *movements* is a related, though markedly different, classification. These great developments in cultural history, like the Renaissance, for instance, are not so easily pinned down within a brace of
historic dates; nor are they the product of restricted groups of
literary men. Such movements are often likened to the growth of
living things, and are looked upon as rooting in the past; then waxing, flourishing, waning; and finally dying out. But the biological
metaphor breaks down when pressed too far in the study of poems
that are looked upon as a part of one of these cultural movements,
for their living relationship is seen to exist largely in the experience
of successive generations of interpreters and critics.

The phrase *historic style* is here used to name another, and related, classification, though the words "mode" and "attitude" and
"tendency" have been used to name the same phenomena.

Each individual has a certain way of doing things, an expression
of his unique personality, that may be thought of as his *personal
style*. So a poet's style will be his particular manner of using language, the expression of his particular personality traits (to use a
now discredited word). He will be predisposed or conditioned to
treat certain themes in certain ways; he will prefer certain forms;
and he will use a certain vocabulary in certain patterns of symbolic
formulation. As the French say, "Le style, c'est l'homme même"
("Style is the man himself"). And the reader may become skilled
in identifying isolated poems as being in the style of Alexander
Pope, of Percy B. Shelley, or of Carl Sandburg.

Now, an *historic style* represents a broad generalization of notable
characteristics to be found in the works of various authors, often
dominantly in the work of a particular literary period or distin-

---

[1] Herrick's "An Ode to Ben Jonson" (p. 437) is one of many poems honoring him.

guishing the work of a certain school or marking the development of one of the broad cultural movements. Such historic styles, however, may be found recurring in various periods, and continuing during the dominance of an apparently incompatible movement. Indeed, a single poet (such as Lord Byron, pp. 529 and 572) may write at different times in two or more of the historic styles; and even a single poem (such as Collins' "Ode to Evening," p. 468) may exhibit elements of different historic styles. Furthermore, these historic styles are to be found not alone in poetry but in all of the Fine Arts.

2. THE CLASSIC AND ROMANTIC STYLES

Classicism (the classic style), romanticism, and realism are usually looked upon as the three outstanding historic styles. But there are a good many other terms sometimes used to designate special historic styles: among them, Euphuism (of Shakespeare's time), neo-classicism and pseudo-classicism (of the seventeenth and eighteenth centuries), sentimentalism (of the eighteenth and nineteenth), and naturalism, expressionism, symbolism, and surrealism (of our own century).

In an over-simplified but helpful essay, Classicism has been defined as "the tendency characterized by the predominance of reason over imagination and the sense of fact"; Romanticism as "the tendency characterized by the predominance of imagination over reason and the sense of fact"; and Realism as "the tendency characterized by the predominance of the sense of fact over imagination and reason." [2] Certainly the words *reason* (for the classic style), *imagination* (for the romantic style), and *sense of fact* (for the realistic) may be helpful in developing a fuller understanding of these historic styles, only the first two of which will be especially illustrated in this chapter.

The *classic style* was, in Western Civilization, the earliest in its development. This style derives from the culture of ancient Greece, which was copied in the arts of Rome. We have already noted some of the work of Homer and Pindar, Sophocles and Aristophanes

[2] William Allan Neilson, *Essentials of Poetry* (Houghton Mifflin, 1921), p. 13.

among the Greek poets, and of Horace and Martial among the Romans. The Renaissance, following the so-called Middle Ages, was marked by a revival of ancient learning and arts; and there were in Shakespeare's romantic time, and just afterwards, poëts like Ben Jonson and John Donne who wrote much in the classic style; and John Milton, in the middle of the seventeenth century, and John Dryden and the Earl of Rochester, of the Restoration, wrote variously, but in the classic style. It was in this Restoration Period that neo-classicism (the *new* classicism), or *pseudo*-(false-)classicism as some have called it, fastened itself upon the body poetic, and leeched it for a century and more, enforcing its metrical rules derived from the formal characteristics (but too often missing the spirit) of the Ancients, and maintaining a stultifying convention of poetic diction. So, in the eighteenth century, one sort of classicism flourished in the work of Alexander Pope and Joseph Addison, in the work of Gay and Prior, and (with modifications) in the work of Collins and Gray, Cowper and Goldsmith. But later in the eighteenth century the neo-classic style, itself changing, finally lost its ascendance to the romantic style. However, in the early nineteenth century, Byron found the classic style agreeable; and so, later, did Tennyson and Austin Dobson, in very different ways. In our own century, the classic style may be seen, for instance, in the poems of A. E. Housman.[3] Classicism, then, has not been confined to one period, though neo-classicism may be viewed as a cultural movement waxing and waning through two centuries.

But now something must be said about the nature of the classic style.

Since Roman times, classicism has been imitative. The Romans copied Greek models, and the Renaissance classicists took their inspiration and examples from Rome and Greece. So, the sub-types of poetry found among the Ancients—and the poetic forms, themes, and moods—are to be found sprouting sometimes rather strange growth in Italian, French, and English soil. Homer's epics, *Iliad* and *Odyssey,* followed by Virgil's *Aeneid,* were the archetype for the later classical epics, of which Milton's *Paradise Lost* is one. It

---

[3] Use the Author Index (the Table of Poems at the front of this book) in finding poems by these men. See pp. 243 ff. for a discussion of neo-classical criticism.

has already been noted that the odes of Pindar and the choral odes of Sophocles set, with some confusion, the pattern for later odes as various as Dryden's "Song for St. Cecilia's Day" (p. 147) and Shelley's "Ode to the West Wind" (p. 133). The very different odes of Horace and the epigrams of Martial served both translators and imitators with models of metrical wit and wisdom. And the satires of Horace and Juvenal (not illustrated in this book) were the fountainhead of later verse satire. But there were other sub-types of ancient poetry: the pastoral idyl and elegy, the verse epistle and verse essay, and the convivial and amatory lyric.

"The tendency characterized by the predominance of *reason* over imagination and the sense of fact." Classicism is the only style in which poets have written much poetry of the so-called expository type, such as Pope's *Essay on Criticism* (p. 244); and there are also a number of distinctively classical sub-types of both lyric and narrative poetry. Among the poetic forms, a number are identified as classic or neo-classic: the closed heroic couplet, in which, for instance, Goldsmith's "The Deserted Village" (p. 492) is written; the stanzaic forms suggested by the Horatian odes; and (again) the so-called Pindaric ode. Some of the divers poetic themes, too, seem to be especially suitable for treatment in the classic style: many of the lighter love-themes, for example, and the praise of wine and friendship; society rather than solitude; urban life rather than rural; the arts rather than wind and birds; mankind and an understandable God. And the classic style seems quite natural to those poets whose moods are intellectual, whether serious wit or light banter.

Such, in broad outline, is the classic style; now for the romantic.

The *romantic style*, unlike the classic, derives from medieval culture, and may be seen in the rich native literatures of Western Civilization, particularly of Italy, France, and England. We have already noted poems by Dante, by Charles d'Orleans, and by (or copied by) John of Fornsete; and the old Scottish and English popular ballads. The Renaissance, which followed, was a cultural movement in which the new learning, the rediscovery of the Ancients, stimulated not only neo-classicism but also (and especially in England) a flourishing of essentially native poetry that was strongly romantic in style. We have remarked the sonnets of

Petrarch and of Ronsard, from Italy and France, and the Elizabethan sonnets of Spenser and Shakespeare. Spenser's *The Faerie
Queene* (p. 251), with its conscious medievalism, is a vast romantic,
rather than classical, epic; and Shakespeare's great tragedies and
graceful comedies are romantic in style. But after the followers of
Spenser, like George Wither (though not in the poem in this book)
and William Browne and (in some ways) John Milton, the romantic style gave way during the early seventeenth century, and
was not to prevail again for a hundred and more years. At that
later date came the revival of interest in the Spenserian stanza and
the sonnet, a closer observation of nature and of common man, and
the numerous other evidences of a change in fashion, as the neo-
classic style gave way to the romantic in what is usually called the
Romantic Movement, centered in the period 1798-1832, and pervading the literature not only of England, but of Germany and
France as well. This was the time of Wordsworth and Coleridge,
of Byron, Shelley, and Keats, upon the basis of whose work it is
usual to define the romantic style. But after their time, later in the
nineteenth century, the romantic style was still a popular one, and
may be observed (with marked differences) not only in the work
of Tennyson and Browning, but also in the work of Dante Gabriel
Rossetti and his sister Christina Rossetti, in the work of Swinburne,
and in the American poetry of Poe, Longfellow, and Whittier. And
in this twentieth century, the romantic style may be seen in Edna
St. Vincent Millay and Stephen Vincent Benét.[4]

Romanticism has been generally more adventuresome than classicism. When it is imitative, it is inclined to choose native or medieval or earlier Renaissance models; but still it may find inspiration in the more romantic of the classics, such as the pastoral elegy.
Later romantic poets have harked back to Milton and Shakespeare
and Spenser, and still later romantics have looked to Byron and
Shelley and Keats for examples of the romantic style.

"The predominance of *imagination* over reason and the sense of
fact." The romantic style has not seemed appropriate for the writing of poetry of the expository type, but it has made ample use of
a number of sub-types both of narrative and lyric poetry—ballad and

---

[4] See the Author Index for page references to works by these poets.

metrical romance; sonnet and song-lyric; ballade, rondel, and triolet—which are sub-types distinguished by being in special form. Among the continuous forms, romantic poets have made wide use of blank verse (as in "Andrea del Sarto," p. 479), and of the open couplet (as in Keats' *Endymion,* p. 585), ottava rima (as in *Don Juan,* p. 529), and the Spenserian stanza ("The Eve of St. Agnes," p. 413), and of a wide assortment of original stanzaic forms. Of the many different poetic themes, romantic poets find certain ones especially congenial: the more serious love-themes, solitude and fellowship with nature, the common man and the noble savage, the social and humanitarian causes, the stormy wind and the sea, creatures of field and air, the pictorial and bizarre, the remote in time and place, the mysterious and supernatural, the ineffable and immanent Deity. The romantic style finds most fitting use by those poets whose moods are of the serious-emotional sort.

Such, then, are two of the notable historic styles in which poetry has been written through the ages.

Classic and Neo-classic

TO THALIARCHUS

ODES, I, 9

Horace, translated by *John Dryden*

Vides ut alta stet nive candidum
Soracte, nec iam sustineant onus
    Silvae laborantes, geluque
        Flumina constiterint acuto.

Behold yon mountain's hoary height,
    Made higher with new mounts of
        snow;
Again behold the winter's weight
    Oppress the laboring woods below:
And streams with icy fetters bound,
Benumb'd and cramp'd to solid
        ground.

Dissolve frigus ligna super foco
Large reponens atque benignius

With well-heap'd logs dissolve the
    cold,

Deprome quadrimum Sabina,
    O Thaliarche, merum diota.

And feed the genial hearth with
    fires;
Produce the wine, that makes us
    bold,
    And sprightly wit of love inspires.
For what hereafter shall betide,
God, if 'tis worth his care, provide.

Permitte divis cetera, qui simul
Stravere ventos aequore fervido
    Deproeliantes, nec cupressi
        Nec veteres agitantur orni.

Let him alone, with what he made,
    To toss and turn the world below:
At his command the storms invade;
    The winds by his commission
        blow;
Till with a nod he bids them cease,
And then the calm returns, and all is
    peace.

Quid sit futurum cras, fuge quaerere
    et
Quem Fors dierum cumque dabit,
    lucro
    Adpone nec dulces amores
        Sperne, puer, neque tu choreas,

Tomorrow and her works defy,
    Lay hold upon the present hour,
And snatch the pleasures passing by,
    To put them out of Fortune's
        power.
Nor Love, nor Love's delights, dis-
    dain;
Whate'er thou gett'st today is gain.

Donec virenti canities abest
Morosa. Nunc et campus et areae
    Lenesque sub noctem susurri
        Conposita repetantur hora,

Secure those golden, early joys,
    That youth, unsour'd by sorrow,
        bears,
Ere withering Time the taste destroys
    With sickness and unwielding years.
For active sports, for pleasing rest,
This is the time to be possest;
The best is but in season best.

Nunc et latentis proditor intimo
Gratus puellae risus ab angulo
    Pignusque dereptum lacertis
        Aut digito male pertinaci.

The appointed hour of promis'd bliss,
    The pleasing whisper in the dark,
The half-unwilling, willing kiss,
    The laugh that guides thee to the
        mark,
When the kind nymph would coy-
    ness feign,
And hides but to be found again:
These, these are joys, the gods for
    youth ordain.

(c. 35 B.C.)

(1697)

THE CONSTANT LOVER
Sir John Suckling

Out upon it, I have loved
    Three whole days together!
And am like to love three more,
    If it prove fair weather.

Time shall moult away his wings
    Ere he shall discover
In the whole wide world again
    Such a constant lover.

But the spite on 't is, no praise
    Is due at all to me:
Love with me had made no stays,
    Had it any been but she.

Had it any been but she,
    And that very face,
There had been at least ere this
    A dozen dozen in her place.
                (1639)

LYCIDAS
John Milton

[In this pastoral elegy Milton (to use his own words) "bewails a
learned friend [Edward King], unfortunately drowned in his passage
from Chester on the Irish seas, 1637, and by occasion foretells the ruin
of our corrupted clergy, then in their height." The name "Lycidas"
comes from Theocritus' "Idyll, VII."]

Yet once more, O ye laurels, and once more,
Ye myrtles brown, with ivy never sere,
I come to pluck your berries harsh and crude,
And with forced fingers rude
Shatter your leaves before the mellowing year.

Bitter constraint and sad occasion dear
Compels me to disturb your season due;
For Lycidas is dead, dead ere his prime,
Young Lycidas, and hath not left his peer.
Who would not sing for Lycidas? he knew
Himself to sing, and build the lofty rime.
He must not float upon his watery bier
Unwept, and welter to the parching wind,
Without the meed of some melodious tear.
    Begin, then, Sisters of the sacred well
That from beneath the seat of Jove doth spring;
Begin, and somewhat loudly sweep the string.
Hence with denial vain and coy excuse:
So may some gentle Muse
With lucky words favor *my* destined urn,
And as he passes turn,
And bid fair peace be to my sable shroud!
    For we were nursed upon the self-same hill,
Fed the same flock, by fountain, shade, and rill;
Together both, ere the high lawns appeared
Under the opening eyelids of the Morn,
We drove a-field, and both together heard
What time the gray-fly winds her sultry horn,
Battening our flocks with the fresh dews of night,
Oft till the star that rose at evening bright
Toward heaven's descent had sloped his westering wheel.
Meanwhile the rural ditties were not mute;
Tempered to the oaten flute,
Rough Satyrs danced, and Fauns with cloven heel
From the glad sound would not be absent long;
And old Damoetas loved to hear our song.
    But, oh! the heavy change, now thou art gone,
Now thou art gone and never must return!
Thee, Shepherd, thee the woods and desert caves,
With wild thyme and the gadding vine o'ergrown,
And all their echoes, mourn.
The willows, and the hazel copses green,
Shall now no more be seen
Fanning their joyous leaves to thy soft lays.
As killing as the canker to the rose,
Or taint-worm to the weanling herds that graze,

Or frost to flowers, that their gay wardrobe wear,
When first the white-thorn blows;
Such, Lycidas, thy loss to shepherd's ear.

Where were ye, Nymphs, when the remorseless deep
Closed o'er the head of your loved Lycidas?
For neither were ye playing on the steep
Where your old Bards, the famous Druids, lie,
Nor on the shaggy top of Mona high,
Nor yet where Deva spreads her wisard stream.
Ay me! I fondly dream
"Had ye been there," . . . for what could that have done?
What could the Muse herself that Orpheus bore,
The Muse herself, for her enchanting son,
Whom universal nature did lament,
When, by the rout that made the hideous roar,
His gory visage down the stream was sent,
Down the swift Hebrus to the Lesbian shore?

Alas! what boots it with uncessant care
To tend the homely, slighted, Shepherd's trade,
And strictly meditate the thankless Muse?
Were it not better done, as others use,
To sport with Amaryllis in the shade,
Or with the tangles of Neaera's hair?
Fame is the spur that the clear spirit doth raise
(That last infirmity of noble mind)
To scorn delights and live laborious days;
But the fair guerdon when we hope to find,
And think to burst out into sudden blaze,
Comes the blind Fury with the abhorrèd shears,
And slits the thin-spun life. "But not the praise,"
Phoebus replied, and touched my trembling ears:
"Fame is no plant that grows on mortal soil,
Nor in the glistering foil
Set off to the world, nor in broad rumour lies,
But lives and spreads aloft by those pure eyes
And perfect witness of all-judging Jove;
As he pronounces lastly on each deed,
Of so much fame in heaven expect thy meed."

O fountain Arethuse, and thou honored flood,
Smooth-sliding Mincius, crowned with vocal reeds,
That strain I heard was of a higher mood.

But now my oat proceeds,
And listens to the Herald of the Sea,
That came in Neptune's plea.
He asked the waves, and asked the felon winds,
What hard mishap hath doomed this gentle swain?
And questioned every gust of rugged wings
That blows from off each beakèd promontory.
They knew not of his story;
And sage Hippotades their answer brings,
That not a blast was from his dungeon strayed:
The air was calm, and on the level brine
Sleek Panope with all her sisters played.
It was that fatal and perfidious bark,
Built in the eclipse, and rigged with curses dark,
That sunk so low that sacred head of thine.
    Next, Camus, reverend Sire, went footing slow,
His mantle hairy, and his bonnet sedge,
Inwrought with figures dim, and on the edge
Like to that sanguine flower inscribed with woe.
"Ah! who hath reft," quoth he, "my dearest pledge?"
Last came, and last did go,
The Pilot of the Galilean Lake;
Two massy keys he bore of metals twain
(The golden opes, the iron shuts amain).
He shook his mitred locks, and stern bespake:—
"How well could I have spared for thee, young swain,
Enow of such as, for their bellies' sake,
Creep, and intrude, and climb into the fold!
Of other care they little reckoning make
Than how to scramble at the shearers' feast,
And shove away the worthy bidden guest.
Blind mouths! that scarce themselves know how to hold
A sheep-hook, or have learnt aught else the least
That to the faithful Herdman's art belongs!
What recks it them? What need they? They are sped;
And, when they list, their lean and flashy songs
Grate on their scrannel pipes of wretched straw;
The hungry sheep look up, and are not fed,
But, swoln with wind and the rank mist they draw,
Rot inwardly, and foul contagion spread;
Besides what the grim Wolf with privy paw

Daily devours apace, and nothing said.
But that two-handed engine at the door
Stands ready to smite once, and smite no more."
　　Return, Alpheus; the dread voice is past
That shrunk thy streams; return, Sicilian Muse,
And call the vales, and bid them hither cast
Their bells and flowerets of a thousand hues.
Ye valleys low, where the mild whispers use
Of shades, and wanton winds, and gushing brooks,
On whose fresh lap the swart star sparely looks,
Throw hither all your quaint enamelled eyes,
That on the green turf suck the honeyed showers,
And purple all the ground with vernal flowers.
Bring the rathe primrose that forsaken dies,
The tufted crow-toe, and pale jessamine,
The white pink, and the pansy freaked with jet,
The glowing violet,
The musk-rose, and the well-attired woodbine,
With cowslips wan that hang the pensive head,
And every flower that sad embroidery wears;
Bid amaranthus all his beauty shed,
And daffodillies fill their cups with tears,
To strew the laureate hearse where Lycid lies.
For so, to interpose a little ease,
Let our frail thoughts dally with false surmise:
Ay me! whilst thee the shores and sounding seas
Wash far away, where'er thy bones are hurled;
Whether beyond the stormy Hebrides,
Where thou perhaps under the whelming tide
Visit'st the bottom of the monstrous world;
Or whether thou, to our moist vows denied,
Sleep'st by the fable of Bellerus old,
Where the great Vision of the guarded mount
Looks toward Namancos and Bayona's hold.
Look homeward, Angel, now, and melt with ruth;
And, O ye dolphins, waft the hapless youth.
　　Weep no more, woeful shepherds, weep no more,
For Lycidas, your sorrow, is not dead,
Sunk though he be beneath the watery floor;
So sinks the day-star in the ocean bed,
And yet anon repairs his drooping head,

And tricks his beams, and with new spangled ore
Flames in the forehead of the morning sky:
So Lycidas sunk low, but mounted high,
Through the dear might of Him that walked the waves,
Where, other groves and other streams along,
With nectar pure his oozy locks he laves,
And hears the unexpressive nuptial song,
In the blest kingdoms meek of joy and love.
There entertain him all the Saints above,
In solemn troops and sweet societies,
That sing, and singing in their glory move,
And wipe the tears for ever from his eyes.
Now, Lycidas, the shepherds weep no more;
Henceforth thou art the Genius of the shore,
In thy large recompense, and shalt be good
To all that wander in that perilous flood.

    Thus sang the uncouth swain to the oaks and rills,
While the still morn went out with sandals grey;
He touched the tender stops of various quills,
With eager thought warbling his Doric lay:
And now the sun had stretched out all the hills,
And now was dropped into the western bay.
At last he rose, and twitched his mantle blue:
Tomorrow to fresh woods and pastures new.

                     (1637)

from THE CHOICE
John Pomfret

If Heaven the grateful liberty would give
That I might choose my method how to live,
And all those hours propitious fate should lend
In blissful ease and satisfaction spend:

I. THE GENTLEMAN'S RETIREMENT

Near some fair town I'd have a private seat,
Built uniform, not little nor too great;
Better if on a rising ground it stood,

Fields on this side, on that a neighbouring wood.
It should, within, no other things contain
But what are useful, necessary, plain.
Methinks 'tis nauseous, and I'd ne'er endure
The needless pomp of gaudy furniture.
A little garden, grateful to the eye,
And a cool rivulet run murmuring by,
On whose delicious banks a stately row
Of shady limes or sycamores should grow;
At th' end of which a silent study placed
Should with the noblest authors there be graced:
Horace and Virgil, in whose mighty lines
Immortal wit and solid learning shines;
Sharp Juvenal and amorous Ovid too,
Who all the turns of love's soft passion knew. . . .
In some of these, as fancy should advise,
I'd always take my morning exercise;
For sure no moments bring us more content
Than those in pleasing, useful study spent.

2. HIS FORTUNE AND CHARITY

I'd have a clear and competent estate,
That I might live genteelly, but not great;
As much as I could moderately spend;
A little more sometimes t' oblige a friend. . . .
A frugal plenty should my table spread
With healthy, not luxurious, dishes fed;
Enough to satisfy, and something more
To feed the stranger and the neighb'ring poor. . .

3. HIS HOSPITALITY AND TEMPERANCE

I'd have a little cellar cool and neat,
With humming ale and virgin wine replete.
Wine whets the wit, improves its native force,
And gives a pleasant flavour to discourse;
By making all our spirits debonair,
Throws off the lees and sediment of care.
But as the greatest blessing Heaven lends
May be debauched and serve ignoble ends,
So but too oft the grape's refreshing juice

Does many mischievous effects produce. . . .
If any neighbour came, he should be free,
Used with respect and not uneasy be
In my retreat or to himself or me. . . .

4. HIS COMPANY

That life may be more comfortable yet,
And all my joys refined, sincere, and great,
I'd choose two friends whose company would be
A great advance to my felicity:
Well-born, of humours suited to my own,
Discreet, that men as well as books have known, . . .
Obliging, open, without huffing brave;
Brisk in gay talking, and in sober, grave;
Close in dispute but not tenacious, tried
By solemn reason, and let that decide;
Not prone to lust, revenge, or envious hate,
Nor busy meddlers with intrigues of state; . . .
In their society I could not miss
A permanent, sincere, substantial bliss.

5. HIS LADY AND CONVERSE

Would bounteous Heaven once more indulge, I'd choose
(For who would so much satisfaction lose
As witty nymphs in conversation give?)
Near some obliging modest fair to live;
For there's that sweetness in a female mind
Which in a man's we cannot hope to find,
That by a secret but a powerful art
Winds up the spring of life, and does impart
Fresh, vital heat to the transported heart.
   I'd have her reason all her passions sway;
Easy in company, in private gay;
Coy to a fop, to the deserving free;
Still constant to herself and just to me. . . .
Averse to vanity, revenge, and pride,
In all the methods of deceit untried;
So faithful to her friend and good to all,
No censure might upon her actions fall. . . .

To this fair creature I'd sometimes retire;
Her conversations would new joys inspire,
Give life an edge so keen, no surly care
Would venture to assault my soul or dare
Near my retreat to hide one secret snare.
But so divine, so noble a repast
I'd seldom and with moderation taste. . . .

6. HIS PEACEABLE LIFE

. . . Lawsuits I'd shun with as much studious care
As I would dens where hungry lions are,
And rather put up injuries than be
A plague to him who'd be a plague to me.
I value quiet at a price too great
To give for my revenge so dear a rate;
For what do we by all our bustle gain
But counterfeit delight for real pain?

7. HIS HAPPY DEATH

If Heaven a date of many years would give,
Thus I'd in pleasure, ease, and plenty live;
And as I near approach'd the verge of life,
Some kind relation (for I'd have no wife)
Should take upon him all my worldly care
While I did for a better state prepare.
Then I'd not be with any trouble vexed,
Nor have the evening of my days perplexed;
But by a silent and a peaceful death,
Without a sigh, resign my aged breath;
And when committed to the dust I'd have
Few tears, but friendly, dropped into my grave;
Then would my exit so propitious be,
All men would wish to live and die like me.[5]

(1700)

[5] Pomfret, a youngish clergyman, married shortly after publishing *The Choice*. Up in London to secure another church, he was called by the Bishop to explain the "witty nymphs" and "for I'd have no wife" phrases in his poem. While waiting for an appointment with the Bishop, he caught smallpox and died.

ELEGY

WRITTEN IN A COUNTRY CHURCH-YARD

Thomas Gray

The Curfew tolls the knell of parting day,
  The lowing herd wind slowly o'er the lea,
The plowman homeward plods his weary way,
  And leaves the world to darkness and to me.

Now fades the glimmering landscape on the sight,
  And all the air a solemn stillness holds,
Save where the beetle wheels his droning flight,
  And drowsy tinklings lull the distant folds;

Save that from yonder ivy-mantled tower
  The moping owl does to the moon complain
Of such, as wand'ring near her secret bower,
  Molest her ancient solitary reign.

Beneath those rugged elms, that yew-tree's shade,
  Where heaves the turf in many a mold'ring heap,
Each in his narrow cell for ever laid,
  The rude Forefathers of the hamlet sleep.

The breezy call of incense-breathing Morn,
  The swallow twitt'ring from the straw-built shed,
The cock's shrill clarion, or the echoing horn,
  No more shall rouse them from their lowly bed.

For them no more the blazing hearth shall burn,
  Or busy housewife ply her evening care:
No children run to lisp their sire's return,
  Or climb his knees the envied kiss to share.

Oft did the harvest to their sickle yield,
  Their furrow oft the stubborn glebe has broke;
How jocund did they drive their team afield!
  How bowed the woods beneath their sturdy stroke!

Let not Ambition mock their useful toil,
 Their homely joys, and destiny obscure;
Nor Grandeur hear with a disdainful smile,
 The short and simple annals of the poor.

The boast of heraldry, the pomp of pow'r,
 And all that beauty, all that wealth e'er gave,
Awaits alike th' inevitable hour.
 The paths of glory lead but to the grave.

Nor you, ye Proud, impute to These the fault,
 If Mem'ry o'er their Tomb no Trophies raise,
Where through the long-drawn isle and fretted vault
 The pealing anthem swells the note of praise.

Can storied urn or animated bust
 Back to its mansion call the fleeting breath?
Can Honor's voice provoke the silent dust,
 Or Flatt'ry sooth the dull cold ear of Death?

Perhaps in this neglected spot is laid
 Some heart once pregnant with celestial fire;
Hands, that the rod of empire might have swayed,
 Or waked to ecstasy the living lyre.

But Knowledge to their eyes her ample page
 Rich with the spoils of time did ne'er unroll;
Chill Penury repressed their noble rage,
 And froze the genial current of the soul.

Full many a gem of purest ray serene,
 The dark unfathomed caves of ocean bear:
Full many a flower is born to blush unseen,
 And waste its sweetness on the desert air.

Some village-Hampden, that with dauntless breast
 The little Tyrant of his fields withstood;
Some mute inglorious Milton here may rest,
 Some Cromwell guiltless of his country's blood.

Th' applause of list'ning senates to command,
 The threats of pain and ruin to despise,

To scatter plenty o'er a smiling land,
  And read their hist'ry in a nation's eyes,

Their lot forbade: nor circumscribed alone
  Their growing virtues, but their crimes confined;
Forbade to wade through slaughter to a throne,
  And shut the gates of mercy on mankind,

The struggling pangs of conscious truth to hide,
  To quench the blushes of ingenuous shame,
Or heap the shrine of Luxury and Pride
  With incense kindled at the Muse's flame.

Far from the madding crowd's ignoble strife,
  Their sober wishes never learned to stray;
Along the cool sequestered vale of life
  They kept the noiseless tenor of their way.

Yet ev'n these bones from insult to protect
  Some frail memorial still erected nigh,
With uncouth rimes and shapeless sculpture decked,
  Implores the passing tribute of a sigh.

Their name, their years, spelt by th' unlettered muse,
  The place of fame and elegy supply:
And many a holy text around she strews,
  That teach the rustic moralist to die.

For who to dumb Forgetfulness a prey,
  This pleasing anxious being e'er resigned,
Left the warm precincts of the cheerful day,
  Nor cast one longing ling'ring look behind?

On some fond breast the parting soul relies,
  Some pious drops the closing eye requires;
Ev'n from the tomb the voice of Nature cries,
  Ev'n in our Ashes live their wonted Fires.

For thee, who mindful of th' unhonored Dead
  Dost in these lines their artless tale relate;
If chance, by lonely contemplation led,
  Some kindred Spirit shall inquire thy fate,

Haply some hoary-headed Swain may say,
   "Oft have we seen him at the peep of dawn
Brushing with hasty steps the dews away
   To meet the sun upon the upland lawn.

"There at the foot of yonder nodding beech
   That wreathes its old fantastic roots so high,
His listless length at noontide would he stretch,
   And pore upon the brook that babbles by.

"Hard by yon wood, now smiling as in scorn,
   Mutt'ring his wayward fancies he would rove,
Now drooping, woeful wan, like one forlorn,
   Or crazed with care, or crossed in hopeless love.

"One morn I missed him on the customed hill,
   Along the heath and near his fav'rite tree;
Another came; nor yet beside the rill,
   Nor up the lawn, nor at the wood was he;

"The next with dirges due in sad array
   Slow through the church-way path we saw him borne.
Approach and read (for thou canst read) the lay
   Graved on the stone beneath yon agèd thorn."

THE EPITAPH

Here rests his head upon the lap of Earth
   A youth, to Fortune and to Fame unknown;
Fair Science frown'd not on his humble birth
   And Melancholy mark'd him for her own.

Large was his bounty, and his soul sincere;
   Heav'n did a recompense as largely send:
He gave to Mis'ry all he had, a tear,
   He gain'd from Heav'n ('twas all he wish'd) a friend.

No farther seek his merits to disclose,
   Or draw his frailties from their dread abode
(There they alike in trembling hope repose),
   The bosom of his Father and his God.

                (1751)

LET THE TOAST PASS

SONG from THE SCHOOL FOR SCANDAL, III, iii

Richard Brinsley Sheridan

Here's to the maiden of bashful fifteen;
　　Here's to the widow of fifty;
Here's to the flaunting extravagant queen,
　　And here's to the housewife that's thrifty.

Chorus.　　Let the toast pass,
　　　　　　Drink to the lass,
I'll warrant she'll prove an excuse for the glass.

Here's to the charmer whose dimples we prize,
　　Now to the maid who has none, sir;
Here's to the girl with a pair of blue eyes,
　　And here's to the nymph with but one, sir.

Chorus.　　Let the toast pass, etc.

Here's to the maid with a bosom of snow;
　　Now to her that's as brown as a berry;
Here's to the wife with a face full of woe,
　　And now to the damsel that's merry.

Chorus.　　Let the toast pass, etc.

For let 'em be clumsy, or let 'em be slim,
　　Young or ancient, I care not a feather;
So fill a pint bumper quite up to the brim,
So fill up your glasses, nay, fill to the brim,
　　And let us e'en toast them together.

Chorus.　　Let the toast pass, etc.

(1777)

Romantic

BALLADE DES DAMES DU TEMPS JADIS

THE BALLAD OF DEAD LADIES

François Villon, translated by *Dante Gabriel Rossetti*

Dictes-moy où, n'en quel pays,
  Est Flora, la belle Romaine;
Archipiada, ne Thaïs,
  Qui fut sa cousine germaine;
  Echo, parlant quand bruyt on
    maine
Dessus riviere ou sus estan,
  Qui beauté eut trop plus qu'
    humaine?
Mais où sont les neiges d'antan!

Où est la tres sage Heloïs,
  Pour qui fut blessé et puis moyne
Pierre Esbaillart à Sainct-Denys
  (Pour son amour eut cest essoyne)?
  Semblablement, où est la royne
  Qui commanda que Buridan
Fust jetté en ung sac en Seine? . . .
Mais où sont les neiges d'antan?

La royne Blanche comme ung lys,
  Qui chantoit à voix de sereine;

Tell me now in what hidden way is
  Lady Flora the lovely Roman?
Where's Hipparchia, and where is
    Thais,
  Neither of them the fairer woman?
  Where is Echo, beheld of no man,
Only heard on river and mere,—
  She whose beauty was more than
    human? . . .
But where are the snows of yester-
    year?

Where's Héloïse, the learnèd nun,
  For whose sake Abélard, I ween,
Lost manhood and put priesthood.
    on?
  (From Love he won such dule and
    teen!)
  And where, I pray you, is the
    Queen
Who willed that Buridan should
    steer
  Sewed in a sack's mouth down the
    Seine? . . .
But where are the snows of yester-
    year?

White Queen Blanche, like a queen
    of lilies,

Berthe au grand pied, Bietris, Allys;
Harembourges, qui tint le Mayne,
Et Jehanne, la bonne Lorraine,
Qu'Angloys bruslerent à Rouen;
Où sont-ils, Vierge souveraine? . . .
Mais où sont les neiges d'antan!

With a voïce like any mer-
    maiden,—
Bertha Broadfoot, Beatrice, Alice,
And Ermengarde the lady of
    Maine,—
And that good Joan whom Eng-
    lishmen
At Rouen doomed and burned her
    there,—
Mother of God, where are they
    then? . . .
But where are the snows of yester-
    year?

Prince, n'enquerez de sepmaine
Où elles sont, ne de cest an,
Que ce refrain ne vous remaine:
Mais où sont les neiges d'antan?

Nay, never ask this week, fair lord,
Where they are gone, nor yet this
    year,
Save with this for an overword,—
But where are the snows of yester-
    year?

(*c. 1450*)   (1869)

TO A MOUSE

ON TURNING HER UP IN HER NEST WITH THE PLOW
NOVEMBER, 1785

Robert Burns

1

Wee, sleekit, cow'rin', tim'rous beastie,
O what a panic's in thy breastie!
Thou need na start awa sae hasty,
        Wi' bickering brattle!
I wad be laith to rin an' chase thee
        Wi' murd'ring pattle!

2

I'm truly sorry man's dominion
Has broken nature's social union,

An' justifies that ill opinion
        Which makes thee startle
At me, thy poor earth-born companion,
        An' fellow-mortal!

3

I doubt na, whyles, but thou may thieve;
What then? poor beastie, thou maun live!
A daimen-icker in a thrave
        'S a sma' request:
I'll get a blessin' wi' the lave,
        And never miss't!

4

Thy wee bit housie, too, in ruin!
Its silly wa's the win's are strewin'!
An' naething, now, to big a new ane,
        O' foggage green!
An' bleak December's winds ensuin',
        Baith snell an' keen!

5

Thou saw the fields laid bare and waste,
An' weary winter comin' fast,
An' cozie here, beneath the blast,
        Thou thought to dwell,
Till crash! the cruel coulter past
        Out-thro' thy cell.

6

That wee bit heap o' leaves an' stibble
Has cost thee mony a weary nibble!
Now thou's turned out, for a' thy trouble,
        But house or hald,
To thole the winter's sleety dribble,
        An' cranreuch cauld!

7

But, Mousie, thou art no thy lane,
In proving foresight may be vain:
The best laid schemes o' mice an' men
   Gang aft a-gley,
An' lea'e us nought but grief an' pain
   For promised joy.

8

Still thou art blest compared wi' me!
The present only toucheth thee:
But oh! I backward cast my e'e
   On prospects drear!
An' forward tho' I canna see,
   I guess an' fear!

     (1786)

LINES

COMPOSED A FEW MILES ABOVE TINTERN ABBEY ON REVISITING
THE BANKS OF THE WYE DURING A TOUR. JULY 13, 1798

William Wordsworth

Five years have past; five summers, with the length
Of five long winters! and again I hear
These waters, rolling from their mountain-springs
With a soft inland murmur.—Once again
Do I behold these steep and lofty cliffs,
That on a wild secluded scene impress
Thoughts of more deep seclusion; and connect
The landscape with the quiet of the sky.
The day is come when I again repose
Here, under this dark sycamore, and view
These plots of cottage-ground, these orchard-tufts,
Which at this season, with their unripe fruits,
Are clad in one green hue, and lose themselves
'Mid groves and copses. Once again I see

These hedge-rows, hardly hedge-rows, little lines
Of sportive wood run wild: these pastoral farms,
Green to the very door; and wreaths of smoke
Sent up, in silence, from among the trees!
With some uncertain notice, as might seem
Of vagrant dwellers in the houseless woods,
Or of some Hermit's cave, where by his fire
The Hermit sits alone.

                              These beauteous forms,
Through a long absence, have not been to me
As is a landscape to a blind man's eye:
But oft, in lonely rooms, and 'mid the din
Of towns and cities, I have owed to them,
In hours of weariness, sensations sweet,
Felt in the blood, and felt along the heart;
And passing even into my purer mind,
With tranquil restoration:—feelings too
Of unremembered pleasure: such, perhaps,
As have no slight or trivial influence
On that best portion of a good man's life,
His little, nameless, unremembered, acts
Of kindness and of love. Nor less, I trust,
To them I may have owed another gift,
Of aspect more sublime; that blessed mood,
In which the burthen of the mystery,
In which the heavy and the weary weight
Of all this unintelligible world,
Is lightened:—that serene and blessed mood,
In which the affections gently lead us on,—
Until, the breath of this corporeal frame
And even the motion of our human blood
Almost suspended, we are laid asleep
In body, and become a living soul:
While with an eye made quiet by the power
Of harmony, and the deep power of joy,
We see into the life of things.
                                        If this
Be but a vain belief, yet, oh! how oft—
In darkness and amid the many shapes
Of joyless daylight; when the fretful stir

Unprofitable, and the fever of the world,
Have hung upon the beatings of my heart—
How oft, in spirit, have I turned to thee,
O sylvan Wye! thou wanderer, thro' the woods,
How often has my spirit turned to thee!

And now, with gleams of half-extinguished thought,
With many recognitions dim and faint,
And somewhat of a sad perplexity,
The picture of the mind revives again:
While here I stand, not only with the sense
Of present pleasure, but with pleasing thoughts
That in this moment there is life and food
For future years. And so I dare to hope,
Though changed, no doubt, from what I was when first
I came among these hills; when like a roe
I bounded o'er the mountains, by the sides
Of the deep rivers, and the lonely streams,
Wherever nature led: more like a man
Flying from something that he dreads than one
Who sought the thing he loved. For nature then
(The coarser pleasures of my boyish days,
And their glad animal movements all gone by)
To me was all in all.—I cannot paint
What then I was. The sounding cataract
Haunted me like a passion: the tall rock,
The mountain, and the deep and gloomy wood,
Their colours and their forms, were then to me
An appetite; a feeling and a love,
That had no need of a remoter charm,
By thought supplied, nor any interest
Unborrowed from the eye.—That time is past,
And all its aching joys are now no more,
And all its dizzy raptures. Not for this
Faint I, nor mourn nor murmur; other gifts
Have followed; for such loss, I would believe,
Abundant recompense. For I have learned
To look on nature, not as in the hour
Of thoughtless youth; but hearing oftentimes
The still, sad music of humanity,

Nor harsh nor grating, though of ample power
To chasten and subdue. And I have felt
A presence that disturbs me with the joy
Of elevated thoughts; a sense sublime
Of something far more deeply interfused,
Whose dwelling is the light of setting suns,
And the round ocean and the living air,
And the blue sky, and in the mind of man:
A motion and a spirit, that impels
All thinking things, all objects of all thought,
And rolls through all things. Therefore am I still
A lover of the meadows and the woods,
And mountains; and of all that we behold
From this green earth; of all the mighty world
Of eye, and ear,—both what they half create,
And what perceive; well pleased to recognize
In nature and the language of the sense,
The anchor of my purest thoughts, the nurse,
The guide, the guardian of my heart, and soul
Of all my moral being.
                Nor perchance,
If I were not thus taught, should I the more
Suffer my genial spirits to decay:
For thou art with me here upon the banks
Of this fair river; thou my dearest Friend,
My dear, dear Friend, and in thy voice I catch
The language of my former heart, and read
My former pleasures in the shooting lights
Of thy wild eyes. Oh! yet a little while
May I behold in thee what I was once,
My dear, dear Sister! and this prayer I make,
Knowing that Nature never did betray
The heart that loved her; 'tis her privilege,
Through all the years of this our life, to lead
From joy to joy: for she can so inform
The mind that is within us, so impress
With quietness and beauty, and so feed
With lofty thoughts, that neither evil tongues,
Rash judgments, nor the sneers of selfish men,
Nor greetings where no kindness is, nor all

The dreary intercourse of daily life,
Shall e'er prevail against us, or disturb
Our cheerful faith, that all which we behold
Is full of blessings. Therefore let the moon
Shine on thee in thy solitary walk;
And let the misty mountain-winds be free
To blow against thee: and, in after years,
When these wild ecstasies shall be matured
Into a sober pleasure; when thy mind
Shall be a mansion for all lovely forms,
Thy memory be as a dwelling-place
For all sweet sounds and harmonies; oh! then,
If solitude, or fear, or pain, or grief,
Should be thy portion, with what healing thoughts
Of tender joy wilt thou remember me,
And these my exhortations! Nor, perchance—
If I should be where I no more can hear
Thy voice, nor catch from thy wild eyes these gleams
Of past existence—wilt thou then forget
That on the banks of this delightful stream
We stood together; and that I, so long
A worshiper of Nature, hither came
Unwearied in that service: rather say
With warmer love—oh! with far deeper zeal
Of holier love. Nor wilt thou then forget,
That after many wanderings, many years
Of absence, these steep woods and lofty cliffs,
And this green pastoral landscape, were to me
More dear, both for themselves and for thy sake!

(1798)

THE BALLAD OF THE DARK LADIE

A FRAGMENT

Samuel Taylor Coleridge

Beneath yon birch with silver bark,
And boughs so pendulous and fair,

The brook falls scatter'd down the rock:
    And all is mossy there!

And there upon the moss she sits,
The Dark Ladié in silent pain;
The heavy tear is in her eye,
    And drops and swells again.

Three times she sends her little page
Up the castled mountain's breast,
If he might find the Knight that wears
    The Griffin for his crest.

The sun was sloping down the sky,
And she had linger'd there all day,
Counting moments, dreaming fears—
    Oh wherefore can he stay?

She hears a rustling o'er the brook,
She sees far off a swinging bough!
" 'Tis he! 'Tis my betrothèd Knight!
    Lord Falkland, it is thou!"

She springs, she clasps him round the neck,
She sobs a thousand hopes and fears,
Her kisses glowing on his cheeks
    She quenches with her tears.

"My friends with rude ungentle words
They scoff and bid me fly to thee!
O give me shelter in thy breast!
    O shield and shelter me!

"My Henry, I have given thee much,
I gave what I can ne'er recall,
I gave my heart, I gave my peace,
    O Heaven! I gave thee all."

The Knight made answer to the maid,
While to his heart he held her hand,
"Nine castles hath my noble sire,
    None statelier in the land.

"The fairest one shall be my love's,
The fairest castle of the nine!
Wait only till the stars peep out,
    The fairest shall be thine:

"Wait only till the hand of eve
Hath wholly closed yon western bars,
And through the dark we two will steal
    Beneath the twinkling stars!"—

The dark? the dark? No! not the dark?
The twinkling stars? How, Henry? How?
O God! 'twas in the eye of noon
    He pledged his sacred vow!

"And in the eye of noon my love
Shall lead me from my mother's door,
Sweet boys and girls all clothed in white
    Strewing flowers before:

"But first the nodding minstrels go
With music meet for lordly bowers,
The children next in snow-white vests,
    Strewing buds and flowers!

"And then my love and I shall pace,
My jet black hair in pearly braids,
Between our comely bachelors
    And blushing bridal maids."

.   .   .   .   .

(*1798*, 1834)

from CHILDE HAROLD'S PILGRIMAGE, Canto IV
George Gordon, Lord Byron

178

There is a pleasure in the pathless woods,
There is a rapture on the lonely shore,
There is society, where none intrudes,

By the deep sea, and music in its roar:
I love not Man the less, but Nature more,
From these our interviews, in which I steal
From all I may be, or have been before,
To mingle with the Universe, and feel
What I can ne'er express, yet cannot all conceal.

179

Roll on, thou deep and dark blue Ocean—roll!
Ten thousand fleets sweep over thee in vain;
Man marks the earth with ruin—his control
Stops with the shore; upon the watery plain
The wrecks are all thy deed, nor doth remain
A shadow of man's ravage, save his own,
When, for a moment, like a drop of rain,
He sinks into thy depths with bubbling groan,
Without a grave, unknell'd, uncoffin'd, and unknown.

180

His steps are not upon thy paths,—thy fields
Are not a spoil for him,—thou dost arise
And shake him from thee; the vile strength he wields
For earth's destruction thou dost all despise,
Spurning him from thy bosom to the skies,
And send'st him, shivering in thy playful spray
And howling, to his gods, where haply lies
His petty hope in some near port or bay,
And dashest him again to earth:—there let him lay.

181

The armaments which thunderstrike the walls
Of rock-built cities, bidding nations quake,
And monarchs tremble in their capitals,
The oak leviathans, whose huge ribs make
Their clay creator the vain title take
Of lord of thee, and arbiter of war—
These are thy toys, and, as the snowy flake,
They melt into thy yeast of waves, which mar
Alike the Armada's pride or spoils of Trafalgar.

182

Thy shores are empires, changed in all save thee—
Assyria, Greece, Rome, Carthage, what are they?
Thy waters wash'd them power while they were free,
And many a tyrant since; their shores obey
The stranger, slave, or savage; their decay
Has dried up realms to deserts:—not so thou,
Unchangeable, save to thy wild waves' play,
Time writes no wrinkle on thine azure brow:
Such as creation's dawn beheld, thou rollest now.

183

Thou glorious mirror, where the Almighty's form
Glasses itself in tempests; in all time,—
Calm or convulsed, in breeze, or gale, or storm,
Icing the pole, or in the torrid clime
Dark-heaving—boundless, endless, and sublime,
The image of Eternity, the throne
Of the Invisible; even from out thy slime
The monsters of the deep are made; each zone
Obeys thee; thou goest forth, dread, fathomless, alone.

184

And I have loved thee, Ocean! and my joy
Of youthful sports was on thy breast to be
Borne, like thy bubbles, onward: from a boy
I wanton'd with thy breakers—they to me
Were a delight; and if the freshening sea
Made them a terror—'twas a pleasing fear,
For I was as it were a child of thee,
And trusted to thy billows far and near, .
And laid my hand upon thy mane—as I do here.

(1818)

THE GARDEN OF PROSERPINE

Algernon Charles Swinburne

Here, where the world is quiet;
　Here, where all trouble seems
Dead winds' and spent waves' riot
　In doubtful dreams of dreams;
I watch the green field growing
For reaping folk and sowing,
For harvest-time and mowing,
　A sleepy world of streams.

I am tired of tears and laughter,
　And men that laugh and weep;
Of what may come hereafter
　For men that sow to reap:
I am weary of days and hours,
Blown buds of barren flowers,
Desires and dreams and powers
　And everything but sleep.

Here life has death for neighbor,
　And far from eye or ear
Wan waves and wet winds labor,
　Weak ships and spirits steer;
They drive adrift, and whither
They wot not who make thither;
But no such winds blow hither,
　And no such things grow here.

No growth of moor or coppice,
　No heather-flower or vine,
But bloomless buds of poppies,
　Green grapes of Proserpine,
Pale beds of blowing rushes
Where no leaf blooms or blushes
Save this whereout she crushes
　For dead men deadly wine.

Pale, without name or number,
  In fruitless fields of corn,
They bow themselves and slumber
  All night till light is born;
And like a soul belated,
In hell and heaven unmated,
By cloud and mist abated
  Comes out of darkness morn.

Though one were strong as seven,
  He too with death shall dwell,
Nor wake with wings in heaven,
  Nor weep for pains in hell;
Though one were fair as roses,
His beauty clouds and closes;
And well though love reposes,
  In the end it is not well.

Pale, beyond porch and portal,
  Crowned with calm leaves, she stands
Who gathers all things mortal
  With cold immortal hands;
Her languid lips are sweeter
Than love's who fears to greet her
To men that mix and meet her
  From many times and lands.

She waits for each and other,
  She waits for all men born;
Forgets the earth her mother,
  The life of fruits and corn;
And spring and seed and swallow
Take wing for her and follow
Where summer song rings hollow
  And flowers are put to scorn.

There go the loves that wither,
  The old loves with wearier wings;
And all dead years draw thither,
  And all disastrous things;
Dead dreams of days forsaken,

Blind buds that snows have shaken,
Wild leaves that winds have taken,
    Red strays of ruined springs.

We are not sure of sorrow,
    And joy was never sure;
Today will die tomorrow;
    Time stoops to no man's lure;
And love, grown faint and fretful,
With lips but half regretful
Sighs, and with eyes forgetful
    Weeps that no loves endure.

From too much love of living,
    From hope and fear set free,
We thank with brief thanksgiving
    Whatever gods may be
That no life lives for ever;
That dead men rise up never;
That even the weariest river
    Winds somewhere safe to sea.

Then star nor sun shall waken,
    Nor any change of light:
Nor sound of waters shaken,
    Nor any sound or sight:
Nor wintry leaves nor vernal,
Nor days nor things diurnal;
Only the sleep eternal
    In an eternal night.

                    (1866)

SUGGESTIONS FOR STUDY

1. *Classic and Neo-classic.* (a) Read the classic and neo-classic group
of poems above. Reread each before going on to the next. (b) Now
review the paragraphs on the classic style in the text. Supplement this
by looking up such terms as "pastoral," "elegy," and "idyl" in the
standard references. (c) Return to a reading of the poems, giving
your attention to the classical elements in their style.

2. *The Romantic Style.* (a) Read and reread the romantic poems in this chapter. (b) Review the paragraphs in the text on the romantic style. (c) Reconsider the poems, now, with special regard to the romantic elements in their style.

3. *Country Churchyard and Tintern Abbey.* (a) Study Gray's "Elegy" and Wordsworth's "Lines . . . Tintern Abbey" together. (b) Consider them as to type and sub-type, poetic form, theme, and mood, and especially as regards poetic style. (c) Jot down in one pair of parallel columns what you consider their similarities, and in another pair of parallel columns what you consider their differences.

4. *Realism.* (a) The realistic style, "characterized by the predominance of the *sense of fact* over imagination and reason," is sometimes concerned with pictorial fidelity and sometimes with psychological fidelity to the fact. (b) Reread the following poems which, in one way or another, may be considered realistic: Denney's "The Hammer-Throw" (p. 8), Sandburg's "Chicago" (p. 216), Frost's "Out, Out—" (p. 30), Eliot's "The Love Song of J. Alfred Prufrock" (p. 319), and E. Merrill Root's "Chicago Idyll" (p. 505). (c) Now work out a paragraph statement of what you consider to be the *realistic style.*

5. *Style Sorting.* (a) Review the poems in Chapters 13-15, with attention upon the poetic style of each. (b) Sort them into five groups: 1. Classic, 2. Romantic, 3. Realistic, 4. Some other style, 5. Undecided. (c) List them, with brief notes about their style, in the form of an outline.

6. *Period Sorting.* (a) The following is a sixfold scheme for sorting poems according to their periods: 1. *Ancient* (850 B.C.-50 A.D.), 2. *Medieval* (1100-1450), 3. *Renaissance* [Early Renaissance, Elizabethan, Jacobean-Caroline] (1485-1650), 4. *Neo-classical* [Restoration, Augustan, Age of Johnson, American Colonial] (1660-1775), 5. *Nineteenth Century* [Romantic Movement, Victorian Era, Early and Later American National] (1790-1890), 6. *Modern* [The 1890's, Pre-War, Post-War, Contemporary, Current] (1890-   ). (b) Leaf through the poems in Chapters 16-18, and classify them according to the six broad periods, listing them chronologically in the form of an outline.

7. *Change in Style.* (a) Read the following brief lyric a number of times in an effort to experience it fully and to catch the elements of its romantic style.

A DIRGE

Percy Bysshe Shelley

Rough wind, that moanest loud
    Grief too sad for song;
Wild wind, when sullen cloud
    Knells all the night long;
Sad storm, whose tears are vain,
Bare woods, whose branches strain,
Deep caves and dreary main,—
    Wail, for the world's wrong!

(1824)

(b) Now consider the question: How might a neo-classical or a realistic poet have treated the same theme? (c) Either write a short paper in which you discuss the possible transformation of this poem into another style, or actually write the lyric over in one of the other two styles.

21

INDIVIDUAL POETS—
JOHN KEATS AND ROBERT FROST

Yet another approach to poetry will be illustrated in closing Part
Five of this book; but, as in the last chapter, it will be only one of
several related points of view from which the reader may look at
poetry.

Each poem is a personal document, a sort of letter from the poet
to his contemporaries and to posterity. Together the works of a
poet stand as an intimate biography, no matter how "objective" he
may have been in his creative work. From the poems stands forth
the man. And the body of this chapter will present two groups of
poems, and invite the reader to look at them as the expression of
two individual poets—which approach, with proper qualifications,
might be called biographical or personal.

I. THE BIOGRAPHICAL AND PERSONAL APPROACH

Biography, in one sense, may be considered as a branch of History, of which there are other branches, such as political history,
social history, and literary history. Now a poem, as has just been
said, may be looked upon as a biographical or personal document;
it may also be looked upon as an historical document, political or
social or literary. For each poet, in one way or another, has been
a part of his times and, consciously or unconsciously, directly or by
indirection, has reflected the life of his times in his poems.

We have already suggested that poems may be sorted out for consideration as regards their historic styles, their relation to the great
cultural movements, literary schools and periods. It remains to observe that poems are also social documents and, in some cases and
to some extent, political documents.

Let us illustrate. We have so far read a number of poems by Lord Byron (1788-1824) and by Percy B. Shelley (1792-1822), English poets both of whom lived their mature lives under the rule of George IV, who was the Prince Regent during the senile lunacy of his father George III and then ascended the throne in his own "right." These were indeed restless times for liberty-loving people. It is true that the American Colonies, which had earlier won their independence, had now established a federal government and a somewhat national if not entirely democratic life. The French Revolution, however, and the popular cause in that country, had eventuated in the Napoleonic empire and then in the restoration of the Bourbons. Both Byron and Shelley were of revolutionary temper. You may recall Shelley's "Sonnet: England in 1819" (p. 116) and his "Ode to the West Wind" (p. 133), Byron's *Childe Harold* (p. 572) and *Don Juan* (p. 529), by no means isolated examples of poetry that may well be viewed in relation to the currents of liberal thought during the Regency Period. Both of these poets were in revolt against the laws and conventions of their own land; both lived their last years in self-imposed exile; both rejoiced in the fall of Napoleon; both encouraged oppressed peoples in other lands, and Byron literally gave his life in the cause of Greek freedom. To understand the political, social, and literary life of their times, one may well read Byron and Shelley. But—to understand Byron and Shelley, one must also read in the political, social, and literary history of this period!

A comparable paradox may be observed when one approaches a group of poems as the work of an individual poet. To read the poems, you must know the man; yet to know the man, you must read the poems. This was seen to be so when, in an earlier chapter, some attention was given to the life and personality of George Herbert in relation to his poem "The Collar" (p. 314). The reader's background was enriched by the presentation of relevant biographical data so that the poem-experience might become more meaningful. Then, in turn, the poem-experience itself shed light upon the personality of the poet.

Modern biography, in its development during the past generation, has added psychological interpretation to sound historiography; and the result has often been the more vivid emergence of the personality of the subject. Knowledge of human behavior has increased markedly since the first Freudian explorations of the unconscious, and the poets have provided a fertile field for such psychological biography.

In studying a group of poems as the expression of an individual personality, it will be important to work within a strict framework of chronology in dealing with the relation of outward events to specific utterances. It is of some importance, for instance, to know the date of Clough's poem "Say Not the Struggle Nought Availeth" (p. 177) if it is to be read against the background of Clough's life and his relation to his times. And it is important to date the possibly relevant events in his life history (which ones precede the writing of the poem?) and the possibly relevant events in the history of his time. Only then can it be said with reasonable certainty that there may be a connection between them and the experience to which the poet gives expression in his poem. It is simple enough to date Shelley's "Sonnet: England in 1819" and Collins' "Ode Written in . . . 1746" (p. 145) and to interpret them in the light of their day.[1] But it is by no means easy to date the first publication of many poems, let alone their composition, as the assignment of dates to the poems of this book may well indicate. The dates of a poet's birth and death are usually accurately known, ascertained from parish and family records, and from the living memory that fastens on such things. But the poet's life, between those vital moments of beginning and end, is by no means so easy to discover. Just what persons influenced the poet, just what incidents affected him, just what books engaged his interest during a certain year of his life—these are most difficult to determine. Yet the systematic and critical interpretation of letters and journals, of various records and testimonies, has allowed the biographer to piece together a chronological account of the subject's life that is often surprisingly complete.

[1] Such reference works as *Annals of English Literature*, Oxford University Press, 1936, and Helen Rex Keller, *The Dictionary of Dates*, Macmillan, 1934, are useful in studying the events of a particular year.

2. JOHN KEATS AND ROBERT FROST

Of John Keats—six of whose poems are presented in this chapter and an equal number in preceding chapters—the biographical data has been patiently gathered and interpreted by such scholars as Sidney Colvin, Amy Lowell, and Dorothy Hewlett.[2] So it is possible, in studying Keats' sonnet "On First Looking into Chapman's Homer" (p. 25), to note the influence of Cowden Clarke, the affecting incident of an evening's reading aloud, the engaging book.[3] But a biographical interpretation would not stop there; it would note possible sources in Keats' reading of such a striking phrase as "the pure serene" (which seems to have stuck in his mind from Cary's translation of Dante) and the stirring similes of astronomer and explorer in the sestet.[4] The date of composition, October 1816, was just prior to Keats' twenty-first birthday and while he was still a medical student. Amy Lowell writes of this sonnet, "The success it met with in the Keats circle must have clinched his resolve to free himself from surgery without delay." [5] It was printed by his friend Leigh Hunt in the *Examiner* of December first to illustrate an article on "Young Poets." The intimate friendship that developed between Keats and Hunt "was really the opening of a new chapter both in his intellectual and social life," writes Sidney Colvin.[6]

Each of Keats' poems read so far—"On First Looking into Chapman's Homer" (p. 25), "Ode on a Grecian Urn" (p. 152), "Ode to a Nightingale" (p. 273), "The Eve of St. Agnes" (p. 413), the sonnet "When I have fears that I may cease to be" (p. 455), and "Ode" ('Bards of passion and of mirth,' p. 469)—may profitably be viewed in relation to the poet's personality and life-history. And each of them, in turn, reveals something memorable about his life and person.

[2] Sidney Colvin, *John Keats: His Life and Poetry . . .*, Macmillan, 1917; Amy Lowell, *John Keats*, 2 vols., Houghton Mifflin, 1925; Dorothy Hewlett, *Adonais: a Life of John Keats*, Bobbs-Merrill, 1938.
[3] For the previous discussion, see p. 25.
[4] Lowell, *op. cit.*, vol. I, pp. 180-83.
[5] *Ibid.*, p. 183.
[6] Colvin, *op. cit.*, p. 41.

The facts about the life of John Keats are readily available and will not be summarized here. Strange as it may seem, however, the biography of modern and living poets is less accessible. The gathering of comprehensive data, the establishing of a complete bibliography, the sifting of private correspondence—these are critical tasks that await not only the completion of the poet's life, but often the conditions of his will and the dissolution of his estate. Yet from many sources come those numerous and stray bits of information, often supplied by the poet himself, that may make for a fuller understanding of the poem in relation to the poet.

We noted, for instance, that Robert Frost's "The Road Not Taken" (p. 209) is usually interpreted as a poem suggesting some experience in the poet's own life, but that it now must be viewed in relation to Robert Frost's assertion that he had in mind the experience of a friend.[7] And so it is in the biographical approach to poetry: the interpretation changes, often radically, as additional data come to light. Keats' sonnet "Bright Star—" was long thought to be his last poem, until it was discovered to have been written seventeen months prior to his final departure for Italy.

Of Robert Frost's life the chief facts are not hard to find; they are summarized in such standard biographical references as *Twentieth Century Authors* by Kunitz and Haycraft, and in *Modern Biography*. A fuller treatment of the poet's life is to be found in an earlier volume by G. B. Munson, and new biographical materials have been gathered by Lawrance Thompson.

The facts about the publication of his poems are to be found in *Robert Frost: a Bibliography* by Clymer and Green; and a rich gathering of critical estimates in *Recognition of Robert Frost,* edited by Richard Thornton.

With these suggestions, then, about the biographical approach—as one of a pair of related points of view from which the reader may consider poetry—we come to two groups of poems which may be used to illustrate it.

[7] See the discussion on pp. 209-11. Two other poems by Robert Frost will be found earlier in this volume: "Out, Out—" (p. 30) and "Mending Wall" (p. 235).

Poems by John Keats

ON THE SEA

[After the publication of his first volume of *Poems* (March 1817), Keats went off to the beautiful Isle of Wight, with its cliffs and seaside, to begin work on his next venture, the long poem *Endymion*. This sonnet was sent to his friend Reynolds in a letter dated April 17, [1817], which says, ". . . the passage in *Lear*—'Do you not hear the sea?'—has haunted me intensely" (*Letters,* ed. Colvin, p. 8).]

It keeps eternal whisperings around
    Desolate shores, and with its mighty swell
    Gluts twice ten thousand caverns, till the spell
Of Hecate leaves them their old shadowy sound.
Often 'tis in such gentle temper found,
    That scarcely will the very smallest shell
    Be moved for days from where it sometime fell,
When last the winds of heaven were unbound.
Oh ye! who have your eye-balls vexed and tired,
    Feast them upon the wideness of the Sea;
Oh ye! whose ears are dinned with uproar rude,
    Or fed too much with cloying melody—
Sit ye near some old cavern's mouth, and brood
Until ye start, as if the sea-nymphs quired!
                        (*1817,* 1817)

Proem from ENDYMION

[The famous opening line of this long poem occurred to Keats as early as 1815, according to his friend Henry Stephens to whom he recited it one night; but he wrote the poem during the year 1817.]

A thing of beauty is a joy for ever:
Its loveliness increases; it will never
Pass into nothingness; but still will keep
A bower quiet for us, and a sleep
Full of sweet dreams, and health, and quiet breathing.
Therefore, on every morrow, are we wreathing
A flowery band to bind us to the earth,
Spite of despondence, of the inhuman dearth
Of noble natures, of the gloomy days,
Of all the unhealthy and o'er-darkened ways
Made for our searching: yes, in spite of all,
Some shape of beauty moves away the pall
From our dark spirits. Such the sun, the moon,
Trees old and young, sprouting a shady boon
For simple sheep: and such are daffodils
With the green world they live in; and clear rills
That for themselves a cooling covert make
'Gainst the hot season; the mid-forest brake,
Rich with a sprinkling of fair musk-rose blooms:
And such too is the grandeur of the dooms
We have imagined for the mighty dead;
All lovely tales that we have heard or read:
An endless fountain of immortal drink,
Pouring unto us from the heaven's brink.

Nor do we merely feel these essences
For one short hour; no, even as the trees
That whisper round a temple become soon
Dear as the temple's self, so does the moon,
The passion poesy, glories infinite,
Haunt us till they become a cheering light
Unto our souls, and bound to us so fast,
That, whether there be shine, or gloom o'ercast,
They alway must be with us, or we die.

Therefore, 't is with full happiness that I
Will trace the story of Endymion.
The very music of the name has gone
Into my being, and each pleasant scene
Is growing fresh before me as the green

Of our own valleys: so I will begin
Now while I cannot hear the city's din;
Now while the early budders are just new,
And run in mazes of the youngest hue
About old forests; while the willow trails
Its delicate amber; and the dairy pails
Bring home increase of milk. And, as the year
Grows lush in juicy stalks, I'll smoothly steer
My little boat, for many quiet hours,
With streams that deepen freshly into bowers.
Many and many a verse I hope to write,
Before the daisies, vermeil rimmed and white,
Hide in deep herbage; and ere yet the bees
Hum about globes of clover and sweet peas,
I must be near the middle of my story.
O may no wintry season, bare and hoary,
See it half finished: but let Autumn bold,
With universal tinge of sober gold,
Be all about me when I make an end.
And now at once, adventuresome, I send
My herald thought into a wilderness:
There let its trumpet blow, and quickly dress
My uncertain path with green, that I may speed
Easily onward, thorough flowers and weed.

(1817, 1818)

LINES ON THE MERMAID TAVERN

[The Mermaid Tavern was a famous resort of Shakespeare, Ben Jonson, and others of the Elizabethan period whose literature Keats read and admired. He wrote the poem early in the year 1818.]

Souls of poets dead and gone,
What Elysium have ye known,
Happy field or mossy cavern,
Choicer than the Mermaid Tavern?
Have ye tippled drink more fine
Than mine host's Canary wine?

Or are fruits of Paradise
Sweeter than those dainty pies
Of venison? O generous food!
Dressed as though bold Robin Hood
Would, with his maid Marian,
Sup and bowse from horn and can.

I have heard that on a day
Mine host's sign-board flew away,
Nobody knew whither, till
An Astrologer's old quill
To a sheepskin gave the story,—
Said he saw you in your glory,
Underneath a new old-sign
Sipping beverage divine,
And pledging with contented smack
The Mermaid in the Zodiac.

Souls of poets dead and gone,
What Elysium have ye known,
Happy field or mossy cavern,
Choicer than the Mermaid Tavern?

(*1818*, 1820)

LA BELLE DAME SANS MERCI

[The title of this ballad, derived from a Chaucerian translation of
an Old French poem, Keats had already used to name an imagined
song in "The Eve of St. Agnes." From a note to the old poem, from
The Faerie Queene, II, vi, 1 ff., and from *Palmerin of England* (according to Amy Lowell, *op. cit.*, II, 221-5) came some of his inspiration.
Amy Lowell dates the poem April 28, 1819.]

I

O what can ail thee, knight-at-arms,
    Alone and palely loitering?
The sedge has withered from the lake,
    And no birds sing.

2

O what can ail thee, knight-at-arms,
    So haggard and so woe-begone?
The squirrel's granary is full,
    And the harvest's done.

3

I see a lily on thy brow
    With anguish moist and fever dew,
And on thy cheeks a fading rose
    Fast withereth too.

4

I met a lady in the meads,
    Full beautiful—a faery's child,
Her hair was long, her foot was light,
    And her eyes were wild.

5

I made a garland for her head,
    And bracelets too, and fragrant zone;
She looked at me as she did love,
    And made sweet moan.

6

I set her on my pacing steed
    And nothing else saw all day long,
For sidelong would she bend, and sing
    A faery's song.

7

She found me roots of relish sweet,
    And honey wild, and manna dew,
And sure in language strange she said—
    "I love thee true!"

8

She took me to her elfin grot,
   And there she wept and sighed full sore,
And there I shut her wild, wild eyes
   With kisses four.

9

And there she lullèd me asleep,
   And there I dreamed—ah, woe betide!
The latest dream I ever dreamt
   On the cold hill side.

10

I saw pale kings, and princes too,
   Pale warriors, death-pale were they all;
They cried—"La Belle Dame sans Merci
   Hath thee in thrall!"

11

I saw their starved lips in the gloam,
   With horrid warning gapèd wide,
And I awoke and found me here,
   On the cold hill's side.

12

And this is why I sojourn here,
   Alone and palely loitering,
Though the sedge is withered from the lake,
   And no birds sing.

                        (1819, 1820)

ODE ON MELANCHOLY

[So different in mood and thought from "Ode on a Grecian Urn" composed at about the same time (May 1819), this ode has been variously interpreted in its relation to Keats' life. Burton's *Anatomy of Melancholy* was amongst his reading, and there was "a fine and culti-

vated melancholy" (as Dorothy Hewlett calls it, *op. cit.*, pp. 331-32)
fashionable at the time; but he was often deeply depressed—by the
death of his brother Tom, by the consciousness of his own illness, by
financial worries, by frustration in his love for Fanny Brawne. However, in January he had written to his friend Haydon, "I do not think
I shall ever come to the rope or the Pistol, for after a day or two's
melancholy, although I smoke more and more my own insufficiency—
I see by little and little more of what is to be done, and how it is to
be done, should I ever be able to do it" (*Letters,* ed. Colvin, p. 214).]

1

No, no, go not to Lethe, neither twist
    Wolf's-bane, tight-rooted, for its poisonous wine;
Nor suffer thy pale forehead to be kissed
    By nightshade, ruby grape of Proserpine;
Make not your rosary of yew-berries,
    Nor let the beetle, nor the death-moth be
        Your mournful Psyche, nor the downy owl
A partner in your sorrow's mysteries;
    For shade to shade will come too drowsily,
        And drown the wakeful anguish of the soul.

2

But when the melancholy fit shall fall
    Sudden from heaven like a weeping cloud,
That fosters the droop-headed flowers all,
    And hides the green hill in an April shroud;
Then glut thy sorrow on a morning rose,
    Or on the rainbow of the salt sand-wave,
        Or on the wealth of globèd peonies;
Or if thy mistress some rich anger shows,
    Emprison her soft hand, and let her rave,
        And feed deep, deep upon her peerless eyes.

3

She dwells with Beauty—Beauty that must die;
    And Joy, whose hand is ever at his lips
Bidding adieu; and aching Pleasure nigh,
    Turning to poison while the bee-mouth sips:
Ay, in the very temple of Delight

Veiled Melancholy has her sovran shrine,
   Though seen of none save him whose strenuous tongue
Can burst Joy's grape against his palate fine:
His soul shall taste the sadness of her might,
   And be among her cloudy trophies hung.

(1819, 1820)

BRIGHT STAR

[This sonnet, written perhaps in February, March, or April 1819, was revised and written out by Keats, when departing for Italy, in a copy of Shakespeare's *Poems*—opposite "A Lover's Complaint"—and given to his good friend and companion Severn. In this form it becomes one of the last things Keats wrote. The earlier version, given to Fanny Brawne, was copied by her into the copy of *Dante* given her by Keats in 1819.]

Bright star! would I were steadfast as thou art—
   Not in lone splendor hung aloft the night,
And watching, with eternal lids apart,
   Like Nature's patient, sleepless Eremite,
The moving waters at their priestlike task
   Of pure ablution round earth's human shores,
Or gazing on the new soft fallen mask
   Of snow upon the mountains and the moors—
No—yet still steadfast, still unchangeable,
   Pillowed upon my fair love's ripening breast,
To feel for ever its soft fall and swell,
   Awake for ever in a sweet unrest,
Still, still to hear her tender-taken breath,
And so live ever—or else swoon to death.

(1819-20, 1848)

Poems by Robert Frost

ONCE BY THE PACIFIC

The shattered water made a misty din.
Great waves looked over others coming in,
And thought of doing something to the shore
That water never did to land before.
The clouds were low and hairy in the skies
Like locks blown forward in the gleam of eyes.
You could not tell, and yet it looked as if
The shore was lucky in being backed by cliff,
The cliff in being backed by continent.
It looked as if a night of dark intent
Was coming, and not only a night, an age.
Someone had better be prepared for rage.
There would be more than ocean water broken
Before God's last *Put out the light* was spoken.

(1926, 1928)

TO EARTHWARD

Love at the lips was touch
As sweet as I could bear;
And once that seemed too much;
I lived on air

That crossed me from sweet things,
The flow of—was it musk
From hidden grapevine springs
Down hill at dusk?

I had the swirl and ache
From sprays of honeysuckle
That when they're gathered shake
Dew on the knuckle.

I craved strong sweets, but those
Seemed strong when I was young;
The petal of the rose
It was that stung.

Now no joy but lacks salt
That is not dashed with pain
And weariness and fault;
I crave the stain

Of tears, the aftermark
Of almost too much love,
The sweet of bitter bark
And burning clove.

When stiff and sore and scarred
I take away my hand
From leaning on it hard
In grass and sand,

The hurt is not enough:
I long for weight and strength
To feel the earth as rough
To all my length.

(*1914, 1923*)

STOPPING BY WOODS ON A SNOWY EVENING

[See the draft of this poem, comment upon the poet's work, and French translation, pp. 603-08.]

Whose woods these are I think I know.
His house is in the village though;
He will not see me stopping here
To watch his woods fill up with snow.

My little horse must think it queer
To stop without a farmhouse near
Between the woods and frozen lake
The darkest evening of the year.

He gives his harness bells a shake
To ask if there is some mistake.
The only other sound's the sweep
Of easy wind and downy flake.

The woods are lovely, dark and deep,
But I have promises to keep,
And miles to go before I sleep,
And miles to go before I sleep.

(*1923*, 1923)

BIRCHES

When I see birches bend to left and right
Across the lines of straighter darker trees,
I like to think some boy's been swinging them.
But swinging doesn't bend them down to stay.
Ice-storms do that. Often you must have seen them
Loaded with ice a sunny winter morning
After a rain. They click upon themselves
As the breeze rises, and turn many-colored
As the stir cracks and crazes their enamel.
Soon the sun's warmth makes them shed crystal shells
Shattering and avalanching on the snow-crust—
Such heaps of broken glass to sweep away
You'd think the inner dome of heaven had fallen.
They are dragged to the withered bracken by the load,
And they seem not to break; though once they are bowed
So low for long, they never right themselves:
You may see their trunks arching in the woods
Years afterwards, trailing their leaves on the ground
Like girls on hands and knees that throw their hair
Before them over their heads to dry in the sun.

But I was going to say when Truth broke in
With all her matter-of-fact about the ice-storm
I should prefer to have some boy bend them
As he went out and in to fetch the cows—
Some boy too far from town to learn baseball,
Whose only play was what he found himself,
Summer or winter, and could play alone.
One by one he subdued his father's trees
By riding them down over and over again
Until he took the stiffness out of them,
And not one but hung limp, not one was left
For him to conquer. He learned all there was
To learn about not launching out too soon
And so not carrying the tree away
Clear to the ground. He always kept his poise
To the top branches, climbing carefully
With the same pains you use to fill a cup
Up to the brim, and even above the brim.
Then he flung outward, feet first, with a swish,
Kicking his way down through the air to the ground.
So was I once myself a swinger of birches.
And so I dream of going back to be.
It's when I'm weary of considerations,
And life is too much like a pathless wood
Where your face burns and tickles with the cobwebs
Broken across it, and one eye is weeping
From a twig's having lashed across it open.
I'd like to get away from earth awhile
And then come back to it and begin over.
May no fate willfully misunderstand me
And half grant what I wish and snatch me away
Not to return. Earth's the right place for love:
I don't know where it's likely to go better.
I'd like to go by climbing a birch tree,
And climb black branches up a snow-white trunk
Toward heaven, till the tree could bear no more,
But dipped its top and set me down again.
That would be good both going and coming back.
One could do worse than be a swinger of birches.

(1915, 1915-16)

THE DEATH OF THE HIRED MAN

Mary sat musing on the lamp-flame at the table
Waiting for Warren. When she heard his step,
She ran on tip-toe down the darkened passage
To meet him in the doorway with the news
And put him on his guard. "Silas is back."
She pushed him outward with her through the door
And shut it after her. "Be kind," she said.
She took the market things from Warren's arms
And set them on the porch, then drew him down
To sit beside her on the wooden steps.

"When was I ever anything but kind to him?
But I'll not have the fellow back," he said.
"I told him so last haying, didn't I?
'If he left then,' I said, 'that ended it.'
What good is he? Who else will harbor him
At his age for the little he can do?
What help he is there's no depending on.
Off he goes always when I need him most.
'He thinks he ought to earn a little pay,
Enough at least to buy tobacco with,
So he won't have to beg and be beholden.'
'All right,' I say, 'I can't afford to pay
Any fixed wages, though I wish I could.'
'Someone else can.' 'Then someone else will have to.'
I shouldn't mind his bettering himself
If that was what it was. You can be certain,
When he begins like that, there's someone at him
Trying to coax him off with pocket-money,—
In haying time, when any help is scarce.
In winter he comes back to us. I'm done."

"Sh! not so loud: he'll hear you," Mary said.

"I want him to: he'll have to soon or late."

"He's worn out. He's asleep beside the stove.
When I came up from Rowe's I found him here,

Huddled against the barn-door fast asleep,
A miserable sight, and frightening, too—
You needn't smile—I didn't recognize him—
I wasn't looking for him—and he's changed.
Wait till you see."

"Where did you say he'd been?"

"He didn't say. I dragged him to the house,
And gave him tea and tried to make him smoke.
I tried to make him talk about his travels.
Nothing would do: he just kept nodding off."

"What did he say? Did he say anything?"

"But little."

"Anything? Mary, confess
He said he'd come to ditch the meadow for me."

"Warren!"

"But did he? I just want to know."

"Of course he did. What would you have him say?
Surely you wouldn't grudge the poor old man
Some humble way to save his self-respect.
He added, if you really care to know,
He meant to clear the upper pasture, too.
That sounds like something you have heard before?
Warren, I wish you could have heard the way
He jumbled everything. I stopped to look
Two or three times—he made me feel so queer—
To see if he was talking in his sleep.
He ran on Harold Wilson—you remember—
The boy you had in haying four years since.
He's finished school, and teaching in his college.
Silas declares you'll have to get him back.
He says they two will make a team for work:
Between them they will lay this farm as smooth!

The way he mixed that in with other things.
He thinks young Wilson a likely lad, though daft
On education—you know how they fought
All through July under the blazing sun,
Silas up on the cart to build the load,
Harold along beside to pitch it on."

"Yes, I took care to keep well out of earshot."

"Well, those days trouble Silas like a dream.
You wouldn't think they would. How some things linger!
Harold's young college boy's assurance piqued him.
After so many years he still keeps finding
Good arguments he sees he might have used.
I sympathise. I know just how it feels
To think of the right thing to say too late.
Harold's associated in his mind with Latin.
He asked me what I thought of Harold's saying
He studied Latin like the violin
Because he liked it—that an argument!
He said he couldn't make the boy believe
He could find water with a hazel prong—
Which showed how much good school had ever done him.
He wanted to go over that. But most of all
He thinks if he could have another chance
To teach him how to build a load of hay—"

"I know, that's Silas' one accomplishment.
He bundles every forkful in its place,
And tags and numbers it for future reference,
So he can find and easily dislodge it
In the unloading. Silas does that well.
He takes it out in bunches like big birds' nests.
You never see him standing on the hay
He's trying to lift, straining to lift himself."

"He thinks if he could teach him that, he'd be
Some good perhaps to someone in the world.
He hates to see a boy the fool of books.
Poor Silas, so concerned for other folk,

And nothing to look backward to with pride,
And nothing to look forward to with hope,
So now and never any different."

Part of a moon was falling down the west,
Dragging the whole sky with it to the hills.
Its light poured softly in her lap. She saw it
And spread her apron to it. She put out her hand
Among the harp-like morning-glory strings,
Taut with the dew from garden bed to eaves,
As if she played unheard some tenderness
That wrought on him beside her in the night.
"Warren," she said, "he has come home to die:
You needn't be afraid he'll leave you this time."

"Home," he mocked gently.

                      "Yes, what else but home?
It all depends on what you mean by home.
Of course he's nothing to us, any more
Than was the hound that came a stranger to us
Out of the woods, worn out upon the trail."

"Home is the place where, when you have to go there,
They have to take you in."

                        "I should have called it
Something you somehow haven't to deserve."

Warren leaned out and took a step or two,
Picked up a little stick, and brought it back
And broke it in his hand and tossed it by.
"Silas has better claim on us, you think,
Than on his brother? Thirteen little miles
As the road winds would bring him to his door.
Silas has walked that far no doubt today.
Why didn't he go there? His brother's rich,
A somebody—director in the bank."

"He never told us that."

                        "We know it though."

"I think his brother ought to help, of course.
I'll see to that if there is need. He ought of right
To take him in, and might be willing to—
He may be better than appearances.
But have some pity on Silas. Do you think
If he had any pride in claiming kin
Or anything he looked for from his brother,
He'd keep so still about him all this time?"

"I wonder what's between them."

                              "I can tell you.
Silas is what he is—we wouldn't mind him—
But just the kind that kinsfolk can't abide.
He never did a thing so very bad.
He don't know why he isn't quite as good
As anybody. Worthless though he is,
He won't be made ashamed to please his brother."

"*I* can't think Si ever hurt anyone."

"No, but he hurt my heart the way he lay
And rolled his old head on that sharp-edged chair-back.
He wouldn't let me put him on the lounge.
You must go in and see what you can do.
I made the bed up for him there tonight.
You'll be surprised at him—how much he's broken.
His working days are done; I'm sure of it."

"I'd not be in a hurry to say that."

"I haven't been. Go, look, see for yourself.
But, Warren, please remember how it is:
He's come to help you ditch the meadow.
He has a plan. You mustn't laugh at him.
He may not speak of it, and then he may.
I'll sit and see if that small sailing cloud
Will hit or miss the moon."

                            It hit the moon.
Then there were three there, making a dim row,
The moon, the little silver cloud, and she.

Warren returned—too soon, it seemed to her,
Slipped to her side, caught up her hand and waited.

"Warren?" she questioned.

"Dead," was all he answered.
(*1905,* 1914)

OUR HOLD ON THE PLANET

We asked for rain. It didn't flash and roar.
It didn't lose its temper at our demand
And blow a gale. It didn't misunderstand
And give us more than our spokesman bargained for;
And just because we owned to a wish for rain,
Send us a flood and bid us be damned and drown.
It gently threw us a glittering shower down.
And when we had taken that into the roots of grain,
It threw us another and then another still
Till the spongy soil again was natal wet.
We may doubt the just proportion of good to ill.
There is much in nature against us. But we forget:
Take nature altogether since time began,
Including human nature, in peace and war,
And it must be a little more in favor of man,
Say a fraction of one per cent at the very least,
Or our number living wouldn't be steadily more;
Our hold on the planet wouldn't have so increased.
(1942)

SUGGESTIONS FOR STUDY

1. *John Keats.* (a) Make a preliminary study of the life of John
Keats using two or more brief biographical accounts in reference works
such as the *Oxford Companion to English Literature* and the *Dictionary
of National Biography.* Pass over the critical interpretations and evaluations of his poems that you may find. Stick to the facts of his life, and
make out a list of the chief events and their dates. (b) Then read the
above group of six poems by John Keats, with their brief headnotes.

Read and reread each one until you feel that you have experienced it fully. (c) Now consider each one from the biographical point of view. What facts from the biography of the poet are of value in the interpretation of each of these poems? What light does each of them shed upon your understanding of the poet? (d) You may well feel that additional biographical data would be helpful, and may wish to turn to the longer lives and critical studies of Keats that are noted in the text of this chapter.

2. *Life and Style.* (a) Review the six poems by Keats reprinted in the earlier chapters of this book, and approach each of them from the biographical point of view. For the interpretation of several of these you may certainly wish to find additional relevant biographical data. (b) Keats is usually considered to be an essentially romantic poet; and, although he did not directly enter the revolutionary currents of his day, he was quite in tune with the general spirit of his times. Give some thought to the poems of John Keats from the point of view of the last chapter.

3. *Beauty and Truth.* (a) In a letter to Benjamin Bailey, dated Nov. 22, 1817, Keats wrote: "I am certain of nothing but of the holiness of the Heart's affections, and the truth of Imagination. What the Imagination seizes as Beauty must be truth—whether it existed before or not,—for I have the same idea of all our passions as of Love: they are all, in their sublime, creative of essential Beauty" (*Letters,* ed. Colvin, p. 41). (b) Consider this statement in relation to comparable thoughts in Keats' poems. (c) Do you recall any other expressions of similar ideas in poetry or philosophy?

4. *Robert Frost.* (a) Without first finding out about his life, read the group of six poems by Robert Frost and also the three in previous chapters: "Out, Out—" (p. 30), "The Road Not Taken" (p. 209), and "Mending Wall" (p. 235). Read and reread them in an effort to glimpse and understand the personality back of them and even something of his life story. Make a few notes so that this first impression of Robert Frost the man, as derived from his poems, will not escape you. (b) Now make a brief study of the events in the poet's life and of his personality as it has been described, using two or more reference works, as suggested in the text. (c) Wherein does this differ from your first impression? Of what help is this biographical data in a reinterpretation of his poems?

5. *Stopping by Words.* (a) Robert Frost's "Stopping by Woods on a Snowy Evening" will repay a closer study. Reread the poem thoughtfully. (b) A facsimile of the poet's draft of this poem occupies the next page. Study carefully the words changed by Frost and other evidences of

The ~~steaming horse~~ think it queer

~~Bo~~   how   ~~must~~
           ~~will~~
The ~~horse~~ ~~begins~~ ~~the~~ think it queer

    To
We stop with not a farm house near

Between a ~~forest~~ ~~and a~~ the woods an a frozen lake

The darkest evening of the year

She
He gives her harness bells a shake

To ask if there is ~~some~~ mistake

The only other sounds the sweep

Of easy wind and ~~falling~~ downy flake.

The woods are lovely dark and deep

But I have promises to keep

~~That bid me~~ ~~give~~ ~~the woods~~ ~~a~~ ~~look~~

And miles to go before I sleep

And miles to go before I sleep

Facsimile of the last three stanzas of Robert Frost's "Stopping by Woods on a Snowy Evening," reprinted by permission of Robert Frost and Henry Holt & Company, publishers.

his creative process. (c) John Holmes has prepared the following extended commentary for this book, corresponding with Robert Frost to verify his observations:

This facsimile is a reproduction of the last three stanzas of "Stopping by Woods on a Snowy Evening" as Robert Frost worked it out. We know from the poet that he had just written the long poem, "New Hampshire," in one all-night unbroken stretch of composition, and that he then turned a page of his workbook and wrote this short poem without stopping. This fact has interesting implications. "New Hampshire" is a discourse in the idiomatic blank verse that is so peculiarly Frost's own style—the rhythms of natural speech matched to the strict but inconspicuous iambic pentameter, the beat always discernible but never formal. It is reasonable to suppose that after the hours spent in writing the long poem, in its loosened but never loose manner, he was ready, unconsciously, for a poem in strict pattern. He had also obviously had in his head for some time the incident on which the short poem was to be based, as well as the use he wished to make of it. He committed himself, as he has said, to the four-stress iambic line and to the *aaba* rime-scheme, in the first stanza, which he wrote rapidly and did not revise. He knew what he had seen, and he knew how he wanted to write it.

> Whose woods these are I think I know.
> His house is in the village though;
> He will not see me stopping here
> To watch his woods fill up with snow.

"That went off so easily I was tempted into the added difficulty of picking up my 3 for my 1-2-4 to go on with in the second stanza. I was amused and scared at what that got me into," Frost says. The facsimile shows what it got him into, how he got out of it, and how he achieved the poem as it meant itself to be written.

It began with what was the actual experience of stopping at night by some dark woods in winter, and the fact that there were two horses. He remembered what he saw then. "The steaming horses think it queer." But the poem needs truth more than fact, and he cancels the line, and begins again, "The horse begins to think it queer," but doesn't like the word "begins," needing in the allowed space a word that will particularize the horse, so writes "The little horse must think it queer." Now he runs into a grammatical difficulty, which must somehow be solved before he gets on into the poem he already feels sure of. "I launched into the construction 'My little horse must think it queer that we should stop.' I didn't like omitting the 'that' and I had no room for 'should.' I had the luck to get out of it with the infinitive." This groping and warming-up has a kind of impatience, an urgency to get on with the poem, but not until all the parts are right. At this point the poet knew and did not know how the poem would end. He knew the feel, and the sense, and almost everything about the form—certainly enough to know when he got off the track.

Whether he revised the third line here or later we cannot know. But we can see in several places in this poem his changes toward particularization. The line "Between a forest and a lake" is a notation, and "Between the woods and frozen lake" is a finished line of poetry. "A forest" is too big, too vague, but "the woods" is definite, and bounded; you get lost in a forest, but you can walk through and out of the woods, and probably you know who owns it—Vermonters do, as he has said in the first stanza. "A lake" has not the specific condition or picture of "frozen lake." This sort of revision, or what Frost calls, "touching up," is what makes a poem—this, plus the first inspiration. Either one, without the other, is unlikely to make a good poem.

The next stanza comes easier, because the rime-scheme has been determined, and one unexpected obstacle has been overcome. But once more there is a delay, as the poet makes a decision as to the "he" or "she"—and the more important and more interesting about the falling snow. In writing "downy flake" for "fall of flake" the gain is great not only for accuracy of feeling and fact, but also for the music of the lines. The simple alliteration in "fall of flake" is canceled in favor of the word, one word, "downy," which blends with the vowel-chords a poet half-consciously makes and modulates as he goes. In this instance, it half-chimes with "sounds" and adds a rounder, fuller, and yet quieter tone.

Now the carry-over rime is "sweep," a fortunate one, really, and important to the final solution of the rime-scheme. It is not too much to assume, knowing all we know about the circumstances of the writing of this poem—the all-night composition of "New Hampshire," and the sudden urge to catch and shape still another saved idea—that the darker, more confident, more rapid strokes of the pen show the poet's growing excitement. The end is in sight. The thing he believed could happen will happen, surely now, and he must hurry to get it onto the page. This is the real moment of power, and any poet's greatest satisfaction.

"The woods are lovely dark and deep/ But I have promises to keep." The first two lines of the last stanza come fast, and flow beautifully, the crest of the poem's emotion and its music. We cannot know whether he had held them in his head, or had swept up to and into them as he felt the destined pattern fulfilling itself.

Then, with success in sight, there comes an awkward and unexpected stumble. He writes, "That bid me give the reins a shake," which may have been the fact and the action. But the rime is wrong. Not only has the rime been used in the previous stanza, but so has the image of the horse shaking his head and reins. Things are moving fast now, no doubt impatiently, but certainly with determination, shown in the heavy black lines of abrupt cancellation. He strikes out "me give the reins a shake," and writes above it, so the line will read, "That bid me on, and there are miles," and then the whole thing comes through! Of course! "Miles to go . . ."

That's what it was supposed to be—the feeling of silence and dark, almost overpowering the man, but the necessity of going on. "And miles to go before I sleep." Then the triumph in the whole thing, the only right and perfect last line, solving the problem of the carried-over rime, keeping the half-tranced state, and the dark, and the solitude, and man's great effort to be responsible man . . . the repetition of that line.

"Stopping by Woods on a Snowy Evening" can be studied as perfected structure, with the photostat manuscript to show that art is not, though it must always appear to be, effortless. It can be thought of as picture: the whites, grays, and blacks of the masses and areas of lake, field, and woods, with the tiny figure of the man in the sleigh, and the horse. And it can be thought of as a statement of man's everlasting responsibility to man; though the dark and nothingness tempt him to surrender, he will not give in. It is interesting to compare this poem with two later pieces of Frost's, in which he uses the same image, "Desert Places," and "Come In," none alike, all on the first level of his poetry, and all three built on the image of the pull of wildness and lawlessness against man's conscious will and the promises he has made to be kept.

(d) A French translation of this poem may serve as the basis for further study:

L'ARRET A LA LISIERE DES BOIS PAR UN SOIR DE NEIGE

Robert Frost, translated by *Edouard Roditi*

A qui ces bois, je crois le savoir,
Mais il habite dans le village.
Il ne me verra pas m'arrêter
Pour voir ses bois s'emplir de neige.

Mon petit cheval doit trouver étrange
Qu'on s'arrête ici, loin de toute ferme,
Entre les bois et le lac gelé
Le soir le plus sombre de l'année.

Mon cheval secoue tous ses grelots
Pour me demander si je me trompe,

Et le seul autre bruit est la poussée
Du vent délié et de la neige duvetée.

Ces bois sont beaux, si sombres et profonds,
Mais j'ai mes promesses à tenir
Et des lieues à faire avant de dormir,
Des lieues à faire avant de dormir.

(*tr.* 1943)

Make an English prose version of the French as a step toward observing what of Frost's poem seems to have been lost in the French translation. (If you do not read French, ask some friend who does not know Frost's poem to translate the French for you.) (e) Listen attentively to the recording of Frost's own reading of this poem (Erpi record VII-VIII).

6. *Himself Speaks.* (a) Robert Frost's own reading of a dozen of his poems has been recorded on a set of four records (Erpi record VII-VIII, IX-X, XI-XII, XIII-XIV). Included are five of the nine poems reprinted so far in this book. (b) Study these recordings thoughtfully. What do they add to your understanding of the poems and of the poet?

7. *Each in His Way.* (a) The six poems in this chapter by Keats and the six by Frost have been selected and arranged so as to invite comparison. (b) Compare and contrast the two poets and these groups of their poems in as many ways as you can.

8. *Frost in Our Time.* (a) Robert Frost is a modern American poet who has been recognized both popularly and critically. (b) What relation do his poems bear to the life and thought of the twentieth century?

PART SIX

Poetry for Intensive Study

22

STUDY WITH RECORDS

In the group of chapters from which we have just turned, poetry was approached from six different points of view: the broad types and sub-types, the several sorts and subspecies of forms, the recurrent poetic themes, the divers moods, the historic styles, and individual poets were passed in review so as to suggest in this *Preface to Poetry* the wide range of considerations that a comprehensive study of poetry would entail.

This concluding group of three chapters will present three techniques that may be helpful in the more intensive study of poetry. Most of the poems forming the bulk of these chapters are of the more difficult sort, and many of them have been chosen from the work of modern poets.

I. POETRY RECORDINGS AVAILABLE

The reader who has made use of the Suggestions for Study in this book is already acquainted with poetry records as a device for preserving and reviving the poem as read aloud by the poet himself or by an interpreter. It now remains to explore more fully this comparatively new technique so that it may serve as an aid to a richer experience and fuller understanding of poetry.

The scratchy mechanical pioneers in phonograph and gramophone reproduction of vocal and musical sound have given way to electrical transcription of high fidelity and to record players with superior amplifiers and speakers. But the value of the phonograph was early discovered for preserving for posterity the voices of historic personalities. So the living speech of Florence Nightingale, of Gladstone, of Tennyson, of every President of this century may be studied today—though the quality of reproduction in these older records is by no means good. Another use of recordings has been to preserve for study the dialects heard in various sections of our country and of the British Isles, and the fast-dying Indian languages. Comparably, phonograph records, early used in the teaching and learning of foreign languages, are now widely used in the learning of dialects by actors of the stage, screen, and radio.

The study of literature with the aid of records has developed rapidly in recent years. Wide, if not always successful, use has been made of them in the teaching of Shakespeare. Recordings by great actors—as early as Ellen Terry, Sothern and Marlowe, and Otis Skinner; and as recent as John Barrymore, Maurice Evans, and John Gielgud—have brought theatrical interpretations of the great speeches into the classroom. And the Mercury Theatre productions of four dramas, directed by Orson Welles, have been recorded complete in sets of nine to twelve records.[1]

It is now possible by means of records to study Chaucer as read in medieval English by such scholars as Harry M. Ayres, F. N. Robinson, and H. C. Wyld; and Shakespeare as read in Elizabethan English by Daniel Jones; and Congreve as read in early eighteenth century English by H. C. Wyld.

Reference was made in earlier chapters to the recordings of choral reading and of songs. However, the poetry records to be considered here fall into two groups: poems as read by an interpreter, and poems as read by the poets themselves.

The professional readers of poetry, whose work is available on records, seem to be more widely different as regards their philosophy of oral interpretation than as regards their vocal skill. A number of them—Norman Corwin, Lowell Cartwright, James Shelley, Edith Evans, John Gielgud, Cornelia Otis Skinner, Basil Rathbone—have prepared albums including recordings of a score or more of poems each. Smaller sets by Clifford Turner and David

[1] See Harry Thornton Moore, "Shakespeare on Records," in *Theatre Arts*, June 1940, pp. 450-54.

Ross, and individual records by Robert Speaight and many others make available a very considerable body of English poetry.

Some readings of these interpretative artists, many of them radio or stage actors, are by no means of much service to the study of poetry. In some cases the "poetic" tone of voice, the sentimental mood, and the independently melodic speech patterns actually obscure the poem rather than illuminating it. Reviewing one of these sets of records, Margedant Peters says it "will serve to fortify the impression among students that poetry is something to be read in a somewhat too-cultivated, and preferably English, accent." [2] But this criticism cannot be made of all poetry recorded by professional readers. The oral reading by Robert Speaight of poems by William Butler Yeats, Gerard Manley Hopkins, Keats, Wordsworth, Blake, Henry King, and John Donne, recorded under the supervision of Professor F. C. Packard, Jr., of Harvard University, will serve as an example of poetry recording that may be helpful in the serious study of more difficult poetry.

The poets themselves, in the oral reading of their own poetry, speak with a note of authority, if not always with voices of wide expressive range and flexibility. More than two dozen of the modern American and British poets have so far made recordings of some of their works; among them are Robinson Jeffers, James Weldon Johnson, and Archibald MacLeish; T. S. Eliot, Walter de la Mare, and W. H. Auden. In the Suggestions for Study in Chapter 13, we noted the record of Stephen Vincent Benét's "Ballad of William Sycamore" and of selections from Carl Sandburg's *The People, Yes;* and, in the last chapter, the recordings of Robert Frost. Through a study of records such as these, one may often come a step closer to understanding the poet's own experience than one possibly can through reading alone. But all poets are not possessed of the vocal equipment and skill that are necessary for good or even satisfactory oral interpretation. And if some of the professional readers are (again in Margedant Peters' words) "hard to take; too dulcet and too dramatic by turns," so the reading of a good many contemporary poets is characterized by an "assertive

2 "New Poetry Recordings," *Poetry: a Magazine of Verse,* December 1942, p. 519.

flatness without clarity or resonance" which adds "no additional shades or depth to the poetry." [3]

2. VARIOUS USES OF RECORDS

Good recordings may be used in a number of different ways in the more intensive study of poetry. (1) Without previous reading of the poem and without following the printed verses at the time, the record may be played repeatedly until the listener feels that he has fully experienced the poem. (2) Or after thoughtful study of the printed poem, including preparation and practice in reading it aloud, the record may be played so that the reader may compare the recorded reading with his own oral interpretation. (3) Or the listening and reading may proceed simultaneously, the responses to auditory and visual stimuli fusing in the receptor's experience of the poem.

Some may prefer an uninterrupted poetry recital, without comment or transition, as the records of one poet or of poems upon one theme are played in succession. Others may prefer repetition of a single record. Yet others will wish to listen and discuss, listen again and interrupt with critical comment, marking the printed poem in such a way as to fix the revealing inflections or pauses of the oral reading. Whether poetry records are used for individual listening and study or for group or class listening, there is certainly no "right" way to use them. But there are a few general suggestions that may be helpful.

In listening to poetry, whether spoken by the live voice or reproduced from a record, one must remember that the oral interpreter (when not the poet himself) is an intermediary, standing between the listener and the printed poem, and that the oral reader is trying to communicate *the poet's experience as he understands it*. When the oral interpreter is the poet, it must similarly be remembered that he is trying to utter the words he has previously set down, in such a way as to communicate his poem-experience. But vocal inflexibility or artificiality may come between the poet-reader and his listener, just as misunderstanding of the poet or elocution-

[3] *Ibid.*, p. 520.

ary speech may prevent clear communication from interpretative-reader to the hearer. He who would use poetry records to profit should bring to them an active and curious attention, rather than the passive attitude which lets the recorded voice flow pleasantly along its musical course.

There are certain advantages in the concurrent listening and reading of poetry. To the auditory stimulus from hearing is added the visual stimulus from "the eye on the page." The auditory and articulatory tied-imagery, the "music" of the poem when it is read silently, is merged with the actual sequence of reproduced speech sounds, and the resulting experience is likely to be the richer. When the ear fails to catch a word as articulated by the reader or poet (and this happens more frequently than one might imagine), the failure is at once supplied by the retinal image of the printed page. And the typographical aspect of the poetic form, observed by the eye, is fused with the rhythmic or metrical form as noted by the ear and the thought structure as it develops in the mind.

It is especially valuable to study two or more recordings of the same poem. Norman Corwin and Marjorie Gullan have both re-corded Milton's sonnet "On His Blindness." John Gielgud, L. E. Armstrong, and Basil Rathbone have all recorded Shelley's "Ode to the West Wind." Edith Evans, L. E. Armstrong, and Clifford Turner have all recorded Wordsworth's sonnet "Composed upon Westminster Bridge." Lowell Cartwright and Norman Corwin have both recorded Arnold's "Dover Beach." David Ross and Basil Rathbone have recorded Herrick's "To the Virgins." Furthermore, Robert Frost's "Mending Wall" has been recorded both by the poet and by Cecil Yapp. His poem "The Runaway" has been recorded by himself and also by Norman Corwin and Cornelia Otis Skinner. Norman Corwin and the poet have both recorded Markham's "The Man with the Hoe." It is unfortunate, however, that more modern poems are not yet available in several recordings for comparative study.

But studying poetry with the aid of recordings may take another turn. Recording equipment, often of excellent quality, is now avail-able for use in most departments of speech and drama, as well as in many radio shops; and records may be made at comparatively low cost. Many home recorders, too, are capable of very satisfactory results. A poetry-record library may well include, in addition to standard recordings, the special recordings of many poems not otherwise available. These may be the oral interpretations of trained and specially skilled readers, or the complimentary recordings of visiting poets or guest lecturers, or recordings of poetry taken from radio broadcasts. Student recordings, also, made as part of the process of studying a particular poem or group of poems, may be added to the collection.

The past few years has seen "the greatest resurgence of interest in spoken verse since the passing of the bards and troubadours and the muting effect of the extension of printing," writes Harry Thornton Moore.[4] The manufacture of poetry records, pretty well interrupted during the war, has been carried on not only by Victor and Columbia, but by smaller or specialized manufacturers such as Musicraft and ERPI, and under the sponsorship of the National Council of Teachers of English and Harvard and Columbia Universities. The Linguaphone Institute (30 Rockefeller Plaza, New York City 20) has not only made its own speech recordings, but also handles the poetry records of other makes, both American and foreign. Its catalogues are the most complete listings available.[5] The Harvard Vocarium records, including the work of more than two dozen contemporary poets, may be procured directly from the Harvard Film Service (4 Lawrence Hall, Cambridge 38, Massachusetts).

The poems that follow have been selected to be studied with records, and will serve to illustrate the use of this technique in the more intensive study of poetry.

[4] "Poetry on Records," *Poetry: a Magazine of Verse,* October 1940, p. 52. See other reviews by Moore of poetry records in the same journal: February 1941 (pp. 338-42), May 1941 (pp. 105-8), September 1941 (pp. 345-48).
[5] The remarkable Phonographic Library of Contemporary Poets at the College of the City of New York is reported by Kimball Flaccus in an article, "An Adventure in Poetry," *Quarterly Journal of Speech,* October 1942, pp. 315-23. See also the report of work at Columbia University, Henry W. Wells, "Literature and the Phonograph," *Quarterly Journal of Speech,* February 1943, pp. 68-73.

Poems with Records

from THE PROLOGUE of

THE CANTERBURY TALES

Geoffrey Chaucer

[Recordings have been made of the reading in Middle English by Harry Morgan Ayres (Linguaphone NCS) and also by H. C. Wyld (Ling. No. 11, rec. 3-4) of Chaucer's "Prologue." Translations of *The Canterbury Tales* into modern English verse have been made by J. U. Nicolson and Frank Ernest Hill.]

Whan that Aprille with his shoures *s*oote	= sweet
The droghte of March hath perced to the roote,	
And bathed every *v*eyne in swich licour	= vein, crevice
Of which *v*ertu engendred is the flour;	= power
Whan Zephirus *e*ek with his swete breeth	= also
Inspired hath in every *h*olt and heeth	= woods
The tendre croppes, and the yonge sonne	
Hath in the *R*am his halfe cours y-ronne,	= *constellation*
And smale foweles maken melodye,	
That slepen al the nyght with open eye,—	
So *p*riketh *h*em Nature in *h*ir *c*orages,—	= prompts, them their, hearts
Thanne longen folk to goon on pilgrimages,	
And palmeres for to seken straunge *s*trondes,	= strands
To *f*erne *h*alwes, *k*owthe in sondry londes;	= distant, hallowed spots, well-known
And specially, from every shires ende	
Of Engelond, to Caunturbury they wende,	
The hooly blisful *m*artir for to *s*eke,	= *Thomas à Becket*
That hem hath holpen whan that they were seeke.	
Bifil that in that seson on a day,	
In *S*outhwerk at the *T*abard as I lay,	= *London suburb, Tabard Inn*
*R*edy to wenden on my pilgrymage	

To Caunterbury with ful devout corage,
At nyght were come into that hostelrye
Wel nyne-and-twenty in a compaignye,
Of sondry folk, by *a*venture y-falle   = chance
In felaweshipe, and pilgrimes were they alle,
That toward Caunterbury wolden ryde.
The chambres and the stables weren wyde,
And wel we weren *e*sed *a*tte beste.   = entertained,
And shortly, whan the sonne was to reste,   at the
So hadde I spoken with hem *e*verychon,   = every one
That I was of hir felaweshipe anon,
And made *f*orward erly for to ryse,   = agreement
To take oure wey, ther as I yow devyse.

(*c.* 1386)

A HYMN TO GOD THE FATHER

John Donne

[A reading of this poem by Robert Speaight has been recorded
(Harvard L-1004).]

Wilt thou forgive that sin where I begun,
    Which was my sin, though it were done before?
Wilt thou forgive that sin through which I run,
    And do run still, though still I do deplore?
When thou hast done, thou hast not done;
       For I have more.

Wilt thou forgive that sin which I have won
    Others to sin, and made my sins their door?
Wilt thou forgive that sin which I did shun
    A year or two, but wallowed in a score?
When thou hast done, thou hast not done;
       For I have more.

I have a sin of fear, that when I've spun
    My last thread, I shall perish on the shore;
But swear by thyself that at my death thy Son

Shall shine as he shines now and heretofore;
And having done that, thou hast done;
I fear no more.

(1633)

THE TIGER
William Blake

[Many recordings of this poem are available in sets of poetry recordings: Norman Corwin (Columbia set E-5), Clifford Turner (Linguaphone, HMV B-3151/2), Edith Evans (Columbia set M-375), Marjorie Gullan (Linguaphone, HAL), Cornelia Otis Skinner (Victor set M-810).]

Tiger! Tiger! burning bright
In the forests of the night, •
What immortal hand or eye
Could frame thy fearful symmetry?

In what distant deeps or skies
Burnt the fire of thine eyes?
On what wings dare he aspire?
What the hand dare seize the fire?

And what shoulder, and what art,
Could twist the sinews of thy heart?
And when thy heart began to beat,
What dread hand? and what dread feet?

What the hammer? what the chain?
In what furnace was thy brain?
What the anvil? what dread grasp
Dare its deadly terrors clasp?

When the stars threw down their spears,
And watered heaven with their tears,
Did he smile his work to see?
Did he who made the Lamb make thee?

Tiger! Tiger! burning bright
In the forests of the night,
What immortal hand or eye
Dare frame thy fearful symmetry?

(1794)

THE WINDHOVER:

TO CHRIST OUR LORD

Gerard Manley Hopkins

[A reading by Robert Speaight has been recorded (Harvard L-1000).
The *windhover* is a sparrow-hawk; *wimpling,* rippling; *sillion,* the
ridge between two furrows of plowed land.]

I caught this morning morning's minion, king-
    dom of daylight's dauphin, dapple-dawn-drawn Falcon, in his riding
  Of the rolling level underneath him steady air, and striding
High there, how he rung upon the rein of a wimpling wing
In his ecstasy! then off, off forth on swing,
    As a skate's heel sweeps smooth on a bow-bend: the hurl and
        gliding
  Rebuffed the big wind. My heart in hiding
Stirred for a bird,—the achieve of, the mastery of the thing!

Brute beauty and valour and act, oh, air, pride, plume, here
  Buckle! AND the fire that breaks from thee then, a billion
Times told lovelier, more dangerous, O my chevalier!

  No wonder of it: shéer plód makes plough down sillion
Shine, and blue-bleak embers, ah my dear,
    Fall, gall themselves, and gash gold-vermilion.

(*1877,* 1918)

THE MAN WITH THE HOE

WRITTEN AFTER SEEING MILLET'S WORLD-FAMOUS PAINTING

Edwin Markham

[In 1938 Edwin Markham, then an old man, recorded "The Man with the Hoe" (Timely recording 1000A). It has also been recorded by Norman Corwin (Columbia set E-5). The text here printed is the revision of 1920, which differs in a number of places from the poem as originally published in 1899 and as recorded by Markham in 1938.]

GOD MADE MAN IN HIS OWN IMAGE,
IN THE IMAGE OF GOD MADE HE HIM.
　　　　　　　　　　　　　—Genesis

Bowed by the weight of centuries he leans
Upon his hoe and gazes on the ground,
The emptiness of ages in his face,
And on his back the burden of the world.
Who made him dead to rapture and despair,
A thing that grieves not and that never hopes,
Stolid and stunned, a brother to the ox?
Who loosened and let down this brutal jaw?
Whose was the hand that slanted back this brow?
Whose breath blew out the light within this brain?

Is this the Thing the Lord God made and gave
To have dominion over sea and land;
To trace the stars and search the heavens for power;
To feel the passion of Eternity?
Is this the dream He dreamed who shaped the suns
And marked their ways upon the ancient deep?
Down all the caverns of Hell to their last gulf
There is no shape more terrible than this—
More tongued with censure of the world's blind greed—
More filled with signs and portents for the soul—
More packt with danger to the universe.

What gulfs between him and the seraphim!
Slave of the wheel of labor, what to him

Are Plato and the swing of Pleiades?
What the long reaches of the peaks of song,
The rift of dawn, the reddening of the rose?
Through this dread shape the suffering ages look;
Time's tragedy is in that aching stoop;
Through this dread shape humanity betrayed,
Plundered, profaned, and disinherited,
Cries protest to the Judges of the World,
A protest that is also prophecy.

O masters, lords and rulers in all lands,
Is this the handiwork you give to God,
This monstrous thing distorted and soul-quenched?
How will you ever straighten up this shape;
Touch it again with immortality;
Give back the upward looking and the light;
Rebuild in it the music and the dream;
Make right the immemorial infamies,
Perfidious wrongs, immedicable woes?

O masters, lords and rulers in all lands,
How will the Future reckon with this man?
How answer his brute question in that hour
When whirlwinds of rebellion shake all shores?
How will it be with kingdoms and with kings—
With those who shaped him to the thing he is—
When this dumb terror shall rise to judge the world,
After the silence of the centuries?

(1899-1920)

from THE CONGO

A STUDY OF THE NEGRO RACE

Vachel Lindsay

[Vachel Lindsay, who devoted much of the later years of his life to the reading of his poems to groups of college students, recorded "The Congo" (Linguaphone NCS [National Council of Teachers of English]) and a number of his other poems. Only two of the three sections may be here reprinted.]

I. THEIR BASIC SAVAGERY

Fat black bucks in a wine-barrel room,
Barrel-house kings, with feet unstable,
Sagged and reeled and pounded on the table,
Pounded on the table,
Beat an empty barrel with the handle of a broom,
Hard as they were able,
Boom, boom, Boom,
With a silk umbrella and the handle of a broom,
Boomlay, boomlay, boomlay, Boom.

*A deep rolling
bass*

Then I had religion, Then I had a vision.
I could not turn from their revel in derision.
Then I saw the Congo, creeping through the
     black,
Cutting through the forest with a golden track.

*More deliberate
Solemnly chanted*

Then along that riverbank
A thousand miles
Tattooed cannibals danced in files;
Then I heard the boom of the blood-lust song
And a thigh-bone beating on a tin-pan gong.
And "Blood" screamed the whistles and the fifes of
     the warriors,
"Blood" screamed the skull-faced, lean witch-doctors,
"Whirl ye the deadly voo-doo rattle,
Harry the uplands,
Steal all the cattle,
Rattle-rattle, rattle-rattle,
Bing!
Boomlay, boomlay, boomlay, Boom,"
A roaring, epic, rag-time tune
From the mouth of the Congo
To the Mountains of the Moon.

*A rapidly piling
climax of speed
and racket*

*With a philo-
sophic pause*

Death is an Elephant,
Torch-eyed and horrible,
Foam-flanked and terrible.
Boom, steal the pygmies,

*Shrilly and with a
heavily accented
meter*

Boom, kill the Arabs,
Boom, kill the white men,
Hoo, Hoo, Hoo.   *Like the wind in*
Listen to the yell of Leopold's ghost   *the chimney*
Burning in Hell for his hand-maimed host.
Hear how the demons chuckle and yell
Cutting his hands off, down in Hell.
Listen to the creepy proclamation,
Blown through the lairs of the forest-nation,
Blown past the white-ants' hill of clay,
Blown past the marsh where the butterflies play:—
"Be careful what you do,
Or Mumbo-Jumbo, God of the Congo,
And all of the other   *All the o sounds*
Gods of the Congo,   *very golden*
Mumbo-Jumbo will hoo-doo you,   *Heavy accents*
Mumbo-Jumbo will hoo-doo you,   *very heavy*
Mumbo-Jumbo will hoo-doo you."   *Light accents*
                                                 very light. Last
                                                 line whispered

3. THE HOPE OF THEIR RELIGION

A good old Negro in the slums of the town   *Heavy bass*
Preached at a sister for her velvet gown.   *With a literal*
Howled at a brother for his low-down ways,   *imitation of*
His prowling, guzzling, sneak-thief days.   *camp-meeting*
Beat on the Bible till he wore it out,   *racket, and*
Starting the jubilee revival shout.   *trance*
And some had visions, as they stood on chairs,
And sang of Jacob, and the golden stairs.
And they all repented, a thousand strong,
From their stupor and savagery and sin and wrong
And slammed with their hymn books till they shook
    the room
With "Glory, glory, glory,"
And "Boom, boom, Boom."   *Exactly as in*
Then I saw the Congo, creeping through the   *the first section*
    black,   *Begin with*
Cutting through the jungle with a golden track. *terror and*
                                                 power, end
And the gray sky opened like a new-rent veil   *with joy*
And showed the Apostles with their coats of mail.
In bright white steel they were seated round

And their fire-eyes watched where the Congo wound.
And the twelve Apostles, from their thrones on high,
Thrilled all the forest with their heavenly cry:—
"Mumbo-Jumbo will die in the jungle;
Never again will he hoo-doo you,
Never again will he hoo-doo you."

*Sung to the tune
of "Hark, ten
thousand harps
and voices"*

Then along that river, a thousand miles
The vine-snared trees fell down in files.
Pioneer angels cleared the way
For a Congo paradise, for babes at play,
For sacred capitals, for temples clean.
Gone were the skull-faced witch-men lean.
There, where the wild ghost-gods had wailed
A million boats of the angels sailed
With oars of silver, and prows of blue
And silken pennants that the sun shone through.
'Twas a land transfigured, 'twas a new creation.
Oh, a singing wind swept the Negro nation
And on through the backwoods clearing flew:—
"Mumbo-Jumbo is dead in the jungle.
Never again will he hoo-doo you.
Never again will he hoo-doo you."

*With growing
deliberation
and joy*

*In a rather
high key—as
delicately as
possible*

*To the tune of
"Hark, ten
thousand harps
and voices"*

Redeemed were the forests, the beasts and the men,
And only the vulture dared again
By the far, lone mountains of the moon
To cry, in the silence, the Congo tune:—
"Mumbo-Jumbo will hoo-doo you,
Mumbo-Jumbo will hoo-doo you,
Mumbo . . . Jumbo . . . will . . . hoo-doo . . . you."

*Dying off into
a penetrating,
terrified whisper*

(1914)

THE CREATION

A NEGRO SERMON from GOD'S TROMBONES

James Weldon Johnson

[Johnson's own reading has been recorded (Musicraft 1083-1084).]

And God stepped out on space,
And He looked around and said,
"I'm lonely—
I'll make me a world."
And far as the eye of God could see
Darkness covered everything,
Blacker than a hundred midnights
Down in a cypress swamp.

Then God smiled,
And the light broke,
And the darkness rolled up on one side,
And the light stood shining on the other,
And God said, *"That's good!"*

Then God reached out and took the light in His hands,
And God rolled the light around in His hands,
Until He made the sun;
And He set that sun a-blazing in the heavens.
And the light that was left from making the sun
God gathered up in a shining ball
And flung it against the darkness,
Spangling the night with the moon and stars.
Then down between
The darkness and the light
He hurled the world;
And God said, *"That's good!"*

Then God Himself stepped down—
And the sun was on His right hand,
And the moon was on His left;
The stars were clustered about His head,
And the earth was under His feet.
And God walked, and where He trod
His footsteps hollowed the valleys out
And bulged the mountains up.

Then He stopped and looked and saw
That the earth was hot and barren.
So God stepped over to the edge of the world

And He spat out the seven seas;
He batted His eyes, and the lightnings flashed;
He clapped His hands, and the thunders rolled;
And the waters above the earth came down,
The cooling waters came down.

Then the green grass sprouted,
And the little red flowers blossomed,
The pine-tree pointed his finger to the sky,
And the oak spread out his arms;
The lakes cuddled down in the hollows of the ground,
And the rivers ran down to the sea;
And God smiled again,
And the rainbow appeared,
And curled itself around His shoulder.

Then God raised His arm and He waved His hand
Over the sea and over the land,
And He said, *"Bring forth! Bring forth!"*
And quicker than God could drop His hand,
Fishes and fowls
And beasts and birds
Swam the rivers and the seas,
Roamed the forests and the woods,
And split the air with their wings,
And God said, *"That's good!"*

Then God walked around
And God looked around
On all that He had made.
He looked at His sun,
And He looked at His moon,
And He looked at His little stars;
He looked on His world
With all its living things,
And God said, *"I'm lonely still."*

Then God sat down
On the side of a hill where He could think;
By a deep, wide river He sat down;

With His head in His hands,
God thought and thought,
Till He thought, *"I'll make me a man!"*

Up from the bed of the river
God scooped the clay;
And by the bank of the river
He kneeled Him down;
And there the great God Almighty,
Who lit the sun and fixed it in the sky,
Who flung the stars to the most far corner of the night,
Who rounded the earth in the middle of His hand—
This Great God,
Like a mammy bending over her baby,
Kneeled down in the dust
Toiling over a lump of clay
Till He shaped it in His own image;
Then into it He blew the breath of life,
And man became a living soul.
Amen. Amen.

(1927)

THE HOLLOW MEN
T. S. Eliot

[Eliot's reading is recorded (Harvard 3).]

MISTAH KURTZ—HE DEAD. . . .

A PENNY FOR THE OLD GUY

I

We are the hollow men
We are the stuffed men
Leaning together
Headpiece filled with straw. Alas!
Our dried voices, when
We whisper together
Are quiet and meaningless

As wind in dry grass
Or rats' feet over broken glass
In our dry cellar

Shape without form, shade without color,
Paralyzed force, gesture without motion;

Those who have crossed
With direct eyes, to death's other Kingdom
Remember us—if at all—not as lost
Violent souls, but only
As the hollow men
The stuffed men.

2

Eyes I dare not meet in dreams
In death's dream kingdom
These do not appear:
There, the eyes are
Sunlight on a broken column
There, is a tree swinging
And voices are
In the wind's singing
More distant and more solemn
Than a fading star.

Let me be no nearer
In death's dream kingdom
Let me also wear
Such deliberate disguises
Rat's skin, crowskin, crossed staves
In a field
Behaving as the wind behaves
No nearer—

Not that final meeting
In the twilight kingdom

3

This is the dead land
This is cactus land

Here the stone images
Are raised, here they receive
The supplication of a dead man's hand
Under the twinkle of a fading star.

Is it like this
In death's other kingdom
Waking alone
At the hour when we are
Trembling with tenderness
Lips that would kiss
From prayers to broken stone.

4

The eyes are not here
There are no eyes here
In this valley of dying stars
In this hollow valley
This broken jaw of our lost kingdoms

In this last of meeting places
We grope together
And avoid speech
Gathered on this beach of the tumid river

Sightless, unless
The eyes reappear
As the perpetual star
Multifoliate rose
Of death's twilight kingdom
The hope only
Of empty men.

5

Here we go round the prickly pear
Prickly pear prickly pear
Here we go round the prickly pear
At five o'clock in the morning.

Between the idea
And the reality
Between the motion

And the act
Falls the Shadow
    For Thine is the Kingdom

Between the conception
And the creation
Between the emotion
And the response
Falls the Shadow
    Life is very long

Between the desire
And the spasm
Between the potency
And the existence
Between the essence
And the descent
Falls the Shadow
    For Thine is the Kingdom

For Thine is
Life is
For Thine is the

This is the way the world ends
This is the way the world ends
This is the way the world ends
Not with a bang but a whimper.
    (1925)

THE FOG
Robert P. Tristram Coffin

[Coffin's own reading is recorded (Linguaphone NCS).]

He knew how Roman legions looked, for he
Had seen the Maine coast fogs march in from sea
For many years now, in the August days.
They came in mighty columns up the bays,
Tawny and gray and silver in the sun;

They trampled out the seaports one by one,
The islands and the woods, with their high hosts,
And pushed the world back inland from the coasts.

This little house was lost, these hills and dells,
Cows in a pasture faded into bells,
The world around a man closed in and in
Till nowhere was ten paces from his chin.
A man drew up and halted with a start
To be so close to his own beating heart
And left so to himself and wholly blind
To everything but what was in his mind.

This was the peril and the comfort, too,
A man who lived in such a region knew;
On any Summer's day, within an hour,
He might be blind and naked to a power
So vast, it might have come from stars unmade,
Undreamt of, even, making him afraid,
So mightier than the night that he could guess
How life was but a name for loneliness.

                                        (1937)

THE COAST-ROAD
Robinson Jeffers

[Jeffers' own reading is recorded (Harvard P-1046).]

A horseman high alone as an eagle on the spur
        of the mountain over Mirmas Canyon draws
        rein, looks down
At the bridge-builders, men, trucks, the power-shovels,
        the teeming end of the new coast-road at the
        mountain's base.
He sees the loops of the road go northward, headland
        beyond headland, into gray mist over Fraser's Point,
He shakes his fist and makes the gesture of wringing a
        chicken's neck, scowls and rides higher.

                                        I too
Believe that the life of men who ride horses, herders of

cattle on the mountain pasture, plowers of remote
Rock-narrowed farms in poverty and freedom, is a good
    life. At the far end of those loops of road
Is what will come and destroy it, a rich and vulgar and
    bewildered civilization dying at the core,
A world that is feverishly preparing new wars, peculiarly
    vicious ones, and heavier tyrannies, a strangely
Missionary world, road-builder, wind-rider, educator,
    printer and picture-maker and broadcaster,
So eager, like an old drunken whore, pathetically eager to
    impose the seduction of her fled charms
On all that through ignorance or isolation might have
    escaped them. I hope the weathered horseman up
    yonder
Will die before he knows what this eager world will do
    to his children. More tough-minded men
Can repulse an old whore, or cynically accept her drunken
    kindnesses for what they are worth,
But the innocent and credulous are soon
    corrupted.

   Where is our consolation? Beautiful
    beyond belief
The heights glimmer in the sliding cloud, the great bronze
    gorge-cut sides of the mountain tower up
    invincibly,
Not the least hurt by this ribbon of road carved on their
    sea-foot.

         (1937)

IN MEMORY OF W. B. YEATS
W. H. Auden

[Auden's own reading is recorded (Linguaphone, NCS).]

I

He disappeared in the dead of winter:
The brooks were frozen, the airports almost deserted,

And snow disfigured the public statues;
The mercury sank in the mouth of the dying day.
O all the instruments agree
The day of his death was a dark cold day.

Far from his illness
The wolves ran on through the evergreen forests,
The peasant river was untempted by the fashionable quays;
By mourning tongues
The death of the poet was kept from his poems.

But for him it was his last afternoon as himself,
An afternoon of nurses and rumors;
The provinces of his body revolted,
The squares of his mind were empty,
Silence invaded the suburbs,
The current of his feeling failed: he became his admirers.

Now he is scattered among a hundred cities
And wholly given over to unfamiliar affections;
To find his happiness in another kind of wood
And be punished under a foreign code of conscience.
The words of a dead man
Are modified in the guts of the living.

But in the importance and noise of tomorrow
When the brokers are roaring like beasts on the floor of the Bourse,
And the poor have the sufferings to which they are fairly accustomed,
And each in the cell of himself is almost convinced of his freedom;
A few thousand will think of this day
As one thinks of a day when one did something slightly unusual.

O all the instruments agree
The day of his death was a dark cold day.

2

You were silly like us: your gift survived it all;
The parish of rich women, physical decay,
Yourself; mad Ireland hurt you into poetry.
Now Ireland has her madness and her weather still,

For poetry makes nothing happen: it survives
In the valley of its saying where executives
Would never want to tamper; it flows south
From ranches of isolation and the busy griefs,
Raw towns that we believe and die in; it survives,
A way of happening, a mouth.

3

Earth, receive an honored guest;
William Yeats is laid to rest:
Let the Irish vessel lie
Emptied of its poetry.

Time that is intolerant
Of the brave and innocent,
And indifferent in a week
To a beautiful physique,

Worships language and forgives
Everyone by whom it lives;
Pardons cowardice, conceit,
Lays its honors at their feet.

Time that with this strange excuse
Pardoned Kipling and his views,
And will pardon Paul Claudel,
Pardons him for writing well.

In the nightmare of the dark
All the dogs of Europe bark,
And the living nations wait,
Each sequestered in its hate;

Intellectual disgrace
Stares from every human face,
And the seas of pity lie
Locked and frozen in each eye.

Follow, poet, follow right
To the bottom of the night,

With your unconstraining voice
Still persuade us to rejoice;

With the farming of a verse
Make a vineyard of the curse,
Sing of human unsuccess
In a rapture of distress;

In the deserts of the heart
Let the healing fountain start,
In the prison of his days
Teach the free man how to praise.

(1940)

EVENING MEAL IN THE TWENTIETH CENTURY
John Holmes

[Holmes' own reading, with some variation in the text, is recorded
(Harvard P-1002).]

How is it I can eat bread here and cut meat,
And in quiet shake salt, speak of the meal,
Pour water, serve my son's small plate?
Here now I love well my wife's gold hair combed,
Her voice, her violin, our books on shelves in another room,
The tall chest shining darkly in supper-light.
I have read tonight
The sudden meaningless foreign violent death
Of a nation we both loved, hope
For a country not ours killed. But blacker than print:
For the million people no house now. For me
A new hurt to the old health of the heart once more:
That sore, that heavy, that dull and I think now incurable
Pain:
Seeing love hated, seeing real death,
Knowing evil alive I was taught was conquered.
How shall I cut this bread gladly, unless more share
The day's meals I earn?
Or offer my wife meat from our fire, our fortune?

It should not have taken me so long to learn.
But how can I speak aloud at my own table tonight
And not curse my own food, not cry out death,
And not frighten my young son?

(*1939,* 1943)

SUGGESTIONS FOR STUDY

1. *Yeats Without Text.* (a) A number of the poems of William Butler Yeats have been recorded by Robert Speaight (Harvard, L-1012). They are suggested here for study from the recordings alone, without · reference to the printed poems. (b) After listening to the recordings several times, alone and with appreciative friends, and when you have begun to hear in your own head the tones and rhythms of the Yeats poems, hunt them up in his *Collected Works,* Macmillan, 1927, and see how much of the pattern you have been able to take in by ear alone. (c) The thought in "Sailing to Byzantium," and "In Memory of Eva Gore-Booth and Con Markiewicz," is of age and loss. Does the tone of the poem, and the reader's tone of voice, suit this thought? Read the poems to your class group, and let your own feelings and understanding mix with the vocal interpretation of the actor Speaight where you think best. (d) Without looking at a printed text, and from what you may know of the imagery drawn from Byzantium, write a page of analysis of this poem. Then do some research into the nature of Byzantine art, and find out why it seemed to Yeats a fitting source of imagery for his rebellious old age. (e) From your experience in listening to recorded poetry, what is your opinion as to the ideal delivery for perpetuation on discs: that of the author, that of a reader who loves good poetry, or that of an actor or actress? Robert Speaight is an actor; do you think he reads the poems as Yeats would have liked to read them, and as they should be read? (f) Imagine that you know no English, and listen to these poems; then say what the sound and the rhythms of line and statement express.

2. *Keats After Study.* (a) The "Ode on Melancholy," studied as a part of the last chapter, has been recorded by Robert Speaight (Harvard L-1006). Listen to it attentively, several times, and write a short comment. Wherein does Speaight's interpretation differ from your own? What in Speaight's reading serves to enrich your experience of the poem? (b) Readings of several other Keats poems included in this volume have been recorded: "On First Looking into Chapman's Homer" (by Marjorie Gullan in Linguaphone set HAL, and by Basil Rathbone in Columbia set E-11); "Ode on a Grecian Urn" (by Rathbone, and by Cornelia Otis Skinner in Victor set M-810); the Proem

from *Endymion* (by L. E. Armstrong, Linguaphone REP 30); "La Belle Dame Sans Merci" (by Edith Evans in Columbia set M-375, and by David Ross in Linguaphone set MC). (c) The Speaight record includes Keats' "To Autumn" and "Ode to Psyche," not reprinted in this book. Study them by means of the record alone.

3. *Donne with Text.* (a) Robert Speaight's recording of "A Hymn to God the Father" by John Donne (Harvard L-1004) might well be studied simultaneously with the text of the poem above reprinted— listening and reading at the same time. (b) Give particular attention to those points at which the oral reading illuminates the text and at which the text makes clear the oral reading.

4. *Markham, Words and Voice.* (a) Study "The Man with the Hoe," at first without using a recording, but with a reproduction of Millet's painting before you. (A two-page reproduction in color appeared in *Life* magazine for July 29, 1940.) The poem has enjoyed wide popularity and abuse during the past half century, and you may be interested in looking into its history and reputation. (b) Now listen to the recording of Edwin Markham reading "The Man with the Hoe" (Timely recording, 1000A). It was made in 1938 when the poet was 86 years old. Note the points in the text at which the poet has further revised his verses. (c) Norman Corwin (Columbia set E-5) has also recorded "The Man with the Hoe." Listen to it carefully, and compare the two readings. (d) Turn back to James Weldon Johnson's "Brothers" (p. 500), and review it. Compare these two poems on the theme of Social Justice.

5. *Congo and Creation.* (a) Listen to Vachel Lindsay's own reading of "The Congo" (Linguaphone NCS [National Council of Teachers of English record]) without following text. (b) Lindsay wrote of this poem:

> The thought of the third section was inspired by a passage in a sermon by my pastor, F. W. Burnham, when he spoke of the death of Ray Eldred, a heroic missionary, who had recently perished on the Congo River. It is logical there should be six lines conforming to the original hymn-theory and set to the tune, "Hark ten thousand harps and voices." But the remainder of "The Congo" is based, however poorly, on the most conventional English tradition of imitative verbal music, going back through Southey's "Cataract of Lodore" to Dryden's "Alexander's Feast." In reciting "The Congo" I unconsciously introduced a new element of chanting, akin to the Gregorian Chant I had heard in the Paulist Fathers' Church, New York. . . . I added this to my usual effort to elaborate the tone-color effects, and as a result of the two "The Congo" became the first recitation of my life to

which big conventional gatherings of people would listen. . . . (*Letter about My Four Programmes,* Springfield, Ill., n.d., p. 5.)

Now read the text of the two sections and listen again to the recording of the entire poem. Comment upon your experience of "The Congo" in the light of the marginal notes and Lindsay's *Letter.*

(c) Read and listen to James Weldon Johnson's poem "The Creation" from *God's Trombones* (Musicraft set 1083). (d) Lindsay, who was not a Negro, and Johnson, who was, have in these two poems written about the religious attitudes and thought of the American Negro. Compare the two in some detail.

6. *Interpretative Readers.* (a) Besides those already mentioned above and in the text, a good many other well-known poems from the earlier chapters of this book have been recorded in the available sets of records: "The Appreciation of Poetry" by Norman Corwin (Columbia set E-5); "Great Themes in Poetry" by Basil Rathbone (Columbia set E-11); "The Voice of Poetry" vol. 1 by Edith Evans (Columbia set M-375) and vol. 2 by John Gielgud (Columbia set M-419); "Anthology of English Lyric Verse" by Cornelia Otis Skinner (Victor set M-810); "Readings in Lyric Poetry" by David Ross (Linguaphone set MC); "Speech, Poetry and Drama" by James Shelley (Linguaphone set 13); other albums or sets by Lowell Cartwright (Linguaphone, BR106), by Clifford Turner (Linguaphone HMV-B3151/2), and by Marjorie Gullan (Linguaphone HAL). *Again it must be pointed out that these readings are not of uniform excellence; that, to some ears, some of them are intolerable.* (The contents of these sets will be found listed in the manufacturers' catalogues, and in the catalogues of Linguaphone Institute, 30 Rockefeller Plaza, New York City 20, from whom these and other records may be purchased.)

(b) Other readings of special interest: Robert Speaight's reading of poems by Blake and Wordsworth (Harvard L-1008) and of poems by Henry King and George Herbert (Harvard L-1010); Ion Swinley's reading of Gray's "Elegy" (Columbia DX594); P. J. O'Conner's reading of Francis Thompson's "The Hound of Heaven" (National Catholic Sound Recording Specialists, New York, set 1056-1059); Paul Robeson's singing of La Touche and Robinson's "Ballad for Americans" (Victor set P-20); Lynn Fontanne's reading of Alice Duer Miller's "The White Cliffs of Dover" (Victor set M-775).

7. *Poets in Waxwork.* Other modern poets have recorded some of their own poems: Archibald MacLeish, "America Was Promises" (Linguaphone 14) and "Frescoes for Mr. Rockefeller's City" (Linguaphone NCS), Carl Sandburg, *The People, Yes* (Decca 273), Walter de la Mare (HMV-B8177/8), E. E. Cummings (HBC and NCS), John

Drinkwater (CL 11115/6), Sir Henry Newbolt (CL D40181/2), V. Sack-ville-West (CL D40192/3), George Barker (Harvard P-1038), Theodore Spencer (Harvard P-1028-30-32), David McCord (Harvard P-1006-8-10), Robert Hillyer (Harvard P-1022-4-6), Richard Eberhart (Harvard P-1034-6), Oliver St. John Gogarty (Harvard P-1040-2), John Gould Fletcher (Harvard P-1044), Edna St. Vincent Millay (Victor set 836), Mark Van Doren (NCS).

8. *Recording Poetry.* (a) Choose a poem or group of poems that may be read in about four minutes, poems that you have not heard read and that you feel are worth your recording. Prepare to read them, following the suggestions given in Chapter 13. (b) Arrange to have a recording made of this poetry. (c) Listen to the record, and make an analysis of your problems in the oral interpretation of poetry.

23

COMPARATIVE ANALYSIS

The use of recordings is one technique that is useful in the more intensive study of poetry; a second will here be called *comparative analysis*. Those who have come thus far have already made use of it. In the opening chapter we paired Leigh Hunt's "The Glove and the Lions" and Browning's "The Glove" (pp. 13, 14); and in many of the chapters and their Suggestions for Study two or more poems have been presented together for the purpose of comparison, or comparative reference has been made to poems previously read. Thus, in the last chapter, two sea-coast poems were juxtaposed; Vachel Lindsay's "The Congo" (p. 620) and James Weldon Johnson's "The Creation" (p. 623) were presented for comparison, and the reader of Edwin Markham's "The Man with the Hoe" (p. 619)—of which two recordings were suggested—was referred back to Johnson's "Brothers" (p. 500); and the thoughts of attentive readers must have darted back and forth, back and forth, from Gerard Manley Hopkins to John Donne, from T. S. Eliot to Hopkins, from Robinson Jeffers to Eliot.

I. SIMILARITIES AND DIFFERENCES

The recognition of similarities and differences is a fundamental aspect of human behavior. Our mental processes are deeply rooted in this capacity to identify like and unlike things. It is a chief function of our thinking machines to point out that *this* is the same or not the same as *that*. We are constantly and inevitably matching up the new with the known, noting resemblances and disparities, making value judgments, accepting and rejecting.

Logical and linguistic processes are based upon this common

function. Definition, as a logical practice, makes use of the concepts of "genus" and "differentiae." The thing to be defined is placed within the class of things to which it belongs and is then differentiated from the other members of the class. And we proposed some working definitions of this sort at the outset of our *Preface to Poetry*. Classification, as a logical means of controlling a wide range of things and experiences, involves the establishing of categories clearly distinguished one from the other. Then sorting places the similar objects within the same group and apart from the dissimilar objects. And this was the basis for Part Five of this book, wherein each chapter made use of a different classification representing a different approach to poetry. Evaluation is another process which may depend upon the recognition of similarities and differences, as we saw in discussing "Good Poetry and Bad" and "Great Poetry and True." And metaphor, too, both in the comprehensive sense, including such language devices as simile and personification, and in the special sense—the use of a word from one universe of discourse to name a relationship or quality in another universe of discourse—metaphor, too, is based upon the recognition of similarities and differences in things as we experience them. The comic element, as well, is based upon the apperception of sameness and unexpected incongruity.

Comparative analysis in the intensive study of poetry, by no means a new technique like the use of recordings, is simply the systematic search for differences in poems that are similar. This chapter, which is intended to give special emphasis to a technique that is already familiar, will consist chiefly of some half dozen pairs of poems that invite comparison of one kind or another. But first a few general observations will be made about the method to be followed in studying them.

It must again be emphasized that the reader will not compare the printed poems except as they are the stimuli for poem-reading-experiences. This is a truism easily forgotten as one pencils his way along in an intensive point for point study. Then, too, the purpose in making the comparative analysis should be constantly kept in focus. Although the purpose will differ from individual to individual, and from time to time, certainly the purpose should be more than the merely curious desire to discover points for comment.

2. PURPOSE AND PROCEDURE

The purpose of such a comparative analysis may be to experience one or both of the poems the more richly and memorably, playing them off against each other so that each is more fully realized and appreciated. So, by comparing it in detail with Watts' "How Doth the Little Busy Bee," the reader may more fully enjoy Lewis Carroll's parody "The Crocodile" (p. 526). And by a close study of Milton's sonnet "On His Being Arrived at the Age of Twenty-three" and of Keats' sonnet "When I Have Fears That I May Cease to Be" (p. 455)—noting widely different attitudes of the two young poets as they take stock of past accomplishment and face the future in relation to the larger framework of their lives—then both poems may be enhanced by the dual study. And the drafts of Keats' sonnet on "Chapman's Homer" (pp. 34 and 25) and of Frost's "Stopping by Woods—" (p. 604 as well as p. 594) were included in facsimile for comparison with the final poems as a means of understanding and appreciating the latter more fully.

Sometimes the purpose of such comparative analysis may be to come, through this means, to a better understanding of poetic types, sub-types, or forms; of poetic themes, moods, or styles; or of the poets as personalities. This use we observed in recent chapters, where it was suggested that Dobson's "Ars Victrix" and Hovey's "Accident in Art" (pp. 486, 488), MacLeish's "Ars Poetica" and Wordsworth's "Nuns Fret Not—" (pp. 89, 87), be studied together as poems upon the themes of Art and Poetry. Gray's "Elegy" (p. 558) and Wordsworth's "Lines . . . Tintern Abbey" (p. 566) were suggested for comparison of the classic and romantic styles. And a number of Keats' and of Frost's poems were so arranged as to invite a comparison that would make each of these two poets stand forth more clearly as an individual personality.

But sometimes the purpose of comparison is the evaluation of one or both of the poems. In an early chapter Felicia Hemans'

"Casabianca" and Robert Frost's "Out, Out—" (pp. 29, 30) were paired in the hope that the former would, even to the unpracticed reader, seem inferior in the presence of the latter. The comparative method of criticism and the related touchstone method were discussed (pp. 247-48), and Stanton's "Keep a-Goin'" (p. 262) and Clough's "Say Not the Struggle Nought Availeth" (p. 177) were proposed in an exercise of judgment.

Whatever the purpose—and in each of the cases cited—*the comparison of two poems proceeds upon the basis of similarity*. It suggests that they are *in the same category* in a certain classification. One can hardly conceive of a profitable comparison of the Parthenon and Shelley's "Ode to the West Wind," of *Paradise Lost* and Jonson's "To Celia," of Dickinson's "I Died for Beauty" and "Lord Randal." There would seem to be no clear basis for comparison; these pairs of things and the experiences that might be stimulated by them do not fall into the same pigeonholes in any of the conventional classifications.

But any two narratives could be compared *as narratives;* or any two ballads could be compared *as ballads.* Stephen Vincent Benét's "Ballad of William Sycamore" (p. 337) and William Rose Benét's ballad of "Jesse James" (p. 429) when studied together, and then in comparison with the folk ballads, would reveal much of interest about this sub-type of poetry. Sonnet may be compared to sonnet in form; the general theme of Death may be the basis for comparing another pair; and so on. Or two poems, as different as "Ode on a Grecian Urn" (p. 152) and "Ode on Melancholy" (p. 590), may be compared as the work of the one poet, Keats.

Once this basis of similarity is established, then the search for differences will proceed along many lines, and it will be noted that *in other classifications they will often fall into widely separate categories.* It is true, for instance, that Keats' two poems are both stanzaic odes; they utilize quite similar stanzaic forms; they are both upon the theme of Love and Beauty—but with what a difference, for the "Beauty that must die" and the beauty that "cannot fade" are diametrically opposed, and the mood of melancholy (whether romantic pose or from the depths of frustration) is the antithesis of the mood of contemplation, classical thought upon a classic object. But these phrases merely suggest a detailed comparison; they do not carry it out.

Without further introduction, the poems for this chapter will be presented; and the reader may proceed at once with his intensive study of them by use of the comparative method.

Poems for Comparison: First Pair

ICH WEISS NICHT, WAS SOLL ES BEDEUTEN
Heinrich Heine

TRANSLATION I, BY LOUIS UNTERMEYER

I do not know why this confronts me,
    This sadness, this echo of pain;
A curious legend still haunts me,
    Still haunts and obsesses my brain:

The air is cool and it darkles;
    Softly the Rhine flows by.
The mountain peak still sparkles
    In the fading flush of the sky.

And on one peak, half-dreaming
    She sits, enthroned and fair;
Like a goddess, dazzling and gleaming,
    She combs her golden hair.

With a golden comb she is combing
    Her hair as she sings a song—
A song that, heard through the gloaming,
    Is magically sweet and strong.

The boatman has heard; it has bound him
    In the throes of a strange, wild love.

He is blind to the reefs that surround him;
　He sees but the vision above.

And lo, the wild waters are springing—
　The boat and the boatman are gone . . .
And this, with her poignant singing,
　The Loreley has done.

(1917-23)

TRANSLATION 2, BY ALEXANDER MACMILLAN

I canna tell what has come ower me
　That I am sae eerie and wae;
An auld-warld tale comes before me,
　It haunts me by nicht and by day.

From the cool lift the gloamin' draps dimmer,
　And the Rhine slips saftly by;
The taps of the mountains shimmer
　I' the lowe o' the sunset sky.

Up there, in a glamor entrancin',
　Sits a maiden wondrous fair;
Her gowden adornments are glancing,
　She is kaimin' her gowden hair.

As she kaims it the gowd kaim glistens,
　The while she is singin' a song
That hauds the rapt soul that listens,
　With its melody sweet and strong.

The boy, floating by in vague wonder,
　Is seized with a wild weird love;
He sees na the black rocks under,—
　He sees but the vision above.

The waters their waves are flingin'
　Ower boatie and boatman anon;
And this, with her airtful singin',
　The Waterwitch Lurley hath done.

(1822, tr. c. 1875)

Second Pair

THE RETREAT
Henry Vaughan

Happy those early days, when I
Shined in my angel-infancy!
Before I understood this place
Appointed for my *s*econd race,   = earthly life
Or taught my soul to fancy aught
But a white, celestial thought;
When yet I had not walked above
A mile or two from my first *l*ove,   = God? Heaven?
And looking back—at that short space—
Could see a glimpse of His bright face;
When on some gilded cloud, or flower,
My gazing soul would dwell an hour,
And in those weaker glories spy
Some shadows of eternity;
Before I taught my tongue to wound
My conscience with a sinful sound,
Or had the black art to dispense
A *s*everal sin to every sense,   = separate
But felt through all this fleshly dress
Bright shoots of everlastingness.
   O how I long to travel back,
And tread again that ancient track!
That I might once more reach that plain,
Where first I left my glorious train;
From whence th' enlightened spirit sees
That shady *C*ity of palm trees.   = Heaven
But ah! my soul with too much stay
Is drunk, and staggers in the *w*ay!   = road
Some men a forward motion love,

But I by backward steps would move,
And when this dust falls to the urn,
In that state I came, return.

(1650)

ODE

INTIMATIONS OF IMMORTALITY FROM
RECOLLECTIONS OF EARLY CHILDHOOD

William Wordsworth

> The Child is father of the Man;
> And I could wish my days to be
> Bound each to each by natural piety.

I

There was a time when meadow, grove, and stream
The earth, and every common sight,
        To me did seem
        Apparelled in celestial light,
The glory and the freshness of a dream.
It is not now as it hath been of yore;—
        Turn wheresoe'er I may,
        By night or day,
The things which I have seen I now can see no more.

2

        The Rainbow comes and goes,
        And lovely is the Rose;
        The Moon doth with delight
Look round her when the heavens are bare;
        Waters on a starry night
        Are beautiful and fair;
    The sunshine is a glorious birth;
    But yet I know where'er I go,
That there hath passed away a glory from the earth.

3

Now, while the birds thus sing a joyous song,
    And while the young lambs bound
        As to the *t*abor's sound,   = small drum
To me alone there came a thought of grief:
A timely utterance gave that thought relief,
        And I again am strong:
The cataracts blow their trumpets from the steep;
No more shall grief of mine the season wrong;
I hear the echoes through the mountains throng,
The winds come to me from the fields of sleep,
        And all the earth is gay;
           Land and sea
      Give themselves up to jollity,
        And with the heart of May
      Doth every beast keep holiday;—
        Thou Child of Joy,
Shout round me, let me hear thy shouts, thou happy Shepherd-boy

4

Ye blessed Creatures, I have heard the call
    Ye to each other make; I see
The heavens laugh with you in your jubilee;
    My heart is at your festival,
      My head hath its *c*oronal,   = garland
The fulness of your bliss, I feel, I feel it all.
    O evil day! if I were sullen
    While Earth herself is adorning,
        This sweet May-morning,
    And the Children are culling
        On every side,
    In a thousand valleys far and wide,
    Fresh flowers; while the sun shines warm,
And the Babe leaps up on his Mother's arm:—
    I hear, I hear, with joy I hear!
    —But there's a Tree, of many, one,
A single Field which I have looked upon,
Both of them speak of something that is gone:

The pansy at my feet
Doth the same tale repeat:
Whither is fled the visionary gleam?
Where is it now, the glory and the dream?

5

Our birth is but a sleep and a forgetting:
The Soul that rises with us, our life's Star,
    Hath had elsewhere its setting,
        And cometh from afar:
    Not in entire forgetfulness,
    And not in utter nakedness,
But trailing clouds of glory, do we come
        From God, who is our home:
Heaven lies about us in our infancy!
Shades of the prison-house begin to close
        Upon the growing Boy,
But he beholds the light, and whence it flows,
        He sees it in his joy;
The Youth, who daily farther from the east
        Must travel, still is Nature's Priest,
    And by the vision splendid
    Is on his way attended;
At length the Man perceives it die away,
And fade into the light of common day.

6

Earth fills her lap with pleasures of her own;
Yearnings she hath in her own natural kind,
And, even with something of a Mother's mind,
        And no unworthy aim,
    The homely Nurse doth all she can
To make her Foster-child, her Inmate Man,
    Forget the glories he hath known,
And that imperial palace whence he came.

7

Behold the Child among his new-born blisses,
A six years' Darling of a pigmy size!

See, where 'mid work of his own hand he lies,
Fretted by sallies of his mother's kisses,
With light upon him from his father's eyes!
See, at his feet, some little plan or chart,
Some fragment from his dream of human life,
Shaped by himself with newly-learned art;
    A wedding or a festival,
    A mourning or a funeral;
      And this hath now his heart,
    And unto this he frames his song:
      Then will he fit his tongue
To dialogues of business, love, or strife;
    But it will not be long
    Ere this be thrown aside,
    And with new joy and pride
The little Actor cons another part;
Filling from time to time his "humorous stage"
With all the Persons, down to palsied Age,
That Life brings with her in her equipage;
    As if his whole vocation
    Were endless imitation.[1]

8

Thou, whose exterior semblance doth belie
    Thy Soul's immensity;
Thou best Philosopher, who yet dost keep
Thy heritage, thou Eye among the blind,
That, deaf and silent, read'st the eternal deep,
Haunted for ever by the eternal mind,—
    Mighty Prophet! Seer blest!
    On whom those truths do rest,
Which we are toiling all our lives to find,
In darkness lost, the darkness of the grave;
Thou, over whom thy Immortality
Broods like the Day, a Master o'er a Slave,
A Presence which is not to be put by;
Thou little Child, yet glorious in the might

---

[1] The allusion is to Jaques' speech beginning "All the world's a stage" in *As You Like It,* II, vii, 139 ff. "Humorous" here means mood or temperament; "humorous stage"—stage peopled with characters of various dispositions.

Of heaven-born freedom on thy being's height,
Why with such earnest pains dost thou provoke
The years to bring the inevitable yoke,
Thus blindly with thy blessedness at strife?
Full soon thy Soul shall have her earthly freight,
And custom lie upon thee with a weight,
Heavy as frost, and deep almost. as life!

9

O joy! that in our embers
Is something that doth live,
That Nature yet remembers
What was so fugitive!
The thought of our past years in me doth breed
Perpetual benediction: not indeed
For that which is most worthy to be blest;
Delight and liberty, the simple creed
Of Childhood, whether busy or at rest,
With new-fledged hope still fluttering in his breast:—
Not for these I raise·
The song of thanks and praise;
But for those obstinate questionings
Of sense and outward things,
Fallings from us, vanishings;
Blank misgivings of a Creature
Moving about in worlds not realized,
High instincts before which our mortal Nature
Did tremble like a guilty thing surprised:
But for those first affections,
Those shadowy recollections,
Which, be they what they may,
Are yet the fountain light of all our day,
Are yet a master light of all our seeing;
Uphold us, cherish, and have power to make
Our noisy years seem moments in the being
Of the eternal Silence: truths that wake,
To perish never;
Which neither listlessness, nor mad endeavor,
Nor Man nor Boy,
Nor all that is at enmity with joy,

Can utterly abolish or destroy!
    Hence in a season of calm weather
      Though inland far we be,
Our souls have sight of that immortal sea
      Which brought us hither,
     Can in a moment travel thither,
And see the Children sport upon the shore,
And hear the mighty waters rolling evermore.

10

Then sing, ye Birds, sing a joyous song!
      And let the young Lambs bound
      As to the tabor's sound!
We in thought will join your throng,
    Ye that pipe and ye that play,
    Ye that through your hearts today
    Feel the gladness of the May!
What though the radiance which was once so bright
Be now for ever taken from my sight,
      Though nothing can bring back the hour
Of splendor in the grass, of glory in the flower;
     We will grieve not, rather find
     Strength in what remains behind;
    In the primal sympathy
    Which, having been, must ever be;
    In the soothing thoughts that spring
    Out of human suffering;
    In the faith that looks *through* death,   = beyond
In years that bring the philosophic mind.

11

And O ye Fountains, Meadows, Hills, and Groves,
Forebode not any severing of our loves!
Yet in my heart of hearts I feel your might;
I only have relinquished one delight
To live beneath your more habitual sway.
I love the Brooks which down their channels fret,
Even more than when I tripped lightly as they;
The innocent brightness of a new-born Day
      Is lovely yet;

The Clouds that gather round the setting sun
Do take a sober coloring from an eye
That hath kept watch o'er man's mortality;
Another race hath been, and other palms are won.
Thanks to the human heart by which we live,
Thanks to its tenderness, its joys, and fears,
To me the meanest flower that blows can give
Thoughts that do often lie too deep for tears.

(1807)

Third Pair

COUNTER-ATTACK

Siegfried Sassoon

We'd gained our first objective hours before
While dawn broke like a face with blinking eyes,
Pallid, unshaved and thirsty, blind with smoke.
Things seemed all right at first. We held their line,
With bombers posted, Lewis guns well placed,
And clink of shovels deepening the shallow trench.
  The place was rotten with dead; green clumsy legs
  High-booted, sprawled and groveled along the saps;
  And trunks, face downward, in the sucking mud,
  Wallowed like trodden sand-bags loosely filled;
  And naked sodden buttocks, mats of hair,
  Bulged, clotted heads slept in the plastering slime.
  And then the rain began—the jolly old rain!

A yawning soldier knelt against the bank,
Staring across the morning blear with fog;
He wondered when the Allemands would get busy;
And then, of course, they started with five-nines
Traversing, sure as fate, and never a dud.

Mute in the clamor of shells he watched them burst
Spouting dark earth and wire with gusts from hell,
While posturing giants dissolved in drifts of smoke.
He crouched and flinched, dizzy with galloping fear,
Sick for escape—loathing the strangled horror
And butchered, frantic gestures of the dead.

An officer came blundering down the trench:
"Stand-to and man the fire-step!" On he went . . .
Gasping and bawling, "Fire-step . . . counter-attack!"
   Then the haze lifted. Bombing on the right
   Down the old sap; machine-guns on the left;
   And stumbling figures looming out in front.
"O Christ, they're coming at us!" Bullets spat,
And he remembered his rifle . . . rapid fire . . .
And started blazing wildly . . . then a bang
Crumpled and spun him sideways, knocked him out
To grunt and wriggle. None heeded him; he choked
And fought the flapping veils of smothering gloom,
Lost in a blurred confusion of yells and groans . . .
Down, and down, and down, he sank and drowned,
Bleeding to death. The counter-attack had failed.

                    (1918)

CONVERSATION PIECE
Smith Dawless

IS THE GATEWAY TO INDIA AT BOMBAY
REALLY AS BEAUTIFUL AS THEY SAY?
    Don't rightly know, Ma'am. Did my part
    Breakin' point in the jungle's heart;
    Blasted the boulders, felled the trees
    With red muck oozin' around our knees,
    Carved the guts from the Patkai's side,
    Dozed our trace, made it clean and wide,
    Metalled and graded, dug and filled:
    We had the Ledo Road to build.

WELL, SURELY YOU SAW A BURNING GHAT,
FAKIRS, ROPE TRICKS AND ALL OF THAT.

 Reckon I didn't. But 'way up ahead
 I tended the wounded, buried the dead.
 For I was a Medic, and little we knew,
 But the smell of sickness all day through,
 Mosquitoes, leeches, and thick dark mud
 Where the Chinese spilled their blood
 After the enemy guns were stilled:
 We had the Ledo Road to build.

OF COURSE, YOU FOUND THE TAJ MAHAL,
THE LOVELIEST BUILDING OF THEM ALL.

 Can't really say, lady. I was stuck
 Far beyond Shing with a QM truck.
 Monsoon was rugged there, hot and wet,
 Nothing to do but work and sweat
 And dry was the dust upon my mouth
 As steadily big "cats" roared on south,
 Over this ground where Japs lay killed:
 We had the Ledo Road to build.

YOU'VE BEEN GONE TWO YEARS THIS SPRING,
DIDN'T YOU SEE A SINGLE THING?

 Never saw much but the moon shine on
 A Burmese temple around Maingkwan,
 And silver transports high in the sky,
 Thursday River and the swift Tanai,
 And Hukawng Valley coming all green—
 Those are the only sights I've seen.
 Did our job, though, like God willed:
 We had the Ledo Road to build.

       (1943)

Fourth Pair

SONG
John Donne

Go and catch a falling star,
   Get with child a mandrake root,
Tell me where all past years are,
   Or who cleft the devil's foot;
Teach me to hear mermaids singing,
Or to keep off envy's stinging,
      And find
      What wind
Serves to advance an honest mind.

If thou be'st born to strange sights,
   Things invisible to see,
Ride ten thousand days and nights
   Till age snow white hairs on thee;
Thou, when thou return'st, wilt tell me
All strange wonders that befell thee;
      And swear
      No where
Lives a woman true and fair.

If thou find'st one, let me know;
   Such a pilgrimage were sweet.
Yet do not; I would not go,
   Though at next door we might meet.
Though she were true when you met her,
And last till you write your letter,
      Yet she
      Will be
False, ere I come, to two or three.
          (1633)

IS MY TEAM PLOUGHING

A. E. Housman

"Is my team ploughing,
  That I was used to drive
And hear the harness jingle
  When I was man alive?"

Aye, the horses trample,
  The harness jingles now;
No change though you lie under
  The land you used to plough.

"Is football playing
  Along the river shore,
With lads to chase the leather,
  Now I stand up no more?"

Aye, the ball is flying,
  The lads play heart and soul;
The goal stands up, the keeper
  Stands up to keep the goal.

"Is my girl happy,
  That I thought hard to leave,
And has she tired of weeping
  As she lies down at eve?"

Aye, she lies down lightly,
  She lies not down to weep:
Your girl is well contented.
  Be still, my lad, and sleep.

"Is my friend hearty,
  Now I am thin and pine;
And has he found to sleep in
  A better bed than mine?"

Aye, lad, I lie easy,
  I lie as lads would choose;
I cheer a dead man's sweetheart.
  Never ask me whose.

(1896)

Fifth Pair

PHILOMELA
Sir Philip Sidney

The Nightingale, as soon as April bringeth
  Unto her rested sense a perfect waking,
While late-bare Earth, proud of new clothing, springeth,
  Sings out her woes, a thorn her song-book making;
      And mournfully bewailing,
      Her throat in tunes expresseth
      What grief her breast oppresseth,
For Tereus' force on her chaste will prevailing.

  O Philomela fair, O take some gladness
  That here is juster cause of plaintful sadness!
    Thine earth now springs, mine fadeth;
    Thy thorn without, my thorn my heart invadeth.

Alas! she hath no other cause of anguish
  But Tereus' love, on her by strong hand wroken;
Wherein she suffering, all her spirits languish,
  Full womanlike, complains her will was broken,
      But I, who, daily craving,
      Cannot have to content me,
      Have more cause to lament me,
Since wanting is more woe than too much having.

O Philomela fair, O take some gladness
That here is juster cause of plaintful sadness!
Thine earth now springs, mine fadeth;
Thy thorn without, my thorn my heart invadeth.

(1590)

PHILOMELA

Matthew Arnold

Hark! ah, the nightingale—
The tawny-throated!
Hark, from that moonlit cedar what a burst!
What triumph! hark!—what pain!

O wanderer from a Grecian shore,
Still, after many years, in distant lands,
Still nourishing in thy bewildered brain
That wild, unquenched, deep-sunken, old-world pain—
Say, will it never heal?
And can this fragrant lawn
With its cool trees, and night,
And the sweet, tranquil Thames,
And moonshine, and the dew,
To thy racked heart and brain
Afford no balm?

Dost thou tonight behold
Here, through the moonlight on this English grass,
The unfriendly palace in the Thracian wild?
Dost thou again peruse
With hot cheeks and seared eyes
The too clear web, and thy dumb sister's shame?
Dost thou once more assay
Thy flight, and feel come over thee,
Poor fugitive, the feathery change
Once more, and once more seem to make resound
With love and hate, triumph and agony,
Lone Daulis, and the high Cephissian vale?
Listen, Eugenia—

How thick the bursts come crowding through the leaves!
Again—thou hearest?
Eternal Passion!
Eternal Pain!

(1853)

Sixth Pair

THE WRESTLING MATCH
Robert Penn Warren

"Here in this corner, ladies and gentlemen,
I now presents 'Mug' Hill, weight two-hundred-ten,
Who will wrestle here tonight the 'Battling Pole,'
Boruff"—who, as insistently the stale

Loud voice behind asserts, is good as hell.
"Is good as hell, I says." And then the bell
Stabs up to life two engines of flesh and bone,
Each like a great and bronze automaton

That by black magic moves tremendously,
Moving with a machine's intensity
To some obscure and terrible conclusion
Involving us, as in an absurd vision

The truculent dull spirit is involved
There to contend above while is dissolved
In sleep the twisted body on the bed.
The barker said—or was it this he said:

"Ladies and gentlemen, I now present,"
(The voice here sank in some obscene intent)
"That which is body, so you all may see
The bone and blood and sweat and agony,

"The thews that through the tortured years have striven
To breach the flesh so sure to spill when broken,
The only breath, a cry, and the dark blood
That forever we would keep if but we could."

(c. 1923, 1930)

A BOXER CALLED PANTHER
Reuel Denney

The girls who made that fighting body love
Remember how those biceps pushed the glove.
He was the bloody scholar of hot speed,
Footloose, shifty, quick to lead,
And swifter yet to draw and weave the blows
Or pivot the dizzy canvas with sure toes.
Relaxing now, his ruined tendons lie,
Whose art was calory braided into eye.
Let's take our hats and go, frail gentlemen;
Those eyes will never chase the arcs again.
Let us go back and yield up to our wives
Our youth, our clerkish labor, and our lives.
Relight cigars. The subway is our goal.
Comes Father Mike to speed the lifting soul,
And wax will guard those level thighs again
When we are lost within the city's rain.
Then, asking about the body, as each goes
—The lovely frame on which we hang our clothes,
Shall we upon our own addresses smile?
Shall we but pause and listen there a while
As for a jaguar roving on that stair,
Death balanced on his eager haunches there?

(1939)

SUGGESTIONS FOR STUDY

1. *Die Lorelei.* (a) As an aid to your comparative analysis of the two translations, the original is here presented for those who can read it:

DIE LORELEI
Heinrich Heine

Ich weiss nicht, was soll es bedeuten,
Dass ich so traurig bin;
Ein Märchen aus alten Zeiten,
Das kommt mir nicht aus dem Sinn.
Die Luft ist kühl und es dunkelt,
Und ruhig fliesst der Rhein;
Der Gipfel des Berges funkelt
Im Abendsonnenschein.

Die schönste Jungfrau sitzet
Dort oben wunderbar,
Ihr goldnes Geschmeide blitzet,
Sie kämmt ihr goldenes Haar.
Sie kämmt es mit goldenem Kamme,
Und singt ein Lied dabei;
Das hat eine wundersame,
Gewaltige Melodei.

Den Schiffer im kleinen Schiffe
Ergreift es mit wildem Weh;
Er schaut nicht die Felsenriffe,
Er schaut nur hinauf in die Höh'.
Ich glaube, die Wellen verschlingen
Am Ende Schiffer und Kahn;
Und das hat mit ihrem Singen
Die Lorelei gethan.

(1822)

(b) If you can read the German, compare each of the translations with it. Which of the two seems to you the more faithful rendering of the sense of the original? At what points do the translations differ markedly? Which seems to you to catch best the spirit of the original? What can you say in justification of Macmillan's Scotch dialect as a medium for the translation?

(c) The well-known melody for this song-lyric was composed by Friedrich Silcher in 1827.

Ich weiss nicht,was soll es be - deu - tèn, dass ich so_trau - rig bin;   ein

Mär-chen aus al - ten Zei-ten, das kommt mir nicht aus dem Sinn. Die

Luft_ ist kühl und es dun-kelt, und ru - hig fliesst der Rhein; der

Gi-pfel_des Ber-ges fun - kelt im A - bend - son -_nen -_schein.___

2. *Recollection.* (a) Wordsworth's "Ode: Intimations of Immortality" is based upon the Doctrine of Recollection, which finds expression in Plato's *Phaedo*: "Your favorite doctrine, Socrates, that knowledge is simply recollection, if true, also necessarily implies a previous time in which we learned that which we now recollect. But this would be impossible unless our soul was in some place before existing in the human form; here then is another argument of the soul's immortality. . . . If the knowledge which we acquired before birth was lost by us at birth, and if afterwards by the use of the senses we recovered that which we previously knew, will not that which we call learning be a process of recovering our knowledge, and may not this be rightly termed recollection by us?" (b) In the light of this note, re-examine Vaughan's "The Retreat" and Wordsworth's "Ode," and compare them in some detail. (c) Another poem on the same general theme was written by a contemporary of Vaughan: "Wonder" by Thomas Traherne (1636-74); the poem, written about 1660, was not published until 1903.

3. *Western Front and Ledo Road.* (a) "Counter-Attack" by Sassoon and "Conversation Piece" by Dawless are poems that give expression to the experience of soldiers in World War I and in World War II. (b) Comment upon the differences in the two wars as revealed through these poems. (c) How do the two poems differ as to type? (Is the Dawless poem narrative? How many characters are suggested?) How do they differ in poetic form? What are the attitudes of the poets toward the wars in which they were involved? How would you characterize the differences in mood? in style?

4. *Song and Plough.* (a) Donne's "Song" ('Go and catch a falling star') and Housman's "Is My Team Ploughing" are here presented as a pair of poems for comparative analysis. (b) What do you assume to be the basis in similarity that would make possible a comparison?

5. *Philomela and Procne.* (a) Sidney's "Philomela" and Arnold's poem of the same title are only two of a good many nightingale poems based upon the Greek legend of Philomela and Procne, two sisters and Athenian princesses, who were turned respectively into nightingale and swallow. The story is one that Ovid retold in his *Metamorphoses.* When Procne married Tereus, King of Thrace, Philomela accompanied her sister to live with her at Daulis, capital of Thrace near the river Cephissus. Tereus fell in love with his sister-in-law Philomela, violated her, and then cut out her tongue to prevent her telling. But she contrived to reveal this horror to her sister, depicting it in a tapestry she was weaving. Procne then killed her son Itylus and served his cooked flesh up to his father. The sisters fled, with Tereus in pursuit. They prayed for help, and were saved by being transformed into birds. (It is romantic legend that birds sing with throat pressed against thorn.) (b) Notice that Matthew Arnold reverses the position of Philomela and Procne in their relation to Tereus. (c) Now proceed with a comparative analysis of the two poems. (d) Other poems on the same theme are Barnfield's "Philomel" and Swinburne's "Itylus." More than a dozen nightingale poems are listed in Herbert Bruncken's *Subject Index to Poetry,* American Library Association, 1940.

6. *Mat and Gloves.* (a) Study Robert Penn Warren's "The Wrestling Match" and Reuel Denney's "A Boxer Called Panther." (b) What different bases of similarity can you suggest for making a comparative analysis? (c) Proceed upon some one of these bases, but search for points of similarity as well as differences: in narrative technique, in poetic form, in theme, in mood and style.

24

CRITICAL INTERPRETATION

The present chapter will not only round out this final group on the intensive study of the more difficult poetry, but will also bring Book Two to a close. In addition, it will serve to conclude the entire volume, *Preface to Poetry*. It will not, then, present new materials, but will recall for final emphasis a number of points made earlier, and review and rearrange them for present use. The reader will then take the techniques of critical interpretation out to the threshing floor, upon which a fresh harvest of poems awaits the flail. For among modern poems, as well as the earlier ones, there are a goodly number whereof it may be said that the hard clear grain of their thought comes free only after rigorous labor.

It is not alone the reader of poetry who finds himself beset with difficulties of interpretation. Most of his problems are the same as those that face the interpreter of other sorts of symbols and signs. But some of the difficulties in interpreting poetry are peculiar to it, and we have already dealt with the complex rhythms of the poem-experience, with the varieties of free imagery, with the several sorts of feeling that may be a part of the response.

I. DIFFICULTIES OF INTERPRETATION

This closing chapter will deal once more with the problem of meaning, with the difficulties that may stand in the way of the communication of thought, and with some of the techniques that are helpful to critical interpretation.

The problem of meaning, the nature of language and of communication, was broached in Chapter 3 and was further developed in chapters 7 and 12, where attention was given to an explanation and illustration of the several functions of language (pp. 43-46, 162-65), the contextual theory of meaning (pp. 49, 165), the process of communication (p. 167), the nature of interpretation (pp. 172, 194), the four phases of meaning (pp. 50, 168-70), ambiguity (pp. 49-50, 170 ff.), metaphor (pp. 173-76), the over-all meaning (pp. 176-81), and the reader's "condition" (pp. 305-11). We shall proceed without reviewing them here, though the reader may wish to refresh himself upon some of them by turning back to the pages cited.

There are several difficulties that often stand in the way of the communication of the poet's thought. Each of us has been conscious of some of them.

First, there is the at times obvious difficulty of not knowing what certain of the words or phrases could possibly mean, not being able to get the sense of it at all. It may indeed be all Greek to the reader; words or phrases—even the title itself—may be in an unfamiliar foreign tongue. Or the words may be English enough, but utterly strange. These difficulties, nevertheless, are not as serious as those involving apparently familiar words used with unusual senses, or words apparently used in a common sense that are really used with rich ambiguity. Proper nouns—names of mythological, literary, or historical persons or characters, places or events—often carry a surcharge of reference which must be caught in order to get the sense of the poet's utterance. Unaccustomed word order, remote connections of thought, metaphors that for a particular reader fail to snap-to, some of the seventeenth century conceits—these may be the most troublesome of the difficulties in this first group, all of which are concerned primarily with the reader's following the sense phase of the meaning.

A second group of difficulties has to do with the other phases of the meaning—tone, feeling, and intention. The clues to the poet's intention may be subtle or they may actually exist outside the framework of the printed poem; so too may the evidences of the particular tone and feeling. Here the more remote allusions may present problems in interpretation. Some of them—verbal echoes and obscure references—will altogether escape some readers' notice, and they will miss the clues that might guide them to the sense of it, as well as to the other aspects of the poet's full meaning. So, too, the larger symbols of the poem may be lost upon some readers, with resultant difficulty in the interpretation of the over-all meaning. Indeed, it is sometimes impossible, as one says, to see the forest for the trees.

Another pair of difficulties deserves brief mention. One is the difficulty a reader sometimes has in seeing that there is any difficulty at all. The meaning of a poem may appear to be perfectly clear, and the reader rests content in a facile interpretation that may be quite inadequate. The converse is also true at times: a reader may make mountains out of the molehills of a perfectly simple and easily interpreted poem—search for and find amazingly complex meanings hidden in transparent song.

So much, then, for a summary of difficulties that may beset the reader. What, now, are the devices and techniques of critical interpretation helpful in the solution of such difficulties?

2. SUGGESTED TECHNIQUES AND DEVICES

Read with your wits and reference books about you—that is the simplest and most direct advice. The alertness demanded of the critical reader is comparable to the reporter's nose for news, the detective's investigative sense, the researcher's keen insights. The interpreter of this sort will add sensitiveness and imagination to eagerness and perseverance. The printed poem will challenge him to bring his best intelligence to bear upon it and to play about it, and he will be satisfied with nothing less than what seems to him to be the very experience of the poet.

Certainly the reader should have at his elbow a good abridged dictionary, such as the *Webster's Collegiate*. He will also need a classical mythology (be it as old as Bulfinch's *The Age of Fables,* or as recent as Edith Hamilton's *Mythology*), a King James translation of the *Bible* and perhaps the Smith and Goodspeed *American Bible,* and a good one-volume Shakespeare (Globe, Oxford, Neilson, or Kittridge text). Only less important will be a comprehensive anthology of English Literature and one of American Literature (like Whiting, *et al., The College Survey of English Litera-*

ture, or Woods, Watt, and Anderson, *The Literature of England,* and Jones and Leisy, *Major American Writers,* or Benét and Pearson, *The Oxford Anthology of American Literature*). Such handy volumes as the *Oxford Companion to English Literature* (and the American and Classical volumes) will be useful, as will Bartlett's *Familiar Quotations.* A reference book on the desk is worth two in the library; but it is not enough simply to have them within reach, it is necessary to explore them to learn their widely varied uses, to enjoy browsing in them, until it is no longer a task to turn to them for very present help in trouble.

To know when to look up a word or phrase, and when the context makes its meaning satisfactorily clear; to smoke out the allusions, and to trace them down when more information will be illuminating; to determine what additional background material is necessary for an adequate interpretation, and where to find it—this calls for nice judgment as well as reference skill, both of which are requisite for the intensive study of more difficult poetry.

How important, after all, is it to know what "a mandrake root" is and looks like in order to read John Donne's "Song" (p. 655) given in the last chapter? The general tenor of the opening lines is clear enough without it: "Go and do any one of these impossible things!" But the critical reader will not content himself with the mere drift; he will want to follow each current and eddy of the thought, and for this the sense and visual image of the forked mandrake root, and perhaps even the legend of its crying out, will be necessary. The two poems on "Philomela" (p. 657) are almost meaningless for the reader who does not bring to them the classical myth upon which they are based; and certainly Vaughan's "The Retreat" and Wordsworth's "Ode" (p. 645) are illuminated by some knowledge of the Platonic doctrine.

The question is naturally asked: If this is so, shouldn't all poems be accompanied by explanatory and glossarial notes? And the answer is: No, not necessarily. Too many notes will tend to do the reader's work for him, and deprive him of the very real pleasure of reading for himself—stumbling, falling, climbing, and seeing with his own untutored eyes. Neatly prepared footnotes may make clear the way and weed the path, but they may also rob poetry of its

enriching ambiguity. Let the reader, equipped with his own mountain tools, break his own way and cut his own footholds up the
rugged cliff. He will gain a practiced eye in spotting the accessible
way and in judging the virtue of each root and stem.

Read, then, with a ready wit and reference books. Read also
with a sharpened pencil. The meat of a more difficult poem may
need to be picked out of its shell. A digging tool recommended,
and made use of in the earlier chapters, is Basic English paraphrase. It is, of course, no open-sesame to the treasure den of
poetry; and other techniques of translation, précis, or commentary
may serve a similar purpose. But the effort to ferret out the sense
of the poem may lead to an understanding of the other phases of
the full meaning and to a richer realization of the other aspects of
the whole poem-experience. From the title of the poem—and how
important the title may be to an understanding of the poem!—
from title to end, the delving process of paraphrase may join some
of the apparent gaps in thought, set straight the unaccustomed
word order, and spring the trap of metaphor, straightening out the
sense of it which, as was said earlier, leads the way in the poem-
reading-experience.

It will indeed take a "scholar of hot speed,/ Footloose, shifty,
quick to lead,/ And swifter yet to draw and weave the blows," to
connect with all of Reuel Denney's thoughts in his poem "A Boxer
Called Panther." Is it an accident that the "Panther" of the title
is echoed by the "jaguar" Death in the close? And what of Father
Mike who comes "to speed the lifting soul" and of his "Then, asking about the body, as each goes"? What is the unusual sense, or
one of the senses, of the possibly ambiguous "addresses"? But such
boxing with ideas, indeed intensive study, will not go unrewarded,
for through it will come an understanding of this unusual poem
upon an important and universal theme.

A good many modern poems are difficult, and will give up their
meaning only after a bout of intensive study. But this is also true
of poems from some of the earlier periods of literature. Each reader
will decide for himself, of course, whether his final experience with
one of these harder poems is valuable, whether the rewards of his
digging are worth the effort. Some who have not acquired skill

with pick and pan will abandon good claims, saying that the dirt is no-pay. But those who have mined with diligence the difficult poetry of our own and earlier times, will prize the dust and nuggets that they have brought back from the realms of gold.

Poems for Critical Interpretation

SO LONG!
Walt Whitman

[A reading of this poem by Ralph Bellamy has been recorded (Victor Album M955).]

I

To conclude—I announce what comes after me;
I announce mightier offspring, orators, days, and then, for the present, depart.

I remember I said, before my leaves sprang at all,
I would raise my voice jocund and strong, with reference to consummations.

When America does what was promis'd,
When there are plentiful athletic bards, inland and seaboard,
When through These States walk a hundred millions of superb persons,
When the rest part away for superb persons, and contribute to them,
When breeds of the most perfect mothers denote America,
Then to me and mine our due fruition.

I have press'd through in my own right,
I have sung the Body and the Soul—War and Peace have I sung,
And the songs of Life and of Birth—and shown that there are many births:

I have offer'd my style to everyone—I have journey'd with confident
    step;
While my pleasure is yet at the full, I whisper, *So long!*
And take the young woman's hand, and the young man's hand, for the
    last time.

2

I announce natural persons to arise;
I announce justice triumphant;
I announce uncompromising liberty and equality;
I announce the justification of candor, and the justification of pride.

I announce that the identity of These States is a single identity only;
I announce the Union more and more compact, indissoluble;
I announce splendors and majesties to make all the previous politics of
    the earth insignificant.

I announce adhesiveness—I say it shall be limitless, unloosen'd;
I say you shall yet find the friend you were looking for.

I announce a man or woman coming—perhaps you are the one, (*So
    long!*)
I announce the great individual, fluid as Nature, chaste, affectionate,
    compassionate, fully armed.

I announce a life that shall be copious, vehement, spiritual, bold;
I announce an end that shall lightly and joyfully meet its translation;
I announce myriads of youths, beautiful, gigantic, sweet-blooded;
I announce a race of splendid and savage old men.

3

O thicker and faster! (*So long!*)
O crowding too close upon me;
I foresee too much—it means more than I thought;
It appears to me I am dying.

Hasten throat, and sound your last!
Salute me—salute the days once more. Peal the old cry once more.

Screaming electric, the atmosphere using,
At random glancing, each as I notice absorbing,

Swiftly on, but a little while alighting,
Curious envelop'd messages delivering,
Sparkles hot, seed ethereal, down in the dirt dropping,
Myself unknowing, my commission obeying, to question it never daring,
To ages, and ages yet, the growth of the seed leaving,
To troops out of me, out of the army, the war arising—they the tasks
    I have set promulging,
To women certain whispers of myself bequeathing—their affection me
    more clearly explaining,
To young men my problems offering—no dallier I—I the muscle of
    their brains trying,
So I pass—a little time vocal, visible, contrary;
Afterward, a melodious echo, passionately bent for—(death making me
    really undying;)
The best of me then when no longer visible—for toward that I have
    been incessantly preparing.

What is there more, that I lag and pause, and crouch extended with
    unshut mouth?
Is there a single final farewell?

4

My songs cease—I abandon them;
From behind the screen where I hid I advance personally, solely to you.

Camerado! This is no book;
Who touches this, touches a man;
(Is it night? Are we here alone?)
It is I you hold, and who holds you;
I spring from the pages into your arms—decease calls me forth.

O how your fingers drowse me!
Your breath falls around me like dew—your pulse lulls the tympans of
    my ears;
I feel immerged from head to foot;
Delicious—enough.

Enough, O deed impromptu and secret!
Enough, O gliding present! Enough, O summ'd-up past!

5

Dear friend, whoever you are, take this kiss,
I give it especially to you—Do not forget me;
I feel like one who has done work for the day, to retire awhile;
I receive now again of my many translations—from my avataras ascend-
    ing—while others doubtless await me;
An unknown sphere, more real than I dream'd, more direct, darts
    awakening rays about me—So long!
Remember my words—I may again return,
I love you—I depart from materials;
I am as one disembodied, triumphant, dead.
(1860-70)

HOUSE

Robert Browning

1

Shall I sonnet-sing you about myself?
    Do I live in a house you would like to see?
Is it scant of gear, has it store of pelf?
    "Unlock my heart with a sonnet-key?"

2

Invite the world, as my betters have done?
    "Take notice: this building remains on view,
Its suites of reception every one,
    Its private apartment and bedroom too;

3

"For a ticket, apply to the Publisher."
    No: thanking the public, I must decline.
A peep through my window, if folk prefer;
    But, please you, no foot over threshold of mine!

4

I have mixed with a crowd and heard free talk
    In a foreign land where an earthquake chanced:

And a house stood gaping, naught to balk
  Man's eye wherever he gazed or glanced.

5

The whole of the frontage shaven sheer,
  The inside gaped: exposed to day,
Right and wrong and common and queer,
  Bare, as the palm of your hand, it lay.

6

The owner? Oh, he had been crushed, no doubt!
  "Odd tables and chairs for a man of wealth!
What a parcel of musty old books about!
  He smoked,—no wonder he lost his health!

7

"I doubt if he bathed before he dressed.
  A brasier?—the pagan, he burned perfumes!
You see it is proved, what the neighbors guessed:
  His wife and himself had separate rooms."

8

Friends, the good man of the house at least
  Kept house to himself till an earthquake came:
'T is the fall of its frontage permits you feast
  On the inside arrangement you praise or blame.

9

Outside should suffice for evidence:
  And whoso desires to penetrate
Deeper, must dive by the spirit-sense—
  No optics like yours, at any rate!

10

"Hoity-toity! A street to explore,
  Your house the exception! *'With this same key
Shakespeare unlocked his heart,'*—once more!"
  Did Shakespeare? If so, the less Shakespeare he!
                   (1876)

from FEARS IN SOLITUDE

WRITTEN IN APRIL, 1798, DURING THE ALARM
OF AN INVASION

Samuel Taylor Coleridge

                . . . Oh! my countrymen!
We have offended very grievously,
And been most tyrannous. From east to west
A groan of accusation pierces Heaven!
The wretched plead against us; multitudes
Countless and vehement, the sons of God,
Our brethren! Like a cloud that travels on,
Steamed up from Cairo's swamps of pestilence,
Even so, my countrymen! have we gone forth
And borne to distant tribes slavery and pangs,
And, deadlier far, our vices, whose deep taint
With slow perdition murders the whole man,
His body and his soul! Meanwhile, at home,
All individual dignity and power
Engulfed in Courts, Committees, Institutions,
Associations and Societies,
A vain, speech-mouthing, speech-reporting Guild,
One Benefit-Club for mutual flattery,
We have drunk up, demure as at a grace,
Pollutions from the brimming cup of wealth;
Contemptuous of all honorable rule,
Yet bartering freedom and the poor man's life
For gold, as at a market! The sweet words
Of Christian promise, words that even yet
Might stem destruction, were they wisely preached,
Are muttered o'er by men, whose tones proclaim
How flat and wearisome they feel their trade:
Rank scoffers some, but most too indolent
To deem them falsehoods or to know their truth.
Oh! blasphemous! the Book of Life is made
A superstitious instrument, on which
We gabble o'er the oaths we mean to break;

For all must swear—all and in every place,
College and wharf, council and justice-court;
All, all must swear, the briber and the bribed,
Merchant and lawyer, senator and priest,
The rich, the poor, the old man and the young;
All, all make up one scheme of perjury,
That faith doth reel; the very name of God
Sounds like a juggler's charm; and, bold with joy,
Forth from his dark and lonely hiding-place,
(Portentous sight!) the owlet Atheism,
Sailing on obscene wings athwart the noon,
Drops his blue-fringèd lids, and holds them close,
And hooting at the glorious sun in Heaven,
Cries out, "Where is it?"

                          Thankless too for peace,
(Peace long preserved by fleets and perilous seas)
Secure from actual warfare, we have loved
To swell the war-whoop, passionate for war!
Alas! for ages ignorant of all
Its ghastlier workings, (famine or blue plague,
Battle, or siege, or flight through wintry snows,)
We, this whole people, have been clamorous
For war and bloodshed; animating sports,
The which we pay for as a thing to talk of,
Spectators and not combatants! No guess
Anticipative of a wrong unfelt,
No speculation on contingency,
However dim and vague, too vague and dim
To yield a justifying cause; and forth,
(Stuffed out with big preamble, holy names,
And adjurations of the God in Heaven,)
We send our mandates for the certain death
Of thousands and ten thousands! Boys and girls,
And women, that would groan to see a child
Pull off an insect's leg, all read of war,
The best amusement for our morning meal!
The poor wretch, who has learnt his only prayers
From curses, who knows scarcely words enough

To ask a blessing from his Heavenly Father,
Becomes a fluent phraseman, absolute
And technical in victories and defeats,
And all our dainty terms for fratricide;
Terms which we trundle smoothly o'er our tongues
Like mere abstractions, empty sounds to which
We join no feeling and attach no form!
As if the soldier died without a wound;
As if the fibres of this godlike frame
Were gored without a pang; as if the wretch,
Who fell in battle, doing bloody deeds,
Passed off to Heaven, translated and not killed;
As though he had no wife to pine for him,
No God to judge him! Therefore, evil days
Are coming on us, O my countrymen!
And what if all-avenging Providence,
Strong and retributive, should make us know
The meaning of our words, force us to feel
The desolation and the agony
Of our fierce doings? . . .

(1798)

THE LEADEN ECHO and THE GOLDEN ECHO

MAIDENS' SONG FROM ST. WINEFRED'S WELL

Gerard Manley Hopkins

THE LEADEN ECHO

How to kéep—is there ány any, is there none such, nowhere known,
    some bow or brooch or braid or brace, láce, latch or catch or key
    to keep
Back beauty, keep it, beauty, beauty, beauty, . . . from vanishing away?
Ó, is there no frowning of these wrinkles, rankèd wrinkles deep,
Dówn? no waving-off of these most mournful messengers, still mes-
    sengers, sad and stealing messengers of gray?
No, there's none, there's none—oh, no, there's none!
Nor can you long be, what you now are, called fair—

Do what you may do, what, do what you may,
And wisdom is early to despair:
Be beginning; since, no, nothing can be done
To keep at bay
Age and age's evils—hoar hair,
Ruck and wrinkle, drooping, dying, death's worst, winding sheets,
    tombs and worms, and tumbling to decay;
So be beginning, be beginning to despair.
Oh, there's none—no, no, no, there's none:
    Be beginning to despair, to despair,
    Despair, despair, despair, despair.

THE GOLDEN ECHO

    Spare!
There ís one, yes, I have one (Hush there!);
Only not within seeing of the sun,
Not within the singeing of the strong sun,
Tall sun's tingeing, or treacherous the tainting of the earth's air,
Somewhere elsewhere there is ah, well, where! one,
Óne. Yes, I can tell such a key, I do know such a place,
Where whatever's prized and passes of us, everything that's fresh and
    fast-flying of us, seems to us sweet of us and swiftly away with,
    done away with, undone,
Undone, done with, soon done with, and yet dearly and dangerously
    sweet
Of us, the wimpled-water-dimpled, not-by-morning-matchèd face,
The flower of beauty, fleece of beauty, too too apt to, ah! to fleet,
Never fleets móre, fastened with the tenderest truth
To its own best being and its loveliness of youth: it is an everlastingness
    of, O it is an all youth!
Come then, your ways and airs and looks, locks, maiden gear, gallantry
    and gayety and grace,
Winning ways, airs innocent, maiden manners, sweet looks, loose locks,
    long locks, lovelocks, gaygear, going gallant, girlgrace—
Resign them, sign them, seal them, send them, motion them with
    breath,
And with sighs soaring, soaring síghs deliver
Them; beauty-in-the-ghost, deliver it, early now, long before death
Give beauty back, beauty, beauty, beauty, back to God, beauty's self and
    beauty's giver.

See; not a hair is, not an eyelash, not the least lash lost; every hair
Is, hair of the head, numbered.
Nay, what we had lighthanded left in surely the mere mold
Will have waked and have waxed and have walked with the wind
    whatwhile we slept,
This side, that side hurling a heavyheaded hundredfold
What while we, while we slumbered.
O then, weary then why should we tread? O why are we so haggard
    at the heart, so care-coiled, care-killed, so fagged, so fashed, so
    cogged, so cumbered,
When the thing we freely fórfeit is kept with fonder a care,
Fonder a care kept than we could have kept it, kept
Far with fonder a care (and we, we should have lost it) finer, fonder
A care kept.—Where kept? Do but tell us where kept, where.—
Yonder.—What high as that! We follow, now we follow.—Yonder, yes,
    yonder, yonder,
Yonder.

                                                    (*c. 1880*, 1918)

THE WORLD
Henry Vaughan

I

I saw Eternity the other night,
Like a great ring of pure and endless light,
    All calm, as it was bright;
And round beneath it, Time, in hours, days, years,
    Driv'n by the spheres
Like a vast shadow moved; in which the world
    And all her train were hurled.
The doting lover in his quaintest strain
    Did there complain;
Near him, his lute, his fancy, and his flights,
    Wit's sour delights,
With gloves, and knots, the silly snares of pleasure,
    Yet his dear treasure,
All scattered lay, while he his eyes did pour
    Upon a flower.

2

The darksome statesman, hung with weights and woe,
Like a thick midnight-fog, moved there so slow,
    He did not stay, nor go;
Condemning thoughts, like sad eclipses, scowl
    Upon his soul,
And clouds of crying witnesses without
    Pursued him with one shout.
Yet digged the mole, and lest his ways be found,
    Worked under ground,
Where he did clutch his prey; but one did see
    That policy:
Churches and altars fed him; perjuries
    Were gnats and flies;
It rained about him blood and tears, but he
    Drank them as free.

3

The fearful miser on a heap of rust
Sate pining all his life there, did scarce trust
    His own hands with the dust,
Yet would not place one piece above, but lives
    In fear of thieves.
Thousands there were as frantic as himself,
    And hugged each one his pelf;
The downright epicure placed heaven in sense,
    And scorned pretense;
While others, slipt into a wide excess,
    Said little less;
The weaker sort, slight, trivial wares enslave,
    Who think them brave;
And poor, despisèd Truth sate counting by
    Their victory.

4

Yet some, who all this while did weep and sing,
And sing and weep, soared up into the ring;
    But most would use no wing.
O fools, said I, thus to prefer dark night

Before true light!
To live in grots and caves, and hate the day
    Because it shows the way,
The way, which from this dead and dark abode
    Leads up to God;
A way where you might tread the sun, and be
    More bright than he!
But, as I did their madness so discuss,
    One whispered thus,
"This ring the Bridegroom did for none provide
    But for His bride."

[I] JOHN, CAP. 2, VER. 16, 17.

*All that is in the world, the lust of the flesh, the
lust of the eyes, and the pride of life, is not of the
Father, but is of the world.*

*And the world passeth away, and the lusts thereof;
but he that doeth the will of God abideth for ever.*

(1650)

NON SUM QUALIS ERAM BONAE SUB REGNO CYNARAE
Ernest Dowson

Last night, ah, yesternight, betwixt her lips and mine
There fell thy shadow, Cynara! thy breath was shed
Upon my soul between the kisses and the wine;
And I was desolate and sick of an old passion,
    Yea, I was desolate and bowed my head:
I have been faithful to thee, Cynara! in my fashion.

All night upon mine heart I felt her warm heart beat,
Night-long within mine arms in love and sleep she lay;
Surely the kisses of her bought red mouth were sweet;
But I was desolate and sick of an old passion,
    When I awoke and found the dawn was gray:
I have been faithful to thee, Cynara! in my fashion.

I have forgot much, Cynara! gone with the wind,
Flung roses, roses riotously with the throng,
Dancing, to put thy pale, lost lilies out of mind;
But I was desolate and sick of an old passion,
    Yea, all the time, because the dance was long:
I have been faithful to thee, Cynara! in my fashion.

I cried for madder music and for stronger wine,
But when the feast is finished and the lamps expire,
Then falls thy shadow, Cynara! the night is thine;
And I am desolate and sick of an old passion,
    Yea, hungry for the lips of my desire:
I have been faithful to thee, Cynara! in my fashion.
                        (1896)

from THE WASTE LAND
T. S. Eliot

2. A GAME OF CHESS

The Chair she sat in, like a burnished throne,
Glowed on the marble, where the glass
Held up by standards wrought with fruited vines
From which a golden Cupidon peeped out
(Another hid his eyes behind his wing)
Doubled the flames of seven branched candelabra
Reflecting light upon the table as
The glitter of her jewels rose to meet it,
From satin cases poured in rich profusion;
In vials of ivory and coloured glass
Unstoppered, lurked her strange synthetic perfumes,
Unguent, powdered, or liquid—troubled, confused
And drowned the sense in odours; stirred by the air
That freshened from the window, these ascended
In fattening the prolonged candle-flames,
Flung their smoke into the laquearia,
Stirring the pattern on the coffered ceiling.
Huge sea-wood fed with copper
Burned green and orange, framed by the coloured stone,

In which sad light a carvèd dolphin swam.
Above the antique mantel was displayed
As though a window gave upon the sylvan scene
The change of Philomel, by the barbarous king
So rudely forced; yet there the nightingale
Filled all the desert with inviolable voice
And still she cried, and still the world pursues,
"Jug Jug" to dirty ears.
And other withered stumps of time
Were told upon the walls; staring forms
Leaned out, leaning, hushing the room enclosed.
Footsteps shuffled on the stair.
Under the firelight, under the brush, her hair
Spread out in fiery points
Glowed into words, then would be savagely still.

"My nerves are bad tonight. Yes, bad. Stay with me.
"Speak to me. Why do you never speak. Speak.
        "What are you thinking of? What thinking? What?
"I never know what you are thinking. Think."

I think we are in rats' alley
Where the dead men lost their bones.

"What is that noise?"
                          The wind under the door.
"What is that noise now? What is the wind doing?"
                          Nothing again nothing.

                                              "Do
"You know nothing? Do you see nothing? Do you remember
"Nothing?"

    I remember
Those are pearls that were his eyes.
"Are you alive, or not? Is there nothing in your head?"
                                                        But

O O O O that Shakespeherian Rag—
It's so elegant

So intelligent
"What shall I do now? What shall I do?"
"I shall rush out as I am, and walk the street
"With my hair down, so. What shall we do tomorrow?
"What shall we ever do?"
                                        The hot water at ten.
And if it rains, a closed car at four.
And we shall play a game of chess,
Pressing lidless eyes and waiting for a knock upon the door.

When Lil's husband got demobbed, I said—
I didn't mince my words, I said to her myself,
HURRY UP PLEASE ITS TIME
Now Albert's coming back, make yourself a bit smart.
He'll want to know what you done with that money he gave you
To get yourself some teeth. He did, I was there.
You have them all out, Lil, and get a nice set,
He said, I swear, I can't bear to look at you.
And no more can't I, I said, and think of poor Albert,
He's been in the army four years, he wants a good time,
And if you don't give it him, there's others will, I said.
Oh is there, she said. Something o' that, I said.
Then I'll know who to thank, she said, and give me a straight look.
HURRY UP PLEASE ITS TIME
If you don't like it you can get on with it, I said.
Others can pick and choose if you can't.
But if Albert makes off, it won't be for lack of telling.
You ought to be ashamed, I said, to look so antique.
(And her only thirty-one.)
I can't help it, she said, pulling a long face,
It's them pills I took, to bring it off, she said.
(She's had five already, and nearly died of young George.)
The chemist said it would be all right, but I've never been the same.
You *are* a proper fool, I said.
Well, if Albert won't leave you alone, there it is, I said,
What you get married for if you don't want children?
HURRY UP PLEASE ITS TIME
Well, that Sunday Albert was home, they had a hot gammon,
And they asked me in to dinner, to get the beauty of it hot—

HURRY UP PLEASE ITS TIME
HURRY UP PLEASE ITS TIME
Goonight Bill. Goonight Lou. Goonight May. Goonight.

Ta ta. Goonight. Goonight.
Good night, ladies, good night, sweet ladies, good night, good night.

(1922)

from THE HAMLET OF A. MacLEISH
Archibald MacLeish

4

Night after night I lie like this listening.
Night after night I cannot sleep. I wake
Knowing something, thinking something has happened.
I have this feeling a great deal. I have

The platform Sadness often. At night I have this feeling.
Waking I feel this pain as though I knew
Something not to be thought of, something unbearable.

The King his I feel this pain at night as though some
father's ghost Terrible thing had happened. At night the sky
appears to Opens, the near things vanish, the bright walls
him Fall, and the stars were always there, and the dark,
There and the cold and the stillness. I wake and stand
A long time by the window. I always think
The trees know the way they are silent. I always
Think someone has spoken, someone has told me.
Reading the books I always think so, reading
Words overheard in the books, reading the words
Like words in a strange language. I always hear
Music like that. I almost remember with music. . . .
This is not what you think. It is not that. I swim
Every day at the beach under the fig tree.
I swim very well and far out. The smell
Of pine comes over the water. The wind blurs
Seaward. And afternoons I walk to the phare.
Much of the time I do not think anything;

Much of the time I do not even notice.
And then, speaking, closing a door, I see
Strangely as though I almost saw now, some
Shape of things I have always seen, the sun
White on a house and the windows open and swallows
In and out of the wallpaper, the moon's face
Faint by day in a mirror; I see some
Changed thing that is telling, something that almost
Tells—and this pain then, then this pain. And no
Words, only these shapes of things that seem
Ways of knowing what it is I am knowing.
I write these things in books, on pieces of paper.
I have written "The wind rises . . ." I have written
    "Bells
Plunged in the wind. . . ." I have written "Like
Doors . . ." "Like evening . . ."
It is always the same: I cannot read what the words say.
It is always the same: there are signs and I cannot read
    them.
There are empty streets and the blinds drawn and the
    sky
Sliding in windows. There are lights before
Dawn in the yellow transoms over the doors.
There are steps that pass and pass all night that are
    always
One, always the same step passing. . . .

8

Ay, sure, this is most brave;
That I . . .
            the live son of a dead father
Doomed by my living breath itself to die

Must, like a whore, unpack my heart with words

Why must I speak of it? Why must I always
Stoop from this decent silence to this phrase
That makes a posture of my hurt? Why must I
Say I suffer? . . . or write out these words
For eyes to stare at that shall soon as mine

Or little after me go thick and lose
The light too, or for solemn lettered fools

Hamlet . . . sole

To judge if I said neatly what I said?—
Make verses! . . . ease myself at the soiled stool
That's common to so swollen many! . . . shout
For hearing in the world's thick dirty ear! . . .
Expose my scabs! . . . crowd forward among those
That beg for fame, that for so little praise
As pays a dog off will go stiff and tell
Their loss, lust, sorrow, anguish! . . . match
My grief with theirs! . . . compel the public prize
For deepest feeling and put on the bays! . . .
O shame, for shame to suffer it, to make
A skill of harm, a business of despair,
And like a barking ape betray us all
For itch of notice

              O be still, be still,
Be dumb, be silent only. Seal your mouth.
Take place upon this edge of shadow where
The stale scene's acted to the empty skies.
Observe the constellations. Watch the face
Of heaven if it change to what it sees.
Spy on the moon. Be cunning.

                       And be still.
We have that duty to each other here
To fear in secret. For it is not known.
The dreams that trouble us may be the shape
Of ill within that by a faulted eye
Abuses us to damn us.

                     I'll have grounds
       More relative than this . . .

13

Why—what men were they that beneath the moon

Ophelia's burial. He quarrels with Laertes in the grave; protests his passion . . .

Had mortal flagging hearts so passionate?
Who heaped these tombs? Who wept so? Who piled up
These brags of marble anguish, these bronze groans,
These cromlech sorrows? Who had griefs so vast
That only mountains evened them, felt so

Deep pain, so suffered, with such iron tongue
Cried Wo that time still hears it? Why, what proud
What desperate nations were they that would leave
No legend after but the unwrit stones
That say they wept here? Or who painted then
These mutilated violent hands that still
Thrust back oblivion from the sad grave door?

What men were they that did protest so loud,
What broken, salty blooded, aching hearts
That could not cease in silence, what hoarse grief
That must be shouted at the narrow stars?
What dying men were they. . . .

                          Nay, an thou'lt mouth
I'll rant as well as thou . . .

                                  I'll swell my gullet,
Leap in the common grave and like a cock
Crow from the carrion. I'll tell the world.
I'll make a book of it. I'll leave my rare
Original, uncopied, dark heart pain
To choke up volumes and among the rocks
Cry I! I! I! forever. Look,
My face here. I have suffered. I have lost
A child, a brother, friends. And do foreknow
My own corruption. There are also stars
But not to listen to. And the autumn trees
That have the habit of the sun and die
Beforetimes often. And at night. And skies.
And seas. And evening. I can read in print
But not these letters. And I was not born
Without a death pain either but that's known,
That's equal and we all go back. I had
No friends but day times. No one called me. There was
No one always underneath the bed.
I'll tell you how I loved too, all my loves,
My bed quilts, bolsters, blankets, my hot hands,
My limbs, my rumps; my wretchedness: my lust,
My weakness later and lascivious dreams.

I'll tell you. Oh, I'll tell you. Lean your ear.
By God, I'll match them at it. I'll be stripped
Naked as eels are, gutted, laid on salt,
Sold in the fish stalls. I'll be ox-chine nude,
Quartered to cold bare bone. Look, behold me
Bearing my dead son's body to the grave.
See how I weep. How many of them all
Have lost a son as I have? Or see here:
The Marne side. Raining. I am cold with fear.
My bowels tremble. I go on. McHenry
Hands me his overcoat and dies. We dig the
Guns out sweating. I am very brave:
Magnificent. I vomit in my mask.
Or here. In Belgium. Spreading on my young,
My three times buried brother's stony grave
The bone-pale scented violets and feeling
Yield at my knees the earth: and crying out
Two words. In agony . . .
                              I'll tell it. Oh
I'll tell it. Louder! Shriek!
                              The sky's there!

14

It is time we should accept,
Taught by these wordy fools, the staged
Encounter and the game-pit rules.
Whilst we have slept we have grown old.
Age is a coldness leaching through.

To whom the eloquent Osrick: communicates the invitation of Laertes to the Playful Bout . . .

We must consent now as all men
Whose rage is out of them must do,
Cancel this bloody feud, revoke
All tears, all pain, and to the drum,
Trump, cannon and the general cheer
Fight with a shining foil the feigned
Antagonist for stoops of beer.
Why should we want revenge of harms
Not suffered in the public street,
Or risk with sharp and hurting arms
The real encounter kept at night

Alone where none will praise our art?

It is time we should accept. . . .

Thou wouldst not think
How ill all's here about my heart!
(1928)

BALLAD OF THE GOODLY FERE[1]
Ezra Pound

(Simon Zelotes speaketh it somewhile after the
Crucifixion)

Ha' we lost the goodliest fere o' all
For the priests and the gallows tree?
Aye, lover he was of brawny men,
O' ships and the open sea.

When they came wi' a host to take Our Man
His smile was good to see,
"First let these go!" quo' our Goodly Fere,
"Or I'll see ye damned," says he.

Aye, he sent us out through the crossed high spears
And the scorn of his laugh rang free,
"Why took ye not me when I walked about
Alone in the town?" says he.

Oh we drunk his "Hale" in the good red wine
When we last made company,
No capon priest was the Goodly Fere
But a man o' men was he.

I ha' seen him drive a hundred men
Wi' a bundle o' cords swung free,
That they took the high and holy house
For their pawn and treasury.

[1] Fere = Mate, Companion. (Author's note, 1920)

They'll no' get him a' in a book I think
Though they write it cunningly;
No mouse of the scrolls was the Goodly Fere
But aye loved the open sea.

If they think they ha' snared our Goodly Fere
They are fools to the last degree.
"I'll go to the feast," quo' our Goodly Fere,
"Though I go to the gallows tree."

"Ye ha' seen me heal the lame and blind,
And wake the dead," says he,
"Ye shall see one thing to master all:
'Tis how a brave man dies on the tree."

A son of God was the Goodly Fere
That bade us his brothers be.
I ha' seen him cow a thousand men.
I ha' seen him upon the tree.

He cried no cry when they drave the nails
And the blood gushed hot and free,
The hounds of the crimson sky gave tongue
But never a cry cried he.

I ha' seen him cow a thousand men
On the hills o' Galilee,
They whined as he walked out calm between,
Wi' his eyes like the gray o' the sea,

Like the sea that brooks no voyaging
With the winds unleashed and free,
Like the sea that he cowed at Gennesaret
Wi' twey words spoke' suddenly.

A master of men was the Goodly Fere,
A mate of the wind and sea,
If they think they ha' slain our Goodly Fere
They are fools eternally.

I ha' seen him eat o' the honey-comb
Sin' they nailed him to the tree.

(1909)

from THE FIRST EPISTLE TO THE CORINTHIANS
Paul the Apostle

CHAPTER THIRTEEN

Though I speak with the tongues of men and of angels, and have not
　　charity,
　I am become as sounding brass, or a tinkling cymbal.
And though I have the gift of prophecy, and understand all mysteries,
　　and all knowledge;
　　and though I have all faith, so that I could remove mountains,
　　and have not charity, I am nothing.
And though I bestow all my goods to feed the poor,
　　and though I give my body to be burned,
　　and have not charity, it profiteth me nothing.
　　Charity suffereth long, and is kind;
　　charity envieth not;
　　charity vaunteth not itself,
　　　　is not puffed up,
　　　　doth not behave itself unseemly,
　　　　seeketh not her own,
　　　　is not easily provoked,
　　　　thinketh no evil;
　　rejoiceth not in iniquity, but rejoiceth in the truth;
　　beareth all things,
　　　　believeth all things,
　　　　　hopeth all things,
　　　　　　endureth all things.
Charity never faileth: but
　　whether there be prophecies, they shall fail;
　　whether there be tongues, they shall cease;
　　whether there be knowledge, it shall vanish away.
For we know in part, and we prophesy in part.

But when that which is perfect is come,
    then that which is in part shall be done away,
When I was a child, I spake as a child,
    I understood as a child,
    I thought as a child: but
when I became a man, I put away childish things.
For now we see through a glass, darkly;
    but then face to face:
now I know in part;
    but then shall I know even as also I am known.
And now abideth faith, hope, charity, these three;
    but the greatest of these is charity.

                            (*c. 52* A.D., tr. 1611)

SUGGESTIONS FOR STUDY

1. *Who touches this.* (a) Study Whitman's "So Long!" and
Browning's "House" as regards the poets' attitudes towards the personal element in poetry. (b) Did you identify the quotation at the end
of "House" as coming from Wordsworth's "Scorn Not the Sonnet"
(p. 460)? Reread the sonnet, and refer again to two of Shakespeare's
sonnets (pp. 159 and 454). Dante Gabriel Rossetti published his sonnet
sequence "The House of Life" in 1870. It is a group of very intimate
and personal lyrics dealing with married love and written largely to
his wife. (The three called "The Choice," p. 237, are less personal
than others in the sequence.) Browning, as Clyde DeVane points out
(*Browning Handbook,* p. 356), did not hold Rossetti in very high
regard. (c) Now reread Browning's "House" in the light of these notes.
(d) Swinburne retorted to "House" by saying, "No whit the less like
Shakespeare, but undoubtedly the less like Browning."

2. *Fears in April, 1798.* (a) Using the *Annals of English Literature*
as a point of departure, make a study of the historical background
that will be helpful in a critical interpretation of "Fears in Solitude."
(b) Using the *Dictionary of National Biography,* find out what you
can about Coleridge's life and character that will serve to explain the
thought of the poem.

3. *Lead and Gold.* (a) Gerard Manley Hopkins, in the Author's
Preface to his *Poems* (London, Oxford University Press, 1930), differen-
tiates the "Sprung Rhythm" (as he calls it) of his own verse from
"Common English rhythm" which he calls "Running Rhythm." He
says: "Sprung Rhythm . . . is measured by feet of from one to four

syllables, regularly. . . . It has one stress, which falls on the only syllable, if there is only one, or, if there are more, then scanning as above,
on the first. . . ." Sometimes Hopkins marked the stress as he intended
it. He says further: ". . . the scanning runs on without break from
the beginning, say, of a stanza to the end, and all the stanza is one
long strain, though written in lines asunder." (b) Read and reread
"The Leaden Echo and the Golden Echo" aloud in an effort to catch
the characteristic "music" of this sprung rhythm. (c) Does the rereading help you to catch the drift of the poem? Write a short prose
statement (in Basic English, if you wish) of the central thought in
each of the two poems. (d) T. Sturge Moore has written a poetic paraphrase or recension of the poem under the same title. It is reprinted
with Moore's comment (from *The Criterion,* July 1930) in Thomas
and Brown, *Reading Poems,* Oxford Press, 1941, which also reprints
Hopkins' poem and a selection from his Preface.

4. *World and Cynara.* (a) Read again the verses from *I John,* 2:16-17
quoted by Vaughan at the end of "The World." (They follow verse
15: "Love not the world, neither the things that are in the world. If
any man love the world, the love of the Father is not in him." (b)
Unless you are pretty well acquainted with the old Ptolemaic cos-
mography, look it up in an encyclopedia. (c) Now reread Vaughan's
"The World," noting the ambiguity of the title. Make a sketch or diagram suggesting Eternity, the spheres, the world. Note the initial and
final use of "ring" in the poem. Who is "the Bridegroom," and what
is the Biblical reference? Write out a summary or paraphrase of the
thought of each stanza.

(d) The title of Ernest Dowson's poem, "Non sum qualis eram
bonae sub regno Cynarae" ('I am not the man I was under the reign
of the good Cynara'), is quoted from Horace's *Odes,* IV, 1 ('To
Venus'), vv. 3-4. In this ode Horace implores Venus not to make him
fall in love again, for he (nearly fifty) is not the man he was when
Cynara ruled his heart; and he suggests that Venus go off to some
younger man who can properly serve her. But the poet admits that after
all he is dreaming of love again. (e) Reinterpret Dowson's poem in
the light of its allusive title.

5. *This Wasteland.* (a) Read the selection (Part II) from *The Waste
Land,* and work out an interpretation of it making use of all the clues
you can find in the text itself. (b) What literary allusions and echoes
did you note? Check back through the poem and make a list of them.
Did you note the opening echo of Enobarbus's description of Cleopatra (reprinted earlier in this book, p. 254)? the "sylvan scene" allusion to the Garden of Eden in Milton's *Paradise Lost* (see p. 411)?
the reference to the story of Philomela (see pp. 657-58 and 663)?

(c) T. S. Eliot added nine notes for this part of his poem: three of them calling attention to the above allusions; three of them cross references to other parts of the poem; and three others—one noting the source of "laquearia" in the *Aeneid*, I, 726, where the word may mean the beamed and paneled ceiling (but the whole scene of Dido's sumptuous feast is suggested). Another notes that "The wind under the door" is an echo of a line from Webster; and a third, on "we shall play a game of chess," refers to Middleton's *Woman Beware Woman*, in which Livia plays a game of chess with Bianca's mother, keeping her occupied while Bianca is being seduced. Eliot indicates as a general source for the symbolism of "The Waste Land," Jessie L. Weston's *From Ritual to Romance*, which deals with the sources of the legend of the Holy Grail. In it the Fisher King ruled over the Waste Land, which was to remain barren and dry until a knight of great purity should come and heal the Fisher King of a genital wound. The hero (Perceval in some versions) undertakes the perilous adventure, and by means of the Holy Grail heals the wounded Fisher King, and fertility is restored to the land. (Additional critical and interpretative notes of interest, and the entire poem, are to be found in Thomas and Brown, *Reading Poems*, pp. 591-603, 716-31, 749-51.) (d) Glance back at the other poems of T. S. Eliot reprinted in this volume; then find out something about the poet. Give some thought to the relation of Eliot's "The Waste Land" to the thought and spirit of its decade.

6. *Hamlet yet again.* (a) *The Hamlet of A. MacLeish* is a poem much longer than the four sections here presented. Reading it presupposes a knowledge of Shakespeare's *Hamlet*. The marginal "stage directions" serve to key the poem to the scenes in the drama from which they take their inspiration: section 4 is suggested by *Hamlet*, I, iv-v; sec. 8, *Ham.*, II, ii (the soliloquy of which is reprinted in this book, pp. 316-18); sec. 13, *Ham.*, V, i, 225 ff.; sec. 14, *Ham.*, V, ii, 1-238. But remember that the poem is "The Hamlet *of A. MacLeish.*"

(b) John Holmes, who has written a thesis based on an investigation of this poem, has prepared for this book a special commentary on the sections that are here reprinted:

This long, dramatic, and subjective poem moves on four levels. The *first* is parallel with Shakespeare's *Hamlet,* and in this way of reading it we recall the castle Elsinore, the ghost of Hamlet's father, the Uncle-King, the visit of the players, the famous soliloquies of the tragically helpless hero, and all the rest of it, including the gloss, or stage directions, which in our time and in the MacLeish poem have the dignity of poetry, and its cryptic meaning. Unless the modern reader can be stirred by subtle allusion, much of the force of this part of the meaning will be lost. The *second* way of understanding the whole poem is through the necessary and intended substitution of another set of symbols. This is the key to the whole poem, and has the author's confirmation. The Uncle-King is the life-force, the sun, the biological urge. The Queen-Mother is the fecund earth. Ophelia is woman, the woman one may be in love with, but not an intellectual equal; in the poem she listens to but does not understand Hamlet's desperate quest for the ultimate truth of life, and breaks down, singing the pathetic mad song. The two well-meaning, easy-going friends, Rosencranz and Guildenstern, are—the people we know, the good, comfortable neighbors and colleagues, who can't see why the philosophical man worries himself about final answers to eternal questions. The most complex symbol is Hamlet's father's ghost. He is that ultimate truth every man seeks, and is at the same time a sort of guilt at the back of man's mind, not so much for a crime of commission as for a crime of omission—some old, very simple, and very important thing once known and long ago forgotten. The *third* level of meaning for the whole poem is autobiographical in a double sense: there is fact interwoven as to Archibald MacLeish's early poetic anguished modesty, and the death of his brother Kenneth in World War I, as well as the poet's own war experience. There is also a *fourth* way of reading the poem: as a record of Everyman's disillusionment in middle age. The MacLeish-Hamlet-Everyman glimpses at first the ghost, comes all but face to face with the ultimate answer to life's greatest question, loses that immediacy, goes mad with frustration, and at last surrenders and accepts life as it is.

The first passage quoted here is one of the subjective parts, the poet himself speaking, the dreaming, seeking youth—

> Reading the books I always think so, reading
> Words overheard in the books, reading the words
> Like words in a strange language. I always hear
> Music like that. I almost remember with music . . .

Part 8, the second quoted passage, is also a personal one. The poet cries out against himself and the hunger he has for public knowledge of his writing, thus of his private emotions. Disgust, pride, and painful sensitivity loose themselves here. There is more of the same self-pity, self-flagellation, and the artist's hurt and hope in Part 13, but here we get Hamlet-MacLeish aching for the ache of time past, mourning for what men have mourned for, and baffled as men have always been. So then he bursts into "mouthing and ranting"—the grave scene with multiple implications, and the nakedest possible personal allusions. This is catharsis. And it is followed by the brief, simple, and most moving final section of the poem. Here Hamlet-Everyman-MacLeish accepts what must be—middle age, consents to the general pattern of the general life, and no more wild hopeful seeking for the answer to the unanswerable. Here the abrupt contrast between the outpourings of

> I'll tell you. Oh, I'll tell you. Lean your ear.
> By God, I'll match them at it. I'll be stripped
> Naked as eels are, gutted, laid on salt . . .

and the short-lined, rimed, controlled, and sadly resigned conclusion of

> We must consent now as all men
> Whose rage is out of them must do,
> Cancel this bloody feud, revoke
> All tears, all pain, and to the drum,
> Trump, cannon and the general cheer
> Fight with a shining foil the feigned
> Antagonist for stoops of beer . . .

is most movingly effective, and here, too, the last echo of Shakespeare's lines comes in with what terrible power, "Thou wouldst not think how ill all's here about my heart."

7. *The Goodly Fere.* (a) Study Ezra Pound's ballad-monologue thoughtfully. (b) Take note, stanza by stanza, of the allusions to incidents in the life of Jesus, referring for them to the chapter and page headings in the Gospels. (c) Consider in some detail Pound's use of the ballad for his narrative, and also his use of folk speech.

8. *Charity or Love.* The version of *I Corinthians,* 13 given in the text is an arrangement of the King James Translation. (a) After rereading the chapter as here given, study one of the other translations: the Douay or Catholic Bible, the Revised or American Revised, or one of the more recent translations by Edgar J. Goodspeed or James Moffatt, or the one in Basic English. (Make a study of the words "charity" and "glass" in the Oxford Dictionary.) Compare the two translations in detail. (b) W. F. Howard says, "This hymn is a lyrical interpretation of the Sermon on the Mount" (*The Abington Bible Commentary,* p. 1187). Read the Abington or another commentary on this the so-called "Love chapter" in the New Testament. (c) The numerous allusions, echoes, and parallel thoughts (as well as variant readings) in this chapter may be traced through a study of the marginal notes to be found in many Bibles. The following are a few of the references that may be of interest: *Proverbs,* 10:12; *Matthew,* 6:1-2; *Matt.,* 7:21-3; *Matt.,* 17:20; *Matt.,* 18:10. (c) There are interesting literary reflections of some of the thoughts of this chapter in Shakespeare's Sonnet 116, Vaughan's "The Retreat," and Thompson's "The Hound of Heaven."

APPENDIX

The Pedagogia

. . . Index-learning turns no student pale,
Yet holds the eel of science by the tail.

—ALEXANDER POPE

Open Letter to the Instructor

Education—paying proper respect to James A. Garfield and Mark Hopkins—may be dramatized as teacher and student teetering on a text.

There are those among us, joint laborers in the academic vineyard, who say that it matters not how bad the book: the good teacher is *all*. And others, with a touch of campus cynicism, say that no teaching, however mediocre, can possibly spoil a really good book. Neither statement is quite true; for both text and teacher must be strong if the process of education is to be successful.

The author and compiler of this *Preface to Poetry* brings his manuscript to a close with the high hope that it will fall into the hands of imaginative and adventuresome instructors, and with some confidence that, despite its shortcomings, it will support the instructor in his efforts to elevate the student.

As a piece of educational machinery, this *Preface to Poetry* is somewhat different from similar equipment now on the market— so its designer and manufacturers might express themselves in industrial terms. For a textbook is, after all, a machine—complex as a lathe, not simple as a log—a machine by means of which the operator may shape his raw material. It is of great importance, therefore, that the instructor familiarize himself with the structure and working parts of this tool for teaching, with its gadgets and adjustments, before he puts it to use.

A book whose purpose it is to encourage the reading and enjoyment of poetry, its understanding and appreciation, would be expected to possess in its substance certain materials that teachers of past generations have found useful in their work. With the respect due to those who have passed on the torch in other times, there is here included a representative body of those prosodic, critical, and historical matters, as well as poetry, such as we have come to expect in works of this sort. And though their orientation may be unusual —there is, however, no generally accepted order for their consideration—most of the facts about English versification and poetics desirable for the introductory course will be found readily accessible within the covers of this book.

However, the novel features that inform this *Preface to Poetry,* and are its reason for being, are as numerous as its traditional materials. Individually, many of these new critical and pedagogical ideas and devices are already in use by eager and experimental instructors, and accounts of their work and success are currently to be found in the professional and educational journals. Separately, several of them have already found their way into the more recent college texts. The present work, by no means a mere synthesis of the pioneering of others, was published in a preliminary edition in 1943 and was subjected to repeated use in the classroom, to candid criticism by student readers and professional colleagues, and to successive revisions and amplification under keenly stimulating editorial advice. It makes its appearance now, no untried fledgling. To all those who have directly or indirectly helped in this venture, my thanks, elsewhere expressed, are here repeated.

The substance of this volume, as a cursory thumbing will show, is of three sorts: (1) the expository discourse of the twenty-four *chapters,* (2) the nearly three hundred *poems,* (3) the more than one hundred fifty *Suggestions for Study.* And this Open Letter to the Instructor will be ordered accordingly.

I

Of the twenty-four chapters of *Preface to Poetry,* the first twelve comprise Book One: The Preface; the second twelve, Book Two: The Poetry. But Book One is not without numerous poems, nor is Book Two without critical discussion. Yet the principal theoretical considerations are to be found in Book One; and the greater number of poems, more than two-thirds of the verses, are to be found in Book Two. In Book One emphasis is placed upon the poem-reading-experience, and an effort is made to help the student to read deeply, to experience fully, to understand richly the individual poem. The direction of this study might be thought of as *vertical,* and it is hoped that the gods will approve the depth of the reading and not expect much breadth. For an age that worships rapidity, in reading as in transport, this vertical reading, creative and critical, can hardly be overemphasized. And the student must be encouraged to make haste slowly, to spend half an hour to two hours on a sonnet, to pause and be refreshed, to stop by words on a snowy evening, to look at the sounds and to listen to the sights. With the willingness established to wrest the full flavor and meaning from the poem, Book Two proceeds, *horizontally,* to survey the broad fields and to wander the paths and bypaths of poetic enrichment.

So much, then, for the two so-called books, whose divisions into three parts each may be observed, together with the chapter headings, in the table of contents.

There are a number of features that distinguish BOOK ONE: THE PREFACE from the discussions in the comparable and in so many ways excellent textbooks in this field. This book puts to use, in a text designed for American undergraduates, a good many of the linguistic principles which stem from the work of I. A. Richards and C. K. Ogden; and it makes active, if unobtrusive, use of that special critical device called Basic English, rather numerous analyses of poems being Basic English paraphrase. This book insists upon the necessity of distinguishing, for critical discussion, the printed poem from the poem-experience; and it proposes, if somewhat tentatively, a relativistic, rather than an absolute, esthetics. For the first time, in a book of this sort, some consideration is given to the seeing-process and the retinal image in relation to poetic form and to the complex rhythms of the poetic experience; and the poetic rhythm, the chief feature of the "music" of poetry, is explored upon the basis of metrical expectancy and semantic deviations. The problems of communication (both of thought and of emotion) are considered in the light of more recent studies of linguistic psychology. Nor does this book avoid—because they are difficult—the problems of goodness in poetry, and truth, and immediacy.

But BOOK TWO: THE POETRY is also distinguished by a number of novel features: It proceeds candidly upon the assumption that skill in oral interpretation must be acquired in order to realize the full potential of poetry; and that one place in which to acquire greater skill in oral reading may be the introductory course in poetry. Nor is there any reason why those instructors who wish to do so should not make use of choral reading and of singing as special aids in this endeavor. For this reason a number of poems for group work and of song-lyrics with their airs have been included.

A systematic approach to the classification of poems provides the basis for considering, in a new light, a number of the traditional approaches to poetry: the broad types of poetry, poetic form, theme, mood, and style are viewed briefly in their relations one to the other and to the sorting factors upon which they are based. For the first time in a book of this sort, special attention is given to the use of poetry records as a device helpful in the study of poetry, and the better-known techniques of comparative analysis and of critical interpretation are given new emphasis.

Novel as some of these features are—and the instructor is under no obligation to use them all—they have already been used by individual instructors, and together they have been subjected to the test of classroom use through the preliminary edition and the successive revisions of this *Preface to Poetry*.

2

The nearly three hundred poems reprinted in this volume are, in the final analysis, more important than the expository substance of the text. They are *it*. For the most part they are complete poems, but with several condensations of, or selections from, longer works. Illustrative scraps of verse have been avoided, for, though such quotations may mean much to the instructor who can recall the full literary context, they usually mean little to the less-well-read student, who only knows what he has experienced. For the same reason, poems not already presented in the preceding pages of the book are not, except in two or three cases, cited in the text. And when the titles of poems already read are referred to for the purpose of illustration, they are usually provided with immediate page references.

Particular attention has been given by the publishers to the problem of typography in an effort to secure a most satisfactorily readable page, free from the distraction of run-over lines except in the poems of unusual verse length. With the same thought in mind, marginal line-numbering has, after due consideration, been eliminated. In some texts it is, alas, the most prominent feature of the page! Certainly no poet ever conceived of pentamerous enumerators as essential to the visual experience of his poem. For some readers they are the stimuli for altogether irrelevant eye-movements. Many instructors never make use of them, or find them an annoyance. However, stanzaic numbering originating with the poet has been retained, with Roman numerals changed to Arabic for increased legibility.

Each poem is presented with title and poet's name as its heading; and each is followed by the date of composition (*italicized*) and/or the date of publication or first book publication (in roman style arabics). Many comparable textbooks either date the poet or, easier yet, omit dating altogether. But dating the poet throws emphasis upon the man rather than upon the work, and omitting all indication of time denies the reader a sometimes very important clue useful in critical interpretation, just as the poet's name, sometimes withheld till the end of the poem, and in one notable instance retired to the notes, also may serve as an immediate aid in the full realization of the poem. There is doubtless error in the dating of a number of the poems; and professional colleagues are invited to communicate corrected dates and their sources to the author for future use in revision.

The selection of the poems is not as casual as at first glance it might appear. Though the poems are chiefly American and English, there are a number of European and Ancient poems, both in the original and in translation. Approximately one third of the poems are modern; one third, nineteenth century; one third, earlier. Most of the famous poets and many of the great poems are included, as may be seen by an examination of the Table of Poems alphabetically arranged by authors in the front of the book. But there are also a good number of favorite and familiar and popular poems—good, mediocre, bad—both of the present and of the past. And there are also many poems of less frequent appearance, contemporary and historical, with a number of poems reprinted here for the first time. The broad types of poetry and the sub-types, the poetic forms, the historic styles, the great themes, the divers moods are also illustrated with some completeness. Most of the older texts have been in some degree modernized in spelling, capitalization, typography, and punctuation; but a considerable selection of *The Faerie Queene* has been printed with the Elizabethan and Spenserian peculiarities.

Poems that are easier of interpretation and those more immediately related to the average student's experience are balanced by poems that are difficult and in some cases remote. A special effort has been made to include a good many poems that will appeal especially to college men. No apology is offered for these poems—athletic verse, war poems, American ballads—which, among others, are of interest to many of the readers for whom *Preface to Poetry* is ultimately intended. But if it is important to take the college student where you find him and to move on from there, the *grading* of the poems, both within most of the chapters and markedly in the volume taken as a whole, will certainly allow the instructor to move from the known to the new, from the familiar to the more remote, from the easy to the hard, from the mediocre to the good.

Certainly there are more poems here included than a student could be expected to experience fully and richly in a one-term course. This will allow for the instructor's selection, which may well be kept realistically in adjustment to the capacity and interests of his particular class. But however numerous the selection of poems in the text, each instructor will certainly wish to supplement it by the bringing in of yet other poems to be read aloud or to be played from records in the classroom.

3

Some one hundred sixty-two Suggestions for Study form an important part of the tool for teaching now in hand. It is quite certain that some instructors will prefer to create their own assignments, but for others the presence of these varied exercises will provide the basis for much of the outside preparation and study, and for class discussion. They may actually free the instructor from the somewhat routine considerations at times, so that he may devote himself more fully to the essential intangibles of poetic appreciation.

As with the poems, there are far too many of these Suggestions for Study for use in any one-term course, and the instructor may wish to vary his choice from amongst them with succeeding classes. Some may suggest to the instructor yet other patterns for problem assignments, written exercises objective or discursive, creative stimulation and expression, group reading and composition, class procedures and discussion. For the study aids, exercises, and assignments here set forth are perhaps of greater variety than those often to be found, and therefore adaptable to a wider range of student interests and capacities. The instructor will therefore not be under pressure to use those teaching techniques that do not seem to him to be helpful.

For instance, one instructor may not be equipped (or may not be inclined) to use poetry records as a teaching device. He will be able, nevertheless, to use the poems reprinted in Chapter 22, and may even find the text of that chapter and some of the exercises in it useful. Other instructors may wish to start right off with records. One instructor may organize an extra-curricular verse choir at once; others may wish to avoid group reading entirely. One may continually encourage the writing of verse; others may discourage the sophomore lyrists.

Certainly the teacher should not be a slave to this or to any text. Although there is, in the mind and intention of the author, a logical progression throughout the chapters in this volume, some instructors may wish to plan their own ordering of the parts and of the poems, particularly as regards the contents of BOOK TWO. It might be useful with some classes, for instance, to move forward simultaneously in Book One: The Preface and Book Two: The Poetry, making assignments in the chapters of Part One and Part Four; then Part Two and Part Five; and finally Part Three and Part Six. The numerous cross references and the Glossarial Handbook with Subject Index would be of especial help to the student in such a case.

The high hopes voiced in the first sentences of this Open Letter are repeated here in closing: May this *Preface to Poetry* fall into the hands of imaginative and adventuresome instructors. And may they, in turn, be confronted and surrounded by enthusiastic and intelligent students hell-bent for the wider reaches of literature and of life. For some of them, at least, a course in poetry may well be the long festal year at Fontainebleau, a time for leaving the ground and putting on the glory.

In the teetering process of education it is hoped that both student and teacher will, at times and by turns, rise above the text upon which for a term they are poised.

C. W. C.

Glossarial Handbook

WITH SUBJECT INDEX

A number of technical terms intentionally excluded from the text have been included for brief consideration in this Glossarial Handbook. The use of *italics* for certain words within many of the entries is an index of *cross-reference,* and the words so distinguished are separately defined or provided with additional page references. ˙

ACCENT, the emphasis given to one or more syllables in a word. See *stress.*

AIR, the tune or melody of a *song.*

ALEXANDRINE, a twelve-syllable or *iambic hexameter* line, as in the *Spenserian stanza;* the *heroic* meter of French poetry.

ALLITERATION, sometimes called initial *rime,* recurrence of a consonant sound at the beginning of adjacent words, 116 ff.

ALLITERATIVE VERSE, the Old English type of *versification,* based upon the four-*stress* line with systematic *alliteration.*

AMBIGUITY, a language symbol used (or interpreted as being used) with two or more references, or possible of being interpreted in two or more ways, 49 f., 58, 162, 170 ff., 178, 233; an exercise, 186.

AMPHIBRACH, the amphibrachic *foot; rocking-triple rhythm;* deDUMM-de; "And lastly, remember the amphibrach's rocking, dear pupil," 106 f.

AMPHIMACER, a *foot* consisting of three syllables, the first and last of which are stressed, DUMMde-

DUMM, and found occasionally as a *metrical variation.*

ANACRUSIS, a sort of *metrical variation,* the addition of an unstressed syllable at the beginning of a verse in *falling rhythm.*

ANALYSES of poems, 25-28, 46-52, 77-79, 112-15, 116-19, 122-26, 138-40 and 159 f., 169 f., 170-73 and 192, 177-81, 182 f. and 184, 188-90, 195-97, 202-04, 206-08, 209-10, 211-13, 214-15, 228-29, 230-34, 250 and 255-58, 272-76, 277-80, 311-15. See *Basic English* paraphrase.

ANAPEST, the anapestic *foot; rising-triple;* dedeDUMM; "Anapestic is rising and three," 106 f.

ANTI-BACCHIUS, a *foot* consisting of three syllables, the last two of which are stressed, deDUMM-DUMM, and found occasionally as a *metrical variation.*

ANTISTROPHE, see *ode, strophe.*

APPROACHES to poetry, 405 ff.; each approach represents the *classification* of *poems* using a different sorting factor. See *types of poetry, poetic form, theme, mood, style, school, movement, period,* personality of the *poet.*

ART, Literature as one of the arts, 53; art-function of language, see *emotional adjustment;* function of the arts, 193; the art *song,* 380; "the Arts" as a poetic *theme,* 478 f., 479 ff.; art for art's sake, 479; art theory, an exercise, 508.

ARTICULATORY TIED-IMAGERY, the feel of the words on the mind's-tongue during silent reading, the consciousness of how the articulators (tongue, lips, etc.) would feel if the words were actually sounded, 92-96; an exercise, 128 ff. See *tied imagery.*

ASSONANCE, the recurrence of vowel sounds, especially in final stressed syllables, but differing from *rime* in that the vowels are followed by dissimilar consonants, 118: "train— James," "town—ground."

ATTITUDE, a psychological posture, readiness to respond in a particular way, 226; *residual attitude,* 226 ff., 304 ff., examples, 228 f., 234; attitudes of various sorts, 229; the attitude of the poet, 213, 216, 236, 237 f.; the mood of a poem, 510. See *tone.*

AUDITORY FREE-IMAGERY, the "hearing" in the mind's-ear of the sounds suggested by the *meaning* of the words, 146 ff.; an exercise, 159 f.

AUDITORY TIED-IMAGERY, the sound of the words in the mind's-ear during silent reading, the consciousness of how the words would sound if actually spoken, 26, 96 ff.; the *poetic rhythm,* most notable feature, 100; oral reading and singing, increase in richness of silent reading, 328, 382; an exercise, 403. See *tied imagery.*

AUTHORITARIAN *criticism,* the judgment of poems by quoting reviewers, critics, historians, 248 f., 258, 259.

BACCHIUS, a *foot* consisting of three syllables, the first two of which are stressed, DUMM-DUMMde, and found occasionally as a *metrical variation.*

BAD POETRY, a bad *poem,* provides the reader with a worthless *poem-reading-experience,* 260; some examples, 29, 211, 250, 262; judgment of a bad poem, 255 ff., 271. See *criticism, evaluation, good poetry.*

BALLAD, a sub-type of *narrative* poetry; a simple folk *story* in simple *poetic form,* 407; (in music, a simple narrative *song,* 378, 409); an exercise, 444. See *folk ballad, literary ballad.*

BALLAD METER, a *metrical pattern* common among *ballads:* (iambic or irregular) $a^4b^3c^4b^3$; example, 337; perhaps developed from *septenarius couplets;* subject to many variations in number of lines, rime, etc., 407, 447; examples, 144, 429. See *quatrain.*

BALLADE, one of the *special forms* (*French forms*), consisting of three *stanzas,* all with the same rimes, ababbcbC, followed by an *envoy* riming bcbC, 449; example, 563.

BASIC ENGLISH, a highly controlled and greatly restricted form of English useful as a critical tool, 177 n., 668; Basic English paraphrases, 27, 45-6, 51, 78, 88, 113, 131, 145, 172, 178, 189 f., 203, 206, 228, 233, 279; an exercise, 190.

BEAUTY, the problem of beauty, 51-54.

BLANK VERSE, one of the *continuous forms,* unrimed *iambic pentameter,* 447, 448; examples, 235, 426, 411, 566.

"BOUND" VERSE, in contrast to *free verse,* the usual sort of *versification* in which the *poetic rhythm* is based upon a *metrical pattern.*

FOOT, (1) the *rhythmic* unit in a *metrical pattern,* 106; it will be *duple* or *triple* (of two or three syllables), *rising* or *falling* (with the unstressed element preceding or following the stressed syllable) or occasionally *rocking* (with unstressed syllables both before and after the stressed syllable), 101 f.; the five common feet, 106: *iamb, anapest, trochee, dactyl, amphibrach;* (2) the uncommon types of metrical unit found as *metrical variations,* 111 ff.: *spondee, pyrrhic, amphimacer, bacchius, anti-bacchius, paeon.*

FORM, see *poetic form.*

FOUR PHASES OF MEANING, a full *meaning* is a complex of *sense, tone, feeling, intention,* 50, 162, 168.

[F]REE IMAGERY, as distinguished from *tied imagery,* consists of mind pictures and comparable goings-on in [t]he imagination, stimulated by the *meanings* of the words, 137 ff.; individual differences, 138 f.; free [i]magery of various sorts: *visual, [a]uditory,* gustatory, olfactory, tac[ti]le, thermal, kinesthetic, equilib[r]al, pain, and visceral, 150 ff.; a [m]eans of communicating emotion, [...]7, 205.

[...] LYRIC, a miscellaneous group of [lyr]ic poems not falling into any of [the] established sub-types, 409.

[...] VERSE, a modern system of [vers]ification; a sort of oral and [wri]tten language falling between [...] and *prose;* not establishing a [metr]ical pattern, the *poetic rhythm* [pro]duces may be as irregular as [...] for prose, though generally [...]er, but in its *typographical* [...] it is like *verse,* 99, 126 ff. See [...]d" verse, continuous form.*

[...] FORMS, a number of complex [...] forms originated by the

medieval Provençal poets, 44, *ballade, rondel, rondeau, villanelle, sestina, triolet;* an exercise, 473.

FULL MEANING, a complex of the so-called *four phases of meaning,* whether of a phrase, sentence, or larger unit of discourse, 50, 162, 168 f., 204. See *over-all meaning.*

FUNCTIONS OF LANGUAGE in poetry: *communication, problem-solving, emotional adjustment,* 43-46, 162 ff.

GOOD POETRY, a good *poem,* provides the reader with a valuable *poem-reading-experience,* 259 f.; *psychological* theory of value, 260; judgment of a good poem, 261 f. See *criticism, evaluation, bad poetry.*

GREAT POETRY, that which has been judged *good poetry* by many of the better readers of the past, 269 f.; some examples, 270; degrees of greatness, 271 f.; judgment of a great poem, 272 ff.; greatness and *truth,* 291; an exercise, 292.

HEADLESS verse, see *initial truncation.*

HEPTAMETER, the *meter* consisting of seven *feet,* 108. See *septenarius.*

HEROIC COUPLET, one of the *continuous forms; iambic pentameter* lines *rimed* in *couplets;* especially the "closed" couplet (with *end-stopped lines* and the longer sense *pauses* coming at the ends of the couplets), but also the "open" couplet (with many *run-on lines*); examples, closed, 38, 244, 554; open, 35, 586.

HEROIC verse, designating the verse form of *epic* or heroic *poetry;* (1) in English poetry, *decasyllabic* or *iambic pentameter* (as in the *heroic couplet*); (2) in French poetry, the *Alexandrine,* or *iambic hexameter;* (3) in Greek and Roman, *dactylic hexameter.*

CACOPHONY, generally harsh or unpleasant combinations of sound, in contrast to *euphony,* 120.

CADENCE, the phrasal unit in the *poetic rhythm* of *free verse,* 127.

CAESURA, a mid-line *pause,* a sort of *metrical variation,* its presence and position in the *verse* determined by the sense, 114; masculine, if occurring after a stressed syllable; feminine, if occurring after an unstressed syllable; epic, if occurring after an extrametrical unstressed syllable.

CARMEN FIGURATUM, the rare instance of *typographical form* so devised as to represent or suggest the subject of the poem, 75.

CATALEXIS, see *truncation.*

CHORAL READING, choral speech, verse choir, 354 ff.; poems for choral reading, 358 ff.; exercises, 375 ff.

CLASSICISM, (1) the classic style, derived from the culture of ancient Greece and Rome, 543 f.; examples, 547 ff.; (2) neo-classicism as a literary *movement,* 544 f.; examples, 554 ff.; an exercise, 577. See *judicial criticism.*

CLASSIFICATION of poems, 405 ff., 639 f., 642; the sorting of *poems* in various ways, 475; exercise, 444-45. See *approaches.*

COMMUNICATION, one of the three *functions of language,* 44 ff., 162 ff.; the process of communicating *thought,* 165 ff.; when successful, 167 f.; communication of poet's *meaning,* 181 ff.; of the poet's emotion, 193 ff., 204, 208 ff., 213; in *oral interpretation,* 329; in *choral reading,* 356. See *utterance, interpretation.*

COMPARATIVE ANALYSIS, the fundamental nature of comparative observation, 639 f.; purpose and procedure, 641 ff.; *comparative criti-*

cism, 247 f., 257. See *pairs of poems, translations, parodies, drafts.*

COMPARATIVE CRITICISM, the use of *comparative analysis* as the basis for judging the worth of *poems,* 247 f., 257, 259; an exercise, 264. See *touchstone method.*

CONDITION, (1) the reader's condition, his unique *attitudes* and psychological needs, 304 f., 305-11; an exercise, 316-18; see poetic *immediacy;* (2) conditioning the reader, providing an enriched *context* for the *interpretation* of a *poem,* 311 ff.; an exercise, 318 ff.

CONNOTATION of words, in contrast to *denotation,* 205.

CONTEXT, the surroundings and circumstances that provide words with particular *meanings,* 49, 162, 165; verbal and vital context of utterance and of interpretation, 165, 178 ff.; an exercise, 190 ff.

CONTINUOUS FORM, the sort of *poetic form* in which the lines follow each other continuously with only occasional paragraphing as in *prose,* 86, 448 ff.; sorts of continuous form: *blank verse, heroic couplet, short couplet, irregular metrical form, free verse.* See *line-scheme.*

COUPLET, a pair of lines *riming,* (1) used successively in the *continuous forms,* (2) used occasionally as a *stanzaic form,* 537. See *heroic couplet, short couplet.*

CREATIVE WRITING of verse: for *choral reading,* 377; of *song-lyrics,* 402; storycraft and poetcraft, 445 f.; a song of praise, 472; sonneteering, 473 f.; a prose poem on a liberal theme, 509; writing *light verse,* 540; restyling, 578.

CRITICISM, literary criticism, the art and/or science of the *interpretation* and/or *evaluation* of poetry, 243; some methods of literary criticism,

HEXAMETER, the *meter* consisting of six *feet,* 108. See *Alexandrine.*

HISTORICAL *criticism,* a method concerned with the interpretation of the *poem* in relation to the poet, his age, his sources, etc., rather than with the judgment of its relative worth, 249, 258, 259; exercises, 264, 303.

HOVERING ACCENT, a *metrical variation* in which the reader's *stress* remains balanced between two syllables owing to the contending pulls of the *metrical pattern* and the *sense pattern,* 104, 114.

HYMN, a species of song-lyric, often *reflective* in character; a religious *song* for group singing, 380; examples, 384, 392; 278, 293.

IAMB, iambus, the iambic *foot, rising-duple,* deDUMM; "Iambic feet are rising twos," 106 f.

IDENTICAL RIME, the sort of *rime* involving syllables identical not only in their vowels and following consonants, but also in their preceding consonants: "bare—bear," "perfection—confection," "sent—consent."

IDYL, idyll, a sub-type of *narrative* or *lyric* poetry; a narrative or descriptive or lyric poem of simple life in the *pastoral* tradition; example, 549; ironic example, 505.

IMAGERY, see *tied imagery* and *free imagery.*

IMAGIST, one of the school of modern poets for whom the evocation of images was a principal purpose, 141.

IMMEDIACY, poetic immediacy, a poem's speaking to the reader's *condition,* satisfying his psychological needs, 304-11, 316.

IMPERFECT RIME, the use, where *rime* is expected, of words that do not strictly rime, either because the vowel sounds are not identical ("good—mood"), or because the following consonant sounds are not identical ("breathe—heath," "river—mirror"), or because both vowel and following consonant are similar but not identical ("pass —was"). See *strained rime, eye-rime,* and *identical rime.*

INCREMENTAL REPETITION, a device in the *ballad,* the repetition of lines or stanzas with slight but significant changes; examples, 411, 690.

INITIAL RIME, see *alliteration.*

INITIAL TRUNCATION, a sort of *metrical variation,* the omission of the unstressed syllable at the beginning of a line in *rising rhythm,* 113; such a verse is said to be *headless.*

INTENSITY of voice, a minor feature of *metrical pattern,* 111.

INTENTION, the utterer's purpose as one of the *four phases of meaning,* 168, 182 f., 215.

INTERNAL RIME, the *riming* of a word in the middle of the line with the word at the end of it, as in this verse, "Marching along, fifty-score strong," 359; or the riming of a word in the middle of a line with the word in the middle of the next one.

INTERPRETATION, the process of reading or listening in an attempt to find out what the utterer's *thoughts* were or are for which the words stand, 170 ff.; guessing and skilled judgment, 172, 194, 210 f.; *context* for interpretation, 165, 178 ff.; more complex for dramatic poetry, 198; *oral interpretation,* 327 ff.; in *choral reading,* 356; *critical interpretation,* 664 ff. See *utterance, communication, meaning,* etc.

INTUITIVE *criticism,* the judgment of *poems* by inexplicable insight, 246, 256, 259.

IRONY, that use of language in which the *intention* is contrary to the direct *sense;* a device often noted in *light verse* and *satire,* 539 f.

IRREGULAR METRICAL FORM, one of the *continuous forms,* using lines of varied *meter* and using *rime* freely, 448 f.; examples, 295, 297.

JUDICIAL *criticism,* the judging of *poems* according to the so-called laws or rules, 243 f., 246 f., 255 f., 259, 544; exercises, 264.

LANGUAGE, words the *symbols* of *thought,* 167; three *functions of language,* 43-6, 162; literature as language-*art,* 53. See *reference, meaning, communication, interpretation, speech.*

LIGHT VERSE, that poetry whose *mood,* whether emotional or intellectual, is gay or whimsical, flippant or frolicsome, witty or satirical, 512; the comic element in verse, 513; the satiric element, 513 f.; sorts of light verse: *epigram,* 514; comic *epitaph,* 515; *limerick,* 516; *triolet,* 517; light amorous verse, 518; comic incidents, 522; *parodies,* 526; *satire,* 529 ff.; *nonsense* verse, 539; *ironic* verse, 539.

LIMERICK, one of the lighter *special forms,* in rough *anapestic rhythm,* aa³bb²a³, 516.

LINE-SCHEME, the way the lines are grouped and related, one of the chief features of *metrical pattern,* 106, 108, and of *typographical form.* See *poetic form, rime.*

LITERARY BALLAD, a *narrative* poem similar to the *folk ballad* in *poetic form* and style, 407; examples, 337, 429, 563, 689.

LYRIC poetry, that one of the broad *types* including a wide variety of *poems* more or less personal and emotional in character, 406, 408 f.; (1) a *song-lyric,* the words to or for a *song,* (2) a short *poem,* neither *narrative* nor *expository,* expressive of a single *emotion* or *mood;* sub-types of lyric poetry: 408 f.: *song-lyric, sonnet, ode, idyl, elegy, epithalamion, French forms, epigram, free lyric;* examples, 435 ff., etc.

MADRIGAL, one of the *special forms* characterized by its particular relation to music, 449; example, 112.

MASCULINE RIME, the usual sort of *riming* in which the repeated sound consists of a stressed syllable, 109: "blast—pass'd," "blue—who," "dark—embark."

MEANING, an aspect of the *poem-reading-experience,* 26 f., · 46-51, 161 ff.; the "true" meaning, what the poet meant, 172, 182 f., 192; less important in *song-lyrics,* 380; three satirical poems on meaning, 539, 524, 526, 537. See *context, reference, ambiguity, four phases of meaning, full meaning, over-all meaning.*

METAPHOR, a device of language in which a word from one field of experience (universe of discourse) is used to convey a meaning in another field of experience, 173 ff.; metaphor, in a broad sense, including *simile* and *personification,* 175; an exercise, 186; metaphor, a means of communicating emotion, 197, 208.

METER, the "measure" or the number of rhythmic units (*feet*) in the line or *verse,* 106 f. See *monometer, dimeter, trimeter, tetrameter, pentameter, hexameter, heptameter, oc tameter.*

METRICAL PATTERN, in so-called *"bound"* verse, the rhythmic *expectancy* established at the outset of the poem; the way the poem "goes," 100; the chief features, 106: *foot, meter, line-scheme;* one aspect of *poetic form,* 446 f.; uncertainty for some *song-lyrics,* 380.

METRICAL ROMANCE, a sub-type of *narrative* poetry; a *poem* of moderate length relating the amorous and valorous adventures of knights and ladies, 408; examples, 251, 413.

METRICAL VARIATIONS, *deviations* from the *metrical pattern* under the insistency of the *sense pattern,* 111 ff.; the sorts of deviation: *substitution* of some other *foot* for the expected one, 113 f.; addition or omission of the expected unstressed syllable at the beginning or at the end of the line, or at a mid-line *pause—anacrusis, feminine ending, truncation, initial truncation,* 113 f.; variation in mid-line pause (*caesura*) and in the use of end-line pause (*run-on line*), 114; the use of *feminine* and *imperfect rime;* the opposition in movement of foot and word (the *dolphin effect*), 114; *hovering accent,* 104, 114; an exercise, 130 f.

METRICS, the systematic study of *metrical patterns* and *metrical variations.* See *prosody, versification.*

MONOMETER, the *meter* consisting of one *foot,* 107.

MOOD, the general attitude of the poet toward his subject matter, 510 ff.; as distinct from the mood of the reader, 511; variety of moods, 510-12: serious-emotional, serious-intellectual, light-emotional, light-intellectual. See *wit, light verse.*

MOVEMENT, literary movements, the general developments in cultural history, such as the Renaissance, 542. See *style, school, period.*

MUSIC, the relation of poetry to music, 378 ff. See *song, air.*

"MUSIC" OF POETRY, the complex of *poetic rhythm, sound pattern,* and *tone color;* that is, the *auditory* and *articulatory tied-imagery,* the sound of the words in the mind's-ear and the feel of the words on the mind's-tongue during silent reading, or the actual auditory and/or articulatory experience of hearing poetry read aloud or of reading it aloud, 26, 91 ff.; the ineffable "music" of poetry, 121 ff.; of *free verse,* 126 f.; an exercise, 132 f.; on *recordings,* 136; an example of *analysis,* 232; relation of the "music" of a *poem* to its *air,* 378 f.

NARRATIVE poetry, that one of the broad *types* including *story*-telling poems, 406 f.; sub-types of narrative, 407 f.: *ballad, epic, metrical romance, dramatic monologue, tale, idyl, fable;* examples, 410 ff.: exercises, 444 f.

NEO-CLASSICISM, see *classicism, judicial criticism.*

NONSENSE VERSE, *light verse* of apparently meaningless character, 129, 539; nonsense *refrains,* 361, 394.

OCTAMETER, the *meter* consisting of eight *feet,* 108.

OCTAVE, a *stanza* of eight lines; the first, eight-line part of a *sonnet.*

OCTOSYLLABIC, eight-syllable verse, usually *iambic* (or *trochaic*) *tetrameter.*

ODE, a sub-type of *lyric* or *reflective* poetry distinguished by being in any one of several variable *special forms,* 409, 451 f.; the Pindaric ode, characterized by its division into *strophe,* antistrophe, and epode, 451, 461; the choral ode of classic drama, 451, 366, 372, 373; the Horatian ode, 451, 547; the irregular or Cowleyan ode, 452, 147, 462; the stanzaic ode, 452, 145, 152; a group of odes, 461 ff.; exercises, 472 f.

ONOMATOPOEIA, words of imitative origin in which the sound immediately suggests the *sense,* as "bang," "buzz," "meow," 120.

ORAL INTERPRETATION, reading aloud, 6, 327 ff.; four steps in preparation, 328 f.; relation to silent reading, 328; poems for oral interpretation, 332 ff.; exercises, 351 ff. See *choral reading, recordings.*

ORTHOLOGICAL *criticism,* the evaluation of poem-experiences with due regard to semantic problems, 258 ff.; psychological theory of value, 260; "good poem" and "bad poem" defined, 260 f.; an example, 261 f.; some critical questions, 267 f.

ORTHOLOGY, one of the several sciences of *language,* the *psychology* of language behavior; concerned with the problems of *communication, interpretation, meaning,* etc.

OTTAVA RIMA, an eight-line *stanzaic form,* abababcc[5]; example, 529.

OVER-ALL MEANING, the *full meaning* of an utterance (such as a *poem*) taken as a whole, 48, 165, 176 ff., 181, 233; the over-all emotion, 196.

PAEON, a *foot* consisting of four syllables, one of which is stressed, DUMMdedede, dededeDUMM, deDUMMdede, or dedeDUMMde, and found very occasionally as a *metrical variation.*

PAIRS OF POEMS for *comparative analysis,* 7 and 8; 13 and 14; 29 and 30; 46 and 52; 55 and 66; 57 and 170; 59 and 60; 66 and 77; 68 and 85; 83 and 35; 116 and 133; 156 and 157; 182 and 184; 195 and 492; 218 and 219; 237, 281, and 285; 239 and 268; 250, 251, and 254; 262 and 177; 265-66; 273 and 657, 658; 293-94; 295-96; 297 and 302; 316 and 318; 334 and 522; 337 and 429; 332 and 343; 362 and 655; 411 and 251; 455 and 455; 479, 486, and 488; 488, 490, and 491; 460 and 87 f.; 498 and 500; 502 and 505; 524, 526, and 537; 558 and 566; 585 ff. and 593 ff.; 620 and 623; 619 and 500; 643 and 644; 645 and 646; 652 and 653; 655 and 656; 657 and 658; 659 and 660; 669 and 672; 672 and 460; 676 and 677; 684 and 316; exercises: 11 ff., 38, 59 ff., 82, 87 f., 264, 267, 292, 294, 297, 323, 539, 578, 608, 636, 661. See also *translations, drafts, parodies.*

PARODY, a poem mimicking the language, style, or ideas of another poem, for comic or satiric effect, 526 f.; exercises, 403, 539.

PASTORAL poetry, poems, such as *idyls* and *threnodies,* dealing with simple shepherd life or incidents after the manner of Theocritus, 549.

PAUSE, the short break at the ends of phrases, clauses, sentences, sometimes indicated by marks of punctuation; the expected stop at the ends of verses and of stanzas; in *oral interpretation,* 330. See *caesura, end-stopped, metrical variation.*

PENTAMETER, the *meter* consisting of five *feet,* 108.

PERFECT RIME, the usual sort of *riming* involving syllables that are identical in their final stressed vowel and any consonants and syllables that follow, but that differ in their preceding consonants, 109; "crop—top," "write—delight," "confession—discretion."

PERIODS, cultural periods, blocks of time bounded by relatively fixed dates for convenience in the study of literary history, 541; an exercise, 578. See *movement, style, school*.

PERSONIFICATION, a kind of metaphor (in the broad sense) in which an inanimate thing or abstract idea is given the attributes of a person, 175.

PITCH of voice, a minor feature of *metrical pattern,* 111.

PITFALLS for the reader of poetry, 5-7.

POEM, the word used in three senses, 22 ff.: (1) poem^p, the poet's experience, 23, 25; (2) poem^v, the printed verses, the poem on the page, 24, 33 ff.; (3) poem^r, the *poem-reading-experience,* 24, 26-28.

POEM-READING-EXPERIENCE, the goings-on in a person as he reads a *poem^v* (printed verses); the complex of the reader's thoughts, feelings, etc., 24; the anatomy of, the six aspects of, a poem-reading-experience, 26 ff., 65-241; an integrated whole, 125, 161, 191, 232.

POET, the *emotion of the poet;* the *emotional adjustment* of the poet; the *attitude* of the poet; the poet's *thought,* the "true" *meaning;* the biographical and personal *approach* to poetry, 580 ff.; examples of biographical approach, 179 ff., 312 ff., 581; life and poems of Keats, 583 f., 602 f., 635 f.; of Frost, 584, 593 ff., 603 ff.; the poet's own *oral interpretations* on *recordings,* 608, 611, 637 f.

POETIC FORM, the complex of *typographical form,* rhythmic or *metrical pattern,* and thought structure, 76, 446 ff.; of three general sorts, 86, 448: *continuous, stanzaic,* and *special.*

POETIC RHYTHM, the chief *rhythm* of poetry, the feeling that results from the apperception of repeated *stresses* at fairly regular intervals in the undulating flow of the *verses,* 100; the poetic rhythm of *"bound" verse,* a sort of compromise between *metrical pattern* and the *sense pattern, expectancy* and *deviation,* 100 ff.; of *free verse,* 126 f.; as a cause of the reader's *emotional response,* 205.

POETIC TRUTH, for the purposes of a *poem-reading-experience* and by the willing suspension of disbelief; a reader's acceptance as *truth* of a system of ideas in which he does not really or necessarily believe, 290-91.

POETICS, a theoretical and critical consideration of *Poetry* as an *art;* sometimes distinguished from *prosody* and *metrics.*

POETRY, working definitions, 53, 508: (1) Poetry (with a capital *P*), used to name all *poems* collectively; (2) poetry (with a small *p*), used to name any one or several or many *poems* or a part of a poem or parts of poems.

POINTERS for the readers of poetry, 5-7.

PRECONCEPTION, an opinion (favorable or unfavorable) based upon insufficient evidence, 4-5. See *prejudice.*

PREJUDICE, an unfavorable opinion or attitude based upon insufficient evidence, 3-4.

PROBLEM-SOLVING, one of the three *functions of language,* 43 ff., 162 ff.

PROSE, the ordinary language of conversation, newspapers, textbooks, history, biography, essay, short story, novel; distinguished from *verse* by the greater irregularity of the *rhythm* induced by it, and by its *typographical form,* 97, 98.

PROSODY, the science of *versification,* the systematic study of *metrical pattern, metrics.*

PSYCHOLOGY OF LANGUAGE behavior, *orthology,* the point of view of this book; psychological theory of value, 260; psychological needs of the reader, 304 ff.

PYRRHIC, a *foot* consisting of two unstressed syllables, de-de, found as a *metrical variation,* 115.

QUATRAIN, various four-line *stanzaic* forms: $a^4b^3c^4b^3$ (see *ballad meter*); aaba⁵, *aaba^5,* 281; aabb⁴, *aabb^4,* 438; and many others.

REALISM, one of the historic *styles,* 543; see exercise, 578.

RECORDINGS of poetry, various uses of, 612 f.; earlier cited in this book, 136, 160, 318; range and extent of, 614; use of records and the making of recordings for improving *oral interpretation,* 351-52, 613; recordings of *choral reading,* 376; of *songs,* 401; of the *poet's* own reading, 608; for intensive study, 609 ff.; for *comparative analysis,* 613; poems with records cited, 615 ff.; exercises, 635 ff.

REFERENCE, the *thought* for which a word stands in a particular utterance, 24, 26 f., 167.

REFERENT, the thing (or experience or other thought) that the *thought* is "of" in a particular utterance; the thing referred to, or pointed to, by the thought, 167.

REFLECTIVE-LYRIC, an "in-between" *type* of poetry, including *poems* that communicate the serious *thought,* as well as *emotion, of the poet,* 406.

REFLECTIVE POETRY, that one of the three broad *types* including *poems*

that are primarily *expository* or *didactic* in character, rather than *lyric* or *narrative,* 406 f.

REFRAIN, a line or part of a line repeated as part of a *metrical pattern,* as in the *rondel,* some of the *ballads,* and many *songs.* See *nonsense* refrains.

RESIDUAL ATTITUDE, see *attitude* and *residuum.*

RESIDUUM, one of the six aspects of the *poem-reading-experience;* (1) in the sense of things remembered, 28, 225 ff.; an exercise, 237; (2) in the sense of residual *attitude,* 28, 165, 226 ff.

RETINAL IMAGERY, the pattern of light reflected into the eye, projected upon the retina, and stimulating the rods and cones, 67, 137; relation to *visual tied-imagery,* 67, 79 f., and to *typographical form,* 75 ff.

RHYME, see *rime.*

RHYTHM, the peculiar sort of feeling that accompanies the perception of repeated points of interest, such as accented syllables and stressed words; rhythmic organization of syllables in twos and threes (*duple* or *triple*), *rising, rocking,* or *falling.* See *stress, verse* and *prose, poetic rhythm, metrical pattern, subsidiary rhythms.*

RIME, RIMING, the repetition of sound often at the ends, and occasionally in the middle, of successive or adjacent verses, 109; rime usually involves words at the end of lines, *end rime,* in contrast to *internal rime;* it usually involves words ending with stressed syllables, *masculine rime,* in contrast to *feminine* (*double* or *triple*) *rime;* it usually involves words that are identical in their final stressed vowels and any following consonants and syllables, but with differing sounds preceding the stressed vowels, *perfect rime,* in contrast to *imperfect rime* (*strained rime, eye rime,* and *identical rime*). See *initial rime, assonance, subsidiary rhythm.*

RIME ROYAL, a seven-line *stanzaic form,* ababbcc⁵, used by Chaucer and Shakespeare and William Morris.

RIME-SCHEME, a *line-scheme* making use of *rime,* 448.

RISING RHYTHM, the *rhythmic* organization of syllables in which the unstressed precede the stressed, 101; *iambic* and *anapestic.*

ROCKING RHYTHM, the *rhythmic* organization of syllables in which the unstressed both precede and follow the stressed, 106 f., 107 n.; *amphibrachic.*

ROMANTICISM, (1) the romantic *style,* derived from medieval European and British culture, 545 f.; (2) the Romantic *Movement,* 546; examples, 563 ff.; an exercise, 578.

RONDEAU, one of the *special forms* (*French*) in which the opening phrase (*R*) is repeated as a *refrain,* (R)aabba aabR aabbaR.

RONDEL, one of the *special forms* (*French*) consisting of two parts riming ABba abAB abbaA; example, 436.

ROUND, one of the *special forms* characterized by its particular relation to music, 449; example, 383.

RUN-ON LINE, or *enjambement,* a sort of *metrical variation* in which the sense carries the reader from one verse to the next without an end-line *pause;* in contrast to the *end-stopped* line, 114.

SACCADIC *eye-movements,* in the *visual process;* bringing successive groups of words into focus upon the retina during the moments of *fixation,* 67 ff.

SATIRE, (1) formal verse satire, in the tradition of Horace and Juvenal, 513; (2) the satiric element, risible criticism of human foibles and faults, 513; examples, 529, 536, 537; an exercise, 539.

SCANSION, the process of marking off the *stresses* and *accents* as they occur, or "should" occur, in *verse,* 97 n.

SCHOOL, literary schools, grouping of poets usually with regard to personal association, as a convenience in literary history, 541 f. See *movement, style, period.*

SEEING the *poem* on the page, see *visual process.*

SEMANTICS, 42; see *meaning, reference, context, ambiguity, metaphor,* etc.

SENSE as one of the *four phases of meaning,* 26, 44 ff., 50; sense leads the way in the *poem-reading-experience,* 161, 177 ff., 183 f., 204; exercises, 184 ff., 186 ff. See *thought, reference, referent, context;* also *denotation.*

SENSE PATTERN, the pattern of *stresses* set up by a consideration of the *meaning* of the verses, and at times opposed to the *metrical pattern.* See *poetic rhythm.*

SENTIMENTALITY, overabundance or lack of restraint in the *emotion of the poet* or in the *emotional response* of the reader, 213; in *song-lyrics,* 381.

SEPTENARIUS, the old seven-stress, *heptameter,* line; relation to *ballad meter,* 73 f.

SESTET, the last, six-line part of a *sonnet.*

SESTINA, one of the *special forms* (*French*) consisting of six six-line *stanzas,* plus a three-line *envoy;*

the six terminal words of the first stanza are repeated in a different order, in each stanza, and all six appear at the middle or ends of the lines of the envoy.

SHORT COUPLETS, one of the *continuous forms, iambic* (or *trochaic*) *tetrameter couplets,* usually *octosyllabic* couplets; examples, 436, 469, 645.

SIMILE, a kind of *metaphor* (in the broad sense) introduced by "like" or "as," 175.

SOCIAL JUSTICE as a poetic *theme,* 479, 492 ff.; propaganda and poetry, 508 f.

SONG, several senses: (1) a musical composition of lyric character, "a song without words," (2) the melodic *oral interpretation* of a poem, (3) a *song-lyric* with its *air,* printed verses and musical notation, (4) a *song-lyric,* the words alone, (5) a *lyric* that suggests musical intonation, 378 ff.; song-lyrics with airs, 55 f., 382 ff., 661 f.; kinds of songs, 379 f.; relation of verse to air, 381; exercises, 401 ff.

SONG-LYRIC, a sub-type of *lyric* poetry; a poem set to music, or intended to be sung, or such as suggests its being sung, 378 ff.; simplicity of, 380. See *song, lyric, hymn.*

SONNET, (1) one of the *special forms* of poetry, consisting of 14 lines of *iambic pentameter,* with any one of several more or less definite *rime-schemes,* 449 ff.; (2) a subtype of *lyric* poetry including *poems* in the sonnet form. The Petrarchan or Italian sonnet, abbaabba cdcdcd⁵ (or cdecde, or cdedce, or cddccd, or cddcee), 439, 266, 12; Shakespearean or Elizabethan, abab cdcd efef gg⁵, 159, 170, 263; Spenserian, abab bcbc cdcd ee⁵, 453: the Miltonic. abbaa-

bbacdecde⁵ (without *octave* and *sestet* divisions), 231; the composite, ababcdcd efgefg⁵, 77; the irregular, 202; the American sonnet, 458; *typographical form* of the sonnet, 78 f.; the *"music",* 232; the *thought structure,* 447; a group of sonnets, 452 ff.; exercises, 472.

SOUND PATTERN, the complex of recurrences and relationship of vowel and consonant sounds that may result in the feeling of certain subsidiary rhythms, 115 ff.; an exercise, 131 ff. See *rime, alliteration, assonance.*

SPECIAL FORM, the sort of *poetic form* of limited scope in which the *poem* is fashioned as a unit, (1) either in one of the traditional *metrical patterns,* 86, 449, or (2) in any unique, non-continuous and non-stanzaic pattern, metrical or free. Examples of traditional special forms: *sonnet, ode, French forms, madrigal, limerick, epigram, epitaph.* See *unique form, line-scheme.*

SPEECH, spoken language, 91, 94 ff. See *oral interpretation.*

SPENSERIAN STANZA, a nine-line *stanzaic form* of *iambic pentameter* concluding with an *Alexandrine,* ababbcbc⁵c⁶; examples, 251, 413, 572.

SPONDEE, a *foot* consisting of two stressed syllables, DUMM-DUMM, found as a *metrical variation.*

STANZA, a formal group of *verses,* usually bound together by a *rime-scheme,* the whole distinguished by its *metrical pattern,* and repeated (usually without variation) throughout the poem.

STANZAIC FORM, the sort of *poetic form* making use of successive *stanzas,* distinguished by their *metrical pattern,* 86, 448 f.; examples: *couplet, triplet, quatrain,* rime royal, ottava rima, Spenserian stanza.

STOCK RESPONSE, the sort of *emotional response* in which the reader reacts to only one factor of a complex stimulus without regard to the other factors, 212; in *song-lyrics*, 381.

STORY, a representation of human beings in a sequence of significant happenings, 407; story elements and devices, 407, 445. See *narrative.*

STRAINED RIME, the use, where *rime* is expected, of words that can only be made to rime by wrenching the *accent:* "die—memory," "sing—burning."

STRESS, the greater emphasis given to the more important words and accented syllables in an utterance; word stress may be distinguished from *accent,* the emphasis given to one or more syllables in a word, 97. See *rhythm.*

STROPHE, in the Greek choral dance, the movement of the chorus from one side of the circular "orchestra" to the other; the part of the choral ode chanted or sung while making this movement; the antistrophe was chanted during the counter-movement, and was followed by the epode; 451-52; examples, 461, 372.

STYLE, (1) the personal style of a poet, his particular manner of expression; (2) historic style, a generalization of notable characteristics to be found in the works of various authors, dominant in the work of a *period* or of a *school,* 542 f.; see *classicism, romanticism, realism;* other notable styles, 543; an exercise, 577 f.

SUBSIDIARY RHYTHMS, as distinct from the *poetic rhythm,* the feelings that result from the apperception of repetitions of vowel and consonant sounds (see *sound pattern, rime, alliteration, assonance*), and of repetitions in the larger movements in the *thought* and *narrative* structure, 115 ff.

SUBSTITUTION of some other *foot* for the expected one, a sort of *metrical variation,* 113 ff.

SUSPENSION OF DISBELIEF, see *poetic truth.*

SYMBOL, words are the symbols of *thoughts;* larger symbols in poetry, 218.

TALE, a sub-type of *narrative* poetry including a wide variety of direct narrative *poems,* usually more artful than the *ballad* and less ornate than the *metrical romance,* 408.

TEMPO, a minor feature of the *metrical pattern,* 111.

TERZA RIMA, a *stanzaic form* consisting of tercets (*triplets*) with linked *rimes:* aba bcb cdc, &c; example, 133 ff.

TETRAMETER, the meter consisting of four *feet,* 108.

THEME, the particular subject matter of the poem, 475 ff.; the universal experiences, 476; thematic categories, 477; two themes illustrated, 478 f., 479 ff.

THOUGHT, that for which the word or words stand; the *reference;* in the process of *communication,* 26 f., 171, 187. See *meaning.*

THOUGHT STRUCTURE, the relationship of the *thoughts* to each other, one of the components of *poetic form,* 446 f.; relation to *subsidiary rhythms,* 115.

THRENODY, a *poem* of lamentation, such as the *pastoral elegy,* 549.

TIED IMAGERY, as distinguished from *free imagery,* is directly "of" or

VERSIFICATION, (1) the practice of verse-writing as of a certain period or of a certain sort—see *alliterative verse, "bound" verse, free verse;* (2) the study of *metrics, prosody.*

VILLANELLE, one of the *special forms (French)* in which the two riming lines are repeated alternately throughout the poem: A'bA" abA' abA" abA' abA" abA'A".

VISUAL FREE-IMAGERY, the "seeing" of pictures in the mind's-eye of what the words stand for, 26, 137 ff.; source of images, 140; the form of mind-pictures, 141; the causes of imagery, 142; examples of visual imagery, 143 ff.; an exercise, 154; visual imagery of motion, 155 ff.; verbal portraiture, 157 f.; an exercise, 158 f. See *free imagery.*

VISUAL PROCESS in reading, seeing the *poem* on the page, 26, 65 ff.; some visual problems, 79 ff. See *retinal imagery, eye-movement, visual tied-imagery.*

VISUAL TIED-IMAGERY, the "seeing" of the words on the page, the direct result of the *retinal imagery,* 26, 65 ff., 79 f., 137 f. See *tied imagery.*

VOCALIZATION, the sounding or mouthing of words during silent reading, 91 f.; relation to *articulatory tied-imagery,* 92 f., 128 ff.

VOICE QUALITY, a minor feature of *metrical pattern,* 111.

WIT, (1) serious wit, that poetry in the serious-intellectual *mood,* 511; (2) light wit, see *light verse,* 512 ff.

First-Line Index

Title Index

[For *Author Index* see the Table of Poems at the front of the book, following the Table of Chapters.]

Poems marked with an asterisk (*) are song-lyrics provided with their airs.